SISTERS IN ARMS

First Harvard University Press paperback edition, 1998

Library of Congress Cataloging-in-Publication Data
McNamara, Jo Ann, 1931–
Sisters in arms : Catholic nuns through two millennia /
Jo Ann Kay McNamara.
p.   cm.
Includes bibliographical references and index.
ISBN 0-674-80984-X (cloth)
ISBN 0-674-80985-8 (pbk.)
1. Monasticism and religious orders for
women—History. 1. Title.
BX4200.M35   1996
271′9—dc20
96-3645

SISTERS
IN ARMS

※

*Catholic Nuns through
Two Millennia*

Jo Ann Kay McNamara

HARVARD UNIVERSITY PRESS
*Cambridge, Massachusetts
London, England*

For John E. Halborg

Contents

Preface

IN SEEKING A TITLE for this book, I found myself torn between two
of the most traditional metaphors for nuns. For a long time, I considered
"Virile Women," relying on the rhetoric of late antiquity. As I plunged
ever further forward in time, however, this title came to seem less and
less viable. To be sure, even the twentieth century has produced its share
of women who were praised by their male companions as manly, at least
in spirit. But while their womanhood clearly defined their vocations, it
was not in their own minds a demeaning condition in need of elevation
to the manly sphere. "Brides of Christ," a male concept of female
spirituality, serves very effectively to anchor women to a traditional
gender role, but women themselves rarely indulge in its implicit eroticism
in their writings. More often, they identify with the Virgin Mary in her
maternal or queenly aspects or model themselves on the heroic virgin
saints, Catherine, Margaret, Thecla, and Ursula.

Accordingly, I adopted a modification of the military metaphor that
has always informed monastic rhetoric. Ascesis (military training), self-
control, obedience, and self-sacrifice are the virtues of soldiers, and they
are most perfectly realized among the soldiers of Christ. Nuns were and
are part of that army even though they tend to be treated as irregulars
in relation to the professional male clergy. Uniformed in veil and
scapular, armed with prayer and good works, they have always been in
the forefront of their religion's battles. They shared the prejudices, the
will to domination, and the fanaticism that characterized the church they
served. They shared too in the founder's vision of an apostolate to the

poor, the sorrowing, the sick, the abandoned children of the earth. They gave their lives, whether in the violence of martyrdom or in the long sacrifice of self-mortification, for those dreams and those ambitions. Some were heroes and some were cowards. Volunteers led daring attacks on seemingly impregnable fortresses. Conscripts sometimes let resentment blight their lives or made their own corners comfortable by slacking off on the discipline. Tyrannical drill sergeants known to generations of children were balanced by generous quartermasters determined to feed the poor and heal the sick.

And, of course, the title *Sisters in Arms* evokes that comradeship which has always given the military life its luster of heroism and virtue. Our sisters have been united in a long war not only against the enemies of their religion but also against the misogynist elements within that religion that have mocked and constrained their efforts. Like Voltaire, I have grown up to be a secular humanist, yet, like him, I must concede that all I am I owe to my Catholic education. The nuns of Saint Cyril's parish school in Oakland, California, and Saint Theresa's in North Tarrytown, New York, gave me my earliest entry into the world of learning and my earliest insight into the world of the women to whose study I have devoted so many years of my adult life. Sister Lillian Thomas Shank, of the Cistercian order, started me and many other women off on the study of nuns when she requested that we write something of their history for the use of her novices. The volumes she subsequently produced with John A. Nichols on medieval religious women have given shape and definition to this field. The sisters (including a handful of honorary lay sisters like myself) who make up the Network for the History of Women Religious have continued this effort into the modern world, bound together through the newsletter regularly issued by Karen Kennelly.

The notes to this text cannot begin to express my debt to my sisters and brothers in the scholarly community for their scholarship and interest. A few people stand out for work shared and insights provided. Among so many, I want specially to mention Connie Berman, Jim Brundage, Vern Bullough, Penny Johnson, Richard Kieckhefer, Asunción Lávrin, Barbara Newman, Bernadette McCauley, Mary McLaughlin, Joel Rosenthal, Jane Schulenberg, Nancy Siraisi, Susan Stuard, Margaret Susan Thompson, Barbara Welter, Suzanne Wemple, and Merry Wiesner-Hanks.

The feminist network of scholarly support and exchange of ideas that flourishes throughout the country and especially in New York City has provided me with regular forums and intellectual stimulation. These include the Coordinating Committee for Women in the Historical Profession, the Columbia University Seminar for the Study of Women in Society, and the now defunct Institute for Research in History, whose daughters, the research groups, live on. From the latter, many staunch friends have listened to my ideas over the years and a few have patiently put up with my obsessions above and beyond the call: Barbara Harris, Sarah Pomeroy, and Marilyn Williams (of the Family History group); Judith Neaman, Phyllis Roberts, Jim Ryan, Pamela Sheingorn, and Marcelle Thiébaux (of the New York Hagiography group).

These feminist networks also brought me the friendship of Joyce Seltzer, who has supported this book from its inception as its editor and helpful critic. Deadlines have come and gone and we have negotiated our way through a change of publisher, but Joyce has firmly kept to our original vision of a one-volume history for the broadly educated public that would at last give the Catholic sisterhood a distinct historical identity.

Medieval recluses were advised to keep no animal near them but a cat. Their instructors presumably made that exception because cats are part of a working household, diligently keeping the vermin at bay. My cat is no exception but in addition, like the hermitage cat, she has been a friendly muse. I doubt I could have kept my patience with this work for so many years without the support of Brumaire, lying across my desk purring.

Finally, I can never sufficiently state my debt nor measure my affection for two men. My son, Edmund Clingan, has from the first moment of his life given me an unanswerable argument against the renunciation of the flesh. His kindly spirit and his challenging intellect have worked their way deeply into my mental processes and inform every page of this book. Father John E. Halborg, my friend and collaborator on several projects, provides a living model for the possibilities of syneisactic friendship. Our quarrels, our respective neuroses and ego trips, and our deep differences of opinion on many important subjects have repeatedly given way before the strength of that friendship, and in gratitude for that fidelity I dedicate this book to him.

SISTERS IN ARMS

Introduction: Chastity and Female Identity

CHASTITY COMBINED with celibacy, the renunciation of biological sex and of social coupling, was virtually unknown to the family-centered societies of antiquity. Unmarried men had a range of sexual choices and made no virtue of self-denial. Few women with desirable assets in property or beauty ever succeeded in reserving their own bodies from the domination, protection, and even the love of men. Poor or aged women who lost their male guarantors were engulfed in obscurity. Unknown disappointments or hopes led women from every rank and economic condition to answer Jesus' call to break old family ties and follow after him. Women and men traveled in chaste partnership, forging a new religion and a new social vision. This apostolic life, transcending gender in pursuit of the kingdom of heaven, gave them the foundation of chaste celibacy on which an autonomous identity could arise. Jesus said that Mary of Bethany, who devoted her attention to his teaching, had chosen "the better part" over her sister Martha's housewifely ministrations. The women who followed him to the cross and kept his memory alive thereafter were determined that it would not be taken from them.

As their faith became a church, a clerical hierarchy arose that, by a process not revealed in our sources, excluded women from its ranks. Women consecrated to the religious life, regardless of the degree and discipline of their commitment, remained part of the laity, arbitrarily barred by their sex from ordination and its privileges, chiefly the sacramental monopoly that qualifies men alone as channels for the saving grace

I

generated by Christ. The church has long taught that the character of priests cannot affect the virtue of their sacraments. Women religious have never enjoyed this exemption. To share in Christ's redemptive mission, they have had to develop alternative spiritualities rooted in prophecy and mysticism or in the imitation of Christ through works of charity. Compassion—the emulation of Jesus' suffering in hope of sharing the distribution of grace through prayer, self-sacrifice, and good works— entitled them to rank in a spiritual hierarchy that has always stood apart from the clerical hierarchy in a dangerously competitive position.

Castimony, which united the religious with Christ, became in time a legitimate alternative to matrimony. Widows, wives living apart from their husbands, repentant prostitutes, and women who had never known a sexual relationship embedded themselves firmly in the core of the infant religion and contested the efforts of conservative authorities like Paul to keep the sexes decorously segregated. An "order" of widows developed a female apostolate to the sick and needy and an educational mission addressed particularly to women. Early Christian communities supported women with notable spiritual gifts in return for prayer and for sharing the revelations that sprang from their intense meditations. These "widows" were the fountainhead from which many springs flowed: communities of virgins, recluses, cloistered nuns, and care givers using various titles experimented tirelessly with the possibilities of the chaste life among sisters.

Scholars have easily perceived men who have served the Catholic Church in their orderly ranks as monks and secular clergy, distributed according to their specialized vocations. Women religious have been torn between lay and clerical status, between episcopal and monastic jurisdictions, between active and contemplative vocations defined by male authorities. Thus, despite the variety of their activities, women's experience of the religious life, as it came to be called, had profoundly different lineaments from men's and merits a separate history stressing the unity of that experience. No human institution is older than this sisterhood. Its impact has been felt throughout the world but, against all reasonable evidence, monastic historians traditionally refused to see anything but their cloister walls and enveloping veils. Reasoning that women do not build institutions or conquer new worlds or make history, the scribes who shape the past have ignored their untidy existence or simply accorded it a hasty nod before pressing forward with the more readily accessible history of male institutions. Still, religious women have a past that has much to teach us, not only about female creativity and accomplishments but about the possibility that women and men may yet enjoy a fuller humanity beyond the barriers of gender distinctions.

Men too came to renounce active sexuality for the sake of unqualified devotion to God. Asceticism was a movement for lay people who cast off all the bonds of worldly commitments. The monastic movement was essentially conceptualized on the primitive model of Jesus' companions, with women as full partners in urban apostolates and desert asceticism. Even in sexually segregated communities, monks and nuns, brothers and sisters, subjected themselves to the same disciplines and shared their labor and its fruits. Chaste celibacy endowed virgin martyrs and desert mothers with the power and authority that nature normally reserved for men by restricting women's autonomy and integrity. The ideology of asceticism argued that manliness was acquired through training and discipline, which women could undertake as well as men. Indeed, the Fathers of the church enjoyed the rhetorical strategy of praising virile women at the expense of effeminate men.

Virginity wiped out gender differences and turned women into men by giving them independence and the authority to pursue a lofty spiritual calling. This ideology was formulated in late antiquity by a cadre of highly articulate men under the influence of wealthy and charismatic women devoted to exploring the chaste life. Based on the ideal of the spirit's triumph over the body, it encouraged a cooperative lifestyle of pooled resources and mutual encouragement exemplified by the desert retreat of Jerome and Paula. They defined virginity by intention and behavior rather than physical accident, resting on a concept of the soul and even the body as malleable to the perfect will. In the circles where the theology of the everlasting virginity of Mary the mother of God developed, it became possible to think of baptism as restorative of virginity. Virginity survived rape when the victim withheld her consent. Widows and married women who left the conjugal bed could enjoy a secondary virginity, and women who had never known sexual activity "became" virgins by taking a vow of consecration.

Even as the Fathers engaged with their female associates in these flights of ideological fantasy, however, they gendered virginity female.

They extended their unqualified admiration to its proponents while bemoaning their own failure to preserve pristine purity. Moreover, they did not accord themselves the forgiving second chances that they held out to women, preferring to gender incontinence as masculine. Chastity, though required, was never the defining characteristic of male monastic life, which extolled obedience, poverty, and humility as its quintessential virtues. Chaste celibacy, originally merely a vehicle for liberating time and energies for divine service, tended to be promoted as an end in itself for women. As the clerical hierarchy incorporated monks into the priesthood and co-opted many monastic virtues, the legal condition of celibacy (the unmarried state) overshadowed the spiritual value of chastity. But for women, all virtues were folded into an engulfing discourse on sexual purity. In the second millennium, praise of virginity degenerated into fretful nagging about keeping all the senses fastidiously unspotted, as well as the mind that controlled them.

Ascetic women became an embarrassing anomaly to a male clerical order. Peer pressure, slander, seduction, and rape have been mobilized to neutralize women who choose a life without sex. At the beginning of our story we will encounter women from puberty to old age who were put to death for refusing to marry. In the Middle Ages, dirty jokes and pornographic fantasies detailing the fictional longings of unwilling nuns gave license to the sexual ambitions of young men seeking wives or just a brief diversion by breaking into convents. Until quite recently, even the handful of modern scholars who have studied nuns have tended to reinforce these ancient slanders, blaming the social conventions that enabled families to determine arbitrarily whether their women would be assigned to a life of matrimony or castimony. Protestants prided themselves on "rescuing" women condemned to languish without husbands, and modern historians have habitually ignored the clear testimony of the women who resisted their assaults. Enlightenment fantasies of the perverted sex to which innocent virgins were subjected behind convent walls are still published, but not the rebuttals of women who went to the guillotine rather than give up their cloisters. In the nineteenth century, anti-Catholic mobs mounted violent attacks on some convents while modern science claimed that rejection of "normal" (procreative heterosexual) sex was a sign of mental illness and might also lead to physical debility. Even today, the true or fictional accounts of renegade nuns readily gain a popular market. The accounts of women who founded new communities or flourished in old ones are too often left to private presses with limited circulation. In our own libertarian age we still refuse to recognize the legitimacy of choosing chaste celibacy, linking it to caricatures of nuns as ignorant classroom tyrants and feminists as angry hags.

Nuns are not only peculiarly vulnerable to outside critics but by nature highly self-critical of their failure to conclude a quest for perfection whose goal always recedes. Religious women who lacked the structural advantages of offices and ordination to enhance their spiritual confidence could rarely trust their own virtue unless they achieved a visionary state in which divine assurances were granted them. Care givers always feared they would fail to maintain their own humility toward the poor made humble by life's cruel oppressions. And the rules of the game were apt to change rudely. Priestly arbiters who equated female perfection with silence and invisibility treated active charity as inherently corrupting. Secular humanists came to value the active life but condemned contemplatives as socially useless. Taught to be obsessively concerned with their own purity, nuns were often driven frantic by the endless pressure to find sources of impurity within the convent and within the soul itself and burn them away through ever more strenuous self-mortifications. They were caught within their own embattled psyches, where no perfect state could ever be gained or maintained.

Obviously, contact with men, always unavoidable, became a terrifying threat to that purity. Clerical insistence on the irresistible power of sexual attraction generated a double anxiety to safeguard not only the unsullied purity of women but also the fragile virtue of men who were said to be prone to lapse into uncontrollable frenzy in their presence. Inevitably, the rulers of the church came to the conclusion that women religious had to be confined behind walls and grilles. But much as they feared sexual temptation, clergymen feared women entirely withdrawn into a world without men even more. This complementary threat of female autonomy always drove them back to the *cura mulierum,* the care (and control) of women.

The entire structure of male authority in any age is rooted in the ideology of gender differences. Religious men and women living together in chastity, recognizing equal spiritual capacities, lay an ax to that root by minimizing those differences. The practice had a name among primitive Christians—syneisactism—a word that has found no modern equivalent. Against syneisactics, sexual temptation has been repeatedly inflated as the devil's snare, leading women and men who imprudently consort with one another to physical transgression at best and at worst to heresy. Thus, the history of nuns is haunted by the presence of men who often admired them yet feared their own admiration; who controlled them but did not trust them; who invested emotional currency in the mythology of mystery and difference rather than the ideal of understanding and equality.

The failure of syneisactism created fertile ground for the growth of a separate feminine sensibility and strengthened the bonds of sisterhood in religion. The trials and triumphs of community resound through the literature of, for, and about nuns in every age and environment. This book provides only an initial glance into the camp behind the cloister redoubts so cunningly camouflaged by the mocking, belittling imagery of popular culture. It does, at least, call attention to foremothers who, for two millennia, have broken new paths for women in a hostile and forbidden world. They served their god and their church and in doing so they fulfilled themselves and laid a foundation for all women. Without the daring and sacrifice of these nuns, it is impossible to imagine the feminist movements of modern times finding any purchase in the public world. They created the image and reality of the autonomous woman. They formed the professions through which that autonomy was activated. They still devote their lives to the care and development of human beings everywhere.

Now at last the ideology of syneisactism based on the erasure or at least suppression of gender differences may have its day. In the modern world, where women and men have at last come to work together and live together in uneasy truce, we are still seeking to expand the areas where gender gives way to individual talent. Wherever women and men struggle to realize their full human potential, they join in spirit with this ancient sisterhood. The history of nuns points to a more integrated life for everyone, transcending gender differences and forging a new personality combining those characteristics so unfortunately divided by sex.

I

THE ROMAN EMPIRE

1

The Apostolic Life

THE WOMEN OF GALILEE were the first Christians. They came up to Jerusalem with Jesus and stayed with him in the bitter hours of his death. They buried him and later announced to the other disciples who were hiding from the Romans that the tomb was empty. One woman testified that she had spoken to him, earning the title Apostle to the Apostles. Having come to believe that their teacher was God himself, who had voluntarily taken a human body to redeem humanity with his own suffering and death, they determined to pursue fulfillment of his mission. Their earthly future was bleak. Jesus' legacy was nothing but a share in his suffering. But they believed that compassion, participating in his sacrifice through imitation, would earn them a place in his eternal kingdom. To that end, they were prepared to take up arms against the empire of this world.

We know some names: Mary, Jesus' mother, and her sister Mary, Clopas's wife; Mary of Magdala, Joanna, the wife of Chuzah, and Susanna, a trio from whom Jesus had exorcised demons; Salome and Mary, the mother of the sons of Zebedee. They were childless widows and separated wives. One had lived for a dozen years with a flow of blood, presumably a menstrual disorder that made her unclean to her Jewish community. Tradition named her Berenice or Veronica. There were other women too, though we do not know whether they were part of the group who followed Jesus to the cross. The Samaritan woman, who confided with shame that she was living with a man who was not her husband, was the first apostle Jesus sent to proclaim him as Messiah. Mary of Bethany, who sat among the apostles listening to Jesus after he refused to send her off to the kitchen, and her busy sister, the practical Martha, provided hospitality for his disciples out of affection for the master. Finally, there was the nameless woman taken in adultery and the Canaanite woman who begged for her child's cure as if for crumbs from a rich man's table.

The women of the gospel had no social identity, though we know that some were rich. They had fallen or leapt through the cracks in a dying order. They lived at a crossroads, a Janus time, that gave simultaneous birth to the Roman Empire and to the Christian religion. The men who should have anchored them to their society had apparently cast them adrift. For centuries, Rome had been engaged in the systematic conquest of the Mediterranean world, engulfing its diverse polities and sapping the power of their oligarchies. In general, these polities shared a socio-political model: the mass of people were ordered and supervised by a ruling class of "fathers" who headed great families of cadets, women, children, and slaves.[1] In addition, the fathers controlled diverse groupings of dependents and clients. In contrast, the simpler unions of humbler people were barely recognized by the empire as marriage at all. The fathers' public life and their family responsibilities were thus mutually dependent. As Rome undermined their public power, they also lost the ability and even the will to protect their private domain from outside intervention. The final victim of this unifying conquest was the Roman Republic itself.

Jesus' contemporary Livy, writing of an idealized and vanished past, believed that the republic's decay began when the Senate failed to heed Cato's warning that uncontrolled women would bring the state to ruin. Its fall, in civil war and anarchy, was ascribed to the failure of old patriarchal virtues, best embodied in the flagrant dalliance of the consul Mark Antony with the seductive Egyptian queen Cleopatra while his good Roman wife languished in neglect at home. Patrician men avoided marriage and the burden of policing women, children, and slaves who were cut loose to shift for themselves. Many sank into misery but others prospered in unprecedented ways. When Antony's brother-in-law, who came to be known as Augustus Caesar, made himself a military dictator under the pretext of restoring the republic, he launched an elaborate program of renewing the old ancestral ways, including the mythical family of the golden age. Accordingly, the first emperor issued laws obliging all men (of the patriarchal class) to marry and all women to have children.

Over succeeding generations, penalties, promises, and finally persecution testified to the importance of the Augustan marriage laws in imperial society and to their failure. The imperial "household" itself destroyed the familial base of society by subsuming the patrician fathers under the patriarchal power of the emperor, who delegated authority to his own wife, slaves, and freedmen rather than to a senate of aristocratic elders. But the miniature imperium of the noble family was needed to maintain gender and class hierarchies. In robbing its patriarchs of the political authority that rewarded their assumption of the familial burden, the empire had weakened their commitment to these social duties. Many aristocratic men simply turned away to a more irresponsible celibate existence, preferring concubinage relationships to lawful marriage.

Many women too opted for a more independent life. They joined angry mobs that forced Augustus to recognize a longer period of widowhood before forcing them to marry again. They secured the steady enlargement of the "right of three children," which gave women free control of their own fortunes after they had borne three children (four in the case of freed women). Whereas Roman observers fretted obsessively about women's sexual license and lack of propriety, Christian writers boasted from the first about their chastity. Indeed, the first fruit of the ultimate Christian victory three centuries later was the extension of the right of three children to women who consecrated themselves to religion as virgins or chaste widows.

The tie between religion and the polity was also breaking. The political crises that produced the empire produced in turn a series of social and psychological stresses that nurtured Christianity. Public religion had generally been the province of men. Increasingly, it was being reduced to the empty forms that Jesus so despised, while private religion—centered on communities of elite initiates endowed with esoteric secrets—came to absorb people's deepest emotional commitments. The fall of so many kingdoms and their attendant gods before the spreading might of Rome convinced many people that the end of the world, or at least its radical transformation, could not be far off. Women seeking a new sense of identity figured prominently among the emperor's disoriented and alienated subjects. Juvenal complained bitterly of women who gave their devotion to emotional and irrational oriental cults.[2] In city streets and desert oases, prophets urged their followers to forsake family and fortune. To Jesus, "the true family of those who hear the word and keep it" included mother, brothers, and sisters but only one father, God in heaven.[3] Although only a few gained a place in scripture, many women stood among the crowds who heard that the last would be first and the meek would inherit the earth.

The women of the gospel came to Jesus out of tragic and broken lives. They needed healing, for their bodies and for their souls. They needed to be relieved of whatever pressures had made them demoniacs or to be forgiven for sexual transgressions. But once restored, they did not simply go home. They joined the family of Christ, which anticipated the kingdom of heaven, where there would be no marriage or giving in marriage but all would be one. The vagabond community whose members contributed their experiences to the compilation of the New Testament commemorated a band of equals. In the aura of Jesus' love and power, other distinctions seemed to melt away. Women and men traveled together freely, shared what they had, and helped one another bear their losses. This ideal of syneisactism, women and men living together chastely without regard for gender differences, was the most deeply radical social concept that Christianity produced.[4]

This principle probably explains Jesus' attraction for many of his female followers. The decay of the old polity based on a union of fathers opened some public space for women. Empresses set the pattern for lesser women to participate in various affairs, particularly in religious associations. Women who had wealth could hold some religious offices and function as patronae. A tomb in Smyrna built by "Rufina, a Jewess, president of the synagogue, for her freed slaves and slaves raised in her house" dramatizes the extent of this leadership.[5] The old laws of inheritance had been designed to keep women in direct dependence on men and isolated from effective alliances with other women. Heiresses, however, found ways to evade the laws imposing tutelage. Divorced and widowed women gained control of their own dowries and other properties. Many women, through the right of three children, claimed recognition as legal persons. Freedwomen could dispose independently of their own property and enter into commercial enterprises that might support them comfortably or even make them rich. While many women were forced to turn to prostitution to earn a living, some Roman ladies actually registered as prostitutes to gain independence from male tutors, a scandal that imperial legislation tried vainly to correct.

Some of Jesus' female companions were among the beneficiaries of these social changes. Joanna was the wife of Herod's steward. With Susanna and Mary of Magdala she supported the little band of vagabonds. In one version of the story, a prostitute extravagantly anointed Jesus' feet with ointment worth hundreds of denarii.[6] John, by contrast, attributes this generosity to Mary of Bethany, who lived with her sister Martha and brother Lazarus in a house large enough to provide hospitality for a fairly large number of peripatetics. Thus, the community of embattled women from Galilee who followed Jesus to the cross should be placed into a context of women from every part of Roman society actively seeking a wider and more purposeful life. Without their money and their labor and their witness, no religion would have been born and no church could have been built.

The Gospels reveal the syneisactic nature of the apostolic life but do not indicate that Jesus gave instruction on the matter. In the first generation, Christianity provoked many debates among its converts about the nature of the gender system in the new order. It was a widely debated topic at the time among the adherents of many religious and philosophical groups. Rejection of established gender roles and of sexuality itself appealed to many individuals outside the Christian milieu. The discussion seems dominated by a notion that gender was fluid, possibly based on the Aristotelian continuum that defined women as imperfect men. The whole concept suggested that women could become perfect by accumulating manly characteristics and that men risked becoming imperfect, or effeminate, if they let their manly self-control and vigor weaken. Writers of the early empire displayed profound uneasiness about society's loss of control over women. They tended to dwell on the sexual license of emancipated Roman women, haunted by Cleopatra and Livia, the seductress and the poisoner, as depicted by contemporary historians. Juvenal satirized religious devotions that took women away from home, claiming that even old established female cults masked orgies of unbridled lust.[7]

These fantasies still represented power channeled through men.

Throughout the first-century world, there were women and men experimenting with a new equation. The syneisactic principle put women on
an equal footing by renouncing the sexual and procreative activities that
made them unequal. Philosophical cults whose members renounced sex
and marriage for the love of wisdom multiplied in the Hellenistic world.
Cynic and Stoic writers recommended that women study philosophy and
men submit to a single standard of morality. The same idea was implicit
in the early Christian communities and made explicit by Clement of
Alexandria (ca. 200), when he defended Christian women who perfected
their philosophical capacities in the Christian mission against pagan
critics.[8]

Pliny identified the *therapeutae*, aging virgins in Hellenized Egypt who
voluntarily chose to devote themselves to wisdom rather than to husbands, as a Jewish counterpart of certain ascetic Greek sects of philosophers.[9] He described the women as serving one another without slaves,
as though all were one family. They segregated themselves from their
male companions solely for the sake of their own modesty, coming
together to sing in choir and then parting to study privately.

Out in the desert, the Essenes were committed to extreme physical
purification. They lived together, kept a common purse, and practiced
manual labor for their own support. Most members of these sects were
male but there were some females among them.[10] References in the Dead
Sea Scrolls confirm that most of them were wives and children of the
members.[11] But the marriages may have been instigated by women
actively seeking a chaste life devoted to worship. Widows of former
members or virgin daughters who remained with their parents past
marriageable age may account for the rest of the female bones in the
cemetery. Thus, though admission to an Essene community probably
depended on the sponsorship of a man, it provided the choice of a
syneisactic life for a few women.

Aside from the freedom from confinement that renunciation of sexuality achieved, there was a pervasive belief that unsullied virginity
commanded certain powers: hence, the consecration of the vestal virgins,
a small handful of women reserved from marriage for cultic purposes.
Ironically, they were among the first women to be endowed with the
right of three children. First-century Christians believed that even in the
Temple of Jerusalem some virgins were maintained in total purity. There

they imagined the young Mary flowering until approaching menarche precipitated her betrothal to Joseph.[12] She had perhaps a counterpart in the aged Anna who is mentioned in the New Testament as a widow who spent her life in the Temple praying.

Other women acted without male support, using religion to free themselves from the sexual demands of men and from the burden of endless childbearing. Juvenal warned husbands against wives who "fill the house with covens of worshippers of strange oriental deities," who encouraged them to torture and mutilate their bodies "to atone for having slept with their husbands the night before."[13] Perhaps he was talking of Isis, sometimes associated with prostitutes, but in another persona a champion of a woman's right to refuse. At the end of the century, the emperor Domitian condemned to death two vestal virgins as well as several Christian virgins who refused to marry. He pursued devotees of Isis even more brutally. Likewise, Roman laws tried to extirpate cults of the Great Goddess that encouraged men to castrate themselves in her honor.

These were the models available to the women of the gospel and other women attracted to the teachings of Jesus in the first century. The band of women from Galilee were the good ground where Jesus' message took root: God loves most the one whom he forgives the most. The seed flourished in them and they gave fruit a hundredfold. Some women may have been among the anonymous "seventy" dispatched to spread the word. Certainly, the Samaritan woman preached effectively, bringing back a crowd of converts. It was Jesus' mother, Mary, who began the instruction of the disciples, gathered together once more at Pentecost, and prepared them for the inspiration of the Holy Spirit. The swift spread of Christianity in the first generation could not have been achieved without an active apostolate of many women and men. They all had memories to contribute to the reconstruction of Jesus' life and message, represented by the four canonical Gospels. Other memories and ideas were embedded in the elusive traditions of the Apocrypha. We cannot know in any detail what they preached and what they sought to make of the new kingdom, but we do know that Christian women and men have never stopped experimenting with the possibilities inherent in the gospel message.

We have only fugitive visions of the fates of a few of the disciples after Pentecost. Collections of apocryphal and Gnostic writings from the second and third centuries may not yield trustworthy historical data but they do illuminate the tradition that passed through many Christian communities. The life of Jesus' mother was enlarged and enhanced as befitted a cult that would swell in importance over the centuries. In the influential apocryphal gospel, the Protoevangelion, she was betrothed to Joseph as a pure virgin, and a midwife named Salome attested to Mary's continuing virginity through and after the birth of Jesus. Other traditions claimed that during her later life in Ephesus with the apostle John she established the first community of Christian virgins. Various apocryphal gospels pay respect to her continuing role as a teacher of the apostles culminating at last in her death and assumption bodily into heaven.[14]

After Pentecost, the original community seems to have split up. The Apocrypha give us glimpses of Salome, Berenice, and the several Marys (gradually conflated into a single figure) as teachers and apostles. In the mysterious Gospel of the Egyptians Jesus promises to save "Mary" by making her a man.[15] Centuries later, as medieval mythology began to take shape, Mary and Martha resurfaced as apostles in Provence, figures of the contemplative life (Mary the hermit) and the active life (Martha the dragon slayer). These powerful mythic figures take us far from the women who swiftly crossed the gospel pages, but they serve to remind us that those women and many others had a life after Pentecost. They were present at the creation of Christianity and, though their testament has been drowned out by the thundering voice of Paul, it was their religion and they had a decisive share in its formation. They were the first in a continuing tradition of sisters who struggled not only to spread the news of the kingdom of heaven but also to translate the teachings of Jesus into new forms of life on earth.

Our meager knowledge about the organization and spread of Christianity in the century after Jesus' death is dominated by the Pauline tradition recorded in the Book of Acts and his Epistles. The work of other apostles and the internal lives of their communities, each seeking to define the Christian life, went unrecorded. The first community in Jerusalem, fleetingly glimpsed in the Book of Acts, attempted to maintain the total egalitarianism of the apostolic life by requiring all members to give up their property.[16] This characteristic may have been unique, resulting from the tie to the temple, or it could have been intended as a model for the mission churches. There is, however, no indication that it was imitated there. Nor is it clear that this Christian communism served to make women equal with men. It may simply have deprived them of the balancing advantage of wealth in the gender equation.

Luke the Evangelist, the probable author of Acts, makes only a passing reference to the women in that community, whom he simply calls "the widows." If Luke was speaking of some or all of the women from Galilee, he may have been using a courtesy title for women living without husbands. In the early days of the Jerusalem community, an altercation arose because the "Hellenists" believed that "their widows were neglected in the daily distribution by the Hebrews." It is not clear why widows should have been singled out like this in a community that boasted of sharing everything. The widows in Acts were not necessarily poor or in need of charity. The community, in fact, may have been financially dependent on them. But it is also possible that once their money had gone into a common purse, the leaders felt that they had better uses for it than the care of "dependent" women. They could have been resisting the recruitment of additional women, hoping to restrict the group to the original followers of Jesus, who would not be replaced as they died out. Already the outlines of a male priesthood were appearing with the inevitable result of limiting the usefulness of women. Paul himself, in defending his right to support from the community, spoke critically of those apostles who expected charitable Christians to support wives accompanying them in their travels.

The quarrel patched over, the group strove to establish a community at least theoretically free of distinctions of wealth, social status, race, and gender, as echoed in the famous formula, "In Christ there is neither bond nor free, Jew nor Greek, male nor female."[17] Possibly part of the original baptismal liturgy, the same attitude appears in other early Christian works like the apocryphal Gospel of Thomas, where Jesus promises entry into the kingdom of heaven when opposites are resolved and male and female are one. A letter attributed to Clement of Rome, Peter's companion and successor (who died about 100), explains that the saying means only that a brother and sister in Christ should not think of each other as sex objects.[18] At the least it defines a minimal syneisactism, the discipleship of equals where all the baptized throw off their divisive identities in favor of new unity and equality. Women prayed and prophesied with men and shared with them in the communal feasts that bound the community together.

The widows may have acted as a particular unit or subdivision within the group, possibly even directed by Jesus' mother and the women who had been with her at Jesus' death. Peter came to be credited with the institution of three orders of widows. Two devoted themselves to prayer for the rest of the faithful and the transmission of revelations arising from their contemplations. The third group attended sick women and looked into the needs of the poor and sick of every sort, securing assistance from the presbyters and deacons in charge of communal goods.[19] In many communities, women who were not necessarily widows were appointed as deaconesses for this work.[20] Thus they gave institutional shape to the tale from Luke, which allotted to Mary and Martha of Bethany the twin roles that women made for themselves within the Christian community: the mystic and the minister. The development of these two roles will occupy the bulk of this history. Women maintained a firm hold on the contemplative life through the development of both reclusive and communal (monastic) lifestyles. The feminine apostolate to the poor and the sick has had a more difficult history because of the reluctance of society to recognize the public roles it allotted to women, but it has been maintained firmly as one of the glories of the Catholic sisterhood.

Jesus' disciples may only have intended the radical communal spirit of the Jerusalem church to last for a short period until they saw him again. As the first generation died away and Jesus did not reappear, Christians began to resettle into the world. Epistles attributed to Peter and interpolations into the Pauline corpus reflect an early attempt to reassert a household code formed on more traditional social values. Though it survived and flourished, the "order" of widows was soon subject to restriction in the more conservative atmosphere. Paul (or whoever wrote I Timothy in his name) attempted to limit the number of "true widows" who had a claim on the community's support. They had to be sixty years old or more, an age that put them beyond the strictures of the Augustan marriage laws. They had presumably fulfilled their obligations to their children and could cut their other ties, take vows of chastity, and devote themselves to prayer and good works. The Jerusalem community did not become the model for the churches of the diaspora and fell into deep obscurity after the Jewish war at the end of the first century. The widows, however, survived and their counterparts soon became a fixture in every Christian community.

Nor was experimentation at an end. Paul's voice, despite its volume, did not have the authority in the first century that it later acquired. Christianity was still being made by its believers. In Jerusalem, members of the original community apparently added their commemorative common meal and perhaps other liturgies to their worship at the temple. In time, Christians seem to have enjoyed choices between some sort of temple worship and home ceremonies suited to local conditions. The lack of established structure may have had special appeal for the women among the gentiles who had already partially broken through gender barriers by heading households and running businesses. Lydia, a dealer in purple dye, was successful enough to support a household that formed the core of the church in Philippi, apparently without a husband present.[21] Perhaps she was one of the freedwomen who, in the early Roman Empire, could amass fortunes and undertake business ventures of their own. Wherever Paul went, he converted numbers of leading women and their populous households, which formed a church in themselves and a nucleus for a larger community.[22] Paul's letters never fail to include greetings to women acting as deacons, apostles, or simply "true yokemates" in the field of the faith. There was also Tabitha, a seamstress in Joppa whose disciples appealed to Peter to raise her from the dead because they could not bear her loss.[23]

House churches—communities of Christians in a single household providing a center of worship, study, and hospitality for wandering preachers—flourished until well into the third century, even in Rome. It was an obvious and convenient way to organize a loose network of Christian congregations springing up around the eastern Mediterranean and even to Rome. As late as the fourth century, Jerome could refer to Marcella's *domestica ecclesia*, though probably as a complimentary reference to an outdated practice. The form suited a widely dispersed and insecure missionary church perfectly. It remained practicable in later centuries when Christians were always under threat of a local persecution or where they were neither numerous enough nor wealthy enough to erect public temples.

We know little about what went on in those churches. Certainly, hospitality for wandering preachers figured importantly in their religious life. As they entertained Paul and his friends so must they have entertained many others, women as well as men, who went abroad to preach the word. By the late second century, nervous priests were warning against the scandal of small sects grouped around wandering preachers behind closed doors. The syneisactic unions of women and men, of charismatic preachers and their supporters, excited the worst fears of prescriptive writers. The foundresses probably preached such idiosyncratic versions of the gospel message as still survive among the Gnostic and apocryphal Gospels that grew up in the second and third centuries. Their liturgy would probably have involved some reenactment of central scenes. Jesus had specifically singled out Mary of Bethany's anointment of his feet for commemoration. The common meal, modeled in some manner after the Last Supper, was always a part of Christian worship and well suited to a house church, though it must have lacked the sacramental qualities that eventually came to require a priest.

The house churches were by nature syneisactic. Paul addressed a few husband-and-wife teams but most women leaders seem to have headed their communities alone. We cannot necessarily conclude that they were unmarried. Women and men often devoted themselves to different religious cults; and Christianity, with its demand for exclusivity, must have appealed far less to men with public lives involving the official worship of the emperor than to their wives. Roman women were often members and patrons of clubs, generally family associations, which strengthened the informal associations among kindred and members of the same households. Such associations, through cultic functions, linked members of various social strata. Paul maintained hopefully that the unbelieving husband might be sanctified by the believing wife.

His communities were ready to think even more radically. Paul's famous Letter to the Corinthians casts an oblique light on the passionate discussions of new social relationships between women, men, women and men, slaves and masters, parents and children. In response to Chloe's inquiries, Paul cautiously suggested that married people might periodically abstain from sexual relations, by mutual consent if that did not tempt either party to look elsewhere for satisfaction.[24] These first Christians, like their apostle, were readily persuaded that the time for marriage and giving in marriage was past, that women would soon come to curse the fate that gave them children in that terrible time.

> The appointed time has grown very short. From now on, let those who have wives live as though they had none . . . for the form of this world is passing away. I want you to be free from anxieties. The unmarried man is anxious about the affairs of the Lord, how to please the Lord; but the married man is anxious about worldly affairs, how to please his wife and his interests are divided. And the unmarried woman or girl is anxious about the affairs of the Lord, how to be holy in body and spirit; but the married woman is anxious about worldly affairs, how to please her husband. I say this for your own benefit, not to lay any restraint upon to you, but to promote good order and to secure your undivided devotion to the Lord.[25]

For unmarried people he was willing to consider permanent celibacy, while stressing that he had no direct command from the Lord. He suggested that widowed women might be happier if they remained unmarried.[26] His caution and reluctance to encourage too radical a rejection of the old boundaries comes through clearly in his ambiguous endorsement of continence for men: "If anyone thinks that he is not behaving properly toward his betrothed and his passions are strong and it has to be, let him do as he wishes; let them marry, it is no sin. But whoever is firmly established in his heart to keep her as his betrothed, he will do well. So that he who marries his betrothed does well; and he who refrains from marriage will do better."[27]

Some scholars have interpreted this passage to mean that there were people in Corinth practicing marriage without sexual relationships or living together unmarried in chaste restraint. Certainly, the women and men who formed one of the first Christian congregations known to us outside the Gospels were engaged in a radical debate concerning the structure of their most intimate personal relationships. Some apparently attempted to practice a form of free love, others to keep themselves from marriage altogether, and still others to form a spiritual union free of physical expression. Paul condemned the first group and cautioned the rest that the ordinary sexual unions of married people were acceptable if carried on with mutual respect and affection. For the heroic few he endorsed but did not initiate the ideal of a syneisactic relationship unfettered by conjugal concerns.

Christianity was widely viewed as a religion of women and slaves, a denigrating caricature but one it shared with the imperial government itself. The Christian "household" was more radical than Caesar's not only because it was based on syneisactism but also because the chaste partnership of women and men often joined upper-class women and lower-class or slave men in religion. It required a rejection of sexuality in the sense that it was not compatible with either the exclusivity or the hierarchy that characterized sexual relationships. At the end of the century, the emperor Domitian tried persecution to stem a tide that swept women, children, and slaves against the ancestral altar of the *paterfamilias*. Christian legend maintains that Domitian's nightmare was realized in the syneisactic union of one of his own relatives, Domitilla, with a pair of male slaves who had converted her to Christianity. Further, the same virgin convinced her betrothed not to consummate their marriage but to join her and the slaves in death rather than to sacrifice virginity.

Women practiced Christianity without need of the clerical hierarchy when the occasion demanded it. A letter attributed to Clement of Rome describes common prayers and scripture readings, rites of exorcism women gave one another.[28] Despite his uneasiness, he was willing to leave them to pursue a full religious life with all the trappings of prophecy, common prayer, teaching, charity, and even ritual if they lacked male partners. Indeed, in writing to male virgins who worked as itinerant preachers, the author advised that, rather than expose themselves to temptation, they should leave women without clerical guidance if there were no men in the community already. Ironically, his caution may well have fostered the spread of female-headed communities.

In sum, the women of the house churches may have been married: some, no doubt, were clerical wives or widows consecrated to chastity. Some of them could have been virgins who had never subjected themselves to husbands and escaped the attention of the law, or penitents, or women estranged from their husbands or abandoned by them. We can never know. But among these congregations composed of widows and their female relatives, friends, dependents, and slaves, we should seek the first communities of celibate women in Christendom.

Sexual renunciation was the key to the new time, with women acting as a metaphor for all the humble and meek destined to inherit the earth. The unblemished integrity of the Christian virgin became emblematic for the victories of martyrs. Although clerical writers attributed the victories of virgin martyrs over their pain and suffering to the glory of God rather than to female strength, they recognized that the virgins' sacrifice won them a special place among the teachers of the new religion. Virgins, whose refusal to marry put them immediately outside the law, gained freedom to preach and minister to their communities, to lead the apostolic life. The four prophetic daughters of Philip the Deacon were remembered for centuries as consecrated virgins whose tombs were honored in Asia Minor.[29]

A network of prophets, both female and male, occupied a special place outside the developing hierarchy, preaching and forming ties among scattered communities. They had their bases in the house churches where they received shelter and entrée into the local community. Itinerant preachers living for brief periods of time in the houses of the faithful were complemented by settled persons upon whom the Spirit chose to alight, like the widows of the first two orders. The women, of course, were not included in the developing clergy, which viewed the uncontrolled prophetic mission with deep misgiving. Their claim to continuing revelation from the Holy Spirit was profoundly incompatible with the clerical effort to establish a stable doctrine based on immutable scripture. The idea of virginity as a source of transcendent power providing access to a higher plane of existence derived from these extrascriptural revelations.

How could an androgynous order of charismatic virgins be absorbed into a church where a married clergy exercised authority over a married laity? A syneisactic order would not be vulnerable, as women alone were vulnerable, to charges of hysteria and foolishness. The presence of women among a moral elite clearly threatened much more than the occasional sexual lapse. Virginity broke the continuum of sexuality,

denying the universal definition of women as imperfect men that rendered a balanced and complementary relationship with men ludicrous.
Ancient Greek traditions had always attributed prophetic power to virgins, and the new Christian communities took advantage of the association to develop a theology based on spiritual illumination. Second- and
third-century pagan philosophers tended to separate mind from body,
freeing the soul from its chains of flesh. Cynic and Stoic philosophers
already recognized that the female mind detached from its bodily restrictions might become equal to the male. Philo Judaeus noted that the
empress Livia had become "male in her power of reason."[30] Clement of
Alexandria argued that women were female only in their sexual and
procreative functions but not in their broader humanity.[31]

Although they substituted the excellence of virtue for the rigors of
philosophical training as authority for their ideas, virgins devoted themselves to the study of various devotional books. These would have
included the scriptures and probably apocryphal Gospels as well whose
authors, women or men, were preaching to the celibate communities.
The Apocrypha originated in the second and third centuries and are now
generally recognized as didactic stories written, like many novels in
modern times, as vehicles for theological ideas. The apocryphal Gospels
are the first works to promote the doctrine of the perpetual virginity of
Mary and the idea of her immaculate conception.[32] Belief in the assumption of Mary whole and incorrupt into heaven also inspired to an
extensive literature on her active apostolate after the death of her son.[33]
Mary's obedience to God's will in bearing Jesus, her embrace of the
choice offered by the angel, positions her as the anti-Eve, the virgin
antidote to the curse suffered by the original disobedient mother. It also
poses her as an alternative to the Gnostic Sophia, the divine woman
brought low by her entanglement in procreative desires. This theology
of Mary provides the basis for a more developed doctrine of virginity
rooted in scriptural or quasi-scriptural traditions.

Paul may have tendered his grudging and cautious approval for some
unmarried women to remain as they were only in view of "the impending
distress," but his name was destined to become indissolubly linked to the
virginity movement. The apocryphal Acts of Paul and Thecla endowed
him with a devotion to virginity not apparent in his canonical writings,

though the same romance relates Paul's dismay when asked to countenance Thecla as an apostle. This female rebel, a noble girl supposedly converted by Paul's eloquence to Christianity and the virgin life together, became the model and patron of the new woman. Whether or not the story is in any respect true, there is no question that by the early second century it was being accepted as a model for women determined to embrace the virgin life.[34] Once Paul rejected her fellowship in his apostolate, Thecla cut her hair and dressed like a man. Threatened with martyrdom, she baptized herself in a puddle of water, challenging the newly developing priestly monopoly over the sacraments. Rescued by a miracle, she broadened her teaching mission and traveled as a prophet for many years before exchanging the active life for the contemplative life of a hermit.

The Acts of Paul, Peter, Thomas, Andrew, and John all display a commitment to the superiority of sexual purity over the most pious marriage. Indeed, a passage from the Acts of John (whom tradition associated with the bridegroom at Cana who was supposed to have converted with his wife on seeing the miraculous transformation of the water into wine) contains a diatribe against marriage in condemnation of the flesh and all its works.[35] Similarly, in the Acts of Paul, the apostle preaches a series of thirteen beatitudes of chastity rooted in the brief remarks that Paul actually made in the Letter to the Corinthians. He concludes that there is no salvation without chastity.[36]

The Acts of John, Peter, Paul, Andrew, Thomas, and Xantippe center on female characters and female interests. Most particularly they portray the pursuit of sexual purity, either in the preservation of virginity or the renunciation of conjugal union, as a heroic undertaking, a quest taken up by inspired women.[37] They focus on chastity as the agent of rebellion against the tyranny of husbands and a path of liberation from the "villainous" plots of parents to drive their daughters into marriage.[38] The refusal to bear children is interpreted as obedience to the gospel command to abandon all to follow Jesus—a virtue rather than a misfortune or even a vice. Not infrequently, the stories feature happy endings for the heroines and violent punishments for their would-be seducers. In brief, the apocryphal Gospels, though generally orthodox in theology, were radical in their social teachings. The message that women, for the sake of chastity, should deny themselves children, defy their parents, and even forsake their husbands struck a potentially mortal blow to the ancient order.

This was a world in which the state reinforced the power of parents or guardians to put women into marriage beds. Inevitably, sexuality itself became revolting to many women. If fastidious men could be disgusted by the physical realities of sex and childbirth, how could women not recoil from a procreative process over which they had no control? The obedience expected of women included their willing participation in the dissolute lives pursued by their husbands, as one Roman woman threatened with martyrdom for refusing that demand knew. What murderous nightmares must have haunted women forced into unwanted fidelity on the one hand and unwilling vice on the other?[39]

Gnostic prophets spoke to this revulsion and fear, proclaiming the flesh itself evil. Their illuminating myth centered on the fall of the divine Sophia (Wisdom) from a higher plane because she had been seduced and raped into the toils of the flesh.[40] The Gnostic message, never intended to be clear to the uninitiated, veered between revulsion for the seductive flesh of women and the hope of undoing Sophia's tragedy. Women were attracted to their sects partly because they offered an active role for the initiates of both genders and possibly because revulsion for the seductions of the flesh was even stronger among them than among the misogynistic preachers who taught that woman was a creation of the devil along with the lower half of man.[41] The extreme asectic sect called Encratites, who welcomed women as leaders, actively worked to end the world of the flesh by refusing to procreate. Their women preachers probably saw men as the principal instrument of flesh, just as men saw women. In any case, they all considered the virgin life a path to a higher stage of existence, an overwhelming justification for women's rejection of marriage and motherhood.[42] They argued that total purity would disentangle trapped souls, reuniting them with the light. Other Gnostics argued that the Resurrection would abolish the procreative works of women or that true marriages would join only the souls of the partners, every sexual act being an act of adultery.[43]

In the middle of the second century, Irenaeus, bishop of Lyons, testified that groups of women from every walk of life were leaving their homes, parents, and husbands—too literally interpreting the gospel commands. Sometimes they went with prophets like Marcus, who was seducing women from the bishop's own congregation. Irenaeus accused him of sexual misconduct ranging even to the use of love potions on women who resisted his blandishments. He said that other Gnostics persuaded women to leave their husbands by promising that they would live as brother and sister while spreading the gospel.[44] Irenaeus, naturally, did not believe that such a promise would be kept, and there is no reason why a modern reader should not be equally skeptical of the intentions of self-appointed cult leaders toward their female companions. Clearly, however, the real risk that bothered the good bishop was not the risk that women ran of sexual exploitation but the risk to the reputation of men like himself if non-Christians should confuse them with men like Marcus. Beyond that, he expressed the fear of a community without any gender barriers.

As the second century ended, the clergy made a concerted attack on the prophets, especially where they produced revelations that altered established doctrine. Preachers like Montanus, who relied on the ongoing revelatory action of the Holy Spirit, were condemned as heretics. Syneisactism, made particularly noticeable by the propensity of male and female prophets to travel together and to regard one another as equals in the prophetic life, became a tentative indicator of heresy. Nevertheless, women and their chaste male partners were making a place for themselves in Christian churches everywhere. In the Syrian church, the syneisactism of the original community had been maintained by requiring both women and men to join a vow of sexual purity to their catechismal promises. Tertullian (ca. 200) often noted the numbers of celibate women in the African church and advised men who wished to enter into living arrangements with virgins to choose from among those who were aged and ugly. Origen in Alexandria is said to have castrated himself so as to include women among his philosophy students without the reproach of seducing them. Having transcended the limitations of gender, such women could join men in a public life forbidden to ordinary married women.

Sexual renunciation was not necessarily bound to the repertory of self-inflicted torments later associated with asceticism. In fact, the virginity movement was primarily an urban women's phenomenon. Its

practitioners did not renounce their property or live in solitary meditation. Instead a network of women lived in their own homes, possibly
forming small house churches with virgin slaves or other dependents.
They scandalized clergymen like Cyprian of Carthage and Clement of
Alexandria with their sociability. They went about the city in their litters
on charitable and devotional rounds, stopping to chat in the marketplace
and sometimes sharing a small picnic at some church where they were
working. They met for prayer, discussion, and possibly common meals
on special occasions. In such communities, some rule of life probably
prevailed, with the older women training the younger in the theory and
practice of virginity. By 200, a prescriptive literature was accumulating
addressed to a defined group of women expected to preserve their
virginity permanently. But no evidence suggests that they were recognized as an order in the sense that they took formal vows, lived in
common, or sacrificed their private property. No one describes any
special costume, though they were urged to veil themselves as was the
custom among matrons.

It is likely that virgins even conducted formal discussions similar to
the fictional encounter related by an early-fourth-century bishop,
Methodius (d. 312), for the edification of a community of virgins in
Lycia.[45] *The Symposium* represents a synthesis of the various doctrines
concerning virginity that would ultimately be incorporated into the
orthodox canon. Ten virgins living in their own homes in a mythical city
gather in the garden of Arete (virtue) to meet with the legendary Thecla
and discourse in the manner of Plato's *Symposium* on the subject of
virginity. Each woman gives a brief speech expanding on some area of
the subject. Among other things, they demonstrate that the virginal life
is the culmination of the new Christian age, superseding the old pagan
family and its procreative purposes. The evening ends with a hymn in
praise of virginity, expressing the women's anticipation of the glorious
day when they will lead all humanity in procession to God's heavenly
court, singing the new song that only they can sing and only God can
hear.

Believing themselves to be so exalted, virgins refused to be silent and
submissive. They boasted of their own superiority to married people.
They advertised their state by dressing in an eccentric manner, refusing
traditional women's veils and sometimes actually adopting male clothes

and hairstyles. They behaved as though they had the dignity of men. Paul sarcastically suggested that if women did not wish to veil themselves when praying and prophesying in church, they might go all the way and shear their heads. By the end of second century, this was no longer a joke. Tertullian complained that virgins refused the widows' veil and tried to argue that Thecla was not a viable model for other women. The virgins answered that Paul's command to women did not apply to virgins. Hardly able to contain his indignation, Tertullian asked whether this perverse logic would oblige male virgins to veil themselves because they were no longer men.[46] He saw their refusal to veil themselves as an effort to claim prerogatives of a sacerdotal nature associated with men alone.[47]

Tertullian had good reason for wanting to anchor the spirit firmly in the body and therefore in physical sex differences. In Gnostic circles, hostility to procreativity had sometimes resulted in the idea that only men could be saved. This notion was countered, however, by the idea that deserving women would be reincarnated as men.[48] In the apocryphal Gospel of Thomas, Jesus refused Peter's demand that Mary leave them: "I myself shall lead her in order to make her male, so that she too may become a living spirit resembling you males. For every woman who will make herself male will enter the Kingdom of Heaven."[49] Ideas about the relationship of body and spirit swirled through such circles, suggesting that the body was not stable but fluid, malleable to the will of the spirit. The ascetic ideal, rooted in the rigors of body building through fasting, spiritual exercise, and discipline began to produce limitless fantasies.

If women ceased to live and act as women, many believed, they could move along the sexual continuum and begin functioning as men. The role of women in prophecy reached its peak in the sect associated with Montanus, whose rigorous teachings and belief in ongoing revelation were ultimately condemned as heretical. Like so many of the Christians excluded from the developing orthodox church, he encouraged the equal participation of women on a syneisactic basis. The prophetesses Priscilla and Maximilla, who claimed to be virgins (though their critics said they were runaway wives), pursued "manly" careers as wandering prophets for many years—not only manly but Christlike.[50] Priscilla had a vision of Christ as a woman who endowed her with wisdom. Epiphanius of Cyprus defended the priesthood of women among the Montanists as an expression of the mystical union of male and female expressed in

Galatians.[51] Thus at the very moment when the clergy was within reach of a monopoly over church leadership, Tertullian feared that virgins might grasp at their sacramental roles. He fiercely castigated those women who followed the model of Thecla and claimed, by her example, the right to baptize.[52]

"Clement of Rome" (or the author of the two letters attributed to him) may have feared more than scandal or sexual misconduct when he tried to prevent the union of male and female virgin prophets. Tertullian knew of a case where a virgin under twenty years of age had been admitted into the order of widows. He thought that monstrous.[53] The whole shape of the developing church was at issue. At the end of the second century, Cyprian of Carthage knew of a prophetic woman in Cappadocia who claimed the power not only to baptize but also to celebrate the Eucharist.[54] Women led gatherings of the Encratites, organizing fasts and feasts, meals of parched grains and repasts of radishes.[55] Irenaeus of Lyons complained that a prophet named Marcus conducted services with a woman who joined him in some liturgy involving a consecrated chalice.[56] Those consecrated women who became wandering prophets did not necessarily sink into poverty. The widows were a vulnerable middle ground. When they transferred their patronage to prophets, they inflicted heavy losses of prestige as well as wealth upon the clergy.

Tertullian himself established three ranks of virgins. To women who had maintained their physical purity from birth he added those who, like the Syrian converts, embraced "virginity" from the moment of their rebirth in baptism by renouncing sexual relations within marriage and those who turned away from remarriage when widowhood gave them a second chance.[57] His was always a divided voice, torn between stiff traditionalism and the lure of Montanist rigor. Even while he condemned virgins who enrolled in the ranks of widows, he praised widows for "becoming virgins." He was increasingly drawn into the ascetic movement and was personally close to some of its female practitioners. He called them his "best beloved sisters"[58] and "handmaids of the living God, my fellow servants and sisters."[59] He did not completely scorn the idea that in some mystical manner virgins were indeed manly: "For you too, women as you are, have the self-same angelic nature promised as your reward, the self-same sex as men; the self-same advancement to the dignity of judging does the Lord promise you."[60]

The intensity of their religious conviction, their prophetic illuminations, and their bold embrace of a new life far beyond the old social boundaries made the virgins conspicuous in the eyes of the Roman persecutors. In one case, we know that they deliberately singled out a young slave girl for special torment hoping to make an example of Christian cowardice. Eusebius wrote that as she hung on her cross, the martyr Blandina "put on Christ, the invincible athlete."[61] Through a literal act of compassion, she became Christ or at least his avatar and blessed her companions, assuring their redemption as they suffered in turn. At the beginning of the third century, Perpetua, a young mother in prison awaiting her martyrdom, recorded her agonies as she systematically stripped herself of all that had made her a woman. Out of her own sense of loss and fear, she experienced transformation. On the night before her final ordeal she dreamed that she entered the arena to fight and was stripped. "And I became a man."[62] Perpetua's virile career was doomed to extreme brevity, but her prison diary provided inspiration for hundreds of women to follow in her painful footsteps.

Virgin martyrs became emblematic of the Christian opposition to worldly power. But where men tended to see a symbol, women lived the harsh reality of suffering and humiliation. After a century of anarchy, punctuated for the Christians by sporadic outbreaks of persecution, the full power of the empire was restored in the final decades of the third century. The imperial program for reform aimed at restoration of the Roman bureaucracy, the Roman army, and the Roman family. Diocletian's laws tried to freeze everybody in their designated places and ordered them to provide children for their own replacement, reinforcing the ancient Augustan marriage laws. He revived and strengthened emperor worship as a state religion to cement this imposing fabric. After several years of toleration, he launched the Great Persecution.

Despite the tendency of ancient chroniclers to use numbers with abandon, it remains clear that the female victims of the Great Persecution were numerous. Although storytellers tend to choose the most attractive subjects—and virgins in peril always make an attractive subject—we cannot ignore the evidence that consecrated women were a favorite target. They were easily caught since their unmarried state could not be hidden and left them vulnerable to both frustrated suitors and jealous neighbors. Moreover, by example and probably by preaching as well, they were spreading sedition against the foundations of the social system.

Christian tradition translated this last and most determined assault into a struggle between naked, helpless women and armed, vicious men. Smashed and mutilated women, like Agatha with her breasts sliced away and Lucy with her eyes torn out, formed the front line of Christ's army. Imperial decree condemned all women who refused marriage to be raped or sent to a brothel.[63] At Antioch, Eusebius said that the bishop was martyred in company with forty-four priests, seven deacons, forty-two acolytes, fifty-two exorcists, and over a thousand widows.[64] Some of these women were far advanced in age and persuaded their tormentors to spare them from rape out of respect for their own aged mothers. Magna, who skillfully avoided the consummation of her unwanted marriage, died among the two thousand virgin martyrs of Ancyra.[65] Future virgins in a safer world enjoyed the legend of three clever martyrs called Agape, Irene, and Chiona, whose lustful jailor was deluded into raping the sooty pots and pans instead of his virgin captives.[66] Another Christian virgin escaped from a brothel by changing clothes with a male sympathizer. When the trick was discovered, they were martyred together, purity intact.[67]

The stories associated with martyrdom capitalized on the idea of bodily transformation. The dead were joined in legend by heroines whose escapes and rescues remained examples for generations. Soteris, an ancestress of Ambrose of Milan, mutilated herself to escape rape by her executioners. In Rome, a generation or so later, when a memorial to a martyr named Agnes was discovered, an author borrowing the illustrious name of Ambrose of Milan popularized her as a virgin who scorned the lustful advances of a Roman aristocrat for the sake of her purity. The thwarted lover went to Diocletian, who condemned her to a brothel. Happily, just when she was most helpless, her long hair miraculously hardened around her naked body encasing her in an impenetrable sheath. Thus, despite the brutal lust of her enemies, the lamb of God achieved her death still inviolate. Romans knew when they condemned Christian virgins to rape that sexual integrity was the key to the transformation of the suffering body into the redeemed soul.

But Christians understood virginity as a spiritual state that embraced the widows and married people converted to chastity. A woman who retained her purity of mind, even though she had been raped, could not be deprived of her virginity.[68] When a judge threatened the virgin Theodora, martyred in 303, with this penalty, she answered: "I think that you do not understand this thing. God sees our hearts and considers only one thing, the will to remain chaste. If, then, you force me to submit to an outrage, I will have committed no voluntary fault but will have suffered violence. . . . God considers the will, He sees all our thoughts and penetrates them in advance. Therefore, if I am violated yet shall I remain pure."[69]

These stories preserve an authentic atmosphere of terror and oppression. Ultimately, Rome struggled to retain its ancient customs and its ancient social system by ferociously attacking women of every age and condition. The triumphant church was always to honor its virgin martyrs, but the church that Constantine accommodated as part of a new Roman order did not preach the doctrine of "neither male nor female" any more loudly than it opposed slavery. Virgins were indeed to have the place they had seized in the dirt and blood of the arena. But the ultimate lesson of the spirit's triumph over the body was to be turned inside out. Virginity of mind was to construed as total innocence of the truth of a soiled and ugly world and therefore to be protected even more ruthlessly than its physical housing. The church of late antiquity prized its respectability and expected its virgins to act with decorum and humility quite unlike the boldness of the heroic days. But the lives and deaths of the virgin martyrs did not go unnoted. They left a living legacy to their sisters. For some, these are stories of terror and threat but for others, surely, they are stories of victory—stories of women young and old whose courage overcame the mightiest empire in the world.

2

⁘✦⁘

Cult and Countercult

BY THE EARLY second century, temple worship had begun to complement and even displace house churches, and a settled clergy—ultimately
to be modeled on the Roman provincial government—was gaining
authority even over charismatic prophets who continued to be the main-
stays of missionary Christianity. Christian apologists cited pagan charges
that the common meals celebrated by Christians in their homes were
really incestuous and cannibalistic orgies to justify a more public and
decorous Christian worship. Clement of Rome ordered that services be
conducted in a proper and settled manner, by appointed persons in the
temple.[1] Resident clergymen provided cultic functions to sanctify the
ordinary cycles of life as against the ecstatic, free-wheeling prophets.
Gradually, a more public and sanitized liturgy celebrating the Eucharist
supplanted the common meal. By the third century, the sacraments were
taking on liturgical centricity. The priesthood was enhanced while bishops
gained structural authority among priests and linked with one another
by the circulation of prescriptive and informational letters. The sporadic
efforts of pagan persecutors to destroy the religion by targeting its
prelates gave them the additional luster of martyrdom.

The shift out of house churches effectively subordinated all the laity,
virgin and married alike, to the male clergy. Women appear to have
resisted for a variety of reasons. Some women wanted to observe Jewish
laws segregating them during menstruation, pregnancy, and childbirth
and others simply hesitated to leave their homes to participate in church
worship. Perhaps some were unwilling to relinquish their active roles in

34

house churches for a more passive position as spectator to a priestly liturgy. By the third century, however, *The Apostolic Constitutions,* compiled for the general church, insisted that women attend public services in church, rejecting any excuse including menstruation or pregnancy that might separate them from the community or cause them to fail in taking the Eucharist.[2]

The church inexorably headed toward the exclusion of women from clerical functions. Gradually, the baptismal liturgy shifted from immersion of the naked body to the more modest practice of aspersion, sprinkling the head, and deaconesses were deprived of their traditional sacramental role.[3] By the middle of the third century, prophecy was no longer admitted as a valid means of creating new orthodox doctrine. The clergy had become strong enough to challenge the whole prophetic claim to charismatic leadership, saying that it sprang all too often from fraud or hysteria rather than divine revelation. Bishop Cyprian of Carthage referred to the participation of women in orthodox services as though it had long been abandoned.

The Christian religion was not predestined to develop into a single church. Indeed, like most religions then and now, it was far more likely that a common faith would act as a loose net for a wide variety of sects. From the time of Paul forward, the episcopacy set itself to weld diverse communities into a single coherent legion committed to fight and die for one God, one faith, and one church. But the enterprise demanded constant negotiation. Even the surviving sources, heavily skewed as they are to the victorious orthodox clergy, reveal many Christianities contending for followers in the years of the persecutions. Prophets, syneisactic sects, and even, in some respects, martyrs represented a radical church increasingly balanced and restrained by a "respectable" church. None of them were obliged to accept the criteria of orthodoxy—in fact, to do so increased the dangers of martyrdom. Even after the legalization of the religion, dissident groups remained immune to serious coercion. Before the fourth century, the clergy had no means of retaliation against nonconformists except to exclude them from the community, which contradicted their inclusionist goal.

In the Roman Empire, women and men, even married couples, routinely practiced different religions. The segregation of Christian women from Christian men would not therefore be wholly unprecedented. In a letter addressed to male virgins only, "Clement of Rome" forbade his readers to dwell with maidens, or eat or drink with them, or sleep in the same house with unmarried or consecrated women, counseling that even aged or servile women be avoided. For safety's sake, he urged his readers to cover their hands and avert their eyes when preaching or praying in public with women in the congregation. Finally, he insisted that if there were no Christian men in the community to safeguard their virtue, they would do better to leave women altogether without priestly services rather than risk their company.[4] Male fear, whether of scandal or seduction, thus encouraged an independent women's cult toward which many women seem to have naturally gravitated.

The diaconate bridged the sexual hierarchy (which ranked virgins, widows, and wives) and the clerical hierarchy. Justin Martyr bears witness that second-century Christians generally attended simple meetings where they heard inspirational addresses followed by a shared meal of bread and wine in memory of Jesus.[5] Distribution of bread and wine at common meals was assigned not to bishops or priests but to deacons and in some cases deaconesses. The pagan Pliny encountered a community led by two deaconesses who administered just such a simple ceremony.[6] Where it was the practice to reserve portions for absent members of the community, it is highly probable that deaconesses administered this communion to sick or housebound women. Deaconesses instructed women catechumens (candidates for baptism) and performed the sacramental service of baptism since it was considered unfitting for the male clergy to have such intimacy with females, particularly in assisting their total immersion.[7] Thus, in the formative early years, women occupied a small but crucial place within the clergy itself, comparable to noncommissioned officers in the embattled *militia Christi*. The formal consecration of deaconesses placed them firmly under episcopal patronage and discipline.[8] The *Apostolic Constitutions* reserved the office for pure virgins or "at least, a widow but once married, faithful and well-esteemed."[9] This prescription gave bishops the power to determine who was and who was not eligible to be classed as a "true" virgin or widow.

As the church developed, unity became an overriding concern. The Christian literature of the second and third centuries increasingly concentrated on the problems of doctrinal, liturgical, and social deviation.

This pressure may have grown from a need to present a united face to persecutors, but it could be argued that unity also heightened the likelihood of persecution. In any case, the clergy moved toward the establishment of a governing hierarchy formed from a clerical elite. The reasons for the exclusion of women and the process of its execution remain deeply obscure. Because women acted as cultic leaders in the ancient world, we cannot simply ascribe the development to unexamined tradition. But ancient cults led by priestesses tended to be segregated from those led by priests, so that the Christian leaders' vision of a unified and hierarchical church may have ruled out women clergy simply because they had determined not to allow a segregated system. This decision might explain the rigor with which the clergy came to attack the syneisactic aspects of the virginity movement.

The renunciation of sexual activity pointed to the development of two hierarchies—one based on ministerial functions and one based on degree of moral perfection—that could have evolved as two different churches. While men enjoyed functional orders from bishop through priest, deacon, and layman, women were ranked as virgins, widows, and wives. Male virgins enjoyed an anomalous position in that they could occupy a place in either hierarchy. The system bred contradictions: male priests might be, as married men, ranked as inferior to female virgins, while male virgins, as laymen, might be inferior to male priests. Moreover, if an ordained male virgin was the highest Christian ideal and virginity was admitted to transcend gender roles, there would seem to be no logical way to bar female virgins from ordination. The clergy, therefore, sought to ensure that women did not transcend their gender through the virginity movement.

Confrontation, however, was not courted by anyone. For a long time, Christian women who enjoyed wealth and status in the urban milieu where the virginity movement had its roots seem to have pursued their own religious callings without much interference from the clergy beyond the occasional prescriptive essay. Within the context of the house churches, they were not dependent on the presence of priests. According to Justin Martyr, Christian women were recognized as orthodox preachers.[10] At the end of the second century, Clement of Alexandria powerfully defended their teaching against the criticism of pagans, because he saw that it enabled women—slaves or their mistresses—to spread the faith in private work quarters.[11] In this setting, a woman could simply form a congregation in her own household and operate without reference to the clergy.

But Christian clergymen, like pagan men, could not view women's authority or women's bonding, or the special union of mistress and slave (male or female), without anxiety. They policed virgins, widows, women living in chaste marriages, and women living with pagan husbands as best they could. On the one hand, clerics warned that the ill-considered fervor of emotional women might provoke a general persecution. On the other, despite the evidence to the contrary, they claimed that an unsupported woman under pagan attack might collapse, losing her own soul and shaming the Christian community. Whether they took all these reasons seriously or not, they certainly did not want to lose women's financial and social contributions. They had no wish to exclude women from the clergy only to find that they had created a separate sect.

The free movement of women who simply desired not to marry, to live alone or together with other women and pursue a vocation of charity and religious devotion in the midst of normal urban life, may have scandalized pagans and provoked persecution. It definitely scandalized male clerics and provoked their resentment. Even women who kept decorously to their houses entertained a regular stream of visitors including itinerant prophets and female teachers. It is unlikely that anything happened at those meetings beyond the regular gatherings of women with their deaconesses and peers, which earlier writers had prescribed to keep them from establishing syneisactic relationships. But the nervous observer who had excluded himself from their community began to fear that they were practicing divination, learning charms and incantations, and carrying on unimaginable liaisons with one another and with the disreputable prophets who came and went in their houses.[12]

Faced with the growing danger of persecution, the clergy devoted its efforts to minimizing Christian differences from prevailing moral standards. It promoted the ideal of a Christian family, sober, loving, and virtuous, where adultery and child exposure were unknown.

[Christians] marry, like everyone; they beget children but they do not destroy their offspring. They have a common table, but not a common bed. They are in the flesh but they do not live after the flesh. They pass their days on earth, but they are citizens of heaven. They obey the prescribed laws and at the same time surpass the laws by their lives. . . . To sum up all in one word—what the soul is in the body, that are Christians in the world.[13]

The ideal of bringing Christian and pagan values into conformity pressured women to move out of the public sphere of church governance and the apostolate, where their appearance often scandalized pagan men. Following Paul's lead, the clergy counseled women to express their faith through their traditional family roles. It cultivated an ideal of marriage as a conjugal union based on affection. Jesus himself promoted a conjugal bond that required a man to forsake his parents and cleave to his wife in an indissoluble bond of one flesh, one bone. Christian women married to pagan men were instructed to try to please their men and attract their affection within the bounds of decency, even to the extent of wearing makeup and seductive clothing. Christian men were encouraged to prefer their wives' company to that of their cronies. Jesus, to the consternation of his apostles, firmly prohibited men from divorce, except in cases of adultery. Women, of course, never had the legal power to initiate divorce, but Paul discouraged women in Corinth who appear to have been leaving their husbands on the grounds that the descent of the spirit had freed them from carnal commitments.

A letter to the Corinthian community by Clement of Rome confirmed the tendency of "Paul's" Pastoral Letters to restore traditional male authority to Christian families. Clement rebuked wives committing sedition against their husbands, threatening them with the fate of Lot's wife.[14] Clement, like the authors of the Pastoral Letters and the household code of 1 Peter, seems to have envisioned a Christian society in which a married clergy would guide a married laity. Husbands would instruct wives and parents would supervise children. The equalizing of genders and social status would be left to the realm of the spirit. Presumably a sort of "love patriarchalism" would rely on the leaven of Christian charity to lighten the burdens of social inequality by integrating it with an ideal of spiritual equality. In brief, a restored patriarchy would be softened by a benevolent paternalism.

Most women, after all, continued to marry and have children, and they profited from the new conjugal ideal advanced by writers like Clement of Alexandria. He lent an air of romance to the ideal of moral equality between married partners and to the vision of virtuous companionship that would woo men away from the temptations of banquets and women from the society of those old crones he so distrusted. Clement scorned the Encratites, the sect that urged self-control and self-mortification, equating them with the hypocrites in the gospel who called Jesus a wine-bibber.[15] Even the orthodox celibates seemed to him to be loveless folk who "let the fires of charity die out."[16]

Christian marriage did reinforce a certain degree of social leveling, which offered advantages to upwardly mobile women as well as men. Despite legal restrictions, slaves were sometimes emancipated as the prelude to marriage with their owners. Women who were of free status but lacking in wealth might prosper by marrying slaves who had accumulated wealth or power by attachment to a great household. Christians spoke with some passion in defense of a marriage of shared love and faith regardless of social barriers—a position demanding courage, considering that the law forbade such misalliances.

Thus the clerical hierarchy began to reintegrate the partially segregated communities of devout women with the larger church. In some areas, churches were constructed with separate galleries for women. It is hard to know whether the prescription in the *Apostolic Constitutions* that women in their ranks (virgins, widows, and wives) should enter church separately from men sprang from a fear of mixing the sexes or a desire to honor women. Clement of Alexandria urged husbands and wives to attend together in partnership, apparently forsaking the idea of physical separation in church. He also noted that women used the churches for gatherings associated with charitable enterprises. Brief glimpses, accidentally preserved, of an idealized Christian society in an age of persecution suggest that women played a larger role in the communal life and worship than we generally suppose. From the beginning, Paul imagined women praying and prophesying in the churches. The prophetic role of Peter's first two orders of widows was apparently still active in Tertullian's African church, where the revelations of a female prophet followed the Sunday liturgy of the male clergy.[17]

Many women may have accommodated themselves to the clergy and its sacraments without really noticing the evolution of their own subordination. If they were wealthy, they could continue to command the respect of their priests. If they were not blatantly heretical, they could freely express their opinions without fear of retaliation. If they were heretical, they could leave the community. If they were martyrs, their courage excused any prior impertinences.

The sexual hierarchy, however, was apparently unshakable, despite the clergy's lack of enthusiasm for its claims. The order of true widows predated the Epistle to Timothy. The author sought to restrict the conditions of membership to elderly and well-tested women to limit an option that was all too popular. Perhaps he feared that the presence in the Christian community of so many women eager for personal liberation from marriage gave credence to pagan charges that they were being seduced away from their husbands. At the turn of the first century, "Clement of Rome" criticized female virgins who lived chastely on their own because they habitually met together to "gossip and chat." He characterized their religious activities as masks for idleness and unwarranted curiosity.[18]

Ignatius, who was destined to perish in the persecution of A.D. 110, expressed the opinion that those who had the gift to remain chaste outside marriage must be allowed to do so. He was aware that, in countenancing a group of unmarried widows and virgins, he was opening the door to women who could neither be instructed nor controlled by their husbands. But he was anxious to assert episcopal control over the widows and virgins who, on every hand, were busy with pious and charitable works. He admonished his congregation at Philadelphia: "let not the widows be wanderers about, nor fond of dainties, nor gadders from house to house; but let them be like Judith, noted for seriousness and like Anna, eminent for sobriety."[19] Elsewhere he expressed himself even more explicitly against chaste celibates for their pride and their boasts of moral superiority over their married fellows, particularly among the emerging clerical hierarchy.[20] The Pastoral Letters attributed to Paul sounded the same note: women who profess religion must be modest.[21] Older women must be reverent, not slandering nor drunk, but sensible, domestic and chaste, kind and submissive.[22] If churchmen agreed to recognize and even honor women who had freed themselves from the responsibilities of their gender, they demanded in return that the women make themselves inconspicuous—quiet, modest, and veiled.

Third-century virgins experimented with the claim that their purity transcended gender and transformed them into functional men. This formulation served well enough for women like Perpetua, whose "manhood" would be tested against wild beasts in martyrdom. But should gender really be reduced to an allegorical conceit, some wondered. If virile women lived like men, then why should they not carry out the functions of men in the church? Theologians were already struggling with the question of whether or not a priest's sacramental virtue depended on his personal morality. If manhood itself depended on spiritual and moral values, however they might be defined, then the priesthood must be open to "men" of either sex. This question underlies many of the doctrinal quarrels of the third and fourth centuries, which ultimately led the church to seal the soul into its gendered casing eternally with the doctrine of the resurrection of the body.

When the virgins of his church in Africa refused to veil themselves because they claimed that Paul's command laid upon women did not apply to them, Tertullian responded sarcastically that he might as well demand that male virgins veil themselves as women. But this pretense that the virgins were simply playing at role reversals masked their real ambition to abandon roles altogether. If all the virgins were set apart in a third gender of their own, the married clergy who served them faced the threat of being downgraded to the lowest rank in the sexual scale. So strong was the growing sentiment in favor of celibacy that clerics themselves had to struggle against the demands of some of their radical communicants that they put aside their wives.[23] They could envisage the sexual hierarchy as a ladder to be mounted. Tertullian still spoke in an orthodox voice when he argued against giving virgins the responsibility of teaching and counseling women, which had traditionally been reserved for deaconesses. He felt that only true widows "who have travelled down the whole course of probation whereby a female can be tested" should take up the task. "So true is this that nothing in the way of public honor can be permitted to a virgin."[24]

Tertullian's solution confirmed virginity as woman's highest aspiration but deprived the virgin of active engagement in the world. Despite his passionate commitment to marital partnership in faith, clerical wives would also be deprived of a pastoral role. At the same time, widows would gain a powerful inducement not to remarry. Starting with Paul, the Fathers who addressed the subject found it difficult to accept the idea of second marriages. They tended to think that chaste widowhood cooperated with God's plan in taking away the spouse. Nor did they want to encourage widows to enter a second marriage at the expense of the children of the first. Tertullian, driven into a frenzy by virgins who joined the order of widows, was even more deeply outraged by the thought of "digamy," a second marriage, which seemed to him nothing less than adulterous given his faith that the original partner still lived in heaven.

It was not a frivolous puritanism that compelled Tertullian to reiterate so obsessively that a virgin is still a woman, subject to the disciplines imposed on women, and to deny virgins public distinction so fiercely. He may have typified the clergy, torn between his attraction to the radical Montanists' uncompromising love of purity and his clerical suspicion of the temptations offered by women. These same bishops who were narrowing their roles in the hierarchy loved and admired their chaste sisters. They had opted for a church that strove to save sinners in the mundane tumble of the world, not the ethereal spaces where virginity crowned an elite who had transcended the fragile senses of men. Their deepest hearts were stirred by virginity as by martyrdom, but their ordinary senses were alert to the snares and delusions of daily life.

Virgins and honorary virgins had their own ideas about their status. They saw themselves transformed and lifted beyond the constrictions of the gender system. They dreamed of winning the triumphal garland as soldiers or athletes in the arena. Some consecrated women apparently felt that, having transcended their physiological differences from men, they could break down all gender barriers. Tertullian himself, in his struggle against "digamy" did not find the traditional sexual division of labor worthy of much respect except in the administration of sacraments. He had no sympathy with men who argued that they needed the domestic labor of women or with women who sought the protection of men by setting up syneisactic households. He refused to concede that any degree of sexual purity could release women from the disabilities of their sex. After much struggle, he borrowed a new metaphor from the family hierarchy that turned the sexual hierarchy into a Moebius strip: "Be veiled, virgin! . . . for you are wedded to Christ. To him, you have surrendered your body. Act as becomes your husband's discipline."[25]

The bridal allegory pinned consecrated virgins to their sexual natures. It joined first to last forever: virgins and wives were one, at the bottom and at the top of the sexual hierarchy, subjected firmly to the decorum imposed on matrons. Moreover, as the attack on prophecy gained ground, it offered a means for interposing clerical men, as representatives of Jesus, between his brides and their spouse. In the course of the third century, bishops assumed a sort of wardship over this harem of virgin brides. The imposition of the veil came to entail a liturgy of consecration that gave virginity and widowhood institutional definition. Women in the sexual hierarchy were no longer simply free of sexual obligations by their own choice. Still worse, if virginity was a state of mind that might be enjoyed by chaste widows and rebellious wives, it followed in the opinion of the Fathers that it might be lost by behavior unbecoming to a virgin. Thus, a bishop could exert regulatory authority over them. A generation or so after Tertullian, Cyprian of Carthage was still haranguing the impudent virgins of the African church to dress and act as became true virgins, to eschew the general bawdry of weddings, to stop flaunting their bodies among men at the fashionable morning bath hours, to refrain from abusing their freedom from the mastery of husbands and the burdens of children.[26]

Virginity lost its transformative power when virgins were thus reduced to allegorical brides. At the same time, consecrated women gained recognition as a discreet order with a constrained but real public role in the developing church. They maintained their charitable activity and probably continued to teach though not in the prophetic mode. Their careers as martyrs had barely begun by the late third century. If they had once believed that the virginal state would wipe out the barriers between male and female or would make them "men," they were disabused as far as any clerical function was concerned. While the clergy gradually conceded that sexual purity was the apex of spirituality, it restricted the liberty appropriate to true virgins. It threatened women who failed to conform with the retaliatory violence of men whose lust might be aroused by their beauty.[27] It warned against even more devastating psychological violation, the loss of that purity of mind which defended their spiritual citadels. Third-century prescriptive literature thus gendered virginity female. Male virgins were absorbed into the clerical hierarchy and enjoyed no special state, no consecration, and no regulation beyond restrictions on their fraternization with virgin women.

If many women left the church in frustration or joined with sympathetic men in syneisactic movements or even attempted to form isolated female sects, our sources have not remembered them. The negotiations that assured celibate consecrated women their special place of honor within the Christian church proceeded in the context of the persecutions. The very bishops who insisted on discipline and decency were stout companions who went with their virgin flocks into that final struggle. That is the truth we cannot forget as they could not forget it. Blood sealed their union. The brides saw their husband all too soon and the guardians were swiftly called to account. In the end, the concept of the bride of Christ was a paradox. It subordinated virgins to their female gender, but it allegorically raised them to the rank of imperial consort, high above the bishops who sought to control them. Moreover, as in any family, love tempered power.

Diocletian's Great Persecution proved finally that the Christians could not be extirpated by violence. In the next generation, their friend and ally Constantine triumphed over his rivals for the empire and not only recognized Christianity as a lawful faith but gave it preference over its religious rivals as well. The dangers of persecution were over, but the struggle between the church and the state, between the clergy and the family, between factions of all sorts, had only been translated to a new and more sophisticated plane. The episcopacy welcomed the privileges and immunities offered by Christian emperors but refused to surrender institutional and doctrinal integrity. Clerics fiercely resisted absorption into the Roman state and the subordination of religious concerns to political priorities. In addition, doctrinal struggles repeatedly divided the Christian community so that every bishop needed powerful allies from the Roman ruling classes to make his view prevail.

The gender gap between Christian women and pagan men became a generation gap in the conversion process. Under the pagan empire, aristocratic and wealthy women were among the most prominent members of the church. The men of the great senatorial families, however, still tied their privileged public life to old pagan ceremonials and offices. They did not uniformly change their faith until Theodosius outlawed all pagan practices at the end of the fourth century. At the same time, many great senatorial families were headed by women, owing to a birth rate favorable to females and a death rate unfavorable to men as the barbarian invasions increased in violence. These women apparently tried in vain to break men's monopoly on public life. The *Historia Augusta* accuses them of forming a "little senate house of women." A law of 370 forbade women who had subsidized the public games to appear with praetorian insignia as men customarily did, which suggests that women were not only performing the civic duties owed by their absent men but also expected to enjoy the public honors associated with them.

The church, in contrast, offered aristocratic women opportunities for influence, intellectual engagement, social service, and experiments in lifestyle as episcopal partisans. Extrasacramental liturgies and devotions attracted their attention. In 311–312, Lucilla, an imposing matron in the diocese of Carthage, introduced the practice of kissing the Eucharist before taking it into her mouth. Helena introduced the pilgrimage as a female complement to the imperial progress. The pilgrim Egeria, in about 400, recorded numerous ceremonial "recipes" for her sisters at home during her pilgrimage to the Holy Land. She noted that the virgin Icelia introduced the custom of celebrating the feast of the Presentation of the Blessed Virgin with candles. Helena's celebrated journey was believed to have culminated in the miraculous discovery of Christendom's greatest relic, the true cross. Virgins chanting in processions became part of episcopal ceremonials, as in Rouen, where the virginal community carried a cross in procession, singing psalms in unison as they advanced to welcome the relics of a saint into their city.[28] This type of public display gave them a quasi-clerical place in the church order, which reached its apogee in Constantinople when the virgin empress Pulcheria, regent for her minor brother, led her community of virgins to communion at the high altar, maintaining that their virginity freed them from the ancient prohibition against women in the sanctuary.

Church politics lured them with the excitement of palace intrigue and intellectual stimulation. Consecrated virgins and widows particularly, a group distinguished in episcopal letters as canonesses, apparently an honorific term, busied themselves in the controversies of the day. Women did not align themselves consistently on one side or the other. Around 370, when the empress Justina attempted to force the orthodox to give up one church to the Arians, Bishop Ambrose of Milan led his consecrated women in demonstrations of resistance that fell just short of violence. The opinionated Melania the Elder put both her fortune and her influence on his side in the same controversy. In the Holy Land, she took up the leadership of the Nicene forces against the Arian bishop of Alexandria, even braving arrest and physical abuse.[29] She and her friend Rufinus, who lived syneisactically on the Mount of Olives, later became even more heatedly involved in the controversy over the ideas of Origen, which put them at odds with their old friends Jerome and Paula. Melania even returned to Rome to support the cause against the opposition organized by Jerome's friend Marcella. Ironically, both women died in the sack of Rome in 410.

The widow Olympias was a friend and champion of three bishops of Constantinople who listened to her advice on ecclesiastical affairs in exchange for generous donations.[30] When she was widowed, at about age thirty, Bishop Nectarius ordained her as a deaconess, helping her to consecrate her life and fortune to the church and resist the emperor's demand that she remarry. She built a house of virgins separated from the episcopal palace by a single wall and organized a group of consecrated women who supported Bishop John Chrysostom of Constantinople in his stormy quarrels with the empress Eudoxia. He addressed his tract on widowhood to her.[31] Olympias followed Chrysostom into exile after his friends were blamed for the burning of the cathedral in Constantinople, and she spent her last years laboring for his restoration with every prelate and royal person she knew.[32] He praised her as a tower of strength "without thrusting yourself into the forum or occupying public centers of the city."[33]

The single concept that appears to have attracted all the active religious women was the power of celibacy to free them from the disabilities of womanhood. Within the greatest of the Roman families a silent struggle raged. Parents, especially fathers, still wished their daughters to marry, to provide alliances and secure the future of their dynasties by having their grandchildren. Bishops and other clergymen began to write biographies and encomia to women who resisted. Parental pressure forced Melania the Younger to marry Pinian. Her biographer wrote that on her wedding night she offered her fortune to her husband and promised to be his personal slave in exchange for her physical integrity. Although he rejected her pleas and insisted that they provide heirs for each of their families, Pinian (who later became a bishop himself) was apparently an advanced thinker and did not require the heir to be a son, for he stipulated only two children.[34] After the children died, he could no longer withstand Melania's "seductions" and agreed to a life of mutual continence. They traveled around the Mediterranean world together for some years before they finally entered separate monastic establishments. Jerome's friend Paula was stoned in the street at the funeral of her daughter Blaesilla, who died of excessive self-mortification as a consecrated widow. Paula had four daughters before she closed her childbearing period with the production of a son. Jerome praised her because the daughters became virgins and the mothers of virgins, breaking the pride of a consular house by ending its antique lineage. Macrina had the support of her mother and brothers in her ambition to remain a virgin, but her father forced her to agree to a betrothal. She escaped only when her fiancé died and she maintained that her betrothal had legally constituted a marriage. As a virgin widow, she claimed that she was protected from forced remarriage.[35] Palladius praised Magna's guile in avoiding the consummation of her marriage until her husband died.[36]

It should be clear from this record that women did not join the virginity movement for the purpose of withdrawal from the world. Through most of the fourth century, moreover, male authorities enthusiastically supported roles in public life for consecrated women. Constantine's mother, the widowed Helena, was the first of a line of empresses to use elements of Christianity to shape an active queenly office. During her celebrated pilgrimage to the Holy Land, she paid special honors to communities of virgins. Constantine was quick to abrogate the Augustan marriage laws and bestow the right of three children on women committed to virginity or chaste widowhood. Damasus, the first aristocratic priest to become bishop of Rome, was famous for his ability to flatter matrons. The church profited enormously as the extravagant charity of consecrated women dissipated vast fortunes and brought the great aristocratic lineages of Rome to an end. Julian the Apostate tried to regain this wealth by marrying them off, but the strength of the movement overwhelmed him. Similarly, when the Christian Theodosius tried to prevent the widow Olympias from diverting her fortune to the church by ordering her to remarry, the combined pressure of the celibate community and the bishop of Constantinople ensured that he soon forgave her. By the end of the century, the Theodosian Code exacted the death penalty from any person who attempted to force a consecrated woman to marry.[37] By the sixth century, Justinian had confirmed that unmarried women who had reached the age of twenty-five were free to control their own property.[38]

Few of the articulate and brilliant bishops of the age were immune to the ideal of purity, the lure of a spiritual victory over the domination of flesh. Ambrose, Augustine, Jerome, John Chrysostom, and Basil of Caesarea, to name only a handful, acknowledged that women "led them in the high emprise."[39] Jerome, who alone of the group was not a bishop, advised Eustochium to pay heed to their authority and to train herself from the works of Cyprian, Damasus, and Ambrose. But he was equally swift to acknowledge his own debt to their instruction. It was perhaps a mixed blessing that these same men invested so many of their own spiritual aspirations in the purity of women. In their writings they lament their own failures of chastity while protesting that women became in some sense the vessels of their redemption.

The lives of the great theologians of the age and their female friends were closely intertwined. Their mothers, sisters, patrons, and in a few cases wives belonged to the virginity movement. Though they lived in an age when women did not write books and did not, like men, circulate their letters for publication, the aristocratic women of the movement were highly educated and took a strong interest in theology as well as church politics. When Jerome came first to Rome, he was amazed to find a wide circle of wealthy noble ladies devoted to study. In 383, when Marcella wrote him about the Montanists' continuing defense of women teachers, Jerome responded that women could not write books in their own names. After the elder Melania and Rufinus broke with him over his ideas on Origen, Palladius claimed that Jerome had perverted Paula's genius to bolster his own inferior intellect.[40] But Jerome had the grace to credit Marcella with some of the biblical exegesis attributed to him because she had modestly undertaken to do some of his work without taking unbecoming credit for it.[41] Gregory of Nyssa stated plainly that the material found in his *Dialogue of the Soul* was dictated by his sister Macrina on her deathbed.[42] Even the silence of these women may be illusory. They wrote letters, though we retain only the answers of their male correspondents. At least one woman, the pilgrim Egeria, wrote a book on her travels, which her community preserved.[43]

The ideas published under the names of male authors were widely discussed and circulated in conversation and correspondence among women and men alike and ultimately represent a theology developed by the whole community. The fragmentary claims of the earlier centuries were molded into a coherent theology of virginity that reinstated much of its transcendent power. In opposition to the traditional claim that women's subordination to men resulted from God's curse upon Eve, Jerome spoke for the virgins, saying that where God had cursed Eve with the pain and sorrow of childbearing, women who avoided Eve's sin were free of her curse. In the case of Blaesilla, who died of anorexia, and even of some of his other friends who fasted to the limits of endurance, this may have been literally true, if the curse can be equated with menstruation. Chrysostom noted that the sexually continent, particularly virgins, retained their health and bloom long past the age when their married sisters withered.[44] Figuratively, Jerome told Eustochium, even the commandment "Thou shalt surely die" did not apply to her because she was free of sexual entanglement.[45] Gregory of Nyssa, echoing the laments of so many of his contemporaries on the fragility of mortal children, reminded his readers that the virgin who lacked carnal children would be spared the grief of their loss while she could rejoice in the children of her spirit.[46] "Death came through Eve, but life through Mary. Thus the gift of virginity has been most richly given to women for it had its beginning from a woman."[47]

Already in the fourth century, the cult of Mary took on that contradictory character which has made it at once a means of subordinating the virgin community to the clergy by glorifying Mary's obedience in contrast to the disobedience of Eve and an instrument for the glorification of women. Jerome in particular took up the old stories circulated in the

Protoevangelion, which henceforth were woven tightly into the fabric of Christian mythology. Mary became the first consecrated virgin, never carnally subjected to human intercourse.[48] She thus conveniently displaced the more aggressive figure of Thecla, whose exemplary role had disturbed even the Montanist Tertullian. Finally, Augustine deemed Mary the first exemplar of consecrated virginity who had married only for the sake of conformity to the customs of the Israelites and maintained a chaste marriage.[49] He maintained that Mary was not the model of matrons because of her virginity but rather the model for women whose purity generated spiritual children.[50] Against the literal force of the commandment "Be fruitful and multiply," he urged the allegorical interpretation of the true mother who adopts slaves and nurtures them to freedom, as did his noble female friends.[51]

The doctrine of Mary's perpetual virginity led ultimately to denial of the claim of Bishop Nestorius that Mary was only the mother of a human Jesus and not the physical progenitor of God himself. Pulcheria, who dominated the government during her brother's minority and who was destined to become empress in her own right after his death, regarded Nestorius's opposition to the special claims of Mary as God's mother as an insult to the special claims of her own virginity. She helped organize the victory for the Marian forces at the Council of Ephesus in 449 and, as the personal representative of Pope Leo I, took charge of the arrangements for the Council of Chalcedon, which saw the final defeat of the Nestorian position. In 453, Pulcheria enlisted the prayers of all holy women for her support. In a letter to a wealthy leader of a women's community in Jerusalem, she outlined a statement of Chalcedonian orthodoxy for their instruction, implying that she was the leader of "all the women dedicated to God."[52]

Pulcheria's theology restored the sexual hierarchy so complicated by Tertullian. Mary's virginity nullified her wifehood and even subordinated her motherhood. This implication echoes the proposition enunciated by the sisterhood of women in Methodius's *Symposium* who reduced the antique family to a lower rung on an evolutionary ladder leading to perfection and an end to procreation. We find deeply embedded in the whole idea a revulsion from the tyranny of the flesh that is peculiar to women. Even more pronounced is a refusal to accept the constricted life that marriage and child care imposed on them. Their disgust, their pain, and their hopes speak vividly from the writings of men, most of them celibate, who could hardly be expected to know anything about the intimate experiences of women. The vivid contrast between the bondage of married life and the freedom of virginity was a favorite topic. Because they condemn a female version of marriage, the Fathers appear to be translating the feelings of the women they knew and loved who were silenced by social convention. Surely, it was his virgin sister Marcellina who supplied Ambrose with his vivid description of the emotions of a woman in the marriage market:

> How miserable is she who, to find a husband, is put up, as it were for sale, so that the one who offers the highest bribe obtains her. Slaves are sold for better terms, for they often choose their masters; if a virgin chooses her husband it is an offense, but if she is not chosen it is an insult. And, though she is fair and beautiful, she both fears and wishes to be seen lest the very fact of her being seen should not be fitting. What fears and suspicions she experiences as to how her suitors will turn out! She is afraid that a poor man may trick her or a noble one despise her.[53]

The literature promoting virginity centered on freedom. Married women, whom Paul himself depicted as distracted from devotion to God by care for husband and family, were repeatedly envisaged as drudges, slaves to the demands of others and to their own flesh. The celibate, however, could move to another plane, devoting herself entirely to religion. The virgins and widows of the Christian empire did not understand their vocation to entail loss of property or status. They had no qualms about doing their business for themselves, despite the criticism that the marketplace was a corrupting influence.[54] They used their wealth to secure clients among the poor and among the clergy. They formed networks and artificial families with other women and some men. It is possible that many of them did not take permanent oaths of consecration but perceived their commitment as one freely undertaken and one that could be ended if they saw fit to do so.

The family system gradually readjusted itself to new types of moral authority. Many widows seized their second chance and brought their virgin daughters with them. Women, delighted to give their daughters the opportunity to remain virgins, which had eluded their own grasp, may not always have been attentive to their children's will. Many Christian fathers came to believe that a virgin in their lineage was essential to their prestige as well as their salvation and had to be restrained from committing children prematurely to perpetual vows. Fathers increasingly prohibited marriage for daughters whom they did not wish to dower or provide with a husband who might rival the father's power. In the imperial family itself, the princess Honoria faced such a fate. Once her son came of age, the adventurous and formidable empress Galla Placidia found a comfortable retirement home in a community of virgins. None of these parties, however, wanted to be restrained by irrevocable vows. After Theodosius died in 395, many consecrated virgins decided to marry. Maybe they had second thoughts as they lived past their first girlish enthusiasms, or maybe they escaped from parental pressure or from the determined zealotry of the emperor himself.

But once bishops had invested so much interest and prestige in the movement, they felt they could not simply leave it open to the changing whims of their clientele. Placed in the first ranks of the *militia Christi*, virgin troops were subjected to training and discipline. The Council of Elvira attempted to impose a binding vow on all prospective virgins.[55] The Theodosian Code gave legal force to these provisions. Some cere-mony of consecration was in effect by the time of the apostolate of Martin of Tours, around 360.[56] It certainly entailed veiling as practiced by Ambrose for his sister Marcellina.[57] The fifth-century virgin Genovefa, among other aspirants, was consecrated by the bishop of Paris with a vow to preserve virginity (or chastity in the case of widows) for life.[58] Sympathy with their vocation fueled the energy of bishops who tried to control these independent women and brake their spontaneity for their own good. Basil urged that virgins who broke their vows be treated as adulteresses, turning Tertullian's concept of the bride of Christ into a crippling legal constraint.[59] Perhaps this smothering concern made the women of Milan reluctant to take the veil, which dismayed Ambrose, who was anxious to crown his episcopacy with a successful community of virgins.

All of this evidence is fragmentary. In the absence of coercive laws or parents, bishops may not have been successful in forcing women who did not marry (or remarry) into solemn vows marked by distinctive habits. As Christian families came to appreciate the strategic value of reserving a daughter for God, they hesitated to make the commitment irrevocable. Even enthusiastic proponents of virginity, were dubious about releasing women altogether from the control and protection of their families. Ambrose encouraged parents to maintain virgin daughters in their households, claiming despite considerable evidence to the contrary that women "are not of the sex that lives in common."[60] The virgin whose parents supported her aspirations could probably spend a fair amount of time in isolation and prayer, while her parents ran the household and provided her with the necessities of life. But she might also encounter difficulties in keeping to her vows. Jerome's friend Asella had been consecrated to virginity in childhood despite her mother's opposition. She acted on her own initiative in selling her gold jewelry and donning a dark dress "such as her mother had never wanted her to wear."[61] Jerome himself was cut off from his aunt and other relatives after he encouraged his sister to embrace celibacy. Ambrose thought that maternal seductions had prevented the girls of Milan from consecrating their virginity to God. Although he complained, he did not take a lead in encouraging children to rebel against their parents. Nevertheless, when familial support failed, or an aspiring virgin needed defense against familial pressure, bishops could impose some degree of regulation as the price of that support.

Inevitable suspicion hounded women who lived alone and unguarded. Marcellina's friendship and the defense of Ambrose himself failed to protect a virgin of Verona, Indicia, from suspicion. As an orphan, she had quite naturally sought a home with her married sister. Her brother-in-law went to the trouble and expense of cutting a separate entrance in the wall of his house, apparently to ensure the privacy of her apartments and, perhaps, to secure his privacy from her. Ambrose suggested that his real wish was to separate the sisters from each other. In any case, her seclusion laid her open to scandal, and Ambrose was roused to write an outraged letter to try to save her from physical examination by the local midwives.[62] These enforced tests to ensure virginity also scandalized Chrysostom, who urged the women under his jurisdiction not to provoke the gossip that would make them necessary.

The whole question of living arrangements became central to the problem of episcopal supervision. Wealthy virgins and widows could maintain a large household whose affairs were relatively open to public scrutiny. The protection and public business usually confided to fathers or husbands could adequately be provided by servants or friends. But virgins of lesser means without a family member or husband tended to make alliances with chaste men (often clergymen) to share their quarters in return for domestic services. As a substitute for second marriage, Tertullian himself once advised priests who felt the need of female services in their households to invite a holy virgin or widow to live with them. Sensitive to the dangers of such a course, he cautioned that the woman in question should be of such an age and demeanor that she could be considered "beautiful only in spirit."[63] But syneisactism was more than a convenient practical arrangement. It was an ideology that challenged its practitioners to transcend the limits of the physical, gendered world.

The sexual hierarchy had an irresistible tendency to expunge gender barriers and join men with women at each point in the scale. The chaste, who continued to observe the social divisions between women and men, were constantly pulled toward one another in a complementary syneisactism. Close association with women among clergy or even pious laymen, however, threatened to unravel the essential male bonding that held the clerical hierarchy firmly in place. Thus, a long and careful tradition was built to deny the faintest possibility that women and men could live together without sexual tension. In 268, the Council of Antioch condemned Paul of Samosata, bishop of Palmyra, for corrupting the virgins he had taken into his household.[64] Cyprian of Carthage at about the same time had to threaten laymen and even a deacon with excommunication for sharing their houses with consecrated virgins and even sharing the same bed with them.[65] The first Council of Nicaea, followed by all the western councils and Nicaea II, repeatedly prohibited the cohabitation of women with clergymen unless they enjoyed a relationship that placed them above suspicion. Sulpicius Severus, who lived with his mother-in-law after his wife's death, defended Martin of Tours's acceptance of a meal served personally by the empress Justina in imitation of Martha despite his lifelong rule of avoiding women. But as a bishop, he warned vain monks who changed their coarse habits for priestly robes not to imagine that the incident gave them license to accept the softest vestments from their intimates among the virgins.[66] Jerome, Augustine, and others complained that some foolish men were in the habit of testing their chastity not simply by living with women but even by sleeping in the same bed with them. Possibly Patrick himself, who launched the mission to Ireland at this time, planted the suggestion that inspired certain monks to take women into bed with them to challenge the devil to combat. The practice became part of the Irish ascetic legend.

Consecrated women who shared households with clergymen tended to slip out of episcopal jurisdiction. Even their partners may have been more influenced by the women they lived with than by their bishops. Basil warned virgins that they could not help the devastating effect of their presence upon susceptible men because it was part of God's plan.[67] The idea that women's heedlessness causes rape, which can be avoided only by their self-effacement, echoes in most of this literature. Chrysostom launched a vitriolic attack against syneisactic households. In great detail he described the romantic temptations, the perversion of normal sexual impulses that must characterize such a relationship. He criticized even successful couples because they scandalized the world with "wise women" running to their houses to assure a gossiping world that the virgin remained intact. He taunted men with their failure to form such relationships with women broken by age and infirmity and sorely in need of money, lodging, and the services of their brethren. Jerome advised a priest, Nepotian, to love the virgins of Christ but avoid living with them.[68] Basil rebuked another syneisactic clerk who was living with a woman on the grounds that the purpose of celibacy was to live without women and that if the pair had really risen above the temptations of carnal desire they would not object to separation.[69] Aphrahat advised monks to marry in earnest rather than attempt spiritual marriages.[70]

Even when the Fathers were willing to admit that there was no danger of sexual transgression, they hated these syneisactic households because they disapproved of the presence of women in what they defined as male space. When one of his monks requested permission to resume his common life with his wife, who had progressed beyond all thought of sex, the old soldier Martin of Tours refused, saying that women did not belong on a battlefield.[71] Ambrose fulminated against the "flood of *agapetae* [companions in holy love], unwedded wives, novel concubines" he saw all around him.[72] Chrysostom charged that men who live with women are made effeminate and unfit for battle, like a captured lion with his teeth pulled. "Women make the men they capture easy for the devil to overcome. They render them softer, more hot-headed, shameful, insolent, importunate, ignoble, crude, servile, niggardly, reckless, nonsensical, and to sum it up, the women take all their corrupting feminine customs and stamp them into the souls of these men."[73]

As the idea of the superiority of the virgin or the honorary virgin over the sexually active became irresistible, the marriages of the clergy were sometimes viewed as a confession of their inferiority to the elite. The relationship between the sexual and clerical hierarchies again came into question, giving new impetus to an old ideal. The decision to transform marriage into a chaste partnership became fashionable among episcopal couples. Pinian and Melania were exceptional in their decision to live apart. In the west, the husband's elevation to the episcopate often signaled the end of sexual relations but not separation. A network of chaste couples drawn from the highest aristocracy of Rome began to form as the episcopate established itself in Italy, Spain, and Gaul. Germanus of Auxerre and his wife took vows of chastity upon his installation as did Bishop Lupus with Pemeniola, the sister of Bishop Hilary of Arles.[74] Paulinus and Therasia wrote to the bishop of Rouen congratulating him on the communities of virgins, widows, and continent couples who flourished in his diocese.[75] These like-minded couples formed a network enlarged by Augustine and his mother, Monica; Sulpicius and his mother-in-law, Bassula; the unmarried Melania the Elder and Rufinus; and Paula and Jerome, who shared the Christian emphasis on the conjugal couple as the center of social life.

Such domestic communities centered on continent couples substituted a cross-sexual bonding for the male bonding of scholarly male communities like Augustine's original retreat at Cassiacum. After the death of their only child, Therasia persuaded her husband, Paulinus of Nola, to take a vow of continence. She turned him away from his old circles of friends and his teacher, the classical scholar Ausonius, who bitterly blamed "Tanaquil" for the breach, naming her after the seductive witch of ancient times who had secured the Roman crown for Tarquin. This incident marks a serious break in the antique gender system, which generally prevented women from exerting much influence on their husbands and partners by the general denigration of female companionship, the solidarity of all-male relationships, and the masculine monopoly of public life. Paulinus turned his back on those representatives of the old pagan nobility who still cherished the cultivated life of their ancient forebears, saying his wife was no Tanaquil but a chaste Lucretia. Therasia cosigned all his letters to his Christian friends, thus evading the strong social prohibitions against married women writing private letters. Within the framework of traditional marriage they were struggling to realize a new coalition. Augustine wrote to Paulinus:

> Your wife is also made visible to your readers, not as one leading her husband into luxury but rather as leading him back to strength in his innermost being. We salute her, also, with the greetings owed to your holiness alone, because she is joined in close union with you, and is attached to you by spiritual bonds which are as strong as they are chaste. There the cedars of Lebanon are laid on the ground; there they are joined by the thongs of charity to be the material of the ark and are incorruptibly floated on the waters of the world; there, glory is despised that it may be acquired and the world given up that it may be held; there, the infants or even the growing children of Babylon are dashed against a stone, that is, the vices of disorder and worldly pride.[76]

Paulinus eventually became a bishop and continued to work in partnership with Therasia until she died, spreading the doctrine of chastity as an antidote to subordination. Writing to another continent husband, Paulinus praised his wife, Amanda, "Who does not lead her husband to effeminacy or greed but brings you back to self-discipline and courage to become the bones of her husband."[77] Those clerical couples who lived together in spirit but separate in body had successfully solved the puzzle presented by the contradiction of purity and marriage. In sexuality they had identified the true source of gender differences and possibly of gender inequality as well. This presidency of women in the secular world reached its apogee in the middle of the fifth century, when the empress Pulcheria, a consecrated virgin queen, occupied the throne, delegating its military powers to her partner in a chaste marriage, Marcion.

The institution of the chaste clerical marriage solved some of the problems confronting women in the development of the priesthood. It seemed to promise the wife an opportunity for personal autonomy and an active role in the church through her husband's position. Some women began to use the titles *episcopissa, presbyterissa,* or *diaconissa,* forever blurring the exact nature of their positions.[78] Some rituals of ordination came to confer a special blessing and habit upon the priest's wife.

Within a generation or so, however, the clerical hierarchy began to seal these breaches. The network of ascetic aristocrats suffered severely in the violence of the early-fifth-century barbarian invasions. Sulpicius vanished in 406. Therasia died in 408 and Paulinus was captured by Visigoths in 410. Marcella and Melania the Elder died in the sack of Rome and its aftermath. By the middle of the fifth century, the exclusion of women from church leadership became more practical with the recruitment of men who recognized the religion so long practiced by their wives and daughters as the avenue to a new public life. As heretic barbarians conquered the western world, the Roman ruling class supplied the flower of its young men to the Catholic episcopate. In 441, the Council of Orange forbade the ordination of deaconesses.[79] Shortly thereafter, the Synod of Nîmes registered the complaint that some women claimed to be deacons and pronounced the idea so indecent that it would invalidate the whole idea of ordination if accepted.[80] In 494, Pope Gelasius wrote to the bishops of Lucca, Abruzzi, and Sicily, discussing the need to control and restrict the pretensions of consecrated women who, he had heard, were being encouraged to minister at the altar and perform services deputed only to men.[81] He prohibited the consecration of bishops' widows to avoid the appearance of ordination. In sum, all this legislation attempted to maintain the sexual hierarchy as a second chain of command reaching down from bishop to laity. It inhibited male and female virgins from joining forces to form a third gender in competition with the sexually active, while allowing bishops to continue enhancing their prestige by maintaining a clientele of unmarried women.

Thus, by the time the Roman Empire was crumbling in the west, women who had escaped the confinement of the gender system by renouncing sexual activity were again restricted to the wife-to-widow cycle in the institutional life of the church. Married to clergymen or partnered with them in separate living spaces, women were distinctly subordinate to the control of the episcopacy. As brides of Christ, they had to submit to the strictures that bound other wives. But their husband was, after all, in heaven and they enjoyed special prestige when dealing with his stewards. Jerome encouraged Paula to make the most of her dignity as God's mother-in-law. This was not enough for Paula, or for Jerome either. As the fifth century opened, they joined the growing exodus of Christians who sought a return to the apostolic life in the desert. There were Christians, as there always would be, who looked back to the old radical days and still sought the transformative powers of the virgin life as exemplified by the Letter to the Galatians. Women as well as men, seeking a higher order of perfection, fled to the deserts beyond the Roman cities. There they submitted their bodies to the discipline, ascesis, that would transform them into contenders for a new martyr's crown. There, still, the vision of Perpetua, whose heroism made her a man, lured her sisters forward.

3

※

The Discipline of the Desert

THE SUBTERRANEAN CHANNELS that bore so many Christian traditions forward through the centuries carried a tale of Mary and Martha of Bethany into the Middle Ages and an enduring place in the history of art and literature. In the harsh and rocky wildernesses of Provence, the story spread that Christianity had come to the Gauls through the preaching of the two sisters who had sailed across the sea from the Holy Land after Pentecost. Eventually, as they made their way up the Rhône valley, the differences in their characters caused them to separate. Ever active, Martha took up the burden of the pastoral ministry culminating in her victorious duel with a man-eating local dragon. Mary, finally conflated with the Magdalene and definitively classified as a repentant prostitute, gradually gave up public preaching in favor of a hidden apostolate. She became the first exemplar of the anchoritic life, devoting herself to penitence and meditation in a remote cave.

The creation of hierarchies, dogma, ritualized activities, and political relationships belonged to the city, the world of the flesh. But the dream and the promise of Christianity was to transcend that world, to break free of the constraints of the flesh. From biblical tradition, this free space meant the desert, the wild place without limit or definition, which represented withdrawal from worldly entanglement, purification, and contact with the divine. In the first three centuries, Christian sources wholly centered on the struggle to build and maintain a church in the cities. Transcendence and withdrawal from the world were all too readily available in the form of martyrdom. With the end of the Great Persecution, however, more heroic souls could no longer triumph in that ultimate contest with the forces of evil. The "desert" that lay outside civilization began to occupy the Christian imagination as a new arena for testing the soul and contesting the world, the flesh, and the devil.

In the early decades of the fourth century, city people began to take note of solitary hermits and whole colonies of spiritual adventurers out beyond the carefully disciplined urban communities, beyond the comfort and control of bishops and sacraments. Multitudes—contemporaries claimed tens of thousands—of ardent individuals felt driven to forsake the world and seek the absolute in those blazing silent places where all dross might be stripped from the eager soul through ascesis, the regime of self-discipline and physical deprivation that prepared athletes and soldiers for combat. It was a complex interaction of soul and body, antagonistic teammates striving for mutual perfection. The soul subdued the mindless lusts of the body through diet, exercise, and sleeplessness. The body disciplined the restless spirit through routines of work and prayer. Sharpened and perfected through rigorous training, ascetics became mediators between God and the world, frontier guards posted in the desert to ward off the forces of evil.

Whereas virginity was essentially an urban movement and gendered female, asceticism was associated with the arena and the battlefield and was originally gendered male. The prototypical *Life of Antony* popularized the exploits of a hermit at the turn of the century who had lived for decades hidden within a desert cave, where he struggled with the weaknesses of his own flesh and the demons that lurked in the darkness. Periodically, he emerged long enough to share the fruits of his struggle and meditations with the aspiring men who camped outside his lair in hopes of instruction. The story, written about 340 by Bishop Athanasius, one of a group of regulators anxious to assure the orthodoxy of the new movement, defined the desert as a place where men could struggle with their sexual longings in the security of a woman-free space. Athanasius claimed that his responsibility for an unmarried sister almost frustrated Antony's vocation until he finally left her behind in a house of virgins.[1] Martin of Tours, the leading proponent of the ascetic movement in Gaul, had been a soldier in the Roman army before he took up spiritual arms against paganism and the devil. His biographer, Sulpicius Severus, said

Martin warned his monastic troops against allowing women, no matter how virtuous, on their battlefield.[2]

These are the voices of bishops, fretful pastors fearful of the effects of syneisactism. But the manly woman had already established her credentials in the arena of martyrdom, and the two movements shared too much ideological ground to remain separate. The sexual renunciation of virgins naturally complemented the physical disciplines of asceticism. The intellectual women of the movement read Athanasius, Sulpicius, and the stream of literature these writers inspired. They made pilgrimages to the east to see the ascetics for themselves. Soon they were practicing the whole regimen of fasting, keeping vigil, and other forms of self-discipline. Male ascetics, in turn, focused on the struggle against sexual desire as emblematic of their efforts to gain total control of their bodies. Transcendence of gender became their garland of victory. As asceticism adapted the language of martyrdom, the female champion again became the perfect metaphor, exalting divine power over the natural order of the world. Magnifying the heroism of the woman who pulled herself up the scale to manliness became a favored didactic device for shaming men who failed to meet their standards as effeminate. Ambrose wrote, "Anyone who does not believe is a woman and should be designated by the name of that sex, whereas one who believes progresses to perfect manhood, to the measure of adulthood in Christ, with the name of the sex, dispensing with the seductiveness of youth and the garrulousness of old age."[3]

For men accustomed to rule, if only within the confines of their own families, the desert represented a playing field where, free of the burden of public responsibilities, they could drive body and soul to the limit of human endurance. Women started from the other end, seeking to be free of sexual subjection, the long captivity of pregnancy, the agonies of childbirth, and the endless distractions of household trivia. They craved the liberation of solitude and the self-imposed physical deprivations of asceticism.

Asceticism was a rejection of the world and the flesh. It was perfectly expressed in the rebellion of women against a family structure designed to maintain and continue an empire based on *patria potestas* (the power vested in the head of a family). Jerome trumpeted the triumph of their chastity over the venerable lineages of the Roman aristocracy as the conquest of time and even death. Even as the barbarian sack of the city in 410 exposed the mortal nature of immortal Rome, he rejoiced that his friends had dissipated their fortunes in charity before the barbarians could steal them. To free themselves from the social constraints arising from female biology, women employed the military and athletic imagery of monks and martyrs, making themselves, as Jerome said, functionally masculine.[4] Gregory of Nazianzus praised the masculine soul of his widowed mother.[5] Gregory of Nyssa wondered whether he could call his sister, Macrina, a woman at all "since she has gone beyond the nature of a woman."[6] Of the elder Melania, Paulinus wrote, "What a woman she is, if one can call so virile a Christian a woman . . . a soldier of Christ with the virtues of Martin, though she is of the weaker sex . . . as a strong member of the weak sex, she might arraign idle men."[7]

Not everyone agreed with this radical assessment of women who had so far overreached their traditional boundaries in the pursuit of holiness. In real life, women faced the constraints of propriety and fear of scandal. The active hostility of the secular world amply reinforced episcopal misgivings about ascetic women. A violent mob accused Paula of causing the death of her daughter Blaesilla by encouraging excessive self-mortification. Eventually she fled from Rome, leaving her whole family behind except for her virgin daughter Eustochium, who shared her ideals. Even at her retreat in Bethlehem, she was continually assaulted by critics and friends who thought her mad and threatened forcible intervention to cure her.[8] Fabiola, separated from a notoriously vicious pagan husband who had been abusive to her, was sharply criticized for a second marriage to a Christian. When he died, she established a chaste partnership running a hostel for poor travelers in Ostia with Paula's widowed son-in-law Pammachius. Their generous charity and work for the poor did not save them from public scandal.[9] The ardor of the friendliest bishops chilled when public scandal forced them repeatedly to adjudicate cases of scandal rising from syneisactic relationships, no matter how innocent they were.

Despite their polemics praising virginity and manly women, bishops could not be easy in their minds about a system that gave women and men too much intimacy. By excluding women from the clergy, they had invested heavily in the logic of a gender system based on female incapacity. Even the fanciful flights of rhetoric which proclaimed that virile women had transcended that system served to reinforce it. Reversing his own praise of the power of women to lead men in sanctity, Chrysostom complained that virgins chose to live with leading clergymen to feed their own vanity, seeking to invert the Pauline prescription by making themselves head of the men and thereby stealing their glory.[10] Careful of their status, bishops feared that the attractions of holy women extended beyond the sexual into the realm of the spiritual and even the practical affairs of the church and therefore the sacred bailiwick of the clergy. They were probably right. The wives of married bishops were clearly partners in their husbands' administrations. Virgins and widows with wealth and influence played crucial roles in most contemporary theological and organizational struggles.

Prudent bishops, concerned for the care of their flocks, could not be indifferent to the proliferation of cult groups in their communities. Nevertheless, the speed with which they came to blend charges of heresy and sexual misconduct where women and men traveled or worshipped together suggests a broader agenda. Sulpicius accused the Spanish heretic Priscillian of holding prayer services at night in the nude with his wealthy and influential female devotees, Procula and Euchrotia.[11] All three were put to death and a year or two later a third woman, Urbica, was stoned in Bordeaux for continuing to hold Priscillian's ideas. Basil of Caesarea charged that the deacon Glycerius surrounded himself with a company of virgins, some of them unwillingly held in thrall, and coerced them into dancing and singing in local festivals, insulting their parents who tried to intervene.[12] Augustine made the same charge against Primus, who, he said, left the orthodox church and became a heretic after being forbidden to have intercourse with a consecrated woman.[13]

As fourth-century men tried to contemplate women who rejected marriage and motherhood, they could not resist the image of the whore. In the elaborately stratified world of the Roman cities, the only women who could legally go abroad with the freedom of men were prostitutes. Women without families or fortunes had no other way to save themselves from starvation, and prostitutes were always a favorite object for Christian charity. But it was a hoary old Roman scandal that some respectable women registered themselves as prostitutes to enjoy sexual, and even social, freedom. Prostitution cut across classes, giving women an opportunity to gain wealth, security, or status through manipulation of their lovers. Literature glamorized the profession, describing the exploits of successful *femmes fatales* who garnered immense wealth from broken-hearted lovers. Men tested their holiness by resisting them and converting them. Conversely, the desert imagery of contest and victory favored the repentant whore over the unspotted virgin as archetype of the holy woman. Melania the Younger gathered ninety women from houses of ill fame and vowed to support and serve them slavishly as long as they refused the company of men.[14]

The conversion or the salvation of the prostitute was, of course, a highly uplifting theme. But it was also a vehicle for the introduction of sex, rejected or repented or regretted, back into the ascetic enterprise. As women went to the desert or made a desert in the city by shutting themselves away from men, men began to develop the idea of the unwilling, sex-starved virgin longing for a manly rescuer. In the sixth century, her unfriendly chronicler accused the empress Theodora of forcibly imprisoning prostitutes so reluctant to repent that they flung themselves into the Bosporus to escape her charity. Men made nervous by the thought of women living independently of men and outside their feminine roles had found a literary device that would serve them well for centuries to come.

For the ascetics, however, the story worked in reverse: the flesh, the sexual world, was the prison from which the manly woman sought to free herself. Pelagia, a fictional prostitute destined for repentance and sainthood, was described in the heyday of her beauty as wearing her clothes with the haughty impudence of a man, her veil thrown about her shoulders in a casual fashion.[15] It was all too easy to imagine the same woman, in disguise, ending her days as a famous "holy man." For to become manly was to lose or disguise those feminine charms that lured men to destruction even against their possessor's will. Women who heard the sermons of the golden-tongued Chrysostom learned that God had given them their sexuality as a weapon to offset their inherent inferiority because, unless men were induced to abandon their good sense in the grip of lust, they would turn from women in disgust and the human race would disappear. Even a generous man like Ambrose had to settle for rebuking men to remember that it was they who were tempted not necessarily women who did the tempting: "But you men say that a woman is a temptation to a man. Yes, this is true and the more beautiful she is, the greater the temptation . . . but it is not a defect in a woman to be what she was born. . . . We cannot find fault with the work of the divine artist."[16] The myth of woman's fatal allure has always been one of the most powerful enforcement agents in the gender system. Women may also have been both attracted and repelled by the mirror images of sexual license and purity. Women who sought an independent religious life, women who wanted to test the full range of their spiritual prowess, and women who internalized male fear of their attractions into fear of scandal or fear of rape all fled to the desert.

The desert was more ideal than real, a landscape of the mind. Its exempla included romances of penitent whores like the irresistible Thaïs walled up in a cell where she practiced penitence while purging herself of her fatal beauty.[17] The "desert" was often a closed chamber or even a discreet household where women lived with other women and male servants. Melania the Elder visited an *inclusa* (an enclosed woman) named Alexandra, who immured herself in a mausoleum to repent having driven a man to suicide for love of her. When the great ascetic Susan had attracted a male discipleship to her desert cave, she wanted to lead her small female community further out into the desert because "it is not possible for our female sex to live among men—since the attack of the evil one against holy men is mostly made through women."[18] Sulpicius mentions an *inclusa* in Gaul who refused to receive Martin of Tours when he broke his own rule of avoiding women in order to pay homage to her chastity.

As a dreamscape, the desert transformed everything. Wild beasts became the docile servants of champions who had tamed their inner beasts. Men found the highest perfection in the humility, silence, and obedience usually allotted to women. Whores became virgins and virgins became men, soldiers of Christ actively contending against the forces of evil. The heroine of the tale of Mary of Egypt was a courtesan who repented when miraculously barred from entering church on a feast day. She fled to the desert to redeem her sin through years of suffering. After many years, she grew old and sun-blackened, so reduced by fasting and exposure that a hermit on a vision quest first thought her to be a shadow and then a wild beast. Her white wooly hair, the emblem of the untamed virgin, hung unkempt to her shoulders. But to instruct the disciple so fortuitously sent, she had to cover her nakedness in the borrowed clothing of the man.[19]

Women who adopted the appearance and lives of men infiltrated the literature of the ascetic movement. Beginning with the perfectly credible proposition that a holy virgin assumes male disguise to protect her from a lusty suitor or from parents determined to force her into marriage, the typical story follows her as she joins a male community and lives among the monks undetected. In some stories, the heroine's sanctity is so outstanding that she is elected abbot, the truth being uncovered when the dying saint confesses to avert violation by her ignorant followers after her death. Other tales lead to a more dramatic denouement. The disguised woman is accused of fathering an illegitimate child or deliber- ately humiliates herself by seeking to convert prostitutes, ignoring scan- dalmongers in perfect confidence of her unimpeachable innocence. Need- less to say, after bearing the punishment and shame rising from false accusations, the heroine always triumphs. Thus the virgin becomes a man, but a chaste angelic man, akin to the great hermits of legend whose asceticism was proof against the attractions of beautiful, lost women. Further to confuse dream and reality, the whole construct depends on the perfection of her disguise, making it impossible to determine the veracity of such stories. Legend associated the famous hermit Daniel of Skete with a patrician lady, Anastasia, who founded a monastery near Alexandria in the sixth century. When the emperor attempted to bring her back to court, she fled and, with Daniel's help, disguised herself as a eunuch and hid in a cell for twenty-eight years.[20] The legend of Hilaria, daughter of the emperor Zeno, provides another example.[21]

Were there really such women in the desert? Hermits in any guise could easily have installed themselves anywhere without leaving more trace in the historical record than these stories. Modern exploration has confirmed the impression given by Egeria in the fourth century and by John Moscas in the sixth that the Egyptian desert and the Jordan valley abounded with small unidentified monasteries. Moreover, we know that in Bithynia, at least, eunuchs were welcomed into monasteries though segregated from the rest of the community. Desert people were solitaries. Even when they organized as a community, they had individual cells where they devoted themselves to fasting and prayer and other bodily mortifications. They shunned bathing and never undressed publicly. They spoke little, gathering only intermittently for prayer or perhaps for meals eaten in silence (wearing hoods designed to protect them from the sight of their companions' chewing). Where they worked together in fields or at small handicrafts, they still observed silence. We have, then, no compelling reason to reject the possibility that anorectic women, clothed in monastic robes, silent and prayerful, could have passed for many years as men.

The stories were intended to illustrate a basic tenet of desert discipline, the potential transformation of women and men into kindred souls. Ancient philosophers held that men could not have friendships with women because of their inferiority. Chaste celibacy eliminated that inferiority. From the beginning, the ascetic movement assumed syneisactic characteristics despite the fears and cautions that accompanied any attempt to translate theory into reality. Devotional collections self-consciously included exempla of holy women among "lives of the Fathers" or the "histories of monks," subtly classing them not only as men but as the highest form of manhood, miracles of self-control and channeled virtue.

If the desert legends were dreams and fantasies, so was the desert itself. Women in particular often found it in their own chamber when they withdrew from marriage, from motherhood, from the social involvements that characterized the "world" of ordinary women. Women and men from every class and every city withdrew to country estates or other areas formally designated as "desert." An elaborate process of trial and error marked the development of monastic communities. Each hermit made up her own rules as she went along. The more successful hermits attracted followers who learned the discipline in their turn. Pilgrims like Egeria toured the fabled hermitages of Egypt and Syria where ascetics were always on display not far from the city and sent back commentaries to their own communities. Saints' lives, literary dialogues, and books of proverbs, "histories" of desert communities filled with edifying anecdotes soon imposed intelligible patterns on the life of the desert. Indeed, hermits often walked a well-beaten path into the marketplaces, where they rebuked the self-indulgent and collected alms from them. Sometimes they came into the city to attack episcopal adherents of a contested point of dogma in the intense theological struggles of the age. When they came from the banks of the Nile, the forests of Gaul, or the women's quarters of a Roman house, their solitude was enhanced by quarreling crowds and their prophetic authority stood sharply against the worldliness of clergy and laity alike.

The desert that these earnest pilgrims went out to see was already shifting from desolate hidden spaces to a network of communities. Hermits who found God there overcame their reluctance to guide others since the adhesion of disciples was an index of their success and disciples, by definition, had to be trained. The great settlements at Nitria and Skete were modeled on the disciples of Antony, training hermits (male and female) for the skills of solitude. The presidency of smaller clusters seems to have fallen to the woman or man who founded or capitalized the enterprise. Susan distinguished herself for self-mortification in a female monastery in Palestine. She fled to Egypt with five heretical nuns who survived an orthodox attack on the community. There she withdrew alone into a cave to be divinely instructed in "struggle and manliness." The fame of her sanctity attracted many disciples including an old man with ten students. After much soul-searching, she agreed to remain with her five sisters in a walled cloister to instruct both monks and nuns, though she never allowed the men to see her face.[22]

Early in the movement, some settlements committed themselves permanently to a communal life. Beginning as a hermit, Pachomius gathered a following of thousands in the Egyptian desert. Legend has it that about 323 an angel gave him a bronze tablet engraved with a rule charting the shift from eremitic solitude to a communal life combining shared living quarters, meals, and manual labor with solitary prayer, silence, and contemplation.[23] From the beginning, the Pachomian rule assumed the presence of women among the disciples. The praises biographers heaped on rich women should not blind us to the spiritual aspirations of the poor. Most of the Pachomian communities were peopled with peasants unable to endow their female dependents in urban houses. Mary, Pachomius's sister, founded a community of women on the opposite bank of the Nile at Tabenisi. It probably mixed women related to the monks and women who made their way to the desert on their own. Men and women alike were subject to the same rule.

Monasticism was a lay movement, a form of religion directed inward, as opposed to the pastoral mission of the priesthood. Its practitioners sought direct ties to God without the sacramental intervention normal to urban Christians. Fed occasionally by a raven, Antony lived beyond the reach of the sacraments. Rejected from the church, Mary of Egypt found God without benefit of clergy or sacraments. Only at the end of her life, on Easter morning, did the penitent receive the Eucharist, rewarding the priest with the gift of her holy death. Thus the Pachomian monks, like the nuns, were not normally priests. They left the risks of female contact to a priest and a deacon who visited the nuns on Sundays when they celebrated mass and excommunicated sisters found to have committed some fault.[24] Pachomius himself stoutly resisted the efforts of Athanasius to ordain him. But the request itself reveals the beginnings of an evolutionary movement toward accommodation with the world and the settled church of the fourth century. I have determined to avoid digressions into the doctrinal quarrels that constantly embroiled the desert folk in charges of heresy against the episcopate and even the imperial power. But we should never forget that throughout this crucial period, the movement was being shaped into an acceptable branch of the Catholic Church. The eccentrics, the rebels, and the high flyers were being winnowed out. The sources we have left are those written by the triumphant orthodox factions that almost completely obliterated their opponents from history.

Doctrinal subtleties shifted and swirled like the sands of the desert itself. But one constant mirage that alerted the orthodox to trouble was the effort to mix women and men. Pachomian monks who had not yet reached perfection could visit their female relatives in the women's monastery by appointment with Mary.[25] Total separation of the sexes, however, virtually defined perfection. The monks' claim to spiritual superiority, which attracted the respect of penitents and the alms of the faithful, depended on their capacity to demonstrate invulnerability to female temptresses. Sexual purity most tangibly set them apart from ordinary poor peasants scratching for a living. They created elaborate physical spaces and even more elaborate personal habits to prove to themselves and to the world that they were completely beyond reach. Except for the priest at Sunday services, the only men who had any contact with the sisters were the monks who went across the river at a

signal to collect their corpses for burial in the common cemetery. Only
in death could temptation be safely discounted.

The traveler Palladius, who wrote a highly influential "history" of the
desert communities at the end of the fourth century, much admired a
woman named Amma Talis, who headed a community of sixty women
in Antinoë. He said she was so loved by her sisters that they held
themselves in check without being locked in.[26] He illustrated the dangers
of over-scrupulosity by a grim anecdote. A man approached a sister and
offered her his services as a tailor. Quite properly, she told him that they
had their own tailors and sent him on his way. But another sister accused
her of breaking the rule by speaking with a man. Factions formed in the
community and the accused sister was harassed into drowning herself in
the Nile. Then the accuser hanged herself in remorse. Both women were
denied Christian burial and the accusing faction was excommunicated for
seven years, remaining in the community as penitents.[27]

Apparently segregation of women and men depended wholly on
self-discipline. The tailor, after all, encountered no barrier to approaching
the nun. Moreover, the superiority of the hermit life was still accepted
dogma, and no bar seems to have prevented women from pursuing it
when they were ready. The hermit Daniel of Skete was admitted into
the sacred female precincts because an angel instructed him to seek out
a particular sister who could give him a lesson in humility. He found her
in the kitchen living off scraps, feigning madness for the explicit purpose
of exposing herself to the scorn and ridicule of the other sisters.[28] Once
subjected to Daniel's praise, the saintly woman disappeared into the
desert, presumably to live out her life in eremitic perfection. According
to the same account, Andronicus and his wife, Athanasia, separated to
pursue their individual perfection. She trained at Tabenisi for twelve
years. Then she disguised herself as a man and went on pilgrimage. By
accident, she encountered her former husband, who failed to recognize
her in her transformed condition. They settled into a hermitage together
and remained there for a dozen years until her death revealed her identity.

When Palladius observed them, there were about four hundred women
at Tabenisi along with two flourishing daughter communities. In comparison with the brotherhoods, these congregations were relatively small,
but by any other standard they were populous. Economic limitation
probably explains why women's communities were so much smaller than

men's. They could not go into the markets and other public spaces preaching and urging repentance. Their comparative inaccessibility would hamper their ability to solicit alms in exchange for prayers. Palladius noted that the brothers shared the proceeds from the sale of handicrafts with the sisters but did not say whether or not women produced some of the baskets and other goods they sold. Certainly, they produced the surplus textiles, which contributed to the joint enterprise. The two communities also exchanged labor services, with the women doing the laundry.

Orthodox writers widely publicized the Pachomian rule, which still ranks as a landmark in monastic history. But only one other community in Egypt adopted it. The "cities in the desert," which multiplied in Egypt, Syria, and the Holy Land, varied considerably in their configurations. Around 390, Egeria wrote home to her community of virgins that she found "countless monastic cells for men and women at the church of Thecla in Silicia."[29] In Thebes, a priest named Elias served as pastor for a community of 300 virgins. One community at Oxyrhinchus was said to contain 20,000 nuns, and Palladius mentioned similar establishments in Syria, Palestine, Asia, and even Rome.[30] Pgol's White Monastery at Panopolis was numbered at 2,200 monks under Abbot Schenoudi and 1,800 nuns under Abbess Tahom, who was forbidden to punish them without the abbot's permission, an odd reflection of the primacy of the father in secular society. This so-called double-monastery system was a pragmatic response to the need of women in the desert for the spiritual and material services of men.

Each community made up its own rules, adapting the examples of others to their unique requirements. A monk named Sinnius formed a "brotherhood" of women and men. "By his revered way of life, he drove out his own masculine desires and bridled the feminine traits of the women by his mastery so that the scriptures were fulfilled: 'In Christ there is neither male nor female.'"[31] His was the sort of social experiment that gave bishops nightmares. Eustatius of Sebaste, who introduced asceticism into Asia Minor about 330, patronized women who cut their hair and wore men's garb as a sign of their asexuality. In 340, the Council of Gangra condemned the practice and rejected his plea for priestly celibacy and the separation of husbands and wives. But it upheld the "purity and holiness of virginity" and endorsed Eustatius's arguments that distinctions between the sexes be eliminated as far as possible.[32] In the last quarter of the century, Jerome warned his female friends against emulating virgins who changed their clothes for the garb of men: "Being ashamed of what they were born to be—women, they cut off their hair and are not ashamed to look like eunuchs."[33] By the same token, he condemned men who dressed as women. He perhaps objected simply to the literal nature of the gender transfer. For he also wrote, "She who has ceased to be a married woman, with the cessation of the function of the menstrual blood, is freed from the curse of God. Nor is she placed under the power of her husband but, on the contrary, her husband is made subject to her and he is commanded by the word of God who told Abraham to obey Sarah."[34]

Jerome was not just playing with meaningless metaphors or flattering his wealthy patronesses. Alone among the great defenders of virginity, he did not become a bishop but threw his cap wholly to the winds to follow Paula and Eustochium in their venture into the desert. In Bethlehem, they formed a partnership that included sharing the burden of material life and the stimulation of genuine intellectual collaboration. Palladius, in his survey of eastern ascetic establishments also praised the joint household of Melania the Elder and Rufinus as a center of pious learning and hospitality. The generation that began to experiment with new communal lifestyles learned to be circumspect in keeping men physically separated from women, but the practitioners were always daring in their inherent syneisactism. Melania trained herself by direct study, touring the Egyptian settlements, as did Egeria. Paula and Melania also made exhaustive trips among the desert dwellers. Macrina had the advantage of her brother Basil's observations.

The house monastery sprang up in place of the vanished house church. Indeed, Jerome used the term *domestica ecclesia*.[35] Sometimes a chastely married couple was at the core. Thomas the Armenian followed up his conversion by building a two-winged cloister for his ascetic household, which included his wife, children, slaves, and servants. Therasia and Paulinus turned their house at Nola into a small domestic monastery of five noblewomen and five noblemen (several of whom were married), several children, and all their servants. Amoun, founder of the desert community at Nitria in Egypt, made a vow with his wife on their wedding night, and the couple lived together in secret virginity for eighteen years. At last, she suggested that he leave and show his virtue to the world. While he went to the desert, she pursued her religious life at home with the privileges of a married woman to her own house and property. The royal Pulcheria and her sisters dedicated themselves to virginity in an imposing public ceremony and transformed part of the imperial palace itself into a female community. When her brother died, she empowered herself to rule the empire by incorporating Marcian, a seasoned soldier, into the community as her husband in an unconsummated marriage.

Pulcheria's alliance with her sisters was even more typical than the marital bond as the core of a house monastery. Formerly, the women of a family had been alienated from one another by the barriers implicit in the *patria potestas*. With the development of asceticism, they became close allies in their joint search for freedom and religious self-expression. Melania the Elder, Albina, and Melania the Younger linked three generations of ascetics. Their cousin Paula justified the loss of her own virginity by that of her daughter, Eustochium. Paula inspired her daughter-in-law Laeta to convert Toxotius to chaste marriage and dedicate their only child, Paula the Younger, to virginity. When her family fled from the barbarians in 410, Demetrias escaped her father's authority and, with the help of her mother and grandmother, broke her betrothal in favor of a life of consecrated virginity.[36]

The foremost exemplum of the female house monastery is the community organized by Macrina, whose virginity was retrieved from the claims of marriage only by her steady and intelligent use of the laws regulating betrothal and widowhood against the authority of her father. Her mother, Emilia, herself had been married reluctantly because she lacked other protection as an orphan. While she was in labor, she experienced a revelation that Macrina's secret name was to be Thecla.[37] The vision relieved Emilia's own stress and designated Macrina as the child who would justify her mother's loss of virginity.

From the beginning—though the texts are not explicit—the shadow of patriarchal power hung over institutional monasticism. We are not told how Antony's sister felt about being put in a house of virgins. We do not know whether it was Mary or Pachomius who decided to establish Tabenisi, though we are told that when Mary made her way into the desert, her brother refused to see her and handed her over to the guidance of an elderly monk. The seclusion of the women there probably gave the monks the power of approval over novices, and they may have favored their own relatives, regardless of vocation. Poor women, unsupported women, driven solely by a vision of God, may have found no place in the Pachomian communities. On the other side, women who had not chosen celibacy may have been subjected to the permanent enforcement of vows. Relatives dependent on the monks may have felt that they had no acceptable alternative but to make the best of their situation. With the legalization of Christianity, it became a crime under imperial law, as it had always been under Christian morality, to expose unwanted children. Febronia's biographer composed a saintly model for women consecrated as oblates (offerings) while still children.[38] To be sure, the child in question was better off in a monastery than exposed to death or slavery, and many oblates made excellent nuns. Nevertheless, the presence of unwilling members must have led to the spread of coercion. This trend may have been palliated by the example of shared voluntary hardships and inclusion in a communal enterprise.

Splendid and rewarding as male-female friendships clearly were, the ascetic movement was perhaps even more revolutionary in introducing women to the great joys and rewards of friendship with one another. Febronia's life, supposedly written by fellow nun Thomaïs, celebrates the love that bound her to the nun who raised her and to her sisters who survived her. After her martyrdom, she was said to have appeared regularly in her customary place at midnight worship. She habitually lectured to the noble matrons of the town from behind a veil. Though a work of fiction, probably written by a nun in a later monastery dedicated to the martyr, her life exemplifies the ideal of modest reclusiveness without formal claustration. The absence of impenetrable cloister walls opened the communal life even to women who could not share their living quarters. Ascetic women added one or more like-minded companions to their *familiae*, providing a much needed refuge for religious women who could not afford to support independent establishments. Young girls offered to monasteries found inspiration and nurture from older mentors, as recounted in the fictional story of Pelagia, who was instructed and baptized by a deaconess, Romana. When Gregory of

Nyssa came to attend to Macrina's funeral, the whole convent met him formally at the church led by a young widow, Vetiana, and Lampadium, "a deaconess in charge of a group of women."[39] They joined freely with pilgrims from the countryside, "hosts of nuns, maidens, and priests" in celebrating the service.

The friendship of a few like-minded women sometimes expanded into a fair-sized community that, like the Pachomian communities, always bore some element of syneisactism, if only because women could not live a religious life without the services of male clergymen and could not live a reclusive life without the mediation of servants and tradesmen. Olympias established the first convent for women in Constantinople in her urban residence.[40] She was joined by two other deaconesses, Elisanthia and Martyria, and the rule they devised kept the community alive for several centuries. Two hundred and fifty women ultimately lived within the house, which shared a wall with the episcopal residence. While no man or woman was supposed to enter from outside, Bishop John Chrysostom gave them spiritual instruction in return for which Olympias imitated Martha by preparing and serving his meals. She had no difficulty in playing a strenuous public part in the bishop's quarrels with the emperor. When Paula went to the Holy Land, she was attended by a "flock of virgins" who intended to settle with her in the desert. Though Jerome said specifically that she refused the hospitality of the bishop's palace in favor of a humble cottage, he did not explain how she housed the retinue of dependents. The cottage must have been of very commodious dimensions: once the whole party was installed in Bethlehem, they numbered about fifty women. Paula's monastery in Bethlehem was complemented by a male community headed by Jerome that she also supported.

No antique *familia* was complete without its servants and retainers. The house monastery was no exception, but its structure was profoundly modified by the rhetoric of social equality that runs back to the partnership of women and slaves embedded in Christian legend. Biographers of ascetics stress that they freed their slaves as part of the whole process of divesting themselves of their wealth. Melania the Younger disposed of eighty thousand slaves. Most of them probably joined the ranks of freedpeople, a recognized social class in the empire that traditionally maintained legal and social ties to former owners. Others expressed the desire not to be freed and went to other masters. But some percentage of the women accepted Melania's offer to support them in monasteries under the same severe rules to which she subjected herself. Macrina's community included her former slaves and servants living a common life with her and her friends on her country estates, "making them her sisters and equals rather than her slaves and underlings."[41] The original fifty women in Olympias's convent included her servants and presumably those of the other women who came from the best senatorial families. "She called her household from slavery to freedom proclaiming them to be of the same honor as her own nobility."[42] What did this mean in concrete terms? In some cases, relationships between women and their servants may have been little changed by the rhetoric of equality. Women had severely limited opportunities to make their own way in the Roman world without male support. Roman women were not independently eligible for the dole, and the private charities of Christian communities seem to have been somewhat unsystematic in nature. Thus women from the poorest classes may have benefited most readily from the generosity of wealthy ascetics, finding shelter and a livelihood from the bounty of the consecrated rich. For poor women with genuine vocations, this arrangement could have proved a real blessing. Other women, however, may simply have taken on the monastic discipline to continue the employment they needed for survival. Jerome noted that the women of Paula's community were divided into three social classes reflecting their rank in the world (though all dressed alike and shared the hardships of the communal life). "If a virgin were of noble birth she was not allowed to have an attendant belonging to her own household lest her maid fill her mind full of the doing of the old days and the license of childhood and might, by constant converse, open old wounds and renew former errors."[43] Prudent as this rule was, it does suggest that noble virgins had lower-class virgins as attendants.

Manual labor was intrinsic to the ascetic discipline, and the sources agree that high-born women did not shirk their share. All monastics received instruction in the importance of avoiding idleness and practicing the humility of domestic tasks. Pachomius introduced manual labor primarily for the practical purpose of concentrating the body so that its native restlessness would not distract the spirit. For that reason, the most monotonous household task and the simplest handicrafts were recommended. But life in the convent was hard and hardest for those unaccustomed to a life of labor. The drudgery of hauling water and scrubbing floors was a physical challenge as well as a powerful test of the spirit. The sixth-century life of Susan by John of Ephesus recorded that the young heroine was initially rejected as a novice because, "Your genteel upbringing does not make you suitable for a convent."[44] Only heroic asceticism convinced the community that she might succeed.

In Paula's community, regardless of class divisions, all the women met together for services. All the sisters dressed alike, using linen only to dry their hands, and none owned anything but food and clothing. Paula chastised each sister according to her nature, humbling the forward, talkative, or quarrelsome, while caring tenderly for the weak or sick.[45] Everyone labored at making clothes and at scriptural study under her supervision. The class division was most likely to make itself felt as the literate and educated ladies applied themselves to work wholly beyond the reach of the humbler women in their midst. But it is possible that some female slaves were literate enough to copy books and fulfill other monastic tasks. Melania the Younger spent her time writing on little tablets according to a fixed schedule of reading and writing each day followed by two hours of sleep. At night she led her virgins in prayer vigils. She instructed novices in chastity and life "above the strife."[46] Presumably the women in this enviable position included her former slaves and those redeemed prostitutes whom Melania had vowed to serve like a slave in return for their chastity.

Throughout this history, the problem of class relations and social stratification within ascetic communities will remain complex and ultimately impenetrable. Melania founded many communities as widely dispersed as her vast estates. There is, therefore, a good chance that the slaves who opted to join these houses enjoyed a high degree of autonomy in governing their own lives under her rule. Her community probably mirrored the stratification of her estates. Moreover, her biographer never explained how gender entered into her arrangements. Were the women mixed with the men in these communities as they had been mixed in the secular world? It is likely that at least some key administrative roles were in fact allotted to former male slaves. Despite the willingness of ascetic women to assume much of the hard labor usually assigned to female slaves, they must have maintained men, whether slaves, freed servants, or lower-class monks, to perform tasks beyond the strength or at least the seemliness of women.

Subsistence was a secondary consideration at best since the lives and sayings of the great ascetics all emphasized that God would provide for those who trusted in him, particularly through the agency of generous and charitable Christians, who in their turn gained the right to participate in the merits of the ascetics by their practice of that greatest of all virtues. The real labor of ascetics was prayer, the *opus Dei*, meditation, broken only by reading and chanting the praises of God. Prayer had more than intrinsic value. It had economic value as well. Asceticism developed the principle of transferable grace, the ability of highly skilled spiritual adepts to accumulate merit to offset the imperfections of well-meaning people left in the world. Gregory of Nyssa gave the superficial impression that his sister and her community lived in complete poverty and seclusion, but he also revealed that Macrina never refused a request for charity, including the important work of hospitality.[47] He noted with satisfaction that they entertained a visitor to their establishment and his wife and their retinue generously, if temperately. Macrina personally entertained the wife and her female entourage. The husband was installed in separate quarters maintained by her brother Peter, with a small community of men. The couple were so delighted with the uplifting atmosphere of the household that they exchanged notes through the servants agreeing to lengthen their stay.[48] Paula once managed two bishops and at least part of their retinues as house guests.[49] In his eulogy for Gorgonia, Gregory of Nazianzus praised his mother for her hospitality, charity, and sympathy, which made her advice law to the men around her.[50] Every desert dweller knew that charity breeds charity. Melania conducted the empress Eudoxia on a tour of the Palestine monasteries. In return for such hospitality, Eudoxia bestowed generous endowments for new desert communities. On at least one occasion, the ascetics were able to show their own generosity by sending ships loaded with grain to starving Rome in the wake of the barbarian invasions. The discipline of the desert demanded poverty of its adherents, but poverty attracted wealth and wealth ideally bred charity and all the prestige and honor that the Lord allows to a generous giver.

The concept of poverty became, like the desert, an assemblage of mirages and complex exchanges. John Cassian, who translated the conventions of the eastern deserts into customs suitable for the west, felt that ascetics should avoid pastoral care for the sake of solitude but warned them not to become heedless of the claims of charity. He praised a noblewoman of Alexandria who attended destitute widows while living as a solitary in the city on her own resources. Of this same woman, he quoted Piamun as saying: "It is enough to shame us, who cannot be at peace unless buried away in caves like wild beasts."[51] Women with fortunes ranging from the comfortable to the vast sought to obey Jesus' command to sell all they had and give to the poor. According to Macrina's brother, she gave her inheritance to the priest who served them and continued to serve God through manual labor. Melania the Younger spent years systematically divesting herself of her wealth. Paula had enough to build and support Jerome's monastery as well as her own, numbering about fifty women, even after she was said to have stripped herself for the benefit of her children—Paulina, Rufina, and Toxotius.[52] In the end, certainly, Eustochium was hard put to keep them all fed.

But all this giving was not a simple reduction to poverty. The charity itself was an act of merit. It also related to the public activities of noblemen, distinguished from pagan times by the numbers and weight of their clientele. The ascetic life opened access to similar prestige to women through patronage of "the poor," who included the clergy and, especially, ascetics. Empress Pulcheria used her consecrated independence to give luster to her theological enterprises. Having built her imperial character on her virginity, she used charity as a means of building a clientele among ascetics who had previously been unremittingly hostile to the established order.

The military imagery so dear to the desert imagination inverted the world order. Where emperors were victorious conquerors leading their soldierly followers against the enemies of Rome, women like Pulcheria could command the *militia Christi* against the more formidable enemies of the kingdom of heaven. Pulcheria, however, resisted ordination as a deaconess, which would have brought her under episcopal authority.[53] Highly unorthodox herself, she sympathized with unruly ascetics who often found themselves doctrinally opposed to episcopal authority and nearly always felt temperamentally antagonistic to what they considered episcopal compromise with the world. She protected them from her brother's government and from the bishop. Similarly, her archrival and sister-in-law, Eudocia, supported rebellious monks against the decrees of Chalcedon even to the point of armed rioting. As late as 417, Melania the Younger gave the heretic Pelagius refuge in the Holy Land, possibly attracted by a vision of translating ascetic Christianity into a spiritual elitism based on the efficacy of works to achieve salvation.

This generation of spectacularly wealthy and influential women lived in a disintegrating world. The fortunes that supported their prestige were being dissipated, and the deserts themselves were in danger from the barbarians who roamed ever more freely within the imperial borders. The secular and ecclesiastical authorities, though indulgent, had little patience. Possibly in retaliation for Olympias's successful defiance of his order that she remarry, Theodosius had legislated that only women over sixty who had already completed their duties to husband and children could be admitted to the deaconess order. He allowed her to devote her own private income to charitable purposes but prohibited the alienation of family property or legacies to anyone outside the family.[54]

Holy men or women could and did mediate for a community with God, with imperial officers and eventually with the barbarians, but in the end the greatest personal prestige melted away without ongoing support to house their relics and surviving communities to publicize their deeds. Unlike the organizational power of the episcopacy, which welded Christian communities together in the face of invasion, heresy, and devastation, asceticism depended on individual heroism and charisma. House monasteries were by nature ephemeral, lacking an institutional base to sustain them when the foundress died or her fortune was exhausted. Charity became a bridge between desert and diocese. Macrina's brother Bishop Basil of Caesarea emphasized works of charity and hospitality as well as mortification in the rule he adapted from the Pachomian model for both monks and nuns, which became the model for mainstream eastern monasticism thereafter. Olympias was famous for her charity, which one of her nuns described as "extending through the entire world of monasteries, convents, churches; beggars, prisoners and exiles." Chrysostom added his praises but discouraged her from going out among the poor personally. He preferred to channel her generosity through his own office to the clergy, the ascetic community, her own convent, and the poor. Cynical as that may seem, it may also be the reason why the community's endowment continued to be replenished from new sources, maintaining the charitable tradition to the time when the abbess Sergia wrote the history of the convent in the sixth century.[55]

After the sack of Rome and the passing of the great ascetics of the early fifth century, the increasing severity of the barbarian threat forced a new solidarity on the contending forces of Christian Rome. Despite Jerome's advice against building churches as a form of charity, women increasingly developed the construction of basilicas associated with the cult of the saints as a public role in which to express their own prestige while supporting episcopal projects. Demetrias had the influential support of Bishop Augustine of Hippo in refusing the betrothal her father had arranged. In return she dignified his diocese with new monuments. Even Pulcheria retained episcopal complaisance in her schemes by building churches, housing relics, and promoting the cult of the saints. She built the first church dedicated to the Virgin Mary and promoted her cult in association with Bishop Atticus, who allowed her and her community of virgins to guide his policies as Chrysostom had formerly listened to Olympias. Raising monuments for the saints became also a chief bridge between the dying Roman world of the west and the new-born barbarian Christendom. In the middle of the fifth century, Genovefa of Paris contributed her formidable spiritual powers to the construction of the first basilica for Saint Denis and his fellow martyrs. Clothild, the first Christian queen of the Franks, swiftly adopted the tradition.

Thus in the fifth century, the desert became institutionalized; the mystical landscape evolved into a system of "cities in the desert." As Roman society closed up under siege, noblemen made peace with the orthodox Christian leaders and increasing numbers of aristocrats joined the ranks of the bishops. Christianity became more respectable and more masculine. Despite the power of Empress Pulcheria and the influence of Melania the Younger, the voices of women faded as their fortunes evaporated and their independence succumbed to the threat of violence. In the east, the virginity movement, while still representing an alternative for women, was increasingly confined and restrained by rules, isolation, and silence. Men regained control of their families even as bishops gained control of the *familia Christi*. Bishops and secular authorities joined to restrain the passions of the desert. Personal discipline was distilled into rules and rules came under episcopal patronage.

The call of the desert was still compelling. The Council of Chalcedon decreed that no monastery would be built in the future without episcopal approval but, once built, no monastery should be abolished or its property diminished. Monks became bishops and monastic principles raised the devotional standards even of married bishops. More than one prelate projected his thwarted longing for eremitic perfection upon his saintly sisters. Gregory of Nyssa wrote Macrina's biography, possibly to advance a specific type of feminine monasticism against the free-wheeling experimentation of the desert. He credited her with initiating three younger brothers into the ascetic life, which involved puncturing the unseemly pride of Basil when he came home full of his scholarship and clerical distinction. Before he was called to the episcopate, Basil established himself in a hermitage across the river from her. Gregory further mentioned many communities in Cappadocia modeled after hers. Later, Basil formed several communities of both women and men using a modified Pachomian rule; he remains famous as the great regulator of eastern monasticism. Basil's system also emphasized cooperation with the bishop and influenced the decrees of Chalcedon that episcopal consent would determine the spread of monasticism. He set an example in numerous pastoral letters to ascetics of various suits, including some urban women styled *Kanonikai*. He was able to reconcile the clergy and the ascetics through a vision of monasticism that wiped out the sharp opposition of desert and city, monk and episcopate, in favor of mutual cooperation.

The Greek tradition, however, grew steadily in the direction of cloistering women and separating them from men, who were explicitly afraid of contact. The virtue of eastern saints came to be measured by their gynophobia. One saint beat a nun who tried to show him reverence, believing it to be a trick of the devil, and the same saint marked the presence of a Latin priest in a convent with horror. Women were barred from the veneration of relics in Greek male houses, and in one story a woman had to adopt male disguise to circumvent the prohibition. Nevertheless, Greek holy men in southern Italy as well as in the east established communities to house their own female relatives and protect them against the greed of secular nobles. In one exemplary tale, the saint warned a nobleman: "If you should die and your wife should wish to live in holiness and becomes associated with another man because she has nowhere to go, the fault will be yours for not taking care that the city should have a monastery."[56]

The Latin tradition remained somewhat freer. Augustine was a bishop who started with ascetic ambitions, inspired by his mother and a sister who founded a community of nuns under his patronage. He wrote several prescriptive pieces for ascetics, some addressed to men, some to women, and others to both. There has been much controversy about the origin and purpose of this collective "rule," which became the base for one of the most influential guides to the monastic life in future centuries. Possibly it was inspired in part by the needs of his noble protégée, the virgin Demetrias.[57] Dissension in his sister's convent after her death precipitated Augustine's corrective letter in 423 to her fellow virgins containing a series of precepts.[58] Whether these pieces represent his original inspiration or whether they are variations on works already written for men, we shall probably never know. In any case, he made no difference between women and men but repeated the same prescriptions for both. The immediate point of the quarrel appears to have been money. He ruled that all property be held in common and distributed according to individual need as determined by the prioress. He ordered those who had formerly been wealthy to give up their privileges freely and told those who had been poor not to try to improve upon their former conditions. This absolute sharing of goods became a keystone of the monastic life, though often debated by various communities.

Augustine also provided general guidelines for the daily routine of the sisters' lives. They were to meet regularly for common prayer. He did not indicate the content of these services but they were likely to resemble the Basilian order that Melania the Younger was introducing in her convents. Food and drink were to be temperate and table manners seemly. The women were to dress modestly and be veiled, taking their clothing from the common store at random. Clothes and bodies were to be washed but not to excess. Each woman was to render regular service to the others by distributing or caring for communal goods, working in the library or the infirmary. Finally, he included a code of behavior. He urged that although they would see men when they were out of the house, they should control their wandering eyes and report any lapses of other sisters. Above all, he forbade quarreling among them and required obedience to the prioress. Augustine's text was known to Caesarius of Arles, and other great rule makers of the west including Benedict and Leander of Seville would draw freely upon it.

Most of the men associated with the virginity movement were eventually moved, even against their wills, into the episcopacy. Pachomius tried to avoid the subordination of charismatic authority to priestly office for himself and his monks by appealing to the overruling power of Christ. It took more than one generation before the men submitted to the hierarchy and then they entered the priesthood. No hagiographer was romantic enough to imagine a woman disguised as a man entering the ranks of the priesthood. Women, however admirable or even masculine, were condemned by virtue of their gender to a secondary state from which no degree of sanctity would lift them.

But ascetics could and did continue to challenge the primacy of the priesthood. Martin of Tours mourned that he had lost much of his power to make miracles when he allowed himself to become a bishop. Augustine tried to live as a monk among his clergy. Like the prophets of early Christianity, the desert dwellers shared an inherently anticlerical ideal, subtly expressed in their ability to remain in the wilderness without the sacraments for decades at a time. In the sixth century, Benedict of Nursia incorporated a warning against ordination into his rule.

Asceticism rivaled the clergy in seeking to define a standard by which Christians must be measured. The clergy was a male precinct, excluding women except in the tentative partnerships of spiritual marriages. As time passed, monastics succeeded in making the ordinary conjugal life of priests seem tawdry and self-indulgent. The clergy in turn pronounced the cohabitation of chaste men and women to be scandalous and tried to force them into segregation from the world and from each other. In practice, however, this rigor continued to be vitiated by the personal ties of clerics to monastic women. Even where women became cloistered, as at Arles in Gaul, Bishop Caesarius remained as interested and familiar as Chrysostom had been with Olympias. Ascetics remained syneisactic at heart because they rejected sexuality and reproduction. Even when they bowed to the reality of physical sexual differences, they stubbornly rejected the idea of spiritual differences. Monks admitted that they were often plagued with sexual temptation—though the problem must have been heavily exaggerated by prescriptive writers or their efforts at syneisactism could hardly have been so persistent. Even when they gave in to segregation, the rules that governed the desert assumed that there was no spiritual feat that women could not perform equally with men.

Monastic spirituality centered on prayer and meditation rather than the sacraments. Egeria spoke of litanies and processions. Melania the

Younger brought Basilian liturgies into her monasteries and devised a special ceremony at the place of the Ascension.[59] Women particularly became interested in devotions associated with graves and relics. The preparation of feasts and memorials associated with family graves, the care of the dead, the anointing of bodies, and the ceremonies of mourning had always been a peculiarly feminine responsibility. The first Christian women had associated themselves in that special way with Jesus and there is evidence that at the time of the Great Persecution, their successors performed the burials and therefore shaped the cults of the martyrs. The Easter scene, the three Marys in search of the Lord, had an abiding liturgical significance that women cherished through the centuries.

Virgins had, of course, occupied a front row as martyrs and therefore qualified for the highest rank among the saints. The new self-created martyrs were also women whose communities tended the bodies of holy foundresses and devoted themselves to promoting their cults. Thus, by the middle of the fifth century, monasticism was becoming tamed and respectable in many aspects, but it always stood outside the clerical hierarchy. Individual holiness, attainable by women as well as men, still distinguished ascetics from the ordained priesthood.

Moreover, the diocese was still primarily an urban phenomenon, and urbanism was far more deeply rooted in the Greek east than in the Latin west. At about the same period as the western cities were collapsing in the face of barbarian invasion, John Cassian began an active collaboration with Pope Leo I promoting monastic communities in Gaul, a province rapidly being turned into desert by successive disasters. In youth, John had been a staunch believer in the superiority of the hermit life, but as he grew older and the conflicts between the eastern bishops and the desert dwellers whom he knew and loved became more fierce, he grew to believe in communal discipline as primary to successful monasticism. His double monastery (or twin monasteries) of Saint Victor in Marseilles became a model, and his books introduced the idea of conferences, discussions and meditations on the meaning of the monastic life for its practitioners.

Cassian's practices governed his sister's monastery also but probably not without modification. It is certainly unlikely that the nuns left their postulants lying naked at the door for ten days to test their contempt for the world before admitting them to the cloister. It is perfectly possible

that they adopted much the same costume, with all the symbolic trimmings that Cassian advised for monks, though a veil must have been
added for women. Cassian prescribed common labor like basket weaving,
gardening, weaving, and cooking for his monks, which would have been
highly suitable for nuns as well. We know that the rotating week of
kitchen service he prescribed was instituted in Gallic convents in the sixth
century. The agent of the transfer was surely Caesaria of Arles, who
trained at Marseilles with an eye to establishing a monastery in her
brother's bishopric. The liturgy revolved around the cyclical chanting of
the psalter with minimal dependence on sacraments. Hence, the women
would have had a substantial round of autonomous spiritual duties
broken only occasionally by the ministry of a priest. The reading Cassian
supplied for his community concerns sins and virtues and his elaboration
of their effects on the soul, which would have been as suitable for women
as for men. Caesaria confirmed that women reached the highest level of
prayer, which Cassian described as stripping the mind to pure concentration by focusing on a simple phrase repeated over and over.[60]

While Cassian's sister and her fellow nuns were learning to focus their
spirits through chanting, chaste episcopal couples were transferring their
house monasteries to the island of Lérins off the Mediterranean coast to
escape the collapsing cities. In Paris, the consecrated virgin Genovefa
organized a troop of matrons to pray the Huns away from the city. An
escaped slave named Patrick headed back to the far frontiers of the west
to convert his captors, including the famed Bridget of Kildare. The
British church withdrew from history itself before the first onslaughts of
the Anglo-Saxons. Europe, in effect, was becoming a society of northern
peoples linked to the heritage of Rome through Christianity. Barbarian
women would soon discover the alternative of the celibate life, their own
legacy from sisters who had labored for centuries against the power of
Roman fathers. They would cherish it and it would spread with the new
religion throughout the western wilderness. A new generation of Christian women would thrill to the example of the women who spoke through
Jerome to men who shirked the final challenge: "Souls have no sex.
Therefore I may fairly call your soul the daughter of hers. For as a
mother coaxes her unweaned child, which is as yet unable to take solid
food, so does she call you to the milk suitable for babes and offers to
you the sustenance that a nursing mother gives."[61]

II

THE EARLY MIDDLE AGES

4

⊹

The Power of Prayer

WHEN MARTIN OF TOURS began to introduce the ascetic life to Gaul in the middle of the fourth century, his disciple, Sulpicius Severus, humorously described his difficulties in a dialogue. He quoted a typical Gaul's response that fasting was simply alien to the nature of his people.[1] John Cassian noted the same differences with a less kindly attitude, attributing lack of zeal to laziness.[2] The cold, damp "desert" of the western forests assuredly lacked the appeal of eastern oases. Women like Paula who decided to attempt the life generally migrated to the Holy Land. The influx of Germanic people intent on carving out new kingdoms from the dismembered empire increased the dangers of the wilderness. Nevertheless, in the twilight of the western empire, many people turned from the transient world to the contemplation of eternity. Monasticism in the embattled west was more likely to be an urban phenomenon, a fortress against the violence of the desert, than a haven from the temptations of the city. When the legions of Rome retreated, the power of prayer became the sole recourse for the women and men who defended the city of God.

Many monks failed to follow Cassian's lead in making provision for women as well as men. The best-documented space in Gaul was the agglomeration around Saint Martin's basilica in Tours, which was restricted to men. Bishop Gregory of Tours's account of the virgin Papula, a typical transvestite saint who had once lived among the monks at Tours, suggests that there was no female community to receive her when she fled her family rather than marry.³ Most consecrated women lived alone or with a few companions, usually close within the orbit of their bishop. Even their largest communities were extensions of households, not designed to survive their wealthy patronesses. Virgins attached themselves to bishops, appearing as a group to chant in public procession as at Rouen. The virgins of Rome marched in a body when Pope Gregory I organized a procession around the city to pray for an end to plague. Contemporary authors wrote little about these women, but their association with episcopal liturgy suggests that they may be related to the *kanonikai* who appear in the letters of Basil of Caesarea and to the canonesses who so proudly and persistently defended their special status in the later Middle Ages.

Even as the Germanic tribes settled down and the Roman and Celtic populations began to assimilate with them and adjust to their rule, they fought incessantly with one another. Loot was their major source of income, and the principle of survival of the fittest dominated their lives. Warfare was a way of life: men died and women went to their murderers' beds. The captive Thuringian princess Radegund lamented:

> The matron was rapt away with streaming hair, bound fast
> Without even a sad farewell to the household gods.
> Nor could the captive press a kiss on the threshold
> Nor cast one backward glance toward what was lost.
> A wife's naked feet trod in her husband's blood
> And the tender sister stepped over the fallen brother.
> The boy torn from his mother's embrace, his funeral plaint
> Hanging on her lips, with all her tears unshed.
> So to lose the life of a child is not the heaviest lot,
> Gasping, the mother lost even her pious tears.
> I, the barbarian woman, seek not to count those tears
> Nor to keep afloat in the melancholy lake of all those drops.⁴

The Germans infiltrated and finally conquered Britain, Gaul, Spain, Italy, and the Rhine frontier. Like the Romans, they too learned to live behind walls. Flight from the world came to be symbolized not by the vast emptiness of the desert but by the monastery, walls within walls. Cassian and his sister established their twin communities at Marseilles between 413 and 416, as the Visigoths were moving over southern Gaul and into Spain. At about the same time, Honoratus established his foundation at Lérins and there he was joined by a number of leading Romans, including Eucherius and Galla, survivors of Therasia and Paulinus's network of chaste couples. Honoratus's sister, Margaret, has traditionally been credited with establishing a separate community for women on the neighboring island that today bears her name. Lérins became famous as a training ground for bishops and monastic leaders where, it is conjectured, Patrick trained before his mission to Ireland.

Our only knowledge of the Germanic peoples before their conversion to Christianity, and indeed for some time thereafter, comes from Roman sources. Even their law codes were translated through the medium of Latin-literate clergy. Bearing this in mind, a few generalizations are widely accepted and appear to apply to the pre-Christian Celts as well. Even in distant Ireland, where there were neither Romans nor Germans, women were habitually enslaved by the raiding enemies of their families. Barbarian society was based on kinship, with a kindred defined by submission to a "father" in return for the assurance that he would avenge any injury to his "family," which included a series of fictive relatives arising from slavery, dependency, and marriage. The kindred accepted collective responsibility for its members before the law and provided collective security under threat of feud and vendetta. Narrative accounts remind us sharply that even this rough-and-ready ideal was more honored in the breach than the observance. But certainly no one who did not have some status, however low, within a kindred had any source of protection or any claim to legal rights.

Obviously, celibacy was not an ideal that attracted them. For men, the *comitatus,* a warrior gang grouped around a powerful lord, provided some alternative to the family and gave some young men the opportunity to establish families of their own by taking captive women and the means to maintain them. Women, on the other side, had a better chance than men of being left alive after a battle and forcibly adopted into a new family. Since important lords were polygamous, they could collect several female trophies. An unmarried man was an unsuccessful man. An unmarried woman simply had no point or value except as a potential wife or concubine. Whether or not she was of childbearing age determined her legal status. Even the Arian missionaries who converted many Germanic peoples to Christianity before they invaded the Roman Empire did not, apparently, promote virginity. At least, Catholic sources make no mention of an ascetic life among them.

Germanic women and the Celtic women of Ireland, Britain and the Gaulish countryside, were, therefore, wholly defined by their familial positions. Within a powerful kindred they often played crucial roles. They had access to wealth through complex inheritance systems that made them eligible for shares in the estates of two families, from fathers and husbands, in addition to lavish gifts from their husbands and clients. They could look for vengeance to their natal families as well as the conjugal unit. If they divorced, they could take their children and their property back to their natal families. If they were widowed, they could take their inheritance from father and husband into a new marriage. Occasionally, slave women could climb into the nobility—some even became queens—through judicious use of sexual attractions.

Although the slippery evidence is difficult to assess, Celtic and Germanic legends that survived into Christian times appear to agree that warrior kings and nobles awarded a high public position to their wives and mothers. Widows sometimes acted as regents for their sons. Contemporary histories reveal some women who were positively frightening in their abuses of power, and the literary heritage of the Germanic peoples, transcribed in later centuries, enhances that image. These viragos, however, were only survivors in a vicious system that gave no quarter to the weak. The respect they earned was real but it was not lasting and it was not structural. The sources do not bear out any notion that women enjoyed power and prestige simply by virtue of their position. They only assure us that some women took advantage of the chaotic world they lived in to wrench what they could from individuals weaker than themselves. Exceptional women made exceptional marks in violent and disordered circumstances, but contemporary chronicles tell too many tales of rape, murder, and widespread terror to give comfort to any hopeful analyst. Successful warriors exhibited their women, dripping with gold and jewelry, to publicize their victories. The woman who appears in one story as a noble queen, giving gifts and hospitality, may well have been forced as a captive into her husband's bed.[5]

In this setting, the idea of a religious woman as a bride of Christ had real social meaning. Many women sought a heavenly marriage to save them from an earthly one they had reason to dread. Many women were given for political reasons to God in a process that mirrored the betrothals and weddings of the world.[6] Once they had entered the monastery, the abbesses, at least, ruled their households and dispensed charity and patronage as became the consorts of a great king. They relied on divine protection and vengeance in the same way that they would have relied on the protection of an earthly spouse.

As these women came to live among a Catholic population, we can only imagine their initial reactions to Romanized peoples and their religion. Relations between the new rulers and the Roman church were uneasy if not decisively hostile. In the days of the conquests, a bishop or some other self-designated religious person functioned as protector and mediator for the flock. As such they strengthened and perpetuated the independence of the church, already well established in the Roman Empire. Women consecrated to religion, sometimes as the wives of the clergy but more often as unmarried women vowed to chastity, shared these mediating roles. Living alone as recluses or in small house monasteries, they opened channels of healing and charity between the peoples. Embattled bishops, even at some risk to themselves, often supported their independence against the demands of their own kindred, and even their own husbands, to secure their services for religion.

The process of recruiting was apparently haphazard, a combination of episcopal initiative and individual vocation. Holy women usually appear in the sidelights of chronicles, offering shelter or assistance to others and sometimes prophesying or scolding wrongdoers. The life of Eustadiola of Bourges, for example, is buried in the more impressive biography of her patron Bishop Sulpicius, who helped the wealthy widow resist family pressure to remarry. When drought threatened the diocese, Eustadiola and her companions walked in a small procession to the church to pray for rain. They barely regained their home before the downpour began. Such proof of divine favor gave her prestige as a mediator in settling local quarrels and helped protect her wealth from vandals so that she could support a household of women engaged in prayer and charitable works.[7]

Only the life of Genovefa of Paris is fully documented, because the Franks who converted to Catholicism in her lifetime adopted the virgin mediator for the Gallo-Roman Christians as patron of their new capital city. Bishop Germanus of Auxerre marked her out for the consecrated life in childhood but he was only able to spare her a single day of instruction and a coin marked with a cross which he hung about her neck to remind her of her promise.[8] There is a high probability that Germanus recruited other women who did not achieve the enormous fame in store for Genovefa. British virgins who might have been consecrated during his preaching missions overseas would have been engulfed in the great darkness that fell on the island during the Anglo-Saxon invasions. Despite Bede's hostile dismissiveness of the British church, it did survive and it is likely that holy women, celebrated in local legend, played an important part in that long ordeal.

Alone and unaided, attacked by suspicious neighbors and angry parents, Genovefa pursued her purpose until she was old enough to secure episcopal consecration.[9] Though other girls received the veil with her, they did not form a community. Genovefa lived at home, subjected to her mother's complaints and beatings when she gave prayer and church attendance priority over household chores. When she moved to Paris after her mother's death, her neighbors questioned her reputation as a wonder worker. On one occasion, they were threatening to lynch her when an archdeacon intervened, swearing that Germanus would vouch for her. She performed the most celebrated deed of her life when she successfully protected Paris from the marauding Huns with a wall of prayer and continued its defense in the critical days when the Frankish king Childeric was conquering Gaul. Genovefa traveled tirelessly around the Parisian countryside, healing the sick, routing demons, freeing prisoners and, once, slaying a dragon that endangered her ship. During the siege of Paris, she persuaded Childeric to allow her to take a fleet of ships up the Seine to collect food for the city. Of all the miracles that accompanied her progress, perhaps the most astonishing was her reckless distribution of the hard-won bread to the poorest and most helpless people in the city.[10] Childeric could not have been immune to her piety and charity. The citizens of Paris long remembered that when he wanted to execute some of his prisoners he locked the city gates to prevent Genovefa's interference. Undeterred, the redoubtable virgin pushed aside the heavy barriers and saved the helpless captives.

Perhaps attracted by such displays of female autonomy as much as by their own charitable feelings, some Germanic women slipped from one side to the other. Queen Clothild, Childeric's daughter-in-law, was the first of many queens and noble ladies to join with Roman bishops as advocates for the downtrodden. Through her efforts the Franks were brought to Catholicism.[11] Much ink has been spilled over why pagan peoples converted to Christianity so quickly and what the religion meant to them once they had done so. Our scant record of the process is limited to the Catholic missions where women were often in the forefront as missionaries to their husbands and sons, a subject I will deal with more fully in the next chapter. Although there is much room for debate as to how far Christian teachings actually penetrated into the barbarian psyche, the record leaves little doubt that the women understood and eagerly embraced the virginity movement. We find highly placed recruits within the first generation of Christian women everywhere and, though the sources do not focus on the subject, the movement clearly reached deeply through the social layers.

Small house monasteries were easily situated to inspire and absorb Germanic as well as Roman converts. So quickly and seamlessly that the process is barely noticeable in the record, the women of the conquering peoples snatched at the opportunity to free themselves from marriage and childbearing and became leaders in the spread and establishment of monasticism in the European west. Clothild's own sister took refuge in a Catholic convent after the murder of their parents by their Arian uncle. After Clovis died, Clothild went into retreat from 511 to 545. Later writers credited her with transitory foundations at Tours, Les Andelys, and other unnamed places.[12] Radegund, the wife of Clothild's son Clothar, began to teach herself the rudiments of religious life while still a child. As queen, she sought instruction in asceticism from local hermits, including a woman who sent her a blessed hair shirt to wear under her royal robes.

The reason for this excess of devotion is not difficult to discern. The violence that threatened Roman women did not spare their Germanic sisters. Radegund was a prize of battle, whom Clothar won by lot from his brothers after they had killed nearly all her relatives in a raid on her native Thuringia. She was forced to marry her captor and to live with him and, presumably, his four other wives, for some years. He complained publicly about being married to a woman with the character of a nun but he would not release her. Finally, after he murdered her brother, she resorted to desperate measures. She fled and forced the unwilling bishop of Soissons to consecrate her by threatening him with divine vengeance if he let her soul slip away. Reluctantly, he consented to make her a deaconess. This revival of an ancient and moribund office was probably the only straw the bishop found to clutch in his deadly dilemma: since neither virginity nor widowhood was a necessary precondition for deaconesses, he left himself a loophole to escape the wrath of the venomous Clothar. After a couple of abortive attempts to get her back, the king resigned himself and subsidized the first large-scale female monastery that we know about among the Franks.[13] Radegund had already read extensively in monastic literature and personally inquired about the life from its practitioners. In 550, when she established Sainte-Croix of Poitiers, she confirmed the west's trend toward the regular life by adopting the *Rule for Nuns* of Caesarius of Arles.[14]

With the worst of the invasions a century in the past, Bishop Caesarius felt it would be safe to return to the desert ideal and selected a site in an old Roman burial ground outside the city for his sister's community. But when the incomplete monastery was destroyed by raiders in 512, he rebuilt within the city walls and, for good measure, surrounded the convent with yet a second set of walls.[15] He stipulated that each nun take a lifetime vow of stability and enclosure.[16] The sisters were to remain indoors and trust others to provide for their needs. Extensive precautions were taken within the monastery to ensure that this claustration would be kept physically and to accomplish the spiritual and psychological changes that would internalize it. Passages to the outside were blocked up and all private conversation, with insiders as well as outsiders, was monitored. Letters and packages were channeled through the abbess. In the context of the age, and particularly in view of Radegund's anxiety to emulate Arles, it seems safe to say that Caesarius's purpose was not so much to keep the nuns in as to keep the world, particularly the men of the world, out. Caesarius's provisions for enclosure probably appealed to Radegund in view of her past history of captivity and her fear of her husband's return. Her patronage would make it intrinsic to the regular life, life under a rule, as formulated for western women.

By its nature, the monastery aimed at becoming a sanctuary, a place of peace and protection. Whereas the desert hermits had fled admirers who wished to emulate them, early medieval monastics were in flight from marauders who wished to rob and ravage them. Even a marriage properly arranged by her parents might force a girl to act as a hostage in an unfriendly household. Hagiographers frequently depicted the heroine's escape from the dual pressures of family and fiancé by praying to be made repulsive. Saint Bridget was miraculously mutilated until safely consecrated, and Saint Angadrisma contracted leprosy, which healed once she had taken the veil. Both legend and reality are full of desperate tales of women fighting to retain their virginity at all costs and enter a walled enclosure that would guard them from the lusts of men and the ambitions of their families. One Irish story, the life of Dymphna, portrays its heroine as fleeing the incestuous designs of her own father. Didactic stories highlight the vengeful power of the heavenly suitor who might execute an obstructive parent or rival. The monastery came to resemble a citadel under siege. A nun of Poitiers, Baudonivia, who wrote Radegund's biography, evoked the queen as a guardian holding the sacred fortress against "a thousand thousand demons," who fled when she made the sign of the cross. The convent was seen as a dovecote to shelter the tender and innocent. On another occasion, the saint's command was enough to silence the raucous nightbird who had shattered the peace and stillness of the night. That is the voice of the cloister itself, protesting violation, seeking peace in isolation from the violent world.[17]

For men as well as women, Germanic as well as Romanized peoples, asceticism came to be associated with walled enclosures rather than huts and caves in the wilderness. Monastic rules, which proliferated in the sixth century, were rarely gender-specific. The regulatory trend aimed at enclosing men as well as women. Radegund's contemporary, Benedict of Nursia, prohibited his brethren from entertaining visitors or leaving the monastery overnight. Stability of place was one of the major features of his rule, designed to prevent monks and nuns alike from gadding about in a dangerous world. The contrast between the old asceticism and the new is strangely illustrated in the life of Benedict himself. Scholastica, his sister, was consecrated to God from her youth but was not confined, as he was, to a monastery. Possibly she simply continued to live in their family home. His rule of stability excluded her and all other women from the monastic enclosure and prohibited him from leaving except on pressing religious business. She came to visit her brother annually, staying at an inn or with friends some hours distant from his monastery. Benedict scrupulously observed his own rule and did not allow his sister to enter his monastery nor himself the liberty of staying with her overnight. When she knew that she was about to die, she begged him to make an exception, but he held firm until a fierce thunderstorm convinced him that God himself had heard Scholastica's prayer. The following day he returned to his monastery and she went back where she came from.[18] Possibly Benedict, like Martin of Tours before him, saw his monastery as a battlefield on which women had no place.

Western monasticism did not simply entail the provision of a wall between the community and the world. It abandoned the basic eremitism of the Pachomian rule for communal devotion. Along with the detailed and practical rule of Arles, the second abbess, Caesaria II, sent Radegund a moving letter of spiritual advice reflecting practices learned by her predecessor at the monastery of Cassian's sister in Marseilles. Cassian already believed that communal life was superior to eremitic in holiness, and all the great regulators and patrons of the early period joined him in attacking wandering prophets or "gyrovagues," restless souls who preferred the undisciplined life of the hermit to the character-building ordeal of community. Benedict echoed this sentiment in the sixth century, as did his patron and publicizer Pope Gregory I, who tried to impose stability and claustration on all monasteries. He ordered that secular officials be entrusted with their business dealings and tried to ban services that would attract crowds into monastic chapels. He banned women from male monasteries and all men but priests and supervised workmen from female communities.

Freed from the conflicted affections and loyalties that detract from a married person's total commitment, the virgin always had a tendency toward self-absorption. Celibates lacked the familial structure that socializes and controls members as components of a larger community. Monasticism disciplined them to the demands of the common life, its trials, its rewards, and its opportunities for virtue. In his rule for his sister, Bishop Leander of Seville (575 to 603) particularly urged the claims of the communal life for women above the reclusive life. In a single cell, he maintained, care for survival, domestic arrangements, and even a decent appearance took too much time away from the service of God, whereas in a convent, the nun had the advantage of other women to emulate and the strength that comes from common prayer.[19]

Patrick probably brought the same sentiments to Ireland from Lérins. Without cities to underpin a diocesan structure, the Irish built their church around monasticism, the form of their mission to the neighboring Scots and the northern Anglo-Saxons. The first generation of Christian women in England soon adopted and spread the ideals of virginity they learned from them. Almost a whole generation of royal women and an unknown number of less exalted counterparts seem to have been in full flight. English historians tend accept the fairly well mannered picture of the Anglo-Saxons depicted by their national historian, Bede, but there is no reason to think those Germanic warriors were less brutal than the Franks.

Among them, polygamy can only be inferred. Bede wrote admiringly of princess Etheldreda of East Anglia, who made a life of total chastity the condition for the financial and political advantages that her marriage brought each of her husbands. She guarded her virginity through two marriages, the second lasting twelve years. Her second husband, Egfrid of Northumbria, was probably sustained in this trial by a co-wife, Jurmenberg, who surfaces in another text as an enemy of Etheldreda's friend, Bishop Wilfrid of York, who supported Etheldreda when Egfrid tried to renege.[20] Bede does not mention Jurmenberg or Wilfrids' exile. The math, however, makes the bigamy inescapable: Egfrid reigned from 670 to 685 and exiled Wilfrid in 678, which has to fall within the twelve years of his marriage to Etheldreda, which took place when he was already king. Etheldreda fled Northumbria and took the veil from her aunt Ebba, abbess of Coldingham. Ultimately, she won Egfrid's consent to her consecration after she had sealed herself in a monastery at Ely, in the impregnable dower lands in the fens that she held from her first husband. There she was succeeded by her widowed sister in 680 and then by her virgin niece, Werburg. After Egfrid's death, Jurmenberg too went on to become a pious abbess.

The church allowed entrance into a monastery as a cause of marital dissolution even when the party forsaken (of either gender) had not given consent, and several English bishops are known to have encouraged women who wished to take advantage of the opportunity.[21] Bishop Aldhelm wrote a tract for the nuns of Barking under Abbess Hildelith about 675. Defining virginity as a persevering celibacy and chastity as the gift of those who "having been assigned to marital contracts, have scorned the commerce of matrimony for the sake of the heavenly kingdom," he praised among other formerly married nuns Cuthburga, foundress of Wimbourne, who left her husband, King Aldfrith, for the monastery.[22]

Monastic literature fostered a vision of the outside world as a glowering, threatening place where no woman might hope to be safe. Irish legends warned against venturing out even in search of food for fear of robbers who beheaded their victims. The same source hinted that fallen nuns would have their guilty pregnancies miraculously aborted once they repented and returned to their enclosures. A collection of exempla from Faremoutiers told of a group of women, unhappy with the restrictions of convent life, who planned to escape over the wall on ropes during the night. Most of them were prevented by divine intervention in the shape of a flaming thunderball, which woke the sleeping community and blocked the exits until the women could be recaptured. Two fugitives resisted making full confession to the abbess and would not allow her to guide them back into the sisterhood. Both died horribly of fever. As the sisters gathered around the rebels' beds with the abbess, praying for them and urging them to repent, the delirious women were distracted by diabolic visions. They screamed that they were being attacked by a horde of advancing Ethiopians and died begging to be released from their rapacious clutches. For a long time thereafter, cries and wailings were heard from the tombs of the lost sisters, who had been buried outside the community. At last Burgundofara had them opened, but nothing was found of their bodies except ashes still warm from some dreadful supernatural fire.[23]

Even the cloister had to be reinforced with strong ecclesiastical legislation to keep women safe. Gregory I punished the bishop of Autun for failing to prevent the forced marriage of a nun to a man who abducted her from the convent. The wicked Eulalius kidnapped a nun after killing her cousin and married her, despite his existing marriage to another woman.[24] The Council of Tours in 567 prohibited the marriage of consecrated virgins and widows under any circumstances. The Second Council of Tours went so far as to apply the law to women who claimed they had taken the veil to avoid rape and alluded to laws of Kings Childebert, Clothar, and Charibert on the same subject.[25]

The wars and political reprisals that embroiled the nuns' friends, families, and patrons sometimes burst into the cloister as well. Rusticula was accused of giving shelter to one of the king's enemies in the course of the endless fraternal wars that afflicted the Merovingian dynasty. True to the tradition of Arles, she invoked the rule of claustration to keep her within her sacred sheepfold, but in vain. Even after one of her assailants was miraculously paralyzed, soldiers forced her from the convent to a distant court for royal judgment.[26] Her deserted flock organized a marathon of psalms, prayers, and mourning to assist her progress, which was indeed so marked by miracles and prophecies that it became at last a triumphal procession.

The only recourse amidst constant peril of fire and famine and disease was their divine spouse and the saintly foundresses who had achieved his presence. When sparks from a burning outbuilding threatened the convent of Nivelles, the spirit of Gertrude, the foundress, was seen on the roof protecting the house with her veil.[27] With these oft-repeated tales of miracles and triumphs, monastics drove home the lesson that theirs was a sacred space, and that Christ their father and bridegroom could well protect and avenge his own.

At first, Germans seem to have respected the idea of sanctuary for Romans better than for their own people. The Goths, for example, boasted that when they sacked Rome they took care not to molest women and children who had taken refuge in the churches. Through the sixth century, the idea expanded and fugitives of all sorts fled for protection to sacred places. Hospitality and enclosure became peculiar partners in the monastic life, as military metaphors depicting nuns and monks as advance guards against the forces of evil were perilously transformed into literal reality. Convents began to present themselves to enterprising bishops and even lay people as solutions to all sorts of difficult social problems. Freeing prisoners, for example, was an important vehicle for holy women to demonstrate the power of their prayers.[28] In a logical development, potential or escaped prisoners began camping out in their sanctuaries under their protection.

Gregory of Tours often mentioned women seeking protection in churches. Although he never described their living arrangements, they probably made use of conventual buildings joined physically or built within the sacred compounds of the churches, a common method of protecting nuns from public exposure while enabling them to go to church. Gregory notes that Ingitrude of Tours built her convent in the courtyard of Saint Martin's church. This would have been a logical place for the daughters of the adventuring nobleman Guntram Boso, who was in the habit of depositing them "in the holy church" at Tours.[29] Was it a convent attached to the church of Saint Saturnin of Toulouse that sheltered the wife of Ragnovald who had already been robbed and forced out of sanctuary at Agen?[30] The same site sheltered Princess Rigunth, daughter of Ragnovald's enemy, Chilperic, who had been robbed of her immense dowry while on her way to a Visigothic marriage. But again, the provision of sanctuary entailed the risk of invasion. A woman claiming asylum at Tours came too close to the door and was snatched out by waiting enemies.[31] No wonder a prudent builder like Caesarius walled up every extra entrance!

Sometimes the need for sanctuary was open-ended. The consecrated community provided a comfortable refuge or depository for elderly or superannuated women. Chilperic's first queen, Audovera, entered a convent when the king determined to devote himself exclusively to the jealous Fredegund. It was a wise choice: his second queen, Galswinth, was murdered by the amorous couple. In turn, some conventual shelter must have been available when the widowed Fredegund took sanctuary in Paris while rallying her husband's allies to her cause.[32] If so, her supporters, coming and going, repeatedly breached the cloister. Queen Balthild was apparently subjected to a certain amount of coercion to give up her regency and devote herself to sainthood. Her biography discreetly hinted that the nuns at Chelles, despite her generosity to them, had some reservations about admitting her among them. Sadalberga, Rictrude, Ita, and many other widows refused second marriages and embraced the conventual life as a logical step in their lifecycles. Most of these widows had some endowment that could be stretched to support the needy as well as themselves. The rule of Donatus of Besançon expressed reservations about the admittance of widows unless they understood that they must forsake all property and all claim to authority upon entrance. A convent where a dowager could rule and her family could continue to wield influence over her inherited lands was a mutually agreeable strategy for them but disruptive for the community.

Widows were not the only women to enter monasteries without a clear vocation for what came to be called "the religious life." The old form of reclusive life or house monasteries clustered consecrated women around their bishops. But as the ideal of episcopal chastity spread, even the mildest hint of syneisactism provoked scandal. The employment of consecrated virgins or chaste widows in episcopal households was attacked by a flood of legislation.[33] Gregory I contributed the exemplary tale of the bishop of Fulda, who maintained a group of consecrated women in his palace where they enjoyed his protection in exchange for household services. One night a Jewish visitor hurried there to warn him that his soul was in danger. The previous night the Jew had been caught on the road and sought shelter in an abandoned pagan temple only to discover that it was a midnight trysting place for local demons. An unwilling eavesdropper, he was shocked to hear them chortling over the report that one devil had induced the bishop to pat his housekeeper affectionately as she bent over her work. They all anticipated that the pat would lead to more familiar embraces in swift order. Without hesitation, the virtuous bishop sent the women to a monastery, and the story ended with the conversion of the awe-struck Jew.[34]

In Frankland and probably elsewhere the wives and widows of clergymen also moved into monasteries as ascetic ideals began to influence episcopal attitudes. The Council of Tours in 567 tried to exclude wives and their female servants from the clerical household at all times except when doing the housework. They were to live in a separate establishment, a sort of convent, and bishops' wives were to receive a special habit and blessing at the time of their husband's ordination.[35] Saints' lives offer some examples of voluntary separation of clerical couples, like Bishop Faro of Meaux and his wife. When Faro would have looked back from the plow, his wife rejected his efforts to reestablish their conjugal life.[36] Again, the inequality between women and men created some ambiguities in this arrangement. Some women may have married priests in hopes of a syneisactic religious life. But when Gallic councils attempted to force clerical couples to do without sex, women had no voice in the decision.[37] Gregory of Tours reported that the frustrated wife of the bishop of Nantes went to his chamber in the middle of the night hoping to catch him with another woman or to seduce him back to the conjugal bed. A vision of a gleaming lamb asleep on his chaste breast deterred her from her purpose.[38] Eventually, Gregory and those of his contemporaries who supported the idea of episcopal celibacy concluded that the couples must separate. Since the Council of Tours had made the wives of priests virtually nuns already by forbidding them to remarry even if widowed, the only logical disposition for them was a convent.

Many women determined to shelter their children by raising them in a convent. Sometimes mothers came in with their young daughters. Some children were given as oblates while still in infancy. Virgin aunts were given charge of their sister's children, as in the cases of Gertrude of Nivelles and Aldegund of Maubeuge.[39] Radegund cured the infant sister whom one nun was raising in her cell.[40] Radegund also raised Baudonivia from the cradle and always referred to the young abbess Agnes as her daughter.[41] Balthild brought her goddaughter with her into Chelles.[42] The fostering of boys by nuns was peculiar to the Irish and came with them to England, at least in the case of the poet Caedmon and others brought up by Abbess Hild of Whitby. The monastery came to be seen as a common option for family strategists. Oblates and property were given, transferred, and taken away as circumstances changed, despite the efforts of church councils to stabilize the situation. Eanfled, the first baptized baby in Northumbria, was consecrated to virginity as an offering of thanks for her father's escape from an assassin on the night she was born. Political interests dictated a change of plan and he married her to Oswy. She in turn consecrated her daughter Elfled in thanksgiving for Oswy's victory over the pagan king of Mercia, and when Oswy died they entered the convent together.[43]

Once outside interests began to dictate the composition of the congregation, the convent was in danger of becoming a dump where indifferent fathers, sons, husbands, or political rivals could deposit women when their presence in the world was an inconvenience. The fathers of Burgundofara and Sadalberga, who were blind, dedicated them to God. Once they were miraculously cured, their fathers tried to take back the promise. The biographer of Odilia of Hohenburg explicitly stated that her father (one of the first Bavarian converts) consecrated her as a substitute for infanticide.[44] Often such children grew into perfect nuns. But some nuns raised children in the convent with no intention of making them nuns. One of the problems raised during an outbreak at Poitiers was that the abbess had married her niece out of the convent.[45] It is not even clear whether vows were understood to be permanent. When Chilperic tried to reclaim his daughter, Basina, from Poitiers, she begged Radegund's protection as supported by conciliar decrees that prohibited any attempt to force a consecrated virgin to marry. But if the girl went willingly, the law would probably not apply. If some women were unwilling brides of Christ, that would be par for the course in this age. For marriage in the early Middle Ages was rarely a matter of choice for women. Sometimes, with a captive bride, it was not even a matter of choice for her own relatives.

In effect, families tended to treat the convent as a convenient solution to their own problems. On the whole, they meant to do well by the young women under their command. Often guardians simply sought to ensure their security and prosperity. A nobleman of Limours, for example, established a nunnery for his daughters and appointed one of them as abbess. Some years later, he and his wife gave the house and its property to the great monkery of Saint-Germain-des-Prés. It probably appeared no more peculiar to him than turning over a daughter with a bride-gift to a husband, who would then control her property and protect her until his death or their separation. The family may have seen additional spiritual and political advantages to this multiplication of ties by the reclamation and redeployment of the property. Nevertheless, the little community of women had lost its independence, and its resources were no longer theirs to be passed to a new generation of nuns.

Early medieval hagiography exalts the superiority of Christ as a bridegroom over mortal men: they age, sicken, and die, but he lives forever and so does his bride; their goods decay or are stolen and they become impoverished, but heavenly wealth only grows. When we look superficially at the spectacle of wealthy women fleeing the world for the monastery and giving their goods to the poor (defined first of all as the church or the monastery), it is tempting to jump to the conclusion that the clergy's commitment to female asceticism was profitable for the church. Responsible bishops were painfully aware, however, that as vicars of Christ they had a special oligation to support even his dowerless brides. The establishment of a cloister often meant, as at Arles, the diversion of a substantial part of the episcopal endowment to assist the nuns. Caesarius broke the laws of two councils and cajoled two popes to fund Saint John's and still the legacy was nearly gone by the end of the century.

The women who most needed this sanctuary were often those least able to finance a withdrawal from the world. One wealthy recruit or generous patron could house many women who were neither safe nor valued where they were. Wimbourne, endowed by the king of Wessex, had fifty nuns; Sainte-Croix numbered two hundred when Radegund died. In the sixth century the Synod of Macon instructed bishops to intervene in secular proceedings on behalf of widows, orphans, and freed slaves. The convent appeared to be an ideal place to shelter helpless and abused women. Six slaves ransomed by Bishop Bercharius in 696 formed the core of his community at Puellemoutiers. When the English missionary Boniface visited Rome in 737, he helped organize a community for English women pilgrims who had fallen into poverty or worse. Women undertook similar charities. The Frankish queen Balthild, who had been captured and enslaved herself before she attracted the attention of her husband, took great interest in ransoming slaves and founding monasteries.

Children, widows, and assorted relatives might not compose an ideal community, but they might settle down together and live a fairly decent and seemly life. Refugees seeking sanctuary did not usually intend to make a vocation of the convent, but they became part of the community while they stayed. Having sought shelter voluntarily, they may have been willing to respect the customs of the place; nevertheless, the comings and goings of the fugitives' relatives and friends, the business and gossip of the inevitable entourage, and the occasional violence of their pursuers brought the world inside the cloister. Even abused wives and freed slaves may not have been enthusiastic about the restrictions and mortifications of a monastery. Oblates offered as children were likely to be even more difficult and, finally, some powerful men could not resist the possibilities of the convent as a prison.

Many a woman unceremoniously consigned to a monastery rather than a husband may have breathed a deep sigh of relief. Most, no doubt, resolved to make the best of it. A few rebelled. Life was accordingly often troubled and sometimes loudly quarrelsome in these holy harems. Theudechild, widow of King Charibert, entrusted her fortune to her brother-in-law King Guntram, who persuaded her that he wished to marry her. He robbed her and confined her to a convent in Arles. When she rebelled against the fasts and vigils and attempted to elope with a Spaniard, the abbess beat her and locked her into a cell until she died.[46] Similarly, Radegund immured a penitent who tried to escape from the convent by a rope over the walls. Her fate was happier since she died in the odor of sanctity. Bishop Felix of Nantes dealt similarly with a niece who wanted to marry against his will. She contacted her lover, who rescued her from the convent despite the penalties of the law.[47] When King Charibert's daughter, Bertofled, escaped from Ingitrude's convent at Tours, the latter was glad to see her go. She said she was a woman "who ate and slept a lot and had no interest at all in the holy office."[48]

The images of sheepfolds and dovecotes beloved by hagiographers are deceptive. Convents often served as hospitals, particularly to shelter demoniacs who raved in locked cells unless a timely miracle were to exorcise them. The noonday demon stalked Arles and captured a lazy girl who had the effrontery to rest from her labors on the sainted Rusticula's bed. Small devils played nasty tricks against any unwary nun who failed to say her proper prayers, bless her food, and cross herself to guard against accidents. The presence within the community of unsuitable recruits and fugitives taking sanctuary aggravated the ever-present threat of violence from without. When Austreberta attempted to impose the full discipline of the rule on her newly gathered community at Pavilly, only divine intervention saved her from poison administered by her nuns. She suffered a further attempt at violence when some of the nuns accused her of encouraging all sorts of disorders to the local count who was their patron. In a fit of rage, he drew his sword to kill her on the spot. Happily, she was inspired to go down on her knees, in the posture of a martyr, and he stayed his hand long enough for reason to prevail.[49]

Intergenerational conflicts between parent and child threatened to drag the whole community into strife. Gregory of Tours's effort to patronize a female community under a holy woman named Ingitrude disintegrated into a family farce. At her mother's urging, Bertegund, Ingetrude's troubled daughter, left her husband and children, defying Gregory himself, who went to the convent and read her the Council of Gangra's decree condemning women who thought that marriage barred them from heaven. Bertegund eventually brought her son into the convent with her and convinced her brother, the bishop of Bordeaux, to annul her marriage. On her husband's behalf, King Guntram attacked the bishop and accused him of sleeping with her servants. Nevertheless, he upheld Bertegund's determination to live as a nun. She quarreled with her mother, however, and after much contention left for another convent. Ingitrude excluded her daughter from her will and forbade her return to Tours even after her death. In retaliation, Bertegund attacked the convent and stripped it of its furnishings.[50]

Scandal broke out in Radegund's own convent of Poitiers some years after the death of the abbess Agnes. Clothild, King Charibert's natural daughter, formed a faction of discontented royalty with Basina, Chilperic's daughter by his first wife, Audovera. Both women were apparently content to be nuns. The princesses felt, however, that they were not being treated as they merited by Leubevera, the new abbess. In all likelihood, one or both of them nursed a grudge because they had been passed over for a social inferior when Agnes selected her successor. Forty or more nuns joined the rebellion and left the convent. Some of them accompanied Clothild to King Guntram's court, while the majority took sanctuary at Saint Hilary's in Poitiers. There they tried to maintain some sort of communal life until Gregory of Tours dispersed them because they were unable to provide themselves with fuel over the winter. Meanwhile some of the nuns got pregnant and some got married. Others recruited a gang of thugs and attempted to break into their old convent to kidnap the abbess.

When the bishops finally gathered to hear the accusations of these nuns, they were treated to a list of grievances that dramatically illustrates the dimensions of the communal problems that probably existed in other convents where Gregory of Tours's pen did not reach. Leubevera was charged with providing poor food for her flock and allowing servants and workmen to use the nuns' bathroom. She was accused of playing backgammon, entertaining lay visitors, and dressing her niece in the altar cloths. Most horribly, she was accused of keeping a lover disguised as a woman in the convent. The man, who was present, claimed that he dressed as a woman to show the world that he was unmanly. To the other charges, the abbess replied that at least the food was plentiful; that the bathroom sharing was a temporary expedient during repairs; that the rule did not forbid backgammon; that she followed the custom of the foundress in giving banquets to Christian travelers but did not eat with them. She admitted that she had outfitted her niece and held an engagement party for her, which the bishop himself had attended. She was acquitted of all charges. Basina returned to the monastery where she can hardly have been a force for peace during the remainder of her life.[51]

The revolt at Poitiers is not an isolated example of monastic disorder in the late sixth and seventh centuries. It may have been aggravated by the long hostility between the bishop of Poitiers and Radegund, which left the monastery without supervision or support from ecclesiastical authorities. Not every prelate was as protective and generous as Caesarius of Arles. We find constant complaints that nuns were too concerned with worldly affairs, but poor communities needed constant shifts to bring in contributions and wealthy ones required as much attention to retain what they had. Laon had seven basilicas in the compound and a smaller enclosure for attendant monks. If the bishop had been a zealous partner he might have done much of the administrative work, but in fact he was intent on robbing Abbess Sadalberga. Even if he were not an enemy, his indifference would not ensure the well-being of the community. Pope Gregory reproached Januarius of Caglaria because his failure to attend to the needs of the nuns in his diocese had forced them to busy themselves with affairs beyond their competence and to spend much of their time outside the cloister.

What should surprise us is not that communities of women, consecrated to Christ, devoted to prayer and self-mortification, should fail to fulfill their ideals. The history of communal movements is a long record of such failures as individual interests and eccentricities grate against the need for harmony and cooperation. The wonder is that, in fact, they solved the problem. During the sixth and seventh centuries, women and men with a call to communal life gradually found a way that worked. Though each monastery was autonomous, the literature of monasticism was avidly read by its practitioners. The rules that proliferated for various houses in the sixth and seventh centuries show considerable cross-pollination. A coherent "monastic" way of life emerged despite differences of detail from one to another. Thus, Caesarius not only had the standard eastern sources to consult but knew as well the practices of Cassian and the various writings dubbed the Augustinian rule. The so-called Rule of the Master drew on Basil, Cassian, Pachomius, and Jerome. It then became the basis for the restructured version attributed to Benedict of Nursia. In the seventh century, the rule of Columbanus from Ireland was added. Elements of all these rules were regularly combined in written house rules like that of the late-sixth-century bishop Aurelian of Arles or the seventh-century bishop Donatus of Besançon. Rules in the confessional tradition of Columbanus usually drew their more practical regulations from Caesarius or Benedict. Conciliar legislation strengthened the ability of episcopal and even secular authority to intervene in the affairs of monasteries.[52]

The monastic ideal was intrinsically contradictory. Claustration meant not solitude but total surrender of personal privacy. The strength of character that enabled women to reject the demands of secular society had to be ruthlessly disciplined if they were to create a harmonious community devoted to self-sacrifice and worship. The proud and adventurous brides of Christ had to learn humility. They had to school themselves to long silences designed not only to promote meditation but to avert the impulses to gossiping and complaining, which irritate any social group. Prayer was not a private meditation but a public chorus. Even self-mortification was stripped of eccentricity. Radegund pursued the most ferocious forms of self-torture but did not permit them in the community. The rule and accompanying exempla were read at meals and other gatherings to inculcate resolve to women who might weaken under the trials of convent life. The religious life came to circle around the three fundamental vows of chastity, poverty, and obedience.

Chastity involved a spiritual transformation, the purification of the entire spirit from the faintest thought of adultery against the immortal spouse to whom both men and women were wed. Men's fear of women's sexual attraction was almost as great (if not as justified) as women's fear of rape. Benedict himself flung his naked body into a nettle patch to distract him from thoughts of a woman he had once known. One Irish saint was said to have been turned away by a wary hermit after she had walked on water to get to his island because he could not trust himself to resist her unwitting attraction. Bishop Leander of Seville urged his consecrated sister to avoid holy men and not to take young pupils because both might incite the banked fires of lust. He also urged her to take special care in reading the Old Testament, applying only spiritual interpretations to some of its racier passages.[53]

Chastity depended on destroying private affections to bind the whole in sisterly comradeship. Although they rarely succeeded, monastic rules tried to prohibit the presence of relatives in the same community. They tried to weaken family attachment by punishing favoritism or special communication with relatives. The abbess and the portress rigidly monitored letters, gifts, and visits from the outside, and all nuns were forbidden to take goddaughters. Individual affection was discouraged in every way. Neither hand-holding nor affectionate nicknames were allowed. Nuns were not to engage in private conversations or visit in one another's cells. Indeed, as the Benedictine rule gained priority, individual cells gave way to dormitories, where the nuns slept under one roof with privacy reserved only to the infirm, the senile, or individuals under punishment. Women as well as men were severely disciplined against "nocturnal visions." In the dormitory, the young women were to sleep near older, tested women for fear of the mutual seductiveness of the young. If young children were being raised in the monastery, they were to be kept apart in sleeping quarters and at table.

Private property was, obviously, the most subversive element against community. Leander of Seville equated it with adultery against the common life. Caesarius's rule forbade any woman to have a chest or cupboard that locked. The nuns had to deny the instincts of ownership even over objects of personal use. Benedict censured a monk he sent to give instruction to a small community of women in a village he had converted from paganism. The monk had absent-mindedly pocketed some handkerchiefs that the grateful sisters had made for him as a personal gift.[54] There were, of course, no limits on the size of a donation to the monastic corporation. Every rule obliged novices to "sell what they had and give to the poor." The poor were, it was strongly suggested, most easily found within the monastery itself. Personal wealth was to be transformed into corporate wealth. The common purse was not only a symbol of solidarity, it was a guarantee of survival in that it aimed at alienating property from the individual sister and from the reversionary claims of her family as well. To each according to her need, from each according to her ability, was the basic tenet of monastic life.

Poverty always loomed, as terrible a threat as armed men. The whole question of how to maintain enclosed women preoccupied most monastic leaders and their episcopal supervisors. Caesarius's order that all nuns share common meals ensured the sharing even of presents of food sent by family and friends. It became one of the basic indicators of good monastic practice. There were some communities of Greek origin in Italy along with other survivors of the invasions whose poverty and distress at the end of the sixth century come to our attention through Pope Gregory's letters.[55] Technically all these little communities came under episcopal jurisdiction, but few of them had the resources or the prestige to be much more than a nagging worry to responsible prelates. The pope was continually concerned to find help for them, ordering support from bishops or from papal property and protecting them against their own families. Sometimes he assured them autonomy from outside interference by using his influence to support the authority of the abbesses. Despite endorsing episcopal jurisdiction in spiritual matters, he readily confirmed privileges that enabled monasteries to preserve their property and pass it on to the next generation by donating it to the monastic corporation.

Increasingly, the turn toward monasticism involved this problem of maintaining the community's economic base beyond the death of the original foundresses when their personal fortunes dissipated or reverted to their families. Radegund also sought the corporate advantages of community identity to safeguard Sainte-Croix economically after her death. Gregory of Tours, who knew her, suggests that in adopting Caesarius's rule, she meant in some way to tie Sainte-Croix to the diocese of Arles in view of her poor relationship with the see of Poitiers. Bishop Maroveus resented the queen's independence and the wealth represented by her relic collection, not excluding her own body, which she had secured from episcopal control by special privileges.

Caesarius followed Pachomius in requiring manual labor as an antidote to idleness. He advised his nuns to take up book production as a suitable means of keeping occupied and earning money. It is unlikely that any large monastery came close to supplying its needs by the handiwork of its members, but at least they could save the money that would otherwise be spent on their care. Much of the work assigned to them was, in fact, housekeeping. The common burden of daily labor made all the sisters equal regardless of origin. Two nuns in Sadalberga's community were both assigned to do the washing and came into potential conflict because one of them had used all the pothooks to lower her cauldron over the inadequate fire. The spirit of community prevailed and she agreed to share her equipment, but both despaired for the lack of fuel to build up the fire. When they prayed together, however, a thunderclap was heard and the fire, fueled by supernatural agency, flickered up and boiled their water.[56] Even the most exalted nuns, like Radegund, showed their humility by applying themselves to spinning and clothwork. God showed his pleasure in the queen's industry when a mouse, which had the temerity to attempt to bite the thread she was spinning, died even as he opened his sacrilegious jaws.[57] She also introduced the weekly turn at kitchen duty from Arles and set an example by her willingness to carry wood and water and clean the latrines and polish her sisters' shoes. One of monasticism's advantages over the eremitic life was that the great must learn to live with the humble. No nun could have a servant or expect service from her fellow nuns. When she was a recluse, Monegund required a servant to supply her with water and the ingredients for the humble unleavened bread she mixed each day with the cold ashes of her fire. When the servant ran away, disgusted with the living conditions, she subsisted on the fresh snow that miraculously covered her window sill until someone discovered her plight and rescued her.[58] But when she turned to a more communal life, she participated equally with her sisters in making small mats to sell as a supplement to her husband's contributions. Laziness and disobedience were also prime enemies of community life. After her death, Austreberta nearly killed a lazy girl by fever because she took a noonday nap on the saint's discarded bed.[59]

Luxeuil on the eastern frontiers of Frankland, and Bobbio, in Italy, promoted the rule of Columbanus, whose chief element was obedience to the superior: "obedience to the death."[60] The bulk of the rule concerned possible infractions of discipline: making noise, allowing externals to distract from prayer, tardiness, gossiping, protesting a superior's decision. The punishments ranged from mild admonitions to extremely severe corporal punishment (as many as fifty blows). No gender-specific exceptions were made to dim the full rigor of ascetic life. Donatus of Besançon's rule for women incorporated virtually the same prescriptions. The abbess was directly responsible for the spiritual as well as the material welfare of her flock. Columbanian rules required confession, daily and even several times a day, to the abbess, who administered the external punishments specified by the rule to secure true internal penitence. Naturally, these confessions were not viewed as sacramental in nature and did not include a priestly rite of absolution.

All the rules aimed at democratic methods in electing the abbess, prioress, cellaress, and portress from among the most sober and steady members of the community regardless of birth or wealth on entrance. Respect for that principle may well have caused Radegund and Balthild to step aside and submit to the governance of their social inferiors. Abbesses were advised to meet daily with the congregation for consultation and advice before proceeding with any plan, to give every sister a chance to contribute to the mutual design for living. Indeed, Donatus urged the abbess to be patient and hear each one impartially, for even the least of the sisters might sometimes hit upon the best plan. But any contention, defense of one's own ideas, or protest against community decisions or the orders of a superior would bring swift punishment running from admonitions to blows to excommunication. In general, however, conventual society appears to have mirrored secular society. Whether duly elected or self-appointed, most abbesses appear to have been the most high-born or wealthy ladies in the community and, when this was not the case, trouble was likely to result.

Sins against sisterhood came from both ends of the social scale. It was, after all, an age in which two slave women had advanced to Frankish thrones. The violence of the period undermined the importance of caste in maintaining the social structure. Slave women and poor women were taken into the convents in large numbers. Once there, hearing that "in Christ there is neither bond or free" may well have inspired them to seek a better material life or higher social status than they had ever known in the world. Writing in the aftermath of the revolt at Poitiers, Baudonivia claimed that the dead Radegund was swift to subject a serving woman who dared to sit in her throne to the fires of purgatory.[61] On the other side, however, high-born women did not so easily lose their pride. Austreberta's successor at Pavilly succumbed to that shameful vice in allowing her sisters to deny a low-born postulant admittance to the community. In despair for her vocation, the woman grabbed the saint's funeral pall and refused to relinquish it until her application was reconsidered. The abbess scornfully rebuked her for attempting to use the convent and its patron saint to raise herself to a rank her birth had denied her. From the grave, Austreberta struck the abbess with a fever that would not leave her until she had "happily remembered what she had so unhappily forgotten; that in Christ there is neither bond nor free."[62]

Humility topped the scale of monastic virtues, a quality best developed under the constraints of community. The rules warn noblewomen against pride and humble women against using religion to better their social status, indicating that they were intended to govern a broad social mix. Sadalberga's community supported both noble and servile women.[63] So did the monastery established by Eustadiola in Bourges.[64] Deprived of every sign of worldly rank by common clothing and customs, each nun was assigned a place in the community based on the date of her entrance. For the rest of her life, she was defined only by that seniority, which controlled her seating at table, her place in procession, and her authority in the chain of deference from "junior" to "senior" nuns. But each woman was exhorted to remember that virtue did not lie even in monastic rank. In Burgundofara's community, a senior nun named Domna had achieved such holiness that, as two little girls in the community indiscreetly exclaimed before the abbess could stop them, rays of light beamed from her mouth when she sang in choir. Unhappily, the news proved her undoing. She became puffed up by the favor and lost her former humility, and when she came to die no choirs of angels attended her passing. The exemplary death once reserved for Domna passed instead to her humble young admirers.[65]

The image of the saint as good shepherdess extends through many exemplary tales in the *vitae* illustrative of their humility and obedience. Famed as a stern taskmistress to her nuns, Austreberta was presumably emulating the abbess Bertofled, who trained her in humility at Laporte before she was entrusted with the community at Pavilly. Austreberta used to patrol the dormitories by night to assure herself that all was well with her daughters. On one occasion, she encountered the equally watchful prioress, who did not recognize her in the darkness. The prioress ordered the abbess to stop prowling about and go to the cross if she could not sleep. In a salutary display of humility, Austreberta did not reveal her identity but went to the chapel and spent the night in prayer before the crucifix, where she remained until relieved by the somewhat embarrassed prioress the next day.[66]

The corporal punishments outlined in the Columbanian rules must certainly have subdued the most boisterous of the nuns, and we have good evidence that they were not neglected. Rictrude's daughter, Eusebia, who was determined to escape her mother's convent in order to take up her inherited responsibilities as abbess in a separate community founded by her grandmother, was so severely beaten for her insubordination that she coughed blood for the rest of her life.[67] Her approving biographer praised the careful mother who did not spare the rod to bring her child to an understanding of the obedience necessary to one who imagined herself fit to rule. Another nun was punished by a hard blow from the saint who appeared in a vision at midnight policing the dormitory to ensure that every sister had joined the community at prayer on her feast day.[68] At Wimbourne, younger nuns were tempted to dance in celebration on the grave of one novice mistress who had been excessively rigid and unforgiving with them. But noting that her uncharitable acts would be severely punished by God, the abbess Tetta instructed her former charges to pray for her forgiveness that her soul might find peace.[69]

Excommunication was the most extreme punishment, isolating the penitent at meals and work and even at prayer. She sat alone and in silence, though the prioress might sometimes judiciously break the discipline to give her a little encouragement. At common prayers and vigils, she would stand apart and humble herself to ask pardon from her sisters. If she were unrepentant, she would lose her place in the choir permanently, being reduced to a junior at the end of the line. In his *Life of Benedict,* an undisguised effort to promote the Benedictine rule, Gregory I told of two nuns whose pride of birth made them incapable of controlling their speech even after threat of excommunication. They died unrepentant and were buried in the local church. Their surviving sisters reported to Benedict that when the deacons came to the point in the liturgy where the excommunicated were ordered to depart, the ghosts of the sisters rose from their tombs and fled the church. Charitably, Benedict reconciled their spirits enabling them to rest in peace.[70]

In the choir, conflicts were resolved and communal love reinforced. For within the convent, for all their irritations, they loved one another. The success of a monastic community depended on the capacity of its director to shape the individual members into a harmonious sisterhood. Monastic liturgy developed into a sort of spiritual drill, molding the eccentric soul into a trained soldier. The constant chanting of psalms in elaborate order was the centerpiece of daily life. Saints' lives repeatedly provide glimpses of choirs of nuns responding to every sort of crisis with an appropriate burst of song. Throughout the day and night, at meals and at work and attending the sick and dying, they sang psalms. When armed men broke into the cloister and threatened them, they stood fast together singing. When greedy lords threatened their property, they rebuked them with psalms. The language of the Bible sank deep into their spirits until their conversation and their writing seemed sometimes to consist of nothing but citations strung like beads on a chain. Caesaria II wrote that individual prayer, focused by the communal chant, should narrow in to a pinpoint, repeating "Help me, God! Help me, God!" until all else was driven from the mind.

Columbanus commanded that a sorrowing member of the community accept the consolation of the rest until she was healed. So it was in Laon when the abbess Anstrude lay prostrate and inconsolable in the chapel mourning for her murdered brother. Night and day her sisters surrounded her, praying with her, comforting her, urging her back into their community. And when the murderers would have pursued her also with their violence, the womanly choir held them back. At a signal, singing and chanting the psalms they knew so well, they advanced steadily upon the men brandishing naked swords at their abbess. Frightened, the soldiers fled the church, as a celestial fireball hastened their departure. When nuns died, their sisters stood around them singing to bind them to the community and celebrate their coming departure. Legend had it that the passing of a saint was heralded to all the surrounding countryside, which often echoed with the sound of angels, conducting the sister to the heavenly choir.

5

The Frontier Outpost

EVEN WHILE Germanic invaders overwhelmed the provinces of the Latin west, the Christian religion of the conquered people was spreading into lands beyond the frontiers, winning converts who had never known the Roman legions. The Irish, converted just decades after the first sack of Rome, led the new missions to the west, to the east, and into the forest wildernesses of the European heartland. Though their converter, the Roman Patrick, left us an autobiography in the confessional form made fashionable by Augustine, he revealed few of the mundane details of his life. We do not know where he got his training, who ordained him, or who sent him back to Ireland after his escape from slavery there. We do know, however, that he coupled conversion to Christianity with conversion to monasticism, a form of religious life particularly suitable to an island with no urban development to support an episcopal organization.

Virgins willing to defy their parents and even to suffer persecution and death to devote themselves to Christ rather than to a husband responded to Patrick's preaching. His strongest partner, Bridget of Kildare, born about 450 to the concubine of a wealthy chieftain, was only one of the women who defied their parents to aid his mission.[1] The Irish mission was advanced by monastic communities, male and female, settled on the lands of their kindred or friendly chieftains or venturing into bogs just being cleared in the fifth century. In addition to "preaching" to family, friends, and visitors, nuns provided shelter for itinerant monks and bishops. They made vestments, altar cloths, and books. They served as catechists for children. Above all, they gave witness in lives of prayer and charity spiced by the occasional miracle.

Patrick came of the generation inspired by the *Life of Antony*, the Pachomian rule, and other accounts that unveiled the mystique of the desert to western eyes. He probably got the ascetic training he brought to Ireland at Lérins or elsewhere in early-fifth-century Gaul. Thus, Ireland nurtured an anachronistic church, in touch with the earliest desert tradition, where saints perfected themselves by inner discipline, refusing the worldly involvements of the priesthood. Itinerant Irish bishops had no necessary functions but to ordain new clergy. Clergymen themselves were cut loose from the firm administrative structures that underpinned their authority on the Continent. Monasticism provided the stable pastoral ministry. As a result, women's prayers were on a relatively equal footing with men's, in contrast to the Roman system, which increasingly relied on sacramental functions.

Famous saints like Monenna and Ita were endowed with land for monasteries in exchange for their spiritual patronage. Indeed, Monenna attracted so many donors that one critic complained that people ignored the clergy and gave their devotion to the nuns. Bridget's seventh-century biographer, Cogitosus, claimed that her monastery at Kildare was the "head of almost all the churches of Ireland standing like a mountain peak over all the Irish monasteries."[2] Bridget was popularly depicted driving a two-horse chariot in pursuit of her pastoral activity, while her monastery stood ever ready to give charity and hospitality. Like her contemporary, Genovefa of Paris, she influenced bishops with spiritual advice and supported the poor with physical food. So powerful was her position, and so strong the memory of her, that a ninth-century biography, probably intended to limit the influence of women in the Irish church, claimed that Bishop Mel recited the wrong liturgy when he gave her the veil and consecrated her a bishop by mistake. The point of the story seems to be in the bishop's ensuing proclamation that it was an honor no other woman would ever share.[3]

Irish monasticism retained the quasi-eremitic qualities of the Pachomian settlements, which made a limited syneisactism more practical than it would be under a communal system. Since women's legal rights of inheritance were generally restricted to life use, permanently endowed female monasteries were rare. Most consecrated women lived in house monasteries on limited tenures granted by their families. Others were associated with male communities, often with their brothers or other relatives. Some embraced the dangerous solitary life, like the holy woman of Leinster who shamed the hesitant Columbanus:

> I have gone forth to the strife as far as it lay in my power. Lo, twelve years have passed by since I have been far from my home and have sought out this place of pilgrimage. With the aid of Christ, never since then have I engaged in secular matters; after putting my hand to the plough, I have not turned backward. And if the weakness of my sex had not prevented me, I would have crossed the sea and chosen a better place among strangers as my home. But you, flowing with the fire of youth, stay quietly on your native soil.[4]

The Irish wedded the ancient spirit of quest and enterprise to the communal monastic form developed under sixth-century rules. In the seventh and eighth centuries, as the new Germanic kingdoms turned away from the Mediterranean and from the Greek and Arab sharers of the Roman legacy, the system seemed perfectly adapted to the problem of founding a civilization in their native northern forests. By Bridget's death in 524, Irish monastic settlements may already have appeared at Tintagel on the Cornish coast. English legends of women like Saint Bee, sailing across the wild western seas on leaves or pieces of turf, suggest that there may have been women among them. Certainly by the seventh century, as Irish missions spread from Iona in Scotland to northern England, at least one recluse, Heiu, lived in Northumbria, where she was associated with the Irish mission. Meanwhile, Gregory I sent a mission to England headed by Augustine of Canterbury in 596. It was the first systematic effort at extending the Roman church beyond the ancient imperial sphere.

The Christian cities of Gaul, Spain, and Italy developed in relatively isolated rural environments where not only their conquerors but also the native populations of the vanished empire remained barely unconverted. Indeed, the same Latin word, *paganus,* served both to designate a non-Christian and a peasant. The seventh-century convent of Jouarre (now engulfed by the suburbs of Paris) derived its name from a local temple to Jove. Two centuries after the pioneering work of Martin of

Tours and one century after the conversion of Clovis, the Irish Columbanus saw Frankland as pagan territory.[5] He founded Luxeuil in a deep
forest where an abandoned fortification was "filled with a great number
of idols worshipped with horrible rites."[6] It became the center of missionary efforts in the Juras, along the Rhine frontier, Switzerland, northern Italy and Austria, not to mention the more settled areas of Frankland.
When Sadalberga led her band of nuns into Laon, one of the bishop's
servants reported a vision of all the pagan demons leaving the citadel in
the guise of wild beasts.[7] Reaching for the swampy coasts of the North
Sea, Gertrude's monastery of Nivelles was founded on an ancient pagan
place of sacrifice. By the eighth century, Anglo-Saxon monastic communities were hacking down the oaks that belonged to the gods of Germany.
The monastic flight to the wilderness heralded the settlement of the
wilderness. Conversion of the pagans involved clearing their sacred
forests and cultivating their wild places.

Practical experience subtly shaped and modified the rules written with
such care and intelligence in the sixth and seventh centuries. Monasticism
developed an elusive prismatic quality. The three great vows and the
virtues they personified continued to dominate the spiritual aspect of the
regular life, but they manifested themselves in shifting colors of the
spectrum that flashed and fractured unpredictably. The enclosed cloister
became the welcoming sanctuary, linking isolation and hospitality. Flight
from the world meant a mission to the pagan. Poverty was achieved
through charity, which attracted donations. Obedience disciplined enterprise, which drew in lands and dependents who required rule and
protection. Chastity opened the way to syneisactism.

Women used the same guidelines as men in regulating their communities. The rule of Columbanus, written for his monks at Luxeuil, became
a popular component of the tailored rules that multiplied in the seventh
century. A typical example written by Bishop Donatus of Besançon for
his mother, Flavia, combined practical features of the Benedictine rule
with the Cassianic spirituality of Columbanus's rule, which Donatus
learned at Luxeuil. He also incorporated parts of the Caesarian rule but
respected the specific preference of the abbess Gauthstruda for the
Benedictine idea of stability over Caesarian claustration, which she
deemed unsuitable for the women of a rural community.[8] His rule was
also adopted by the first female monasteries in Auvergne: Royat, Marsac,

Beaumont, Chantoine, and Chamalières. Similar Columbanian influence appears in the rule attributed to Waldebert of Luxeuil for the use of Sadalberga at Laon.[9] The Frankish queen Balthild probably favored the Benedictine rule at her female foundation of Chelles as she did for her male foundations. But her first abbess, Bertilla, was trained in Columbanian practices at Jouarre, and her biography indicates that she continued to be guided by his principles. Gertrude of Nivelles worked closely with Irish monks and established a constitution designed to use them as outside workers to ensure the enclosure of the nuns within, though this arrangement did not inhibit them from running a hospice for travelers and receiving dinner guests. A similar system appears to have been established by Romaric, founder of Remiremont.

Queens carried missionaries in their wedding trains to pagan Anglo-Saxon kingdoms, who spread the message of monasticism. The first women with vocations were sent to Frankland.[10] Two daughters of the first Christian king of East Anglia, Saethryth and Aedilberga, joined Princess Earcongota of Kent at Faremoutiers. In the next generation, Balthild, by birth an Anglo-Saxon, introduced her compatriots to monastic life at Chelles. About 640, Aidan, the Irish missionary bishop of Lindisfarne in Northumbria, established the hermit Heiu with a small community as a nun at Hartlepool. Aidan then diverted the princess Hild, destined to join her sister at Chelles, to Hartlepool, where she succeeded Heiu in 649. Hild went on to found her own monastery at Whitby and the system grew.[11] There in the north, the virgin queen Etheldreda observed it. After a sojourn with Ebba at Coldingham, she returned to the south and established her own foundation at Ely on land inherited from her first husband.

From the establishment of Lérins forward, the episcopate was slowly monasticizing. The process accelerated with the pontificate of the first monk-pope, Gregory I, who tied the English episcopate to monasteries. Legislation to procure clerical celibacy, or at least continence within marriage, failed but the example of monastic chastity cast aspersions on a married episcopate. Popular opinion opposed continuation of normal marital relationships when a man entered the episcopate. Gregory of Tours, scion of a whole network of episcopal dynasties, associated continuing marital relations with a fatal failure of self-control. For example, he contrasted his own granduncle, the chaste Nicetius of Lyons, with his successor Priscus, who allowed his wife, Susanna, the freedom of his chamber. They produced idiot children; the bishop died suddenly; Susanna ran mad through the town.[12] Gregory shared the prejudices of the age against spiritual marriage. He preferred self-control partnered with prudence and urged that the episcopal wife rule other women in a monastery, thereby forging a religious partnership between women and men that surpassed the old marital bonds. A larger pattern of cooperation between nuns and bishops with an affinity for the regular life developed. Sometimes the partners were brothers and sisters mutually drawn to religious life as were Florence and Leander of Seville or Erconwald and Ethelburga of Barking in Sussex.

Each monastery became a recruitment and training center. Gender was disregarded in the mentoring process. Abbesses were trained at Luxeuil or one of its daughter foundations, from which they drew cadres of recruits for new colonies. Nuns educated children of both sexes, whether or not they were destined to enter the community. Ita, "foster-mother of the Irish saints," ran a school for boys where, among others, the voyager Brendan received his initial education. A few women managed to form a small community in an Italian village that Benedict had converted from paganism, and at their request he sent them one of his monks to live with them and give them instruction.[13] Fara (also called Burgundofara), the protégée of Eustasius of Luxeuil, collaborated with her brother Faro, bishop of Meaux, whose wife also entered religious life. Her monastery at Faremoutiers became an important center for educating Anglo-Saxon women. Hild devised a communal discipline at Hartlepool and later at Whitby from her own spiritual sense, wide reading, and consultation with Aidan and other experienced men who took an interest in her project. There she taught scripture to such good effect that many of her pupils received holy orders and five became bishops. Cuthbert maintained a long association with Ebba, abbess of Coldingham, residing for some years in the monastery to help train the nuns in "the way of righteousness." He also maintained friendships with other abbesses, particular Verca, whose gift of cloth he kept for his shroud out of affection.[14] The missionary bishop Boniface installed his cousin Leoba at Bischofsheim, where she trained German nuns to be the future abbesses of a spreading network.

In this context, the pastoral responsibilities of an abbess assumed the highest importance. Eangyth, abbess of an unknown monastery in England, complained that the demands of persons of both sexes for care of their souls added to the disastrous economic condition of her monastery.[15] Despite Pope Gregory's desire to keep the laity out of monastic churches, rural monasteries and even some urban communities took the place of parishes in the religious life of the surrounding neighborhood. Nuns maintained priests for their own sacramental needs and shared them with the world at large. Each monastery had several churches or oratories attached to them. Nivelles had the church of Saint Peter, where Ita and Gertrude were buried, and an oratory dedicated to the Virgin, where the saint had died. Abbess Agnes added a third church for the relic of Gertrude's bed. Laon had seven basilicas to house various relics and devotions. For her neighbors at Chelles, Bertilla reinforced the occasional excitement of visiting preachers by offering frequent confessions and communion. At Laon, Sadalberga instituted a program of baptisms in collaboration with the local clergy. The presence of the holy woman, said her biographer, converted an idolatrous population, given over to gaming and homicide, to the holy cleansing of baptism.

Monasticism was a lay movement. The pastoral work of nuns did not differ in quality from that of monks. Indeed, Benedict's rule prohibited or at least strongly discouraged the ordination of monks because he thought the two states incompatible. For basic sacramental needs, monks might provide priests from among their own community. Nuns commonly admitted men into their communities to achieve the same end. Priestly prayers, however, were not privileged over monastic. It is impossible to judge how often anyone, even nuns, attended mass. In any case, the mass itself was a rather private ceremony. The priest performed his rites in a language that few people (sometimes including the priest himself) understood. The elevation of the host had not been introduced and the congregation apparently shuffled about, sometimes cut off by the monastic choir from the altar. Even exceptionally religious people rarely received the Eucharist. Once consecrated, it was apparently reserved for administration in times of need by the abbess or another nun if a priest were not present. In a vision from her sickbed, Aldegund saw Saint Amand in heaven consecrating communion for her so she could take it freely in her own hands. Similarly, Saint Odilia, as related in her ninth-century biography, gave herself communion just before her death from the chalice brought by her mourning nuns.[16] Monks as well as nuns devoted most of their energies to nonsacramental religious services.

The hierarchical character of the clergy was greatly diminished, reflecting the horizontal kinship organization of the aristocracy and the provincialization of secular as well as ecclesiastical administration. The edges between secular and ecclesiastical personnel blurred as secular nobles sought clerical places for their sons. The nonclerical nature of monasticism encouraged nobles to seek places there for their daughters as well, causing the clerical hierarchy and the monastic community to overlap. The Irish model, where the absence of cities and a Roman administrative class reduced bishops to wandering preachers empowered to ordain priests, suited the European frontier. Columbanus himself had notoriously little respect for Frankish bishops and even viewed himself as the equal of Pope Gregory. The monks at Luxeuil worked to secure independence from episcopal authority for the monastery and most of its daughters. Monks turned bishop, like Amand, fostered autonomous male and female monasteries. Immunities from episcopal authority were especially associated with the widespread patronage of Queen Balthild, and they were given equally to nuns and monks. Hild assumed a prestige usually reserved for bishops when she presided over the synod where the Irish and Roman churches competed for the allegiance of the Northumbrian king. The situation was exceptional because the contenders were bishops. Even so, it illustrates a larger truth. Wealth and status commanded power and, in seventh-century conditions, abbesses had both. Accordingly, they enjoyed many of the administrative (but not the sacramental) prerogatives associated with bishops and expressed by the shepherd's crook, which they bore as an iconic attribute.

Seventh-century abbesses were generally safe from the envy of bishops like Maroveus of Poitiers, who had refused to install the relics Radegund collected in her convent and even avoided conducting her funeral when she died. In contrast, however, their sanctuaries were less impervious to the political struggles of their families. When Anstrude of Laon, for example, was physically threatened by Bishop Madalgar's attack on her property, she called on the powerful magnate Pippin for protection. Eangyth tried to enlist Boniface as an influential protector against the claims of local nobles and clergy to heavy burdens of service. She attributed her dilemma to the loss of all reliable family connections but her elderly sister, a nephew with his own problems, and a daughter, herself "bereft of all that was dear to her."[17]

As cities dwindled into relatively small and shabby administrative centers, Romans and Germans alike settled into agrarian estates. A decentralized monastic church was more compatible with this rural aristocracy. The communal organization devised by Benedict and his contemporaries suited the northern geography as well. A European ascetic could hardly go naked into the "deserts," even in the summertime. Simple fare like dates and nuts, even honey and locusts, were not easy to find in western forests. They were rich in game, but the blood-lust of the carnivore was expressly forbidden to monastics. Without good husbandry, the winters brought famine as well as frost. Clearing and cultivating the soil were ideal forms of manual labor for contemplatives with an ideology of work and thrift. Common ownership also fitted the capital-intensive agriculture of plow and cattle that the heavy soil required. Only exceptions like the early Irish saint Monenna and her nuns tilled their land with their own hands. Elsewhere, slightly hypocritical monastic rhetoric gave the characteristics of rugged pioneers to aristocratic women (and men) who certainly never shouldered a shovel themselves. In seventh-century Frankland, bishops like Amand collaborated with wealthy women to establish frontier monasteries spreading in a fan from Normandy across Belgium toward the German borders. About a third of the monasteries that evangelized that frontier were women's communities.

Solemn vows of poverty were not yet obligatory, but an entrant to monastic life was expected to give her goods to the poor. Nuns who theoretically owned nothing were often generous to a fault. The process of giving up their wealth sometimes extended over a lifetime or more. It often went in tandem with the acquisition of more wealth. Ownership rarely meant absolute rights of alienation. Obligations to kings and other donors went with land-holding. Most gifts had strings attached to the original giver. Families had various claims over individual holdings, and even strangers had certain claims to use rights. The transfer of land usually meant the transfer of the people who derived a living from the land. Ownership then entailed jurisdictional rights, which also came with grants of use by kings or great lords to smaller nobles. A nun who surrendered all her possessions to Christ still had to fulfill these responsibilities in his name, and she collected dues and rents to support the burden.

Seventh-century families tended to favor living kindred over future progeny. Their strategies aimed at amassing wealth, influence, and support through a wide network of extended family rather than concentrating wealth with a view to future preservation. Women in their various roles were seen as important players in the game. All the Germanic nations made provisions for female inheritance and ownership of property, possibly under the influence of Roman Law transmitted through church authority. Seventh-century women could amass considerable fortunes from their parents and their husbands, legacies from any benevolent party, and gifts from friends or strangers hoping to win their influence. When they were married, their husbands usually controlled the disposition of this property, but if they entered religion their property went with them.

The same woman might still have inheritance rights to further wealth at a future date, or her relatives might have rights to inherit from her. Though Gregory I forbade religious persons to make personal testaments, the normal practice in Merovingian Gaul was to do so and several testaments from nuns have survived. The noble Abbo, for example, got a legacy from Ricuberta, described as a woman consecrated to God.[18] The testament of Fara, foundress of Faremoutiers, tentatively dated 633–634, is an early type of *laudatio parentum,* an instrument ensuring that family members would not interfere with bequests.[19] Fara left her interests in one town, Louvres, to her siblings in exchange for their agreement not to contest the endowment of her convent with the rest of her considerable property. Sadalberga also designated her community heir of her patrimony and performed a disciplinary miracle on her deathbed to force her brother to hand it over. Such women founded monasteries (or in some cases several monasteries) and supported less well endowed women. They gave lavishly to the poor and spared no expense on the furnishings of chapel and library. Radegund used her wealth and her connections with the Frankish royal family to good effect by sending to Constantinople for choice relics, including the fragment of the cross that assures her convent continuing popularity as a cult center even to this day. Generosity was the very mark of nobility, and few women of this period whose lives are celebrated deprived themselves of the opportunity to practice the virtue.

In the sixth century, women may have been avenging their own abuse when, with the encouragement of the Roman episcopate, they attempted to redistribute barbarian wealth. Warriors came home with loot and shared it with their comrades. They displayed it on their women, who in turn exercised their own patronage among the troops of beggars, vagabonds, and refugees who came to their doors. Their men were often actively hostile to this open-handed gift giving to people outside their usual circles of exchange. Bridget of Kildare, born a slave to her father's concubine, had no scruples in stripping him of all the goods that came to her hand to help the poor. Only a miracle saved her finally from his vengeance. What Clovis and his Frankish warriors amassed in loot his queen and her successors seemed determined to dissipate. Radegund, in particular, was so energetic in her distribution of gifts to churches, holy persons, and any needy beggar who came in her way that Clothar's alarm at the inroads she was making on his treasure may finally have persuaded him to let her go. On her progress to Poitiers, she ostentatiously heaped up gold and jewelry on every altar she visited, but she retained plenty to endow her own foundation. The Anglo-Saxon princesses of East Anglia massively turned the wealth of husbands and fathers over to their lavish convents and associated charitable projects. In this diversion of wealth, they had the strong support of the church.

Legacy hunting became a thinly disguised aspect of monastic recruiting. Caesarius of Arles left his fortune to his sister's convent and stipulated that their endowment be supplemented regularly by required donations from every postulant.[20] But a generation later they were out of money. The fourth abbess, Liliola, claimed that the sainted Caesarius of Arles had come to her in a vision to reveal the hiding place of Rusticula, the only surviving heir of a prominent Gallo-Roman family. She had been kidnapped by an ambitious suitor who had entrusted the child to his mother to raise as his future wife, apparently confident that he would get her dowry and her inheritance in the end. Having balked this nefarious plan, the saint produced further visions and miracles to

ensure that he would get her (and her fortune) for the convent. Her
mother grieved bitterly, "Give me hope for my child. Who now will care
for my old age? She was the only one I had left. I seek my little sprout
and cannot find her. Where can I run? Where to turn, I do not know!
I pray grace and call on God to witness that you should have mercy on
me, struck with such sorrow and order the restoration of my only child
in my widowhood."[21]

Nevertheless, the child was installed at Arles, nurtured there, and
eventually raised to its abbacy. She brought enough with her to build a
new church and maintain the community comfortably. Rusticula became
a famous saint, and the tale of conspiracy between the abbess and the
dead bishop encouraged other heiresses to follow her example. To a
family threatened with extinction or a fortune-hunting suitor, Christ must
have seemed a ruthless competitor.

Slowly, the situation changed. The ability of the church to maintain
its rights stabilized, and the new barbarian nobility began to merge its
interests with those of God. Columbanus and his successors at Luxeuil
actively encouraged girls to defy their families and refuse to marry, but
they offered them an impressive career that came to appeal to men as
well. In his wanderings, the missionary found the house of Chagneric
near Meaux, where he singled out the child Fara, who vowed herself to
the monastic life. When Columbanus left, he took one of her brothers
as his companion. No doubt on his recommendation, his successor,
Eustasius, returned and supported Fara's resistance to the betrothal her
parents had arranged. Her rebellion was marked by periodic illness and
timely miracles, which her biographer offered as a lesson to anyone who
might attempt to prevent a wealthy young heiress from giving herself,
with her worldly goods, to God. The girl's example also inspired her
brother Faro and his wife to separate and enter the monastic life.[22] A
substantial portion of a noble fortune was thus diverted from secular to
ecclesiastical uses, while ecclesiastical offices fell into the family's hands.

Eustasius himself initiated the recruitment of at least one other heiress.
He healed the young Sadalberga, who had been blind from birth, after
she had declared her desire to join the ranks of consecrated women.[23]
The next abbot, Waldebert, however, was not on the scene to prevent
her from being pushed into marriage by her parents. Her husband
enjoyed his victory for a mere two months before he died. Pressured into

a second marriage two years later by King Dagobert, she repaid her debt with interest. With Waldebert's help, she brought her husband with her into the monastic life, and eventually all her surviving children followed, as well as the disappointed suitor of her daughter Anstrude. A boy, Baldwin, pursued a secular career but was murdered while still young by his political enemies.[24] The remainder of her parents' fortune was secured when her brother turned to a monastery, sending his wife, Odila, with a generous endowment into Sadalberga's house.[25] Waldebert kept up the tradition by encouraging Aldegund to maintain a vocation. Her parents sickened when they sought to oppose the divine will. From that conversion stemmed the further conversion of her sister Waldetrude with her husband and her two daughters and even their mother, who had long opposed the virgin's determination to live unmarried.[26] In England, it was the same: Etheldreda established Ely on the dower land she inherited from her first husband, and its possessions swelled under her sister and niece.

While the image of the maiden resisting threats and blandishments to keep her faith with her heavenly lover never lost its attraction for hagiographers, hard evidence suggests that great aristocratic families of the seventh and eighth centuries were easily reconciled to the match, if not in some cases its initiators. They generously endowed their daughters with lands and powers. Aldegund had a series of visions in which Christ wooed her while King David negotiated her dowry with her family. A family might well be pleased to have a daughter's substantial inheritance in the hands of a husband who would not sire children likely to take the property into a new lineage and would not leave the young woman a widow who might marry again.

As nobles settled and consolidated their position with the native population, they gradually usurped jurisdictional powers that belonged to the king. In the early seventh century, when royal power attempted to reassert itself, Dagobert pursued a policy of marrying the heiresses of his greater nobles to his own friends at court to strengthen them and weaken the great provincial nobility. More than once, he was stopped short by the preemptive action of a virgin or widow who declared herself consecrated to God. Gertrude of Nivelles, daughter of the powerful Pippin, was still a child when Dagobert attempted to impose a betrothal on her. Her biographer scarcely concealed the complicity of her parents in her precocious declaration that she loved Christ alone. When her father died, mother and daughter barely waited until the tomb was sealed before they transferred their wealth into a monastery. She pursued her vocation and her family retained a lien on her inheritance through patronage of her monastery. The king was left with empty hands and an unrewarded courtier.

The natural administrative talents of aristocratic women could be put to good use by their families. Vast acres, dozens of villages, came under monastic government. Great families could extend their grasp through the dedication of their daughters, and their luster attracted other women with good dowries of their own. Some daughterless lords sought out likely women with vocations from the lower nobility, educated them, and endowed them handsomely. Women embracing poverty, humility, and obedience willy-nilly became the lords and protectors of whole peasant populations. Their aristocratic rank and self-assurance enabled them to administer estates and hold court over their subjects. Such women served patron families by allowing them to influence abbatial elections and the admission of candidates for the future, as well as giving them a special place in their prayers. In the complex system of property ownership that characterized the age, monastic land alienated to God was paradoxically never alienated at all. Places vacated with every generation could be filled and refilled to the patron's profit. Every gift and every favor brought rights of proprietorship, and every exercise of those rights increased the indebtedness of patrons. Dynasties of abbesses developed. Sadalberga was succeeded by her daughter Anstrude. Gertrude raised her niece Wulftrude at Nivelles to be her successor, and the young abbess successfully defended her dynastic rights against royal intervention. Etheldreda was succeeded at Ely by her sister and then her sister's virgin daughter. Bede lamented this tendency to turn church property and institutions into extensions of secular estates.[27] Still, where such a family connection existed, a well-endowed establishment might have a long and prosperous history. Many convents from his age endured until a general dissolution of the monasteries in modern times. Some of them are still in operation.

Even while monasteries profited from the economic strategies of aristocratic families, they routinely shielded themselves from the power of secular potentates under the privileges and exemptions confirmed by church councils. These freed people under the broad banner of "the clergy" from most of the taxes and services owed to their lords. This share in immunities granted to the church by secular powers made monasticism attractive to many ordinary people. It did not, after all, require ordination to make a person a religious, and the requirements were still far from standard for an institution fundamentally laic in nature. Spanish sources make casual references to transitory monasteries supported by sheep herding, which flourished in Galicia among peasant and even slave families in contrast to the "deluxe" version revealed in the rule of Leander of Seville. Fructuosus of Buaga called the family monasteries of Galicia *falso nomine monasteria*.[28] Other bishops cited these unregulated nuns and monks as simple tax dodgers. In Ireland, monastic families were sometimes literally kindred with abbots and abbesses presiding over communities of their own descendants. A similar impulse was apparently widespread in seventh-century England, where Bede complained that married couples with their families only posed as religious communities to evade military service.

We may actually be looking at an adjustment to the lifecycle. Couples who lived together during their childbearing years could have converted to spiritual marriage in old age or embraced celibate widowhood, turning the farm into a house monastery. In the case of the peasantry, it is possible that the monks and nuns were religious only by some legal courtesy, as at Remiremont, where the former serfs of the founder, Romaric, were assigned to the aristocratic sisters to undertake the heavy work of clearance and cultivation. Monasteries, like all medieval estates, needed their laborers. Eangyth in England complained of her monastery's poverty resulting from the uncultivated state of much of her land. Possibly monastic status (with protection from taxes) was sometimes offered to peasant families as an inducement to settlement or donation. Such families were very difficult to define legally, as they belonged to the church but in most cases lived the lives of ordinary seculars.

Benedict assumed that religious would work for their keep.[29] But none of these communities could have raised large sums by their own industry. Christianization and fund-raising went hand-in-hand. The most conscientious and unworldy nuns aggressively cultivated the friendship of people from their neighborhood. Monasteries encouraged visits from their neighbors and may have offered some auxiliary share in their devotions. On great feast days, a meal called a charity was often offered to friends and supporters of the community. According to one story from Nivelles, a matron who often visited the convent expressed a lack of faith in the patron's powers of advocacy. One of the nuns hotly defended Gertrude and promised that she would prove herself on her feast day. The matron, with her young son, attended the charity and, while the party was still in the refectory, the child began to play in the cloister. He fell into the well and drowned there. Happily he was restored to life by the power of the saint, and amends were made to the community by his repentant mother.[30]

Monasteries regularly incorporated children into monastic life. The constant reading intrinsic to the religious life recommended nuns as educators for youngsters of both sexes. Rusticula, raised in the convent at Arles, was early trained to letters by a nun who sat by her bed nightly and whispered in her ear as she slept. Gertrude of Nivelles was said to have memorized an entire volume of divine law.[31] The English Leoba, vowed to the monastery from birth, entered when she was old enough to be educated. She devoted herself to carrying out the precepts of her reading, spurning jests and "girlish romance," and preferred reading and listening to Scripture to every other task.[32] It was not, however, a matter of dumb rote. Girls destined for the monastic life learned to propagate Christian doctrine by instruction of the young as well as the occasional admonition or impromptu sermon to adults. A good sound stock of theology was a necessity in a world where a heretic might arrive uninvited at a convent, as one did at Faremoutiers, and attempt to seduce the nuns with his smooth tongue. A few sharp lessons from Abbess Fara soon won his repentance and reform. Education was thus a requirement for missionary activity, a necessary component of the religious life, and a means of strengthening the network of gift and countergift.

Book production, recommended as a suitable craft for nuns in Caesarius's rule, soon became the single activity most closely associated with the monastic life. Manuscript illumination and other artistic efforts were, in fact, an extension of the Christianizing mission. Gregory I championed Christian use of images against contemporary iconoclasts because of their effectiveness as a teaching device for the illiterate. In Belgium, nuns studied calligraphy, painting, and embroidery as well as chant and divine and human law. Gertrude, great-aunt of the emperor Charlemagne, was a notable teacher who assembled an important library with books brought from as far away as Rome. Such a legacy not only provided nuns with the means to educate themselves and others but also gave them books to copy and send to grateful friends and patrons. The English Eadburga supplied Boniface with books for his German mission from her convent scriptorium including a portion of the gospel in golden letters.

This education fostered a sense of history among nuns and fortified them with the memory of their glorious predecessors. Letters and lives of sainted foundresses provided examples and illustrations for future generations. Along with devotional homilies of all sorts they were also read in monasteries during meals, nourishment for the mind to accompany the feeding of the body. In the dedication of his *Treatise on Virginity* to the nuns of Barking, Aldhelm listed Scholastica, Eulalia, and Thecla among the Germanic names. Indeed, the intrepid apostle was a fairly common namesake for her Anglo-Saxon sisters. Agnes, Agatha, and other women from the earlier ages of the virginity movement were commemorated in this manner as well. Unfortunately, we do not know if these were names given to women at birth (which would suggest maternal hopes for their futures) or whether the women had changed their names at baptism or upon entering religion. While neither practice was standardized, we have examples of Germans in the sixth century who took new names on baptism and cases in England itself in the eighth century.

Nuns sometimes wrote compositions of their own, though few have survived the vicissitudes of time. Caesaria II's letter to Radegund on the spiritual life may actually have been but one of many such treatises, lost to us because of the general disrespect for women's writings that has characterized every age in the past.[33] Baudonivia wrote the *Life of Radegund* and an anonymous nun is probably responsible for the collection of short biographies called the *Life of Fara* incorporated into Jonas of Bobbio's biography of Columbanus and his successors. Nivelles became an important center of hagiography with the *Life of Gertrude* and its continuations as well as the *Life of Aldegund*. A nun of Chelles is believed to be the author of the original *Life of Queen Balthild*, and nuns probably wrote the original biographies, now lost, used as primary sources by the Carolingian hagiographers of some other foundresses. Rudolf of Fulda, for example, used memoirs by four nuns, Agatha,

Thecla, Nana, and Eobba, of Leoba's community at Bischofsheim in writing her biography. Leoba herself wrote several surviving letters and a poem following the rules of composition she had learned from Eadburga.

Through book production and composition, through correspondence, and through the education of young people of both sexes, with or without a monastic vocation, nuns extended their sphere of influence far beyond their immediate environment. Huneberc of Heidenheim's *Hodoeporicon,* narrating Willibald's adventures on his pilgrimage to Rome, is the most ambitious work to survive from an eighth-century convent. An Anglo-Saxon nun, she, like many of her sisters, had joined Boniface's German mission. In a gender-specific version of the usual self-deprecating introduction common to monastic authors, Huneberc said that her privileged position as "a humble relative" of her hero must excuse her impertinence in preempting the literary task that might have been undertaken by one of the "many holy priests" in the saint's company. As so often happened, Willibald was part of a larger party staying at the hospice of her convent in Eichstätt when he regaled her and her sisters with his account of his travels, for she cited "two deacons who will vouch for its truth."[34]

It was a matter of common courtesy to offer shelter and food to travelers in the hospice, often the only inn for miles in any direction. This constant flow of visitors and pilgrims helps explain the continual need of communities with ample endowments and connections. Land endures but its products are finite, and estate managers worried about having sufficient supplies and ready money. Moreover, they could not predict outlays. The burden of hospitality entailed feeding and sheltering the impressive entourage (including animals) that followed every important person. Paradoxically, the very burdens that drained the community's resources were its best sources of income. Monastic charity was no exception to the rules of an economy based on gift and countergift. The unusually forthright biographer Baudonivia stated boldly that a certain magnate cured of an eye disease by Radegund's hair shirt gave the princely sum of 100 solidi to establish an oratory.[35] But petitioners knew the importance of gratitude: even the poor man in search of a cure knew that saints would smile more sweetly on one who brought a fresh fish for the nuns.

There was no end to the stream of indigent and invalid pilgrims who crowded monastic public spaces. The tomb of a certified wonder worker soon became the camping ground for innumerable sick people. They spent nights at vigil in the basilica itself as well as in the hospices designated for the purpose. In one case, a saint's biography mentions a man with a putrescent affliction of his nose who considerately kept himself back from the tomb to avoid giving offense to the crowd installed there. Possibly the saint also found the stench hard to bear, for she acted quickly in his favor.[36] Whether or not a miracle was vouchsafed, the sick could count on more homely nursing. Radegund and her nuns undertook to provide bathing facilities, food, and shelter to anyone who asked for them. The queen herself bathed the women invalids, oiling their sores and combing the lice from their hair. She served food and drink to all, though she did not personally partake of the lavish banquets she spread. Even on Sunday morning, when the nuns attended mass, one woman was assigned to stay behind to provide for chance supplicants.

Even Radegund, with all her wealth, found the burden heavy. Her biographer claims that she had divine assistance in the form of a wine jar that miraculously filled itself after every use. Monastic hagiographers often claimed food multiplication miracles for abbesses. This is particularly true in Ireland, where Bridget and Monenna are both associated with extravagant charity. When Saint Ailbe tried to emulate a holy woman who miraculously milked a steer, an angel advised him to leave these little miracles involving the food supply to women and be content with moving mountains.[37] Similarly, on the Continent, a charitable saint was encouraged to believe that she could rely on last-minute providence if she did not stint her hospitality. Thus while Aldegund's biographer criticized her prudent mother, he praised the open-handed saint, whose scanty supplies of money and clothing were multiplied as she gave them out to beggars at the door.[38] When in need, a saint always found a fish willing to jump into the net or obligingly leap to dry land. Loaves and fishes for the multitude always multiplied in the world of exemplary literature.

In reality, of course, the food supply was finite. The stocks used to feed the poor did not multiply miraculously for hungry nuns. When the rebels at Poitiers complained of the poor food, the abbess snapped that they should be happy that they were always fed. At dinner, nuns must often have been encouraged to suppress their discontent by reading from

lives of saints famous for their fasting. At Faremoutiers and elsewhere
in the chain of Irish establishments where Jonas of Bobbio's collection
was circulated, they heard warnings against gluttony in the example of
Beractrude, a compulsive eater who habitually raided the pantry when
the other nuns were not watching. Her punishment was a food phobia,
restricting her diet to tree bark and dead leaves washed down with the
dregs from the brewing. And whenever the unfortunate sister sat down
to this miserable fare, she found herself facing a phantasmic boar for her
dinner companion who snuffled and grunted over his slops throughout
the meal, a mirror of her own gluttony.[39] Greed for food and drink was
a sin against sisterhood. It deprived the other nuns and mocked their
fasting and scrimping to divert their resources to the poor.

Charity means love. The net spun between the convent and the world
stretched over great spaces. Called from England to Germany, Leoba
sent her own nuns ever further out into the German wilderness. She
allowed her German nuns to visit their families and kept a witless pauper
in the house permanently. She kept open house for all, washed the feet
of her guests, and gave banquets when she herself was fasting. Leoba
traveled often to court after Boniface's death and became so friendly with
Charlemagne's wife, Hildegard, that the latter tried to keep her there
permanently. But her villagers were her flock. When they took shelter
in her church from fire and storm, her prayers warded away the light-
ning.[40] She regularly visited the daughter houses founded from Bischofsheim to ensure their continued discipline in following the Benedictine
rule. One night she dreamed that she drew a purple thread that came
from her very bowels out of her mouth and wound it into a never-ending
ball. An old nun who had the spirit of prophesy explained that it
represented the truth in her vitals, which would come as counsel from
her mouth and be put into practice like the thread in her hands. The ball
she made was divine truth turning perpetually between the works of
earth and the contemplation of heaven.

The greatest monastic work was prayer, which absorbed women and men
alike. Prayer was a form of preaching and of charity as well. Columbanus agreed to pray that Duke Waldolenus and his wife, Flavia, would
have children if they would promise the first-born to God. The resulting

child, Donatus, educated at Luxeuil, became bishop of Besançon and made his own mother the gift of a monastic rule. Prayer entwined the seemingly contradictory concepts of enclosure and mission. Monenna's group abandoned the site where Patrick placed them to support his preaching, because they wished to rid themselves of the interruptions of well-meaning visitors. Having determined that their prayers were of more help than their physical labor, they enclosed themselves so strictly that, in dry seasons when their well did not supply their needs, they suffered severe thirst rather than venture out for water. Despite that, or because of it, they prospered well enough to found three large daughter monasteries and to support at least one other poor community in need of charity. Even in the work of supervising estates and their laborers, prayer was more efficacious than physical exertion. Sadalberga superintended the gardening by spiritual vision, correcting the gardener from within her walls when he became careless with the lettuce. Gertrude's prayers protected her fishermen from attack by a whale. The frontier between earth and heaven, heaven and hell, had ultimately more meaning for the lives they led than the wilderness of the time-bound world.

The object of the common endeavor was to mold each individual into a part of the whole and to create for each a life constantly informed by prayer. Nuns prayed when going out and coming in, before and after meals. While occupying their hands with menial labor, they made frequent signs of the cross. When the signal sounded during sleep, or interrupted work, they hurried to the chapel for the praises of the hours. Every rule centered on the *synaxis,* the order in which the full course of the psalms would be divided to be sung throughout the turning year. The short summer nights and the long winter darkness would be fittingly filled with the sound of women's voices chanting. Donatus emphasized that the work of God came before all other activity.[41] The chapel was never to be used for any other purpose, so that any nun could go there, day or night, to pray, decorously, silently, never distracting her neighbor but never ceasing to be attentive to her principal duty. The pettiest distractions (like clicking teeth against the chalice at communion) were punished. During Lent special observances could be instituted by individual initiative. At Remiremont, Amatus, a monk sent from Luxeuil to train the nuns, divided them into seven groups of twelve each to work in relays. They formed a prayer chain to ensure that the praises of God never ceased at any hour, the *laus perennis*, which became the centerpiece of many a contemplative house.

The mission aimed for internal revolution. Each nun sought to develop awareness of her own failures and promote her own desire for perfection. Discipline only reinforced self-discipline. The sight of an excommunicated sister, begging for pardon and restoration to the community, was a burden and a punishment to everyone. Fighting boredom, discomfort, discouragement, and all the abrasive difficulties of intimacy, they sought divine signs and portents in the events of daily life, magnifying and embroidering their defeats as well as their victories. The abbess was responsible for the souls entrusted to her and even too much fondness, resulting in their dependence on her care, might be held against her. Fara was sent back to life from the very judgment seat of God because her nuns prayed for her restoration, fearing that they would be lost without her guidance.[42]

Sisterly love demanded the subordination of selfish interests to the end of community. Donatus began his rule with a reminder that his reader should treat everyone as she hoped to be treated herself. The nuns at Besançon were penalized for wasting kitchen supplies or trying to hide food and drink in bed so as to get more than their share.[43] Every rule provided that packages from outside first pass through the portress and the abbess, who had the right to disburse their contents among the community as she deemed most expedient. Love of God was expressed by love for the sick, for the poor, for the traveler, which was expected to flower out of the cultivated soil of sorority. Hild modeled Whitby after the example of the primitive church where everything was held in common and nothing was considered to be anyone's personal property. Sisters were exhorted to believe that God would look after his own. Aldetrude, Aldegund's little niece who was being raised in the convent, accidentally set fire to a pot of candle wax that she was melting down. Demonstrating her faith, she plunged her bare hands into the fire and rescued the community property without any injury.[44] Likewise, when Austreberta was taking her turn at baking the community's bread, her inexperienced companion failed to clear the fire completely out of the heated oven. The bread would have burned, leaving the sisterhood without food, had not the saint intrepidly reached into the fire and pulled out the smoking loaves with her sleeves, miraculously free of injury.[45]

Shared food expressed sororal love as nothing else could. The common table was central to monastic life. A sainted sister's body represented the ultimate act of sharing by converting itself into food as it generated income through miracles. Moreover, the body multiplied and extended its powers incessantly through the vehicle of associated relics. Monegund's mourning sisters implored her to bless a quantity of oil and salt as she lay dying so that they might use it to relieve sick petitioners when she was no longer with them.[46] Oil, because of its dual association with healing and with holy anointment, became associated with saints who caused lamps to overflow or even spouted oil from their own bodies. Many years after her death, Gertrude of Nivelles sparked fresh interest in her cult through quantities of healing oil flowing from her tomb.[47] Cloth objects—clothing, funeral palls or grave cloths—were also popular as relics. In addition to her hair shirt, Radegund's funeral pall and even the water it was washed in proved to be vehicles of grace. Dust from Anstrude's tomb provided the chief ingredient in a healing potion, as did the washing water from Rusticula's tomb. Dust and water of this sort, of course, were particularly convenient types of relics because of their infinite capacity for multiplication and maximum portability. Pilgrims came to these shrines seeking help. They left gratuities behind and carried tidings to the world that there lay one with the power to answer prayers.

Armed with prayer, nuns guarded the frontiers of life and death. The Irish particularly developed the idea of purgatory, and their writings yield more than one account of the afterlife and the punishments to come. In 716, Boniface wrote to Eadburga, describing the visions of a man who had died and been restored to life in Milburga's convent at Thanet. Abbess Hildelida had written that the man had seen angels wrestling with demons for the souls of the dead. Other souls on their way to the heavenly city had first to purge themselves of every small stain of sin in a river of boiling pitch.[48] The idea of salvation as something attainable by human effort underpinned the monastic life, and it became part of the unalterable dogma of the Catholic Church. Once it was accepted that every sin could be counterbalanced by an equivalent act of virtue, it did not take long for religious philosophers to propose that the superabundance of virtue accumulated by holy people could be transferred as charity to weaker souls with a superabundance of vice to repay.

This concept of purgation, of cleansing the soul to make it fit for heaven, became the centerpiece of the monastic economy. It generated a penitential system modeled on the monastic rule aiming to impose uniform penalties on moral infractions. The idea that this spiritual debt could be paid by the generosity of a wealthy patron flowed naturally from the underlying premises of penitential spirituality. Unlike the sacramental system, the expiatory prayers that generated transferable grace depended for their efficacy on the virtue and self-mortification of ascetics. It was the surplus of grace they generated that was available to help suffering souls in need of assistance. Thus Ita prayed her father into heaven. Leoba's nuns expressed their sisterhood and overcame their own sin of anger by learning to pray for the soul of a dead novice mistress who had been so strict that they wanted at first to dance on her grave. The prayers of monastics, men or women, depended on the purity of the inner self gained from self-denial, self-control, and the self-knowledge learned in the hard school of daily confession to the abbess and the chapter of fault where a nun not only accused herself but submitted to the judgment of her peers concerning every aspect of her behavior.

Nuns and monks performed basically the same services and said the same prayers. With a spirituality designed for lay people, priestly duties almost dwindled to the consecration of hosts, apparently kept in reserve to be administered, if need be, by the abbess. The archbishop of Canterbury, Theodore of Tarsus, authorized women to read the lessons and perform altar ministries excepting sacramental functions.[49] Most rules were not gender-specific, and there are no elements in any of them unsuitable for women. Some manuscripts of the Benedictine rule were copied with feminine designations replacing masculine (*sorores, abbatissae,* and so on). Queen Balthild used the Benedictine rule to govern loose conglomerates of cells she endowed at basilicas of well-known saints and at her larger male and female foundations.[50] Leander of Seville assumed that it would supplement his short rule for his sister Florence, which slighted the details of government for the general admonitions and exhortations that would inspire the spiritual life. Similar clothing minimized distinctions between monks and nuns. Gertrude of Nivelles (and probably other women trained in the practices of Luxeuil) cut her hair in the round Irish tonsure.[51] Fara was said to have raised a child in such perfect innocence that her biographer said she could not distinguish women from men.[52]

These similarities promoted a cautious syneisactism among religious. Monks learned to fear and shun women as nuns learned to fear men and fear their own sexual attractions. All sensible people agreed that the abilities of the chaste to withstand temptation should not be put to gratuitously harsh tests. They took precautions to prevent intimacy between the sexes but they were equally uneasy about the perils of attraction within the same sex. Female monasteries normally had a fairly large cluster of men attached to them as priests or laborers, and fellow monastics were obvious candidates for these places. Indeed, many factors promoted cross gender identification between monks and nuns. Benedict hesitated to have priests in monasteries, and Pope Gregory maintained the separation between monks and clergy where he could, seeking to keep monks out of the world and clergy within it. Thus, religious women and men shared a lay spirituality as well as a common way of life. Monastic theorists tended to conceptualize a third gender, apart from the two sexually active genders, harking back to the old view that, without active sexual and reproductive activity, gender did not exist. Jonas of Bobbio commemorated Farn as one of Columbanus's successors in his history of the abbots of Luxeuil. Aldhelm mixed women and men in his hagiography, as did Gregory of Tours. Pragmatists did not go so far but they apparently took the sensible position that, with care, women and men could control themselves sufficiently to endure the contacts that their mission forced upon them.

Modern scholars have given much attention to abbeys where women ruled nuns as well as resident monks, which they have dubbed double monasteries. They have labored long over the origins and structure of the institution. One of the most popular theories connects the Irish both at home and in their missionary work in Scotland, England, and on the Continent to syneisactic practices that nineteenth-century scholars sometimes linked to a putative Celtic matriarchy. Theorists look back to a mysterious pre-Christian social system to explain the preeminence of abbesses (in some houses) over monks. The rule of the abbess over both women and men has naturally given rise to feminist speculations as well.

The double monastery, however, seems to be fundamentally a scholarly invention and one that is fast losing its usefulness.

For it was not a system but a convenient arrangement haphazardly adapted to the needs of frontier missions. The amount of daily contact and socializing between monks and nuns varied greatly. Coldingham apparently allowed very casual association between its female and male members, for which Bede criticized them sharply. The allotment of authority also varied. At Remiremont, there was a joint community with Amatus as abbot and Mechtafled as abbess. Pavilly and Jumièges began as one community but separated, though they preserved cooperative links. Bezé became a double monastery in 657 when Adalsinda, abbess of Doriaticum, asked her brother, Abbot Waldelen, to take her community under his protection, to avoid injuries from strange men. Generally, the nuns dominated in England, and the same pattern emerges at Laon and Jouarre, which Faro transformed from a male monastery to a double one under Theudechild. Chelles became a double monastery because so many men sought entry. Nivelles and Maubeuge had men subjected to abbesses. Marchiennes and Hasnon had separate abbots for the men. An abbess was generally the dominant party where she was the social and economic superior of the monks as at Remiremont, where the farm laborers were monks of some sort. At Nivelles, a small male community had its own director, but all obeyed the abbess in performing the external tasks that threatened to distract the nuns from their devotions. The nuns at Barking lived in an inner cloister but were infected with the plague when they nursed their monks. At that abbey it is difficult to discern whether the superior was Abbess Earcongota or her brother Bishop Earconwald. And what do we say of the nunnery founded by the hermit Patroclus, who gathered a flock of female disciples and lived in chastity among them?[53]

Monkeries normally had a cohort of women, often relatives, associated with them, which scholars have tended to ignore. One of Patrick's foundations brought together three brothers with their sister, a community that was considered normal in Ireland, where women did not inherit permanently and therefore generally joined with their male relatives or protectors.[54] They often extended their blood bonds to spiritual brotherhood as well as sisterhood. Abbess Egburg described herself as Boniface's disciple, "once my brother, now brother and father in the Lord," when she offered mutual consolation in the loss of "my own brother

Oshere" and "my dearest sister Wethburga," who vanished from this life to become a recluse in a Roman cell.[55] Such associations have attracted less attention because the idea of dependent women cared for by authoritative males is inherently less dramatic and because the sources on male monasticism are prone to conceal cross-gender associations. Sexual purity was clearly a fundamental requirement for a monk, yet it was difficult to describe it or even to admire it. Christianity opened the way for a positive ideal of womanhood as the repository of the virtues most prized in Christian teaching, meekness and humility oddly paired with the manly virtues of courage and perseverance when God's will ran counter to that of man. The concept of chastity provided a new source of potency.

The whole Christian vision rested on role reversals, gender transformations, revolt against nature. Monastic men were brides of Christ as women were soldiers of Christ. But the womanly man was a far less popular image than the virile woman. The male virgin was a difficult concept to elucidate. Pope Gregory's exemplum of Galla, a Roman matron who grew a beard because of the manly heat built up by her chastity, rested upon the venerable and noble concept of the virile woman. Gregory of Tours had a more difficult time presenting an exemplary picture of Gallus, who cut his hair (an emasculating act for Franks) and remained a virgin. He also conspicuously abstained from simony. His singing voice remained sweet and agreeable, which attracted royal patronage. Yet, in contrast to the virile Radegund of Baudonivia's biography, he was something of a coward, running away when a mob protested his destruction of a pagan shrine.[56] As if to underscore the ambiguity, at his funeral women dressed as though mourning husbands and men as though mourning a wife.[57] Yet Gregory considered Gallus a "Father," as was Monegund, a wife and mother before God marked her for his own.

The Pauline formula, neither male nor female, probably relied on sexual inactivity. The third gender combined the classical virtue of self-control and the Christian virtue of self-abnegation. God delegated authority to those who subordinated their will to him. Self-control was thus measured by obedience and sacrifice, not by domination and violence. Chaste men could absorb the positive qualities of both men and women. Gregory of Tours illustrated the idea in the lives of Lipicinus and Romanus, two brothers who founded a monastery and acted as parents nourishing their monks. Gregory inverted their birth order to make a gender point.[58] He assigned Lipicinus, who had been sullied by a betrothal (apparently unconsummated) in the world, the role of elder brother, while calling the virgin Romanus the younger brother. Lipicinus played the father of the monks, mortifying himself heroically, shunning women, and disciplining his "children" remorselessly. The maternal brother, Romanus, never mortified himself but continued to bestow blessings and charity on men and women alike. He comforted and reconciled the monks driven to anger by Lipicinus. Finally, the saintly brothers determined to be separated when they died. Lipicinus was buried in the monastery to continue watching over the monks, and Romanus, though sorrowing that they could not rest together, chose a tomb well apart from the monastery so that women as well as men could benefit from his healing powers.

The saintly bishop Salvius, who lived as a virgin for many years before entering a monastery and then a hermitage had a vision of heaven as filled with "a throng of people, neither men nor women . . ., not angels but holy saints."[59] Bones have no sex, and the mixing of the sexes in heaven was often symbolized by the mixing of their bones on earth. Gregory of Tours wrote of two couples who lived in spiritual marriages only to have their tombs miraculously joined after they died. Aldhelm said Hildelith mixed the bones of the dead nuns and monks in a single sepulchre at Barking. Scholastica joined her brother Benedict in his monastery after she died. Guthlac was emotionally close to his sister Pega, though he divided himself from her on earth as a mortification. Leoba traveled in triumphant death to Fulda, where she performed many miracles in tandem with Boniface, united at last in a world where there is no marriage or giving in marriage.

The creation of a third gender depended on the painstaking elimination of sex, and monastics expected to complete the task only when they had abandoned the earth. But, with care, women and men collaborated in the missionary age on earth. They respected one another as equals in prayer. In the apostolate and its monastic virtues they achieved a circumscribed but workable syneisactism in the wilderness. But in the city and the empire, papacy and crown overcame the desert and its lack of boundaries. The religious climate changed by the middle of the eighth century. Conceptually, monks found a world without women more hospitable to their own aspirations.

6

The Bonds of Castimony

AT THE BEGINNING of the ninth century, Bishop Amalarius of Metz undertook to write a rule intended for all Frankish nuns. Reflecting the considered opinions of the combined authorities of church and empire, gathered in council, he wrote:

> Let no petitioner be too easily admitted to a monastery. Be sure that she understands the requirements of the life of castimony. She must understand that, once enrolled in the lord's militia, she may never again follow her own counsel or engage in secular business or enjoy the company of men or chat with familiars except for unavoidable reasons. So let her scrutinize her inmost heart and meditate painfully on the sentences of the fathers lest in the end she render herself up to Satan like a dog returning to its vomit.[1]

Until the eighth century, monasticism was shaped by its practitioners. They conformed to dogma as defined by church councils and to the moral norms of other Christians, distinguishing themselves by striving for perfection within that common framework. Religious women and men represented a lay alternative to the hierarchical church, with its married clergy and its preoccupation with the affairs of the Christian world. Renunciation of sexual activity enabled them to maintain a spiritual parity, which I have characterized as a third gender. Though physically separated to satisfy the demands of modesty, they minimized differences in dress, worship, and way of life to the point that, at least in theory, slightly disguised women could live in monkeries without discovery. While the female monk may have been only a hagiographical construct, it is certainly true that sixth- and seventh-century authors credited both genders with an equal capacity for sanctity in equal living conditions. Among the exempla so abundant in seventh century hagiography, there is little evidence of anxiety that the congress of women and men would lead to sexual disorder.

Yet once the pressures of conversion abated, gynophobia spread again among men familiar with the monastic scene. The missionary Boniface typified his age in turning from the sibling models of monasticism, with its strong New Testament roots, to the more patriarchal spirituality of the Old Testament. Instead of a brother to his sisters, he became a bishop and as such a father to his spiritual daughters and a vicar for their husband, Christ. Modifications to women's entry into monastic life reflected this change in status. Originally, a simple vow given under the Benedictine rule to the abbess, followed by the taking of a veil, seems to have sufficed to consecrate a woman to God. In the middle of the ninth century, the word "castimony" appears in some texts to distinguish this chaste matrimony, and by the middle of the tenth century an elaborate ceremony had evolved. High Mass with a special episcopal blessing of veil and habit paralleled the growing solemnity of the secular wedding ceremony. The prospective nun's male guardian gave her away. She was married to Christ with ring and crown. She was interrogated and her oath confirmed, and finally she proceeded in her new habit to the altar carrying a lighted candle in memory of the wise virgins.

Between 700 and 900, even in areas still experiencing a substantial growth in the numbers of monasteries, the proportion of female to male foundations declined steadily. Historians have tended to attribute every failure and disappearance to Saracen marauders active in the Mediterranean and throughout Iberia from the beginning of the eighth century, joined by Magyars from the east and Vikings from the north in the ninth century. But even in relatively well protected parts of Frankland, female monasteries dramatically declined. Nor did they have the elasticity to revive characteristic of male monasticism. By about 850, only 17 of the 167 foundations known to have been established in earlier times survived. In many areas, communities whose disappearance has been attributed to Viking destruction in fact fell from the historical record at a substantially earlier date, apparently sandbagged by conflicting theories of corruption and reform.

The monastic system, with its self-regulating autonomous houses, was ideally suited to the maintenance of religious observance in chaotic conditions. Boniface had maintained the closest ties to English abbesses who supported his Frisian mission with money, prayers, and personnel. In 722, with the conversion of Hesse and part of Frisia, he began establishing both female and male communities to consolidate their Christianization. But in the same year, the abbesses Eangyth and Bugga wrote to him from England that, like many of their friends and relatives, they were making plans for a pilgrimage to Rome. Although they had the approval of their former abbess, Boniface advised them to stay home, saying that the brothels of Italy were filled with English nuns who had never completed their trips. Concern for their safety on the road probably inspired this rude reaction, but Boniface also believed the rumor that King Aethelbald of Mercia was in the habit of fornicating with nuns who, he hinted, were not victims of rape. To their shame, he compared the English with the heathen Wends, whose women refused to survive their dead husbands. Comparing Aethelbald's alleged sin to the crime of adultery against a lord (Christ), he coupled the admonition with a lengthy description of the horrible deaths visited by pagans on adulterous women.[2] He most likely had in mind Repton, a community of women and men presided over by abbesses known to be enterprising. In 755, Aethelbald chose that monastery for his final resting place, with all the financial advantages that accompanied a royal tomb. In 832, the abbess Cunewara leased the lead mines of Wirkswork to an entrepreneur named Humbert. By that time Boniface's successors had gone a long way in tightening episcopal authority over monasteries.

To Boniface and his contemporaries, the Frankish church was in severe need of reform. After the great councils of Merovingian times had regularized the practice of Christianity in newly converted territories, legislation had largely fallen off, and in a period of civil war and invasion enforcement of existing legislation no doubt had grown lax. The new Carolingian dynasty and its cohort of energetic bishops, however, apparently meant something quite new when they set out to reform the church, particularly religious life. The reformation and regulation of female communities was carried out by men who made no discernible effort to consult the women concerned. Their program followed a systematic vision drawn from centuries of episcopal irritation with women living a free-lance spiritual life, but it cannot be called a reform in the sense of restoring a recognized and accepted standard for female monasticism. Basically, it had two unstated but clear objectives: to separate female and male religious and to subject all religious to episcopal authority.

This regulation grew out of the ongoing reform of the episcopate itself, which dated back to the period of Gregory the Great. Lay potentates, who exercised growing influence over episcopal appointments, actively cooperated in the frustration of any clerical trend toward a hereditary caste. Bishops, stung by adverse comparison or challenged by the celibate ideal, adopted the lifestyle of monks, separating from their wives upon their elevation. Cathedral chapters in newly converted lands like England and northern Europe were based on monastic communities, and bishops doubled as abbots. Increasing numbers, like Boniface himself, had begun as monks. The advancing intrusion of monasticism into the hierarchy paralleled the priesthood's infiltration of the monastery, particularly where a monastic community doubled as a cathedral chapter. The combination effected a schism between monks and nuns, who were barred from the priesthood.

In Spain, Isidore of Seville tried to subordinate the monastic movement to his episcopal authority and ruled that monks and nuns must live separately, each house having its own superior under episcopal supervision. His brother, Bishop Leander, wrote a rule intended to standardize the nuns of the diocese.[3] The effectiveness of the effort was cut short by the Muslim invasions of the early eighth century because episcopal control of monasteries required strong royal support to be effective. In the middle of the eighth century, campaigning for Pope Zacharias to give his imprimatur to the Carolingian usurpation of royal authority, Pippin II encouraged Boniface, with the assistance of Bishop Chrodegang of Metz, to undertake a large-scale reform that eventually encompassed much of modern France, Germany, the Low Countries, and northern Italy. Boniface also successfully urged his English compatriots to accept the decrees of the Frankish Council of Soissons for their own church. The reforming Synod of Cloveshoe in 747 enhanced episcopal authority, and in turn the English bishops demonstrated their willingness to increase their dependence on papal authority.[4] These councils sought to place all monasteries under the bishop's direct supervision, giving him visitation rights to ensure that the regular life was observed. They made particular provisions regarding the policing of nuns' drinking habits, gossiping, and preoccupation with their clothing and recommended measures to ensure that nuns were not letting secular persons wander in and out or employing servants of too worldly a cast of mind.

In 789, Charlemagne, guided by the papal law called Dionysio-Hadriana, forbade abbesses to usurp episcopal functions, not only in Frankland but also in the newly conquered territories of Saxony in the north and Lombardy in the south. Presumably these included administrative and possibly liturgical functions with no sacramental authority. Logic points to activities involved with the government of religious women. Charlemagne deprived abbesses of the power to veil nuns, reserving the exclusive right to the male clergy, who also had power to approve and regulate recluses.[5] By 829, even veiling by priests required episcopal permission. Women who had veiled themselves were accused of tempting priests and barred from churches, and their general services to the altar were severely limited.

Reforms advancing the agenda of the clerical hierarchy were not always compatible with the monastic ideal, increasingly defined as strict adhesion to the Benedictine rule. When Louis the Pious succeeded his father in 814, he gave charge of all the monasteries in the realm to the reformer Benedict of Aniane. Benedict put strict enclosure and devotion to God through prayer and study at the center of his conception of monasticism. He structured community life around a liturgical reform that greatly expanded the devotional tasks of the religious life. Long elaborate chants, processions, and prayers were woven into the daily routine to enhance the religious' sense of closeness to God and focus their intensive study of Scripture. Expertise in book production, which favored literate monastics above those engaged in physical labor, became essential. The lengthy liturgy outlasted the reform itself. Religiously minded individuals gained much spiritual profit from its observance, and it made monastic worship far more tangible to prospective patrons.

Monastic spirituality was nonsacerdotal in nature and equally suited to nuns and monks. The Carolingian age threatened a transformation

that would be highly disadvantageous for women. The reforms segregated women from clerics and reiterated their exclusion from clerical
activity. Pope Zacharias exacerbated the split when he canceled Theodore
of Tarsus's allowance of a nonsacerdotal ministry of women on the altar.
The Council of Soissons repeated that consecrated women could not
serve at the altar.[6] Some women are known as a matter of course to have
performed quasi-liturgical services involving caring for vestments, supplying oil, wine, and other ingredients for the ceremonies, lighting
candles, and ringing bells. It is highly probable that women in a number
of parishes and monastic establishments also filled in as acolytes and in
other auxiliary capacities for priests. In 829, the Council of Paris cut
back traditional activities involving decoration and housekeeping, accusing women of polluting altar vessels and linens by cleaning them.[7] The
council forbade nuns to ring bells or light candles. Obviously, if these
liturgical changes were to be imposed on female communities, nuns
would have to depend more heavily on the services of men, not only
priests but sacristans and acolytes too. Yet the capitulary assumes the
shift from a weekly mass to a daily mass in monasteries. This schedule
was also stipulated for English monasteries at the Council of Cloveshoe
in 747, where all monastic persons were instructed to keep themselves in
a constant state of preparation for the reception of the Eucharist.[8] By
adding the offices of the dead to the mass and stipulating that the
benediction following compline be given by a priest, Benedict ensured
that these new rituals could not be performed by nuns alone. This reform
heavily compromised women's ability to lead a satisfactory spiritual life,
and it handicapped them in competition for donors. Naturally, nuns
strove to rise to the challenge and maintained priests to ensure a full
range of services. When the abbey took the Benedictine rule, Remiremont created a necrology to facilitate remembrance of the generous dead
during their daily masses. But women's devotions lacked sacramental
power, and they themselves suffered from the increasing perception that
nuns were no more than feeble dependents burdening monks. The first
known confraternity of prayer was formed by Chrodegang of Metz
among the twenty-seven bishops and seventeen abbots gathered at the
Council of Attigny. The exclusion of abbesses from the reforming
councils kept them from access to these spiritual associations, which were
gaining popularity in the late eighth century.

  This growing sense of the church as a male club may account for the

snide attitude of the biographer of Bertha of Blangy.[9] Writing a fiction-
alized account of the seventh-century foundress of the monastery whose
relics had already been appropriated by enterprising monks engaged in
a "sacred theft," the author claims that every bishop of Dagobertian
Frankland came to honor Bertha by assisting at the dedication of her
monastery. When they had all assembled, the officiating bishop asked if
she had the ingredients prepared for the ceremony of consecration. She
assured him that she had but was publicly humiliated when it turned out
that she was too ignorant to have provided hyssop for a necessary
ointment. Despite God's miraculous help in sending a timely hyssop
salesman to the door, the story implied that women were too incompetent
to serve the altar even in this ancillary capacity.

In 813, the Council of Chalons issued a special set of rules designed
for maximum separation of nuns from all men, reinforcing the earlier
prohibitions on the movements of abbesses (even within the precincts of
an episcopal city) and limiting the times of speech with all men, clergy
or lay, to the daylight hours in the presence of witnesses.[10] Though this
latter injunction may seem like a perfectly reasonable one, its very
existence suggests a snide and probably undeserved suspicion of the
inclinations of nuns, which may provide more insight into the minds of
reformers than of their subjects. The genuine difficulties of establishing
a communal celibate life, particularly for women who could not separate
themselves entirely from men, clearly justified some precaution. But so
systematic and widespread an attack on the least hint of a syneisactic
accommodation to secure the spiritual and temporal powers the system
denied to women stemmed also from the episcopate's dislike for a
religious system independent of its own authority. While the need for
disciplinary regulation grew out of the inescapable frictions that arise in
a community still striving to blot out class and gender distinctions, we
cannot acquit male clerical leaders from acting out of dislike for the
liberties enjoyed by monastic women.

The ninth-century bishop of Metz firmly maintained:

They who devote themselves to castimony should be careful that their
minds are as unspotted as their bodies, wearing a veil on their souls as
well as their heads. Freed from conjugal slavery which subjects them to
their husbands, how much more must the brides of Christ devote them-

selves to the religious life, the discipline of subjection to Him with all humility and chastity? How could anyone be so mad as to believe that what was not allowed to her in her father's house or in the bonds of matrimony could be allowed in a monastery? It would indeed be wicked if the fragile sex and imbecile youth were allowed to abuse their own wills and make licit what is illicit. But this can never be.[11]

Among their many reforms between 742 and 747, Boniface and Chrodegang imposed the Benedictine rule on all monasteries. This step should have stemmed the tide separating male and female monastics. Benedict had advised that monks should not be ordained priests and that priests should be excluded from the monastic community. His precepts should have kept women and men alike pure of the worldly involvements that clerical ordination entailed. They would thus be equally dependent on the clergy for the sacraments but equally lay in their spirituality. The Council of Verneuil in 755 placed all monastic persons, female and male, under episcopal jurisdiction.[12] It threatened nuns who resisted the imposition of the rule with excommunication, imprisonment, and forced labor. Why was this necessary? For women who had already chosen communal life, the rule should not have required any great change. The various rules from the preceding century would have become more standardized, but Benedict was flexible and brief and the longer rules of the Columbanian monasteries simply built upon his ideas. Except the Caesarian rule being used at a small handful of nunneries, no extant set of regulations deviates significantly. Yet in 787, Charlemagne wrote to Monte Cassino for an authentic copy of the rule.

Perhaps Charlemagne was looking for legislation that did not exist in the Benedictine tradition. In fact, by silent consensus, the Benedictine rule, with its non–gender-specific requirements of stability and obedience to the abbess was treated as unsuitable for women, though it remained the norm for monks. From 789 forward, imperial decrees and conciliar decisions attempted to impose strict claustration on all nuns. Benedict of Aniane began his reform by compiling the *Codex Regularum* from all the monastic rules available. His special section devoted to women collated portions of the rules of Augustine, Donatus, Leander, Caesarius, and Aurelian of Arles with Benedict's.[13] He ostensibly sought to show that all the great monastic leaders said the same things. But this is perhaps a little disingenuous. By claiming that all the rules were mutually compatible, Benedict could draw upon Caesarius to interpret Benedictine stability as strict enclosure for women. Perhaps inadvertently, the system isolated women from their male partners while simultaneously depriving them of the direction of their own community life.

After the middle of the eighth century, the boundaries between clerics and monks became ever more blurred and porous, while the lines separating nuns and monks were institutionally and even physically strengthened. The whole concept of castimony and the revival of a developed analogy of nuns as brides of Christ set them apart from monks. Theoretically, male virgins were brides just as female virgins were soldiers of Christ, but in fact the imagery was never applied. The matronal model for nuns was couched in terms of male guardians keeping the lord's wives from rape and adultery. Boniface may not have intended for his policy to fall most heavily on women, but his letter to Bugga suggests that he was not averse to having his policies subject women to a system of claustration that, as far as we know, had formerly been found only at the Caesarian monasteries of Arles and Poitiers and specifically rejected for the Benedictine and Columbanian monasteries of the rural frontier.

Rudolf of Fulda, in the ninth century, idealized Wimbourne, a double monastery endowed by the king of Wessex where Leoba trained. He claimed (and we cannot check him) that in the eighth century each community was surrounded by strong walls so that neither could be breached by members of the opposite sex except for priests who went to celebrate mass in the nuns' chapel. The abbess conducted her business with the outside world by speaking through a window. In contrast, Bede, who generally admired the abbesses of England, expressed concern with the consequences of the easy congress of nuns and monks, which characterized monastic establishments everywhere. When Coldingham accidentally burned down, the venerable historian chalked it up to retribution for the nuns' lax life. His accusations, retailed through the vision of a holy man who lived in the monastery, included too much eating, drinking, gossip and other amusements, which left the inhabitants sunk in exhausted sleep "or awake only to sin." He observed himself that the nuns were preoccupied with their own adornment.[14] Bede's impressions of one convent seem to have been generalized by the prelates who adapted Boniface's Continental reforms at the Synod of Cloveshoe.

Spain, too, embraced an ideal of strict segregation within paired communities. Possibly prelates there were responding to a problem that Bede also saw in England: that monasteries had been converted from family farms, perhaps as nothing more than a tax shelter. Isidore of Seville decreed that nuns would be allowed to produce clothing for their associated monks and that one monk could live in the nunnery to supervise their property and supply sacramental needs.[15] The presence of non-Christian rulers favored the continuing autonomy of these institutions. In the ninth and tenth centuries, as the Muslims gained a tighter hold on the peninsula, double monasteries continued to expand. Eulogius, bishop of Toledo (859), spoke of their foundation as everyday events praising Tabanos, where the abbess gave orders to the monks through a window. Penna and Mellaria grew up in the vicinity of Cordoba. Eulogius himself joined the many martyrs from these monasteries that he praised.

Writing, like Bede, in the eighth century, Cogitosus idealized Kildare in his *Life of Bridget:*

> The number of the faithful of both sexes increasing, the church was enlarged, having three large oratories within it separated by wooden partitions under one roof. One partition extended the entire breadth of the eastern part of the church from the one party wall to the other with the two doors at its ends. Through the one door on the right side, the chief prelate enters the sanctuary accompanied by his followers in the rule and the ministers of the altar; through the other, the abbess and nuns enter when they communicate. Another partition divides the floor of the house into two equal parts. There are two main doors: one for the men and one for the women.[16]

Even this cautious pairing was threatened by the wave of reform legislation, beginning with the Council of Verneuil in 755.[17] It imposed heavy restrictions on the movements of abbesses outside their monasteries, which were confirmed by the Council of Heristal in 779 and most of the later councils of Charlemagne and Louis the Pious. Moreover, bishops tended to be stricter in enforcing stability on women than on men: Bishop Lull of Thuringia excommunicated Abbess Sitha for allowing two nuns to travel without his permission, though abbots generally could permit monks to go out at will. The Council of Friuli in 796–797 forbade abbesses to go to Rome on pilgrimage, which would also have ruled out chances of direct appeal to the pope against episcopal decisions.[18] Abbesses (as opposed to abbots) could leave their convents only once a year when the king commanded it and only with episcopal permission.[19] At other times, they were supposed to send any message they had to the king or synods through couriers. This may have been intended as a barrier to pluralism, an abbess's capacity to govern more than one monastery, which the same chapter forbade. But pluralism was equally condemned for men and it was not enforced by isolating them. Instead, it deprived abbesses of the power to supervise daughter convents, as Leoba had always done, transferring the responsibility to men. And they could make no appeal against episcopal decisions unless the bishop himself gave them permission to do so. By 803, young boys were forbidden to enter female monasteries as pupils. The loving relationships between nuns and bishops nurtured during these educational years were to be no more.

Amalarius of Metz's ninth-century rule for nuns clearly rested on a premise that, left to themselves, women would simply run amok. Many shared this assumption. The male biographer of Boniface's fellow missionary, Leoba, writing in the ninth century from eighth century sources which cannot now be checked, claimed that the devil tempted her and her sisters with thoughts of the flesh and tried to destroy their reputations when he failed to destroy their virtue. A crippled girl, a lay woman who was supported by the nuns, committed fornication and threw the resulting baby into a millpond, where a local woman coming to draw water found it. The furious villagers mobbed the monastery and accused the nuns of aggravating unlawful motherhood by encroaching upon the sanctity of the priesthood with their murderous baptism. Their suspicion focused on Agatha, whom the abbess had given leave to visit her parents. Hearing the accusation, Agatha returned and the whole community prayed through the entire psalter with arms outstretched and then carried their cross in procession around the monastery three times until God exposed the real criminal. With her confession, the innocent nuns were reconciled to the neighborhood.[20] Boniface remained a dear friend to Leoba and her companions until his death, but he became increasingly concerned about regulating nuns, and one of his reforms even included penalties for murdering illegitimate children born to nuns. He was one of several episcopal monks whose continued interest in their female companions, many of whom were their sisters and mothers, tended to smother them with killing kindness.

At the same time that these restrictions were being placed on the large nunneries, smaller communities and hermitages were curbed. Ninth-century bishops tended to look askance at any form of amateur spirituality. The Carolingian kings also promoted a more highly structured ecclesiastical organization that did not encourage a diversity of religious life. Women who lived religious lives outside the monastic system, attached to cathedrals or to the households of priests, as recluses, or simply as self-consecrated widows or virgins in their own homes faced sustained attack.[21] After Pippin promulgated the canons of the Council of Soissons, Boniface wrote to England urging the monarchs there to prevent women from living in priests' houses. Both nuns and monks were required to wear habits and both were to be punished for any lapse of chastity.[22] In 779, women who took a religious vow (clerical wives and widows) and then fornicated or resumed marital relations were ordered to be confined to convents.[23] Men were prohibited from marrying nuns, and all women who took vows of virginity or chaste widowhood were ordered to join convents.[24] In 796–797, the Council of Friuli declared private vows of chastity binding, but eventually they were prohibited altogether by Louis the Pious, who attempted even more far-reaching organizational control of the church than his father.[25] Convents were also used increasingly in the ninth century as prisons or repositories for unwanted women. Louis the Pious began his reign by banishing his unmarried sisters, who had been living with their lovers in the royal palace under their father's indulgent eye. Naturally, it seemed to the pious king that their amorous history qualified them for a convent, fully in accord with his legislation against private vows of consecration, which forced unmarried women into convents to prevent widows from using their "fraudulent" vows as a shelter for sexual freedom.

The Council of 829, probably in the same spirit, discouraged the establishment of small monasteries, which were most likely to be communities of women in their own homes. Subsequently, Bishop Hrabanus Maurus encouraged the closing of *monasteriola nonnarum*. (little monasteries of nuns).[26] This legislation prevented most new foundations for women while abolishing many older ones. The available evidence appears to indicate that women simply did not have as much property at their disposal in the ninth century as they had had in earlier periods.

The loss of these small independent arrangements damaged women's spiritual aspirations in two ways. It meant they had fewer convents to join at the same time that conventual affiliation was being strengthened by secular as well as ecclesiastical authority. The king joined with the episcopal establishment to take control of vocations, to ensure that persons who had entered the religious life not attempt to reenter the secular world and disturb its arrangements, and to draw and maintain a firm defining line between secular and religious persons. In 726, Gregory II wrote Boniface strictly prohibiting children, male or female, who had been placed in a cloister by their parents to leave and get married.[27] Monastic persons were declared to be civilly dead, which was intended to prevent them, particularly women, from being held in reserve as religious until it suited them or their families to change their state. Charlemagne prohibited entrance to the convent until a woman was twenty-five years old. He kept his own daughters equally from matrimony and from castimony. Louis the Pious, in 817, penalized priests who tonsured boys or veiled girls without the permission of their kin and ordered widows to delay taking any vow of chastity for at least thirty days and then not to act without counsel.[28] This loss of fluidity had to do with a desire to place women firmly under the appropriate ecclesiastical or secular men who would prevent their erratic tendencies to move from one way of life to another at their own will.

Episcopacy and monarchy alike were prepared to uphold parental authority to choose between cloister and marriage for their daughters, but they were determined to hold women to that original choice. Many children, like Leoba, grew to love their conventual life and to embrace its opportunities. But many others must have created ongoing disciplinary problems in convents. Moreover, while the male oblate who hated his monastic calling was unfortunate if he could not support the need for perpetual chastity, he could aspire to a career outside the monastery by moving into the clergy and aiming for a bishopric. He could travel widely as a missionary or in a variety of diplomatic capacities. He might busy himself with the life of the court in the capacity of confessor or advisor. None of these options were open to women unwillingly snared into a life they had not chosen.

Women gave Benedict of Aniane considerable material help in the early days of his foundation, and he returned the favor by being an active supporter of widows and nuns in his neighborhood. But when he joined the imperial administration, his reforms tended to discourage the spread of female monasticism and increase the difficulties of established houses. With the capitulary of Aachen, Louis the Pious gave imperial sanction to the form in which he applied the Benedictine rule. Cornelimunster was designated as *schola monachorum:* two monks from every monastery would be sent there to be trained in the practice of the new rules.[29] In addition two of Benedict's works praising and defending the rule's virtues circulated widely among the monkeries. But despite his clear interest in the regulation of female monasticism and the specific imposition of the rule on nuns, he established no school for their training. It is, of course, possible that monks were simply more in need of training since, as we shall see, most abbots were unfamiliar with the rule. The stronger implication, however, is that nuns were not expected to govern their own affairs and therefore needed no special instruction in how to go about it. It may be, too, that the reformers were conscious that the Benedictine rule, if closely studied by nuns, might provide too many arguments against the new interpretations being imposed upon it.

Whether or not the reformers intended it, they had split the third gender. Castimony represented a form of monasticism restricted to women, separating them from their brothers in Christ and subjecting them directly to bishops as the proxies of their absent and jealous husband. It made the simplest and most practical forms of syneisactism unthinkable. Double monasteries evolved into single-sex institutions or died. Heidesheim began as a joint venture by Wynnebald and Walpurga, the brother and sister of Bishop Willibald; and when Wynnebald died, it was carried on by Walpurga on her own. By 790, it had become a monkery. In some communities, like Remiremont, the male component shrank away, replaced by small communities of canons who served the spiritual needs of the sisters. Although the canons did not share the common rule or the common life, their clerical status gave them a certain authority even, in some respects, over the abbess.

In the end, all this legislation had but one purpose for women: the imposition of external controls over them combined with internal claustration. The reformers seem to have been largely indifferent to what they made of the life that resulted. Yet they set the pattern for the church's treatment of nuns in every major reform thereafter. Consciously or unconsciously, they swept women out of their way as they reorganized their official world. The monarchy based on a Christian ideology of kingship tended to become a male union. The visions and ambitions of reforming bishops, monks, and kings were dazzling. By the eighth century, the initial task of converting the Germanic invaders of the empire was nearly complete. The first outline of a "Christendom," institutionally and ideologically amalgamated, was taking shape. The monastic system had even bridged the opposition between city and countryside. From Ireland in the west to the Rhineland in the east, from Italy to the northern lowlands, monasteries formed the strong web that held Latin Christendom together. The Carolingian dynasty based its revived empire on divine sanctions. Men began to dream that the City of God might come to life on earth.

Nevertheless, the Carolingian reforms had little lasting effect beyond their ideological impact on monastic life. The new empire was born in warfare and peace never came. The chaos of the age did not allow for untroubled islands of contemplation. From 711 on, Europe was threatened by new invaders who were not susceptible to the Christian mission. Muslim armies crossed the Straits of Gibraltar and destroyed the Visigothic kingdoms of Spain. Massive and successive attacks ravaged Italy and Frankland as far north as Le Mans and Troyes. The faith and its monastic outposts sorely needed a defender. In the whole of southern Frankland, the only certain monastic survivor was Saint Victor of Marseilles. In Italy, a few of the more powerful Lombard nunneries, like Saint Julia of Brescia, founded in 753 by Queen Ansa, and a couple of royal foundations in Pavia, whose composition is unclear, survived. But some of the greatest monasteries of the early period were destroyed (though Monte Cassino and a few other male institutions were reestablished as soon as possible). A few nunneries in and around Rome housed fugitives from the Saracens, but they probably did not last beyond a generation.

Ecclesiastical land-holding reached its peak in the eighth century and diminished fairly steadily thereafter. In 732, Frankland's most powerful noble, Charles Martel, stemmed the Muslim advance at Poitiers. Once crowned by the pope as emperor, his grandson Charlemagne posed as David come again. But, as defender of the faith, this new David had no easy task to perform. Through the ninth century, the danger expanded as the Carolingian empire fell prey to intestine warfare and Viking and Magyar raiders fed on the carcass. Everywhere, nuns and monks fled with the bones of their saints. Despite all the efforts of reformers, they lodged themselves haphazardly wherever they could find shelter. Communities dissolved and reassembled, distinctions of gender and the niceties of the rules forgotten. Defensive wars, even when successful, did not bring in new land, while the increasing cost of more advanced weaponry bloated military expenditures. Charles Martel reversed the trend of aristocratic endowment of monasteries and financed his wars by giving the revenues of ecclesiastical properties to his soldiers.

The inclination to be generous with God diminished dramatically. Charlemagne founded no new abbeys. Limits on new foundations and closings of small monasteries prevented the tax sheltering of fortunes that Charles's own ancestors had practiced in the time of Dagobert. Many monasteries passed from private patronage to royal protection through conquest (as in Italy) or because the noble proprietors gave them up as gifts or lost them through confiscation. Protection, then as now, was something of a racket. Under the Carolingians, the system of benefices of land (with attendant revenue and jurisdictional rights) to support the military nobility became firmly established. Superiors of both nunneries and monkeries diverted their revenues to enrich the royal fisc or support their own military commitments. Thus, the reforming interests of the Carolingian monarchs conflicted with their military needs.

Wala, abbot of Corbie, complained that monastic disorders stemmed from the presence of the laity in monkeries and nunneries. He tried to limit and define the military use of church property and to prevent prelates from actively engaging in military service.[30] But in the end neither Wala nor any other superior could prevent patrons backed by the king from commandeering all but a bare subsistence for the religious. Charlemagne's restrictions on ease of access to religious life for women and men, both nobles and serfs, reduced the number of chanting mouths that needed feeding. Louis the Pious, at least once, in the case of Poitiers, limited the ability of a convent to accept new recruits because the endowment could not support them. Meanwhile, secularization of the office of abbess diverted the revenues out of the community. The historian of the miracles of Saint Rictrude at Marchiennes was particularly critical of the abbess Judith, who ruled the monastery during the same civil wars. "She began to dissipate the possessions of this church, daring with marvelous boldness to pass the farms into the hereditary right of her nephew, a soldier."[31] The king completed the despoliation in 876. The double monastery of Hasnon came under imperial control when Charles the Bald secured the election of his daughter as abbess. Secularization also damaged the female monasteries of Hamaye, Aldeneyck, and Odilienberg. Maubeuge, Hautmont, and Andenne were made royal abbeys by the Treaty of Meersen, in 870. Even monarchs who continued to show generosity in making donations to the church also secured abbeys for their followers, who diverted the revenues to their own purposes. Reforms imposing the Benedictine rule with its careful election procedures have a mocking tone in the light of lay abbacies. The abbess's absolute authority under the rule was balanced by her pastoral responsibilities and by the fact that her flock had chosen her after full deliberation. The secularization of the office turned nuns and their superiors into hostile camps.

Where the revenues of a single monastery were not enough to support the needs of a military lord, he (or even his wife) might be given several offices. Pippin attempted some legislation against pluralism, but it was nullified by his inability to depose lay abbots. Although reformed abbesses were prevented from supervising more than one monastery by legislated claustration, pluralism allowed lay abbesses to be installed for the sake of skimming off revenues. Charles the Bald's wife, Ermentrude, certainly acted as abbess of Chelles and probably Soissons and Faremoutiers as well, though the claim that Jouarre should be added to her holdings was stoutly denied by the abbey's historian, who gave another Ermentrude that distinction. Schanis, a Benedictine convent founded in the early ninth century, prospered through possession of a relic of the holy cross donated by the emperor. In the difficulties of the century's end, the convent lost its relic, which somehow turned up at the male foundation of Reichenau in 923. The convent dwindled and failed to secure a steady patron. It was torn between the claims of conflicting noble families. The empresses Bertha and Richardis were imposed as abbesses on the community and treated it as a private estate. Finally, the property was divided into incomes for nuns from local noble families, who were released from the requirements of the common life.

Even these flagrant abuses were preferable to the situation that sometimes occurred with the collapse of the Carolingian empire when the military aristocracy took over entirely. Some women's monasteries were subjected to lay abbots.[32] In the worst cases, they moved in with their wives and families and encouraged the monks and nuns also to marry, passing the monasteries to their children. A diploma of Charles the Bald in favor of Saint Julien d'Auxerre ordered that the religious women there be given a defined and inalienable subsistence allowance. The act was requested by Hugues, abbot of the monastery and probably count of Sens, to secure sufficient food and clothing for the nuns against the anticipated depredations of his successors.[33]

In Spain, a reform was attempted based on the family monastery. Fructuosus of Buaga ordained that all husbands and wives who converted their holdings into a monastery had to live separately and never talk together without witnesses. They had to turn the administration of their property over to others and even entrust the feeding and physical discipline of their children to others (though they could interest themselves in the monastic training of the children).[34] At least one monastery, Cuteclara, tried the system: the abbess and abbot were a married couple following the rule of Fructuosus.

Bishops claimed to figure among the great patrons of monastic establishments. This was clearly not an unmixed blessing. Charlemagne and Louis the Pious affirmed bishops' authority and strengthened the metropolitan organization based on the parish system. This geographical administrative hierarchy imposed incompatible boundaries on the alternative piety and decentralized organization represented by monasticism. It would have been beneficial if centralization offered religious houses protection from local nobles who preyed upon their properties. However, episcopal founders and patrons often acted from family or personal interest just as secular donors expressed pious intent. Like lords seeking lands and offices for their followers, bishops also had many people to reward for services. Few women numbered among the claimants. Often bishops competed for the control of monasteries with the founders and with the congregations themselves. They could use their authority over the disposition of relics, the consecration of altars, and the appointment of priests to secure advantages over the community, especially over nuns, who could not secure spiritual services from one of their own group. The role of bishops was further compromised by their alliance with the Christian monarchy.

Monasticized bishops, who left no legal heirs behind them, made perfect candidates for royal office. The Carolingians used them as ministers of every sort, in which capacity they had to subordinate themselves and the properties they held from the king's gift to his military needs. Royal demands transcended simple greed for loot when the very existence of the Christian commonwealth was threatened. These episcopal officials secured control of convents from imperial or royal charters. The practice of basing bishoprics in monastic communities in missionary areas meant that some were installed in a double monastery, as at Ely, where women originally predominated. Ely's history after the first generation of royal abbesses is lost to record, but when the wealthy monastery was reconstituted after the Viking invasions, a community of Benedictine monks attached to the episcopal see took over the dower of Saint Etheldreda and enjoyed its revenues.

Emperor Henry II gave the nunnery of Kitzingen as a donation to the newly founded bishopric of Bamberg in 1007.[35] But episcopal commitment to religion was constantly compromised by the demands of the fisc. Notker the Stammerer said Charles hid one of his episcopal nominees behind a curtain so that he could watch friends and family, particularly his beloved queen, Hildegard, try to secure the office for their own candidates. The candidate thus learned where to give his true loyalty.[36] The divided spirit of a monk bishop looked restlessly from contemplative to pastoral concerns. The conflict of a prince bishop, torn between the demands of church and secular government, loyalty to a clerical hierarchy and to a monarch who characterized himself as the defender of the faith, was even more appalling.

Bishops who saw their estates diminished by lay warriors often looked to the monasteries for compensation. The archbishop of Sens, for example, made up for his own loss of income by seizing the goods of monasteries in the diocese. It was rare indeed when a monastery had an abbess as successful as the emperor Lothar's daughter, Bertha of Avenay, whose territorial claims against the powerful archbishop Hincmar of Reims were sealed in the peace treaty between the warring sons of Louis the Pious in 851. Pope Sergius III saved the nuns of Santa Maria in Tempuli from starvation by a timely donation, for the sake of the convent's most valuable possession (a painting of the Virgin Mary said to have been done by Saint Luke). But it required a miracle to prevent Sergius IV from removing the painting to the papal palace. The relic generated enough income to enable a small congregation of an abbess and five nuns to survive until 1221, when the icon was given to the Dominican nuns of Sisto (presently La Madonna del Rosario). Benedict of Aniane complained of widespread attack by prelates on monastic goods.[37] Religious women, of course, could not compensate themselves by seeking bishoprics

The need for monastic reform grew directly out of these abuses, yet in reading the acts of the various councils one would hardly guess their existence. Charlemagne wanted a well-run church with well-behaved clergy, but he saw his military responsibilities as having priority in God's service. The bishops he appointed were not likely to be offensive to their patron. Indeed, in the troubled reign of Louis the Pious they showed themselves loyal to the ideal of a united empire above all other considerations. After the early ninth century, as fratricidal warfare within the ruling family intensified the threat of non-Christian invaders, the secularization of abbots and the movement of monastic estates into the hands of local magnates surged. Religious women and men tended to find themselves under the direction of strangers who had little care for their spiritual interests and upon whom there was little restriction on the disposition of their endowment.

Charlemagne's capitularies restricted monks and (by implication) nuns to stability and prohibited all involvement with commerce. Enclosure inhibited nuns from soliciting donations or promoting cults. When they did not observe the restrictions, the breach of the regulations tainted their reputations. They were forbidden recourse to lay justices, and the crown undertook to enforce their vows. Increasingly, they had to depend on advocates, lay officials who attended to the secular affairs of monasteries, theoretically to protect the inhabitants from worldly concerns. Lay officials were supposed to secure the immunities granted to monasteries by royal charter. But Charles the Bald allowed royal immunities and other benefits to revert to local lords even as he treated abbeys as part of the fisc, to be distributed as benefices to his followers. The office of advocate fell into the same hands and lords used it to their own profit.

From 755 forward, councils commanded bishops to ensure nuns the necessities of life. Even to avert hunger, the nuns were told to go through the bishop to appeal for aid to the king, and any nun who broke the rule would be confined in a special part of the convent until she corrected herself. The Council of Tours protested that monks were being forced to leave their cloisters to beg on the roads because of poverty, and this complaint was repeated at Aachen.[38] The councils did not mention nuns, but the situation must be imagined as worse for them since they were not even allowed to appear at councils or make direct appeals. We do not know where women went when their small convents closed.

In these circumstances, the demands of reformers that the Benedictine rule be observed by all monastics stung. The diversion of monastic goods to lay abbots and abbesses, to advocates and other officials, mocked the ideal of community of goods and equality of provision. The installation of a male superior over a monastery of women made the rule's require-ment of a common table more scandalous and dangerous than any private arrangements. The Council of Aachen's decree that the abbess must share the life of the community was just short of a dirty joke. The only realistic recourse was to secure what private property each nun could command to guarantee her own subsistence and then share it as she saw fit. Yet in 847, Amalarius of Metz insisted that no nun seek to provide herself with any food above the subsistence level allowed to the entire community.[39] Complaints multiplied that nuns ate in separate quarters and entertained company there. Clearly, they were living on gifts from friends and relatives in whatever style their connections could provide. In addition to the loss of goods, the loss of the common table dealt a sharp blow to the whole concept of sisterhood. The drive to secularize their property worked against the drive to enclose nuns. The communal solidarity that gave sweetness to the concept of an enclosed life was smashed.

We do not know what, if any, improvement was made to the morals of nuns by all this legislation. It does seem clear that the longer and more firmly religious women were segregated from religious men, the more deeply the men fell prey to gynophobia. In the end we are forced to conclude that Louis the Pious and his bishops wanted not to expand the monastic system for women but only to maintain it in a rigidly constricted form. The tendency to secularize the abbatial office, added to restrictions on other income-producing activity, ultimately meant that there would be fewer nuns in an institution and that entrance would become increasingly difficult for any woman who could not bring in some income for her own support. Any effort to wipe out class distinctions and provide for impoverished women with vocations was doomed. Financial necessity turned surviving houses into exclusive communities that could not afford to support poor women and were increasingly unwilling to accept non-noble women. In brief, the most lasting and meaningful effect of a century of effort to "reform" women's monasteries under the direction of the male hierarchy of the Carolingian church and state was the end of the long struggle to realize the ancient Christian dream of establishing a community of neither bond nor free nor male nor female.

The Carolingians approved this outcome, as they viewed convents as a convenient place to store women not serving as wives or mothers. Royal women often found convents comfortable and attractive places for permanent or temporary retirement. The sisters and mother-in-law of Louis the Pious resided at Chelles. Queen Richardis entered Andelau. Queen Ermengard, first wife of Louis the Pious, died in a monastery at Angers, where she had stopped when taken ill on the road with her husband. Only Charlemagne's learned sister Gisla, who entered a convent voluntarily and became renowned for her brilliant education, may have made some small effort to live with the rest of the community as an equal.

Based on the concept of military and administrative function as the legitimator of power rather than blood right, the Carolingian monarchy tended to be more resistant to sharing influence with women than the Merovingians had been. Women who were once seen as peace weavers and mediators were transformed into evil geniuses. Where Merovingian kings often relied on their queens because they were the only people totally dependent on the king's good will for their own prosperity, Carolingian queens carried a lot of political baggage of their own. They became targets for political enemies reluctant to defy kings directly. When this happened, confinement in a cloister seemed an ideal solution.

Each house was expected to maintain an "interior cloister" reserved for women of chronic disobedience and intractibility in following the rule.[40] During the rebellion of Louis's older sons, his second wife, the empress Judith, was imprisoned in a convent on the grounds that she was sexually depraved and a practitioner of sorcery and therefore must be kept from her husband. Lothar tried to force his unwanted queen, Theutberga, into Avenay after he had accused her of incest, sodomy, and abortion. His mistress, Waldrada, ended at Remiremont as a penitent. If these women had been guilty of only a portion of what their enemies accused them of, they would have needed strict security indeed to keep them out of mischief. Apparently a ninth-century convent, suitably chosen, seemed capable of imposing that security even on women who had powerful political supporters. But we may well ask why it was believed that women accused of terrible sexual crimes—women who unquestionably did have a taste for worldly power and wealth—were thought to be suitable company for consecrated virgins.

Partially, at least, it must have been because both lay and ecclesiastical authorities nursed a secret suspicion that nuns had little innocence to protect. Abbesses were ordered to ensure that nuns not use lack of food as an excuse for sexual misbehavior.[41] Was it a guilty conscience or specific information that led the prelates at a council of 836 to report that some nunneries seemed to have become brothels?[42] The ongoing reforms imposed on the Frankish church tended to aim at keeping women out of sight and out of mischief. And, of course, separation could only enforce fear of pollution.

Within the monastic movement, a disastrous imbalance was developing. Houses for men grew steadily, and when their inmates failed to live up to their ideal, they were enthusiastically reformed and stimulated. Charges of laxity and unruliness against women in monasteries, by contrast, multiplied and led to the closing of houses or the virtual confinement of the nuns under close episcopal supervision. Half of the thirty-six early women's monasteries in central France that can now be traced failed: six perished utterly; three were given to canons because of their convenient location near churches; and nine went to monks.[43] Of the eighteen that survived, Sainte-Croix of Poitiers, the oldest, still flourishes today in a new location.

Whether nuns were voluntarily engaging in sexual affairs for personal or financial reasons is beyond our power to discern. We do know, however, that they were vulnerable to unwanted assaults. Gerberga, the sister of Bernard of Septimania, was dragged from her convent and executed as a witch by her brother's enemies. Hincmar of Reims condemned a man named Nivinus, who ravished a nun and took her to live in a far-off region. The Council of Aachen imposed lifelong penance for the ravisher of a religious, the Council of Meaux (845) strengthened the penalties. In 853, the Colloquy of Valenciennes instructed officials of Charles the Bald and Lothar to enforce the right of sanctuary for widows and orphans and refer cases of rape (which meant abduction and even elopement in early medieval law) to royal courts. Still in 851, Count Eberhard of Alsace repudiated his wife and married a nun whom he had abducted from the convent at Erstein. In the time-honored spirit of blaming the victim, Amalarius of Metz, about 847, devoted several chapters of his rule to punishments for sexual misconduct both with outsiders and among the sisters.[44]

Whether or not the nuns of the ninth century strove to honor the bonds of castimony into which they had entered as willingly or unwillingly as other women entered the bonds of matrimony, we can never know. Possibly poverty drove them, as it drove many a married woman, to supplement their incomes in the one manner always open to women. Possibly they called their hunger fasting and made the best of it. What is certain is that the civil wars of midcentury left the most prosperous communities in jeopardy. Laymen, prelates, and their erstwhile brothers in religion all cast hungry eyes on the remnants of what they possessed and let greed reinforce the competitive process of misogyny.

By the last quarter of the ninth century the secular and ecclesiastical hierarchies responsible for reform had virtually collapsed. The church, like almost every other institution, fell prey to the unbridled rapacity of marauders and pretended friends. Lack of income discouraged vocations and shrank communities. Rapine and negligence both destroyed the communal economy. The nuns of these reduced foundations still had something to lose and still had a chance of recovery. Even a devastated community, even one whose nuns had all fled or been martyred, retained a legal existence. The land itself, however ravaged, remained an object for greed. The bones of dead saints continued to be potential revenue enhancers once a cult was restored. Some communities endured and some returned from exile to their old houses, struggling with want and fear to maintain the religious life. Strange weapons came into play: maledictions and reports of vengeful miracles were abundant. Saints, long dead, experienced a new burst of life in defense of their worshipers. Even more wondrous was the discovery of new saints, hitherto unknown to all. Women and men alike tried to manipulate supernatural powers to their advantage.

Santa Bibiana in Rome was saved because the abbess Eufrosine succeeded in restoring the cults of the saints whose relics she possessed. Often, however, success only bred envy in jealous competitors. An exemplary tale was fabricated by a monk in the community of Humblières. The nunnery was believed to date from a seventh century foundation by a virgin named Hunegund, whose dowry of estates and slaves maintained a small congregation until the Viking invasions. Apparently at that time, the nuns buried the body of their foundress in an unmarked grave, since the elaborate tombs of saints in their chapels were favorite targets for marauders. Then they fled, leaving the site abandoned. In 945, the archbishop of Reims appointed a pious widow, Berthe, from the convent of Saint Peter to reform the nuns who must have returned at some unknown time. Berthe "located" the body of the saintly foundress thanks to a timely vision and had it solemnly translated to the church, where it could be observed for some weeks intact from corruption. She registered a series of miracles attesting to the saintliness of the relics and before she died in 948 or 949, she had persuaded the archbishop to establish a feast and endow the cult with privileges aimed at improving the revenues of the community. The helpful saint provided a show of power by causing grain harvested on her feast day to drip with blood, punishing the peasants for failing to attend the services. Despite Berthe's success, the nuns were soon removed from the site on the grounds that their morals were past repair. According to the hagiographer, one of the nuns was carrying on a regular affair with a nobleman who was ready to repent after a reproachful vision from Hunegund. His lascivious paramour, however, persuaded him to return by assuring him that the vision was only a rival in disguise hoping to gain his love for herself. After that, Hunegund appeared again and punished the lover with a blow to the groin from her spear.[45] Presumably his readers would conclude that nuns who allowed the sinner in their midst deserved expulsion.

Men, who controlled better access to communication and a more effective support network, had a record of co-opting the cults established by nuns. A community of monks in flight from the Vikings took refuge at Blangy. During a new invasion, they encouraged the nuns to flee with the relics salvaged from the monkery and those of their foundress, Bertha. They found shelter in a convent at Mainz. Once the danger was past, the monks installed themselves on the old convent lands. When they went to Mainz to collect their own relics, they claimed that Bertha had been appearing in visions to a woman back at Blangy demanding restoration to her original resting place, and they took her relics as well.[46]

In this context of rivalry we should not be surprised to find criticism of the morals and competence of the sisters offered not with an eye to reforming the institutions, as would be the case where male monasteries were involved, but to justify the conversion of a formerly female house into a male institution. For example, the rich lands commanded by Marchiennes from the inheritance of Saint Rictrude and her children remained in the abbey's possession despite the destruction of its buildings and records by Vikings in 879. When the danger was over and the abbey had been restored, it was taken from the nuns and given over to a community of monks, one of whom wrote a memorandum of the latter-day miracles of the foundress. In support of this usurpation, he maintained that the founder had originally intended to settle monks in the place and had only brought in nuns as an emergency gesture. By his account, the nuns managed to hold on for many years past the time of the invasion, though he charged that "they were all of the infirm and imbecilic sex, powerless to maintain the affairs of the church because of womanly slothfulness." Because of this "insolence and womanly impotence," they allowed their revenues to be lost and dissipated until they "had hardly enough to sustain their miserable lives."[47] He expected his readers to believe that neither the burning of the abbey by the Normans nor the depredations of a secular nobility followed by a royal pillage in 876 caused the abbey to decline; rather, the incompetence and dissolute behavior of the women did. It seemed logical to the monk, accordingly, that the count was justified in removing the nuns (to an unnamed location) and reforming the monastery by the installation of men.

All of this thievery of reputation as well as property went on under cover of overt violence. The lure of treasures ill-defended by women and men whose profession forbade the bearing of arms proved irresistible to marauders. In 870, a Viking fleet landed in Scotland and moved south making "an utter desolation" of England.[48] At the news of their approach, Ebba, abbess of Coldingham (the very monastery that had inspired Bede's criticisms), assembled the virgins "of whom she had the pastoral care and charge" and warned them of the danger of rape. She then proceeded to cut off her own nose and upper lip with a razor to make herself horrible to the attackers. As day was dawning and the Vikings reached their gates, the rest of the community followed her "maternal lead." The horrified marauders shrank back from the sight of the mutilated and bloody women and left the premises, content to burn the monastery and remit the virgins to the reward reserved for martyrs.[49]

The same army proceeded down the coast, burning and destroying the nunneries at Tynemouth, at Whitby, and in the marshes of Northumbria. They pressed into the fens of East Anglia and broke into Ely, violating the tomb of Etheldreda (who promptly blinded her attacker) and burning the buildings. Despite the recovery of Derby after the victory of Ethelfleda, Lady of the Mercians, over later invading forces in 917, the double monastery of Repton vanished.[50] The scarcity of remaining records supports the claim that monastic life disappeared from "western Mercia and southern England as well as the east and the north."[51]

The Continental story is equally bleak. In 857, Charles the Bald ordered repairs of Viking depredations graphically described by Hincmar of Reims, but he could hardly compensate for the rape of consecrated nuns and widows, which the archbishop lamented.[52] A "great army" of Vikings went out again from Louvain in 884. In 892, they moved around Belgium, burning Blangy and other monasteries. Some Belgian foundations, notably Hasnon and Hautmont, survived to be ravaged by Magyars in 954. The lives manufactured to accompany the relics of Saints Gudula and Berlinde describe the devastation of Moorsel, originally a prosperous convent of noblewomen. Invaders drove the nuns away with the body of Gudula. They lost their building to the Vikings and their land to the count who was their advocate.[53] An eleventh-century fiction called *Vita Berlindis*, probably written to repair the later poverty of the community, depicted a noblewoman whose father disinherited her in a fit of anger when she entered the same monastery, a poor shelter scarcely able to support six nuns.

Also at the end of the ninth century the Saracens, who retained their hold on Spain, widened their raids in the south, devastating Italy and southern France. In a relatively rare burst of intolerance, the Muslims of Cordoba demanded that Christians abandon their faith, and a number of nuns died as martyrs. In Italy, monasteries vulnerable to Saracen raiders fell. In Switzerland, the recluse Wiborada was but one of many victims of the invading Magyars. Female monasticism was particularly vulnerable to this onslaught and to the internal attacks of the Christian military. Most of the larger and wealthier houses perished. Those that survived were poorer than before, but they had become effectively free of the limitations placed on them by the reformers of the earlier age.

7

Family Ties

HOHENBURG was an old foundation but the Carolingian biographer of the foundress, Odilia, who described her as offering her nuns a choice of rules, may have wished to defend a relatively new way of life by creating an old legend. "Dearest sisters," he has her tactfully state,

> "Do you know that the climb [to the monastery] is so hard that few of the pilgrims and invalids who want to can come up to us? If it please your holinesses, I want to have a hospital for their reception built on the lower slope of this mountain." Then they all answered that this was best. With their blessing, she first constructed a church there dedicated to St. Martin and then provided for the reception of the poor. Moreover, . . . they asked that a monastery be built there also because the higher monastery was situated in a very arid place. And giving heed to their counsel, she built a monastery there, which remains to this day. Having finished both monasteries and collected nuns in them, she convoked all the sisters and asked them whether they wished to live the canonical or the regular life. All unanimously responded that they wished to follow the regular practice but humbly and mildly she said: "I know dearest sisters and mothers that you are most swift to endure every hardship and difficulty for Christ's name. But I fear that if we choose the regular life, it will put a curse on our successors because, as you know, the great difficulty of procuring water makes this place inconvenient and improper for the regular life. Whence it seems to me, if it is pleasing to your gentleness, that it would be better for you to live the canonical life."

Taking her advice, they all chose the canonical life in which rule that monastery perseveres, even today.[1]

The trend to reduce or eliminate quasi-clerical functions was bound to meet resistance from religious women who did not envision their vocation as a cloistered one. The reformers' failure to designate a nunnery for training in the Benedictine rule may have stemmed from the refusal of religious women to accept the rule as reformers interpreted it. In 796, the Council of Frankfurt offered consecrated women a choice between the Benedictine rule or the canonical life, theoretically splitting contemplative devotion from the active practice of hospitality and charity.

Scholars have long debated about the history of the canonical way of life. Basil of Caesarea used it to describe *kanonikai*, women who seem to have been consecrated to religion and the active life in the urban dioceses of the fourth century. Those women, in turn, do not seem dissimilar to the virgins and widows of earlier times. Other scholars have preferred to date the institution from the first appearance of the word "canon" in western sources: an English penitential by Egbert of York (732–766). Chrodegang of Metz produced a rule for men only, possibly intended to transform at least portions of the secular clergy attached to cathedrals into celibate communities thus excluding women. Once the idea was advanced, however, communities of women living under episcopal supervision in cathedral precincts as at Mons, Ely, and Milan may have assumed a parallel order for themselves. The architectural fashion for double churches, joined on either side of two baptismal fonts, suggests a system of separating women and men in joint worship. Such churches spread in Frankland, Lombardy, Switzerland, and the Rhineland in the ninth century.

In 803 the Council of Mainz directed women who made a profession of the Benedictine rule to live "regularly" and the rest to live "canonically" under the diligent care of a custodian.[2] In the same year, the Council of Tours recognized "those who have lived the canonical life from antiquity" and instituted reforms for clerks, canons, and *sanctimoniales canonicae* (canonical nuns).[3] Canons and canonesses had begun to claim ancient association with the rule attributed to Saint Augustine, a brief set of directions which assumed that the women and men it governed would customarily be abroad on community business and normally see one another in their daily routines.

Except in Spain, where Carolingian authority did not reach and Muslim conquest impeded episcopal regulation, the old monastic system, mixing women and men, pastoral and contemplative works, disappeared in the wake of the Carolingian reforms. Many of the monasteries that modern scholars have classed as "double" and that appear to have become single-sex establishments at this time adopted the canonical way of life. Where the community shifted from lack of male recruits, chapters of canonesses supported ancillary clerical communities just outside their enclosure or in the church they all served. One of the advantages of Hohenburg's extension at the bottom of the mountain was that Odilia could meet holy pilgrims from all over Christendom, some of whom she recruited as priests for her monastery.

Monkeries ceased to contain formal communities of nuns, but nuns were attached to loose groupings of consecrated women who, despite the legislation, took vows as recluses, widows, and virgins living in their own homes or in the homes of clerical relatives. In the early tenth century Odo, abbot of the famous reforming monastery of Cluny, which rejected association with female houses, helped a young girl to defy her parents and escape marriage by installing her "at an oratory for women near his monastery." There he supplied her with food and protection until he could find her a place in a nunnery.[4]

In the eighth century, secular abbots encouraged confusion between monks and canons, who retained control of their own property, because it lessened their responsibilities for the support of the community. Thus, even monasteries not associated with a cathedral or large parish church might become canonries. At Chalons in 813 the council published a set of regulations for canonesses. In 816, at the Council of Aachen, Benedict of Aniane attempted to make canons and canonesses virtually indistinguishable from monastics, even addressing his section on canonesses to sanctimonials, the customary term for nuns.[5] He imposed common sleeping and meals, regular offices, and absolute obedience to their superiors on both women and men. Canonesses had more restricted claustration and relations with the outside world than canons. They were discouraged from going on pilgrimage, and visits—even from clergymen—were strictly monitored.[6] Modern historians have great difficulty distinguishing between "canonesses" and "sanctimonials" when the sources do not address the subject, and the religious seem often to have avoided definition. Still, many old double monasteries like Nivelles, a canoness house for some time before 877, insisted on the difference. The nuns there believed that their abbess joined with Mons, Maubeuge, Cologne, and Mainz in an appeal to the pope against episcopal attempts to impose the Benedictine rule.[7]

As canonesses, they claimed three distinctions between themselves and Benedictine nuns. First, they performed a variety of public liturgical and charitable services, which freed them from strict claustration, though they accepted a degree of enclosure for the sake of security. Second, they did not take permanent vows of chastity and could leave and get married. Finally, they did not take vows of poverty or common property, retaining the right to their own wealth, though they entrusted its administration to the monastery's advocate or to a relative or friend to avoid distraction with worldly affairs.[8] They had their own dwellings within the walls of the monastery, either in the form of small houses or private apartments, and they employed servants.[9] These conditions tended to foster continuing close relationships between individual canonesses and their friends and relatives outside, which must have weakened their communal bonds considerably.

Against the ecclesiastical effort to regularize the monastic system, secularization continued undeterred in the tenth century, but the effects were not uniformly damaging. Indeed, despite the ravages of war and invasion, new communities formed and old ones revived. Association with aristocratic and royal patrons often made them wealthy and exceptionally powerful. In spite of all the odds, Wimbourne and even Saint Milburg's convent at Thanet survived in England until the last great Danish invasions of the eleventh century, when Leofruna, the abbess, was captured and held for ransom. Barking also remained a reasonably prosperous community for women in the next century. The successful foundation of Wilton probably belongs to the period of Alfred the Great, whose house for women at Shaftesbury developed steadily into the great monastery of Athelstan's time.

In what is now central France, a similar picture is gradually emerging. Thanks to the patronage of the aristocracy and bishops, at least eighteen houses were maintained from the Frankish period and thirty-eight new houses were added in the tenth and eleventh centuries. Saints' lives indicate that many women led their male relatives into religion. The more abundant documentation of the eleventh and twelfth centuries reveals numerous syneisactic groupings centered on familial ties. Sisters paired in contiguous establishments with their brothers, and mothers who had nourished their sons' vocations became the daughters of these spiritual fathers. In Anselm's time, three women, including Abbot Herluin's mother, resided at Bec. The mother of Johannes of Gorze attached herself to his monastery as a seamstress, despite the brothers complaints that the place was turning into a "gynecaeum" (a women's workshop).[10] Adelviva followed her son to Saint Vanne and went into service to the monastery but then left to become a recluse.[11] Premonstratensian houses established between 1120 and 1150 formed around nobles seeking to reform themselves and their families. Sometimes the women of the family may have had no choice. Whole families were received into Saint Martin's of Tournai and Saint Sulpice la Forêt when men donated the lands to support their wives and children after their deaths.

On the frontiers, female monasteries again proved their usefulness. A house for women was the first important abbey to appear in Holland with the foundation of Dirk II in 922 at Egmont and the double monastery of Thorn. In the same period, the evangelization of Bohemia began around 970, when Princess Milada and her brother established the first monasteries in Prague. In Spain, a "powdering" of small male and female monasteries remained faithful to their old traditions while a few great abbeys began to organize new institutions. Along the Castilian frontier between the ninth and eleventh centuries, a "pactual" form of monasticism developed. All the members of a community (generally comprising both women and men) signed an agreement specifying the conditions of their submission to the abbess or abbot, complemented with a statement of the rights of the nuns and monks. Communities may have needed such agreements because peasants who became monks or nuns had to be set free but also had to be bound to work for the monastery. The Riojan rule for nuns attempted to bring the pactual tradition into conformity with the Benedictine system. In the twelfth century, however, married couples who followed "the counsel of the Apostle that it is better to marry than to burn" formed the Order of Santiago and kept their children as members of the order until they were old enough to decide whether to remain or go out into the world.[12]

Noble patronage was also vital to the renewal of female monasticism in Italy. In 932, only three communities for women survived in Rome after a long and exhausting period of devastation by Saracens and local noblemen. Santa Bibiana appeared on a survey of 806 and surfaced again in 981. The nuns of Santa Maria in Campo Martis and Tempuli were saved from immediate starvation by a donation from Pope Sergius III in 904. The three senatrices Marozia (junior), Stephania, and Theodora (junior), with their cousin Alberic, lord of the city, founded the convent of Saint Cyriacus in Via Lata. They also helped endow lesser female and male monasteries.

The German nobility was spectacularly active. Between 919 and 1024 it endowed at least thirty-six communities of women in Westphalia alone, dramatically outnumbering male foundations. Indeed, some tenth-century Saxon families would not be known to us at all but for the lavish foundations of their women. The "proprietary church" system was developed by lay magnates as they gradually reconstructed a working social hierarchy out of the ruins of the Carolingian state. The new aristocracy was founded upon military force. Some descendants of the old dynasty secured a fragment of the strife-torn empire as the base of a new principality. Elsewhere, their officials, who were sometimes descended from servile families, took up the lands and duties abandoned by former lords. New families rose and old families crumbled. Free nobles reduced themselves to vassalage, while former slaves grew rich from the performance of public duties and bought their freedom. The resulting sense of anomie was reflected in a confusion of responses: cynical translation of public trust into private power did not prevent a craving for legitimation that could be satisfied only by extreme generosity toward a heavenly judge. Nobles, anxious to assuage their sense of guilt or to secure some firm footing in a swiftly turning world, were eager to be generous but at the same time viewed monasteries as providers of offices for family and friends and a haven for their own souls when their final accounting was due. Thus, monasteries became dependent upon secular magnates who funded them and protected them in exchange for the right to appoint their officials and manage their legal and financial affairs.

In the post-Carolingian age, women had unparalleled access to wealth and status, and their marital relations were exceptionally unstable. At least in Saxony, an area relatively late to convert to Christianity and center of the revived Holy Roman Empire, the birthrate apparently favored the survival of female infants over male, and in many families several girls seem to have been born before a surviving boy appears. Although women ranked below men in the order of inheritance in the *Lex Saxonum,* their greater survival rate favored the accumulation of property in their hands. Similarly, the *Sachsenspiegel* provided that daughters shared even in legacies that originated outside the family. Moreover, where the only son was a clergyman, his sisters were entitled to half the family inheritance as well as the whole of their mother's furnishings. In addition, when they married, women retained their own property while taking precedence over their sons in their husbands' inheritance and again over their younger sons when the elder died. Accordingly, a lot of land concentrated in the hands of women, who often invested it in monasteries to ensure a comfortable and productive life. For example, the sisters Friderun and Imma, foundresses of the nunnery of Kemnade, came into control of their father's entire estate after the death in 994 of their last brother, whom they survived for at least thirty years. Lammspringe was founded by a noble for his daughter and Herzebrook by the widow Walburga for her daughter Duda. A founding abbess might make an endowment for other nuns from her own inheritance. Godesti, daughter of Duke Bernhard Billung, disposed of a huge inheritance by founding a Benedictine monastery while she herself continued to act as secular abbess of both Metelen and Herford.

Without strong and consistent institutional protection, however, few monasteries could retain their endowments under the proprietary system. What was so generously given in one generation was all too vulnerable to repossession in another. Bishops occasionally intervened to restore goods to a ravished community, particularly when they were related to an abbess, but these were acts of random charity compared to the consistent pressure of the episcopacy to control all monastic property and offices. Lay patrons and even abbesses were equally destructive.

Under the proprietary system, they viewed monastic income as part of the family fortune and disposed of it with little regard to the common mission or the individual needs of the sisters within the community.

The ravages of invaders and protectors alike created a severe economic hardship for many houses that can only be described as a monastic subsistence crisis. To protect themselves from their superiors, monastic communities and cathedral chapters revived and extended the practice from sixth- and seventh-century Spain and Italy, where bishops divided the offerings of the faithful into three or four equal parts to support the bishop or abbot, sustain the clerks or monks, maintain the buildings, and fulfill obligations of hospitality and alms. Income earmarked for the support of the community of clerks, monks, or nuns, as distinct from income controlled by the bishop or abbot, went into a conventual mense (from the Latin for table). Ownership of the common property still belonged wholly to the institution but a distinct part of its revenue was reserved for support of the community while the superior retained the rest. The growing popularity of the conventual mense may help explain women's choice of the canonical over the Benedictine rule. Most abbeys designated as canoness were held by secular superiors who had no incentive to impose the Benedictine rule, considering that wherever it was reestablished, the community income had to be increased.

The system was most effectively established for "royal monasteries"— those attached to the crown regardless of what family was in power— though others often followed suit. In 814, Louis the Pious combined the immunities normally enjoyed by bishops, which gave them autonomy in taxing and doing justice on their estates (and eventually over whole areas assigned by the crown), with the protection usually extended to monasteries founded by the crown.[13] He thus integrated both bishoprics and abbacies into the whole royal system of governance and regularized the secularization of their property, which extended back to the time of Charles Martel. The monarchy was not insensitive to its spiritual responsibilities, and endowment of a royal monastery often included the establishment of a mense to protect the community from the king's own appointed lay superior, who could then help herself to the remainder of the income. Episcopal or noble patrons often did the same, and some superiors even established a mense to constrain abuses by their successors.

Once established, the mense tended to take on a life of its own and could diminish or increase separately from the common patrimony. It acquired donations from individuals concerned with securing spiritual services who wanted to bypass the abbess or bishop. It also got legacies from patrons grateful for hospitality and charitable service. In some places the abbess strengthened the community by donating her own property to it. The abbess Ermengard endowed a conventual mense at the ninth-century royal foundation of Buchau before advancing to the Benedictine convent of Frauenchiemsee as abbess. She was probably trying to save the community from the effects of losing a royal abbess. The monies could be stretched to supporting *conversae*, nuns of humbler condition like those in Saint Cyriac's necrology, working as servants or, more important, contributing the physical labor attached to the charitable mission of the community. Such women could be supported by a conventual mense with little personal endowment though, at least in England, a few were admitted to full status as an act of charity.

In 877, the canonesses of Nivelles created a conventual mense and shared their portion of the patrimony with the hospice, which got a small estate, a vineyard, and the tithes of the abbey. They were thus reduced to the portion intended for the "poor of Christ" and in addition the cares of hospitality were laid on them. The lay abbess, usually a Carolingian princess, exercised the abbey's dominion and became one of the richest landlords in the area, disposing of fiefs for her vassals from the abbatial mense. Gisla, a daughter of Lothar II and Waldrada, was also "abbot" of Fosses, the old monkery once attached to the double monastery. She gave it to the bishopric of Lièges under terms that enabled her to enjoy its revenues in her lifetime. At her death in 907, the bishop got complete control. Queen Mathilda as lay abbess showed none of the generosity to Nivelles that she showed to her own foundations in Germany, and Empress Theophanu simply spent the income she received as a betrothal gift from Otto II. Meanwhile, however, the canonesses tended to their vocation of ministering to the poor. Grateful clients and admiring friends routed legacies and donations to the conventual mense, and ultimately the hospice and the congregation grew wealthy and outshone the abbess.

Despite such exceptions, the mense rarely supported the religious adequately when it was administered by bishop or abbess. The community could protect itself only when it managed specific income and property, which was more difficult for women, who usually had to trust to an advocate to do any public business for them. The best solution often was a royal abbess, who kept the crown actively interested in the continuation of the monastery. The Saxon emperors energetically tried to control the dispersal of land and power to the aristocracy. To diminish struggles over his inheritance, Otto I married off only one daughter and made the other one an abbess. Similarly, all but one of Otto II's daughters were made nuns and the granddaughters followed the same pattern. Unlike Charlemagne in the previous century, whose unmarried daughters remained in his palace to make embarrassing liaisons with various courtiers, the German emperors made the celibacy of their daughters a positive advantage by employing them to administer the proprietary church system. Otto I's provision for his mother's foundation of Quedlinberg stipulated that proprietary rights over the abbey should revert to whomever should be elected emperor in future.[14] Princess Hildegard established Zurich on royal estates succeeded by her sister and then the empress Richardis, who also ruled Sackingen. Royal foundations like Brescia and Zurich were secured from alienation by a sort of appanage: after the death of the foundress (and her daughter in the case of Brescia) the house reverted to the king so that another daughter of the royal house could be provided for and its lands would not fall into a stranger's hands. In the second strong monarchy of the age, England, an even more systematic policy was followed with all female monasteries put under the supervision of the Queen. Aethelred in his charter for Wherwell carefully respected the proprietary rights of his mother, who used all her royal prestige to protect the nunnery from incursions.

During the eighth and ninth centuries model account books advised the rational division of the conventual mense itself into portions for support of its personnel, upkeep of the establishment, and maintenance of charitable obligations. The chapters assigned its administration to a prioress who directed the cellaress, chamberlain, portress, hotelier, infirmarian, and treasurer in their tasks. Nivelles, like many royal monasteries, was governed by a resident abbess under monastic discipline, Adalberine, whose reign (966–992) runs through the lifetimes of both royal abbesses. At Santa Giulia in Brescia in the ninth century, the abbess Ermenberga was similarly paired with the empress Judith. Even so, the communal life expressed by the communal table, with its inspirational readings and exemplary punishments and exhibitions of sisterly equality, did not flourish under these conditions. Calculations of necessary revenues were always connected to the number of people to be supported. Documents generally assigned part of the goods to the exclusive use of the religious *ad stipendia* ("to assure their subsistence"). Sometime during the ninth century, the word "prebend" appears, meaning the amount of food and drink needed to nourish individual religious; it gradually expanded to mean an individual's income. The system, which prevailed for centuries, clearly favored women who could bring their own prebends into the community or women (usually relatives) who stood to inherit a designated prebend. In most cases, they lived on their personal resources, leaving the common endowment for the upkeep of the churches, hospitality, and alms.

The property of the mense was also carefully separated from the private property of individual members. The conventual mense was not expected to furnish the religious with more than the austere daily rations stipulated in the rule. The decrees of Aachen suggest that canonesses could be given a mense containing less property than nuns because they could keep their own property.[15] Endowments of land and wealth brought in by individuals reflected the communities' attractiveness as appropriate places for noble kinswomen. This system produced rather small communities, overwhelmingly drawn from the daughters and widows of local nobles. Many were probably ephemeral, perhaps never gaining a place among the records at all. Others accumulated property from satisfied members. Canonesses were eligible to increase their property through inheritance following the usual allotments for daughters and sisters. Thus Azela, a nun at Elten, received a share of the property left by her mother. Nuns could will their estates to anyone they liked but seem usually to have left them to their convents, where they still had to protect the legacy against other claimants.

This was an age of open-ended, horizontal kinship, in which each alliance by marriage or even gift exchanges and fraternity associations widened the net of mutual assistance even as it multiplied personal feuds. While violence left many women bereft of men but rich in material wealth, the desire to prevent or contain violence dictated that many of them be withheld from marriage. The custom of endowing monasteries for women enabled nobles to avoid too many costly marriages and too many kin without infanticide. It also avoided the risks of incest, misalliance, and promiscuity threatening unmarried girls at home. Sonless nobles established convents to house one or more daughters, keeping them out of the control of kings who would transfer royal land grants from the family by securing the heiress's marriage. Gandersheim, for example, was built by Liudolf, ancestor of the Saxon royal family, who endowed it with lands and relics and installed his daughter Hathumoda over the community, to be followed in her office by two of her sisters in turn. Similarly, the first three abbesses of Remiremont were daughters of the founder, Romaric.

The establishment of a nunnery also provided means for keeping property as a pool of prebends and powers available to the same extended network. Where there is documentary evidence of actual elections in France, the claim of the nuns to elect the abbess is invariably balanced by the confirmation of the noble patron. Aeddila inherited the money to found Hilwartshausen from her dying sons. The widow Helmburg, foundress of Fischbeck about 955, also gave a donation to Aeddila's foundation about 960, suggesting that they may have been sisters. Adalbero sponsored her appeal to the royal court for approval of the foundation, and his daughter Rotgard eventually became abbess of Hilwartshausen. Two of Helmburg's daughters also entered that house and two went to Gandersheim, having been provided for from other parts of the family inheritance. The problem then was to protect the legacy against other claimants. Many nuns gave their property to the bishopric in return for annuities and money rents called "precaria." By exchanging the original inheritance for these precaria they were assured a fairly steady income without the perils of dealing with relatives and advocates. The exchange also introduced the problem of episcopal claims to individual endowments, however.

Time proved that nuns were not safe from the depredations of their own relatives without a royal charter to remove them and their endowment from the patronage of the founding family. Royal abbeys for women multiplied. Sometimes a foundress turned a community over to royal protection. Sometimes the emperor acted unilaterally to manipulate elections or confiscate their property. Hathumoda's biographer, Agius, described the nuns at Gandersheim as haunted by nightmares of the abbey collapsing at her death and vastly relieved when she secured royal privileges through the use of her influence with her family and with the bishop of Hildesheim.[16] But the later account by the nun Hroswitha, written while the abbess Gerberga was struggling with the bishop's successor, omits all reference to the event.[17] Nuns who lacked influence and whose property was overly modest found that they could not protect themselves or their pious purposes. The small community founded around the cell of Liutberga at Wendhausen, for example, struggled along under the Benedictine rule for some years but finally welcomed Queen Mathilda's proposal to transfer them to Quedlinberg as canonesses under royal protection. Otto I endowed them with villages, lands, and serf families, which yielded sufficient income to support a rump Benedictine community to guard Liutberga's old hermitage at Wendhausen with the church she built in honor of Saint Michael.

But while royal intervention protected communities from others, it cost them heavy dues in the form of hospitality, military, and other services for the monarchy and exposed them to imperial or royal interference in their elections. According to Hroswitha, after Otto I took Gandersheim under his protection in 946, he granted the monastery immunity from the dubious assistance of an advocate and from episcopal power.[18] She also claimed that Gandersheim was protected by the pope, because he had given relics to the founders, and by the king of France, who had married the foundress's sister. The chronicler thus provided historical support for her community against the aggressive bishop of Hildesheim. Despite imperial guarantees of free abbatial election, however, politics dictated the choice of the fractious princess Sophia, whose pride aggravated the quarrel with the bishop. Faced with such difficulties, convents attempted to maneuver their way between conflicting powers and interests.

In Germany in the tenth century and somewhat later in England the possibility arose of playing royal power against local lords and bishops. In England, as in Germany, noble foundations rarely lasted long. In at least two cases, Leominster and Saint Osyth, convents had to be restored in the tenth century after some calamity had driven the nuns out and left only a community of chaplains to occupy their former double monastery. Chatteris and Leominster survived but in the hands of Edward the Confessor's wife, Edith. From 850 on, charters of immunity from episcopal jurisdiction were secured by German women's communities. In 973, Elten received freedom to elect its own abbess without episcopal intervention, and in 993 Metelen appealed to Otto III against episcopal usurpation of its liberties. But the communities did not always succeed. The foundress of Odingen commended her abbey directly to Otto III, who allowed bishops to control the elections. Borghorst, Molenbeck, and Neuenherrsee succeeded in placing their goods under royal protection but that did not include the right of free election. Widigenberg, Epinal, and Heiningen actually lost their electoral rights through episcopal manipulation of royal protection.

At Neuenherrsee (founded by a bishop), royal bailiffs intervened to keep land out of the bishop's hand. We have every reason to suppose, however, that where the candidate was a member of the royal family, the claim of free elections was a sham. The heads of the great royal abbeys were of princely status *ex officio,* and we can be fairly certain that their patrons and protectors made sure that they came of suitable families. In England, home of a sweeping reform in the tenth century, provision for election in conformity with the Benedictine rule was modified by the proviso "with the king's advice and consent so as to ensure the best people."[19]

Ottonian church policy withdrew church lands and offices from local secular power and assimilated them to crown lands. This process diminished the power of the nobility, and by appointing members of his own family, the emperor could secure the effective support of the ecclesiastical hierarchy. The emperor controlled the office of abbess by giving royal women as oblates, brought up to the service or naming them as abbesses on entry. The royal princesses Mathilda and Sophia entered into castimony at age eleven, when their contemporaries were getting married. Since many girls were placed in convents before or at puberty, the question arises as to whether or not they were forced into the monastic life against their will. Many surviving deeds of gift by noble founders and donors from France include language that might be interpreted to mean that the decision was entirely in the power of the novice's guardian, who could choose to "make her a nun" or "dedicate her" to God. But this language may be entirely misleading. In one case, the donation is earmarked so that if the daughter proved unsuited to the monastic life, it could be used to endow another novice from the same family. Fathers probably preferred to settle their daughters comfortably, and daughters certainly were raised to identify their interests with those of their families.

When prospective abbesses were to be endowed with far-reaching powers and entrusted with substantial amounts of the family wealth, their commitment to the monastic life was made firmer than that of most canonesses. The eleven-year-old princess Sophia, destined to become abbess of Gandersheim, was solemnly asked whether she wished to be received into the convent, and her brother, the emperor, was asked whether he agreed to transfer his guardianship to the convent. The young woman was ready enough to agree and even ready to make submission to the bishop of Hildesheim, who was the official supervisor of the community. But this did not prevent her from threatening violence if she could not be consecrated by the archbishop of Mainz rather than the less exalted bishop. Once the point was established, she was eager to enhance her prestige with an elaborate castimonial ceremony, though her convent did not follow the Benedictine rule.

The abbess of Gernrode had the power to select her novices and train them from childhood. Presumably she would have considered it to the advantage of the abbey to select girls of a willing and pious disposition, but there must have been times when more worldly considerations intervened. For example, legacies tied to prebends or conventual menses, were liable to depend on possession of a place. On the other side, Adelheid of Vilich, who turned her canonry into a Benedictine convent, was praised by her biographer for refusing to take children because she wanted nuns with genuine vocations. In brief, in an age when young people were universally considered to be primarily instruments of family policy, the decision of a young woman's father often determined her future. Whether he placed her in marriage or in a convent might be equally conducive to her future happiness or misery. But if a woman were old enough to marry by the time she entered the cloister, she could not be considered too young to have a mind of her own. Even at eleven, many young women proved to be determined about having their own way.

The oblate, a woman offered by her parents to God, became a popular hagiographical model in this period, displacing the older type of virgin heroine who gained the convent only at the risk of alienating parents and friends who urged her to marry. We may be seeing nothing more than a shift in the fashion toward a sanctity that emphasized humility and obedience in preference to rebellion, even for the sake of God. Finally, many women might have chosen or been chosen by simple default. Virgins who did not participate in a castimonial ritual might live on as canonesses or quasi-nuns in the convent indefinitely. In Yorkshire as late as 1267, episcopal visitors complained that lay sisters wore the black veil of the nuns. Out of twenty-three women at Villarceaux in the same period, the archbishop of Rouen noted that only four nuns were professed.[20]

Canonesses always maintained that they took no permanent vows and retained both their property and their freedom to marry.[21] A convent might provide a setting conducive to respectable courtship or seek out the limits of the permissible. A canoness of Cologne held a salon that attracted many admirers and eventually married one of them. The abbess and the bishop forced her back, and when she escaped again, she and her husband were excommunicated. In a poem from the second half of the twelfth century, a clerk of Toul described a court of love held for the amusement of an assemblage of nuns and clergy at Remiremont. After a lecture on Ovid and a recital of love songs, the canonesses compared the advantages of clerics and knights as lovers, a popular debate topic of the period, and each lady was advised to secure a clerical lover and be faithful to him. Girolamo Priuli, in his journal, said that beautiful Venetian nuns, skilled in music and needlework, attracted the visits of foreigners to whom they granted their favors in return for legacies.

Critics were always concerned by the prospect of frivolous women taking advantage of the freedom of the nunnery. The Roman synod of 1059 criticized secular canonesses as degenerate, requiring them to conform either to the Benedictine or Augustinian rule. The more serious problem was always the predatory suitor. Promulgating the decisions of the Council of Soissons, Pippin forbade men, under all circumstances, to marry nuns. Women in these troubled centuries were pitifully vulnerable both to rape and to seduction. Monastery walls increased their security, but no woman seems to have been safe from the pressures of powerful suitors, who probably made little distinction between nuns and canonesses. In 901, while Edward the Elder was distracted by a struggle with his cousin Ethelwold, his heir married a religious from Wimbourne without his permission. The king had her arrested and restored to her monastery. Abbess Mathilda of Quedlinberg successfully sued the Landtag of Magdeburg to restore Liutgard, who had been abducted by the son of a Saxon nobleman, pleading that the girl was a nun, despite Quedlinberg's almost certain status as a canoness institute. These stories must be set in the context of the marital instability that characterized tenth- and eleventh-century society. Efforts made by bishops to enforce marital indissolubility ceased with the collapse of the Carolingians, and marriage became a matter of political strategy, to be made and broken almost at will.

Hatheburg, who had been seduced by the future German king Henry I, was restored to her convent and her broken vows declared an impediment to marriage, but only after she had borne a child and Henry had decided to marry someone else. One cannot but wonder if the future queen Mathilda ran a similar risk when she allowed him to woo her in the convent of Herford, where the abbess herself undertook to act as chaperon for the young couple and arrange the terms of their marriage. Naturally, her biographer did not suggest that she should have remained in the convent, but later she reverted to a nun's life and took on the responsibilities of a secular abbess. Ultimately, she was rewarded with sainthood.

King Edgar of England attempted to seduce Wulfhild with the connivance of her aunt, the abbess of Wherwell. The young woman escaped him and returned to her convent school at Wilton, where he tried unsuccessfully to abduct her. She received the veil in that community, where Edgar struck again, seducing the young Wulftrude who bore him a child, the future saint Edith. After Edith's birth, her mother was restored to the convent and apparently took up her life as a nun smoothly. Edgar's generosity to her and her daughter's status, at least in legend, as a possible heir to the throne suggest that the misfortune was a failed marriage rather than a love affair. Edgar's generosity to Wulftrude in later years also implied a continuing regard. He made her abbess of Barking and endowed her with churches at Horton, Shaftesbury, Wareham, Wilton, and Southhampton. Edith was endowed with the royal abbey of Wilton. Sometimes women who grew up in a convent and intended to take the veil were forced out against their will. Hroswitha maintained that the abbess Gerberga was forced to honor a betrothal her father made "for the peace of the country." When her fiancé refused to set her free, Christ intervened by killing him.[22]

This prevailing confusion about the status of women in convents may shed light on a famous case from the end of this period. The Anglo-Saxon princess Edith (later Mathilda) wished to leave Romsey abbey to marry Henry I of England. Despite her claim that she had only put on the veil under her aunt's coercion after she entered the abbey to take refuge from the invading Normans, she had great difficulty persuading ecclesiastical authorities to approve this politically desirable union. Edith was stepping out of her monastery into a newly reformed age and, though she won her case, definitions would be much stricter for her contemporaries and successors.

Widows also found monasteries convenient refuges in their bereavement, though they rarely seem to have undertaken castimony. The widow Oda lived to be 107 years old, according to Hroswitha. Despite the ravages of childbirth, the survival rate for married women was far higher than for men, possibly as a result of women's relative immunity to the violence of warfare and even travel. Where information is available about the communities, anywhere from a quarter to a third of the women in French convents were widows or even married women, and there is no reason to imagine that the percentages would be different in other areas. Elsewhere in Europe, widows were equally long-lived and faced the problem of safe-guarding their rights to liberty and property. In England, Aethelred's laws took them under the direct protection of God and the king, a combination best expressed in the monastery. The empress Adelheid lived for many years after both her husbands died. Even the empress Theophano, who died young, outlived her husband by some years. Ealswith, Alfred's widow, founded Nunnaminster at Winchester, where her granddaughter Eadburga was abbess, and she is believed to have retired there after Alfred's death.

The formation of a religious house probably provided the best security a widow and her daughters could get against the importunity of ambitious suitors and greedy co-heirs, who were always ready to challenge their inheritance. After her first marriage in Italy, the empress Adelheid had been mercilessly pursued by fortune hunters and even imprisoned. She often told of her escape after she found security with Otto the Great, her second husband. When he died, she spent most of her time with her daughter at Quedlinberg, from which she governed the empire as regent for her grandson Otto III.[23] In two instances, Borghorst and Elten, a mother and a father respectively had established monasteries to endow their daughters as abbesses. In both cases, a second married daughter challenged the endowment as soon as the parent was dead. Property invested in a monastery continued to serve its dead proprietor when his or her earthly ambitions had been thwarted. Thus the margrave Gero intended to use property given him by Otto I for his family seat, but when his two sons died childless, he transformed the lordship into the canoness institute of Gernrode headed by his eldest son's widow. His earthly lineage gave way to a monastic family whose prayers profited him in eternity.

Like many widows of the period, Gero's daughter-in-law was very young. Where it is traceable, childbearing appears to have been closely spaced and ended early. Most women were through by the age of thirty, by which time they were often widowed as well. Often they joined forces with their virginal daughters in the family monasteries. Oda helped Gerberga guide Gandersheim, making the nuns her foster children. She pressured her grandchildren to give gifts to Gandersheim and, with King Louis's permission, left her own property to the monastery, while her daughter Liutgard, who married the king of the Franks, persuaded him to increase the endowment. His successor, Arnulf, was likewise persuaded to contribute vineyards. Oda was still living when Gerberga's sister, Christina, succeeded as abbess; and when Oda died, she was buried in the church with her kindred and daughters. Aeddila's daughters Berthild and Emma were with her in Hilwartshausen and Emma became abbess in 990. A widow, Marcswith, joined forces with a kinswoman, Emma, in 940 to found Schildesche in Westphalia. These unconsecrated but religious women resembled the general class of convent inhabitants called "vowesses" in England. We have no way of knowing how many of the women who lived as nuns in convents actually confirmed their position in a formal and public way. Presumably widows and married women did not do so, though they may have taken some less elaborate vow. At her foundations of Erstein and Saint Julia of Brescia, Empress Ermengard prohibited the consecration of married women, as did Richardis at Sackingen and Zurich. But both allowed such women to enter, administering their goods under a usufruct formula.

Women found themselves in the thick of the dynastic politics of the tenth and eleventh centuries, even to the point of leading armies. Naturally, they often became political casualties. Some married women or widows were clearly placed forcibly or at least by persuasion in convents to get them out of the way. Count Alberic's foundation of the nunnery of Saint Cyriacus coincided with his overthrow of the Roman government of his mother, Marozia, and grandmother, Theodora, which a gynophobic contemporary labeled a "pornocracy."[24] It was probably a refuge for Theodora, who had attempted to regain power while Marozia, whose eventual fate has never been known, had been tentatively traced to Santa Maria Campo Martis. Henry I's widow, Mathilda, was forced into a convent by her son Otto I, who confiscated her dotal lands because he resented her extravagant charities. Thus, the convent was viewed as a punishment even for a woman who lived like a nun in her palace, founded two great royal convents where she spent most of her time, and always traveled with a contingent of nuns for company.[25] But Mathilda and Marozia were confined in the end because they had enough power to make them a threatening force in the affairs of the world. And Mathilda, at least, was never completely isolated from the center of the political scene. The princess Sophia showed particular adeptness at playing the archbishop of Mainz against the bishop of Hildesheim for the advantage of her convent.

If Benedictine reformers tended to think of nuns as pure and unsullied brides of Christ, canonesses were apt to interpret castimony as a more practical matter of housekeeping and hospitality. Their devotions were incessant, we are often told, though carried on in the hustle and bustle of a busy world. Some widows took over their husbands' powers intact and used them to play an active role in the church as patrons of all sorts of ecclesiastical offices and of monasteries for both women and men.

Eilika Billung became *advocatissa* (advocatess) of the monkery of Gosbeck and did not hesitate to throw out one abbot and choose his successor. In 929, Adelheid—sister of Rudolf of Burgundy, widow of the duke of Burgundy, and mother of the king of France, Raoul I—gave Romainmoutier to Cluny for reform. As landlords, abbesses also had the right to present candidates for ecclesiastical benefices and thus wielded enormous influence over the formation of the parish system. Uncloistered canonesses or unconsecrated vowesses could travel on any kind of business. They got leave for extended periods to visit their families and friends. During marriage and in widowhood, they formed strong alliances with abbesses, which involved them in the most momentous affairs of the day. The great abbeys were expected to serve the royal court as a chancery, provide embassies and counsel to their rulers, and offer a site for large meetings. They entertained guests of every position in the monasteries and the abbesses frequently traveled on affairs of state, taking several nuns with them as chaperons. The abbess Hathui of Gernrode was the emperor's guest at the consecration of the new cathedral of Halberstadt in 992, and in 999 she took part in the installation of the emperor's daughter Adelheid as abbess of Quedlinberg. In 1004, she entertained the empress Cunegund at Gernrode. The abbesses Adelheid and Sophia of Gandersheim, sisters of Otto III, secured the election of Cunegund's husband, Henry II, after their brother's death and took a leading role in her coronation. In her turn, Cunegund was a generous patron during her reign and retired to Kaufungen, her own foundation, after Henry's death.

This system tended to restore some of the cross-gender cooperation lost in the wake of the Carolingian reforms. Even the opposition between episcopal interests and those of nuns was often dissolved by family concern. The clergy did not constitute a separate social class. At every point in the hierarchy, church personnel were drawn from a corresponding level of secular society. Therefore, the great bishops of the tenth and eleventh centuries were generally born into the ruling class and often related to the great abbesses of the proprietary monasteries. Canonesses identified themselves with the secular clergy and its liberties. Remnants of the old syneisactic monasticism still survived in these partnerships. An institute was generally attached to a cathedral chapter or large parish church. If not, the "collegial" church was itself a ceremonial center. The canonesses of Überwasser, for example, were named *consorores* (co-sisters) with the canons of Münster.

The rule of Aachen prescribed modulation of the psalms as a principal liturgical activity, probably included in the public rituals celebrated in the churches. Canonesses became known as choir ladies, and members of a chapter had to have intensive training and study before admission. The evidence for canonesses chanting the services, making processions, and playing ceremonial roles of various sorts is largely negative but persuasive. Beginning with the Carolingian prohibitions against altar service, reforms frequently tried to restrict women's participation, and reformers complained about their loud voices and elaborate modulations. The Second Lateran Council of 1139, for example, forbade canonesses to sing psalms with the canons in choir.[26] If the ceremonials prohibited in the twelfth century were ever performed, it must have been in the heyday of canoness prestige in the late ninth, tenth, and eleventh centuries. Even without the magnetic power of a cathedral, many canoness institutes were important pilgrimage sites. Like Ermengard of Jouarre, some abbesses were able businesswomen, exploiting the new interest in relics to promote cults that helped to support the community.

Class overrode gender as aristocratic abbesses assumed temporal as well as spiritual jurisdiction of their holdings. When Henry III founded Überwasser in 1040, he named the abbess archdeacon and episcopal vicar for the diocese. Mathilda of Quedlinberg had the most dramatic abbatial career of the period. Promptly at the age of eleven, she was "elected" to *suae metropolitanae sibi haereditariae,* a title that suggests episcopal powers, which she certainly wielded in nonsacramental matters. As an adult, acting as regent when her brother Otto II went to Italy, she governed, as the approving chronicler said, "without female levity, using the skills of her talented ancestors and parents to restore the stubborn officials of barbarian kings to peace and obedience." The annalist praised her because she achieved her aims through prayers and inspired actions, though swords were at her disposal.[27] She held a reforming synod for the German church at Dornberg during her regency and in 984 held an imperial diet at Quedlinberg, where Duke Henry the Wrangler challenged the claims of the infant Otto III to his father's imperium. With her mother, Empress Adelheid, and her sister-in-law, Empress Theophano, she succeeded in breaking his bid for power and holding the empire together. Her inspired energy has even been credited with a role in the formation of the ideal of sacral kingship, which dominated the monarchs of the next century. Quedlinberg, in fact, became the center of a small monastic empire with several dependent houses, one as far away as the Slavic frontier. Henry II appointed the abbess of Quedlinberg as abbess of Gernrode and its dependency at Frose.[28]

This extension of royal control was typical of the eleventh-century monarchy both in England and the empire. Previously, Gernrode had been a stronghold of noble privilege, and its election records indicate that only the noble canonesses including the sisters from their dependency at Frose were entitled to vote for the abbess and other convent officials, excluding the male clergymen of lower rank who served them. Royal privileges for convents often included the community's right to choose new nuns and elect abbesses according to the rule, which would give the canonesses power to alienate family land and episcopal land as well. Perhaps because of this power the interest of nonroyal patrons shifted before the end of the century to male institutions. In the royal abbeys of Erstein and Andlau, royal charter guaranteed the right of free election as a tool to prevent the intervention of noble donors against royal interests. This weakened hold of the nobles on property they had entrusted to monastic government forced them to settle for somewhat limited prebends, or "dowries," to support themselves or their female relatives in the community.

Despite this decline in rich endowments, the old communities continued to flourish. Their great princess abbesses and noble sisterhoods settled into a comfortable life not undistinguished by both liturgical and charitable services. In addition, we should remember that while history is built on the great institutions with a grand documentary legacy, real life often escapes our records. There was always something rather porous and flexible about the female monastic experience, which gives us every reason to believe that a far greater number of *monasteriolae*, recluse establishments, and family foundations must have survived the general devastation of the ninth century. Similarly, we may at least speculate that many communities weakened by lack of donations in the eleventh century endured in a humbler form, perhaps reemerging in the hermitages, hospitals, and informal communities that appear so dramatically in twelfth-century sources. Many such communities were probably ephemeral but some, like Metelen and Mollenbeck, appear in the sources only after they had formed a common life together without a secure endowment, seeking charters of recognition at a later date. Great houses often had members whose status was problematic, like the girl mentioned in the *Miracles of Saint Verena* who appealed to the saint for protection against the oppressive vassal who had usurped the saint's endowment and was forcing her serfs to work on his fortress. When the tower collapsed and killed the duke, the girl gave herself voluntarily into servitude to the saint to show her gratitude.[29] Such women might, like Saint Liutberga, be loaned out to work for wealthy families or they might eventually become the center of a small hermitage engaged in pastoral work for some remote rural community.[30]

From the outside, tenth-century monasticism appears indeed to be a rather squalid history of money quarrels with little spiritual value. Female monasticism in particular has too often been seen as a rather inconsequential instrument in the larger power politics of the male relatives of the nuns. It is not surprising that many writers on the subject have been tempted to dispose of it briefly and hurry on to the more exciting study of Cluny and the other reforming congregations with their impressive array of liberties and institutional innovations. But though all too firmly rooted in the material world for the peace and comfort of the most saintly of their contemporaries, the nuns of the tenth and eleventh centuries, who were closed firmly out of the reforming movements of their brethren in most countries, lived a deeply satisfying life by their own account.

Not the least of the convent's attractions was the opportunity for an intellectual and artistic life. Practical and religious concerns required them to have a good education. Reading was one of the prescribed activities in the rule of Aachen and most canonesses had other skills, particularly in music and the art of copying and illuminating manuscripts. A woman who could not read her psalms and her music would not be accepted into a socially desirable canonry.[31] Liutberga in her hermitage, Queen Mathilda in her visitations as secular abbess, and the Benedictine abbess Adelheid of Vilich, who often visited the schoolroom to question the girls on their grammar, took a keen interest in the educational mission of monasticism.[32] Boys as well as girls continued to come as pupils in the ninth and tenth centuries. Paschasius Radbertus, abbot of Corbie

(844–851), expressed his gratitude for his education at Soissons in the dedication of one of his works.[33] The chronicler Thietmar learned his letters from his grandmother, who died in the convent of Quedlinberg in 991. Most communities housed virgins who were simply pupils, as was presumably the case with the future queen Mathilda when Henry of Saxony came to woo her. In France, at least, some unconsecrated women served as teachers and left to get married, apparently without prejudice. They may have been pupils who had never been intended for consecration but just stayed on without taking castimonial vows.

This education produced several authors whose work survives, most notably Hroswitha, a nun of Gandersheim (d. 1001 or 1002), who called herself a "strong voice" raised to defend the virtue of women.[34] She referred lovingly to the education she received from her abbess Gerberga II and to the critical skills of the others in her community who helped her with her work, which included a volume of plays, a book of poetry, a history of the reign of her relative Otto I, and an account of the founding of Gandersheim. She knew the liberal arts and a good selection of patristic literature, all reflective of the excellence of Gandersheim's library. She knew the old stories of the desert mothers and the apocryphal Gospels. She wrote in Latin, which she did not blush to oppose to the popular classical playwright, Terence, and she may have known some Greek perhaps owing to the monastery's connection with the Greek empress Theophano.

Scholars have often speculated about Hroswitha's work and her audience. Secular abbesses and patronesses came freely into religious houses and remained there for long stretches of time, conducting their normal business as though they sat in their own great halls. Gandersheim, like the other great royal abbeys of the age, was open to visits from its imperial patrons and the noble relatives of the nuns. Hroswitha certainly intended her historical work to be read by a secular public. In the plays and poems she made the case for religious women as worthy objects of respect and, by extension, investment. As far as we know, Hroswitha was the only playwright of her age; and it is improbable that she would have chosen so rare a form if she had not intended to provide an alternative to the ancient farces, which based their humor on feminine frailty. Her material was drawn from the readings about the virgin life familiar to generations of nuns. If the plays were performed outside Gandersheim, which is likely, lay actors were probably hired. There is, however, every reason to suppose that the sisters and their invited guests were Hroswitha's primary audience, and there is no reason to rule them out as producers and actors. Convent drama was a well-established activity in later times, though often criticized by reformers. This may explain the prohibition of Aachen against nuns wearing male attire. For younger sisters in particular, the act of aping men in lustful pursuit of women who victoriously repel them may have provided relief from many of the pressures of castimony. The drama itself fostered pride in their common way of life, and its production would create a sense of common endeavor.

Such a reaffirmation of their distinction and their dedication must have been very important in reinforcing a sense of sisterhood. Nuns, canonesses, or religious women with no distinctive title went in and out of their living quarters to visit family and friends, to do monastic or personal business, to fulfill their liturgical or charitable functions. The lives of their saints and the testimony of their poet, Hroswitha, indicate that they enjoyed a life of companionable and supportive sisterhood. Royal abbesses still found time to act as mothers to their monastic families, and the sisters still learned the lessons of harmony in their chants of endless praise. Evidence is not lacking for their spiritual achievements, while contemporary annalists testify to the energy and potency of the more worldly of their company. If we change our point of view and attempt to see with the eyes of their foundresses and sisters, we may understand that these communities, integrated into the social and political world of the age, provided a germinal environment for female talents and female piety.

8

The World, the Flesh,
and the Devil

THE CHURCH OF the first millennium incorporated clergy and laity at every level. Its flaws and its virtues stemmed equally from this bonding with the encompassing society. On the one hand, the domination of the nobility readily undermined the ancient principle of canonical election of bishops by clergy and people. Princely bishops, on the other hand, were best suited to defend the interests of their churches against interfering lords. Kings raided church coffers and filled church offices with their own friends, but they also took a devout interest in the quality of spiritual services and personnel. Moreover, female and male partnerships progressed in various dimensions. A celibate clergy tightly enclosed within its own order had not yet consigned all laity to the world and the flesh. Chapters of canons and canonesses regularly formed a mixed community. Clerical wives bound priests to their parishioners, while the option of spiritual marriage opened a higher plane to clerical as well as secular couples. Monasticism attracted women and men with vocations for celibacy and accommodated a controlled syneisactic lifestyle. Priestly monopoly of the sacraments was balanced by monastic devotions like the *laus perennis,* which offered nuns a satisfying liturgical life. The autonomy of each convent guaranteed its local ties, while episcopal and secular authorities alike reined in any tendency to eccentricity. Changing times and radical idealism brought the old church under attack. Canonesses, in particular, offended reformers anxious to close the circles of the clergy to women:

In imitation of the canons . . ., there are women who call themselves secular canonesses or domicellas, for they do not wish to be called nuns as canons regular are not called monks. They do not like to receive any but the daughters of knights and nobles in their college, preferring the nobility of the world to nobility of manners and religion. They put on purple and fine linen and gray furs and other frivolities with their clothes and twist various nets and jewelled ornaments in their hair. . . . When they want a break or are troubled by infirmity . . . they are easily conceded relief and recreation in their own homes where they may remain for some time, or they ride abroad visiting friends and relatives. . . . On solemn occasions, secular canons sing on the other side of the choir with the aforesaid domicellas in the same church, striving to balance their modulations with responses. . . . They hold processions with canons on one side and the ladies on the other.[1]

The rhetoric of reform has continued to drown their voices. As a new millennium approaches, however, we should reconsider the virtues of that decentralized church, with its bonds to family and patrons and its hospitality to women's aspirations. From Merovingian times through the tenth century, women actively occupied the spiritual domain, feminizing charity and mercy as foils to the warrior character of men. Radegund was a favorite model for women of the proprietary church like Queen Mathilda, who played supplicant for the poor and for criminals condemned by the avenging justice of her husband and son.[2] Living in retirement at Quedlinberg, she gave travelers shelter and bathing facilities. She kept a table prepared at all times for pilgrims and paupers, spreading food under the trees in summer and within, near the fire, in winter. She celebrated the anniversary of her husband's death with a banquet for all who came to pray for him. Her biographer claimed that one year the crowd was so great that she had to climb to the peak of the mountain and shower down bread, which miraculously multiplied and distributed itself as it landed.

Mathilda represented secular abbesses at their best, moving easily between the convent and the world outside, supervising foundations they did not rule directly. Care for nuns was one of the clear duties associated with the sacral queenship of the age. The empress Adelheid frequently visited female monasteries and resided in one or the other of them most of the time after her husband died. Possibly Hroswitha was competing for her patronage when she praised her dramatic resistance to the Italian suitors who literally had her under siege when Otto the Great arrived to rescue her.[3] Empress Cunegund frequently visited her foundation at Kaufungen and did not hesitate to administer physical punishment on one occasion when she discovered the abbess, her niece Uta, dining too frivolously with her friends.[4]

This queenly role was formalized in tenth-century England when King Edgar, naming himself "father of the monks," determined to "drive out negligent clerks and replace them with monks and nuns under abbots and abbesses."[5] New regulations, codified like those of Benedict of Aniane from a collation of all extant rules called the *Regularis Concordia*, continued the Carolingian trend toward standardization. Modeled on Benedictine reforms at Ghent and Fleury in France, they allowed monks and (by implication) nuns to travel abroad particularly to supervise dependent priories and other monasteries and to have men into the chapter room on business.[6] Tenth-century reforms created networks of houses under the same rule, but only in England was the queen appointed "mother of the sanctimonials" and empowered to protect their interests. Despite her rather dubious reputation, Queen Aelfthryth defended her abbeys fiercely against all depredation and founded at least four new establishments in the 980s. Abbesses were given unlimited access to the queen whenever the good of the house required it and were free to meet persons for business reasons within the monastery or outside it (though never for social purposes).[7] English women could thus participate directly in the religious life of the kingdom. Assembled under a single authority, they formed a congregation linked, through the royal couple, with the male houses.

Despite the queen's position as a secular abbess, the convent community continued to nurture the solidarity of the nuns. The *Regularis Concordia*, like many contemporary Continental sources, included the daily chapter meeting prescribed in the rule, which consolidated communal life through readings and prayers followed by public confession and penance for offenses against monastic discipline. The chapter's conciliar functions balanced the power of the abbess. German hagiography gives us a more anecdotal view of the common life. Hathumoda, foundress of Gandersheim, ate at the common table together with her nuns and wore identical habits of wool, "neither especially well cut nor especially vile."

They came together for the course of offices and did their own work without servants or any man in the cloister except a priest to perform the sacraments. Hathumoda herself slept in the common dormitory, last to bed and first to rise.[8] She died of a plague raging within the cloister because she had nursed her sisters until the strength had left her. Then her nuns took turns tending her in her last illness, while those who could not fit into the room where she lay prayed in the chapel. They made and remade her bed, putting pillows under her head, rubbing her hands, feet, and stomach to keep her warm in her chills, fanning her, and washing away her sweat during fever.[9] Similarly, Bertha wrote that the older nuns at Vilich remembered Abbess Adelheid for her maternal care. She fed the sick as though nursing them at her breasts, and on cold mornings she warmed the nuns' feet with her hands.

The Benedictine rule, which dominated all these reform concordances, did not impose strict claustration, though it discouraged leaving the monastic precinct for frivolous reasons. Adelheid of Vilich breached her cloister willingly in time of famine, when she led her nuns into the streets to seek out starving supplicants too weak to get to the convent.[10] In ordinary times, however, she simply expanded the rule's provision for guests to include the poor. Before she converted her community to the rule and endowed them with her property, she made all her sisters swear to provide perpetual support for fifteen paupers with food, clothing, and a gold piece each Christmas. An additional fifteen paupers were to be given alms during Lent. In England, the *Regularis Concordia* stipulated that every nun, including abbesses, take a turn in the daily formality of serving the poor assigned to their convent and washing their feet.[11]

Charity was part of the special vocation of canonesses and the rule of Saint Augustine, which they embraced. The Council of Aachen had determined that every canonry should have a hospice for travelers, asylum for the poor and unfortunate, shelter for virgins and widows supported by the church, a hospital, and an orphanage.[12] Beyond the great endowed canonries, women living in houses clustered around monkeries or in *monasteriolae* and recluseries shared the labor of charity. The hospice clients themselves helped one another and helped the sisters. Thus, a continuum of ill-assorted women consistently irritated the orderly minds of early medieval reformers, a spiritual matrilineage for the Beguines, middle- and lower-class women pursuing religious life outside the convent, who emerge so dramatically in thirteenth-century sources. Because they appear so late, we are accustomed to dismissing claims that trace their origin back to Begga, the secular sister of Gertrude of Nivelles, who has always been a contender for the title of eponymous foundress. Recently, however, scholars have become more sensitive to the vast histories that left no written record and are readier to conceive of a common origin for the canonesses and the Beguines. Both groups had property (or the right to earn money), houses and servants, the right to leave and marry, a semienclosed life, and a common routine of work and prayer in architecturally similar enclaves of small cottages and chapels. Both were subject to such barbs as the satirical poet Rutebeuf aimed at thirteenth-century Beguines: "Last year she wept; this year she prays; next year she will take a husband."[13]

Sources tied to property tend to eliminate all but the owning classes from history, but we can readily imagine a continuum reaching from the great proprietary houses down to those too humble to be recorded. Communities that survived the violence of the age or returned from exile to their old houses often floundered. Others soldiered on as best they could, struggling with want and fear, maintaining the religious life by adapting to their circumstances. Where the reformed Benedictine system increasingly linked male houses together, women were more apt to maintain ties with friends and family, to depend for their support on the immediate neighborhood, and to direct their pastoral impulses to local needs.

Many small, forgotten communities are probably typified by the group that surrounded Liutberga's cell at Wendhausen. A nun without endowment, she had supported herself as a business manager for an aristocratic family, traveling widely on behalf of her widowed employer without a breath of scandal. Indeed, her biographer suggested that her status as a nun guaranteed her safety. At last, her patron's son agreed to pension her off with a hermitage, where she put her convent-learned arts of cloth making and dyeing to such good use that she was called "Daedala," a complimentary comparison to the legendary artisan of Greek myth. She received visitors and educated girls and conferred with bishops and other clergymen about local ecclesiastical affairs. Probably as a result of her travels, she was helpful with liturgical innovations promoted by Rome (particularly the Sabbath fast) and, as a community grew up around her, she took up the *horarium* (the offices marking the hours of the monastic day). Her relics continued to support her small following after she died.[14]

Liutberga's life reminds us that the most definitive agent of monastic life was the chant. Liturgical competence had recognized value, exchangeable for more mundane countergifts. The Carolingians had restored the practice of public penance for major sins, but sinners incorrigibly sought vicarious relief by subsidizing the sacrifices and prayers of others. Charters expressed the hope that donations would secure a share in the benefits of religious life. Nuns had to offer services that could compete with those of monks. Hroswitha, who knew the political and financial importance of such considerations, introduced a note of penitential spirituality into her plays on the harlots Thaïs and Maria. By glorifying the desert mothers who cleansed their souls through self-mortification in isolated hermitages she may have been promoting nunneries like Gandersheim as asylums for women to complement monastic retreats for men. For example, although the duchess of Burgundy belonged to Cluny's confraternity of donors entitled to the prayers of the community, she could never have become a full-fledged brother as her husband did when he died. Or perhaps, like the nuns of Quedlinberg, who took over the support of Liutberga's community, Hroswitha was paying homage to those humbler and more heroic women who occupied small penitential hermitages around the fringes of the great monasteries.

Religious communities offered their patrons care of the bodies of the dead and the vicarious salvation of their souls through prayer. Odilo of Cluny stimulated this unique service when he instituted the Feast of All Souls.[15] To remain competitive, Remiremont employed mass priests to commemorate donors listed in its Book of the Dead. Gernrode observed special vigils and feasts for the patron Gero, his two deceased sons, and eventually, at the end of her extraordinarily long life, Abbess Hathui, his widowed daughter-in-law.[16] Over time, additional patrons and dead sisters joined the founding family on this list. The *Regularis Concordia* devoted close attention to the celebration of special feasts and prayers in English communities for the dead as well as for the king and queen as patrons. These special commemorative services must have taken up much of the nuns' time, distracting them from the contemplative rhythm of the Benedictine life, but a saint's tomb was a steady income producer. Bertha of Vilich complained that the crowds who came to pray at Abbess Adelheid's tomb within the cloister were so great that they gave the nuns no peace. The nunnery, however, gladly distributed the offerings that these pilgrims left there for the poor. Even the tomb of an important lay person, particularly a royal corpse, guaranteed a steady income from grateful descendants in return for continual prayer for the deceased's eternal well-being.

Where they could, women continued the intrusion into sacramental services that had so enraged Carolingian reformers. Canonesses may have enlarged their participation in the choirs and processions of cathedral and collegial churches. The small dialogue, *Quem Quaeritis*, enacting the discovery of the empty tomb as part of the Easter liturgy, which made its appearance at this time, would seem to fit with Hroswitha's theatrical interests. In later years, it was a favorite pageant for canonesses (in their own chapels) and perhaps, in this period, they took part in some of the performances in their cathedrals. For example, at Sainte-Croix, on Holy Saturday, a nun playing Mary Magdalene participated in several dialogues with a priest playing the angel as she met him at the church door, conducted him to the window where she revealed the relic of the cross, and then led him out a different door.

They could emulate the elaborate chants and processions that marked the early period of Cluniac spirituality. In time, however, the *laus perennis* and other elaborate liturgies specific to the monastic movement gave way to sacramental observances as more monks sought ordination. The mass, increasingly a private ceremony between the priest and God, sometimes even without acolytes, began to dominate devotional life to the obvious disadvantage of women. Because many convents served also as parish churches, however, the expense of supporting a priest was shared with local people, and support could be enlarged by the cultivation of special feasts and ornamentations added to the basic services. Queen Mathilda's life may shed some light on this inventiveness in embroidering sacramental services so as to soften priestly domination. At daily mass, she was in the habit of presenting the bread and wine in a golden ampoule for the Eucharist at the altar.[17] Similarly, nuns performed a ritual involving a crystal reliquary as Hathumoda lay dying. The bishop appeared with the brothers attached to the community only when she was at her last gasp to give her sacramental anointment.[18] But such embellishments could not stem the evolutionary tide in male institutions.

The substitution of the mass for the gender inclusive chant was but a single step in the redefinition of the church as a body of professional male clergy encompassing monks but not nuns. When Odo of Cluny (927–941) was searching for a compatible monastery, he found only Baume, headed by Abbot Berno in Burgundy, observing the rule as prescribed by Benedict of Aniane. From there, he launched the Cluniac movement, to target the abuses of secularization that had ruined the original reform. Cluny sought to free itself from the world as thoroughly as had the ancient desert hermits but not from the gifts the world had to bestow. Odo gained a charter from the duke of Aquitaine for a monastery to be owned by Saint Peter alone, free of both secular and episcopal authority. Enabled to elect their abbot as the rule stipulated, the Cluniac monks could again be confident of the holy power of their vow of obedience. Many monkeries were eager to share in the reform and Odo obliged, sending monks to train them in the restored Benedictine life and the elaborate rituals that drew the admiration and contributions of the faithful. In return, Cluny demanded a guarantee from the proprietor and bishop that any newly reformed house would be granted the same privileges and immunities. Thus, a far-flung network of exempt houses ultimately submitted to the supervision of Abbot Odilo (994–1048) and his representatives. Although this network should not be mistaken for an institutionalized "order" like those of a later age, its solidarity and collective reputation for purity served to enhance the privileges of all partners and strengthen their resistance to lay and episcopal powers alike.

A peculiar belief took root that the Benedictine rule was inherently too demanding to be observed by women. Hundreds of Cluniac monasteries in France, Lorraine, England, and Spain were in communication with other reforming abbeys like Ghent, Hirsau, and Marmoutier, which grouped monkeries, dependent priories, and collegial churches into "congregations" supporting one another under a common set of customs supervised by the abbot of the mother house. Gerard de Brogne organized twenty houses spreading from Germany to Normandy. Germany was the center of the reformed congregation of Gorze, and the emperor Henry II patronized the congregation of Stavelot-Malmédy. The customs of Fleury spread to reformed abbeys in France, Lorraine, and England. All these bonds were exclusively male. To the Cluniacs and the generations they inspired, reform meant freedom—freedom from the world as exemplified by the proprietary nobility and freedom from the flesh, best exemplified by women.

Women's exclusion from the liberties and privileges bestowed on affiliates of Cluny obviously handicapped their aspirations for reform. When individual male reformers took an interest in the needs of women, they acted outside the emerging structure of their congregations. Odo once risked his own life to rescue a virgin who was being forced into marriage. When Berno had him caned for his recklessness, he proclaimed that he would gladly endure the like for every woman in the province if they should make the same request.[19] Still, he could not bring his protégée to Baume but left her in a nearby oratory of women. And when he came to establish his own great house at Cluny, he made no provision for those women he so professed to love. The one nunnery he did reform, at Bauxières, was not associated with Cluny, nor was Saint Jean d'Autun, where Abbot Odilo placed his mother. This negligence is astonishing in view of the belief they continued to promote under Abbot Hugh (ca. 1050) that a house fit to receive a woman who genuinely wished to renounce the world for God's service could scarcely be found.[20] Rather than seeing nuns as partners in the spiritual enterprise of shedding gender, the Cluniac monks equated manliness with self-control, producing a rhetoric dominated by the implication that women were simply not capable of conforming to the demanding Benedictine rule.

Tied to the world by their inability to escape secularization under Cluny's wing, and to the flesh by male systems of classification, women were easily demonized. Carolingian reformers had attempted to split male and female monastics, and their successors continued to teach their brothers to define women as a source of corruption and to treat their presence as an onerous and dangerous intrusion. The voices of tenth-century monks turned shrill when they tried to confront man's presumed inability to maintain his self-control against the destabilizing magnetism of female sexuality. Odo of Cluny, in his biography of Gerald of Aurillac, ascribed his hero's intention to rape the daughter of one of his serfs to her unconscious but deadly seductions. Liutprand of Cremona blamed the corruption of the papacy on the inability of the popes to withstand the sexual powers of Roman noblewomen. Where Hroswitha indicted lusting men for their persecution of women, raped, brutalized and driven to death, men complained that they could not help themselves. Women, for their part, could never enclose themselves so tightly as to bar male advocates and male clergymen from their cloisters.

Greed reinforced the competitive process of misogyny. Even wealthy houses with royal connections like Gandershcim felt the chill. Hroswitha pictured herself as fighting under the command of her abbess Gerberga, to whom she dedicated her five plays testifying to the heroic chastity that, in her view, characterized true womanhood. She discreetly focused her attack on a contemporary vogue for the Roman playwright Terence, with his emphasis on the looseness and immorality of women. But, living as she did among the great folk of the world, she must have been aware of the upsurge in misogynist attitudes that characterized monastic writing throughout this period when the power and wealth of women was equated with the degeneracy of the age. Odo of Cluny was fond of remarking that if men could only see the disgusting reality that lay under the smooth skin of women, revulsion would replace lust.[21] Hroswitha might have wished that they would take his advice. She was, as she said, a strong voice raised against men's criticisms of the seductive powers of women. She spoke uncompromisingly of the capacity of all women for virtue, even those most deeply enmeshed in carnal sin. One of her plays praised the determination of a princess to maintain her virginity in spite of her suitor's urgency and her father's wishes. Another centered on the miraculous rewards flowing from a married woman's prayer for death before dishonor. A mother's willingness to die with her virgin daughters before seeing them sullied by a lustful soldier was actually turned to black comedy in her deft hands.[22]

Despite Hroswitha's "strong voice," non-Benedictine women seem to have felt insecure and apologetic about their vocations. They clearly believed that the Benedictine rule represented a harder choice; to embrace it was seen as an indication of special holiness in an abbess. The tenth-century *Life of Odilia of Hohenburg* depicted the seventh-century saint as vetoing her nuns' choice of the rule on the grounds that their successors would not have the courage to maintain their standards.[23] A similar choice was recorded about 1000 by the abbess Attala of Saint Stephen's in Strasbourg. Mathilda of Quedlinberg maintained a Benedictine house separate from her own canonry, which attracted some noblewomen but had a majority of common women and may have been viewed by the abbess as an exercise in piety by proxy. Or she may have been perfectly secure in her own piety but convinced that the Benedictine rule had value for her dependent abbeys because it ensured the nuns freedom of election of their own officials, which would protect them (and their patroness) from the intervention of local nobles. This freedom may also have been the principal attraction for the French convents founded in the early eleventh century. Those women's communities, though classed as Benedictine, never gained the exemptions and liberties that strengthened Cluny and its emulators. At best, they could play off secular authorities, often their own relatives, against episcopal interference. But that required a more active public life than most people were willing to allow Benedictines.

As Cluny definitively tied the idea of monastic corruption to any deviation from the Benedictine standard, religious women eagerly embraced reforms that would bring them closer to the old ideal of the common life. The count of Barcelona reformed the Spanish pactual monasteries on the Cluniac model and placed them under the jurisdiction of French monasteries. Elsewhere in Spain, in the early eleventh century, the Benedictine rule was introduced for nuns at Oviedo and the double monastery of Ona. By 1050, the Council of Coyaca had imposed the Benedictine rule on all Spanish houses not already organized on the rule of Isidore. Following the Merovingian practice of setting house rules on the abbess's own reading of the models, many houses agreed independently to take up the reformed customs. Kaufungen, founded in 1017 by Empress Cunegund, submitted to the rule from the start.

As charters, saints lives, and chronicles indicate, most abbesses were trained before shouldering their responsibilities so that the basics of the reform could be passed from house to house. Modesta was a nun at Remiremont before being elected abbess of Ören at Trier, and Duda trained at Liesborn before taking over her mother's foundation at Herzebrook. Often female houses came under the informal guidance of men's reformed houses. The foundress of Herford was first at Soissons, and her monastery was attached to the male house of Corvey, where her uncle was abbot. In turn, Herford trained Hathumoda before she took up the rule of Gandersheim. Once installed, according to her biographer, she issued commands, counsels, and persuasion under the guidance of the Bible and her instinct for charity.[24] Sometimes, female reforms occurred under the inspiration of male congregations but not as part of the brotherhood. In the early tenth century the widowed countess Adelinde undertook to reform Zurich during her virgin daughter's abbacy and made it a Benedictine convent associated with the male foundations of Saint Gall and Reichenau. Nuns of Admont swore to live in poverty, cloister, and community according to the customs of Hirsau. In 1020, Abbess Ava of Saint Maur of Verdun, through the intervention of her friend the reformer Richard of Saint Vannes, was allowed to visit Cluny to observe the reform in action. At least once, it worked the other way. In England, Alfred the Great's single male Benedictine foundation failed to survive because it had to be staffed by foreign monks, whereas the nunnery of Shaftesbury succeeded and acted as model of the *Regularis Concordia*. Some nunneries even formed small networks on the Cluniac model. The abbess Wirade of Nonnberg (998–1027) reformed her monasteries "according to the spirit of Cluny" and inspired emulators like Hemma of Gurk all over Austria.

Even where reform was successfully accomplished, propagandists claimed that it was excessively hard for women. But the real secret of success was immunity from outside interference. When a noble widow founded Vilich in 987, Otto III endowed it with the same privileges as the canoness institutes of Gandersheim, Quedlinberg, and Essen, giving the abbess control of the judges and advocates who conducted her legal and business affairs. The widow entrusted its direction to her husband's sister, Adelheid, who had been trained as an oblate at Santa Maria of Cologne in the "rule of Saint Jerome."[25] Once in charge of the convent, Adelheid became convinced of the superiority of the Benedictine rule, and she practiced its austerities in secret for a while to assure herself of her powers of endurance. When she announced that she intended to impose it on the convent, some members of her congregation left her in anger. But the rest were retrained by her example. Later she was invited to return to Cologne to repeat the reform, and she ruled both monasteries until she died. Then Abbess Hildegund submitted her abbey to the archbishop of Cologne. These modest congregations show that women were headed in the same direction as Cluny, spreading reform through association, but their institutional capacities were to be thwarted repeatedly by the frameworks of male authorities.

Reform on the Cluniac model aimed at securing autonomy of election and vocation but in the eleventh century episcopal authority over autonomous monastic communities grew. The convents of Saint Glodesind and Saint Peter in Metz, for example, were reformed by their respective abbesses, Himiltrude and Hauwide, in imitation of the reforms of Gorze. But they depended on the support of the bishop to maintain their discipline, and no question ever arose of gaining liberty from his authority. Many female institutions were being subjected to bishops even as Cluny gained freedom from their authority. Bishops received supervisory power over elections and, in 1039, the bishop of Minden deposed Abbess Alberada of Wansdorf. Some bishops who controlled convents did not reform them but handed them over to reforming monks. Henry II patronized German reformers and, from about 1024, growing closeness to Robert the Pious in France inspired him to extend Cluniac influence in Germany. As a reformer, he could also move against the proprietary power of noble families invested in monastic communities. Without regard for canonical election, he appointed and deposed abbesses and abbots on the excuse that he was reforming the cloisters. In addition, royal support shifted toward the episcopacy, and Henry II was generous with nuns' property in endowing the bishopric of Bamberg. Gurk, one of the most important reformed nunneries in Austria, was suppressed to provide an endowment for a new episcopal diocese. As monks grew closer to priestly cadres, they taught themselves to believe that women were by nature their spiritual inferiors and therefore should not share in their exemptions. As the twelfth-century Cistercian Idung of Prüfenung summed it up: "It is not expedient for that sex to enjoy the freedom of having its own governance because of its natural fickleness and also because of outside temptations which womanly weakness is not strong enough to resist."[26]

By the eleventh century, even family associations could not protect the privileges of proprietary nunneries. Despite his debt to the abbesses Sophia of Gandersheim and Adelheid of Quedlinberg for their help in

securing his imperial election, Henry II sought to replace the independence the abbesses had enjoyed under the Ottos with stronger imperial control over their goods and powers. The emperor did not hesitate
to subordinate Gandersheim to the bishop. He ended the practice of
appealing for papal exemptions from episcopal authority for Quedlinberg.
The fractious Sophia constantly challenged her ecclesiastical superiors in
defense of Gandersheim's privileges and her own royal prerogatives
against episcopal aggression utilizing a strong working knowledge of law.
In 1011, when Henry began to incorporate small foundations into larger
institutions, she got Essen, and Adelheid of Quedlinberg got Gernrode
and Vreden in 1014. But these enhanced institutions were pressed under
episcopal control, and Henry III combined Quedlinberg and Gandersheim into one enormous princely estate for his daughters, despite the
abbesses' strong resistance. We should, therefore, look for a subtext in
Hroswitha's writing, particularly in her version of the foundation of
Gandersheim, defending nunneries from the attacks of misogynists and
greedy authorities.[27] Whether they liked it or not, women religious in
this age of massive institutional reform had to struggle with the paradox
of an unwanted subjection to episcopal authority coupled with an unwanted liberty from the organizing efforts of the monastic networks.

Had women internalized their own demonization? Notwithstanding
their close relationships with many communities and their continuing
responsibilities as secular abbesses, women patrons increasingly favored
monks. The proven merit of Shaftesbury in maintaining the Benedictine
rule did not stop King Athelstan's niece, Ethelfleda, from allowing the
reformer Dunstan to use her enormous legacy to establish five monkeries.
Queen Edgiva and other women did the same, and the number of English
nunneries declined precipitately as much from neglect as from a new
round of Danish invasions in the early eleventh century. Later in the
same century, as the Reconquista (reconquest) progressed in northern
Spain, noblewomen enthusiastically patronized male reforms. Bertha, the
mother of Empress Adelheid, introduced Cluniac monasticism to Germany, and Adelheid herself was a major benefactress of Cluniac foundations without pressuring the congregation to accept female houses.
Even that famous "pornocrat," Marozia, may have preferred the prayers
of men to those of women. If she can be correctly identified with the
nun Marozia who ended her life in the convent of Santa Maria Campo

Martis, then we know she said plainly in her will that she would rather give her wealth to a male monastery than let women have it.[28] As *advocatissa* of Gosbeck, Eilika Billung did not hesitate to throw out one abbot and choose his successor, but neither she nor any other female patron gave any monkery, however corrupt, over to nuns. The widowed empress Agnes, an energetic supporter of the reform that imposed celibacy on the clergy and attacked all secular patronage and influence in the church, financed the importation of reforming monks from Fructuaria in Piedmont to Germany but gave no support to the aspirations of religious women.

Men who feared their own impulses would not be very likely to place themselves in the hands of women. As for the women, they must have been doubly vulnerable to the tensions of anomie. If patrons were searching for sanction and legitimacy by pinning their hopes for salvation to the old established rule, they may have felt that women were too insecure as investments. If Odo, Liutprand of Cremona, and Peter Damian are any fair indication of the attitudes of their male contemporaries, the fear of women ran very deep among men of the time. The self-control that gave Cluny moral power depended on emphasizing the seductiveness and vulnerability of women. In the eleventh century, the revulsion against female power in the world and in the church developed on many fronts. Women themselves may have come to associate their sexual and procreative roles with the flesh and the devil who controlled the world. Perhaps, like their most misogynist male contemporaries, many women feared their own freedom and viewed it as an unnatural condition to be regularized or atoned by support of male notions of reform and right order.

The cult of the Virgin Mary became a focal point in this shift in gender relations. From the second generation of Carolingian scholars an interest in Mary as queen and helper complemented the growth of the queenly office. Hroswitha's account of the foundation of Gandersheim started with the rather aggressive reflection that the convent was consecrated exactly 881 years "after a virgin, without loss of her maidenly chastity, brought forth the king," a variation on the theme of *anno Domini*. Her poem on the life of Mary drew principally on the old apocryphal Protoevangelion, which promoted the idea of Mary as co-mediatrix with Jesus, a partner in the work of Redemption.[29] In her preface, she acknowledged that its veracity had been called into question; but with, perhaps, a disarming show of pretended naïveté, she added that she determined not to change it because what is sometimes thought to be false later turns out to be true. In Hroswitha's hands, female martyrs like Agnes became active opponents to their persecutors, in sharp contrast to the passive victims of male hagiography. One wonders if this spirited defense of women's capacities caused the mistrust of women's writing imposed on the Cluniac nuns at Marcigny a generation later and the upsurge of books of advice by men for the guidance of nuns as women's religious enthusiasm grew.

In the eleventh century, queenly power weakened dramatically. Royal partnerships became unbalanced by the cults of saintly kings, which may have arisen from the Cluniac equation of masculine power and sexual self-control. Biographers of Henry II in Germany, Edward the Confessor in England, and Robert the Pious in France, modeled their subjects on an idea of sacralized kingship that co-opted the queen's traditional mediating role. Even in spiritual marriages, suspicions that the fragility of women could not withstand the stress of chastity undermined queenly sanctity.[30] Mary became a consolidated stereotype of feminine virtue comfortably ensconced in heaven and exquisitely malleable to monkish visions and fantasies, which filled the yawning gaps in the sources. With the Blessed Virgin Mother to play Other to their manhood, monks found they had no need for religious women on earth to offset the demonized flesh. The remaining role between whore and heavenly virgin went to the repentant Magdalene, another rich fantasy creature whose cult was blossoming. The dedication of monasteries to the Virgin Mary was one of the devices unifying the Cluniac network. By contrast, the only female house, Marcigny, was pointedly associated with Mary Magdalene. Abbot Hugh of Cluny prayed that Jesus, who had honored Mary "the sinner, after the filth and iniquity of her body," would grant the sisters a share in her apostolic destiny.[31] Under Cluniac patronage, the cult of the one perfect virgin tended to co-opt the powers and presence of all the others. The one mediatrix with a special tenderness for monks who followed the example of her son pushed aside earthly queens. When Abbot Hugh founded Marcigny in 1056, he provided for no abbess. Her place (the seat of the hundredth sister) was delegated to the Virgin Mary.

Drawing on Caesarius rather than Benedict, Hugh followed the Carolingians in making enclosure the defining core of women's monasticism, paradoxically making observance much more difficult for women while reinforcing the appearance of weakness. Hugh's determination to ensure that his nuns could pursue their spiritual concerns undisturbed may have been laudable, but he also claimed that their "glorious prison" would not only protect them from temptation but prevent them from tempting men, which was otherwise inevitable. The idea that women had to be locked up to save men from raping them was becoming a monkish cliché. In time, however, the nuns of Marcigny became deeply committed to the idea of themselves as penitents immured in a living tomb. When fire threatened the convent and the papal legate himself urged their evacuation, they refused to move, trusting in divine protection for their cloister. And indeed, observed Peter the Venerable, the flames did spare them.[32]

Cluniac monks praised Hugh for his heroism in undertaking the supervision of women in the religious life.[33] To ensure successful enclosure, Hugh risked the revival of something resembling the double-monastery system of an earlier age. Marcigny's ninety-nine places were allotted to women of noble status. Hugh's sister and then his niece were prioresses in succession. His mother was also in the house, as was William the Conqueror's daughter. But he treated these noblewomen as incapable of conducting their own affairs as nuns had generally done before. With the Blessed Virgin as abbess, the nuns had no active administrative responsibilities. Their names appeared only in the initial charters relating to their donations and dowries, in strong contrast to contemporary convents. A priory of monks shared the church at Marcigny, separated by a wooden screen from the nuns. The prior, the abbot of Cluny himself, was responsible for their temporal goods, which in addition to Hugh's own family lands included extensive endowments from the nuns' noble families. Three times during the next century, the influential abbot was able to enlist papal legates to intervene on the convent's behalf against local nobles. This strong commitment of time and energy was too strong, as time would show, to be extended beyond the limitations of a single house.

In return for his care and constant vigilance, Hugh instructed the nuns to commemorate him in chapter at their five principal feasts and supplied his own memorial to be read at those times.[34] In his *Imprecatio*, Hugh urged the sisters to keep their thoughts on otherworldly things and confess anything that preyed on their minds to the claustral prior responsible for their spiritual needs. This seemingly simple piece of advice reveals a cataclysmic change in the community life of religious women. Formerly, the abbess and, in hard cases, the whole chapter heard, judged, and corrected the errors and difficulties of the sisters. In the future, the chapter of faults and the governing powers of the abbess would still be used for blame and punishment. But the compassionate, intimate elements of confession—its healing and strengthening quality—shifted to the priest as the sacramental element superseded the personal. Thereafter, the figure of the confessor began to intrude into the lives of nuns with a power whose ultimate effects can, perhaps, never be measured. Hugh's desire to protect the sisters' spiritual commitments may have been quite genuine, but his reform served to nurture psychological dependency and to alienate them from their own community and their own gender.

Limited as it was, Marcigny was not intended to grow as a subsection of the order. Despite a long waiting list, no effort was made to absorb women with vocations by expanding the convent or establishing a chain of daughters. Cluny's missionary instincts never extended to women. Still, some growth was inevitable. Ulrich, one-time prior of Marcigny, who established German Cluniac monasticism in 1090, imitated Hugh by founding a single nunnery at Bollschweil. In 1086, when the Cluniac movement was expanding in Italy, one house for women was founded, Santa Maria de Cantú. By 1115, nuns transferred from Bollschweil staffed at least one other convent, Seleden, and Marcigny itself had at least one priory in England. Nuns' efforts to join the reform were restricted by the unwillingness of the male reformers to accept their houses and by the tie of women's reform to claustration, which made them incapable of organizing their own networks. Yet, apologists have preferred to claim, even in recent times, that the system of prebends and the recruitment of women without strong vocations led to supposed irregularities and decadence that prevented the customs of Marcigny from spreading.

In fact, it was the dependence of cloistered convents upon men that inhibited their growth. With Marcigny, eleventh century reformers had at last found a solution to their sexual dilemma. If women were thoroughly "protected" from the world, their sanctity could be praised and even harnessed for the salvation of men without threatening the integrity of the individual or collective man. The nuns of Marcigny, as members of the Cluniac communion, were supposed to be included in the prayers of all the houses and contributed their own prayers to the penitential practices of the congregation.[35] Women who had always been partners and even leaders in the monastic enterprise were treated as mere sources of temptation, helpless dependents who drained monastic resources and energies. As reform ideology spread, fear and hatred of women spread with it. In the eleventh century, zealots transformed the respectable relationships of the married clergy into a swamp of corruption and led at last to a revolution in the structure of the church itself, forever separating the male clergy, monks and seculars, from the imperfect laity, stigmatized by its association with women. The reformers were the first to articulate the Frauenfrage, the question of "surplus" women, which came to be called the *cura mulierum,* the care of women: the clergyman's burden.

The foundation of Marcigny (1056) coincided with the Roman Synod of 1059, which launched the transformation of the church and the world it inhabited for the next millennium. The pope and his supporters condemned simony, clerical marriage, lay participation in papal elections, and the canoness rule of Aachen, in one fell swoop.[36] The reform redefined the Catholic clergy as a womanless population. Nuns were caught in the dangerous space between the celibate priesthood and the sexually active laity. As Marcigny showed, however, they could be contained and their spiritual powers cleansed of the inherent pollution of their gender through enclosure. Abbot Hugh, like the other reform leaders, felt empowered to resist the fatal attractions of powerful secular women like Empress Agnes and the countesses of Tuscany, who played so crucial a role in the revolution that would reorder the Christian world under papal leadership. But the characteristic gender system of the new church was built on the myth of a clergy sealed off from dangerous intimacies. Where men were not willing to support enclosed women or women were not willing to be enclosed, the only solution was pragmatic blindness. The real and continuing presence of women around monkeries like Bec, Saint Vannes, and Saint Albans was treated as a series of unique accidents. They were dismissed as dependents, harmless female relatives doing laundry or cooking for the monks in return for their protection. When an abbot like Geoffrey of Saint Albans allowed his respect for the saintly Christina of Markyate to lure him into spiritual intimacy, he was subjected to cruel gossip.

Women were irreducibly lay people and the thought of their trespass into sacerdotal ground was increasingly intolerable. Tenth-century Germany may have tolerated the sight of the *metropolitana* Mathilda of Quedlinberg but by 1078, with Gregory VII in the papacy, abbots who bore episcopal paraphernalia were required to be ordained. Though Abbot Hugh continued to value monasticism as a higher calling than the priesthood, many Cluniac monks became bishops and even cardinals to assist with the purification of the clergy. Canonesses, who remained publicly attached to both worlds, disturbed the clarity of the intended separation. Their control of property came to be associated with simony and their freedom to marry became infinitely more insufferable as it was denied to priests. Reformers complained of irregularities to justify their dissolution for the profit of male institutions. The only major nunnery in the eastern Pyrenees, Saint Joan de las Abadessas, was turned over to Saint Victor of Marseilles, and by 1099 it had become a community of canons. Pfalz and Deggingen in Germany; Ely, Whitby, Repton, and Wimbourne in England; all went to monks. Unknown numbers of others were declared to be incorrigible and were dissolved in favor of monkeries. Canonesses were evicted from their choir stalls in Milan and Monza. The Lateran Council of 1139 prohibited them from occupying their own houses.[37]

The same council condemned women who called themselves religious without submitting to a rule.[38] The only available choices were the Benedictine and Augustinian rules, both of which were widely interpreted as requiring some form of claustration. Recluses and Beguines, women who worked for a living and made a virtue of poverty and service, were thus placed beyond the pale: "Women everywhere had come to such corruption and defect of cloister that [genuinely religious women] had no refuge anywhere. For none who was aware of the thousand arts and *maleficia* of such women doubted that they made it too dangerous and difficult to preserve chastity from uncleanness."[39] In the mid-twelfth century, their bishop denounced the canonesses of Kazis as a *synagoga Satanae,* because they failed to practice community of property and claustration. Nuns and canonesses in older monasteries, noblewomen who practiced the virtues of their class—hospitality, charity, and display—were branded as hopelessly corrupt.

The post-Gregorian clericization of monks, drove a wedge between them and nuns, who remained of necessity the only practitioners of the old lay monasticism. Though free with its criticisms, the clergy preferred to leave women "unreformed" rather than give them a place in the hierarchical church distinct from that allotted to the passive laity. Women who undertook a public pastoral role in the traditional monastic fields were regarded simply as nuisances or even actively harmful. Their processions were branded as acts of vanity. Caesarius of Heisterbach condemned an abbess of Cologne for leading a "fatuous parade of canonesses and canons" in the streets, contesting the right of way with the dean of Saint Andrews, who happened to be leading a crowd of the poor.[40] Even Hildegard of Bingen was criticized for dressing her nuns in elaborate costumes, probably to perform her "opera" *De ordo virtutum,* which depended on the singing in high voices that offended many male reformers.[41] Nuns in Zurich put a high price on retention of a place in public religious life. But the processions they joined deteriorated into drunken brawls, and men gave themselves license to break into the convent and steal the Christ figure.

Not every attack ended in defeat for the canonesses, however. In the twelfth century, the count of Hainaut became "abbess" of the collegial church of Saint Waudru at Mons and tried to allocate its prebends to men. One morning, he locked the canonesses out of the church; from outside they could hear the inexperienced men chanting the wrong proper for the day, and they responded by singing the correct liturgy, which persuaded the count to change his mind.[42] Faremoutiers had sadly declined since Charlemagne's daughter Rothild was the abbess in 840. In the ensuing anarchy it had been secularized, maybe even as a subfief for some noble's men-at-arms. But the nuns had held on and were still struggling when Philip I, in the late eleventh century, proposed to give it to the monks of Marmoutiers because the infirmity and neglect of the inhabitants had caused all religion to vanish "and we fear it has become a brothel." He may have gotten his information from the reforming bishop Ivo of Chartres, who had an extensive record of hostility to canonesses.[43] For unknown reasons, the plan failed and Faremoutiers endured as a female institution for centuries. Jouarre, too, managed to survive the burning of the house by Vikings in 887–888. Afterward, it slipped into the hands of the count of Blois. By the end of the eleventh century, Philip I had claimed the right to protect the abbey. Maintaining that the nuns were living in disorderly manner, again with supporting criticism from Ivo of Chartres, he tried unsuccessfully to turn it too into a male priory of Marmoutiers.[44] A similar incident favorable to canonesses appears in the records of the bishopric of Verona, where a Benedictine abbess was replaced by an abbot assigned to reconstitute the "mismanaged patrimony." Monks and nuns alike were driven out soon after for having turned the monastery into "a brothel of Venus, a temple of the devil more than of God," and all replaced with canonesses. Despite these small victories, however, the reforming church did its best to eliminate the way of life that distinguished the canonesses by making the common dormitory, the common purse, and the common table a requisite of religious life for all women. The Council of Reims in 1148 ordered "women called canonesses" to take either the Benedictine or Augustinian rule, and Rome continued to attack the "shocking" canoness rule throughout the Middle Ages.[45]

The fifteenth-century Cistercian visitor for Savoy noted that the nuns of Bonlieu "wear peculiar habits. They never eat in community but, being all noble, they live privately with two or three servants and eat and drink with their friends. They chant badly and not according to the rite: they sing the hours of the Virgin Mary in loud voices. They do not live as religious but as sequestered ladies who avoid marriage but do not free themselves from the lineage or fortune of their relatives."[46] Throughout the revolutions, reforms, and declines of the high Middle Ages, that old female monasticism went on in many guises. Family life and family ties endured and intervened in the communal life at many points. Related women, like seven sisters in Cologne, often went to the same convent. Women generally entered institutions within a couple of days' traveling time from their original homes. Gentlemen often preferred to endow a new house for their daughters than to send them away. They could therefore visit often and call them home for a variety of reasons.

With nuns or canonesses, Benedictines, Augustinians, or secular choir ladies, the great old noble houses of the early Middle Ages lived on. Most survived until the French Revolution and a few still function today. Their fate as religious institutions, however, was sealed when they lost the opportunity to enter into the great reforming congregations. In the second millennium, they tended to function primarily as elegant homes for unmarried ladies. In 1059 Henry III divided the conventual mense at Nivelles into specific prebends to support seventy-two nuns and assigned the remainder to a third mense for the work of the hospice. This arrangement cut the ladies off from the services they had performed so successfully, but soon a beguinage surfaced under the protection of the abbess. The noble character of the house intensified, and by 1112 the canonesses were each called domina. Many of the German houses took to calling themselves Benedictine but continued to live the same life they had pursued as canonesses. Perhaps deliberately, many houses became difficult to classify. Quedlinberg's dependents, Wendhausen, Walbeck, and the Marienkloster of Munzenberg, claimed to be Benedictine in some documents and canonical in others. The English female foundations that survived until the conquest were uniformly regarded as Benedictine, but the nuns went in and out, married and returned, and apparently continued to enjoy private property. The enclosure imposed at Marcigny did not seem to affect most houses. There is no reason to regard these shifts as frivolous. Abbesses needed to move with flexibility among the conflicting claims of male authorities over them.

Sometimes a change of rule may have been part of a complicated strategy to maintain the privileges of the house. Remiremont had lapsed from its first "reform" in the tenth century. Abbess Oda got a charter of immunity from the reforming pope Leo IX in 1049 and a second charter in 1050 from the emperor Henry III. In 1070, the abbess Gisla secured a diploma from Henry IV confirming her liberties, but she turned to Gregory VII in 1076 for support against the bishop of Toul. At that point, the community moved from the mountain where it had been established to Chamoussey, where the abbess believed conditions were more favorable for rigid observance. She may have had a genuine desire for reform, but her strategy also included appeal to the pope against the bishop, who was using the convent's failure to reform against her, despite the bishop's own loyalties to the emperor over the pope. By 1114, when Gisla's niece Judith succeeded her, the convent had reverted to a canoness institute again and the nuns had become uncompromisingly dominae. The convent secured its liberties, but gradually the sense of communal life decayed and each lady occupied her own house and led her own life.

All of this maneuvering, reforming, and renegotiating of vocations fit into the struggle that involved the whole of Christian society at the end of the eleventh century. The decrees on clerical celibacy and the battles against lay people investing clergy with ecclesiastical offices were designed to define and separate the clergy from its flock. The imposition of rules and episcopal supervision on monastic communities strengthened the structure of the clerical hierarchy against any competition from men or women claiming a more perfect form of life. Obviously, the impact was different for women because they could not cross over into the clergy, which ever more fiercely protected its ranks from feminine infiltration. This was a heroic age, with pope and emperor locked in a legendary competition for supremacy over a newly organized Christian world. The old society of family ties and great proprietors who used church offices with worldly estates in their dynastic designs was dying. There seemed to be no place for the great abbesses, whatever rule they embraced, to maintain their position in the order emerging for the second millennium.

The reforming church advertised its goal as the liberty of the church from bondage to proprietary lords. Unlike some secular noblewomen and many women of the lower classes, few nuns or canonesses could have viewed the Gregorian revolution as an instrument of liberation for female monasticism, and many of the great abbesses resisted it as firmly as they could. Nuns at many convents resembled those at Remiremont in seeing the bishop as a principal source of their difficulties. The wars between papal and imperial forces provided ideal opportunities for bishops and advocates to help themselves to monastic estates, particular those belonging to women's institutions, in the name of security. Political reality reinforced family loyalties for many abbesses who assessed the need to maintain imperial protection as vital to their survival.

Saxony and its wealth of nunneries was an imperial power base. Beatrix I (1044–1061), and Adelheid II (1061–1095), abbesses of Quedlinberg now combined with Gandersheim, were both daughters of Henry

III, and they held true to the imperial cause throughout the great struggle with the papacy. This position required some courage: at one point Quedlinberg was forcibly occupied by the emperor's enemies, who held a synod there against the abbess's will to humiliate the king's sister. Then Henry IV used it in 1088 for the trial of Egbert of Meissen, who had unsuccessfully laid siege to the convent. The nuns did not always agree with their abbesses when they saw their own prebends and the corporate property being wasted. One of the canonesses of Gandersheim (perhaps still unreconciled to the convent's absorption by Quedlinberg) complained that the abbesses had laid waste the goods of the community, that Beatrix and Adelheid after her had quartered soldiers in the abbey and given them benefices from the conventual mense.[47] Again in 1119, Calixtus II excommunicated the abbess Agnes of Quedlinberg and Gandersheim for her loyalty to the king, which she and her predecessors had expressed by reverting to the worst excesses of secularization. Herford, a sister institution of the papalist monkery Corvey, took a firm stand on the imperial side.

But the great proprietary abbesses were not simply slaves to family loyalties. They played the power game with everyone else, relentlessly seeking the survival and enhancement of their communities. Thus in 1105, Gernrode, trying to free herself from enforced submission to Quedlinberg, admitted the rebel Saxons to communion within the cloister at Easter time and received confirmation of their new abbess from Pope Calixtus.[48] Even Gandersheim and Quedlinberg got feudal grants from Paschal II. With the pope's effective victory in the 1120s, they lost this opportunity for maneuver. Nevertheless, over the centuries, many of the old imperial abbeys maintained their prestige and property under high-born princesses who took the veil and joined the community or even secular abbesses. In the sixteenth century, Martin Luther observed that women still came and went freely from Quedlinberg, and he actually advocated the preservation of the secular canonries for women when he was engaged in destroying the religious life for everyone else.[49] The proud old houses of Merovingian Gaul mostly still stood, still inhabited by women, when the French Revolution came. The abbess of Quedlinberg sat high in the imperial diet until Napoleon abolished the diet itself.

Medieval reformers would persistently focus on canonesses as examples of corruption. Attacks on the moral standards of nunneries often ended with their conversion into monkeries. Suger of Saint Denis, for example, justified his seizure of Argenteuil by calling the nuns corrupt, though the best proof rests on the testimony of Abelard, who became a monk at Saint Denis after the end of his own tragic love affair, which included a quick bout of lovemaking with his wife at Argenteuil. His story certainly suggests that the nuns were lax in the security they imposed on their guests, but Abelard wanted to show how compelling was the grip of their madness.[50] The Cistercian order took particular pride in recovering nunneries "too secularized" to be reformed. Saint Bernard called the convent in Laon a house of debauchery and, in 1128, the nuns were replaced by monks.[51]

Convents under episcopal jurisdiction sometimes had to cope with the bishop's conviction that reform was synonymous with their subjection. In the early twelfth century, Abbess Rissende of Faremoutiers asked for nuns from the abbesses of Chelles and Jouarre, who had successfully reformed their own houses. Instead of approving the initiative, the bishop of Meaux took advantage of the move to impose his own authority over the convent and the abbess. When they resisted, the reformer Ivo of Chartres called them "real demons."[52] The conscientious archbishop of Rouen used reform as an excuse to expand his authority over the exempt abbey of Montivilliers, which registered formal complaints.[53] He accused the nuns of giving leftover food and clothing to the maids rather than as alms. He said that they were lax in fasting and keeping a common table and that they sang scurrilous songs at certain feasts. He ordered them to stop having public processions.

The papacy itself did not hesitate to "reform" abbeys friendly to its enemies. The imperial abbey of Gernrode, for example, was twice a victim of papal reform politics. In 1156, Hadrian IV gave the bishop of Halberstadt, one of his strongest champions against Frederick I, visitation rights over Gernrode with power to reform it and remove the abbess "if she is found to be as useless and pernicious as they say." In 1245, Innocent IV sent the Bishops of Naumberg and Mainz to investigate the same abbey, thus weakening a less friendly bishop of Halberstadt.

Women who ventured to make themselves conspicuous in public were subject not only to suspicions but also to charges of structural flaws because of their private property. The attack on simony ultimately broke the power of great patronesses and cast a denigrating shadow over female monasteries, which required contributions from their novices to survive. Critics consistently conflated them with nuns and professed to be scandalized because they were not bound by permanent vows, promising only chastity and obedience while remaining in the convent with the right to leave and marry.

Indeed, women in many houses had ill-defined roles. Pupils stayed on without consecration and married, and widowed women simply took up residence. It was not always clear what rule bound them or what vows they had taken. As the world of monks grew better delineated with each reforming wave, the world of nuns gave a scandalous appearance because of their vague and often lax supervision by bishops who considered them a nuisance or a ripe source of aggrandizement. The attack on clerical marriage transformed the clergy into a quasi-monastic body from which women were excluded. Monasticism itself was severely challenged by this clerical encroachment on its peculiar virtues. A growing percentage of monks were ordained as priests while growing numbers of priests became canons regular. Legally prohibited from following this route, female monastics became increasingly isolated, with an outmoded and discredited liturgical life and a new set of standards structurally formed to impoverish them and bind them to ever stricter rules of claustration.

The reform rewrote the history of the church of the first millennium in such a manner that the presence of women was either obliterated or seen as a sign of corruption. Local saints suffered in contrast to the cult of the Blessed Virgin, and other universal saints and patronage turned from the cults of family saints as the reform leaders turned from local powers and local churches. This shift dealt a special blow to women's houses, which depended so heavily on the relics and example of resident saints for their income and their inspiration. Idung of Prüfenung wrote in the twelfth century that Benedict had not intended his rule for women and justified this argument with the outrageous claim that in the sixth century all women's monasteries were directed by abbots. The intrusion of the world (simony) and the flesh (clerical marriage) were equated with abandonment to the devil. The new church, a clerical monopoly organized in an institutional hierarchy that excluded women throughout its ranks did not prevail unchallenged. The human Jesus, who took his flesh from his mother Mary, inspired a new apostolic movement whose syneisactic participants strove to reassert that old ideal of subsuming both male and female in Christ. Women passionately embraced new forms of religious life involving charity, contemplation, and mysticism, but they would never succeed throughout the second millennium in reviving the third gender of early monastic life. The framework of new institutions was built and rebuilt to ensure their exclusion from a shared spiritual life.

III

THE HIGH MIDDLE AGES

9

---✦---

The Imitation of Christ

REFORMED AS A hierarchy of professional male clerics, the church of the second millennium provided an ideal framework for shaping the proliferating institutions of a rapidly maturing European civilization. The twelfth century was a time of stunning change, precipitate transformations of every aspect of life. Society was literally on the move. In the early Middle Ages, a growing population had been readily absorbed into the wilderness. The gift of underutilized land to a monastery normally meant that the land would be made productive and settled. But by the twelfth century, the situation was reversed and great lords made laws to protect their hunting grounds from the inroads of the plow. The "wilderness" so beloved of monastic legend had become a lost fantasy. The roads teemed with pilgrims and peddlers, wandering scholars and preachers, knights errant and prostitutes. With the launching of the first crusade in 1095, this energetic, bursting population reached beyond the boundaries of Europe for new opportunities, adventures, and spiritual inspiration. But the fleeting promise that a new frontier might be found in Muslim lands barely outlasted the crusaders' first exposure to the civilizations of the Near East.

The younger children of every class crowded into burgeoning cities as surplus land vanished and families sought to consolidate their holdings. Internal violence combined with the crusades left many upper class women unmated and without sufficient cash to support them in convents. Displaced younger sons of the landed nobility sought service with greater lords and in their turn employed displaced peasants in their own retinues. The ecclesiastical hierarchy developed legal and administrative needs while young men, entering the lower ranks of the clergy, began to evolve the university system that would offer professional training in law, medicine, theology, and other areas. Barred from the clergy and the professions that were developing to employ clerks, forbidden to seek husbands among the men thus absorbed, women contributed disproportionately to the unskilled labor pool. In the late twelfth century, Jacques de Vitry complained that scholars and prostitutes brushed against one another as they ran up and down the stairs of their city lodging houses.

The real new frontier was the city, and the new commercial and professional classes, the bourgeoisie, took root there. For the first time, Europe was beginning to resemble the world where Jesus once walked, giving vivid and passionate reality to the theology of his humanity. The urban patricians appeared, seeking to buy nobility by adorning their cities with churches and displaying their prestige by acts of charity. The urban poor also emerged, the "huddled masses" who haunted the consciences of the rich. Few concerned observers could escape the conclusion that the rise of the one group was causing the depression of the other. The gospel message resonated in the hearts of new disciples fearful of the fate of the rich young man in ancient Galilee. Wandering preachers appeared in marketplaces and public squares, berating the prosperous for their devotion to filthy lucre and their lack of charity for those who had fallen by the wayside.

Ancient condemnations of usury took on new life with the appearance of the monetary instruments of capitalism. Preachers condemning trade and interest as immoral and unnatural thundered against usury. The sins of lust and greed were woven together as a lash to the hard-hearted. Every wandering preacher, it seemed, prodded his listeners on behalf of repentant prostitutes in need of food and shelter to keep them from a life of sin. If some of these "penitent" women were in fact the abandoned wives of the reformed clergy, how much greater was their claim to Christian charity? Driven by the desire to find their way back to the religious fervor of the first Christians, charitable people in the twelfth century became increasingly enamored with their own impoverishment.

The reform that enclosed the ordained clergy in a womanless space was mirrored by a grass-roots movement that partnered women and men in imitation of the apostolic life. They sought the key to Christian perfection, not by liberating the church from the world but by making themselves as one with the unfortunate, the weary, the grief-stricken, naked to follow the naked Christ. They resolved to share the fruits of the earth in common, to elevate the humble and cast down the proud. Their favorite models were Mary Magdalene and her supposed brother Lazarus, whom tradition had made into a repentant prostitute and a cured leper. The spirituality of service brought out the nurturant qualities of many men. The successful pursuit of wealth preyed upon their consciences until a midlife crisis convinced them to abandon their worldly goods and devote themselves to the poor. Women unable to undertake other clerical activities tended to preponderate in the care-giving vocations. Many wealthy and powerful widows joined their humbler sisters as "Magdalenes," repenting for sins hardly to be named. Women who may well have associated the abuse of money with their own position as merchandise in the marriage market, expressed their horror of usury. Yvetta of Huy was impelled by suspicions that her husband's money could not have been obtained honestly in the first place.[1] While he lived, she persuaded him to give up his conjugal rights. When he was dead, she had to be forcibly prevented by his relatives from giving away his estate and impoverishing her sons as well as herself. Marie d'Oignies refused to eat the food given by charitable patrons to her hospital for fear of defiling herself with the fruits of usury.[2] In the fourteenth century, Birgitta of Sweden incorporated a rejection of all donations of usurious money into her rule.

Hermitages, *monasteriolae*, convents, canonries, abbeys, and beguinages multiplied as fledgling saints sought union with the divine, and penitents—eaten with remorse for unknown sins—sought to make reparation by caring for the sick, the weak, and the bereaved. Mingling of the sexes was commonly seen as intrinsic to the *imitatio Christi*. Twelfth-century humanistic scholarship placed new value on the Gospels as a historical record. Robert d'Arbrissel reminded the world that Jesus traveled with women and lived with them. Abelard began his history of nuns with a discussion of the women around Jesus. He stressed the equality of both sexes in the apostolic life and even tried to revive the female diaconate, reminding his readers of the sacramental services of New Testament women.[3] By midcentury, clerical observers had already begun to attack the syneisactism that joined religious men and women in a common enterprise and that defied the carefully nurtured fear of women at the base of the clerical reform. By the thirteenth century, the forces of separation had successfully equated syneisactism with heresy. Throughout the Middle Ages and into modern times, however, a variety of charitable activities, particularly the care of the sick, continued the movement on the fringes of the clerical church.

Throughout the twelfth century, observers everywhere commented on the numbers of women who devoted themselves to religious life. For the historian, the multiplication of written evidence that accompanied the growth of literacy in this age is an immeasurable boon but, like so many gifts, it must be handled with some caution. The growth of documentation may easily be mistaken for the growth of the thing documented. Women's religious communities tend particularly to be invisible until a male preacher, cleric, or monastic community adopted them into the world of account books and charters. Thus, the sudden appearance of large numbers of recluseries, hospices, and beguinages may be a figment of the surviving record, the abrupt uncovering of a phenomenon with a long but hidden history. Nevertheless, it seems safe to say that with the growth in population, the settlement of virtually all the arable land in the European heartland, and the expansion of cities, such establishments must have grown proportionately. They seem often to have begun outside the usual conventual bounds, establishing themselves as formal communities only after a growth of recruits and endowments assured their viability. In part, this pattern resulted from the limited endowments available for nunneries but, more important, it grew out of the emerging ideal of the apostolic life as a life of service to the poor in imitation of Jesus.

The wide range of partnerships between women and men resemble the affectionate alliances of late antiquity. Recluses formed spiritual friendships of extraordinary fruitfulness with hermits, or even with abbots of male monasteries. Eva, a hermit who trained at Wilton in England before she entered a reclusery near Angers close to the retreat of Herväus, a preacher from the monastery of Trinité-la-Vendôme, had a wide circle of male admirers.[4] The abbot of Meaux resigned his office and lived at Watton as a recluse "next to the church," depending on the nuns for his care. In these relationships, the female recluse was often the guide and inspiration of the active man. Marie d'Oignies had extensive relations with Cistercians around Nivelles. Her biographer, the famous preacher and cardinal Jacques de Vitry, maintained that he merely publicized her doctrines.[5] Hildegard of Bingen, one of the greatest religious writers of the age, relied much on the help of her nephew and the monks of Trier and Disibodenberg. The monks of Villars, a house heavily committed to the guidance of women, sent her Guibert to act as her amanuensis. In turn, she answered difficult theological questions for them by using her visionary powers and gave them a copy of her book on the meritorious life. She had a mutually enlightening correspondence with Bernard of Clairvaux, the leading monastic figure of the age. Even Franciscan and Dominican friars in the thirteenth and fourteenth centuries, when women's relationships were more carefully circumscribed, actively pursued friendships with female mystics.

There were many reasons why women might choose a reclusery over a convent. Sometimes they simply could not afford entry into a convent or could not find a convent with a place for them. In the great secular houses, even the pretense of abiding by the equality demanded in early medieval rules was dropped. In fact, as ignoble wealth sometimes outbid noble blood, snobbery became more intense. Thus, Hildegard of Bingen wrote to the abbess of Andernach defending the exclusion of non-nobles from noble convents: "The lower class should not elevate itself above the higher. What man gathers all his livestock into one barn?" She argued that accepting everyone equally would give rise to snobbery and social climbing within the community.[6] Those who were barred from the canoness houses by social prejudice or lack of the necessary dowry found it easy in the twelfth century to set up their own establishments roughly following the same model.

Often the convent life simply failed to match a woman's vocation. Eva, who had been wed to Christ in splendor at Wilton, chose to remove herself to a reclusery in Anjou as her spiritual life progressed. Christina of Markyate was supported in her early struggles by a whole network of local religious people. Her childhood friend, the hermit Sueno, arranged male disguise and a horse for her flight from her family. A recluse named Alfwen gave her shelter. While one hermit, Eadwin, persuaded the archbishop of Canterbury to dissolve her forced and unconsummated marriage, another named Roger took her into his cell and hid her from her pursuers.[7] Ultimately, she took Roger's place and formed a community of women around his cell. Ensconced in a circle of Saxon hermits and recluses, she may have been conscious of acting as a bridge from the days before the great reform, easing their transition into a new church dominated by Norman bishops and a Roman pope. In her full spiritual maturity, Christina became the guide and inspiration of the abbot of Saint Albans, whose monastery assumed the spiritual care of her group. She declined invitations to join several established female monasteries, including the socially exclusive Marcigny, preferring "our monastery" where Roger and other of her friends were buried.[8]

Similar groups of women, relatives or simply pensioners, formed an aureole of recluseries and women's communities around many, perhaps most, male monasteries. A range of shared foundations probably evolved from the old proprietary system, though they shared no single formal constitution. New foundations also paired nuns and monks in various ways. In England, more than forty monasteries housing men and women together could be found between 1130 and 1165. In Germany, there was hardly a single great house of monks without a nearby female house linked to it informally by exchanges of services and spiritual friendship. In France, Saint Sulpice (ca. 1120) had one male and one female house both under an abbess. Local hermits and wandering preachers drew women repudiated by their husbands or priests' wives driven from their homes by reformers, repentant prostitutes, impoverished widows, and aspiring virgins into their orbits. The hermit Salomon built a nunnery at Noiseau in 1109 on the river Oudon. Robert d'Arbrissel gave shelter to his female followers at his home monastery of La Roe and then moved them to uncleared land at Fontevraud donated by Countess Ermengard of Brittany. At first they were all mixed together, living in small huts with minimal sex segregation. They worked for their living, clearing and cultivating their land, while also receiving contributions and supplies begged from pious devotées of Robert's preaching. The group attracted generous donations as well as hysterical criticism of its syneisactic practices from local prelates. As a result, it was soon housed in more comfortable and decorous quarters with men and women, lay devotees and consecrated religious, carefully segregated under the command of the abbess.

Similarly, the evangelical preacher Norbert of Xanten settled some of his female followers in a community under Ricwere de Clastres in 1120. They took no formal vows but lived under the protection of the nearby monastery of Prémontré. Within twenty years, they numbered in the thousands, by far the majority of his followers, adapting the canoness tradition of freedom and hospitality to their service to the sick. Under Norbert's guidance, they worked in urban communities as nurses and lived in rough partnership with the canons of the Premonstratensian order, ruled by an adaptation of the Augustinian rule. Some were housed in the curacies and priorates that depended on Premonstratensian monasteries but were not physically incorporated into them, while others may have had no accompanying male community at all. Many female communities took on an apparently autonomous life in the documents simply as a result of their later severance from male communities originally formed to serve the nuns. Women without the organizing inspiration of a famous preacher grouped themselves together for mutual support and charitable endeavors.

The apostolic life rested on individual effort rather than the regular life of monastic communities. Independent of sacramental liturgies, it was particularly suitable for women, who frequently established themselves without any formal connection to the hierarchy. Jacques de Vitry publicized groups of saintly Beguines in the area around Liège in 1213.[9] In his subsequent travels he saw similar groups living in poverty and self-mortification in Italy, Greece, and the Latin kingdom of Jerusalem.[10] Lacking the institutional firmness that aids a historian, their origins have been hopelessly obscured. The enthusiasm of male reformers may well have brought to light a women's movement that reached far back into the early Middle Ages, whose adherents were growing along with every other segment of the population. Women far outnumbered men in the reclusive life in Lorraine, England, Italy, and Bavaria. When the friars began to preach in Germany in the thirteenth century, they found many consecrated women living near chapels and in their own homes.[11] Indeed, modern historians have been tempted to speak of a "women's movement."[12]

By the twelfth century, the wilderness (or desert) so central to ascetic thinking had in fact practically disappeared. Recluses were not expected to live in genuine isolation. In fact, they generally resided in public places, near or even in the heart of cities. Their cells often had room for servants and disciples, an enclosed garden, and a window open to the street. Grimlaic, in an earlier century, had advised that two or three solitaries live together, encouraging one another through their windows.[13] Sometimes a partition was installed in an anchorage originally meant for one to ensure privacy for meditation. The three sisters for whom the *Ancren Riwle* was written in the thirteenth century shared a house where each had a separate cell. The smallest of Cologne's ninety-nine Beguine communities contained only two women, while the largest could support fifty; the curtis beguinages of Belgium were often good-sized villages within the larger city. The recluse world pictured in Christina of Markyate's life suggests communities, and it is difficult to see where to draw the line between a recluse, several recluses, and a small convent. The matter is further complicated by the presence of recluse-servants and by the grouping of recluseries in adjacent lots.

The reclusive ideal combined Mary's meditative life with Martha's charity. Their "solitude" as individuals or in groups was continually tempered by their involvement with their social communities. An anchorage was commonly built against the church wall so that the churchyard served both to isolate the recluse and provide space for people seeking spiritual guidance and practical assistance from her. Anchoresses acted as arbiters and prophets, interpreting dreams and foretelling the future. Hildegard of Bingen, who took over her teacher Jutta's reclusery, operated a small dispensary to cure the physical ailments of local people and healed spiritual ailments through her preaching and her far-flung correspondence. Loretta, once countess of Leicester, went into retirement as a recluse at Hackington. But she continued to give advice to many applicants, including King Henry III.

Networks of religious women and male sympathizers assisted the broad spread of the movement. Elisabeth of Thuringia was inspired to experiment with the communal life by her confessor Conrad of Marburg, who was connected to the circles described by Jacques de Vitry. Her desire for a life of active service was reinforced by an exchange of letters with Francis of Assisi, who was also connected to Clara of Assisi. She, in turn, sent letters of advice to Elisabeth's relative Agnes of Bohemia, who introduced the Clarisses, nuns following Clara's rule, to eastern

Europe. News must have traveled from north to south with the movement of sympathetic preachers as well as laymen attached to the Albigensian and Spanish crusades. Similar foundations appear in the twelfth and thirteenth centuries in Catalonia, Castile, and Aragon, where the women were called Beatae. Finally, we have reports of semimystical communication among devoted individuals: in southern France, Douceline de Digne formed two groups of Beguines after she had a dream-vision of three northern sisters who advised her about their habits and rule of life.[14]

Charity bound all their activities together. Since neither recluses nor Beguines were bound by monastic vows of poverty, they could dispense alms and services freely to their neighbors. When she was still a child, Ida of Nivelles joined a group of pious women who lived a common life, not dissimilar to that of the noble canonesses of Nivelles, who retained free use of their property. Individual recluses often educated children, particularly young girls, from their cell windows. Widows like Ermentrude de Harzi and her cousin Ida of Boulogne dispensed regular poor relief. Noble widows under the protection of the church sometimes took over the care of isolated oratories and other sacred buildings. Some recluses acted as bankers, guarding deposited treasures and securing loans, possibly to safeguard their clients from the ravages of usury. Aelred of Rievaulx, stiff with disapproval, complained of recluses leaning out their windows to carry on their personal business, directing their representatives in the care of their flocks and chattels. He scolded them for gossiping with casual guests and gathering the news of the community, giving advice and intervening in everybody's troubles.[15]

As in the original apostolic community, many holy women shared inheritances or endowments with their companions. Since recluses lived by their own rules, they had great latitude in choosing companions and living conditions. Beguines have even been seen as primarily communities of women formed for economic reasons in a world where self-support was almost impossible. Many had nothing but a slender income from sewing and other cloth work, or cooking and cleaning as domestics. Recognizing such economic realities, women often grouped the houses according to class; some foundation charters stipulated that wherever possible the inhabitants be selected from the founder's relatives. Other circumstances encouraged Beguine houses to cut across classes and draw women together. Throughout the thirteenth century, Beguines willed their houses to other Beguines. A recluse ordinarily lived in great intimacy with her servants, who were occasionally male. Loretta, countess of Leicester, had a male servant who was exempted from jury duty. Katherine of Saint Albans was served by a couple, Joan and Philip Gerard. Aelred of Rievaulx, writing for his recluse sister, told her to be content with two servants, a discreet old woman to keep the door and a strong girl for the heavy chores.[16] Sometimes the maid succeeded to the anchorage, its endowment, and the anchoress's position in the community, which suggests that during their lives together they had overcome class distinctions and the mistress had provided for the maid to take her place. Presumably the anchoress supported the servant either from her private income or from what she took in as alms. The servant supported her mistress physically and eventually took her place as an almsgiver.

At least in the early years of the apostolic movement, its practitioners were eager to blur the lines between almsgivers and alms takers, both in terms of class and wealth. Even poor spinsters might act as conduits, receiving wealth and funneling it to the needy of the community. Wealthy patrons eased their consciences by supporting religious women in decent poverty. When Saint Louis established the Paris beguinage, he saw himself as performing an act of charity for poor gentlewomen. But the women themselves were always involved in charities of their own. Uncloistered religious women were often classed as *conversae*, a somewhat confusing parallel to the unordained and illiterate members of male communities assigned to do the rough labor for the ordained monks. Numerous lower-class men and women gave up their liberty in exchange for protection and support by becoming serfs to a saint. In the late eleventh century, Gualbert, founder of the Vallombrosian hermits, introduced *conversae*, probably women of this class, into his male community to do the housework. Gilbert of Sempringham classed laymen and illiterate women (women who could not occupy themselves with the holy offices) as "converts" in his rule.[17]

The distinction only added to the prevailing confusion about classifying women religious. The Premonstratensians, for example, were called canons because they took the Augustinian rule to cover the active work they embraced. The Premonstratensian sisters were normally called canonesses, and at least some of them must always have been occupied with the chanting of the offices (a role that would have expanded as they became a cloistered order). But because the Premonstratensian sisters provided manual service to the brothers in addition to nursing the sick, some observers considered them only *conversae*. The bishop of Laon, however, claimed that there were ten thousand Premonstratensian nuns, most from noble and wealthy families.[18]

Among them, as at Fontevraud, the word may have designated well-born women who had been (or perhaps were still) married. Robert d'Arbrissel, founder of Fontevraud, insisted that the abbess be chosen from among the lay *conversae* rather than from among the virgins who were supposed to know nothing but psalm singing. He preferred "one who covers her light with a rough cloak and manfully sustains the tempests of external things."[19] Presumably the noble widow Petronilla de Chemillé, who was appointed abbess, accepted the characterization of herself as a *conversa*. In any case, she and her successors did not hesitate to take advantage of their immunity from the rules applied to "nuns" to lead an active public life. Petronilla traveled among the daughter houses placed under Fontevraud's supervision and accompanied Robert on his later preaching tours. By the end of the twelfth century, Eleanor of Aquitaine, who had been queen of France and England in turn, installed herself among the Fontevraud *conversae*, which did not hinder her continuing interest in public affairs. The only consistent use of the word, therefore, is in the distinction between choir nuns and coarser workers in the vineyard. Women who were noble but no longer virgins may deliberately have sought to humiliate themselves with titles normally describing servants or laborers.

Charity came to have a penitential quality that apparently stemmed from uneasiness with the growing money economy. Disgust with money itself inspired a reevaluation of poverty as a warranty of purity. Queens like Eleanor and other noble ladies gradually lost their public duties in favor of salaried officials trained in law and other bureaucratic skills. The taxes required by state-building rulers to pay for their expanding governments were universally abhorred. Many women linked the passion for renunciation to social criticism. While she was married, Elisabeth of Thuringia had practiced traditional charity: feeding the hungry, burying the dead, washing feet on Holy Thursday. But after she was widowed, she evolved an ideal of flinging herself after her despised and homeless savior, taking no thought for the morrow. She opened the landgrave's granaries during the famine of 1226, trying to force the ruling family into which she had married to share the starvation of the poor. Her maid testified that her excessive fasting was a protest against the landgrave's taxation, and she fled the castle with her children "to avoid participating in the exploitation of the poor too often practiced at princely courts."[20] She may also have equated her brother-in-law's political greed with his aggressive control of her own dowry. She lived as a penniless beggar on the roads until her confessor procured the restitution of her income, money from Hungary, presumably unpolluted by usury, which she could use to establish a hospital at the foot of the Wartburg. There she lived among the poor, attracting ever more of them to the castle neighborhood until she died, prematurely worn out by her self-mortifications.

Examples of oppression for the sake of profit came readily to hand, and many women associated control of money with control of their own bodies. They fled from property as they fled from becoming the property of others. In 1146, the prior of Steinfeld wrote to Saint Bernard against women who left their husbands to take up with religious fanatics, many of whom worked by weaving.[21] They turned their backs on wealth because they equated poverty with freedom. How should we assess this opposition of the spiritual and corporal worlds, which seems to equate avarice and lust as dual sources of corruption? If we look back to the violence with which some women were herded into marriage, perhaps we can understand the connection of money and rape as joint threats and understand their flight from both. This complicated phenomenon seems to connect purity and poverty, freedom and chastity, rebellion and renunciation.

In earlier centuries the epic adventures of heroines in flight from marriage ended with their enjoyment of their hereditary wealth in the autonomy of the monastic life. The association of chastity and poverty was a new ideal expressing a practical ambition to escape the corruption and coercion of people greedy for women's bodies as they were greedy for money. Christina of Markyate's parents thought nothing of exposing her to the illicit lust of Ranulf Flambard when she was still a young girl. When they learned of her personal vow of virginity, they attempted to get her drunk at a public party to arouse her sexual desires. They pressured her into marriage. When she persuaded her husband to undertake a chaste marriage, they taunted his lack of manliness and sent him back with instructions to rape her if necessary. They even offered to help him if he needed it. She finally escaped out the window only to find that even the church was reluctant to help her out of her forced marriage.[22] Both Agnes of Bohemia and Isabella of France had to struggle to escape marriage to Frederick II, who was widely reputed to be the Antichrist himself. Agnes de Harcourt's *Life of Isabella* recounts the saint's miraculous intervention to save a young girl from parents who were planning to force her into prostitution.[23] This apparent willingness on the part of their "protectors" to see women forcibly subjugated by rape and abuse readily suggests an explanation for the eagerness with which they gave away whatever money or goods they could wrest from their relatives or husbands.

The laity's enthusiastic endorsement of the Gregorian attack on a corrupt and simoniac clergy intensified the idea of the poor as the victims of greed. The ideal of imitating Christ came to rest on the concept of apostolic poverty. Moreover, it was joined to a revival of apostolic syneisactism. A little before 1050, Gaucher of Aureil built a house for women near his own cell explicitly to "share" his poverty.[24] By the late twelfth century, groups of men and women, some married and others celibate, joined in communities devoted to manual labor and charity. Under a variety of names, they lived in self-imposed poverty in order to serve the poor by example as well as preaching. Membership cut across all social classes. Many were fustian workers seeking protection from merchants who often demanded labor as interest on usurious loans. Others were Lombard nobles who took up wool working on principle. One such group, the Poor Catholics, associated with Durandus of Huesca in 1209, combined care of the sick, the poor, orphans, and pregnant women with prayer and preaching. The apostolic life of charity, poverty, and chastity was an adventure principally associated with lay people who sought to return the church to its humble and ardent origins.

As almsgivers, religious woman had always acted as bridges between rich and poor, the powerful and the powerless. But Elisabeth and her contemporaries sought to cross over and make themselves poor. If the central quality of the *imitatio Christi* was poverty, then it followed that poverty was in itself a virtue. This sacralization of the poor was a sentiment to which the New Testament gave poetic support. For the first time, the poor themselves became serious candidates for sainthood. As the rich made themselves poor, the poor made themselves rich in the sense that they too became charitable. Margaret of Cortona (d. 1297), a repentant prostitute who had no money of her own, lived on alms herself but reversed her status by starving herself and her son while giving away everything that was given to her.[25]

As the twelfth century progressed, however, the ideals of these lay reformers revealed themselves to be ever more at odds with those of the priestly hierarchy. The exaltation of women and the poor that characterized the apostolic movement was inherently anticlerical as the church, if not its individual clergymen, became ever more wealthy and powerful. The charity and poverty of wandering preachers and their followers contrasted starkly with a bureaucratic clergy intent on supporting their institutional endeavors with taxation, exemptions, and privileges. Most especially, the preachers' ability to maintain virtuous and fruitful partnerships with women contrasted sharply with the hysterical and often unchaste celibacy of the parish priesthood.

Misogynist clerics responded with charges of hypocrisy and scandal. Guibert of Nogent in 1124 and Peter the Venerable in the 1130s were already warning their readers against false monks practicing the *vita apostolica*. Gaucher of Aureil's willingness to undertake the care of women drove his disciple Stephen of Grandmont away to found a monastic order that strictly excluded women. Bernard of Clairvaux, who claimed that no one who associated with women could remain chaste, charged that the syneisactics were deliberately causing scandal, proving them to be secret heretics despite their pose of sanctity.[26] Paschal II, in 1101, complained to Bishop Didacus of Compostella that monks and nuns were said to be living together throughout his province and ordered them to be separated.[27] The charge of scandal accompanied the association of monks and nuns even as far as the Arrouaisian houses of Ireland.[28] Marbod of Rennes accused Robert d'Arbrissel of teaching the brothers contempt for the canonical life for the sake of the sisters.[29] He reported that Robert was said to keep watch among his sleeping disciples of both sexes. Marbod condemned Robert's practice of sheltering women in his hospices who mixed with impunity among paupers and pilgrims because, he said, their services often ended with the flight of the women or a child born secretly in their cells. Geoffrey of Vendôme also warned Robert that he was accused of excessive intimacy with women, talking privately and even having them into his chamber at night. Abelard, comparing his enemies to the critics of Jerome and Paula, complained that he was blamed for neglecting Heloise and then criticized for not being able to leave her alone, though he had supposed that his castration had entitled him, like Origen, to teach women with impunity.[30] Christina of Markyate was also compared to Paula because of the criticism she endured until a suspicious monk received a vision that cleared her name.[31]

Books regulating recluses proliferated. The biographer of Hugh of Cluny credited him with instituting both cenobitic and eremitic customs for women, but no special rule has survived.[32] In the early twelfth century, Goscelin wrote the *Liber Confortatorius* (Comforting book) for Eva, a nun of Wilton who became an anchorite at Angers. Aelred of Rievaulx's rule adapted a Benedictine model for his sister to guide her in training younger recluses. He advised a prudent division of the day between manual labor and brief simple prayers with reading in ascetic literature to avoid idleness, the mother of evil. The book continued to be read by English recluses (or anchoresses as they were often called) and influenced the enormously popular thirteenth-century *Ancren Riwle* (A rule for anchoresses). Aelred's sister had already received training as a nun but the *Riwle* was written for three women who had not experienced a novitiate. It outlined a liturgical day providing a simpler ritual of prayers (some in the vernacular) and offices than that of the Benedictine rule. The author urged recluses to minimize outward observances in favor of strict attention to the "inward rule," stressing enclosure from the world. Most of the book is directed to this internal rule: meditation on control of the senses and on the problems of the deadly sins, emphasizing anger.

A true anchoress was expected to avoid unseemly conduct that might cast doubt on her profession. Even confession, the delight of the meditative soul, was dangerous. Since only men could hear them, "candid" confessions might undermine the standards of modesty imposed on women. Thus, Aelred conceded that recluses could speak to a confessor for limited spiritual direction. They could also speak occasionally in the presence of a third person to an abbot or prior or other estimable person. But meetings with the same person should not be frequent for fear of temptation. Male ascetics writing for women were often fanatically preoccupied with their chastity. Aelred bade his sister compare their two destinies, for she was able to keep the chastity that he had lost.[33] A similar concern tormented Godric of Finchale, who enjoyed vicarious virginity by guiding and protecting his recluse sister. In contrast to the muscular concept of heroic chastity that informed the spirituality of women, Aelred used images of incarceration, even of the tomb, to describe the ideal life of the recluse. Even her furnishings were to reflect her purpose. No vanity of pictures and hangings but pure white linen for the altar, washed and bleached with its purpose always in mind. She should eat only with pain and shame, fearing violation through the ears or a vile word from her own mouth. She was not allowed to sully her purity even by excesses of self-mortification.

Aelred's ever-deepening defense of every possible threat to his sister's purity tended to destroy not only the active relationships of recluses with men but networks with women in the community as well. He forbade the common practice of teaching children from the cell window. He complained that it was hard to find a single recluse alone, before whose window a talkative old woman was not sitting keeping her "busy with tales, feeding her on rumors and detractions, describing the appearance and face and deportment of this or that monk, clerk, or religious, throwing in a spicy anecdote or two, telling of the infatuation of young girls, the license of widows to do what they please, the ingenuity of wives in deceiving their husbands and satisfying their desires."[34] A more sympathetic observer might have noted that it is a charity to listen to talkative old women and to join in the formation of a network that might indeed intervene in the daily life of the community. But Aelred feared that this would make the recluse a chatterbox who, even when avoiding impropriety, would spend the day spreading gossip. He did not add, though it was probably in his mind, that it might also make her a critic of the local clergy. Approvingly, he praised his sister, "You sit and keep silence, you suffer things to happen."

The life of prayer, however, had always had a pastoral dimension. No one questioned the teaching role of recluses, though a rigorist like Aelred preferred it to be restricted to exemplary silence. Preaching was an extremely delicate concern. It lay outside the forbidden sacramental preserves of the clergy but well within the ministerial preserves that they increasingly monopolized. The amateur efforts of lay people to combine gospel lessons in the vernacular with works of charity tended to emphasize the subversive elements that always lay close to the surface of Christian teaching. Alexander III, a lawyer pope, condemned their emphasis on preaching and poverty as heretical. Peter Waldo's plea for his vernacular Bible was denied, and the Waldensians were ordered not to preach except by invitation of the local clergy. The canonist Ivo of Chartres urged preachers to ground themselves in the gospel. But the aspect of Christ that reformers most wished to imitate was his defiance of authority, his criticism of the rich and greedy. In the northern beguinages, many a holy woman, exhausted from fasting and prayer in her chaste and enclosed cell, had visions of clergymen fouled with sin or suffering in purgatory. Recluses busy in their vast networks of charity and counseling denounced the secret sins of clergymen, which came to their knowledge either through gossip or through visions. Innocent III noted with displeasure that Spanish nuns undertook "clerical" activities of preaching, bestowing blessings and hearing confessions from one another.[35] By 1210, when he licensed Francis of Assisi, the pope had formulated the idea of obedience to the Holy See as the test of orthodoxy. Soon after his death, Lutgard of Aywières saw him in a vision pleading with her to pray for his release from purgatory.

The same women often proved to be powerful defenders of clerical authority. Hildegard of Bingen was licensed to preach because Innocent II was impressed with her arguments against the Cathar heresy. Similarly, Jacques de Vitry stressed Marie d'Oignies's commitment to orthodoxy and the powerful effect of her prayers against the growing force of Catharism. The hierarchy nevertheless concluded that the dangers outweighed the benefits. In 1184, in his bull *Ad Abolendam*, Lucius III proscribed the Waldensians and Humiliati as heretical because they preached without license. In 1210, Amalrician heretics were accused of penetrating the homes of pious women and widows, using the confessional to spread heresy informed by Joachite beliefs in the coming invalidation of the sacraments in the age of the Holy Ghost.

By 1215, a regular procedure excluded all unlicensed preachers as heretics. Women, who could never expect to receive a rule authorizing them to preach, were almost prohibited from talking at all. Bishops took over the *cura monialium* (care of nuns) from wandering preachers and independent hermits. They required recluses to receive episcopal license—not always easy to obtain. Innocent II reinstated Carolingian regulations making private vows permanently binding. Critics said Waldensians justified entering women's communities and preaching to them on the grounds that the apostles did it. Stephen of Bourbon criticized women who preached in their homes, in the streets, and even in church.[36] He called it heresy to say that the sex of the preacher is irrelevant to good teaching.[37] Anchoresses were accused of heresy or incontinence if they left their retreats for any purpose or even relaxed their fasts without permission. Men were criticized for their willingness to consort with women, preach to them, and hear their preaching.[38] Many men, in fact, argued that whatever women might say constituted heresy simply because they said it. Even teaching by example was becoming dangerous.

Among the virtues that comprised the active *vita apostolica*, neither charity nor voluntary poverty was prized above silence and obedience for women. Aelred of Rievaulx condemned recluses concerned with their flocks and money making who followed the fluctuations of the market and cultivated avarice under the illusion that they should give alms and hospitality. "She should have no beast but a cat," said the *Ancren Riwle*. Both writers said that recluses should not take charge of anyone's goods or even of church vessels or vestments because evil would follow. Aelred believed that a perfect recluse would support herself with hand work or find a benefactor before becoming enclosed. He said her cell should not be besieged with beggars or orphans or widows crying for alms, but she should give freely the better alms of her compassionate prayers. The *Ancren Riwle* stated that a recluse should not have enough of her own to dispense and should be suspicious of taking on the task for others. Generosity was to be viewed as a snare that leads to greed.

While women saw money as a pollutant, their critics located the threat to their purity in a life of begging. Even the most radical men agreed. When Peter Waldo converted to poverty, he left his wife at home and provided for his two daughters by installing them at Fontevraud, after which he gave all his property away to the poor. William of Saint-Amour, the strong partisan of the rights of the secular clergy, criticized able-bodied persons who lived on alms and particularly young women who tried to preserve chastity outside the cloister. Though it goes without saying that all too many women were reduced to begging for their living, voluntary begging was considered too dangerous to female chastity to be allowed.[39] Humbert of Romans, a thirteenth-century general of the Dominican order, said that begging was so dangerous to women that no woman should be regarded as a religious who could not support herself in a cloister without begging.

Even women's liberty to dispose of their own property was confined. When Yvetta of Huy, in guilty gratitude for her widowhood, stripped away her possessions in acts of unlimited charity, her father feared she would destroy her sons' inheritance and took steps to put her in tutelage. He, like the landgrave of Thuringia, regarded women's property not as their own but as family property in trust for male heirs. Clara of Assisi remained determined to accept wealth from no one but to cling to her poverty grimly until her death, despite the discouragement even of her mentor Francis and the disapproval of several popes. By 1220, religious poverty was being associated with heresy and Beguines were commonly accused of hypocrisy that amounted to heresy. The archbishop of Mainz condemned women who called themselves religious and did not live in cloistered convents. He ordered them to cloister themselves at home if they were too poor to gain entrance into a community. German synods of the 1230s prohibited wandering women from preaching poverty. In 1261, a group of Swabian nuns rebelled, arguing that God could be better served with a free spirit than through mindless obedience to orders.

Fear of scandal outweighed any evidence of innocence or guilt as the reformed church began to channel and regulate the passions of Christ's imitators. Under pressure from their own consciences or from their ecclesiastical superiors, monks put both literal and psychological distance between themselves and their female partners. Fontevraud abandoned the active life of social service before the first generation died out, leaving its hospitality to lower class *conversae* on the model of the older abbeys. In 1134, after Norbert became bishop of Magdeburg, the Premonstratensians turned away from their commitment to nursing. Innocent III, himself an admirer of the *vita apostolica* who patronized hospitals, licensed the Humiliati as a male order in 1201, carefully distinguishing them from a second order of unmarried lay women and men called *religiosi,* without full monastic status, and from a third order of married lay people whom the pope instructed in the precepts of a Christian family life. The Poor Catholics of Durand de la Huesca were similarly reconciled at the price of limitations on the role of their women. Even Francis of Assisi, widely admired then as now as the perfect proponent of the *imitatio Christi,* sacrificed the partnership of Clara for papal recognition of his order. She and her sisters were segregated in a second order, and women who worked in the world were classed with married men as Tertiaries (members of a third order).

Neither legislation nor the prescriptive literature aimed at recluses actually prevented women from embracing an apostolic life combining charitable work with prayer and preaching by example or advice. But such restrictions obscured their efforts, withheld institutional support, and cast doubt on their competitive claims to sanctity against the established clergy or the male orders. Individual anchoresses and Beguine communities, like more formal monastic communities, were still committed to the provision of hospitality, shelter to travelers, and care for the sick. Some retreats had a guest house for the rich and an almshouse for the poor. Almost unnoticed in the general outcry against women preaching and tempting sexual predators by conspicuous giving or taking of charity, a new vocation centering especially on the care of the sick emerged from the apostolic movement. Toward the end of the twelfth century, Jacques de Vitry said:

> In western lands, there are innumerable communities of men and women who renounce the world and regularly live in houses of lepers and hospitals for the poor, humbly and devoutly ministering to the poor and infirm. Men and women separately and with all reverence eat and sleep in chastity. They do not omit to hear the canonical offices day and night as much as hospital work and the ministry to Christ's poor permit. . . . They take infirm people or healthy guests into their houses where they eat and sleep, segregating the women. Their chaplains, ministering with all humility and devotion to the poor and infirm, instruct the unlearned with preaching the divine word, console the pusillanimous and debilitated and exhort them to patience and grace. They celebrate divine offices, which all the infirm may hear in their beds. . . . They administer confes-

sions and Extreme Unction and other sacraments diligently and carefully to the infirm and give fitting burial to the dead. . . . For them, the Lord changes the filthy shit which they are forced to clear into precious stones and the stench becomes a sweet aroma.[40]

The first monastics with a special nursing vocation were attached to the hospitals under the knights of Saint John and the ladies of Mary Magdalene, respectively, in Jerusalem after the First Crusade, which subsequently grew into the order of the Knights Hospitalers. The original Premonstratensian women formed a corps of professional nurses who tended their own hospices and went abroad to tend the bedridden sick. A group of sisters established Saint Katharine's hospice near the Tower of London. In Paris, the Hôtel Dieu was founded by the Sisters of the Holy Ghost. The women involved were by no means exclusively from the lower classes. Elisabeth of Thuringia, who was particularly associated with the hospital movement, came from an eastern family that produced two generations of saintly women instrumental in the conversion of the Slavs. Her mother Gertrude, queen of Hungary, and other relatives were abbesses and foundresses of hospitals including Agnes of Bohemia, the confidante of Clara of Assisi. Her aunt, Queen Hedwig of Poland, devoted herself to leprous women by sending them money, food, and clothing. In England, Queen Mathilda, who had abandoned the monastery of Romsey to marry Henry I, founded a leprosarium in 1101, where she tended personally to the patients.[41] Robert d'Arbrissel included a leprosarium among the four buildings at Fontevraud.[42] Clara Blassoni set up a hospital for lepers in Milan and formed a group of sisters to care for them. The author of *Ancren Riwle* allowed for the reception of guests in the anchorage "in great necessity" without specifying where they would sleep. Marie d'Oignies persuaded her husband to embrace a life of marital chastity and devote their property to a leprosarium. Hospitals of unknown origins show up regularly in every sort of record.

In 1194, Celestine III prohibited nuns from going out to visit the poor and restricted their charity to distributions from the convent gate. The "gate," however, was often a capacious hostel providing food and shelter to pilgrims who voluntarily exposed themselves to the hardships of the road, vagrants who had no choice, and sick people without help at home. In cities, the hostels sometimes acquired a semipermanent set of residents.

Sometimes the abbess or prioress managed these institutions through a bailiff. Elsewhere, as at Nivelles, the chapter controlled the hospice. We cannot tell how intimately nuns were ever engaged in the actual care of the poor. They certainly engaged actively in the administration of the hospital and the supervision of the nurses. It is generally assumed, for example, that few of the well-born nuns of the hospital of Saint Margaret's of Augsburg would have undertaken menial nursing work, but when the institution was secularized in the sixteenth century, a lay official complained of the loss of training, responsibility, and long-term planning they had supplied. In the same city, Abbess Eilibirg von Thurheim of Saint Stephan's founded cells for "four honorable women and soul nuns" to care for the sick and dying of the foundation. This evidence suggests that upper-class nuns may have supported lower-class sisters, perhaps *conversae* not bound by permanent vows, in soul houses for the deserving poor. The sisters at the French hospital of Aubrac, however, were noblewomen who made the beds and cleaned, washed, and deloused the sick. Noblewomen of the Order of the Hospital of Saint John of Jerusalem, who worked at the hospitals associated with the Commanderies as lay women, eventually took the habit of the order as widows and retired within. The Teutonic Knights admitted women as *consorores* because they considered them necessary for nursing their wounded, specifying that they have a separate domicile to protect the chastity of the knights and that they recruit *conversae* for the heavy work of the hospital.[43] The Templars, on the other side, firmly rejected the recruitment of women in any capacity: "The company of women is a dangerous thing, for by it the devil has led many from the strait path to Paradise."[44]

Franciscan and Dominican Tertiary rules, recognized by Nicholas IV in 1289, were commonly used by women who wished to serve from their own homes. Small communities like the Sisters of Saint Agnes, Augustinians of Galilee, or other local groups named for the patron saint of the parish formed a common life in the world devoted to visiting the sick. In the late fourteenth century, the Gray Sisters of Saint Omer, undertook to beg food for the poor. By 1500 they had nearly a hundred groups in Flanders and Burgundy and one in Scotland, combining care for the sick with spiritual comfort. They visited the sick in pairs and refused to enter dishonest houses or to keep watch with the sick for more than two or three nights. Otherwise, their rule forbade them to go out at night or eat outside their homes. When not occupied with care of the sick they worked for the common support. In Bologna, Tertiaries nursed the sick and at Modena, they took impoverished gentlefolk under their protection. At Mons, they taught children and in many places they opened homes for prostitutes. In 1353, when the Franciscans gained control of the four holy places in Jerusalem associated with the life of Christ and his mother, Sofia of Florencia organized a group of Tertiaries to run the pilgrims' hospice.

Observance of a monastic way of life, not professional standards of health care, was the first concern of patrons, supervisors, and even, to some extent, inmates of hospitals. But strangely enough, there was little of the concern noted elsewhere for segregating women and men. Perhaps the excessive anxiety to preserve the mental purity of recluses simply did not extend to the physical purity of women whose bodies had already been so thoroughly vilified by monastic misogynists. Caretakers or recipients who intended to remain in a hospital took vows of poverty, promising to make all their property available to the community. Where a formal rule was imposed by ecclesiastical authorities, the brothers and sisters were strictly segregated but where it was not, women and men shared the common rooms and refectory.

Women who served the poor and sick directly were generally refused status as nuns. Following the lead of Innocent III in his shelters for pregnant women and foundlings in Rome and Montpellier, lay sisters or conversae came under the Augustinian rule. Nevertheless, in 1248 the archbishop of Rouen, who worked for many years to impose a monastic orderliness on the hospitals in his diocese, found nuns staffing Salle-aux-Puelles, a leprosarium for women established by Henry II in 1183.[45] He complained that they did not hold regular chapters nor audit their accounts on a regular basis. Lay people entered the cloisters, kitchens, and workrooms talking with the sisters. At another hospital with a male and a female community under a prior and prioress using the Augustinian rule, chapters of males and females met separately for spiritual matters and together for secular affairs.[46] Though everything was orderly, he complained that they talked too much in the refectory and issued a formal directive regulating their diet, their bathing (which was to be more frequent), and distribution of charity to the poor and sick. Elsewhere, he complained of hospitals that allowed gift shops to flourish at their gates. He complained of maidservants eating in the bake house for fear of scandal and prohibited nuns from selling thread and spindles. In England, a brother and sister at Croydon convicted of soliciting alms were ejected from the hospital and others were expelled for excessive chattering and gossip provoking quarrels within the community.[47]

The inevitable mingling of women and men in hospitals, which involved the most intimate bodily contact, though viewed with disfavor, did not seem to elicit the horror that moralists felt at the sight of a gossiping recluse. Assuredly, the hospitals needed supervision. They often appear to have fostered an atmosphere of laxity. The abbess of Barking expelled a leper from the hospital at Ilford for introducing a prostitute into his chamber under the pretext that she was his sister. The prioress of Bondeville took advantage of her situation as hospital supervisor to keep her own table and visit outside the priory, letting the sisters drink in the granges and go to Rouen often.[48] In 1257, the brothers and sisters of the Maison Dieu attached to Gournay priory commonly ate together, and some of the men slept with their wives.[49] Some hospitals gave little attention to the sick though they received healthy travelers as guests.[50] And supervisors constantly suspected that hospitals abused their funds.

Many religious women continued to serve the poor directly by enclosing themselves in hospitals, sometimes in association with male orders devoted to the care of the sick, thus blurring gender as well as class lines when we seek to analyze their populations. The flexible Augustinian rule provided institutional cover for the double order of the Holy Spirit, which had houses everywhere in Christendom. Brothers and sisters maintained hospices for travelers, sick people, pregnant women, abandoned children, and repentant prostitutes. The sisters did laundry and prepared the food. They lived in separate quarters and had their own chapters. Their rule forbade them to do any domestic work for any brother not too sick to care for himself. The sisters wore habits and took the three vows. They regulated their work to combine spiritual and bodily care of the sick with their own spiritual improvement: on Tuesdays they washed the inmates' hair; Thursdays they washed their feet. The brothers did heavy work and jobs that required leaving the institution, particularly begging for donations. Conversely, the Trinitarians and the Mercedarians, who were devoted to the ransoming of prisoners, had female branches for fund-raising. The Cellite sisters partnered with the Alexian lay brethren and organized plague houses for victims of the Black Death in Belgium. The Jesuate sisters, or Sisters of the Visitation of Mary, were founded under the same rule in 1367 by Katharina Colombini at Siena to assist the Poor Brothers in serving the sick and dying. Eustochia of Messina, a leader of the Observantine Franciscan movement, organized her sisters to nurse the sick.

Some houses were exclusively for women under a prioress and some were mixed. Special prayers were added at the consecration of a virgin or widow and chastity was imposed even on married persons. Female servants who did laundry and other sorts of work at all hospitals, even when all the patients were men, were treated as quasi-religious. Some hospitals had only enough income to support their staff, and the brothers and sisters could take in no patients at all. Though patients were supposed to be separated from their attendants and women from men, admission as an inmate or a caretaker both required a religious ceremony. Sometimes the sick and the healthy serving them were equal in numbers and sometimes they were indistinguishable. Transient patients or attendants gave donations or made wills in favor of the hospital. Patients and staff wore religious habits. In one hospital under the supervision of the bishop of Rouen, a lay sister had a child. Although she was listed as one of the lepers, she claimed to be in good health and the bishop sent her home.[51] Leprosaria appear frequently in episcopal visitation records as trouble spots and possibly as targets for clerical greed. For example, the bishop deprived Santa Croce, the leprosarium of Verona, of control over its own income after he claimed to have found unbridled fornication among the lepers, resulting in the birth of illegitimate children.

The inhabitants of hospitals were not necessarily incapacitated. Healthy people could retire into hospitals for shelter in old age or widowhood. Even formally enclosed convents were sometimes paid handsomely for education of the young or shelter of the old, but too often such arrangements proved to be losing propositions. Hospital work offered poor people the opportunity to engage in selfless acts of charity and share the profits of grace. Inmates were customarily treated as quasi-religious and subjected to the Augustinian or Hospitaler rules with provision that they could leave or be expelled for bad behavior. The hospices of the Knights of Saint John were not only served by women attached to the order but also maintained women as inmates in the Holy Land and elsewhere. Portuguese leper houses were usually self-contained communities with chapel, garden, and several small houses. Members contributed their possessions to the community and placed themselves under the warden's discipline. They could go out on pilgrimage, begging their way to sacred sites, or undertake the licensed begging that supported these small charitable communities. Donors were more prone to donate support to hospitals where the poor and their caretakers lived in a quasi-religious way, which was supposed to make their prayers more efficacious to the donor. Indeed in the fourteenth and fifteenth centuries, this form of foundation was so highly favored in England that decayed monasteries were frequently converted into hospitals where inmates lived as a religious community and ministered to the parish poor. Often hospital workers were oblates supported by life annuities, as at Figeac, in southern France, where widows gave themselves with their goods to the hospital in return for food and shelter, living thereafter as religious in a community. After they had seen to the needs of their brothers, many Venetian hospitals, called *scuole,* sheltered widows and dowered unmarried girls. A majority of the city's small hospitals housed women exclusively.

Among the sick, leprosy, which apparently grew to nearly epidemic proportions in this period, gained a peculiar, perhaps illusory, preeminence. Enthusiasts who aspired to the apostolic life may have tended to confound certain venereal diseases with the familiar biblical affliction. Lepers were unaccountably associated with lust and "excommunicated from society" as much for their suspected moral failings as for their physical contagion. Ironically, however, their social death closely paralleled the ascetic ideal of becoming dead to the world. For hospital communities driven by spiritual ambitions as much as concern for healing the sick, the cure of a leper was a moral reform as well as a physical regime. The hagiographic conventions, which make the physical caress of lepers a signifier of sanctity, thus hide a strange enigma within the nauseating trappings of the narrative. Certainly for a woman fearful of rape, or at least forced marriage, the taint of leprosy may have seemed a shield for her chastity.

Why did women obsessed with the polluting power of money and sex willingly expose themselves to the contagion of such a disease? Why did the men who admired them and recommended their deeds successfully for the approval of the hierarchy praise them for courting infection? Jesus himself was identified with the despised and rejected and popular tradition transformed Lazarus, the resuscitated brother of Martha and Mary, into a leper. Thus, in some fashion, the leper came closer to the *imitatio Christi* than anyone else. Alice of Scharbeck, a nun suffering from leprosy, converted her disease into a vehicle of almsgiving by offering her lost limbs to God for various causes. Alice may be understood as a person valiantly striving to bring something meaningful out of a doomed life, but other women actually prayed to become lepers. Yvetta of Huy did her best to contract the infection from her charges. Intimacy with lepers became the hallmark of the mendicant orders of the thirteenth century, culminating in the fourteenth with Catherine of Siena's heroic determination to overcome her personal revulsion by drinking the water in which she had washed the sores of a leper. Indeed, it may be argued that as long as the poor were prized as the meek and humble exemplars of the evangelical vision, impoverished women who were well secured from inheriting much on earth were especially prized as the inheritors of the kingdom of heaven. By turning their flesh, so often allegorized as corruption, filth and dung, into a literally contagious putrefying mass, women may have hoped at last to allay the anxieties of the men whose aspirations they strove to share. By turning their bodies into objects of self-mortification they unquestionably sought to liberate their spirits and render them eligible for the true imitation of Christ in his complete humanity.

10

⋆

Cura Mulierum

THE DESERT ANCESTORS of medieval monastics were said to live on faith alone. Honey and locusts, dates and water sufficed the biblical prophets. God sent a raven from heaven with bread in its beak to relieve Antony's years of fasting. But as Paula, Melania, and other imitators soon learned, apostolic poverty cost money. From the beginning, western rhetoric glowed with visions of wilderness to be cleared and cultivated, simple handiwork exchanged in a local market, self-sufficiency won by the blessed sweat of the monastic brow—in short, a dream of what never was. And by the twelfth century, Europe's expanding population had plowed the wilderness away. The hermitages of hagiography turn out, on closer examination, to be in well-populated and economically productive areas. Ailred of Rievaulx's sarcastic picture of a recluse hanging out the window to discuss her investments and flocks was far more realistic than his advice that she remain screened by a pure linen curtain from all mundane concerns. Hospitals and shelters, food for the hungry and support for the devoted woman who distributed it all cost money. Women who wished to follow the radical path of voluntary poverty were swiftly frustrated by clerical efforts to keep them in cloisters. Even Christ lived from the purses of Joanna, Susanna, and the rest; his imitators, who sought to live on the alms of the faithful and in turn serve the needy poor, were soon endowed with buildings and incomes by an admiring public or restrained by the threat of heresy.

With urbanization, a new class system began to replace the old kinship networks. Cash hungry fathers saw their daughters as drains on their resources rather than assets. Bachelors seeking to marry up precipitated dowry inflation, which forced women to remain unmarried or accept the humiliation of marrying down. Working boys learned trades and skills, whereas girls got jobs as servants. Boys pinned their ambitions on entry into a guild, whereas girls tried to save enough for a dowry. Charities also subsidized training for boys and dowries for girls, though eligible husbands were sometimes difficult to find. As guilds gradually limited opportunities for men also, apprentices and journeymen stayed unmarried for years or for life if they failed to get a mastership. The church opened many avenues for upward mobility to talented men, whatever their origins. Excluded from the clergy and, since clerical orders were a requirement for university study, from professional training as well, women were rendered uncompetitive. Clerical celibacy made them un-marriageable as well. Begging was a sign of abandoned, involuntary poverty, when even prostitution had failed to support them. Having steadily outstripped male demand for marital partners while their chances for self-support dwindled, women became a pressing social problem: that is, men had the problem of finding a satisfactory way to dispose of the surplus. The woman question was rooted in ideas about status and propriety. There were not necessarily more women than men alive in the twelfth century, but there were more women than men could suitably maintain in their proper sphere. Affection and pride forced men to find suitable provision for their female dependents in tune with the complex myths of fragility, vulnerability, and incompetence that disguised the structural realities denying women self-sufficiency. The woman problem was posed as the *cura mulierum*, the care of women.

Women's voices on the subject are rarely heard, but presumably most women thought that they had something to offer that repaid the costs of their care. Heloise rejected Benedict's requirement of manual labor as unsuitable for women. Urging the model of Mary at the lord's feet, she asserted that silence, contemplation, and perpetual prayer earned them the right to be served and supported by priests as deacons served true widows in apostolic times. Her monastery, the Paraclete, was one of the success stories of the age, rising from a humble endowment to become a wealthy royal monastery in the thirteenth century. But such a rise was as exceptional as Heloise herself. Men who accepted the proposition that women must be supported nevertheless sought ways to shift the burden to other men.

Secular men agreed that the *cura mulierum,* like the care of the poor, properly belonged to the clergy. From northern England to the communes of Italy, in the Rhineland and every French province, the story is the same. Although new communities were always being opened, there were never enough of them and they never accommodated enough women. Convents ranged in size from ninety-nine places at Marcigny or a hundred at Fontevraud to two or three in the smallest houses. All sorts of influential people sought places for daughters or protégées. Women with powerful vocations and adequate financial qualifications might be denied consecration because donors, even resident nuns, had a waiting list of "nieces" to whom the available places had been allotted. Beguinages drew recruits in greater numbers than bishops could supervise. Endowed anchorholds had a waiting list. Women everywhere set up communal households with or without ecclesiastical license. Noblewomen monopolized places in more desirable nunneries. Women from urban patriciates filled the remainder. In some areas, nobles and patricians pushed lower-class women out of beguinages and even houses originally intended for repentant prostitutes. Healthy women took hospital places meant for the sick.

Everyone saw convents as obvious places to park women in need of assistance or shelter or even a timely vacation. Founders demanded hospitality and even had special sets of apartments reserved for indeterminate stays. Impoverished widows, cheated of their dower rights or grown burdensome to their children, widows of nobles defeated in private wars or pauperized by confiscation of their estates, had no alternative but to seek shelter in the church.[1] Girls who left before professing were educated in convents and it is not clear that they paid their way. In 1260, the archbishop of Rouen ordered secular girls to leave Saint-Saëns except for one who was not a burden on the house. But in 1269 he had to repeat the same order.[2] They often became nursing homes for aged and diseased persons whose contributions, called corodies, might be a significant addition to the endowment or might be speedily eaten up by their living expenses.

Conversae were sometimes lower-class servants earning their keep in the convent and sometimes upper-class women almost indistinguishable from the nuns. Cluniac nuns grouped *conversae* and oblates separately from the professed nuns, adding an incalculable number of inhabitants to the designated places. Eudes of Rouen in 1252 registered twelve nuns and twelve lay sisters at Saint-Saëns, but the following year he listed eighteen nuns and three lay sisters in the same convent.[3] Nun Coton had thirty nuns, ten *conversae*, three chaplains, and twelve lay brothers, almost as many servitors as nuns. Gilbert of Sempringham began his order with a group of well-born virgins, adding a sisterhood of *conversae* to serve them. Wealthier convents also accommodated personal servants who worked for wages and may not have lived in the convent. Every community gambled that this human bookkeeping of endowments and liabilities would balance in the end.

The clergy accepted the burden of the *cura mulierum* grudgingly, with the proviso that the women be self-sufficient and not drain resources needed for the church's more important responsibilities. Men agreed that women needed less material wealth than men and that self-mortification was especially becoming to the vainer sex. Women's houses founded in the high Middle Ages were generally smaller and poorer than men's houses.[4] The donations they received were often intended for the support of individual members of the community rather than the whole, reflecting the difficulty of promoting women's religious activities as worthy of support for their own sake. Finally, despite all the devices confining women to a dependent condition and despite all the warnings that the slightest hint of worldliness would defile their precious purity, religious women were generally left to take care of themselves whether they liked it or not.

The growth of the cash economy was but one more complication in the thick texture of goods, services, rights, and exemptions that defined wealth in the Middle Ages. Religious communities, whatever their size or purpose, did not exist outside the economic fabric. The land they occupied cost money and was liable to taxes. Their buildings needed repairs and their furniture replenishing. Even productive enterprises undertaken for the support of the community needed capital investment. Abbeys, like all landlords, responded to inflation, which put pressure on incomes from fixed rents, by tightening old dues or converting services into money payments. They profited from higher prices for goods produced on their estates and resisted higher taxes and new demands from ecclesiastical as well as secular authorities by seeking exemptions and privileges. As lords, they collected customs duties, tolls, and fines levied in judicial proceedings from tenants, particularly market towns on their estates, and in turn resisted the merchants' demands for liberties where they could. The price of consumer goods went up but so did the price of spiritual services. Burial rights, commemorative services for the dead, ceremonies concerning relics, and feast days were all part of a nunnery's economy. Ascetics had to enter into the marketplace of capitalism directly as entrepreneurs or indirectly as competitors for donations from charitable persons who were rapidly learning to think more precisely about the value they could expect for their money.

Older monasteries generally possessed a landed base, though it was often scattered into small and distant holdings reflecting the patchwork character of the original donations. The grants carried jurisdictional and tax rights with them. For example, the twin monasteries of Gernrode and Frose shared about a dozen villages from their original endowment. By 1207, when Innocent III confirmed their rights, they controlled twenty-four villages, nearly a thousand hides of arable land and four hundred hides of hay meadows. They had the income from judicial fines in all those villages and tithes from twenty-one parish churches. Comparable grants were not made in the high Middle Ages. As the lineage-oriented society of the early Middle Ages gave way to institutionalization, magnates depended less on family members to administer and conserve their property. Cash payments rewarded professional men for more narrowly defined services. Prayer and charity, the designated functions of monasteries, did not require such elaborate support.

The ideal of self-sufficiency still guided Benedictine, particularly Cistercian, foundations. They strove to build a patrimony of agricultural or pastoral rights, pieced together from gifts and investments of money saved by careful management and an ascetic life. Neither nuns nor monks customarily cleared land with their own hands, but contrary to legend, Cistercian monks exploited established holdings more often than they pioneered the wilderness. Nuns tended to get the less desirable, uncleared acreage and thus may have been the order's true pioneers. In one area around Chartres where monks cleared the tenants from land already cultivated, nuns are known to have used tenants to clear uncultivated land. The abbesses of three nunneries founded in the early thirteenth century on decidedly inferior land consolidated their holdings and acquired rights of forage in waste and forest. English nunneries often occupied lands that might have to be abandoned periodically because of flooding or the unpredictable eruptions of border fighting. Around 1236, the countess of Flanders donated uncultivated land for a convent at Ter Hagen. Over a thirty year period, despite periodic flooding from the sea and recurrent deaths from polder fever, the nuns got it cleared and cultivated. Though most prescriptive writers denied the possibility, some women actually cultivated modest land grants personally. Francesca da Romano and her community supported themselves by working daily in a small vineyard that had originally been part of her dowry. In his charter for Havenholme, the bishop of Lincoln praised nuns who were thus attempting to fulfill the Cistercian ideal of clearing the wilderness on land so poor that the monks had refused the gift: "the faithful nuns of wonderful religion. . . . Seizing on the narrow life, the strict life, the life of the monks with Cistercian religion, so far as the weakness of their sex permits they strive to keep it and they do keep it."[5]

Most nuns, like monks, hoped that these dramas of early hardship would swiftly resolve themselves into an austere but economically stable life, and they directed their efforts to that end. Around 1131, when Abelard installed Heloise and a group of Benedictine nuns dispossessed from Argenteuil by the monks of Saint Denis in a convent called the Paraclete on his modest estate, she argued that the field work prescribed by the Benedictine rule was inappropriate for her and her gentle companions from Argenteuil. Being a bookish, urban woman, she certainly showed no inclination to go out and till the fields herself, but there may be a subtle irony in her complaint, considering how seldom Benedictine monks were found in the fields. Revenues pieced together from individual donations were scattered and diverse, difficult to administer and to collect. Either they had to be exchanged for more convenient possessions or farmed out in exchange for rents lower than the original income. The inflationary economy threatened even great landed endowments. Like secular nobles, some abbesses responded successfully to the challenge and others succumbed to mounting debts and incompetent administration. For example, Nivelles's domain was almost swallowed up by the growing town whose secular officials resisted the convent's manorial authority. But despite some difficult times, the abbey gave up direct exploitation of its domains and supported itself as a rentier until the late eighteenth century. Abbess Gertrude of Quedlinberg systematically exchanged distant lands for nearer ones. At the end of her incumbency, she thanked God that she had been able to relieve the abbey of the heavy debts and burdens incurred in the wars of Frederick II. The reprieve was only temporary. Her successor, Abbess Bertradis II, 1270–1308, did far more selling than buying to pay her current debts. But Quedlinberg survived, though greatly diminished from its former glory.

The Cistercian system was a model for all contemplatives. They supported themselves from estates organized as granges exploited by lay monks, or *conversi*. The system ideally suited cloistered women, but monastic and episcopal authorities seem to have manufactured objections. Where the land was close to the monastery, supervision was relatively easy, but nuns seem to have had fewer and smaller consolidated holdings. When Saint-Saëns kept two nuns at its grange at Saint-Austreberta, the archbishop ordered them back, fearing the danger in their separation from the community.[6] Where Cistercians often incorporated small male communities into their order as granges, they rarely accepted women's communities as granges, leaving them instead as small monasteries that had no political, financial, or spiritual clout to acquire granges of their own. Generally, therefore, women had to rent their farms to tenants rather than exploit them directly with *conversi*.

The Cistercians, who prided themselves on their primitive purity, sometimes created their own wilderness by evicting villages of farming tenants from their lands in favor of sheep, which would not disturb their solitude. Wool was a cash crop much in demand for the growing cloth industry. Cistercian nuns shared the *privilegium commune*, which excluded their goods from episcopal control and gave them papal protection. In Yorkshire, they settled on moors and the Pennine fringes, cultivating some land and raising sheep. The order's pasturage and enclosure rights protected the nuns' flocks. The order successfully rationalized distribution for markets in nearby towns and long-distance trade. Italian and French merchants rode out every spring to buy the wool crop while it was still on the sheep, negotiating with the order's business agents in bulk. Even modest convents could thus maximize their profit on a small flock, though a higher percentage went for subsistence than for the venture capital generated by the great monkeries. Stixwould, a prosperous convent, exported about fifteen sacks of wool a year through the Cistercian trade network.

But the order's *cura* was not always benign. Riffredo, an old Benedictine foundation, led a general land-clearing effort in Italy. The valley remained a stronghold of the manorial system, and the nunnery lived on its own produce, manor dues, and services with minimal cash flow long after most of northern Italy had embraced the capitalist economy. The expanding Cistercian monastery of Staffarda contested the nuns' rights, and Riffredo joined the order in the 1240s, hoping to nullify the threat. But the monks resented having to act as the nuns' agents in the neighboring communes and resumed litigation in 1279. When the abbess's procurator resisted, the abbot of Staffarda excommunicated the nuns. The abbess denied his visitation rights and in 1291 the pope reinforced the excommunication. Eventually, however, the nuns freed themselves from the Cistercian connection, which had impoverished them, and reverted to managing their own reduced affairs, several small communes and at least one substantial grange, with fair success. One of the nuns took over an outlying domain originally managed by a layman. By 1289 she had become prioress of six nuns living there with her who sometimes went to the chapter of Riffredo. By the fourteenth century, Riffredo employed nuns or lay sisters to supervise the business originally entrusted to Staffarda.

As Cistercian institutions, many nunneries claimed to share in the order's tithe exemptions. Abbesses in greater houses were frequently given the highly prized exemptions from episcopal authority that entitled them to revenue-producing rights of public and ecclesiastical jurisdiction: tithes, justice fines, tolls, and other forms of taxation. Many convents held parish tithes along with alms and mortuary rights. The prosperity of the Benedictine community of Brindisi and its daughter house at Lecce, founded by Guiscard and his wife, Sichelgaeta, in the late eleventh century, depended on the exemption that gave the abbess jurisdiction over clerks and parishes on their estates. In Spain, Las Huelgas de Burgos's exemption empowered the abbess to confer benefices on clergy and invest them with care of souls, establish new parishes, and discipline priests suspected of heresy. Presiding over her courts, she promulgated decrees and indulgences from Rome; the third abbess, Sancha García (1207–1230), even claimed she could hear confessions. Parish tithes were lucrative and many towns formed communes to resist them. Abbesses drove hard bargains over the splitting of justice fees and rights of high justice with secular lords. Well instructed in the law, Abbess Thebalda personally supervised Riffredo's litigation to maintain its parish tithes. She enlisted the lord of Saluzzo and even the monks of Staffarda, who hoped to appropriate her rights. She got the pope to excommunicate the recalcitrant parishioners, but they continued their defiance even when two nuns and their notary stood at the door of the nearest parish church taking the names of the excommunicated people going to the forbidden mass.

The greater houses fought fiercely and not always hopelessly for their rights and exemptions. Jouarre struggled from 1128 to 1225 to maintain its claim over the town, the bourg, and the parish against the bishop. In 1201, Innocent III ordered the abbess Agnes to submit, excommunicated her, and interdicted the town. She persisted, fighting for each privilege separately. Finally, she conceded a package of specific rights to the bishop but not complete jurisdiction. In 1219, the abbess Hersende took up the fight again and ultimately got her exemption confirmed by the pope. At Überwasser, the original abbess and her brother, the bishop of Münster, had transformed the family estates into a Cathedral chapter closely tied to a canoness institute. The bishop and abbess continued to be allies with canons and canonesses sharing the income of the original endowment. The bishop supported the convent's resistance to the Benedictine rule until 1460.

All this litigation increased the power of that peculiar guardian created by the *cura,* the advocate, the community's legal representative. The advocacy evolved from the patronage and protection the original proprietor gave a monastery into a highly profitable, often hereditary, office in the twelfth century, as canon and feudal law strengthened prohibitions on clergy and women sitting in various court cases. The advocate's exactions to compensate for his legal services burdened both the abbey smallholders and the abbess herself. The abbesses of Lindau and Buchau complained of advocates who forged privileges to deprive them of their income. Some advocates used the pretext of holding court to overwhelm the nuns with force. They customarily withheld the justice fines they owed the abbesses. In 1114, the abbess of Remiremont complained to the king that the advocate had dissipated the nuns' allowances and even stripped the parish church bare. At Waldkirch, the lord of Schwarzenberg stole all the convent's property and the abbess was powerless to control him. At Metelen, the advocate was the bishop of Münster, who used a forged deed to become the convent's landlord.

Some abbesses struck back as ruthlessly as they could. About 1200, the abbess of Nivelles forged imperial deeds restricting the powers of the count who held the advocacy and incorporated similar restrictions in specific charters of donation and wills. She obtained genuine imperial letters and papal restrictions. But inexorably, the count's power grew. At the same time, he did nothing as advocate to protect her temporal powers against the growing communal movement in the town. In 1212, in pursuit of her rights against Quedlinberg's advocate, who was supporting the imperial claims of Frederick II, Abbess Sophie allied herself to his opponent, Otto of Brunswick, and endured a siege. The nuns, led by the prioress, rallied the town, which favored going over to the Hohenstaufens rather than standing a second siege. Even her dependent monasteries opposed her, as shown in an order of 1220 from the pope commanding them to obey their abbess. In 1223, the Reichstag in Nordhausen deposed her and the advocate forcibly installed the prioress as the new abbess. That year, papal investigators charged that "robbers, incendiaries and persons excommunicated by us and proscribed by the emperor [Otto] have been received within the walls" and destroyed the convent's goods.[7] In 1218, Frederick destroyed the defenses of Quedlinberg and compensated the abbess with money for the remedy of his soul. Fines and taxes from courts, fairs, mills, woods and other manor dues, mint rights, rents, or tolls could be fractionated among many claimants. A gift to Ronceray, for example, consisted of one-eighth of all offerings of money, candles, tithes, rents, and first fruits at "the altar of Saint George."[8] Abbess Gertrude of Quedlinberg divided the advocate's income and functions into fragments, which she loaned, mortgaged, or sold to subadvocates. By the late thirteenth century, Quedlinberg had many advocates and the power of the office had dissipated. Abbess Gertrude gradually bought most of the advocacies back into her own hands.

Many houses suffered a fatal blow to their independence when Innocent III and the Fourth Lateran Council made visitation obligatory for all monasteries. Nunneries with ties to the developing orders would be subjected only to the discipline of their monastic partners and sometimes, at least, these were women. Fontevraud and the Gilbertines had regular provisions for female visitors. The Cistercians had some female affiliates who did the job, and other orders haphazardly improvised similar systems. However, as we shall see, women were not always able to find stable relationships with an order. When their order neglected them, Dominican women asked the bishop of Strasbourg for protection while utilizing cunning delaying tactics when he claimed authority over them: "Lord, we know that we are bound to obey our bishop but we are ignorant of so many things and know not in what cases. Whence we ask you humbly to suspend your authority over us for a while so that we might investigate in what things we are bound to obey you." The bishop agreed. They then alerted the friars to the episcopal threat to their prerogatives, persuading them to appeal to the pope. In the end, the pope incorporated them into the order with all its privileges.[9]

Non-ordered houses were subject to episcopal visitation, often entailing an expensive and tyrannical abuse of the *cura*, which they resisted as far as they were able. The rich Norman abbey of Montivilliers had enjoyed immunity from episcopal control since 1035, thanks to privileges won by Abbess Beatrix, the duke's daughter. It was the only female house in Normandy with baronial status, owing knight service equal to the greatest male abbeys. In 1203, Abbess Alix de Vaierville got a confirming privilege from Innocent III. But in 1259, Archbishop Eudes Rigaud insisted on a complete visitation despite the community's charters and privileges.[10] When the community resisted, he ordered the nuns to do penance for disobedience, rebellion, and contempt. In 1260, they submitted, but not without registering a letter of protest.[11] The archbishop responded with a formal denial of their privileges, citing the law of Innocent III, made some liturgical adjustments, and deprived them of their keys. Thereafter, he visited them regularly (at their expense).

Abbess Sophie von Wettin of Quedlinberg appealed to the pope when the bishop of Halberstadt abused his customary rights of hospitality during Palm Sunday by increasing his entourage to an unmanageable size. The pope renewed her old proprietorial privileges but refused new ones in deference to episcopal authority. The abbey steadily lost ground over a century-long litigation until the bishop finally consolidated secular power over it. Similar struggles with mixed results involved most of the great old German institutes. Leo IX supported episcopal claims over Gernrode, which had been independent in Ottonian times. The monastery's resistance ended only in the fourteenth century with the forcible imposition of episcopal visitation. Gandersheim apparently used a forged document to secure Innocent III's recognition of its claimed exemption, which did not prevent subsequent struggles. Herford and Fischbeck also struggled against episcopal jurisdiction over their property though they recognized the bishop's authority in spirituals.

Episcopal carelessness contributed to intramural difficulties, and when bishops tried protect nuns, they sometimes killed them with kindness. Archbishop Thomas Corbridge of York repeatedly insisted that claustration be enforced in his diocese and tried to relieve the resulting poverty of his nuns by appeal to men who had already demonstrated their unwillingness to support women and who had in some cases cheated them. He asked a local noble to intervene for the nuns of Swine who, he said, had been left without counsel when their enemies acted unjustly toward their monastery because the fragility of the feminine sex "needs subsidy," thus reinforcing their helplessness.[12] The enforcement of inappropriate rules seemingly made the regular life a genuine impossibility for many women.

A new nun took the veil and wore a ring to seal her marital union with Christ. The bride was metaphorically empowered as consort of the lord of the universe. In this role, nuns shared the problems of secular women, who were being idealized by poets while losing the power they had formerly enjoyed within their family setting. Thus, in his correspondence with Heloise, Abelard made much of her superiority to him as his master's consort. But in his "rule" for the Paraclete, he appointed the monks' provost as advocate, to serve the abbess as a queen. The "servant" effectively controlled the community resources, though he had to swear "not to consent to oppression [of the sisters] in any form and to guarantee their bodily purity." Heloise was a match for Abelard and for any provost. But elsewhere monks sometimes treated the *cura* as a source of profit, having only a tenuous commitment to the good of the community they served. Nunneries commonly complained that canons and *conversi* fed themselves by depriving the sisters of money and even food. Priors to whom the Cluniacs had consigned the care of their enclosed nuns diverted donations, even of food and clothing, to themselves. The nuns of Feldbach rebelled against their prior in 1297, as did the nuns of Solden in 1311 and Marcigny itself in 1321.[13] The chapter general of 1314 attempted to answer the problem by appointing a prioress to regulate internal discipline. But the prior remained in control of the community's resources. After the monks robbed the refectory of its linens, the prioress led the nuns in the destruction of the monks' choir stools during Christmas Mass.[14] In 1315, nuns of Huy physically fought with the prior of Bertree over the goods of deceased sisters.

The monks of the Gilbertine order were originally brought in to support and protect nuns who were too tightly cloistered to administer their property. Yet, the archbishop of York wrote to the Gilbertine monks of Watton as though their sisters in religion were incompetent dependents:

> We have seen how the nuns in your house, permanently and strictly cloistered from its first foundation, have shown themselves devoted servants of God. This makes it incumbent on you to support them with the greatest solicitude because the fragility of the female sex would threaten them if they were dispersed. Plague has destroyed the animals of those nuns who resided at the grange at Ravensdale and the poor soil has yielded little fruit for seven years. Meanwhile the poor flock looks to your monastery for help which you cannot give them. And because of this you are heavily burdened to divide your own necessities with the nuns. As an act of charity we will assign the church of Hitton near Watton to you with all its appurtenances in present and future so that its fruits will support the nuns to serve their creator in all sanctimony and the fruits are to be used in no other way under pain of excommunication.[15]

Belief in women's financial incompetence has always been an important component of the capitalist gender system. One of the burdens associated with the *cura mulierum* was the fancied need for men to supervise the bookkeeping and conduct the external business of cloistered women. Geoffrey of Vendôme's donation to Fontevraud of a salt revenue was administered at his abbey by monks sent from Fontevraud. Gregory IX ordered that monastic accounts be open to episcopal audit. The archbishop of Rouen repeatedly ordered these accountings in his visitation records and often noted that the abbess "does not care to compute." The abbesses in question, however, may have been moved by a spirit of independence rather than incompetence. In one case, the archbishop sent the prioress of another convent to do the audit. In the fourteenth century, the Godstow Register had to be translated into English because the nuns could no longer read the Latin.[16] But ignorance of Latin did not make record keeping impossible. Godstow was a modestly wealthy monastery, having an income listed at £258 10s. 6½d at the dissolution, and its abbesses pursued a sober if not imaginative financial course. Most of the endowments from the twelfth century remained in abbesses' hands in the sixteenth.

Nevertheless, the incompetence of nuns at running their financial affairs was a standard complaint in the Middle Ages and, until recently, modern authors have also believed it. Where close studies have made some comparison possible, nuns do not seem to have been worse than monks in their managerial abilities. Moreover, earlier critics may have misread the evidence. Nuns were much more intensely involved in capitalist enterprise than they imagined. They made loans and borrowed money, mortgaged land for investment capital and took interest on mortgages they granted to others. This ebb and flow of cash often explained the apparent financial decline of some well-endowed houses. Credit operations fitted easily into a cloistered environment and, however offensive it may have been to their spiritual image, nuns made long-term productive investments. When the abbess of Godstow signed Wycombe church over to two local gentlemen, she kept the church's flax and hemp tithes.[17] Some nunneries capitalized mills and other enterprises or operated them after receiving them as donations. In large-scale credit transactions with local businessmen acting as their agents, they acquired a variety of properties, including mills for cloth finishing and tanning. The abbess of Clairets pursued properties associated with the growth, production, and distribution of wine.

Transactions on this scale rested on the long-term commitment of the entire monastic corporation, that rational planning economists associate with the rise of capitalism. But an abbess had serious problems predicting and controlling her revenue sources. Willful obfuscation of ownership compounded the vagaries of charity. Theoretically the community controlled all the goods brought in by individuals, but in fact the abbess probably could not invest money from a dowry without consulting the contributor. The ideal of claustration, which increasingly dominated the whole notion of women's vocations in the thirteenth century, rendered their very existence impossible without an assured income. This myth that women could, and should, sequester themselves from economic concerns, supported the whole concept of the *cura mulierum*. The myth of women's financial incompetence may well have been encouraged by women who knew that their eligibility for future donations rested on a reputation for otherworldliness that sat badly with demonstrations of financial acumen. Canonesses and Beguines, who never took vows of poverty and lived on their personal incomes, always attracted popular suspicion and reproach.

Determined to purify his new church, Gregory VII included the vow of poverty in his revision of the old ninth-century rules for canons and canonesses.[18] Nuns were, of course, assumed to have embraced the vow of personal poverty incorporated into Benedictine and Augustinian rules. The entry gift most orders required women to bring with them into the convent was supposed to be absorbed into the community property. But women rarely lost all control of their own property and, indeed, a careful abbess never neglected to keep nuns' ready cash securely in separate bags or chests. The corporate finances, computed for the visitor's audit, hid the "under the table" revenues that provided most of the individual members with running expenses for food, clothing, and other goods. Friends and family supplemented the nuns' income with gifts and entertainments. Theoretically, and often in practice, the revenue from gifts went into the common funds, but nuns usually retained personal items of clothing, books, and furnishings in locked chests, for which visiting bishops constantly rebuked them. Without these personal emoluments, it is plain from account books and visitation records, most convents could not have maintained even the relatively modest numbers of nuns who depended on them.

By the end of the twelfth century, the men who had undertaken the *cura* agreed that it required that women be secluded from public money-making activities. Women were neither to make money in the marketplace nor to beg it on the street. The alternative generally adopted was to enter the cloister with an endowment sufficient for self-support. The refined sensitivities of canonists, however, came to equate entry gifts with simony. In 1215, the Fourth Lateran Council specifically associated it with women: "since the simoniacal stain has infected so many nuns to such a degree that they scarcely receive any as sisters without a price and then seek to palliate their crime by a pretext of poverty, we prohibit entirely that this be done henceforth."[19] The council sentenced the receiver and the received to be transferred to a stricter monastery for perpetual penance, a punishment obviously designed to place a double burden on the unoffending monastery. In 1236, Gregory IX ordered the bishop of Amiens to send the "simoniac" nuns of Villencourt to stricter houses. The bishop of Lincoln received a similar order in 1239 but relented when the designated houses objected to the cost and burden of being used as prisons.

None of this legislation had any practical effect except to cast a shadow on the profession of nearly every nun in Christendom. In 1225, the Premonstratensian order openly, and perhaps maliciously, demanded dowries from its unwelcome female applicants. In 1273, the Dominican order refused to admit any woman who could not support herself in a cloister. The bishop of Mainz ordered women to cloister themselves at home and live by handiwork if they were too poor to dower themselves into a cloistered community. Sporadic efforts were made to enforce the law by popes and bishops who never seemed to understand the location of the problem. Honorius III suggested that simony could be eliminated if each candidate were approved by the entire chapter, preventing favoritism in selecting novices. The Cluniacs stated, in the chapter of 1317, that limiting the number of nuns would prevent the poverty that led to simony. The Augustinian provincial synod of 1310 determined that convents should be open to all but allowed an applicant's friends and families to give alms to the community.

The pious fiction that endowments were spontaneous offerings of alms made rational calculation of the amount of an entry gift virtually impossible. Probably each convent had some standard estimate for entry fees, but they varied wildly. In England, Nun Monkton in 1468 was said to require an entry fee of £3 from everyone. At Godstow, in about the same time and place, £13 6s. 8d was mentioned as a usual amount.[20] Other factors also interfered with rational accounting. Many houses were probably little more than houses where women pooled their narrow resources. Dominican preachers moving into Germany in the early thirteenth century encountered groups of women living under simple rules of their own making. "When any of the ladies wishes to come to them she presents all her movables and immovables and never cares about them again. She remains with the order for a probationary period and if the convent displeases her she departs with all her goods; if she displeases the convent, they return everything to her. If she apostatizes after some years of profession, she can have nothing back except by grace."[21]

The money upon which a woman's livelihood rested could not be so lightly absorbed. The archbishop of York ordered the prioress of Sinningthwaite to accept the final vows of Mathilda of Grimston, who had been wearing the white veil of a novice for too long. After every nun in the house told him that Mathilda was unwelcome, he finally agreed that she should go elsewhere. But the cost of her habit, her entry feast, and her admission fee to table had to be fully refunded, without regard to her expenses during her long novitiate.[22]

The process of receiving new members, like a marriage, involved negotiations and contracts. Donors as well as nuns kept a sharp eye on their money. A woman entered Ronceray in 1080, where her niece was already consecrated, offering the income from a woodland. Her nephew disputed her gift but compensated the convent with the lump sum of £10, which he refused to pay when his aunt died. Then, when his second daughter entered the same convent, he returned the £10 and dropped his claim to the woods. Let us hope that the added meadow and his waiver of customary "sales tax" on certain goods compensated the convent for its legal expenses.

The question of new recruits was therefore more complex than one might imagine. Even when dowries supplied adequate support for individual nuns, they did not defray the expenses of maintaining the infrastructure, which often made the recruitment of additional nuns an aggravation to a convent's economic problems. Bishops sometimes refused to consecrate novices where resources were overburdened. In response, individual nuns shared their prebends with protégées, often called "nieces," while they waited for admission. In 1259, the archbishop of Rouen rejected the "nieces" of various sisters at Saint-Saëns. Five years later, however, the community had increased by four nuns.[23] Obviously, they could not or would not refuse the claims advanced by their sponsors.

Some donors to nunneries thought only of the immediate problem of support for female dependents rather than long-term endowments. They frequently attached more binding conditions to gifts for nuns, preferring annuities or assigned revenues, which had less immunity to inflation and did not lend themselves to economic enterprise in the growth market of the thirteenth century. Grants of land or income-producing properties were often stipulated as support for an individual while she lived, only to revert to the community with her death. In practice, many nuns turned the prebends thus created into hereditary incomes so that they could will their place in the convent to a "niece." Friction among women with different standards of living tore at the communal fabric. The archbishop of Rouen found houses that could not support a refectory for common meals. Not surprisingly, such groups of independent boarders did not hold chapter meetings.[24]

Perhaps it hardly mattered to them who held office but certainly they formed factions who socialized together. Wealthy nuns were always prepared to treat their friends to gifts and suppers. They may also have bonded with sincere friendships and mutual undertakings. The mystic Beatrice of Nazareth, who was so poor that she had to borrow a veil from one of the other nuns to receive visitors, was maintained by her community as a common asset. Other narrative sources seem to indicate that women in difficulties found welcome in women's religious houses. The hospital of Mont Cornillon, though governed by a prior, put a prioress in charge of the women. The first prioress donated her own fortune and the dowries of her two daughters, whom she brought in as child oblates. In 1237, when one of the daughters, Juliana, succeeded, a new prior attempted to seize their wealth and title deeds, causing the nuns to flee with their documents. After they had been virtually homeless for nearly three years, the bishop of Liège restored them. In 1247, however, the deposed prior returned and Juliana and her companions were hounded from one monastery to another, begging for food and shelter, until they took refuge in the beguinage of Namur. Imène, abbess of Salzinnes, finally rescued them and gave them a house and pension.[25]

More modestly, the chronicle of the miraculous graces visited on the nuns of Unterlinden notes that they added several poor and dowerless nuns to their community of noble ladies.

The system contributed to the conversion of the convent's goods into something like negotiable shares in a cooperative venture. Occasionally ladies held prebends in more than one house. Such incomes often shrank, owing to inflation, leaving the community with the problem of apportioning the property to assure that no more nuns were admitted than the institution could support. In a single house, the prebends were sorted into bundles to support the expenses of officials and individuals. There must have been a great deal of brokering as individuals bought additional prebends to maintain their standard of living or sold out when they needed ready cash. At Remiremont, 36 of a total of 144 prebends were held by the abbess and 79 by the ladies in packages of 2 to 5 each. The titleholder could share these with "nieces" whom she personally sponsored as novices, or she could keep them all for her sole support. The remaining prebends went to the canons, officers of the chapter, and perhaps general expenses.

Harmonious communities may well have made joint investments or agreed to assessments for capital improvements and repairs. Agreements were certainly not guaranteed. The abbess and chapter at Nivelles quarreled over the assignment of revenues from the conventual mense and the maintenance of the walls. Throughout the thirteenth century, as count and commune steadily attacked the convent's corporate rights, the nuns fought the abbess over the division of revenues from temporal jurisdiction. At times the abbess suspended the prebendial revenues and the chapter interrupted the divine offices in retaliation. At one point the abbess and chapter even required outside arbitration over the distribution of cheesecakes. In 1286, the chapter complained that the walls were fractured and that people turned their animals out to graze within the cloister, coming and going at will. Moreover, the clocks were all broken and silent, and taverns had opened all around the abbey. In 1287, the abbess fixed the clocks and the buildings but claimed that the chapter was responsible for the walls.

The regulation of prebends, an ongoing cause of disunion and strife within many communities, caused much official concern in the thirteenth century. The nuns of Gandersheim complained that their prebends were not respected. The abbess of Swine was accused of diverting funds from the other nuns. The process sometimes facilitated secularization. German abbesses got imperial support in diverting community property to themselves, which they then parceled out as benefices to imperial vassals. The abbess of Saint-Antoine near Paris used the conventual mense as prebends for impoverished noble nuns when the entrance of wealthy patrician women, particularly the spectacularly endowed Blanche of Paciac, put the whole establishment on a sounder footing. Neither Blanche nor any of her patrician sisters were chosen to hold office in the community, but their wealth clearly established the common endowment until the French Revolution.

Women did not make their careers in the broad reaches of an order as monks did. They tended to enter houses close to their homes and to maintain an active role in the neighboring community. Nuns entertained their families and friends within the convent on a regular basis.[26] They also returned the visits, particularly when the family had need of their personal services. Indeed, there is some reason to believe that the main purpose for the endowment of women's communities was to support their economic, social, and charitable activities within that tight local network of influence. Several ladies from the same family often resided in the same convent. One noble German girl named Mathilda entered the Cistercian convent of Fusinnich and soon rose to abbess. Her widowed sister Aleidis joined her there and became prioress. Another relative who had fled from her parents in Utrecht in male disguise joined them, and a third sister was caught attempting the same feat and forced to marry.[27] Donations to Shaftesbury show a pattern of endowment and recruitment for the daughters of local landholders. In the late twelfth century, the sheriff dowered his daughter as a nun with land he had previously wrested from the abbey. Local families repeatedly served the abbess as seneschal and steward while their daughters became nuns.

Women of local magnate families might be imposed as abbesses on the community even without prior service as nuns. Controlling the goods and powers of the community, these abbesses had considerable political power. Even in England, where the monarchy was generally strong and stable, a patron's rights tended to be combined with the rights and responsibilities of a feudal lord to license elections and consent to the results. The king of England prevented a traitor's daughter from

being elected abbess of Shaftesbury fearful of her control of the convent's knight service. Instead Henry II's half-sister Mary strengthened
its links to the crown and the monastery prospered until the dissolution.
In other cases, self-proclaimed guardians used convent goods as their
own, even moving into the estate with their families, servants, and
animals. The duke of Lorraine seized one house, with the nuns' grain
and beasts for taxes. He dug a lake on their land and fortified one of
their buildings. An abbey's relationship with its "protector" was complicated by the abbess's own political connections. At Gernrode, imperial
charters gave the abbess full control over appointing the advocate. But
by the thirteenth century, all the abbesses came from the noble Anhalt
family and the advocacy gradually became a hereditary perquisite of the
same family.

As men vied for the wardships of wealthy heiresses in the secular world,
so they were eager to undertake the *cura* of wealthy nunneries. When
they saw nothing to exploit, however, they registered long complaints
against the burden of women. A bishop's care of the orphaned establishments whose buildings were in disrepair and whose nuns were going
into debt to feed themselves tended to be brusque. Some nuns received
permission to break their claustration to beg for the necessities of life.
Veronica de Binasco, for example, led a double life combining exalted
mystical contemplation with begging in the city and environs of Milan
to support her community.[28] Fourteenth- and fifteenth-century guides for
recluses advised that alms could be collected more easily in a city.
Gertrude of Delft, a Beguine so poor that she depended on a local
farmer's miraculous inspiration to provide a piece of bread and cheese,
enhanced her begging by singing with her companions on the town
bridge.[29] Bishops sometimes went so far as to grant impoverished nuns
the exemptions they denied to wealthy houses. Letters of indulgence
forgiving tithes for female houses and episcopal letters supported fund
drives by houses suffering dire poverty. Bishops occasionally even gave
up their right to charge the nuns for the expenses of their visitations.
But their most common response was to try to limit the number of such
women in their care.

In 1249, Eudes of Rouen visited the small convent of Saint-Aubin and forbade the nuns there to take novices without his permission. He complained about gifts from friends and threatened to send them back to the world if they did not observe community of property. Five years later, he attempted to impose uniform habits on them instead of the clothing given them by friends. Then he complained that they had no parish priest and neglected the sacraments while still entertaining friends and family in the convent and simoniacally receiving new nuns. By 1256, he had become so disgusted that he deposed the cellaress and threatened to deprive the nuns of their veils. That year the nuns were a thousand pounds in debt. The new parish priest the archbishop had sent them was living in their house and they had no provisions. They pleaded that they could not afford wine for communion. The roof of the main monastery leaked so badly that they were driven into the outbuildings, and the nuns were quarreling over the distribution of eggs from their privately owned chickens. The archbishop scolded them again in 1267 because three nuns were out of the house working in a vineyard, but he noted that their debts amounted only to thirty pounds and by 1268, though he was still complaining, the women had somehow reduced the debt to eight pounds.[30]

What disturbed the bishop was not that women were working but that they were doing it in public. All the rules prescribed domestic labor, though it is likely that the grander choir ladies confined themselves to administrative and liturgical work suitable to their station. But the cloistered Gilbertine women made all the community's clothing except the men's underwear. The monks brought food to the window and ordered the day's meals from the cellaress, who then supervised the nuns in cooking for the whole community. The lay sisters brewed ale, sewed, washed, spun thread, and wove wool. Cleaning, cooking, sewing, tending the sick, and a thousand associated household chores had to be undertaken by some of the community's women whether nuns, conversae, or servants.

Moreover, from the time of Caesarius of Arles forward, it was assumed that nuns would work for their livelihood, preferably at enterprises adapted to a cloistered life. Urban industry provided work for local cloisters and beguinages. As expected, they raised sheep for wool and worked at every level of the cloth industry. Although a surprising number of German Beguines were dowered daughters of the city patriciate, many supported themselves by handiwork. In many cities, notably Strasbourg, Beguines regularly worked in industry, and indeed the beguinages were primarily cooperative communities where working women pooled their resources. Houses that prided themselves on a high level of spirituality sought ways to combine work and prayer. At Töss, all the nuns took up the common labor of spinning. Dominican nuns at Unterlinden made constant reference to the workhouse as a central part of their lives. Sister Gertrude of Colmar prided herself on her fidelity both to divine offices and to the common work.[31] Anna von Klingenow continued to spin even when bedridden, meditating on pious sentiments she had engraved on her distaff.[32] Even on her deathbed, Clara of Assisi had herself propped up so that she could continue to inspire her sisters to labor without cease.

Many monasteries undertook small manufacturing enterprises. An English Franciscan house became well known for its rose water. Book production, embroidery, and cloth work of every sort were most common. In Hildegard of Bingen's monastery, the nuns copied books, made liturgical garments, and did other handiwork. From nothing she had raised enough money to build commodious buildings for the inmates and guests with water pipes in all the workrooms. Her administration provided enough for fifty nuns and guests.[33] Engelthal was founded by a harpist in Elisabeth of Hungary's wedding party who gathered the Nürnberg Beguines together to pool their common goods and skills.[34] One sister, Reichgard, was a fine artist and another, Alheit, was credited with knowledge of several crafts, which they shared with the other women.[35] Nuns copied books and did miniature paintings. In the fifteenth century, the nuns of San Jacopo di Ripoli in Florence had a printing shop. Some convents educated girls who did not enter the community, though teaching was not generally considered a suitable function for women.

It is difficult to know how profitable this industry was. In the thirteenth century, women were fairly free to labor, particularly at low-skilled and low-paid jobs like spinning. Franciscan Tertiary rules popular with Belgian Beguines and at least one English house assumed that members would live in their own homes and support themselves by work. A typical rule, that of 1288 from Trier, prohibited begging but encouraged female Tertiaries to seek employment.[36] This new social structure, however, in its every joint and dovetail, reinforced the feminization of poverty. Women participated in manufacturing and trade in a family setting but as the guild system developed, they were shut out from independent access to the training and licensing required for most skilled jobs. It was generally assumed that women would be paid only half the wage given to men on the grounds that they ate less. This put Beguines, who were willing to live a life of severe austerity to compensate, in a strong competitive position against men. In the fourteenth century as overpopulation led to land exhaustion and finally the Black Death, as depression, crop failure, bank failures, and increasing war and internal violence worsened, women's labor was attacked by unemployed men. Guilds restricted the work available to them and subjected them to guild standards without guild privileges.

To make the problem of financial security infinitely complex, money-making enterprise might well be counterproductive for nuns. The rents that replaced direct exploitation of estates were often disguised mortgages, interest on loans, and therefore a circumvention of Alexander III's usury legislation in 1179. Sensitive nuns felt that the usurious practices men could sometimes get away with were particularly dangerous to them. The reformer of the Franciscan order, Colette of Corbie, demanded her convents refuse any money even mildly tainted.[37] Birgitta of Sweden (or Jesus speaking through Birgitta) made elaborate precautions to ensure that no usurious or simoniac money taint her order.[38] Aside from a laudable desire to be virtuous and obedient to canon law, this reluctance to handle "dirty" money probably arose from the peculiar vulnerability of nuns in respect to ecclesiastical revenue. Donors wanted spiritual profits from their investments and therefore judged the moral reputations of nuns severely. As a result, nuns had to bow to donors' concepts of what feminine holiness involved, which certainly meant that they had to curtail the amount of work they did in public, particularly work intended to earn money.

Immoral priests could still deliver good sacraments but nuns had to be personally holy to help their patrons. The pastoral services performed by priests in connection with the sacraments were relatively immune to the effects of simony legislation. Critics might call it simony when confessors accepted "alms" or even assigned penances that obligated the sinner to pay for masses said by the confessor. But the church firmly held that no personal sin could affect the sacerdotal powers of the clergy. Accusations of simony attached to their entry gifts threatened to invalidate nuns' spiritual services, which lay outside the sacramental area and therefore were not protected by the threat of Donatism. Being barred from Holy Orders, nuns were limited in the spiritual services they could offer potential donors. In England, at least, they usually shared their churches and services with the surrounding parish, the nuns occupying the west end (unlike monks who took the east end and blocked the participation of the parishioners).

Burial rights and the related advantages of possessing relics were the most important staples in the sacred economy. In 1156, Hadrian IV gave Heloise permission to inter charitable lay people in the nuns' cemetery at the Paraclete, a popular money-raising device to give them the benefits of monasticism in death. In the last year of her life, Hildegard of Bingen braved an interdict to keep the body of an excommunicated young man in consecrated ground, arguing that he had received the sacraments on his deathbed and Hildegard had seen in a vision that he was in heaven. Burial rights acquired further dimensions when the body was a blessed one. Abbess Petronilla insisted on moving Robert d'Arbrissel's body to Fontevraud from Orsan, where he died, and entombing it in the main church despite his modest wish to be buried in the monks' cemetery.

Relics drew many pilgrims. At Jouarre, a hospice for guests and pilgrims was established under the abbess Mathilde de Coucy. Its position as a devotional center was heightened in 1111, when the abbey acquired the relics of Saint Julle, a virgin martyr of Troyes, and of Saint Pelagia, the repentant sinner; by the thirteenth century a great fair had grown up around their feasts. The reforming abbess of Faremoutiers, Rissende, organized a tour to raise funds for rebuilding the convent after a fire in 1140. The nuns carried several of their relics of Saint Fara and the head of Saint Agnes to various places. At Tours, several miracles were attributed to this traveling show, and the monastery's debts were cleared. Public rituals also advertised the presence of nuns in a city's spiritual economy. In the thirteenth century, the nuns at Frauenmunster in Zurich paid handsomely to maintain their prestigious place in the city's Palm Sunday processions, escorting the figure of Christ on a donkey back to the great church.[39]

Personal virtue, mystical insights, and spectacular piety thus became important items in the community's economy. Gertrude van Oosten waited with other Beguines in the parish church at Delft while her patron's army battled on the Meuse. When she knew that danger threatened, she said: "Sisters, now is the time for prayer and great need because at this moment a great battle is being waged on the waves of the Meuse." And when she perceived that the battle was ended, she said: "Sisters, praise the Lord, for we have obtained our prayer and the battle is over."[40] On several occasions she took credit for saving Delft from the flooding Rhine by praying with her fellow Beguines.[41]

The knowledge that families spared the expense of finding a mortal husband for their daughters by entering them into religion whether they were suited to it or not had a severe negative effect on nuns' ability to attract support. Bernardino of Siena summed up the accumulated opinion of several centuries when he characterized the unmarriageable girls put into convents as the "scum and vomit of the world." William de la Pole left money to endow a house of Clarisses in 1366, but his son canceled the license in favor of a Carthusian house because he thought men would serve God with more vigilance than women. The community that finally settled at Engelthal was endowed by a nobleman grateful to them for nursing his only son. He made his gift of land and money contingent on their cloistering themselves under the Benedictine rule, however. This condition was not good enough for a second patron, who was distressed because his holy ladies were only "nuns." He had to be comforted by a dream vision of a heavenly voice saying, "Nuns are suns."[42] Despite this endorsement, the convent soon sued for entrance into the Dominican order, whose master was so struck by their austerity that he ordered other cloisters of the order to follow their example.[43]

In the fourteenth century, German nuns sometimes published records of the spiritual assets of their communities. These probably helped to attract donations to the communities beyond the rather meager dowries of the sisters. Thus, we sometimes hear that the very convents most distinguished for their austerity were able to provide generous temporal alms. Katherine Guebeswihr, chronicler for the strictly enclosed nuns of Unterlinden in Colmar, contrasted the oppressive greed of their "protectors" with the provident grace that enabled them to prosper and give charity to others. In 1282 during a famine at Colmar, they fed 1,600 poor people for six weeks even though the prefect of Alsace took eight tonneaux of wine from them by force that same year. In 1288, King Rudolph's son lodged with a hundred horses in their court, but the following year they completed the third wall of their cloister. In 1294, when a new disease struck the country, their charity rose equally to the challenge.[44]

The poverty of the sisters, particularly when combined with charity, exerted a powerful attraction in donors. Elspeth Stägel maintained that at Töss, the sisters kept extra habits and other things that friends gave them as gifts in the community as common goods.[45] A widow who had entered the convent in comfortable circumstances eventually reduced herself to beggary, eating and clothing herself from the common store.[46] Elsabet von Cellinkon was raised at Töss, so poor that she had no money to buy what the other children got in the refectory.[47] Once, when a sister went around the convent collecting alms for the poor, she gave the kerchief from her head, saying, "This is worth a dollar." But when she was older she gave away all the money she earned through writing for a life-size cross for the convent chapel. As a child, according to the nuns who wrote her biography, Clara da Gambacorta could not be restrained from giving away everything she got her hands on, even passing her own clothes through the window. As a Dominican prioress, she diverted donations to her convent for the maintenance of a foundling hospital. Beguines stripped themselves of their property giving it directly to the poor and then struggled to sustain themselves and their companions by manual labor.

Charity thus became associated with self-mortification. Obviously, the immediate advantage of the austere life was the saving of food, money, clothing, and other goods, which could be distributed to the poor. In addition, cloistered nuns were especially generous with spiritual alms. Even when their deprivations did not produce a tangible surplus, they were accumulating vast capital assets in the spiritual economy. A widow at Töss, Ita von Sulz, gave away her entire fortune and then deprived herself further by pouring cold water over her food and choosing the food she liked least. When she had exhausted all the money at her disposal, Yvetta of Huy continued to put herself among the almsgivers by adding her self-inflicted sufferings to her store of alms.[48] In the thirteenth century, women turned their sights on purgatory as an appropriate arena for their patronage. The belief that prayers could be offered for the relief of specific individuals, living or dead, became highly systematic in this age of double-entry bookkeeping. As it became a more familiar and conventional part of the spiritual repertory in the late thirteenth century, prudent people with an eye to their salvation invested in prayers for their souls much as they invested in earthly securities. Beginning with Christina of Saint Trond and Lutgard of Aywières, around 1200, women became specialists in the economy of suffering. In their cloisters and recluseries, they undertook heroic self-mortification, reporting regularly on visions of souls thanking them for their salvation from hell. Lutgard, indeed, had the satisfaction of granting her assistance to the deceased Innocent III, who begged her to save him from suffering in purgatory until the Last Judgment.[49]

Fathers were often the first beneficiaries of their daughter's holy generosity, perhaps indicating that there could be no simony attached to her endowment. Aemilia de Bicchieri, prioress of a Dominican convent in Vercelli around 1273, introduced a penitential routine for the entire community, restricting drink as well as food between meals for all her nuns. The happy result was revealed in a vision of a dead nun who announced that all the drinks voluntarily forgone on earth were given to her by her angel to extinguish fires in purgatory.[50] Through this means, convents recovered much of their early importance as focal points for depositing spiritual wealth and then dispersing it, not only to the immediate patrons of the community but to the anonymous poor who thronged purgatory. Aemilia's own fasting and mortifications were specifically connected to the alms she was able to send out from her closed convent to the poor.[51]

Smaller and poorer than the great monkeries, nunneries seem to have been dedicated principally to the material and pastoral service of the nuns' families and friends. They did not enjoy spectacular careers in the schools, the professions, and the hierarchy. But neither did they deserve to be sloughed off as the useless vine that takes its strength from the mighty oak. When their prayers and mortifications are added to their other services, it may be surmised that many fathers saw Christ as a desirable match and placed a high value on the spiritual profit his daughter might bring him. The clergy tended to complain much about the burden of the *cura mulierum*, but perhaps envy informed their complaints. Many secular people and many nuns may have translated their situation as the care of women for others. The sisters of Töss competed regularly with one another to reduce themselves to poverty and to increase their spiritual offerings. Mezzi Sidwibrin, a sister who was not only poor but feeble-minded, had little to contribute but her industriousness at the common work. "And so she sat and spun and did it devoutly so that she sat and spoke with our lord as though there were no one there but she and he. She would say, 'Lord, I will dedicate every thread that I spin, so a soul rises to you,' and then the tears ran freely down her cheeks."[52]

11

Disordered Women

A PASSION FOR ordering characterized the twelfth and thirteen centuries. The loose social divisions of the early Middle Ages, porous and easily penetrated, gave way to precisely defined, licensed professions. Costumes, manners, communal activities, and legal privileges marked their boundaries. The wide spaces on the gender continuum where collaboration, blending, and role reversals could occur among women and men who had forsworn sexual activity were gradually occupied by men alone. As monks bonded ever more closely into the ordained clergy, the gender gap that separated them from nuns widened. The Benedictine and Augustinian rules, which had governed monks and nuns alike for centuries, were elaborated and modified in the name of "reforms" supported by coalescing orders, each claiming to have recovered the purest form of the original monastic vocation. As time went on, separation from women became the hallmark of this purity. Some monastic writers denied that nuns had ever been true yokemates with monks, and others confessed that the deteriorating moral standards of their own age did not produce men heroic enough to withstand the temptation of propinquity.

Ecclesiastical authorities, who always frowned on double monasteries, encouraged paired and mutually dependent communities to draw apart. The apparent spontaneous blossoming of autonomous women's houses in local archives probably documents the separate endowment and institutional recognition of female communities once attached in some informal way to monkeries. In other cases, small communities of hermits or canons who had originally acted as chaplains and general supporters to nunneries broke off, sometimes simply to go their separate way. Occasionally, they succeeded in getting control of the original endowment and subordinating the nunnery to their "protection."

Outbursts of misogyny exaggerated the dangers of contact with women; impulses of genuine affection prompted fear for women. The secular clergy, headed by the pope, understood the danger but adamantly insisted that nuns be supervised by men. No branch of the clergy could escape the *cura mulierum* (or, strictly speaking, *cura monialium*), though both monks and bishops complained that it drained their energies and resources. Meanwhile, science itself proved that women could not be easily kept safe from their own weak natures. By the end of the twelfth century, the orders were trying to exclude women as far as possible, but the pope was equally energetic in demanding that they bear their share of the burden. Ultimately, they settled for women's institutional invisibility by inserting strict claustration into their rules. A turntable for passing material objects back and forth without physical contact was widely adopted for the outer gates of convents along with a grille to separate nuns from visiting relatives or friends or even confessors.

Practically, this isolation would have made nuns a genuinely insupportable burden. However, cloister was more a state of mind than a physical imprisonment. Despite legislation to the contrary, the nuns were readily available to family, friends, and potential donors. Nunneries tended to be on the edges of towns where sisters had access to country lanes and fields. Often the enclosure itself contained acres of park and farmland. Even small recluseries had gardens and windows to the outer world. No cloister could bar workmen, officers of the advocate, bishops, patrons, or, above all, priests whose monopolies ultimately included preaching and the entire complex of pastoral care involved in confession and spiritual counseling. Even the strictest orders were generous in practice. Gilbertine and Cistercian nuns attended their order's general chapter meetings, and nuns of all orders participated to some degree in visitations and other legitimate outings.

If women were averse to cloistering, the sources have silenced them. Men and women alike viewed the contemplative as the most perfect life, and thousands of people considered meditation on and with God their vocation. Many autonomous nunneries still clung to the Caesarian rule as a guarantee of their security and their own purity. Heloise, abbess of the Paraclete, mistrusted the results of propinquity to such an extent that she asserted that she could not eat with pilgrims and guests, as Benedictine abbots were supposed to do, citing Jerome and Ovid about the immodesty of the table. She complained that even female guests could corrupt women with flattery and worldly thoughts.[1]

As the genders polarized socially in the twelfth century, nuns and their male mentors viewed details of costume and liturgy as hallmarks of a refined identity within the contemplative life. Among prescriptions written by men, with or without feminine consultation, one precious work from the literary dialogue between the famous lovers, Heloise and Abelard, gives us a woman's view. Heloise claimed that she could not follow the Benedictine rule because it was insensitive to women's special needs. "Through lack and need of this it is the practice today for men and women alike to be received into monasteries, to profess the same rule, and the same yoke of monastic ordinance is laid on the weaker sex as on the stronger."[2] Heloise wanted a rule that would define her as a woman in particular ways, prescribing dress, food, and daily routine. She claimed, for example, that the male costume prescribed in the rule was inappropriate to women because menstruation made woolen garments impractical next to the skin. She stressed that Benedict himself left the arrangement of the psalmody to the discretion of each house. The recovery of classical science fortified the opposition of male to female with proofs of natural differences, and like other self-conscious women at this time, Heloise customarily utilized the clichés of Aristotelian philosophy stressing the weakness of women compared to men. She complained about the Benedictine diet because Aristotle demonstrated that women naturally eat less than men and are almost immune to inebriation because of their humidity and holes.

Abelard responded by producing a rule modifying Benedictine prescriptions. He particularly wished to reconcile the need for priests with cloistering. The rule for the Paraclete combined an exemplary vision of the parity of male and female vocations with an institutional pairing of male and female communities under the final authority of the provost of monks, who was depicted as the loyal steward of his lord's wife, the abbess-queen (as bride of Christ).[3] His first duty was to safeguard the cloistered meditations of the nuns. While the provost controlled all external affairs, the abbess governed the women, though she took counsel from the assembled chapter in all major matters and a few senior nuns in others. She had the decisive voice as to what the men might impose on the women, but Abelard stated that abbesses who ruled clergymen were acting against nature, "leading them on to evil desires in proportion to their dominance."[4] He referred in passing to the head of his female community as a deaconess, looking back to apostolic times to solve the dilemma of an abbess who was not entirely cloistered, involved in worldly business, and, in Heloise's case, not a virgin.

This associated system never developed. The Paraclete remained a nunnery with a few chaplains and lay brothers serving the nuns. Priests from the nearby male monastery came through a hidden entrance to say mass for the sisters when they were not busy with their own offices, leaving an elderly priest to administer communion after the deacon and subdeacon had withdrawn. The infirmary was arranged so that priests could give the sacraments unseen behind a screen even when the whole convent was attending their dying sister.[5] The abbess of the Paraclete became a successful entrepreneur who followed the patterns of the older proprietary monasteries. Heloise increased the convent's possessions and constructed a fine cloister. A small congregation developed under her authority with three or more daughter houses. Such local groupings distinguished many female houses, informally sharing a common rule and authority but not organized as an order and usually confined to a single neighborhood. Abelard's specification that the abbess not be chosen from a noble family was abandoned. The Paraclete expanded as far as it could in its own neighborhood and then, in 1196, the abbess Melisand had to limit the admission of novices.

Despite pressures to Benedictinize themselves, most canoness houses kept to their own ways and some, like the canonesses of Saint Victor, colonized congregations of daughter houses following the old Cluniac model of houses under the same rule but without the "ordering" paraphernalia of a constitutional superstructure. They often successfully adapted under the double-monastery pattern, which disguised the heavily female elements. The Congregation of Saint Sulpice la Forêt joined convents and priories under a common observance and even held chapter-generals for their priories. Nuns attached to Admont spread the reforms of Hirsau to Paulinzell, Gottweig, and Petershausen, forming a sort of female congregation within a male congregation. Admont was the most prominent center for the education of nuns in the twelfth century. Its most famous pupil, Herrad, later abbess of Hohenburg, 1160–1170, wrote an encyclopedic history of the world, *Hortus Deliciarum*, illustrated by her sisters. The abbesses of these houses did not meet as an order, but they attended cathedral chapters and diocesan synods, which at least kept them actively involved with the larger church if not with an order of their own.

Of all the proponents of the apostolic life, only those at Fontevraud tried to institutionalize its radical syneisactism. Within Robert d'Arbrissel's lifetime, the vision of an apostolic life of physical labor, charity, and preaching shared by women and men, laity and clergy, had vanished. In its place was a cloistered community of women, ruled and protected by *conversae*, served by a subordinate male membership, under a modified Benedictine rule.[6] As a *conversa*, the abbess was exempt from the claustration to which all the virgin nuns were subjected by Robert's rule.[7] She was empowered to receive novices and regulate all relations with the outside world. She could designate male novices for the priesthood and send them to study. The monks were protected from temptation by the strict enclosure of the nuns. The abbess screened all visitors, both lay and monastic, and was ordered to get the residents out of the way when tourists wished to see the cloister. Even the offices for the dead were carefully designed to preserve the segregation of nuns and monks.[8] The sisters were never given the kiss of peace but kissed a piece of marble passed through the window. The cloistered women were forbidden to work outside or even to attend services with the brothers without a grille or wall separating them.

In 1115, during an illness, Robert d'Arbrissel admonished the brothers that they must subordinate themselves economically and socially to the nuns.[9] They took an oath to obey the abbess in all things, but after his death they rebelled periodically against the unnatural tyranny. The subordinate condition of the Fontevrist monks was always something of an offense to the hierarchy. As early as 1106, Paschal II's bull of protection for Fontevraud masked the problem by treating it as a simple nunnery. Despite the generous privileges enjoyed by her order, Petronilla de Chemillé was continually forced to defend Fontevraud's rights and property against Bishop Ulger of Angers, who used the discontent of her subordinate monks to undermine her authority. Most especially, he opposed the abbess's power to appoint priests to her oratories. Nevertheless, the houses of Fontevraud maintained their institutionalized requirement that the brothers existed for care of the nuns. Though she required an impeccable escort, the abbess was expected to travel abroad on the business of her associated houses. Indeed, in Robert's lifetime, the preacher rarely went abroad without the company of his female companions, always the keepers of his apostolic dreams. The first abbess, Hersend, was a daughter of the count of Champagne and Agnes of Clairvaux, while the men, lay and clerical, were probably of a lower social origin. Petronilla de Chemillé, a noble widow, succeeded Hersend as prioress. These stouthearted noble ladies managed not only to maintain their independence and keep their property but also to expand Fontevraud as an order.

Paschal II's privilege approved five daughter houses. Calixtus II in 1119 confirmed the abbess's full jurisdiction over both men and women in spirituals and temporals. Following the lead of the Cistercians, the abbess of Fontevraud held chapter-generals after 1149. The order even spread to England, where nuns from the mother house were imported to replace the "corrupted" nuns of Amesbury. On the other side, houses established in southern France by noblewomen inspired by the apostolic movement tended to lose their attendant monks and therefore the Fontevrist association. They either became autonomous Benedictine houses or, as in the case of Nonenque, ended in the Cistercian order where they were subordinated to their former male partners. Though far from its original apostolic inspiration, Robert's solution worked insofar as the abbey survived, the rule was extended to a series of priories, and the independence and authority of the nuns was maintained against every pressure by its noble abbesses until the French Revolution.

The leaders of the reformed church concentrated their resources on administrative structures to reinforce and define their authority. The papacy developed comprehensive legal machinery to subject the laity to the clergy and to subject both secular and regular clergy to the ecclesiastical hierarchy. The Second Lateran Council in 1139 required all monastic houses to adopt either the Augustinian or the Benedictine rule and sought to subject them all to the authority of bishops and ultimately the pope. Monastic orders were organized to resist this aggrandizement through corporate negotiation. Houses with common characteristics grouped together to secure protection and privileges, particularly their exemption from episcopal authority, from both clerical and secular powers. The abbot of Cluny said that by 1200 his houses could boast, "we are one congregation and one order and we should conform in all things."[10]

Cluny had, of course, led the way in hiding the women of its order. In the poor and struggling years, most orders were willing to make common cause with women's houses to establish their privileges. But as their own bonds to Rome became stronger and women were put at a greater disadvantage, they tended to break those bonds or, in turn, appropriate the women's rights, as in the case of Riffredo. Men's houses were consolidating to make themselves competitive in an increasingly crowded field. They avoided the inclusion of women who would undermine their claims to heroic austerity and interfere with their sense of solidarity.

The problem of the *cura monialium* stemmed from the larger problem of monasticism's relation to the clerical hierarchy. Male monasticism gradually ceased to be primarily a lay institution as the male Christian population divided into clergy and laity. The secular clergy became increasingly monastic in its commitment to celibacy and obedience while the regular clergy became increasingly clericized, reducing its lay brothers to *conversi*. Religious women shared the subordination of monastic houses as a whole to bishops and papal control but were confined to lay status, equating them with a strictly subordinate class of male religious. If they were successful in generating support from the laity, the hierarchy tended to think that the funds would be used more efficiently by men. If they were poor, voluntarily or involuntarily, they nevertheless had to be supported and directed by men. Otherwise, they might escape the institutional framework of the church altogether. Though bishops tended to take up the supervision of unattached houses, the papacy preferred to incorporate nunneries into the developing orders of monks. Monks were rarely receptive to the *cura monialium*, but the organizing imperatives of the age worked against them. Despite constant struggles between the heads of orders and the curia in Rome in the thirteenth century, a mounting number of women's houses were jurisdictionally classified as members of one or another of the emerging monastic orders.

Competing orders refined their identities to exemplify spiritual perfection. The proximity of women constituted a measure of corruption that nearly every articulate reformer recognized. Even when open scandal failed to erupt, it proved that the rival's standards were low enough to accommodate the weaker sex. The contenders were not always truthful. All of the twelfth-century orders started with female affiliates. Some houses sprang from women's foundations; sometimes women outnumbered the men. But they shaped a history that hid the fact. Thus, the official Premonstratensian story was that, after an initial syneisactic experiment where the female followers of Norbert devoted themselves to nursing under the spiritual guidance of the canons of Prémontré, their houses split into segregated communities where women were virtually quarantined within their monasteries. Next, female and male monasteries were separated and finally, in 1137, the order suspended female recruitment altogether.[11]

In fact, Innocent II in 1138, Celestine II in 1143, Eugenius III in 1147, and Hadrian IV in 1154 ordered the Premonstratensians to give adequate maintenance to their women members, noting that they had received a large part of their property from them or from friends on their behalf. Although the men of the order took vows of poverty, they retained their own incomes. They could buy, cultivate, and lease lands under papal protection while exempt from papal taxation. The Premonstratensian convent of Averbode was founded about 1134 by an aristocratic couple for their daughter, who took the habit there. The original Premonstratensian community at Oignies consisted of women and men who were relatives. The second generation of monks evicted the women from their common property, obliging them to move to the town, where they continued to have meals and devotions in common.

Despite such instances of aggression against women's property, the order complained that women drained resources that ought to be directed to their primary mission. In 1198, they tried to remove women from the order altogether but the women continued to practice their rule and, in the mission fields of the east, their active nursing vocations. Many thirteenth-century convents calling themselves Premonstratensian were only loosely affiliated with the order, founded without its recognition, without submission to abbatial authority or material assistance. By 1240, the order capitulated with a statute limiting female houses to twenty sisters under a *magistra* (a female master) to enforce the decisions of the abbot. He controlled the choice of new postulants, who were obligated to bring a dowry. In 1270, the order tried and failed again to get rid of the nuns.

Gilbert of Sempringham, a typical reforming preacher, failed to recruit men for a new religious community because his demands were too rigorous. In 1131, he reluctantly agreed to supervise seven young women eager to accept his restrictions. Gilbert never intended to join women and men in a syneisactic relationship but concluded that women had to be incorporated into a male order. In 1147, he asked the Cistercians to take on his growing community. They flatly refused to take charge of the women, but the ubiquitous Bernard of Clairvaux assisted him in writing a rule designed to segregate them from the canons who supplied the sacraments and other services. The resulting rule closed off Gilbertine buildings housing the canons from the women and partitioned the church during mass. On Good Friday, two canons entered the nuns' church and placed the cross on the ground. After they had gone, the nuns and sisters entered to venerate the cross. Six brothers carried the "stone of peace" to a turntable so that the sisters could give them a vicarious kiss of peace, a practice introduced at Fontevraud. The porteress guarded the turntable through which she also received the holy water. The Gilbertine canons could see the women only to give them last rites.

The Gilbertines adopted the visitation system that was the hallmark of all the new orders. The master visited each house with two male canons and a lay brother, and two nuns and a lay sister (scrutators and scrutatrices). The rule also provided for sisters to attend general meetings. Gilbert envisioned the whole order as a four-wheeled cart: nuns and monks; and *conversae* and *conversi,* having different but equal roles to play. When Gilbert died in 1189, his biographer counted 700 monks and 1,500 sisters in his order and praised him for "this miraculous unity both of persons and of churches, this unheard-of communion of all things which thus makes one thing all and all things one, in a diversity of so many hearts and of such great monasteries."[12] The symmetry, however, was illusory. True to the prevailing notion that women were unsuited to the active life, Gilbert imposed the Benedictine rule on his nuns and the Augustinian rule on the canons of his order. Before long, the Gilbertine monks, like the Premonstratensians and Cistercians, began to appeal for relief from the burden of women. Gilbert himself was never comfortable with his commitment to nuns, and in later years as his order gained popularity with donors and male applicants increased, he excluded women from his new foundations. Already in the 1160s rebellious lay brothers criticized the mixing of the nuns and canons. The master had the right to summon members to the chapters by name, excluding all others. Though we have no information, it is unlikely that the sisters were summoned after the first years. After the first generation, the Gilbertines ceased to recruit women altogether.

While the secular clergy and the monastic orders struggled to control women's spiritual lives without shouldering the *cura monialium*, nuns went from one order to another looking for entrance. The number of female houses that sprang up spontaneously nearly kept pace with male foundations, and existing houses filled to bursting both in rural and urban areas. As did men, women needed the shelter of an order urgently. The possessions of unprotected houses were fair game to the greedy. The insoluble problem of obtaining the sacraments always hung over women, and unregulated enthusiasts were increasingly viewed as heretics by an unsympathetic hierarchy. The majority of women's houses ended by maintaining the Benedictine or Augustinian rule under the supervision of the local bishops, who were always on the lookout for protectors for female communities. If a nearby male house would accept them, they joined its order or at least adopted its name. Nuns were transferred from houses they had outgrown and recluses were grouped together.

Concurring that the cloistered contemplative vocation most suited women, the representatives of the hierarchy particularly pressed the Cistercians into service to care for them. Of all the monastic communities growing out of the apostolic movement, none was destined to expand so widely or leave so heavy an impact upon the medieval world as Cîteaux. From humble beginnings, the monastery mothered a far-flung family of daughters that still stretches over the continents of the earth. The mystic and preacher Bernard of Clairvaux, whose imprint marked nearly every important event of his age, formed and dominated its charism, the spiritual and physical expression of its identity. The order evolved a constitution, the *Carta Caritatis*, which became a model for all orders by the early thirteenth century, when it was probably completed. Based on the Benedictine rule, devoted to the contemplative life, the *Carta*'s chief innovations were in the direction of binding solitary houses into a single order. The order adapted the visitation system from Cluny. In the 1120s and 1130s it began the practice of bringing representatives from each house together annually in chapters-general. Through this device they could maintain conformity of discipline enforced by visitors who also solidified the network. The chapters-general added statutes binding on the entire order to the basic rule and formulated policy for the whole order in dealing with both ecclesiastical and secular powers. The abbot of Cîteaux could then negotiate for everyone in seeking exemptions, privileges, and other benefits. The resources of the order were at the disposal of houses threatened with outside aggression. Other orders followed the Cistercian model, adopting a common master guided by chapters-general.

These institutional lines were not rigorously delineated in a day. By the early thirteenth century, with the introduction of filiation, they became fully structured. Every house was related as a daughter to a mother house in a series of lineal relationships leading back to Cîteaux itself. Mothers were responsible for the training and visitation of daughters. But the matrilineages thus established were largely mythical: they tended to obscure the folding of houses of independent origins into the order at various rates. Their affiliation obeyed administrative convenience more than any sentimental foundational tie. In the process, women's houses often became subordinated or dropped out of the order's relationships. Many a house founded as Cistercian was effectively kept from the order by lack of a formal filial tie. Cistercians claimed that women could not bear the austerity of their life and installed their female relatives in Benedictine convents at Jully and then at Tart, implying that the Benedictine life was suitably effeminate. Ignoring the presence of Cistercian nunneries already sharing the exemptions of the order, they tried to close their ranks in 1134 by legislating that no abbot could receive or bless nuns.[13]

In 1147, though it had just refused admittance to the impoverished Gilbertine sisters, the order merged with the older and wealthier congregations of Savigny and Obazine, accepting the nuns already affiliated with those houses. The order's purists opposed this step violently and, in a sense, still do through historians who see it as the first lapse from their original purity.[14] Only partially enclosed, these nuns remained free to go out to work and attend chapters. In 1184, Pope Lucius III imposed a stricter rule, but as late as 1194 and even 1220, the chapter-general criticized the "excesses" of nuns who visited Cîteaux and Savigny and joined men in singing the office. An abbess or cellaress could easily gain permission to leave the cloister to do her convent's business. As late as 1240, the Cistercians ordered their nuns to give up their elaborate carriages for covered two-wheel carts drawn by two horses and forbade them to ride horseback unless the path were too narrow to accommodate a cart.

In 1242 the chapter-general allowed nuns a place within the convent for visitors such as patrons and relatives to whom they felt they could not deny entrance. Between 1190 and 1210 many other convents secured recognition in the order and, through persistent lawsuits, defended the interests and endowments of their convents when the order threatened to absorb them. They were not always successful, but the effort was worth the gamble because inclusion enabled them to claim the Cistercian *privilegium commune,* confirmed at the Fourth Lateran Council of 1215, guaranteeing free election of abbesses and immunity of the cloister and its granges from episcopal jurisdiction as well as from universal interdicts. In 1228 the order again shut the door but the pope constantly forced new admissions, while

> sanctimonial religion was multiplied as the stars in heaven and grew up in the great Cistercian order. . . . Convents were replenished, virgins flowed and widows ran and married women with their husbands' consent changed carnal for spiritual matrimony. Nuns from other monasteries changed their habits drawn to the fruit of a harder way of life. Noble matrons, potent in the world, forsook their earthly inheritance and immense possessions, preferring to be abject in the sight of the lord rather than live in the tabernacles of sin. Wise and famous virgins disdained offers of matrimony, left their parents and the blandishment of earthly delights, expensive ornaments and precious clothing.[15]

The order as a whole regarded new female institutions not as a sign of health and growth but as a cancer. In 1213 the chapter-general issued a statute signifying its willingness to recognize "nuns who are incorporated into our order," if they were strictly cloistered with a sufficient endowment supplemented by dowries from every entering nun. Male supervisors, at least in theory, approved professions of novices, *conversae* and *conversi*. They presided over the election of abbesses and had the power to invest the abbesses with spirituals and temporals. Confessions could be made only to designated confessors with whom the nuns were to communicate through a window unless they were sick. Visitations ensured conformity of customs and abbesses were obliged to execute the decisions of male visitors, who were given primacy over female visitors. Visitors tended to limit the number of nuns and stop new settlements.

Even when the order denied their membership, many houses maintained a firm grip on the religious life by claiming its privileges. In 1230, the Cistercians agreed to take up the *cura* for monasteries incorporated de facto in 1213. While prohibitions against new female affiliates were repeated in 1239 and 1241, popes and other important persons continued to press on behalf of specific foundations. Each house had its own historical development. Often the incorporated convent was a community of some age, either an unregulated group like a beguinage or a Benedictine or a Premonstratensian house changing its rule. The order published an incorporation procedure that required a commission of the chapter-general to inspect the abbey in question to ensure that it was established in a suitable place, strictly cloistered, and in possession of sufficient goods for its own support. The order complained of a shortage of monks and lay brothers to undertake the *cura monialium* and accepted novices destined only for that service, who spent their lives in the convent under the authority of the abbess. In 1251, the order secured a bull from Innocent IV dispensing it from further incorporation of women's houses. But where the order would not or could not oblige them, women made their own arrangements with a bishop and adopted the rule, the habit, and the name of Cistercian.

Many convents calling themselves Cistercian existed for decades before ever requesting incorporation. Often they were founded by nobles and rich burghers for their relatives. Helfta, for example, was founded in 1229 by the count and the countess of Mansfeld, who spent the years of her widowhood there. In 1258 when the saintly Gertrude of Hackborn was abbess, the community moved to her brother's estates. The original charter assigned the convent to the Cistercians, and it was first colonized by Cistercian nuns of Saint Jacques de Halberstadt. Sophie von Stolberg, the fifteenth-century historian of the convent and its great saints, said it was always Cistercian though the house was never formally incorporated into the order.[16]

Its confessors were, in fact, Dominican, and one of its trio of famous mystics, Mechtild of Magdeburg, always associated herself with that order. By 1262, it had over a hundred nuns and could send out a daughter house of twelve sisters. Such well-endowed houses had no real need and probably no desire to join the order. Using its name, they could be virtually free of supervision while claiming some sort of share in its privileges. Cistercian foundations for women remained generally proprietary in nature. A noble family could continue to reap the benefit of its donation (however thoroughly alienated) by judiciously exploiting family ties with local prelates. In that sense, the anomalous, unofficial quality of Cistercian nunneries in the twelfth century suited the nuns' families and patrons and falls well into line with the thesis that local ties rather than international networks best delineated their spiritual and material lives.

The chapter-general was the heart of the Cistercian web, the stage on which the great business of the order was played. In 1215, the Fourth Lateran Council imposed the chapter-general system on all monastic orders. It was the one place where an abbess might hope to appeal decisions of the visitors or make a case for the interests of her own house. But an abbess who made the long and difficult trip would likely find herself friendless among abbots more inclined to criticize the behavior of nuns than sympathize with them. French abbesses attended but could not prevent the discriminatory legislation that the brothers constantly passed against them. On one occasion, they loudly protested and staged a walkout. Even when barred from the meetings, they often remained outside the meeting rooms with their nuns lobbying the abbots.

Clearly, they needed some device for uniting against their brothers rather than for entering common cause with them. In Spain, they evaded attendance at the chapters and held their own meetings. In 1190, the chapter-general voted to write to the king of Castile and say, "we cannot force his abbesses to go to the chapter . . . but if they wish to go—and we should advise them to do so—it would please us greatly."[17] The offending women were the daughters of the royal abbey of Las Huelgas de Burgos. In 1188, the abbot of Cîteaux recognized Las Huelgas as mother of the order's Spanish convents at the request of Alfonso VIII and Queen Eleanor of Castile. In fact, monasteries independently endowed by the king of Aragon never succumbed to this attempt at Castilian aggrandizement. Nevertheless, Las Huelgas got control of about twelve houses and their abbesses apparently turned their backs on the male chapters, holding their own chapter-general meetings from 1187 on. There the abbess of Las Huelgas presided and four abbesses of Perales, Gradefes, Canas, and Saint Andrés de Arroyo were designated as her visitors. They were scheduled to meet annually at Las Huelgas bringing no more than six servants and six horses each to be boarded by the abbey. The third abbess, Sancha García, took on abbatial powers to give benediction and preach followed by other abbesses of the diocese of Burgos and Palencia.[18]

The example of Las Huelgas may have inspired the French house of Tart, chartered in 1125 by the founder of Cîteaux, to insist on stronger ties with its own priories. In 1189, the abbot of Cîteaux empowered the abbesses of Tart to call chapter-generals of their prioresses with the abbot of Cîteaux or his vicar presiding. By the beginning of the thirteenth century, these included about eighteen houses in the Burgundy region, at least some of which were founded independently of Tart. The abbess also imposed common discipline by annual personal visitation. In 1290 the chapter-general confirmed the visitation rights of the abbess of Tart, though the terminology suggests two sets of visitations: perhaps the abbess took care of simple and "feminine" problems in advance of the more formal visitation by the abbot of Cîteaux or his delegates. Just like the male Cistercian chapters, the abbesses made their proclamation in the abbot's presence and took steps to correct abuses among themselves and to take important decisions.

This quasi-order was not a success. The chapter-general could assert discipline and restraint on the nuns. It took resolutions in 1268 and 1269 against elaborate dress and food for nuns and *conversae* alike. But it could provide no privileges or powers in return. In 1268, the abbess of Montarlot was deposed for failing to attend the chapter-general for three years. The abbess of Ounans, whose excuses were unsatisfactory and delivered by an impolite varlet, was given penances to be administered by the abbess of Tart. The problem of missing abbesses recurred, and in 1290 apparently none appeared at the chapter-general. The order to meet regularly was renewed in 1302, but after 1308 there is no sign of any further meeting. Possibly, the tightening of cloister in 1298 with the bull *Periculoso* and Clement V's *Attendentes,* imposing male visitors on most nunneries, dampened the zeal of abbesses for attending chapters or visiting their daughter houses, though Las Huelgas apparently kept up visitations through the fourteenth century.

In effect, these efforts to form what might have been a second, female, order of Cîteaux collapsed. In the end, Las Huelgas was disciplined by the pope himself, who was horrified by the independence of the abbess, and Tart failed to maintain its independence. Rightly or wrongly, most houses hewed out a line of their own to solve the problems of their anomalous position within the great orders. Theoretically at least, they were cloistered and dedicated to prayer and meditation. Presumably their numbers were limited by the order's capacity to provide them with the services they needed to protect their solitude. In fact, they often managed their own economic enterprises and ruled *conversi* and clergy assigned to the *cura*. Their subjection was limited by their own enterprise and by the order's indifference to them. Whatever the name they gave themselves, whatever habit they wore, most nuns rose or fell by their own efforts.

This independence, even neglect, was always bounded by the hierarchy's imperatives for control. Orders may have been reluctant to spare the time and energy, but the pope—always concerned with defining and securing orthodoxy—pressed them. Some women seem to have perceived the need for their own unified organizations by the end of the twelfth century. But the way was barred by the Fourth Lateran Council, which prohibited the introduction of new monastic rules and the organization of new orders without papal approval. The apostolic movement, fueled by the growth of a literate urban laity, kept generating new groups of people who brought the monastic vow of poverty out into the world as the core of the gospel. Concern with purity and chastity led to Catharism, a heresy that condemned all fleshly indulgence as allegiance to an evil God. The founders of the great mendicant orders, Francis and Dominic, gained exceptions to the new law largely because of their unreserved demonstrations of obedience to the hierarchy.

The two great founders, like many contemporary sect leaders, also had a marked tendency toward syneisactism, generally considered to be an indicator of incipient heresy. The mendicants, heirs of the apostolic movement, organized a new form of religion tailored to the need of urban society to supplement the overloaded parish system. Their vocations centered on relieving the spiritual and corporal needs of the poor by preaching and practical charity. Vowed to chastity, poverty and, above all, obedience but not to stability, they lived by begging alms from the faithful, taking no thought for the morrow in imitation of Christ. A heavy part of the price they paid for church approval was separation from the aspiring women who partnered and encouraged their idealism.

It is perhaps simply a defensive topos that hagiographers later ascribed warnings to the friars against the companionship of women to both Francis and Dominic on their deathbeds. Francis's friendship with Clara of Assisi was a source of nourishment to them both in their respective battles to embrace the ideal of apostolic poverty. Dominic not only encouraged Diana d'Andalo's plan for a companion order to his Preachers but became a familiar figure in their convents. Clara and Diana, however, were not allowed to become members of the mendicant orders whose active lifestyles were deemed unsuitable for women. Papal prohibitions against new orders balked their efforts to found their own orders tailored for women's vocations. Nevertheless, they left behind the first rules and guiding visions for the autonomous women's orders and communities that would eventually emerge, and their aspirations provided inspiration for the development of the Tertiaries, men and women of a vaguely conceived third order who lived in the world under special religious guidelines.

In 1216, Jacques de Vitry encountered the followers of Francis of Assisi dispersed in small groups throughout Italy.[19] In the daytime, the men went to preach and do charitable works in the towns and villages. The women kept hospices near the town, where they supported themselves in their religious works by manual labor. Once a year the brothers and sisters of various houses gathered together to dine and pray in common. This early glimpse of the Franciscan order contrasts sharply with the later official history, which represents only a male group of disciples tightly bound to Francis complemented by the single shining figure of Clara of Assisi, named for her pregnant mother's vision that she would illuminate the world.

Clara was a heroine out of legend. In full bridal regalia, she escaped from her family to join Francis at his retreat. He himself may have been somewhat alarmed by her haste, but he helped her cut her hair and gave her the penitential habit in which she confronted her pursuing uncle.[20] Her younger sisters, Agnes and Beatrice, a cousin Pacifica, and finally her mother followed so that all the women of the family eventually resided in the sanctuary at Saint Damiens. Thomas of Celano reported that when their pursuers dragged Agnes from the convent, her body miraculously became so heavy that they could not carry her over a stream. Clara chased after them and rescued her sister.[21] Agnes became abbess of a convent in Florence, followed by their cousin Benedetta.

Throughout her life, Clara insisted on fully sharing Francis's commitment to poverty and the apostolic life. Francis, however, was embarrassed from the first by the daring and ardent women who had forced his hand. He commanded the women to accept the Benedictine rule and moved them from one Benedictine convent to another before settling them at Saint Damiens and giving way to Clara's entreaties for a *formula vitae* in 1212. Even so, they still lacked an approved rule several years later when the Camaldolese nuns of Vallegloria joined them. Clara's own lost *formula vitae* of 1215 probably imitated Francis's first rule in depending on evangelical texts stressing personal and corporate poverty. The sisters of Saint Damiens had an informal relationship with the brothers at the Portiuncula. At first, Francis visited them every day, and once they even went for a picnic at the friary. Many sick people came to Saint Damiens and Francis himself had great faith in Clara's thaumaturgic powers. Their life probably resembled the union of peripatetic men anchored by women in hospices that Jacques de Vitry saw in Perugia in 1216. But, though Francis continued to visit until the end of his life, he prudently withdrew from any hint of a partnership even when the sisters complained that they were being imprisoned.[22]

In 1214, when Francis proclaimed Clara abbess of the growing group he was trying to monasticize at Saint Damiens, he was struggling with the pope on one side and his own brethren on the other to establish a rule reflecting his apostolic vision. The tension between institutionalization and spontaneity was resolving itself in new bursts of legislation and theological rigor. Innocent III increasingly inclined to find heresy in any innovative religious expression. Whatever he meant at the beginning,

Francis insisted that Clara obey the Fourth Lateran Council's prohibition against new rules, stranding her in a highly ambiguous situation. Her community was not encompassed in the exception granted to the friars, and Francis himself had judged that she and her sisters could not live their life. She spent the rest of her life fighting for a rule that would reconcile her Franciscan vocation with the claustration he had demanded. Within six months of the Fourth Lateran Council, she was besieging the pope for a privilege of poverty, which she secured from Innocent III just before he died.[23]

Cardinal Hugolino, the future Gregory IX, took a particular interest in the Humiliati, the Poor Catholics, the Dominicans and other groups of women and men practicing apostolic poverty in Italy at this time. He energetically devised rules to co-opt these groups into the orthodox camp against heresy. He gained immediate exception from the Fourth Lateran Council's prohibition of new religious orders for Francis, who impressed the pope deeply with his commitment to obedience to Rome. But, in every case, Hugolino saw the claustration of the women as an index of orthodoxy. In 1219, Francis assured him that the order would not accept further female communities.[24] In 1219–20, he based the "Hugolino" rule, composed for the Clarisses in Florence and elsewhere, on the Benedictine rule, emphasizing claustration and silence. The Franciscan "first rule" of 1221 (actually the second, following a now lost document) ordered the friars to avoid women and never converse with them.

Francis died in 1226, leaving Clara to her lifelong struggle to defend her privilege of poverty.[25] By 1228, she still had a resisting grip on her own house and that of her sister Agnes. When Hugolino, now Gregory IX, offered to absolve her of her vow of poverty, she retorted that she would gladly be absolved of her sins but not of her vow. In 1228, he renewed her *privilegium paupertatis* for Saint Damiens alone, keeping twenty-three Clarisse houses in Italy and four or more in France under his own rule. He forced the sisters of Monte Lucido at Perugia to accept donations of books and estates against their will and forbade them to give them away.[26] In 1239 and again in 1245 the pope confirmed the imposition of the Hugolino rule upon the other Clarisses.[27]

Still, Clara clung to poverty and the idea that sisters served outside the monastery, though neither the curia nor Francis himself regarded woman as eligible partners in the preaching mission. Clara's rule of 1253 (written just before she died) provided for a grille to separate nuns from visitors and restricted traveling outside except for necessary and good purposes, but these included work outside the convent. It insisted repeatedly on poverty, requiring all novices to dispose of their goods as they saw fit and forbidding unprofessed women to live in the monastery, thus compelling the nuns to do the work done elsewhere by *conversae*. But "those who serve outside the monastery" were allowed to wear shoes and were dispensed from the strict rules of fasting. They were warned not to speak much and to avoid conferences with men.[28]

The friars were torn by bloody internal strife for more than a century over the poverty question. Occasionally, renegades determined to maintain strict poverty against the more moderate body of the order appealed for help to the sisters. The brothers were also discouraged from visiting the sisters, a custom included among the charges against Elias of Cortona in 1239. After being deposed as general, he continued his visits to the Clarisses of Cortona and chose excommunication over their discontinuation. Clara also maintained her friendship with Angelo da Clareno, around whom the nucleus of the strict observance group formed. He was with her when she died. When the chapter-general of 1266 ordered the destruction of the "ancient legend" (the original life of Francis extolling his absolute commitment to apostolic poverty) in line with the order's modification of its ancient ideal, Friar Leo left his copy at Saint Damiens and the sisters hid it with their other papers.[29] The monastery and other Clarisse convents in Italy were pillaged and emptied many times, and the papers suffered accordingly, though the nuns succeeded in preserving the crucial poverty privilege of Innocent IV.

When Gregory IX forbade the visits of preachers, Clara sent back the quaestors who managed their temporals, saying she would not keep the friars to care for their bodies if they were to be deprived of those who cared for their spiritual good.[30] Her makeshift rule was based on work both in the household and in the city, as well as care of the sick and begging. She fought the pope for her vow of poverty but apparently took enough contributions to enlarge Saint Damiens to include a dormitory and refectory for about twenty to thirty nuns and a charity hospital. Bedridden for many years, Clara had herself propped up so that she could continue to work, vindicating her right to call herself poor and Franciscan. She and her companions performed manual labor and begged leftover food, preferring broken to whole pieces. Bound to strict silence even when going out to beg, the sisters could preach only by example. Clara promoted greater fasting in compensation for the prohibitions on her active services. The sisters of Saint Damiens sometimes suffered hunger because of shortages rather than fasts, but Clara still demanded reconfirmation of the privilege of poverty on her deathbed in 1253.[31]

Bright as it was, her example was not enough to bind the sisters of her order into a single institution. In 1237–38, Gregory IX imposed a new version of his own rule on Clara and her houses featuring cloistering on the Cistercian model. In 1244, the curia placed a number of the independent communities that had sprung up in central Italy as in the north, Germany, and France, under the Benedictine rule with Franciscans responsible for the *cura*. Thus attached to Franciscan charism, they had no formal tie to the order. Clara tried to keep up some sort of network, as shown by her surviving correspondence with Ermentrude of Bruges on one side of Europe and Agnes of Bohemia on the other.[32] The inspiration spread to Poland, France, England, Belgium, Germany, and finally Bohemia, where the powerful queen Agnes enrolled as Clara's chief ally in her pursuit of a compatible rule. Clara even encouraged Agnes to resist the order's general, Elias of Cortona, in anything that would hinder her perfection as a poor virgin embracing the poor Christ.[33] In 1238, after Gregory IX denied Agnes's petition to use Clara's rule for Saint Damiens, Clara wrote giving her advice about fasting and feast days. Given this lead, Agnes somewhat speciously got the pope to agree to let her make modifications of the Hugolino rule in deference to the cold climate. With Clara's support, Agnes gained the *privilegio pauperum* from the pope in 1240 after a long campaign. He still refused to recognize the new rule Clara had based on it.

In 1245, Innocent IV tried to subject the Clarisses to the Benedictine rule but withdrew in the face of Clara's and Agnes of Bohemia's protests. He ordered both mendicant orders to oversee care of souls and supervise discipline but leave the women free to elect prioress and abbess. Mendicants were to hear confessions, give communion, provide a chaplain for all emergencies, and ensure material well-being. Clara's rule of 1253 insisted that the visitor be Franciscan and requested that the brothers and sisters always share the same supervisory cardinal.

At last, Innocent was forced both to provide a new rule, releasing the

Clarisses from the restriction of the Fourth Lateran Council, and to recognize that they were Franciscans, not Benedictines. In 1253, in respect for the dying foundress, Innocent IV confirmed her own rule but restricted its use to Saint Damiens and a few other houses, which adopted it with papal permission. As documents from the Clarissan house in Milan show, most of her communities could not preserve the privilege of poverty or the life of begging. But the far-flung sisters did not submit willingly. In 1250, Innocent IV warned the English that true Clarisses were enclosed and did not wander as beggars. Similar letters to the bishop of Salamanca and bishops in Italy indicate the existence of a movement of wandering friaresses on an international scale.

In their long struggle to maintain the founder's principles, the sisters had little support from Franciscan friars. Popes expressed concern with the growing reluctance of the friars to share their alms with the sisters. Distracted by their own priorities the friars found the sisters a burden and struggled to free themselves from them in imitation of the Dominicans, who had rejected their nuns in 1228. Alexander IV allowed the friars to stem the growth of the Saint Damiens order at the chapter-general of Narbonne in 1260. The tie of the Clarisses to the Franciscans was finally confirmed in the "Isabella rule" for French and English houses, based on that of Saint Damiens and altered slightly by Alexander IV in 1259. Isabella de Valois (1225–1270) was the daughter of Blanche of Castile and sister of Louis IX of France. She refused marriage, preferring to live a nun's life at court, and took her dowry to a convent at Boulogne after her mother's death.[34] Devout as she was, however, the royal princess and her noble sisters lacked Clara's fierce dedication to Franciscan poverty. Isabella's acceptance of enclosure dictated the Benedictine rather than the Franciscan model of poverty. Her rule required dowries, and individual wills indicate that the nuns continued to own books, cups, and other personal things. Within the monasteries they supplemented their income by embroidery and illuminations; one house made rose water.

Urban IV, in 1263, ordered the friars to take up the *cura monialium* and gave the protector of the two orders power to appoint friars as confessors and visitors to the nuns (though he could use other priests for the work). He recognized Clarisses, or Poor Clares, as a discrete order but did not impose the rule of Saint Damiens, nullifying Clara's long struggle for its approval by issuing his own rule. Agnes of Bohemia (d. 1274) remained true to her old friend and clung to the Saint Damiens rule, but few houses had the resources to defy the pope. Urban's rule governed the order outside France and England, where the Isabella rule maintained its dominance.

By 1400 there were about 400 houses: 250 in Italy and most of the rest in Spain and France, with a few scattered in England, Germany, and eastern Europe. One or two houses may have held more than 200 women but most ran between 50 and 80, with a few numbering only 2 or 3. In all probably 15,000 women belonged to the order. Abbesses were generally elected for three years but some continued in office for life. Some had broad dispensations and one had even inherited an abandoned abbey's privilege, allowing her to perform episcopal functions. Their institutional status remained unstable. The Clarisses lacked the constitutional unity and corporate ties to make them an independent order but they were not incorporated into the Franciscan order either. Abbesses could not attend the chapter-general nor hold chapters of their own. They were strictly subjected to legislation the friars passed. In turn, the order had to supply substantial numbers of men to live with the sisters as chaplains and advisers. But the sisters had to support and maintain a number of lay brothers for work not suitable for the friars.

By the early fourteenth century, no house received approval unless it made adequate provision for the support of all those members. The popes even allowed individual sisters to enjoy "all possessions, goods, and rights which came to them by inheritance and which they would have enjoyed had they remained in the world."[35] Conforming to the much debated practice of the friars, this property was managed by *conservatores*, trustees appointed by the pope to represent them in court, collect funds and fees, and manage their domains. Some of the *conservatores* were lay women, as evidenced at Genoa. But they made all property decisions in consultation with the friars. The sisters who had said so much and struggled so long became silent. Meanwhile, at Saint Damiens they proudly maintained the privilege of poverty. In the fifteenth century, when the memory of Francis inspired his order to make another attempt at the life of poverty, it was a woman, Colette of Corbie, who took up Clara's standard and launched the Observantine reform of female and male houses.

The mendicant charism inspired another pair of ardent founders in the early thirteenth century, Dominic and his friend Diana d'Andalo. A Spaniard preaching against Cathar heretics in Toulouse, Dominic found the lines dividing heretic from orthodox women thin and their presence on either side sometimes entirely accidental. Cathar religion taught that members who hoped to be saved would eventually have to become *perfectae,* perfect ones, by renouncing the sexual activities that assisted the victory of the flesh over the spirit. Raymond VI's first wife, Beatrice of Béziers, left him and took her goods to a Cathar nunnery. His fourth wife, Eleanor of Aragon, became a perfect, which automatically dissolved the marriage and left her goods with her husband. Philippa, wife of the count of Foix and sister-in-law of the famous heretical leader Esclarmonde, headed a *perfectae* convent to which another lady of Foix, the widow of Jourdain II de l'Isle Jourdain, retired. Heretics in southern France, like the orthodox of the north, faced problem of excess daughters, and Dominic converted "certain noble women whose parents had been forced by poverty to entrust them to heretics to be educated and brought up."[36] They complained to him that if they embraced Catholicism they would be paupers with nowhere to go. To house such women, Dominic founded the nunnery at Prouille in 1206, and by 1212 they were enclosed under a monastic regime supported by the crusader Simon de Montfort.

Ironically, Cathar women, accustomed to a doctrine that, however heretical, stressed sexual purity and a strict observance of gender divisions in order to maintain it, seem to have fitted readily into the enclosed Dominican convents where they took refuge after their conversion. By 1216, he had placed them under a modified version of the Augustinian rule devised for the brothers, apparently recognizing them as partners in his developing order. Again, in 1218, Dominic gave the habit to some nuns in Madrid; a year or so later he ordered the friars to abandon their properties to the sisters who had not yet been introduced into the rule for lack of proper housing. In effect, he had determined that in the absence of sufficient resources, the sisters would have to be enclosed in the available buildings and the brothers would have to go out and shift for themselves. In the interim, Dominic urged the women to fast, maintain cloister, and obey, stressing the importance of silence, an ironic commandment for even the most marginal members of a preaching order.[37]

In Rome, Honorius III recruited Dominic to carry out a plan formed by Innocent III for consolidating all Roman nuns in a single enclosed and reformed establishment. He persuaded the nuns of the old foundation of Santa Maria in Tempulo to join his new community of San Sisto. Friends and relatives urged the women to refuse, but after he preached to them all but one agreed on condition that they could take their miraculous picture of the Virgin Mary (supposedly by Saint Luke) with them. Once they agreed, Dominic enclosed them without further opportunity to speak to anyone else.[38] The establishment of Prouille and Madrid suggests that Dominic was particularly impressed by the urgency of the apostolate to women, as some of his admirers have claimed. But neither house was in the order when it was approved by the pope in 1215 and San Sisto, which was established later, was enclosed under the Augustinian rule. Therefore, none of the original women's houses were under the Dominican rule and none enjoyed official incorporation into the order, though Dominic may have seen them as part of his flock.

Primarily, Dominic viewed women as the fruits of his preaching and did not shirk the burden of their *cura*. They could have supported the preachers much as Leoba and her sisters had supported Boniface and his missionaries. With Simon de Montfort's endowment, Prouille provided an economic substratum for the preaching friars who joined Dominic's mission, housing nuns and attendant friars as well as transient preachers, but the sisters adopted Cistercian usages, though a few engaged in exceptional educational work. Sister Cecilia of San Sisto wrote fondly of his visits and his thoughtfulness toward her community. Dominic did not focus on the question of women in his order, however. By early 1217 he had determined to commit the preachers to university studies in Paris to train them to preach "throughout the world." Women, of course, were constitutionally barred from the university and consequently from preaching as well. The decision strengthened the order's later resentment of the *cura monialium*.

The concept of a second order of Saint Dominic originated in

Bologna with the eighteen-year-old Diana d'Andalo (d. 1236). She had already vowed herself to religion when she met Dominic in 1219 and suggested to him the idea of a female order partnered with the Dominicans. With other young noblewomen, she took personal vows from Dominic and began plans to build a new monastery, Saint Agnes of Bologna. Dominic entrusted four friars, drawn from a separate community at San Sabina, with the task of establishing a monastery for them. Between 1219–1221, Dominic personally worked with these friars and spent much time on the female apostolate. He secured the chapter's approval for Diana's foundation in 1220, but her antagonistic family raised unexpected obstacles. In 1221, the year of Dominic's death, Diana took a party of friends to an Augustinian convent to celebrate the feast of Mary Magdalene and put on a habit, refusing to leave. Her relatives removed her by force, breaking a rib in the process, but they gave up after she made a second escape. The injury may well have shortened her life.

Not only did Dominic nourish Diana's spiritual progress, he continued to visit San Sisto and numerous individual recluses. Cecilia, the first of a line of Dominican nuns to record their own history, said Dominic spent his days preaching and doing good works while in Rome, but in the evening he and other brothers visited the sisters and preached to them.[39] The rule he finally provided for Prouille and San Sisto in the last year of his life bears marked resemblance to that of the Gilbertines.[40] Cecilia cited one of Dominic's letters to the newly established sisters in Spain prohibiting their supervising prior from receiving women into the community without the specific approval of the prioress, to avoid strains on their resources. He gave his brother, whom he charged with direction of the sisters, the authority to remove the prioress if a majority of the sisters agreed.

His successor, Jordan of Saxony, was a friend of Diana's and helped her open her house in 1223, vainly trying to get nuns from Prouille to train the novices. But initially he accepted the chapter-general's rejection of her application for admission.[41] Although Jordan continued his correspondence with Diana on ascetic subjects until her death in 1236, and even recruited the nuns at Bologna to pray for the success of his efforts to convert Paris students, he delayed affiliation of the women until 1227, when Honorius III ordered him to do it. Meanwhile, he wrote worried notes to Dominican provincials in Lombardy concerning whores or frivolous girls who cut their hair and took habits without supervision.

In 1228 the chapter-generals of both the Dominicans and the Cistercians forbade further acceptance of new convents. At the same time the Cistercians and the Franciscans raised the wearisome objections that the development of the apostolate of women would absorb and distract their energies, presumably from the all-important apostolate of men. The Dominicans particularly complained that the care of women diverted them from the university studies that were to fit them so brilliantly for their work as inquisitors in the years to come. In 1229 the provincials of Lombardy again tried to bar the nuns from the order, but Jordan protected Saint Agnes (only) from their decision, writing Diana that the prohibition did not cast aspersions on her group. Jordan explained that he intended only to prevent German friars from bringing converts from sinful lives or untested women into the order, which he clearly thought Diana would understand.

In defense of the unnamed German women, we should note that they were probably the loosely organized groups of Beguines and holy women that the first Dominicans found living praiseworthy lives when they began to evangelize Germany.[42] In the 1230s and 1240s the convents of Töss, Unterlinden, and Engelthal, and others, destined to be among the brightest glories of the Dominican order, were incorporated in this informal manner. The Beguines of Nürnberg had been established by a woman troubadour in the wedding party of Elisabeth of Thuringia. When they removed to Engelthal to avoid the interdict on Nürnberg for supporting Frederick II in his long struggle with Gregory IX (1227–1241), a debate arose about "nunning" the community to get monastic privileges. Gregory, as Cardinal Hugolino, had been deeply involved in organizing groups of free-spirited evangelicals under monastic regulation. The women at Engelthal considered the Cistercians first, but in 1244 they entered the Order of Preachers under the Augustinian rule used by San Sisto in Rome. Similarly, the independent community of Unterlinden resisted when the bishop of Colmar tried to assert his authority over its property.[43] The community delayed, saying it had to investigate the exact terms of the relationship, and began negotiations with the order to secure monastic privileges.

Diana d'Andalo wore herself out in the struggle to gain recognition for her community within the Dominican order. Its status was still anomalous when she died. She never fully realized her ambition of founding a second order, nor did her sisters attain full incorporation into the Order of Preachers. As with the Clarisses, various communities of women serving under different versions of the Augustinian rule were bound by a common charism, by the assignment of Dominicans to their *cura,* when they could accomplish it, and by their own determination that, silent and cloistered though they were, they belonged to the Order of Preachers.

By 1242, there was a new general and Gregory IX was dead. The nuns at Prouille and at Madrid complained that the order had abandoned them to secular priests. The chapter-general of 1242 prohibited all friars from giving religious women the last sacraments and acting as their spiritual directors. It forbade friars to translate scriptures, sermons, or conferences into the vernacular for them. It also withdrew the confessor and lay brothers from San Sisto, until Innocent IV (elected 1243) forced it to bring them back. A string of German cloisters followed in 1245, at papal orders, but the order retaliated by giving them incompetent brothers. When Simon de Montfort's third daughter, Amicia, founded Montargis in 1245, she was obliged to embark on a struggle that went on for decades to maintain her privileges in the order. The pope forced the Order of Preachers to take on Montargis and the German convents, but in 1252 they appealed again to restrict their service to Prouille and San Sisto.

Even with reasonably sympathetic generals, Hugh Saint Cher followed by Humbert de Romans, the chapter-generals, to which the women were not invited, responded by stiffening conditions for approval, particularly strengthening claustration and property requirements. Dominican sisters never participated in chapter-generals, but they were not reduced to servants as at Prémontré, nor abandoned. The order made admission difficult, but each nunnery was paired with a friary and governed by their prior supporting the immediate authority of the prioress with spiritual services. Male and female communities sometimes shared farms, cellars, and other facilities. Instead of participating in academic studies, which the friars enjoyed, Dominican nuns worked on community projects, mainly sewing and embroidery, which complemented their choir service. Nevertheless, some of the nuns knew Latin and could even write or speak it, while others wrote impressive works of mysticism and local history in the vernacular. Despite the order's reluctance to receive them, Dominican nuns formed an important and expanding part of the preaching order.

The common theme that runs through the history of the relationship of each of these orders with their sisters is the determination of the papacy to force the orders to take up the *cura monialium* despite their reluctance. Moreover, the shape and end of that *cura* was the same in every case. Nuns did not enjoy the refinement of vocation open to men. Insofar as they might shape a special sense of their Fontevrist or Dominican identity, they had to do so within the conditions of claustration and the contemplative life. By the end of the thirteenth century, the orders had taken on a hefty share of the burden of religious women, but nothing could stem the tide of vocations or family strategies that filled established houses to the bursting point and caused new, informal foundations to burgeon everywhere. Many nuns, Beguines, and recluses still lived in relatively independent circumstances under the jurisdiction of bishops, using a variety of rules, wearing different habits, and devising their own religious routines. By the end of the thirteenth century, the church could not tolerate this "anarchy." In 1298, Boniface VIII, in his bull *Periculoso*, decreed that all religious women everywhere must be cloistered. He stressed the peril of men's inability to resist raping women and women's natural inability to refrain from tempting men. The bull was immortalized in Boniface's addition to the canon law (the *Sext*) and extended to include Beguines, Tertiaries, and other less formally consecrated women by Clement V *(De quibusdam mulierem)*. Although the bulls did little to change the actual daily lives of most religious women, they remained in force and were reinstated at the Council of Trent and again at the First Vatican Council in the nineteenth century.

The final attempt in the Middle Ages to found an order for women centered from the beginning on the contemplative life. In the fourteenth century, with the pope "captive" in Avignon and charges of corruption shaking the entire church, a powerful Swedish noblewoman, Birgitta, claimed direct orders from Christ to reform the church by means of a new order of women. He dictated a rule, complete in every detail from architecture to daily discipline, which she included in the wider body of her *Revelationes*. She limited the community to sixty nuns and made provisions for a sufficient endowment to avert poverty, the nuns were deprived of personal control of their own wealth, with its attendant inequities.[44] Unwilling nuns and oblates too young to know their own minds were sternly rejected.[45] The exact proportions of men to women were outlined in symbolic order.[46]

Fundamentally, Birgitta followed the Benedictine or Cistercian model, but she sought to avoid some of the problems faced by other religious women by reverting to the old pattern of the double monastery. The plan was somewhat risky because double monasteries had again been condemned in the fourteenth century. Birgitta, doubtless, hoped that the authority of Jesus himself would support her argument in their favor as the only means of surmounting the ever pressing problem of the *cura monialium*. Her rule almost obsessively detailed the placement of grilles and turntables connecting the nuns' court to the monks' court and to the world outside, to ensure the strict claustration of the nuns and of priests who would be devoted to none but sacramental duties. Lay brothers would serve consecrated women and men alike in supplying their earthly necessities.

Like a Fontevrist *conversa*, Birgitta herself remained at large throughout her active life but she (or Jesus) failed to make similar exceptions for the abbess of her order. Her daughters Katherine and Ingegard—who actually established the order—were virgins and subjected to its claustration requirements, a mistake that doomed its future as a united institution. Under Jesus' instructions, women and men were to live as equals under direct episcopal supervision, thereby evading the problem of a separate hierarchy within the order and, at the same time, keeping the women free of the brothers' jurisdiction. In fact, within the cloister itself, the abbess had complete authority over all the members and pastoral responsibilities for the women.[47] In a later vision, the Virgin Mary herself soothed Birgitta's doubts about putting a woman over men. In the later history of the order, Katherine of Vadstena demonstrated her clear opinion that the abbess of Vadstena was intended to rule the entire order.

The resulting system should have satisfied the strictest regulations, but Birgitta's scheme was long delayed by papal reluctance to lay aside the pronouncements of the Fourth Lateran Council and the Second Council of Lyons (1274) against the proliferation of rules and orders. Several years passed until Birgitta reported that Jesus said:

> I am the Son of God. This rule which you have heard must be confirmed by the Pope, my vicar, who has the power of binding and loosing. I am he who told Moses I am that I am. The one who was pleased to enter into the body of a human virgin. I am the one who said that I came not to break the law but to fulfill it. I want this rule which was not dictated by any man to be confirmed as were other rules which were composed by men under the same inspiration.[48]

However we choose to read these supernatural pronouncements, this one is particularly interesting because it indicates how carefully Jesus, or Birgitta's subconscious, or the clerk to whom she dictated her visions, strove to reassure the ecclesiastical establishment about his orthodoxy.

Birgitta's campaign to establish her order closely paralleled her campaign to restore the pope to Rome; she had long prophesied that his presence in the city would be the sign that confirmed her visions. In spite of that, the pope would not set aside the ruling of the Fourth Lateran Council against new rules. In 1370, Urban V gave her permission to build two Augustinian monasteries (one for men and one for women) rather than the double monastery of her revelation. She was allowed to add details from her own rule.[49] Birgitta bowed to papal authority, but at the same time she handed Urban a written transcript of a revelation from the Blessed Virgin accusing her "second son" of turning his back on her. The pope was warned that if he ever tried to return to Avignon he would have a stroke. When she was dying, she dictated a final vision in which Jesus forgave her failure to secure approval of his rule and promised that she would appear before him as his bride in the dress he had prescribed for his new order.[50]

Despite the fulfillment of this dire prophecy, Birgitta's rule was not confirmed in her lifetime. She did not like the revision and though the building at Vadstena continued, it was only after her death that her daughter Katherine (d. 1381) was able to obtain its approval as a constitution under the Augustinian rule, respecting the Fourth Lateran decrees. Despite this outcome, the Brigittines have always called themselves the Order of the Most Holy Savior.[51] Rome's insistence on the Augustinian rule, however, crippled the concept of an order. Birgitta had asked that constitutional details be supplied from the Cistercian constitution, but this was not done. Accordingly, though the rule was adopted by the Porta Paradiso in Florence in 1395 and Syon, a royal English foundation around 1400, the order lacked an overarching constitution.

This confusion about the nature of the rule created tension between the monks, who generally favored centralization, and the nuns, who were necessarily jealous of each abbey's autonomy because their enclosure prohibited their attendance at chapter-generals. Syon sought and secured independence from Vadstena and the chapter-generals, though the abbess retained the prerogative to attend if she saw fit. The double system was expensive and difficult to maintain. The monks resented the authority of Vadstena and the local abbesses. In one house after another, the monks died out and the house became entirely cloistered and female.

Even as early as 1378, papal presentations of the Brigittine system undercut its claim to be an order and obscured the primacy of the women over the men. The papal translation of the revealed rule into a bull removed the revelatory prologues that stressed the importance of female control and placed the religious women at the center of the rule. Throughout, the pope referred to separate monasteries of women and men living under the Augustinian rule, which split a community that Birgitta saw as a spiritual whole. When the pope insisted on separate churches as well as separate living quarters, the original concept of common worship was lost. They remained legally united under the abbess but the male head of the monks was called a prior, suggesting autonomous authority. In 1378, the pope added an oath for the monks to a "confessor-general" who never appeared in the original revelations. Thus, subtly the pope raised the community of brothers and the confessor general to legal equality with the sisters and the abbess.

The nuns at Vadstena fought to retain control of their order, but they were defeated by the crippling effects of claustration and the prejudices of the male hierarchy. In 1400, Birgitta's granddaughter, Ingegard, sent one of the Vadstena monks, Lucas Jacobi, to Rome to secure a bull giving her control of the confessor-general. Ingegard was attacked from two directions. The brothers at Vadstena said that she had used Jacobi, whom she had even kept in the women's cloister, as her instrument for their domination. Then, within a year, Jacobi abused the authority she had given him to take control of the Florentine convent. In 1403, the monks at Vadstena got Ingegard deposed by claiming that she had alienated church property. Jacobi, however, continued to advance himself in Rome and was elected confessor-general in 1418. He did not forget his original mission but ordered the brothers in Genoa to admit the sisters for whom it had been built into a house they had occupied for eighteen years. The brothers got the city fathers of Genoa to complain to the pope that "scandals and suspicious might arise as a result of the admission of women into the same buildings with men."[52]

Martin V issued a bull prohibiting the double-monastery system as too expensive and morally dangerous, ordering the brothers in existing houses to leave. At Vadstena, where the rule was believed to have been directly revealed by Jesus, the nuns mobilized the king and queen of Sweden and the king of England, patron of Syon, arguing that the order could not survive separation because the cloister of the nuns required the services of the clergy. They could neither afford to support priests not of their order nor trust them so completely. In the end, like the sisters at Fontevraud, they effectively gave up the idea of partnership, claiming that the brothers had no function without the nuns who, in fact, owned all the property. In that sense, the monasteries were not double at all but essentially women's communities. In 1423 the pope revoked his bull. Vadstena, Syon, and a few other great houses in Scandinavia, the Netherlands, and Germany continued to flourish until the Reformation.

The Brigittine system solved the question of the *cura monialium* by supporting its own contingent of priests. It could not solve the problem of establishing a viable woman's order. Because of claustration, the houses remained autonomous, like the canoness institutes of an earlier age. Finally, the order's expansion was severely limited because the combination of claustration and syneisactism proved far too expensive for any but the most wealthy and munificent patrons. The "woman problem"—the problem of too many women for the inadequate spaces allotted to them in religion as in society at large—remained unsolved.

The development of orders and their clericization fractured the once-solid monastic movement along deep and jagged gender lines. Women were not encouraged to cultivate manly qualities but redefined as guardians of perfect purity. Men who did undertake the *cura monialium* were often enthusiasts, more than ready to dedicate themselves to broadcasting the private revelations and hidden mortifications of holy women. Often they depicted the virgin bride in her spotless purity as an idealized portrait of the soul itself, in a sense, perhaps, their own better selves, kept eternally new and untouched by time and its inevitable corruption. Individual Cistercians were enthusiastic about the spiritual capacities of women and active in their promotion. Even Bernard of Clairvaux, who adamantly opposed any active involvement with the *cura monialium*, endorsed Hildegard of Bingen's preaching, and many abbots asked her to obtain divine approval of their elections.[53] The Cistercian chapter-general itself requested her to use her visionary powers to discern any defects in the order and subsequently issued statutes responding to her criticisms. Marie d'Oignies and Juliana of Mont Cornillon had a special devotion to Saint Bernard, and his order encouraged their remarkable mystical powers. Occasionally brother and sister teams developed between Cistercian monasteries, as can be found in the letters of spiritual encouragement from Thomas the Cantor to his sister at Parc-aux-Dames. A Cistercian monk, Eckhardt, served as amanuensis to his visionary sister, Elisabeth of Schönau. The monastery of Villers in Belgium fostered many close connections between the brothers and holy women in the area.

The same men who claimed that the rules of their orders were too harsh for women were often charmed by individual women who proved capable of extraordinary courage, as Gilbert of Sempringham had been charmed by his original seven virgins. Jacques de Vitry, a cardinal, was the first to publicize the special holiness of the northern Beguines. Douceline de Digne, sister of a leading Dominican preacher, established the first beguinage in the south. Even as the female branches of the mendicant orders were more heavily cloistered, the same orders promoted the idea of Tertiaries. Gregory IX approved Dominican Tertiaries in 1235. They got a uniform rule under Munio of Zamora (1281–1291) and received papal privileges through the fifteenth century.

Partnerships between mystical women and learned friars like Christine of Stommeln and Peter of Dacia, Catherine of Siena and Raymond of Capua, produced a rich treasury of feminine spirituality. Holy women like Margaret of Cortona and Angela of Foligno did not join the

Clarisses, though they lived in towns where convents existed. As Tertiaries, they established intense relationships with the friars. Outside the
material and psychological protection of an order, their lives were often
dangerous, particularly after the publication of *Periculoso*, followed by
De quibusdam mulierem. Nevertheless, in small houses or colonies within
the heart of a city, and in secluded recluseries attached to local churches
or on the outskirts of the towns where the hospices were built, disordered
women pursued the religious life in company with men who saw in them
the embodiment of their own best aspirations.

Many men were moved by the romance of the virgin life and composed inspirational literature for women to read or hear, pondering their
lessons late into the dark and silent night. Even in the day, nuns were
advised to sew or spin continually while praying and mesmerizing
themselves with thoughts of their heavenly bridegroom. Gilbertine nuns
were told to sit with each facing the other's back. The literature written
for their use encouraged romantic fantasy, which presumably reflects the
imagination of the men who wrote it. The *Ancren Riwle* culminates in a
courtly allegory of Christ wooing the soul. About 1230, Thomas de Hales
wrote a "love song" for a "maid of Christ" on how to be a true lover
to her heavenly husband.

They promised a mystical fusion into the divine essence and convinced
some ecstatic women that they had become one with God in a soporific
dream of love. The spiritual marriage, a vision of a formal betrothal and
wedding, rewarded a few rare souls. But always and above all, in men's
writing for women the dominant vision was that of virginity. Like Aelred
of Rievaulx, men who wrote for the guidance of women tended to see
female virginity as a pristine condition that could only deteriorate if not
scrupulously guarded from every source of pollution, making it a device
for the virtual immobilization of women. "Virginity is the gold, the cell
is the furnace, the blower the devil and temptation the fire. The flesh of
the virgin is the earthen vessel in which lies the gold to be purified."[54]

12

$$\cdot \ast \cdot$$

The Alchemy of Mysticism

KATHERINE GUEBESWIHR, describing the ascesis, the training of her sisters in the Dominican convent of Unterlinden, sharply reminded her readers that the real life of a nun did not center on the management of money or the direction of an order or even the care of the poor but on the service of God:

> Some afflicted themselves by laboring through many genuflections adoring the Lord's majesty. Others melting in the fire of divine love could not contain their tears but a more devout plangent voice was heard. Nor did they draw back while they burned with new grace and sought "him whom the soul loveth." One with bundles of twigs, another with knotted cords, or two to three palm branches, or iron chains, or thorny sprays, afflicted the flesh, lacerating it harshly. After matins, during Advent and the whole of the Lenten season, sisters in chapter or elsewhere cruelly and fiercely lacerated their bodies until the blood flowed so that the sound of their whipping resounded through the whole monastery, ascending to the ears of the lord of hosts as the sweetest of songs. Such humility and devotion pleased him greatly. Nor did he despise the tears of the penitent. Some of them, burning with the desire of divine love, kept vigil through the night until matins in urgent prayer, then assisting with solemnity at the service. One of them throughout her whole life, no matter how weak and infirm, never returned to her bed after matins but remained immobile in prayer. Nor was she cheated of her desire but abundant drops of grace infused her. So in all these many ways did they approach the Lord: their

hearts were illuminated; their thoughts were cleansed; affection warmed; the conscience soothed; their minds raised to God. Whence some of them were seen to be elevated in prayer between heaven and earth, the spirit of grace and grave devotion acting upon the earthly body.[1]

No languishing bride nor far-away princess sighing for her knight, a nun was a soldier resolutely guarding the cosmic frontier, a dragon-slaying Martha rescuing souls in peril. Entering as raw recruits, with varying degrees of enthusiasm, the sisters strove under the guidance of their rule and their superiors to transform themselves into a worthy Christian militia. Through self-mortification and the daily discipline of silence, self-control, manual labor, and reading cloistered women trained to perfect their skills.

The soul's lessons were learned upon the body. Nuns rarely saw themselves as passive guardians of virgin gold, preferring the role of smiths hammering its carnal vessel on the anvil. Virginity was a desirable condition, but widows and married women could overtake and surpass a woman who merely lacked sexual experience. Purity might come from the flagellations and fasting that purged the body of every uncleanness. Or it might come by engaging with dirt, taking on the more repulsive jobs in the convent, spoiling one's food to make eating an ordeal. The sick turned their afflictions into wounds of battle, heroically borne to advance the cause of religion. Alice of Scharbeck, a leper isolated from her community because of contagion, systematically treated her lost limbs as sacrificial prayers.[2] The alchemy of mysticism that consecrated women sought to activate involved the transformation of flesh into spirit in a mystery analogous to the original incarnation of the spirit as flesh. Cloistering and self-mortification compressed their physical experience until their minds sprang free, breaking into insight and understanding expressed in visions and voices speaking to all their senses.

We are fortunate to have abundant testimony from the twelfth century on about the spirituality bred by these exercises. Nuns are well represented among the major mystics of the high Middle Ages. Nevertheless, Hildegard of Bingen, Elisabeth of Schönau, Gertrude of Helfta, and Birgitta of Sweden among others can be understood only as figures in a far more complex pattern. They shared common themes with the Beguines, recluses, and Tertiaries who wrote or dictated their revelations to learned churchmen, but the literature produced in convents, particularly "nunbooks" (collected accounts of "special graces," the supernatural illumination or comfort granted to members of the community), put less emphasis on spectacular public demonstrations of individual sanctity. Visions and miracles were clearly meant to inspire discouraged sisters with promises of rewards to come for those who maintain the honor of their holy regiment. The log of daily wonders set a standard for novices and even veterans struggling with the regular discipline of obedience, endurance, and charity.

The struggle for change or transformation, essential to the Christian vision of life, was inherent in the nun's spiritual quest. Young girls obeying family decisions, grieving widows forsaking the world, weary laborers, and incandescent virgins were thrown together to forge a common salvation. They had to learn to live with one another in intimate quarters. Ideally, they had to learn to love one another and help one another. The cloister was designed as a haven where silence bred devotion, meditation produced intense fantasy, and even the simplest souls might sometimes feel touched by a divine finger. Some sources suggest that the results were often far different. But when nuns spoke for themselves, they recalled visions of one another transmuted into gold, crystal, pure light. They saw themselves singing, dancing, flying into the glory of the heavenly choir.

Whether in an order or supervised by bishops, most nuns experienced their community as a secluded space where they had responsibility for their own governance and their own style of life. The Premonstratensian rule of 1143 required that the cloistered sisters be actively supervised by the *magistra disciplina*.[3] At compline, the Dominican nuns of Engelthal went to their mistress and asked how they should spend the next day, and she determined their tasks.[4] The Cistercian Gertrude of Helfta placed her vocation for "care of souls" above the seductions of mystical ecstasy. She strove to teach her flock that disobedience was the root of sin because it resists the order and lawfulness inherent in divine nature.

Abbesses had no easy task instilling this decorum in children or even grown women who often took up their service less than whole-heartedly. Hildegard of Bingen complained that her nuns resisted her discipline and continually disturbed her work with their frivolity. At the other extreme, unrestrained devotion was also a distraction. Nunbooks rarely admit that the sisters succumbed to the attacks of screaming or loud weeping common among uncloistered mystics. Adelheid von Trochau of Engelthal, however, enjoyed attacks of grace which made her so giddy that she would burst into laughter, run around embracing the trees in the woods, and do other silly things. When the mistress called her a goose, she disrupted the choir by flapping her arms and honking until the mistress took it back.[5] Ida von Wezzikon of Töss must have been equally hard to bear as she sought to compensate for her poor singing by the energy with which she bowed, stood, and knelt. The customs of Unterlinden directed that novices be trained to live in the community in an orderly manner, in modesty and silence, avoiding gossip, slander, and contention. Guebeswihr exulted: "So there was among them great peace, concord and charity which is the chain of perfection for that the busy tongue was stilled. For as heat is held in when the mouth of the oven is covered, so silent service retains the Holy Spirit in the heart."[6]

Within the cloister there were long hours to fill and the danger of acedia, the most deadly of all monastic sins, was grave. Salvation lay in discipline and *esprit de corps*, the suppression of individual eccentricities. "Regimental" identity was marked by the peculiar habit and emblems of the orders. The archbishop of Rouen, like many reformers, was distressed when the sisters of an impoverished convent could not wear uniform scapulars and went around in civilian hand-me-downs. Indeed, popular sobriquets such as Gray Sisters and White Ladies distinguished religious by the colors of their habits. The writers of rules for women obsessed over details of costume. White veils distinguished novices from the black veils of nuns. Abelard wanted to distinguish widows from virgins at the Paraclete by their headgear. Birgitta received lengthy communications from Jesus concerning the four-cornered crowns embellished with red tassels that her nuns were to wear. The Virgin Mary, whom the Beguines claimed as their foundress, sent Douceline de Digne a vision so that her Beguines in Provence could emulate the costume worn in the north.[7]

More important than common appearance, however, was the discipline of the *opus Dei*, the daily office. The choir spent many hours drilling to achieve perfect harmony. This aim had cosmic significance, reflecting as it did the heavenly choirs that nuns hoped one day to join. Hildegard of Bingen's *Ordo Virtutum* opposes the voices of women representing the various virtues twined together in harmony to the rough, raucous male voice of the devil, which disrupts the musical fabric. When Hailrat, the singing mistress at Engelthal, sang the German verse "I have loved thee with such love and this I have shown thee with my compassion," one nun remembered, "the convent was almost senseless with devotion, lying like the dead until they came to themselves again and sang Matins with great devotion."[8] The choir was commonly the scene where earth and heaven met. Nuns reported that they saw Jesus, the Virgin Mary, or the saint whose feast was being honored moving among them with signs of approbation. Sister Berta von Herten saw a golden pipe rise from one sister's mouth up to heaven. She also saw a red rose fall from another sister's lips.[9] Geri Heinburgin of Katharinenthal witnessed a golden globe descend from heaven into the choir with the names of all the sisters singing there inscribed upon it.[10] On Pentecost, while the sisters chanted *Veni creator Spiritus*, one saw divine fire illuminating them as long as the hymn lasted.[11] But as always danger threatened. Gertrude of Colmar encountered a former chantress suffering horribly in purgatory, who confessed that she had abused the noble voice God gave her by seeking worldly glory in her solo song and sparing her throat during the common chant to God's glory.[12]

These performances, designed to shape the community's own worship, also constituted its visible public service. The friends and families who relied on the spiritual services of individual nuns as well as the neighboring communities supporting the monastery were vicarious participants in their rituals. Nuns had liturgical roles in public religious celebrations, such as their role in the Palm Sunday processions in Zurich. They could also invent processions for special occasions. During a siege of Colmar, one of the sisters of Unterlinden, bearing an image of the virgin, led the nuns weeping bitter tears on a circuit three times around the monastery. At the end of the final procession, she was assured that they would be protected from all anguish and danger. They could thus take credit when the discord was quelled and peace came to Colmar.[13]

Small convents often doubled as parish churches, and even large communities offered special devotions during the liturgical year. Jesus dictated the proper observances of certain feasts to Gertrude of Helfta, Birgitta of Sweden, and other abbesses. In many convents, sepulchers were built in chapels to implement the liturgical drama called Paschal

Matins, a reenactment of the encounter between the women and the angel on Easter morning. The elaborate painted chapel at Wienhausen still conveys the flavor of the ceremony. The Customary of Barking, which outlines the annual rituals, indicates that Abbess Catherine de Sutton, who had pastoral responsibilities for the people of the parish as well as for her nuns, instituted its celebration on Easter Sunday to stimulate the devotion of her flock.[14] In 1207, Innocent III prohibited theatrical spectacles in church, but Honorius III made an exception for Franciscans to establish a Christmas pageant in 1223. Nuns' reenactments of the nativity involved much fondling and kissing of figures of the baby Jesus, which easily induced visions like that given to Anna von Klingenow at Töss, who saw the child Jesus descend from the altar to sit on her spread habit as she knelt. Many convents had a small industry making such figures out of various materials, which were often included in trousseaux.

The sisters also cultivated the feasts of saints, particularly patrons of the community or the city or those who intervened in local historical events. Elisabeth of Schönau seems to have been the first to track the calendar in her visions of saints being feted by their celestial friends in their places before the heavenly throne.[15] At Töss, Ita von Sulz saw Ursula and all her virgins arrive in their choir "beautifully and finely dressed" to celebrate their feast day. When they realized that, at the orders of the provincial, the nuns were omitting their office, they turned away contemptuously.[16] Veronica de Binasco, in a series of ecstasies that began with the Annunciation and continued through the liturgical year, witnessed the events of the New Testament, gaining mystical understanding of their meaning. She particularly enhanced the roles of the women in the gospel with her own experiences, which were incorporated into the prayers and meditations of her fellow nuns. Veronica revealed, among other things, the details of Mary Magdalene's conversion by her convent's patron, Martha. On Martha's feast, she was rapt into a celestial crowd of nuns dressed in white, whom the angel described as women specially devoted to imitating Martha's life.[17]

The saints appearing most frequently in visions are those most popular with the artists of the period drawn from the Golden Legend and the New Testament. Martha and Veronica as well as early martyrs like Agnes and Ursula gave nuns a focal point for their imitation. The newly awakened cult of Catherine of Alexandria may have promoted respect for educated women, drawing together the twin qualities of purity and female inspiration and preaching. Relics, which were more widely distributed in private possessions than ever before, stimulated even broader areas of devotion.

Some nuns with a special talent for the work put their mystical abilities to work as authenticators of relics. Elisabeth of Schönau was commissioned to use her visionary powers on the supposed relics of Ursula and her 11,000 virgins, which had been discovered in Cologne in 1106. Gradually she filled out the dramatic details of their passion and provided a number of the bones with specific names and personalities. Lutgard recognized a hitherto unknown saint, Princess Osanne of Ireland, whose unmarked tomb lay in the crypt of Jouarre.[18] She also had conversations with Elizabeth, Catherine, John the Baptist, Mary Magdalene, the mother of James and John, Agnes, and some of the 11,000 virgins of Cologne.

Herrad of Hohenburg included an account of the legendary foundress of her convent, Saint Odilia, in her compendium of historical and scientific knowledge with a drawing of the abbess Relinda giving the community a copy of her monastic reforms.[19] Herrad's emphasis was exceptional. In this period, local cults of foundresses and patrons so popular in earlier periods were giving way to more universal saints. In such spheres of activity, the nun's life of public service intersected with the intense inner life that fed her powers. The joining was not always harmonious and sometimes it was dangerous to the community or to the sister. Most of the mystics who brought the saints closer to earth did not aim to be distinguished themselves. Nor were their communities apparently eager to promote them to sanctity as they had been in the past. A saint long dead seemed willing to fit peacefully into a routine of public ceremonial with an occasional special event when a crisis called for some miraculous demonstration. Living or recently dead saints had trouble settling in with decorum. After her death, Hildegard of Bingen soon ceased to produce miracles at the request of her sisters, who feared the loss of their peace. Even sanctity came second to a breach in the communal harmony.

Religious communities, always threatened by invasive forces from outside, had also to guard against internalized sources of hostility, which insinuated themselves in a variety of metaphors. A sister of Unterlinden recognized a sow and her piglets as diabolic agents fouling the chapel. A swarm of flies threatened the chalice during mass until they were routed by the sign of the cross. Adelheid de Torolzheim was accosted on the choir steps by a devil in the shape of a pig rubbing its back and sides vigorously on the newel. On the other side, she saw a sister who had recently died aping the pig. To reach her station in the choir she had to conquer her fear and cross between them.[20] Christina of Markyate and her congregation had to bypass a gruesome headless phantom to go into their chapel for worship.[21]

Visions sometimes healed psychic rifts in the community. The devil often acted as a device for externalizing the bad feelings of individuals. At Unterlinden, there was a sister who had been baptized and brought into the convent straight from her mother's womb, never to be contaminated by the world. Nevertheless, she allowed the devil into the community through her jealousy of a sister who had precedence over her in procession. Sisters envious of the special attention Jesus paid to Veronica de Binasco found her bruised and bleeding. They learned that a jealous demon attacked her, stamping his feet, farting and snorting like a cow, whenever she meditated on the Passion. For three years, they nursed her bruises and headaches. When she subsequently began to be cured while in ecstasy, they could make a mild joke, saying Sister Veronica had been taken to the doctor.[22] A nun at Katharinenthal was similarly attacked by the devil whenever she meditated on the Passion, yet she summoned the strength to ignore the attacks and by her persistent prayer protect a tempted sister. Lutgard saw a demon tormenting a dying sister but he told her that his power would evaporate when the community arrived. Humans who allowed themselves to be the devil's instruments could be punished, but the demon, not the sister, was the enemy, the tempter who attacked even Jesus in the wilderness.

Hours were set aside for private prayer and meditation, and silence governed the workrooms. Affective meditation, stressing identity with Jesus, his companions, and his saints, was perfected by the Cistercians in the twelfth century and promoted by the mendicant orders in the thirteenth and fourteenth centuries. Books of devotion and the realistic depiction of legendary scenes in painting and sculpture focused the contemplative. As with Anna Wansaseller at Töss, it was not unusual that Jesus, Mary, or particular saints appeared in the same dress and pose as a particularly cherished image, a form of authentication that alleviated fear of false visions inspired by the devil. Adelhait Pfefferhartin of Katharinenthal particularly loved to pray before a picture of Saint John resting on the bosom of our Lord, and once a sister saw her swept up from the earth and suspended in air while she knelt there.[23]

The tension between inward meditation and the bonds of sisterhood was always in play. Fantasy or revelation, the extraordinary experiences that broke into a life of routine and petty irritations could be dangerously addictive. The chronicle of Unterlinden claimed that the younger sisters had to be restrained lest immoderate vigils, fasting, and other forms of self-mortification render them needlessly weak and unable to do the regular works.[24] Bernard himself once warned a nun of the dangers of solitude for the untrained or unwary. The abbot of Clairvaux was principally concerned with temptations to sin, but more subtly the devout nun was tempted to retreat away from the community and sink into self-involved brooding. To protect her solitude, Lutgard refused election as prioress of Saint Catherine's and transferred to the Cistercian convent of Aywières, where the nuns spoke French, a language she never learned.[25] Werntrudis von Bern could speak to only one of the nuns at Kirchberg, who reached her with a psychic language that was neither German nor Latin.[26]

One means of restoring the mystic to the common life was the transformation of visions into liturgies. Drama gave a tangible communal form to individual mystical experiences. Hildegard of Bingen's songs and playlets invited all her fellow nuns into the private world of her visions. New devotions, often focused on Mary, spread among a network of nuns. The "psalter of the virgin," a popular recitation, which eventually gave way to the Rosary, provided the stimulation of repetitious ritual organized around a series of mysteries, which led the praying woman through the life cycle of Jesus by identifying her with Mary. Christine of Christ saw her rosaries materialize as roses surrounding the baby Jesus as he grew into the suffering man. The shadowy tradition of the Protoevangelion, stretching from the first generations of Christian virgins, continued to be reflected in art and legend. Many nuns had visions promoting the Marian feasts of the Assumption and the Immaculate Conception, though the hierarchy long resisted enshrining these popular beliefs as doctrine. Juliana of Mont Cornillon promoted the singing of the *Magnificat* in northern convents. As Sunday was devoted to Jesus, Saturday became Mary's day at least as early as the twelfth century. Night and day, the nuns at Unterlinden sang the offices of her feasts with solemn devotion, their voices echoing even to the infirmary, where sisters lying sick in bed joined the prayer.[27] The Virgin instructed the Brigittines to sing the mass of our Lady on all her feast days followed on Saturdays by the *Salve Regina*.[28] Birgitta reported that Jesus named the abbess head of his proposed double order in honor of the Blessed Virgin, who "was after my ascension, head and queen of my apostles and disciples."[29]

Yet, liturgy without inner commitment engendered little respect in an age credited by modern scholars with the discovery of the individual. Mary was a powerful role model for nuns because of her humility and obedience. These are the two virtues most commonly associated with monasticism from the beginning of its history. Monks and nuns alike are far more fixated on them than on chastity simply because they were relatively so hard to achieve. The eccentricities and excesses of devotion that might sanctify women working out their vocations in the world were poisonous to community life. Mechtild of Magdebourg, a former Beguine, needed divine reassurance to survive the constraints of cloistered life, even though she had entered seeking shelter from the harassment and threats of heresy charges that pressed mystics in the outside world. Yet individual passions cried out for distinctive expressions, and no wise directress would discourage them altogether. Therefore, within the community the individual subtleties of each woman's inmost thoughts were scrutinized and each special virtue polished, each special vice countered in line with the developing science of intention and motivation.

The Cistercian Beatrice of Nazareth imagined each personality as an "interior monastery" with God as the chief.[30] Reason was the abbess, wisdom and prudence the prioress and subprioress. Charity was cellaress, compassion infirmarian. Gratitude and constancy were chantresses. Faith and hope were sacristans. Sobriety and patience governed the refectory while chastity commanded the gates ready to welcome guests and reject evil thoughts. Humility and obedience were the novice mistresses.

Every nun regularly appeared before the "chapter of guilt" to accuse herself or her sisters of the smallest infractions that might indicate lurking sin or faults against the spirit of community. Gilbertines had three chapters a week under the prioress. The Premonstratensian *magistra* held one each morning. The Dominican chronicler of Unterlinden described Gertrude of Colmar, who had the office of administering correction, as manfully rising against any negligent sister. Once in chapter she accused as many as twenty sisters.[31] The prospect of such relentless criticism explains why Alheit at Engelthal tried to use her blindness to avoid chapter meetings until corrected by a divine voice.[32] The novice Irmgard von Roth once fell into a faint when she was with other children at table and saw an evil spirit writing down every word of their chatter while the mistress was absent.[33] Christine of Christ was beaten in the chapter for her lateness to choir, and Jesus himself told her to learn obedience rather than cultivate her personal devotions.

Nunbooks stress sororal assistance. Neither the chaplain nor the official visitor figures in the accounts. Abbesses are included only on an equal basis with the other nuns. Some care is taken to bring the *conversae*, the aged, the illiterate, and even the feeble-minded into the foreground. Even the most severe austerities are treated as part of a common ethos. Sisters at Töss regularly took turns in groups of twelve beating one another before the chapter house after matins on appointed days. According to their individual notions, some used chains, whips, or juniper branches.[34] The "special graces" they received often rewarded humbler and simpler exertions. When Adelheid du Huterin interrupted her games with the infant Jesus in the choir to obey the porteress's call to work in the kitchen, she found the baby awaiting her there.[35] A nun of Saint Martha's in Milan appeared after her death to admonish the other sisters against making complaints.[36] A young sister accused of a fault in the Unterlinden chapter dreamed of a dead friend carrying a burning candle and a rope of hemp. The rope turned to ashes in the flame and the dead sister said, "So by the fire of punishment in chapter all your sins are consumed and burned like the rope to nothing. Therefore, do not complain when you are accused in the chapter and punished."[37] Ghosts of dead sisters returned to encourage those who still lived with a glimpse of the rewards prepared for them. Margret von Klingenberg appeared wearing golden shoes earned by her care in keeping the chapel altar lighted at night.

Many nuns were mothers, widows retiring into the convent, or even women whose relationship to the heavenly spouse was not entirely exclusive. The women at Obazine, who were married to the monks but living apart, kept their daughters, transferring sons to the monks when they were five. Widows brought their virgin daughters into the convent. A Premonstratensian convent in Cologne was endowed by a patrician widow who entered as a *conversa* while her three daughters became nuns. The paradoxes sometimes fed into a spirituality devoted to the Virgin Mary and the child Jesus. Adelhait von Frowenberg struggled to avoid interfering when the novice mistress at Töss punished her daughter.[38] She substituted devotion to the child Jesus, praying that she could give her skin to make him a diaper and her veins for threads in his shirt. But the prioress of Unterlinden, Adelheid de Rivelden, "sorrowed vehemently and prayed to the glorious virgin for the forgiveness of the sins of her daughter, sister Sophia."[39] Past sin may have haunted the career of the mystic Margarethe Ebner, who had a vision of the child Jesus coaxing her to cuddle him. Another nun wrote on the same night that she dreamed that Margarethe was suckling her own child and expressed her surprise at the "shameless" display of affection.[40]

Many nuns and more novices were children themselves. Some of these children, like Irmelin, raised at Engelthal, successfully embraced the mystical tradition of the convent.[41] They tried to introduce Mary and the child Jesus actively into their communal life by sharing visions. The Virgin brought her baby to them, gave her blessings to their spiritual marriages, and came to take away their fear at the hour of their death. The child came to comfort Willi von Kostentz on her deathbed, while Mary appeared to Elisabeth Bechlin bringing the child for her to play with when she was sick. Sisters began to compete over the numbers of Ave Marias they could say in a day but transformed the contest into a cooperative venture when Beli von Lutisbach saw Mary in a white dress that still required fifty Ave Marias to complete the sleeves.[42] At Töss, she appeared to Adelheit von Frowenberg to thank her for a beautiful new blue mantle woven of the convent's prayers. When the child Jesus appeared to Ite von Hollowe, a lay sister, while she was drying the vegetables, she made a ball and played with it while an angel cooked the dinner.[43]

Jesus and the women around him became models for creative role-playing as nuns inserted themselves into key incidents, sharing the results in conferences with other sisters. When a nun at Töss complained that she could not develop her meditations on Jesus in the wilderness,

Elisabeth Bechlin volunteered that she imagined herself holding Jesus by the hand and warming his feet while he shared with her his torment in the face of the devil's temptations. She even confessed that his hair was too tangled for her to manage.[44] Gertrude von Winterthur contributed a vision of a bleeding Jesus who assured her that every word of their common prayer soothed his wounds. Thus, piety forged a consortium in the work of salvation, which seems to have reflected the way that nuns understood their lives as the lord's wives.

No trial was more terrible and no success counted more than the offering of love and service to sisters whose daily habits grated on the sensitive soul.[45] Christine of Christ was chronically impatient and intransigent with the sisters. She defeated her acedia by flagellating herself and going without heat in the winter. She cured herself of pride, anger, and a tendency to wound others with her tongue by becoming infirmarian. Elsbeth Schefflin at Töss was singled out for praise because she called no sister by her proper name and said only "sister." A record of miracles expanding the wine supply, keeping cups full, and multiplying the available food, reminds us that often convents had a real problem supplying the table properly. At Töss, Saint Catherine was seen with supernatural food to supplement the poor diet. Cecilia of San Sisto saw angels multiplying their food to accommodate the early Dominican preachers.[46] Giving up food turned material poverty to spiritual wealth, and sharing could heal communal wounds. Sophia von Klingenow was inspired to pass on a fruit she had been given to a sister who had snubbed her, thus expressing love for the offensive sister.[47] Reformers complained consistently against women who shunned the common table to eat separately with their chosen friends, a sin against the basic principle of community.

These women also missed their spiritual food. The rule was read two or three times a year during meals. The Brigittine monastery of Vadstena broke long silences for table conversation about spiritual matters and the order's observances.[48] In some areas, reading in the vernacular accompanied meals and then silence began again. On Sundays when the Gilbertines rested, one of the nuns read to them and spoke to them of the good of their souls. For the guidance of her flock, Beatrice, prioress of the Cistercian convent of Nazareth, systematically charted the soul's progress through purifying ascesis and freely rendered service to wisdom and understanding through triumphant love.[49] Hildegard of Bingen analyzed the roles of the vices and their opposing virtues in the development of the psyche. Convent literature stressed mutual assistance as the highest ideal. Adelheit von Holderberg's mystical insight informed her that God preferred her to comfort a disturbed novice than to commune in silence with him.[50] A sister in the workroom at the same house lost her vision of the infant Jesus when she turned away another sister who asked for help in learning her skills.

For the purpose of all their gifts of enlightenment was to create a vehicle for the education of the other women. Before the twelfth century, intense study in monastic libraries produced an unstandardized "prescholastic" learning characterized at its best by women of impressive intellectual scope. In 1173, Herrad of Hohenburg composed an encyclopedic collection of sources and readings to educate her sisters, grouping texts around the Old Testament, the New Testament, and "modern" scholarly treatises.[51] Hildegard of Bingen compiled a collection of books ranging from herbal treatments for various complaints to the cosmic plan of creation, combining empirical observation with divine revelation. As university education replaced monastic learning, nuns lost access to the new scholarship, which was monopolized by the clergy. They continued to pursue the understanding of God and his creation as energetically as men by the physical discipline and intense meditation that produced spiritual insights. Gertrude of Helfta, in the thirteenth century, exhausted the resources of her convent library before a physical and intellectual crisis precipitated the development of her mystical talents.

Mysticism is a manner of perceiving and organizing knowledge about the forces that control the world. Monastics cultivated it through long years of discipline and silence and prayerful focus on the teachings of the Bible, the incidents in the life of Jesus celebrated through the liturgical year, and the ecstatic language of the psalms, chanted incessantly in choir. Scholasticism taught university men to think in Aristotelian chains of proofs and syllogisms, forging their intellects in the rough and tumble of debate. Monasteries formed women's thoughts in silence, surrounded by the vivid illustrations of biblical and historical scenes that decorated their walls. Where scholastic method proceeded by breaking down complex phenomena into their parts and categorizing them, mysticism tended to be holistic. In their more fluid world, mystics did not so much aspire to write books as to become books. The intellect, the body, and the soul were tightly bonded. Sisters praying at all hours mesmerized themselves into a trance state that opened their senses to illumination. They performed repeated genuflections, wept or sang verses from the Song of Songs. They whipped and starved away all impurity. Then they were filled.

A nun who had grown up at Engelthal questioned God to learn how he could be contained in a vessel so small as the host. He "opened the eyes of her mind," so that she understood that he was in the whole as in each particle and enabled her to share her understanding with the community.[52] The Beguine Douceline de Digne impressed theologians with the understanding of the Trinity she had gained through supernatural instruction and shared it with her sisters. At Töss, one winter day, Anna von Klingenow talked so long about God with the sisters who came out to her in the garden that she froze into position. Many nuns claimed to be unable to read or write, though they may simply have been expressing the insecurity generated by lack of the intensive Latin grammar and rhetoric provided at universities. Certainly, choir nuns spent much of their time reading or, at least, looking at books and listening to readers while they spun or sewed or ate. Kunigund von Vilsek saw a crowd of childlike souls begging the nuns to share their psalters while they read about the Resurrection.[53]

This constant study of material long heard and long recited may account for the frequent miraculous acquisition of spontaneous literacy. Lutgard of Aywières was enlightened when Saint John as an eagle flew down to touch her lips. A vision of physical transformation sometimes signified transformation of the intellect. When Hedwig von Regensburg received the ability to read the offices, the whole choir saw that her heart shone through her habit as the sun through glass. Agnete de Ochsenstein's entombed body appeared in a vision as a life-sized crystal.[54] She had been granted not only the capacity to read the writings of the prophets word for word but the ability to comprehend the incomprehensible essence of the deity enfolded in their cryptic messages.

The attribution of their knowledge to a direct gift from God commonly resolved psychological stress for women who lacked institutional and even intellectual tools to validate their experience and convictions.

The stress of enlightenment and the pressure to reveal their knowledge often caused intense physical and emotional pressure before mystics bowed to irresistible divine command. Hildegard of Bingen preferred to pose as a nearly illiterate woman dependent upon divine revelation for every decision, though it has been conclusively demonstrated that she was learned in a wide variety of patristic and contemporary theological sources. After she had concealed her visions for half her life, severe illness and torment gripped her in 1141 until she obeyed a divine voice commanding her to write her experiences.[55] Thereafter, her far-flung correspondence and her four preaching tours spread her fame and influence. Elisabeth of Schönau's visions began in 1152, five years after Hildegard's vindication by Eugenius III and one year after *Scivias* appeared. She visited Hildegard in 1157, frantic with anxiety that Hildegard (and the rest of the world) should misjudge her and condemn her as a hypocrite or hysteric.

Elisabeth excused herself for infringing on men's monopoly of preaching on the grounds that God put his revelations into her mouth and, through an angel, promised to help her if she acted manfully and preached against sin on earth. He had singled out her book from a library of occult heavenly knowledge, which he intended to reveal through dictation to his predestined saints before the world ended. Though wary of uncontrolled religious emotion, the hierarchy welcomed the support of mystical women and men in defense of orthodoxy against the heresy and schism that uncontrolled intellectual enthusiasm often generated. Repelled by the chilly techniques of logic, Bernard of Clairvaux attacked more than one university scholar with the conviction that knowledge of God can be reached only through the heart, not the unloving intellect. As scholastic productivity increased in the high Middle Ages, so did the dissemination of mystical accounts. Women anxious to serve the cause of God through the church generally spoke through books dictated to men and conceded without complaint when their confessors or other church authorities asked for revisions that conformed more closely to received Catholic tradition. Scholastic authors were equally restrained, however. Few escaped official demands for revision of their books to avoid heresy. Their insecurity with the reach of logic beyond the safe limits of received revelation made mystical revelation a welcome validation for an ever-broadening body of theological knowledge.

As time went by, however, the risks for women grew. In the twelfth century, the church welcomed mystical women like Hildegard and Elisabeth, nuns whose works had successfully passed the scrutiny of church officials, in opposition to the wandering men and women whose anticlerical and often heretical sermons had attracted a frightening number of adherents. But in the thirteenth century, with the establishment of the preaching orders carefully trained at universities in the technical subtleties of theology, mystics of both sexes were marginalized. Humbert of Romans composed a systematic argument against women preaching that reinforced the "scientific" fact of women's natural ignorance and seductiveness with reminders that Eve's foolish preaching had destroyed the world.[56] From Innocent III through Clement V, popes forbade women to preach. Marguerite de Porete was actually burned at the stake while her book, falsely attributed to a male mystic, lived on in approved orthodoxy. Mechtild of Magdebourg bitterly complained to God that the same people who sought to burn her books because she was a woman would have fawned upon a priest honored with her revelations. The threatening atmosphere drove Mechtild into the convent of Helfta, where, despite the spiritual atmosphere that produced at least two other contemporary mystics, she felt severely constrained by the pressures of the common life. For all its pressures, the cloister offered greater space for ordinary women to develop their intellectual and spiritual capacities than the hostile world outside.

Within convents women's flights of mystical insight apparently did not carry them beyond the bounds of orthodoxy. Their constant discipline, self-examination, and common conferences must have suppressed or silenced heretical inclinations. The simple effort to bring meaning and validation to the restricted religious lives offered to them involved considerable imaginative effort, however, much of which was unavoidably anticlerical. Already in the twelfth century, women were wrestling with the problem of their place in the plan of creation. Trotula, the gynecologist, saw the creation of woman as bound to God's procreative plans. She placed woman with man above all other creatures because of the "freedom of reason and of intellect" they shared.[57] This view was supported by the mirror-image anatomical theories of sexuality current in the twelfth century. To Hildegard of Bingen, another medical specialist, the sexual component of life fitted women and men together into a larger humanity, making woman's talents desirable complements to man's. Her identification of the church as mother feminized the very activities monopolized by priests acting for her. Elisabeth of Schönau had a vision of a woman clothed with light, weeping when clouds of iniquity shadowed the sun. An angel told her that the woman was Jesus appearing in a female rather than a male form so that Mary could be comprehended in the image.[58] This vision was soon modified under the guidance of Elisabeth's cautious Cistercian brother into a simple vision of the Blessed Virgin. The Virgin herself took on new dimensions in women's devotions as the symbolic cosmos was being debated and realigned. As men tended to set her apart from Eve or at best make her the opposite side of the feminine coin, women tended to blend the two representatives of their gender.

Hildegard made creative use of the allegorical clichés identifying woman with flesh to bind women to the humanity of Christ in the generative and suffering body. The opposition of Eve's disobedience as the instigator of the Fall to Mary's obedience as the spring of the Redemption was a popular devotional theme of the age. Cathars and other Docetic heretics allegorized a dichotomy of flesh and spirit as the opposition of evil and good. Heretical denial of the flesh also entailed denial of the humanity of Jesus and the transubstantiation of bread and wine into his body and blood, which had been declared dogma at the Lateran Council of 1139. Hildegard declared that "the one who made flesh and blood in the womb of the Virgin also makes the bread and wine on the altar flesh and blood."[59] Hildegard joined Eve and Mary in their mutual fertility, emphasizing women's central role in the drama of salvation. The serpent hated Eve for her children, who would replace his followers in heaven. Her softness made her vulnerable to his attack, but the same softness gave her the transformative power that leads to redemption. Eve's sexuality resulted not just from the Fall but also from the fount of fertility, which culminated in Mary's virginity. Eve's sinful eating was justified when Mary bore the fruit of her womb.

Thus through flesh, and woman as flesh, redemption was achieved. Hildegard elaborated the idea of Mary, the mother of Jesus, as *mediatrix* and *salvatrix*, as a sharer in the mission of Jesus. Mary alone endowed him with the body whose suffering made salvation possible, and in her cooperation and her compassion with his death on the cross she brought all women into the great work. The affective meditation promoted by the Cistercians, identifying with Christ's humanity, laid the basis for the practice of compassion, taking part in his suffering. Mary's agreement to the original incarnation, her obedience, complemented the obedience of Jesus in the sacrifice of the cross. Mary's intense sharing in the redemptive agony of her son made her the principal mediatrix between God and humanity. Devoted contemplatives shared the passion in the same manner and, in proportion to their suffering and sacrifice, they assisted in the redemption. Holy women of the thirteenth and fourteenth centuries sought, through compassion, to reverse the mystery of the incarnation whereby Mary transformed God into flesh.

The prejudice against women preaching led them to teach primarily by example. By the thirteenth century, deliberate self-inflicted suffering had become central to the imitation of Christ. Jesus rebuked Margaret of Faenza for concentrating her devotions on his birth, taking only honey and not the gall. Thereafter she focused her meditations on the cross. When Dorothy of Montau's confessor told her that "it is more perfect to imitate Christ in suffering than in action," she devised a series of postures to accompany her prayers and meditations on various stages of the Passion. The elaboration of homegrown rituals led from mimicry to the actual infliction of pain. Bronislava, a Premonstratensian, specifically understood her vocation as marriage to the crucified Christ, who taught her to share his sufferings by beating herself with thorns. A nun at Unterlinden pressed a great wound in the shape of a cross with sharp wood on her breast, which she renewed when it showed signs of healing.[60] At Katarinenthal, Hilti Brunnsinn meditated before a picture of Jesus bound to the pillar. Her prayer that he would share with her his bitterness and suffering in that moment was answered and she retained that grace for two weeks.[61]

Their bodies thus became slates, cleansed and clear, to be written upon. "So they bore the stigmata of Christ on their bodies and were not cheated of the glory of martyrdom and for love of Christ shared in his passion."[62] The Beguine Marie d'Oignies is the first person whom we know to have suffered the stigmata through intense pain without the open wounds exhibited by Francis of Assisi a few years later. About three-quarters of the hundreds of stigmatics who have multiplied since the early thirteenth century have been women. Where Tertiaries and recluses living in the world, like Margaret of Cortona or Christine of Stommeln, exhibited supernatural wounds or had themselves publicly tortured like Clara of Rimini, nuns often asked that their suffering be internalized, lest they be singled out from the common worship.[63]

Devotion to the Sacred Heart grew out of this intense compassion and became the ultimate expression of the interior quality of this feminized religion. Alice the Leper had taken particular comfort from visions of Jesus' bleeding heart, and Lutgard of Aywières envisioned an exchange of hearts with him.[64] An autopsy after the death of Clara of Montefalco revealed the instruments of the Passion embedded in her heart. Helfta, with its three great mystics—Mechthild of Hackborn, Mechthild of Magdeburg, and Gertrude of Helfta—became a center for disseminating the worship that would so distinguish women in centuries to come. Gertrude had a vision of John the Evangelist confiding the mystical secret of the pulsating heart he had known when resting on Jesus' bosom. He told her that the first age of Christianity had been launched by the Word become flesh but the second age would experience a rekindling of faith through the fiery love of the heart of Jesus.[65] Through this ultimate feat of purification and mystical imagination, these women had almost surpassed a condition of union with God. They became God, his redemptive suffering inscribed upon their bodies.

This alchemy both complemented and contradicted the hierarchy's approach to salvation, which focused on the clergy and the sacraments they alone could administer. Twelfth century monks, influenced by Cistercian hostility to elaborate liturgies, condemned the processions and endless chanting that characterized the Benedictine tradition, preferring to emphasize mass and other priestly activity. But for nuns, the daily offices acquired greater importance as the sacraments were limited. Hildegard of Bingen was criticized for dressing her nuns up in crowns and fancy costumes to act out allegorical performances, but acting enabled them to share the mystical transformations generally monopolized by the priesthood. As mysticism furnished an alternative to scholasticism for penetrating cosmic mysteries, it also offered a devotional alternative to consecrated women denied the right to celebrate the sacraments, a right becoming more broadly defined as hierarchical power tightened in the thirteenth century.

Within convents, nuns carried on many quasi-sacerdotal activities. After the Fourth Lateran Council these came under the close scrutiny of bishops and their representatives, who were instructed to visit all monastic houses not under the discipline of an order. The bishop directed the prioress of Easebourne to appoint one nun each week in turn, beginning with the eldest as chaplain *(capellanissa)* for divine services. Other visitations, service books, and the records from the dissolution in England as well as Germany also refer to women as chaplains. Presumably their chief task was to keep vestments and vessels in good order in the chapel for the use of priests, but even these ancillary services came under attack. In the thirteenth century, when the old Carolingian laws were revived, prescriptive literature criticized the fine needlework employed in making altar cloths as vanity. *Ancren Riwle* warned anchoresses against taking charge of church vessels and vestments, a practice that Premonstratensian nuns always followed in their double cloisters. The chaplain-nuns may have recited the "inferior" services in the chapel, but if so they too clung to the edge of the acceptable. The abbess of Las Huelgas caused a scandal that reached as far as the pope's ears because of her practice of giving benediction to her nuns. After the nuns of Prébayron, who had been consecrated as deaconesses from the sixth century on, joined the Carthusian order, visitors complained that they wore the priestly maniple when reading the epistle at mass and the stole when reading the gospel at evening offices and even further overstepped their bounds by serving at mass. In the mid-thirteenth century, the archbishop of Rouen found that some of his nuns assisted the priest at mass and ordered an end to the improper practice. Similarly, the privilege of administering eucharists kept in reserve (called "masses without priests") was being steadily restricted to the most extraordinary conditions.

One response was certainly to focus devotion elsewhere. In female communities attached to monkeries, in double monasteries, and even in nunneries used as parish churches, the nuns were architecturally alienated from the mass by the walls, grilles, and turntables, the monks' choir stalls and lay people's galleries that stood between them and the altar. They tended to become absorbed in meditative devotions even while the celebration proceeded. Small pictures and inspirational sentences, like those that modern archaeologists have found beneath the choir stalls at Wienhausen, must have stimulated private devotion even during common offices. Elisabeth of Schönau regularly fell into trances and dictated lengthy accounts of her visions while the brothers were saying mass beyond the window where she was listening.

The bull *Omnis Utriusque Sexus* issued by the Fourth Lateran Council in 1215 made annual confession and communion at Easter time obligatory for all Christians, but male aversion to the *cura monialium* often meant that nuns had no priest to provide them with services. Ordained monks celebrated as many as three masses daily, a practice that must have enhanced their growing disdain for women, who could neither say mass nor even hear it without their assistance. Visitors rebuked them for failure to fulfill the Easter duty. They had to suffer priests who were often ill-trained and sometimes immoral. The archbishop of Rouen relieved one debt-ridden house of the burden of a pension for a chaplain but made no alternative provision.[66] Elsewhere he ordered the replacement of an incontinent confessor but did not send a new confessor for eight years. A nun at Engelthal considered it proof of God's protection that a rich and sinful priest reformed when he came to live among them as their chaplain.[67] Cistercian and other monk-priests enjoyed the privilege of daily communion. Most nuns were not encouraged to expect the sacraments very often. Communion was generally given no more than once a month and often less. The convents Eudes of Rouen visited averaged six or seven times a year. Only a few female saints, after displays of supernatural intervention, were able to secure daily or even weekly communion.

When hostility or simple neglect of the *cura* caused priests to restrict their access to the sacraments, women were driven to go over the heads of the clergy. Adelheid von Trochau at Engelthal had a mystical encounter with the souls of unbaptized children who warned her that her own baptism lacked some element of correctness. She defended herself to Mary Magdalene, John the Baptist, and Saint Peter on the grounds that she had not committed any fault, reproaching Peter in particular that he could not say the same for himself. The saints relented and corrected the priest's error with a miraculous baptism, a stream of water that poured over her when she was chanting in choir with the other sisters.[68] Mechtild of Magdeburg was transported to a heavenly ritual in which John the Baptist read the mass. Clerical critics complained that, as a layman, he had no right to do so. They were cut of the same cloth as the curial representatives who never blushed to tell Birgitta to explain the canon law to Jesus when he demanded that they recognize her new order of nuns.

In retaliation for the reluctance of priests to give them frequent communion, women often claimed to have received the Eucharist from Christ himself. Twice Jesus fed the Eucharist to Catherine of Siena when priests refused. Clearly, some overlap existed between the confessional responsibilities of priests and the abbess's pastoral responsibilities, which had long included hearing daily confessions from the nuns as well as supervising the chapter of guilt. Deprived of the sacramental power of the confessional, superiors sometimes seemed to have mystical gifts for seeing into the hearts of sinners. Ida of Nivelles identified the temptation to blasphemy, which one nun suffered at La Ramée. Christine of Mark-yate could discipline her nuns by knowing their secret thoughts and acts.[69] Gertrude of Helfta even had quasi-priestly powers to gain forgiveness for her own and her sister's sins directly from Jesus. When their confessor failed to arrive before a scheduled communion service, she received assurances from Christ that her own sins and those of her sisters had been forgiven. Following her visionary instincts, she examined the sisters to learn whether they were in a state of grace and could receive communion. Such alternatives and reassurances must have been particularly important to nuns in times of interdict when they might be cut off from all access to sacraments and forced to live on their own resources.

When they did not enjoy an order's exemption from the spiritual siege that might be laid to their province, they developed protective spiritual mechanisms. In the beguinage of Delft, Gertrude van Oosten often consoled penitent women by telling them that their tears would wash away their sins. "And on God's part I say to you that you shall never be damned."[70] Mechtild of Hackborn saw Jesus rescue a dead nun suffering in purgatory by saying the mass she had missed in her last illness. Similarly, when she was obliged to miss mass because of illness, Jesus instructed Gertrude of Helfta on meditations that would garner her equal amounts of grace.[71] Even though Christ provided her directly with sacramental services, the abbess of Helfta was careful to teach that the priest should not be bypassed. She had a vision of one nun suffering in purgatory for pretending to be asleep when the priest was hearing confessions. In short, nuns sought to develop orthodox forms of devotion that would satisfy their need for active worship without alienating them from the grace-giving sacraments of the church. Mechtild of Hackborn had a eucharistic vision during a time of interdict and Christ gave her communion with the understanding that she would confess later. Jesus appeared visibly to the sisters at the death watch of one nun and administered communion and extreme unction to her. But then he said, "Although you received the sacraments of the church from me, take them again from the priest lest you seem to refuse ecclesiastical rites."[72]

In the thirteenth century, women's ecstasies increasingly centered on the sacramental yoking of confession and communion. Penance was at the axis of several spiritualities. It involved the sacramental cleansing, which God administered only through the agency of his priest, and sometimes mystics used their power to reinforce the principle. Veronica de Binasco saw a demon enumerating the faults of a dying nun, every light word or failure to observe silence "which mortals think of no moment," but he fled, confounded, when her helping angel responded that she had confessed to all of them.[73] Gertrude of Herenkem, an illiterate and somewhat feeble-minded lay sister, saw the Virgin Mary and her baby moving through the choir greeting each of the sisters with an embrace save for one sister with an unconfessed sin from whom she averted her face.[74] Jesus appeared to Christine of Christ as a ray of sunlight that vanished before she could touch him. After she made a general confession to the vicar, the vision returned and descended straight into her heart.

Mystics sometimes paired themselves with the priests as controllers of grace. Her confessor-biographer stressed that Catherine of Siena sent everyone converted by her prayers to a priest for confession.[75] This respect for their powers might have also forced priests to be more attentive to their penitents. Priests often complained of the overscrupulosity of nuns. Moreover, modesty and fear of their own seductiveness inhibited the full disclosure essential to a good confession. In response, nuns apparently added the examination of conscience and the process of penitence to their private meditations with relatively perfunctory regard to the confessional. Mid-thirteenth-century mystics received elaborate instructions from Jesus himself, which they expanded enthusiastically, concerning their preparation to receive the sacrament. Elspeth Stägel believed that God himself had sent her Heinrich Suso for a confessor. The famous mystic became intensely attached to his "Magdalene" after she sent him a wax tablet recording her self-examination, but she related that when he hardened his heart against another woman who interrupted his devotions for confession, God punished him by drying up his capacity to pray.

More actively, mystical women moved the focus of penance away from the sacramental absolution obtained in confession to the process of penitence more in tune with the monastic tradition. The penitential services of nuns bypassed the sacramental powers of priests and extended beyond the gates of death. Hildegard pioneered a type of piety stressing guilt and repentance. She claimed repentance, compassion, and mercy as the feminine virtues contained in the androgynous godhead.[76] Repentance cleansed and perfected the sinner, making her fit for acts of compassion through which she became an active agent of God's own mercy, by her accumulated merits securing the salvation of sinners. Thus, excluded from the celebration of the sacraments, the devoted woman could partake even more intimately in the process of distributing God's grace.

At Watton, it was the custom of the nuns to pray incessantly for the soul of every nun who died until she gave them assurances that she no longer needed their prayers.[77] At Engelthal, Anna von Weiterstorf appeared to a sister and asked her help to repair something unconfessed that still separated her from God.[78] Beli von Liebenberg saw four bright lights shining at the window and a voice told her that they represented four sisters recently saved by her prayers.[79] A nun with difficult family relationships was likely to record visions of relatives recompensed for their support of her vocation. The prioress of Unterlinden, Adelheid de Rivelden, like her contemporary, Dante Alighieri, saw many of her deceased acquaintances suffering in purgatory, but her vision served to reassure her of the efficacy of her sisters' efforts.[80] Even more directly, Jesus explained to Gertrude of Helfta how his satisfaction when nuns received communion and performed other good works was transformed into graces, which he distributed to suffering souls.[81] Mechtild of Magdebourg made frenzied efforts to free souls from purgatory and even, against all theology, from hell.

Purgatorial visions often anchored the seer in the bedrock of orthodoxy by entrusting her with messages to priests. Thus, a soul in purgatory explained to a nun that she could be freed by thirteen masses by six priests, whom she named.[82] The process seems to put the priests at the service of the dead and, by implication, of the nun chosen to receive their messages. Birgitta of Sweden, a royal lady who well understood the ways of patronage, claimed to be able to discover who was in purgatory and transmit to the living what alms and sacrifices might free their suffering friends and relatives. One lady, for example, instructed her that her friends should have chalices made for the communion offering if they would set her free of suffering.[83] In effect, these women transformed the process of receiving the sacraments into a distribution agency that carried their accumulated merits to Jesus and thence to their clients in purgatory. Moreover, they often saw priests in hell or procured their salvation when they cried out from purgatory. Lutgard of Aywières in particular was solicited by the suffering soul of Innocent III.[84]

Though not systematically anticlerical, this sacramental mysticism entered dangerous areas. Priests could separate their human selves from their priestly offices. No matter how sinful the individual celebrant might happen to be, his sacrament was irreproachable. But in the end he would pay for his sins like any layman. In their intimate moments, Christ urged Veronica de Binasco to learn a lesson in patience by emulating his sufferance of priests who handled the sacraments with polluted hearts and unclean lips.[85] Demands for reform were particularly effective in the mouths of women whose ecstasies, trances, and stigmatas vouched for their personal purity. Mystical women, endowed with clairvoyant gifts, avoided priest whose sins had been revealed to them. More dramatically they often reversed the uses of the confessional by urging the priest to repent. A cleric who seduced an honest woman died without the sacraments when he scorned the rebukes of Yvetta of Huy to make him repent. Her sensitivity to the moral condition of others enabled her to expose priests who were suffering from avarice and other mortal conditions.[86] When her priest refused to give her the sacraments, Saint John revealed that the priest had feared that she would see that he had polluted himself with a prostitute.[87] Francesca of Rome saved a priest celebrating mass in a state of mortal sin by telling him that she saw him rotting with leprosy. When Clara da Gambacorta heard anything scandalous she would berate priests under cover of confession.

Clergymen and nuns and even ordinary lay people ultimately stood equally before a judging and merciful God. The vast majority of nuns were loyal to the church and obedient to its laws, but a few of them energetically employed their mystical relationship to Christ as a tool of reform against corrupt clergymen. Hildegard of Bingen saw the church as a bride threatened with the corrupting and seductive powers of greedy prelates. She described them as effeminate, but not womanly, people who have breasts and will not nurse, who have the vices of both sexes and the virtues of neither. She equated the feminine with frailty but argued that God chose the weak to shame the strong, a sentiment repeated in the lives of many holy women later in the century. This sense that God made use of women for the highest ends validated Hildegard's activity as his instrument: "For when learned and powerful men are sunk into feminine levity, then men are scandalized by the preaching of women."[88] Elisabeth of Schönau claimed that God reveals himself to women when men are sluggish.[89] She addressed sermons to clergymen whose unclean condition scandalized the faithful and forced God to turn away.

Tension centered strongly on the eucharistic devotion, which gave priests their authority as vicars of Christ and women their fulfillment as his compassionate hosts. The mystic receiving communion could distinguish unconsecrated from consecrated wafers. The infirmarian of Kirchberg reprimanded the chaplain when he attempted to give her an unconsecrated host: "Dear brother Conrad you are not bringing me God but only bread."[90] A priest attempted to curb Francesca of Rome's frequent reception of the Eucharist by giving her an unconsecrated wafer, but she perceived it and told her confessor, who straightened out the priest. Such conflicts could be embarrassing all around. Lidwina exposed the priest who gave her an unconsecrated host as a test. The priest retaliated by denying her claim that she had received a host from Jesus. A mysticism so free of clerical authority and yet so centered in the sacraments inevitably presented challenges to ecclesiastical authority.

The tension between brides and ministers, givers and receivers of sacraments, was sometimes dangerous. God channeled grace through priests into the Eucharist, but the grace he channeled into women in a sense made them eucharists themselves in a variation on the incarnation. The sacramental drama focused on women as the receivers of eucharistic grace, a complex union mixing bridal and maternal components that climaxed in a compassionate sharing of the redemptive experience of the

Crucifixion. The process of penitence and purgation, fasting, and other forms of self-discipline prepared them for the ultimate ecstasy in communion, which entirely blotted out the performance of the priest upon the altar. They elaborated an intense sense of intimacy and union with Christ through a mystique of reception. Gertrude of Helfta was accustomed to carry out conversations with Jesus while the mass was proceeding. The reception or even the immediate perception of the sacrament was commonly the signal for mystics to fall into states of trance that sometimes continued for several days. Elisabeth of Schönau began having ecstasies at the moment when the chalice was elevated, though her accounts suggest that she could not even see it. She did see the crucified Christ pouring blood into the chalice and later had a similar vision with a dove. The church was under intense pressure to increase the laity's access to the Eucharist. The consecrated host was raised during mass and ringing bells were added by the early fourteenth century. Ultimately, more general public exposition in a monstrance was introduced. Juliana of Mont Cornillon, with the enthusiastic support of other female mystics followed heavenly instructions in promoting the feast of Corpus Christi.

At the same time, the hierarchy drew back from encouraging what appeared to be the excesses of women recipients. Priests were forbidden to give the Eucharist to women in a state of ecstasy. Legislation of the thirteenth century prohibited too frequent communion, and by the fourteenth century the laity was deprived of the wine, much to the distress of Catherine of Siena, who often made pointed references to the clergy's surrogacy. Mysticism was always subversive of the ecclesiastical hierarchy even when it was most supportive of the sacraments of the church. As early as the middle of the thirteenth century, Albertus Magnus preached to the Augustinian nuns of Cologne against visions and miracles. At the Council of Lyons in 1274, more than one German bishop warned of the trend among German nuns to place their union with God above the sacraments of the church. Lamprecht of Regensburg's *Daughter of Syon* attacked women for adherence to the ideal of inner light with its attendant ecstasies and visions.

Obviously the more exposed women who lived outside cloisters suffered most readily from these persecutions. But even the public services performed by cloistered nuns were somewhat restricted by *Periculoso*, though the bull was never seriously enforced. Many of the nunbooks of the late thirteenth and early fourteenth centuries were collected in an atmosphere of repression against women's mystical experiences. Women were a marked presence among the growing body of critics who attacked the papacy at the end of the thirteenth and through the fourteenth centuries. Against a church widely perceived as dominated by worldly, vain, ambitious, and greedy men, humble women and men calling themselves the Friends of God advocated a classless, genderless, rankless spirituality. At the Council of Vienne in 1311, Clement V condemned "certain women commonly called beguines who, though they promise obedience to no one and neither renounce property nor live in accordance with an approved rule . . . wear a so-called beguine habit and cling to certain religious men to whom they are drawn by special preference."[91] The bishop of Strasbourg acted against his Tertiaries, harassing those who kept to their sober habits with threats of heresy prosecution unless they dressed in bright colors.[92] It was no idle threat. Elsewhere, uncloistered Beguines and Tertiaries were persecuted and even burned at the stake.

By 1320 the papacy was caught in that long sojourn in Avignon that alienated loyal Catholics outside France. Birgitta of Sweden and Catherine of Siena prevailed upon the curia to return to Rome in 1378, advising Urban VI to replace the College of Cardinals with a parliament of mystics when their resistance precipitated a schism that was to last until 1415. In the discussions of order and hierarchy that grew out of the debacle, the place of mystics in the church was questioned. The influential chancellor of the University of Paris, Jean Gerson, blamed Catherine and Birgitta for the schism and attacked the fundamental idea of inspiration outside and superior to the institutions of the church. The art of exposing false visions became a new prerogative of prelates and theologians. As we have seen, Birgitta's rule was never recognized as a genuine revelation from Christ. Moreover, another alchemy was at work throughout the age. As women grew ever more determined to transform their bodies into vehicles of supernatural knowledge, it seems that men became ever more focused on those bodies as vehicles of carnal knowledge. The mystical voice of the convent was always challenged and often drowned out by a strident male critique of worldly or even sexually abandoned nuns.

13

※

The Tears of the Magdalene

FROM THE TWELFTH CENTURY forward, women's determination to live without sexual involvement was treated as an indicator of heresy and some women were actually burned because of it. At the same time, hagiography in praise of heroic virginity lost in popularity to bawdy literature gleefully celebrating clerical frailties. The image of women starved for a "natural" sex life roused both sympathetic and salacious thoughts. The sexually greedy nun became the delight of pornographers, reflecting late medieval notions about the uncontrollable nature of the female sex drive. Attacks on religious women always accompanied the rhetoric of reform and critiques of decay in the clerical hierarchy. In the religious enthusiasm of the twelfth century the unreformed secular canonesses were regularly savaged. Unworldly syneisactics were generally treated with an attitude of "Where there's smoke, there's fire."[1] The long quarrels over the *cura* expressed clerical gynophobia through a pair of truisms. There were no men so virtuous that they could withstand the temptation roused by the mere presence of the most blameless woman. There were no women whose virtue could compensate for the risk to men's souls. Peter the Venerable had a partition erected at Marcigny to separate the nuns from the priests in their own church. The Carthusians called their five female monasteries "the five wounds of their order."[2]

Perfectly sober historians have tended to mistake satire for reality or to generalize from a few well-publicized incidents that the forced recruitment of nuns led to indifference and even hostility to their vocations. In 1460 Emmeline de Ramstein stood in the public courtyard at Saint Madeleine in Basel "to show the world that her parents had forced her entry and she had never consented."[3] The Dutch reformer Gerhard Groote (d. 1384) maintained that the provision of dowries encouraged donors to use monasteries for incapacitated and unwanted children. The evidence that dowry inflation and other family strategies impelled parents to place their daughters in chronically overcrowded convents remains compelling. In 1481, an advocate complained to the Parlement of Paris that the wars had beggared the nobility so that they could not marry their daughters fitly and had to make them nuns. From the Middle Ages to modern times, observers have not failed to find a source of humor in the thought of these nubile women outwitting their captors and finding sexual gratification. But by now, the laughter should have died down, allowing us to transfer our commiseration to the living women who suffered slander and sometimes violence as a result of the misguided fantasies of men about languishing virgins.

The very virtues of women, particularly when accompanied by tangible marks of divine favor, reproached clergymen who failed to achieve sanctity despite the advantages of ordination. In the late thirteenth century, as the worldly power and wealth of the established church eroded its spiritual prestige, the ecclesiastical hierarchy became steadily more anxious to keep its nuns silenced and out of sight. *Periculoso* was issued by a pope accused of causing the abdication and possibly even the death of his sainted predecessor, Celestine V. At least in part he may have been stung by the criticisms of mystics who idolized the former hermit as a patron and hero. The continuing criticism of "spirituals," whose ranks encompassed many uncloistered women, provoked the bulls issued by the Council of Vienne and the violent persecutions that followed. For three-quarters of the fourteenth century, the papal court remained at Avignon, attracting so many prostitutes that a special office was set up to register those who wished to repent. The anticlericalism that would ultimately lead to the Protestant revolution took root and spread, winning the allegiance of a number of publicly vociferous women. Such women were especially vulnerable to the vengeance of the hierarchy whose imminent ruin they often prophesied. Women of the most irreproachable orthodoxy fared no better. They easily became scapegoats, attracting the barbs of critics reluctant to attack the powers behind them.

Thus, the papacy's "Babylonian Captivity" in France ended in 1378 with a schism that the French blamed on Catherine of Siena and Birgitta of Sweden, active proponents of the papacy's restoration to Rome. For a generation, two popes competed for control of a shattered hierarchy. Loyalties divided along emerging nationalist lines, undermining the whole international structure of monasticism. Orders split between French houses and houses loyal to Rome, disrupting every aspect of their unity and discipline. Communities under episcopal jurisdiction were neglected or harassed as their dioceses were drawn into the dispute. Individual houses ruptured internally or suffered the imposition of superiors whose political views conformed to those of the prevailing secular lord. At the same time, the lords themselves were involved in an unending series of wars attended by civil conflict and brigandage.

Within the walls that embraced medieval towns, riots and civil strife targeted convents as peculiarly vulnerable representatives of the ruling class. The sisters of Unterlinden moved to the suburbs of Colmar to avoid riotous townspeople but moved back inside in 1252 because of the repeated depredations of soldiers. When Juliana of Mont Cornillon and several of her nuns were expelled from their hospital by a greedy prior, they lost their endowments. They were saved from penury by the abbess Imène of Salzinnes, but in 1256 that community was forced from Namur by rioting townsmen enraged that they had secured the intervention of the empress to quell disturbances emanating from a nearby house of debauchery.[4] The years 1315–1321 brought drought, cattle plagues, and land exhaustion. Famine set in and supplies were particularly hard to get for cloistered nuns whose tenants conspired with their agents to cheat them. Charters were lost in peasant uprisings. Supplies and crops vanished; mills and farm buildings burned. The misery was deepened by the onset of the Black Death. Tenants died or were driven away; their lands were left uncultivated. Monastics were particularly vulnerable to plague because of their communal life and their hospitality; women, perhaps because they were relatively undernourished or because they were less able to run away, suffered the most. For a period in the fifteenth century, normal demographic relationships reversed: women were in short supply, leaving only the most undesirable for convents.

In England, from the troubled reign of Edward II through the War of the Roses, marauders and greedy lay lords raided convents and their estates. In 1383, local men broke into the close at Brodholme and stripped it of timber and food, besieging the nuns in the priory. In 1367, the abbess of Shaftesbury received permission to crenellate her abbey for defense, but hired soldiers often caused as much violence as they prevented. Soldiers mustered for the war in France ran amok at Saint Albans and carried off the nuns with other townswomen. Blaming the nuns for the storm that subsequently struck at sea, they threw the women overboard after the baggage. Mercenary soldiers in Spain, Italy, and Germany, border raiders in England and Scotland, Hussites in Bohemia, and outlaws everywhere considered nuns valid objects of loot. A gang of violent men broke into Rothwell in 1421, carried off a boarder, and raped her. She escaped but the men came after her, and when the nuns tried to protect her, the brutes threw them down, kicked them, and dragged off their clothing.

The Hundred Years' War obliged nuns in France to abandon cloisters for years at a time. Embattled secular lords claimed their temporals to support armies that alternately protected and threatened their peace. Many convents were reduced to total penury and then stripped of their land by the powers that should have protected them.[5] The rich convent of Pace de Maria in Laon was so beset "by the growing malice of the times, the turmoil of war, fire, plague and other calamities which afflict these places, particularly oppression by armed men" that the buildings collapsed. The nuns lost their books and ornaments. Revenues and provisions were so diminished that they could provide for no new novices, and divine services ceased when the abbess died. In 1428, some local knights requested that the derelict place be incorporated into the male preceptory of Saint Antony.[6] The nuns of Renaud fled when their buildings were leveled. The prioress lived at Agen in deepest poverty while the land was given to the cathedral chapter.[7] The prioress of Jully asked the chapter of Molesmes for help. The monks took over the property and determined that no new nuns would be recruited, but they cared for the survivors until they died.[8]

Again and again, nuns made appeals to Rome, to princes, to orders: buildings rotted and collapsed, starvation and infirmity decimated the community, and finally divine services could not go on. War, plague, and financial disaster destroyed works of charity and turned almsgivers into beggars. Pope Eugenius wrote on behalf of the Hôtel Dieu:

> Because of the war, nobles, citizens, merchants and other powerful people have despoiled them and ejected them from their houses, possessions, and captured some and mutilated others, wounding and even decapitating them. Hunger, plague and destruction lay all about increasing the numbers of poor and infirm who have consumed all that remains of the goods of the hospital, the masters, brothers and sisters. In the course of one year 30,000 people have died in the hospital. They cannot support themselves or anybody else. They have been forced to desert the hospital, which has brought Christian religious and professions of the church into offensive opprobrium and scandal and set a vicious example to many.[9]

A realistic discussion of the sexual scandals fitfully revealed in various sources cannot ignore this background. No rigorous or systematic study can be carried out, given the haphazard character of the available records, but notes from visitations provide some estimates. Between 1430 and 1450, 12 out of 220 nuns in Lincoln were found guilty of immoral behavior. In eight out of twenty-four houses in York and Lincoln there were serious lapses. In 1514, a general visitation in Norwich found only 1 nun of Crabhouse who had gone wrong out of eight houses with 72 nuns. The extensive visitation records of Eudes of Rouen in the thirteenth century yield comparable results. Some nuns in some houses were incorrigible and some houses were disgraceful, but the great majority of communities at any given moment were free of sexual misconduct. Moreover, the records of episcopal visitors generally concerned the most fragile communities, which, through poverty or lack of influence, could not recommend themselves to the *cura* of an order. These same communities did not benefit from the presence of a colony of experienced nuns to train them at their foundation. To be sure, what was successfully concealed then will not be exposed now. Even so, it behooves the most skeptical modern reader to remember that the bishop, the secular patron, the superior, and the nuns themselves with their families had a strong vested interest in a good reputation and a decorous life. Rather than follow the lead of all too many writers in assuming disorder where the only evidence stems from the overheated imaginations of social satirists and entertainers, we should allow some presumption of innocence to prevail.

Just as some convents were crucibles of mystics, others were barrels of bad apples. Saint Michael's in Stamford is the worst house recorded in late medieval England. Under an aged and infirm prioress, one nun ran away with a friar, came back, and eloped again with a harper. Two other sisters were notorious and may have borne children. In thirteenth-century Normandy, the most disorderly house was Saint-Saëns, which the busy archbishop could not correct after ten years of effort. The prioress was suspected of a liaison with a friend whom her brother often brought to stay in the convent. Later, she was accused of having frequent rendezvous with the local priest and mingling with unsavory company. Nicola the Chantress was rumored to have had an abortion after dining with her sister at the rector's house, though the other nuns swore that the tale was false. Petronilla had a long-standing relationship with the priory's harvester, who was married.[10] In Venice, where nuns' sexual activities were crimes against the state, evidence from police blotters has produced a fairly clear picture. The diarist Priuli complained of fifteen nunneries as "public bordellos which shame God and the Republic. The noble daughters of the first families have become public prostitutes."[11] It is true that nuns from at least thirty three convents were prosecuted for fornication and others may have escaped uncharged. The greatest number, however, were heavily concentrated in one particular convent. Nuns from the notorious Sant'Angelo di Contorto entertained lovers in their private cells, and their abbess occasionally took them out for picnics and other excursions with their lovers.

Criticism often went hand in hand with correction. Even Sant'Angelo was closed down in 1478. Nicholas of Cusa, embarking on a program of visitation and reform, accused noble Tyrolean nuns of living the freest and most luxurious life under cover of the veil. But the records of the reformers in fifteenth-century Germany do not often expose sexual transgressions. "Chastity is not always their strength," said a tactful Cluniac visitor in Auvergne, but again smaller sins of vanity and comfort fill up the records.[12] At the dissolution of the English monasteries, when Cromwell's visitors pressured nuns to reveal cases of incontinence, they found few serious sins, though many nuns were all too worldly. The visitors explained their failure by maintaining that the nuns had taken an oath never to expose their sisters.

Most of the time, normal piety and normal laxity were probably the rule. Episcopal or monastic visitors charged with supervision indicate that nunneries were considerably more decorous than monkeries. They usually found the weaknesses we might expect of ordinary women living humdrum lives: they wore coquettish clothing, made themselves comfortable, lavished affection on pets. Relatively small breaches were often blown up because the standard was so high or because ecclesiastical reformers and secular satirists rejoiced in female fragility. A fifteenth-century English visionary saw her vain sisters in purgatory wearing dresses made of hooks and headdresses of adders.[13] She witnessed one nun being torn to bits by the spirits of a dog and cat she had loved too well. The visionary also saw specific sisters purged of gluttony, wrath, envy, oath breaking, back biting, and slander. Christine de Pisan described a visit to her daughter, a nun at Poissy. The nuns entertained her and her friends with a good dinner and good conversation and set her maternal heart at rest by showing her the comfortable quarters and solid furniture they enjoyed.[14] Was this happy occasion similar to the "little drinking parties" noted peevishly by the visitor to Godstow?[15] Elsewhere, nuns were in the habit of slipping out to the tavern for a drink. At Villarceaux, the archbishop blamed a fistfight on the prioress, who got drunk every night.[16] The nun of Engelthal resented the visitor's implication that the prioress of Aurach's ecstasy was a drunken stupor.[17]

Perhaps the penitential practices at these same convents manifested the internalization of criticism. At Töss, one sister was nicknamed "man of sorrows" because an "evil spirit" gave her a terrible thirst and, while she held the office of cellaress, made her hallucinate serpents and worms on her bed. The sister warded off the demon with a crucifix and beat herself strenuously.[18] Even within the stoutest walls, nuns had to fear their own thoughts, the stray desire that might expose them to the deadly charge of hypocrisy, against which there was no effective defense. It threatened their whole claim to society's support. The spiritual services of women were less objectively quantifiable than those of men. The church guaranteed the efficacy of sacraments regardless of the virtue of the priest. By contrast, the efficacy of nuns' prayers depended on their personal influence with their heavenly spouse, which depended on the unknowable condition of their inmost souls.

Whatever we may think we know about the probabilities of sexual transgressions in women's communities, it is worth repeating that when women of that milieu speak to us in their own voices, they speak fiercely in defense of their own chastity. Christine of Markyate's parents and friends offered to help her husband rape her when she was a reluctant bride. After her escape, one of the priests who gave her refuge attempted to seduce her by showing her his naked body. No wonder that, when she had a vision of being exposed to the horns of a field full of angry bulls, a heavenly voice promised that if she stood perfectly still they would not touch her.[19] A nun at Engelthal remembered when King Konrad "gave his mercenaries authority over the spiritual women." In flight, fearful for her honor, she heard Christ promise to make her an angel.[20] Mechtild of Hackborn, during Good Friday services, saw Jesus give each of the nuns a shield and buckler, promising that their prayers would protect them from rape and pillage.

Fear and horror of carnality even shadowed virgins who had never been threatened with matrimony. Elisabeth of Schönau and Hildegard of Bingen condemned marriage in almost heretical terms.[21] At best, they saw it as servitude in contrast with the virgin's liberty to serve God. Gertrude of Helfta called it bloodless martyrdom. Catharism, which promoted an end to sexuality and procreation, attracted women in southern France who were prepared to burn at the stake for their faith. Even the northern Beguines, who supported the struggle against the heresy with prayers, fasting, and other self-mortifications, lived at the edge of orthodoxy. In 1224, Henry Minneke, provost of the Cistercian nunnery of Neuwerke, was convicted of Catharism and of teaching his flock that it was a sin to marry. Having learned to regard him as greater than any man born of woman, his credulous nuns risked sharing his fate by supporting his appeal to Rome. A girl at Reims in 1180 was actually burned at the stake because her steadfast refusal to surrender her virginity convinced her would-be seducer that she was a heretic.

Let us then remain heedful of these voices as we confront the cynics drawn by the magnetic appeal of poorly cloistered virgins. Their aspirations were trivialized by poets, polemicists, and preachers who claimed that the female nature was too fragile, if not inherently vicious, to support a full religious vocation. Men who gave their time to the instruction of women or who listened to their ideas were slandered, and the women were left vulnerable to the designs of the unscrupulous. The Dominicans, who took the *cura mulierum* most seriously, bore the brunt of the attack. William Saint Amour, leader of the secular clergy's opposition to their pastoral programs, used their association with nuns and Beguines as a weapon.[22] The troubadour Rutebeuf accused the Paris Beguines of intimate relations with the friars.[23] Jean de Meun implied that Beguines enticed friars to visit, preach charming sermons, and come so close in confession that "often their two heads were in one hood."[24] Instead of defending the women under their care, the Preachers tended to defend themselves by joining the attack. Their rule for the sisters limited social visiting between friars and nuns. It restricted nuns to weekly confession and warned priests against wasting the time of women who depended on their handiwork for a living. Giles li Muisis, the French moralist, said that the very men who consorted with religious women criticized and vilified them when they were done with them. In 1336, the Cluniac chapter general attempted to force its nuns to discontinue working with monks, even at offices. When they resisted, the pope excommunicated fifty nuns and threatened to transfer the most recalcitrant. Archbishop Peckham prohibited nuns of Godstow from conversing with Oxford scholars, for fear that unclean thoughts might breed. At the priory of Saint Radegund, the nuns earned notoriety for conversing with Cambridge scholars, a scandal that finally justified the dissolution of the priory in 1496.

Women depended upon the friendly cooperation of male confessors and spiritual directors to express and channel their religious experiences. Dominican control of the Inquisition had always been balanced by a willingness to promote some women as champions of orthodoxy. Frozen out of that necessary intimacy, women suffered an intensifying threat of heresy. Moreover, growing misogyny increased the pressure to avoid the least breath of scandal. When Catherine of Siena applied to the sisters of Penance or Mantellate, a group of Dominican Tertiaries, they agreed to accept the young virgin only if she were not too pretty because they feared scandal. Fear of gossip frustrated the syneisactic rapport that gave women their only credible voice and led priests to despise nuns and discourage their aspirations. Sympathetic confessors and potential hagiographers began to shun close connection with religious women, and their own voices competed poorly with the increasing gynophobia.

Critics blamed failure to keep cloister for every crime, complaining that nuns strolled about town marketing, collecting tithes, doing business or going out to beg in cases of penury, and even absenting themselves for years to visit sick relatives, attend family celebrations, or go on pilgrimages. The simple irony was that nuns may often have been safer outside their cloisters than within them. Convents were open to all sorts of casual visitors. Some nuns petitioned for enclosure to avoid the burdens and disturbances of hospitality, which could be very heavy indeed. For example, in 1371, John of Gaunt obtained a papal grant to enter any monastery, male or female, once a year with thirty persons of good repute. Parish churches sometimes stood within a convent's enclosure, or the nuns' church might double as a parish church. Workmen, agents, and episcopal visitors were men whom the nuns could not keep out. Engelthal received knights as oblates to protect them from marauding soldiers.[25] The same convent had a reformed rake as chaplain. Families, friends, and notable persons treated monasteries as hotels or refuges.

Most communities housed women who had never taken vows of chastity and never intended to do so. During political upheavals, women were confined to convents to protect them from enemies or prevent them from joining friends. Convents were commonly used as asylums for women who had to hide their shame from the world. Embarrassed families and even the state used them as respectable prisons. A noble Venetian woman pregnant by her lover was condemned to a convent for two years at her husband's expense. After her child was born, her lover rescued her and resumed the relationship. Temporary lodgers awaited resolution of their marital problems, sometimes without much regard for the sensibilities of their hostesses. Heloise took shelter at Argenteuil after her secret marriage with Abelard, who later boasted that they continued to enjoy their conjugal pleasures even in the convent.[26] The principle that mutual consent constituted binding marriage caused much litigation at the beginning and the end of unions. Unions that had never been formalized sometimes dissolved, and repudiated wives sought shelter in convents.

Castimony was as unstable as matrimony. Nuns' voluntary vows lacked the absolute definition that ordination conferred on priests. A nun might or might not come solemnly before a bishop to dedicate herself to Christ. Many were veiled by female superiors. Many veiled themselves in some manner. Many denied that they had taken permanent vows or that their particular vocation demanded such vows. Women often dressed as nuns hoping for protection from abduction or rape. They could leave and marry once the danger had passed if they could prove that they had never intended to be nuns. Virginity itself required legal and theological definition. Sometimes its loss was defined by intention rather than physical state; at others it depended on a rigid interpretation of a woman's physical condition.[27] Some women even claimed to regain their virginity through self-mortification. Young, untutored virgins might not always understand where the limits on their behavior lay.

Visitors and reformers persistently complained of children in nunneries being brought up by their mothers, aunts, and cousins, who left them their bibelots, books, and sometimes prebends. When, if ever, did their virginity become a matter of vocation? A girl raised in a community might stay as a nun or she might marry whenever her parents chose to withdraw her. In Florence, at the beginning of the fifteenth century, parental strategy generally determined whether women would be nuns or wives by age six or seven. Oblates were distanced from their families by being educated in the convent and took vows at age twelve or thirteen. After the Black Death, particularly, vacant places often went to young pupils. Such young women were frequently awaiting marriage, even seeing suitors. Others were tentatively earmarked for the cloister but not permanently consecrated.

Many of the children may well have been the illegitimate offspring of the sisters. So many of the nuns of Saint Aubin had children that their disgusted archbishop refused to regard anyone in this convent as a nun.[28] Our records rarely mention the fate of these children. Often nuns sent their infants to relatives. Fathers sometimes took responsibility, but frequently they were local priests or officials living on the convent goods.[29] It seems probable that others simply blended in with the foundlings, pupils, and relatives. I have already described mothers and daughters in some of the most rigorous convents. Documents do not always indicate the marital status of the nun or the intentions of the daughter. Where the pupils are male, there is even more reason to wonder about their parentage. The nuns of Bival in 1255 were bringing up ten boys. The nuns of Villarceaux were ordered in 1258 to expel the young boy they were rearing.[30] In any case, the routines of silence, chanting, and prayer that dominated the conventual rule had to be greatly modified by the presence of healthy and restless children among the sisters.

A community often housed unwilling children offered as nuns at puberty or girls utterly unsuited to religion. Mad or deformed women were stashed away to secure care or simply to relieve their relatives. Well-meaning efforts to take care of unwed daughters or orphans of guild members or widows of conquered enemies filled convents with women who sometimes wanted nothing but to flee. In sad contrast to the ardent saints who disguised themselves as men to seek the monastic life, Agnes de Flixthorpe escaped her convent and was caught attempting to live in the world in male disguise. Luckier individuals got their vows nullified on the grounds of duress. In 1383, the pope dissolved the vows of a woman who had fled from her convent and married. She testified that she had been carried into the church by force and consecrated despite her loud cries that she was unwilling. A similar case in 1304 ended with the excommunication of the woman who refused every pressure from the archbishop to part her from her lover and child.[31] Women like this clearly found the cloister permeable and made opportunities for rearranging their fate.

The presence of young girls of marriageable age, not yet consecrated or perhaps actively courting, may explain some of the more frivolous instances of merrymaking. Cloistered women sometimes got into difficulties participating in secular celebrations, particularly weddings and christenings held in convent churches. Contemporaries criticized nuns acting as godmothers or bridal attendants who sometimes took the lead in the singing, dancing, playing of musical instruments, and even drinking. Visitors objected to women who donned the habit without formal consecration. The ladies of Saint-Cyr near Rouen, however, wore elaborate dresses and colored veils and acted in "farcical performances" on the feasts of the Innocents and Mary Magdalene when they danced with lay people.[32] The nuns of Sainte-Croix in Poitiers, and probably numerous other communities, indulged in the popular Feast of Fools, when they chose their youngest and silliest novice as "abbess" to lead in merrymaking generally aimed at relieving social tensions by turning the world upside down for a day. Bishops tried in vain to prohibit such lapses of decorum. Even where the prioress was a reformer, their charges did not necessarily obey. From 1230 to 1237 Juliana and her sister Agnes strove to discipline the hospital community of the Augustinian double monastery of Mont Cornillon but failed to curb the younger women intent on meeting men.[33]

Torn between competing male needs to acquire them and to protect them, women suffered from a subliminal identification with "filthy lucre." Unlike money, however, women had wills of their own, contributing to the highly perishable nature of their chastity as a commodity. To secure a desirable suitor or simply to break a girl's determination to remain a virgin, parents might ruthlessly expose her to the lusts of chosen suitors. Or they might sell her outright rather than dower her for marriage. Saint Isabelle appeared in a dream to a girl who was about "to be handed over" to a brothel and directed her to a convent, where the nuns took her in, barefoot in her shift as she escaped.[34] Overly sheltered girls were caught between the need to attract a husband in such confining circumstances and the danger of seduction and ruin. Sequestered and guarded, or vulnerable even in church to the rudest manhandling, some dowerless girls must have evolved "Cinderella" schemes to escape their fate by snaring a husband with their unaided charms.

Meanwhile young men were encouraged to think of women as prizes to be rescued or stolen from behind forbidding walls. Subjected to an unwanted celibacy by families anxious to concentrate their lineage and property by bidding for an elder daughter with a highly inflated dowry, young men turned their gaze toward convents filled with extra daughters, often languishing unwillingly because of the same family strategies. A bride's dowry was paramount in a young man's plans for his future, but poorer, younger sons were willing to settle for less from well-born girls whose parents had ambitions that outstripped their resources. They paraded outside windows and sought amorous encounters in churches.

Popular tales and songs encouraged them to believe that women in convents longed for sex. Rape was only beginning to be understood as a crime of violence against women. In an older sense, it meant the theft of a woman. Young men went out in the world looking for an heiress whom they could attract or even coerce. Yvetta of Huy, an attractive and well-to-do young widow, enclosed herself in a beguinage after a suitor introduced into her home by her relatives tried to rape her while everyone slept. Mechtild of Colmar saved herself from a violent suitor by promising that she would marry him if she ever married anyone. When he later tried to force her in court to marry him, she became a nun.[35] Women with justified fear burrowed deeper into seclusion but often to no avail. Ecclesiastical courts resolved a fair number of cases of abduction of a nun or novice by ordering marriage. If some women cooperated in their own abduction, they served to encourage further attempts of the same sort. If they did object, it is unlikely that their testimony would be given much credit by men convinced that women secretly lusted after them. Gratian applied the most extreme penalties for rape to men who abducted nuns, while the woman who succumbed was punished as an incestuous adulteress. But in practical fact, a nun's flight from a convent could result in a court order that her seducer marry her, providing an enterprising man with a wife and her fortune.

Other men were not looking for marriage but viewed sex as a joke, a competitive game. They could not resist the challenge of scoring against nuns and seemed to think that Christ was a husband they could safely cuckold. In fifteenth-century Venice, the seduction or rape of nuns became a fashion among a certain set of raffish young men. Sisters abetted one another in their love affairs, and in one Venetian convent a sister helped her brother seduce one of the nuns. Lutgard of Aywières, an unwilling nun at first, was courted in her convent by an amorous young man, which the nuns apparently permitted. When she went outside to visit her sister, another wooer tried to kidnap her. She escaped but had to return home through a curious and mocking crowd. Thereafter, she enclosed herself seriously though her fellow nuns ridiculed her exaggerated piety.[36]

Such notions may also have weakened the resolve of young girls to resist seducers. Just as any convent at any time was likely to house a nun with mystical talents, any community might include a sister who had fallen from grace. Unless they had eloped permanently, repentant nuns had to be reintegrated into the community. Around 1160, Aelred of Rievaulx witnessed the outcome of a case involving a Gilbertine nun of Watton who had been pressed into the nunnery as a child and did not develop a religious vocation.[37] One of the brothers of the double order who came into the cloister to work persuaded her to meet him and raped her. She then agreed to an elopement, which the community managed to foil. The nuns beat the girl and shackled her. The brothers beat the guilty man and gave him to the nuns, who forced their pregnant sister to castrate her lover. As she lay in chains, near the time of her delivery, the dead archbishop who had consecrated his niece to the convent appeared in a vision and told her to recite the psalms. As she did so, the pregnancy disappeared and the shackles fell off one leg. When her second foot was liberated, Aelred, whose investigation convinced him that no trickery had been employed, pronounced that God had determined to save the convent from disgrace. Presumably the young woman lived out her life among the same sisters who had punished her sin. Let us hope that the miracle softened their anger at her for jeopardizing their hard-won reputation for sanctity.

The prioress of Thicket vainly protested an order from Thomas Corbridge, archbishop of York, to receive Alicia Darel back after her long wandering in the world whether or not she was repentant:

> We fear that it is probable from the way she talks that if she should return because of heaviness of heart she will not behave herself as her status requires nor ever live peacefully with her companions. Whence for the love of the crucified and restoration of peace we unanimously ask that if it is possible she be placed elsewhere. . . . For if we enclose her alone in the house as you ordered we think that she will deteriorate rather than improve and when she finds it possible to get out she will behave more terribly than she has now. May your paternal feelings always control your government of your daughters in Christ.[38]

Corbridge also forced the prioress of Escholt to restore a nun who left the convent to have a child in her father's house.[39] He may have understood that life is, after all, longer than the smiles of a summer night and that genuine repentance could follow a youthful lapse. At Wilton, in 1528, Cardinal Wolsey objected to the election of an abbess who had once borne two children by two different priests. But he ended by approving the convent choice as "wise and discreet," despite the scandal of her youth.[40]

Moralists who had occasion to confront inevitable sexual misdemeanors tended to stress the possibilities of repentance and redemption. Caesarius of Heisterbach, for example, offered an exemplum that has remained popular for centuries in which a foolish nun, seduced into the world by a dashing stranger, clung to her devotion to the Virgin Mary. When at last she returned to her convent, worn and sick from the abuses of a sinful life, she discovered that the Blessed Mother had kept her place for her, allowing her to return with no one the wiser.[41] These kindly stories, however, put other women who suffered violence in double jeopardy when they proved not to have sufficient virtue to warrant a corrective miracle.

Literature and disciplinary records agree that the vast majority of the nuns' sexual partners were priests. As late as the fifteenth century, the German reformer Johan Busch (d. 1479) said that the lay brethren of his own Augustinian monastery had private property and kept nuns in the monastery with whom they slept and sometimes had children.[42] Presumably, the "nuns" were lay sisters; their status may have been open to debate. All nuns, however, had to maintain chaplains for their sacramental needs—chaplains, who, as we have seen, were often men considered unfit for better work. Visitation books often charge that chaplains performed their rituals badly, behaved in rude or immoral fashion, and did not deal honestly with their charges. Students from Oxford and Cambridge were criticized for cheating nuns whom they served as priests. In 1478, the bishop of Chicester recorded that the chaplain of Easebourne, with a secular accomplice, abducted two nuns with whom they had long-standing relations resulting in children. In collusion with "brother William Cotnall," who boasted of relations with several of the nuns, they persuaded the prioress to pawn the house jewels, spent the money, and used the monastery seal to acquit themselves.

The familiar techniques of sexual harassment were all too readily available. The biographer of Lutgard of Aywières warned nuns to spit in the faces of men soliciting the kiss of peace or to punch anyone, even a priest, who tried to fondle their bosoms. But when Lutgard refused her bishop, who was kissing each nun in turn, the other nuns jokingly forced her to "suffer the violence."[43] Young women of all sorts, but most especially nuns, learned to be obedient and yielding to their superiors, particularly to priests, who heard their most intimate confessions and who sometimes claimed the power to chastise them physically as penance. Johan Busch praised one prioress for her lack of good sense, which made her obedient to her superiors. He happily noted that if one of the fathers ordered something that seemed to her harmful to the nuns, she would point it out humbly but would always obey if overruled.[44]

The power men enjoyed institutionally intimidated women who feared the intentions of their clergy. A priest at Huy pretended to be a disciple of Yvetta to gain access to a young woman living with her. Warned by friends who suspected that she had carelessly encouraged his love for herself, she did not know how to drive him from the place without scandal. Happily, a modest miracle caused the priest to repent and leave.[45] Eudes of Rouen ordered the removal of the priest at Saint-Saëns because of ill fame. Yet it was no small matter to solve the problem. At Bival, in 1248, Sister Isabelle had a child by a priest, who was finally dismissed in 1256. In 1265, the archbishop wanted to recall him to save the £30 they paid him as an annual pension, a heavy sum that was running them into debt. But the nuns complained that the man was "worse than ever" and that they feared his return and his way of life. The archbishop relented and ordered them to keep him away.[46] And when women were not meek and mild, men had greater powers of coercion. Consider the unseemly scene at Marienzee, where the nuns were threatened with expulsion because they refused to adopt Busch's "reform," which the duke of Brunswick promoted. The women resisted angrily and resorted to blows. The duke wrestled one to the floor while the priests watched in amusement before carting the nuns away.[47]

Between clerical "protectors" and secular "attackers," the very existence of many convents was constantly under threat. Spiritual disruption mirrored physical distress. Nuns from houses closed for moral delinquency were routinely distributed among communities with unblemished reputations, spreading suspicion. The sense of family and the intensely particular spiritual practices that marked an established community were utterly unbalanced. Reduced communities were grouped together regardless of order or commitments to patrons. Thus, a handful of impoverished Cistercian nuns from Maguelonne joined the Dominican priory of Prouille.[48] The nuns of Saint Verana of Avignon, desolated by war and flooding, were assigned with their incomes to another monastery. This change gave such offense to the donors of masses for the faithful buried there that they were divided up again.[49] The hierarchy's concern with claustration seemed not to extend to the real hardships of dispossessed nuns. The Dominicans of Saint Praxedis had to go some way down the street for water because the only house where they could afford refuge had a common well with a fish seller, whose filth and stench polluted the water.[50] When war destroyed the buildings of a community in Arles, the sisters caused scandal because they had to shelter in a profane house among priests and laymen.[51]

Gynophobia aggravated the social violence that was driving women out of the fragile shelter of their cloisters. In the fourteenth and fifteenth centuries, consumers of popular literature craved fantasies about vices lurking behind the locked and mysterious doors of the cloister. Nuns became the heroines of a new sort of literature ranging from the gentle cynicism of Chaucer's *Canterbury Tales* through the outright pornography of Giovanni Boccaccio.[52] Men generally agreed that they had drawn the criticism upon themselves. The English social critics John Gower and William Langland attributed the problem to the fundamental weaknesses of women. Nuns were paired with priests and monks in fabliaux. In one story, when a reluctant woman told her suitor that she would become a nun, he countered that he would become a priest and get her that way. "The Crafty Nun," from the *Cent nouvelles nouvelles,* pictured a whole convent of sisters commanding priests and monks to sleep with them because their abbess needed to be cured of love sickness and they all wanted to support her. A genre of anonymous lyrics called "nuns' songs" became popular throughout Europe. They featured the complaints of nuns as unwilling prisoners longing for love. On the other side, the poem, "Why I Can't Be a Nun" turned on the proposition that a young girl striving for a religious life against her father's opposition gave in when a vision of Lady Experience showed her the vices that flourished in nunneries.

Reformers from Carolingian times colorfully described many convents as *lupanaria,* or brothels. The idea may say more about the male imagination than female behavior, but the likeness between prostitutes and nuns became a commonplace of misogynist humor. In the twelfth century, Duke William of Aquitaine, irritated by the success of Fontevraud, where his former wife had taken shelter, threatened to build a "convent" of whores.[53] The resemblance struck the fancy of men made uneasy by the presence of women outside the boundaries of family controls. Jacques de Vitry wrote angrily that some Dominican priests betrayed religious women who confessed their weaknesses and lapses by preaching publicly that congregations of holy virgins were brothels rather than religious convents, "attributing the faults of a few women to all, so far defaming the order approved by God and God-fearing persons that they shocked many people."[54]

Jacques himself was shocked to see prostitutes who plied their trade in the houses where the young clerics of Paris were being educated for the church. Cathedral chapters and other ecclesiastical establishments repeatedly and vainly tried to keep prostitutes out of the small houses around the closes. They haunted church yards and porches and even solicited business inside churches. The sisters of the Hôtel Dieu in Paris, whose refectory looked out on the street, complained of the unsavory exchanges that they unwillingly heard whenever they opened the windows for fresh air. Preachers tried to discourage young men from physically molesting honest girls in church, but more powerful officials looked for a solution in the confinement of all women. Even concerned protectors agreed that respectable women would not expose themselves to danger. The public places belonged to men.

Thus whether beggary, routine business, charity, or soliciting drove women into the streets, the rudest of men felt free to give them "what they asked for." Women's need for money in the face of desperate, involuntary poverty involved them in webs of sin and deception spun by men who tended to think that pure women could live on virtue alone. Their charities were classed as theft from their husbands or their children. Every unmarried woman who supported herself in the various trades was suspected of occasional prostitution by anyone who knew the insufficiency of their wages. Beguines who solved the problem by self-starvation were accused of hypocrisy. Men simply deemed women were inscrutable, secretive, devious. They were social shape-changers, one day virtuous maids or matrons, the next bewitching whores or lascivious nuns.

Nuns were already tainted as simoniacs by the dowries they brought for their support into the convent. When that money did not suffice, or when it was lost through violence, houses vanished because the nuns could not feed themselves. In some cases, they left the monasteries to beg and at times may have tried to support themselves by prostitution. The fifteenth-century jurist Franciscus de Platea determined that convents should not retain fees collected by nuns acting as prostitutes but spend them to support pious causes.[55] Perhaps only a lawyer's exercise, this view mirrored popular fancy. Prostitution was seen not as a means for poor women to support themselves but as a necessary, regrettable, outlet for men. The plague's ravages among women and escalating dowry costs left many young men unmarried. Moralists and civic authorities considered prostitution a defense against a consequent rise in homosexuality and rape. The same disproportionate mortality of women, however, caused a prostitute shortage, which may in part account for an escalating attack on nuns.

Nuns and prostitutes shared certain characteristics. Above all, they were independent of parental and conjugal discipline. They had some claim to economic and social independence. In the twelfth and thirteenth centuries, private brothels might be owned by any entrepreneur, including the clergy and even nuns, though they did not necessarily run the business. In time, however, just as monasteries came under clerical control, brothels were taken over by public powers. Popular tradition credits Louis IX with the assignment of eight particular streets in Paris to vice. By the fourteenth century, it was the general practice throughout Europe to limit prostitutes to particular "red light districts" and to punish them if they strayed beyond. They shared houses or bought them with the proceeds of their trade. In 1489, the *filles publiques* of Amiens asked the city fathers to charter a place where they could live and work together. By the fifteenth century, when the public brothel was a recognized institution all over Europe, female ownership had given way to masculine management. An inmate of a brothel had become a "public woman" rather than a private entrepreneur.

Like convents, enclosed brothels challenged enterprising men with thoughts of mysterious and forbidden women. They resembled cloisters in that the women were rarely allowed out (only for mass) and had to eat in the community. Their clothing was strictly regulated. Prostitutes were prohibited ornaments or elaborate trimmings for their clothes and the list of forbidden items grew. At first, the sergeants who caught the offending women could confiscate the finery and enrich themselves with it. After 1420, proceeds went to the city and at least one court diverted a prostitute's jewelry and fur trim to the Hôtel Dieu. Finally, they were commanded to observe the sexual fasts of the church and forcibly exposed to sermons during Holy Week. Through the fourteenth and fifteenth centuries, even legal documents routinely used the terms "abbess" and "abbot" for brothel managers. Not uncommonly, the houses had to be fortified to protect the women from attacks.

But prostitution was not a permanent stigma. Mary Magdalene—popularly depicted as a repentant prostitute, the first hermit, and the exemplar of the contemplative life chosen by Mary of Bethany—typified the tendency for women from one stratum to melt into another. She gave her name to a quasi-order of repentant prostitutes. Just as marriages could be annulled, prostitutes might nullify their sin by confession and follow the penitential path laid out by dozens of mythical saints. Popular preachers of the twelfth century portrayed prostitutes as the victims of an avaricious society that turned poor women into disposable "surplus." Innocent III and other church authorities encouraged their marriage and promoted the charity of giving poor girls dowries. For many reformed prostitutes, convents served as rehabilitation centers. In 1186, an Augustinian nunnery formed in Cologne around a penitent woman who wore a religious habit and ministered to her former lover, who had enclosed himself in the church. In 1198 two priests, Fulcon and Pierre de Rossiac, specialized in the conversion of prostitutes for whom they founded the monastery of Saint Anthony near Paris. Fulk of Neuilly founded an abbey in 1206 for prostitutes converted by his preaching. A German preacher named Rodolphe persuaded a group of prostitutes to reform in return for food and drink. He enclosed them in a house and set a servant to beg food for them while he went on preaching in other towns.[56]

Some refuge had to be maintained for the prodigal daughter when she repented, if no husband could be found to bear the burden. In 1215, Bishop Fulk of Toulouse gave Dominic, who had previously specialized in rescuing women from heresy, buildings to house "women reclaimed from the streets who embraced the religious life." In 1226, the bishop of

Paris established a new house for penitents whom he called the Daughters of God because they had lost the protection of their earthly kin. Sometimes a convent took in abandoned wives, reclaiming the cost of their support from their husbands when possible. Catherine de Lizé's husband left her penniless. She supported herself by prostitution for a while and then gained admission to a convent for penitents. Twenty years later, in 1476, when her husband attempted to reclaim her, she was head of the house.

In 1227, Gregory IX chartered a penitential house in Mainz for prostitutes who, after a short trial period, were to choose marriage or the cloister. They were commonly known as White Ladies from the color of their habits. In 1232, the pope ordered German houses of the "order of Saint Mary Magdalene" to adopt the Cistercian, Augustinian, or San Sistan rule. This rather loosely conceived order spread in the Rhineland and central Germany, Italy, and Bohemia. By the late thirteenth or early fourteenth century, most major towns in southern France had such communities. In 1286, the entire order of penitents was transferred to the Dominicans, who succeeded in freeing themselves from the undesirable *cura* within five years. Some houses remained Dominican and others went to other orders. Some remained under episcopal supervision. The Magdalenes dissolved among the other loosely defined communities of women supervised by various orders or ecclesiastical officials.

Colette of Corbie, the fifteenth-century Franciscan reformer, worked with her confessor to convert "poor women, dissolute and deviated from the way of purity and honesty."[57] She saved them by her preaching and he gave them a house and the necessities of life. Colette, it was said, "never abominated sinful women or held them in horror whether they were religious or of another state but carefully guided and piously reminded them how our savior came from heaven for sinners' sakes."[58] Her tolerance drew women who "confidently came to her exposing enormous excesses of sins to her never disclosed to any other. And she so admonished them that they became their own accusers and were brought to true penance."

A repentant women's convent functioned as a retirement home as much as a genuine religious community. Sometimes prostitutes entered a convent as a group, supported by a society concerned with preventing "retired" prostitutes from engaging in more criminal activity. At one point, the whole municipal brothel of Albi converted and lived on public alms. Possibly for that reason the charter of a house for penitents in Avignon specified that they would receive "only young women of 25 years of age who had been lubricious in their youth and who by their beauty and charm might still succumb through their fragility to worldly pleasures and attracted men to them."[59] They were directed to behave modestly and humbly, eschewing all idle or involved conversation. Except for the rectrix and her chosen chaplain they were to be strictly cloistered, and any nun who tried to go out was to be imprisoned. They were to sleep clothed and penalties were provided for any who slept naked and with a younger sister. They could have visitors at a grille with a chaperon but were particularly forbidden to speak with men who had been their partners in crime. But even penitence implied the will to sin. Images of lustful nuns and repentant harlots dissolved back and forth into one another and flowed into other darker images still. The dichotomy of Eve and Mary melted into a single image of woman as the carrier of sexual disorder, the temptress, agent of the ancient enemy, always alert to pollute unwary men.

Former prostitutes shared the penitential experience with the sexually fragile and even with ordinary nuns. As we have seen, women who fled and returned, women who had children as a result of seduction or even rape, were generally reintegrated into their communities for lack of a better solution to their problems. Penitents were often empowered to introduce nuns from other orders to instruct them in observing the rule. Or they could delegate women from their houses to go to other orders for instruction. Moreover, convents of penitents often housed perfectly respectable virgins or widows who exchanged their goods for a place at the common table and a private room, going and coming freely without being constrained by the rule. In 1347, the director of the Magdalene in Avignon was the widow of one of the leading nobles in the city, whose family had produced many consuls. She had sufficient funds to buy two good pieces of land for the convent. The convent of the White Ladies of the Penitential Order of Mary Magdalene was founded by certain patricians in Cologne for repentant prostitutes around 1229. But by 1250 the pressure for places was so great that nuns from the propertied class, predominantly middle class with a few patricians, had displaced the original inhabitants.

There is no reason to suppose that these respectable ladies had any great difficulty in classing themselves as penitents. Medieval people, after all, knew that everyone sinned and all must repent. Mary Magdalene was also the patroness of contemplative virgins. Penitential manuals contained a systematic apparatus for the definition and discovery of sin, aimed specifically at exposing the inadequacy of the sinner. Confessors emphasized scrupulosity in order to promote penitence in more hardened souls. Unscrupulous confessors could easily play on a woman's fear of her own unworthiness. One of Yvetta of Huy's companions was seduced out of her cloister by her confessor, who convinced her that her reputation for unstained chastity had snared her in the deadly sin of pride.[60] The late Middle Ages were characterized by extravaganzas of guilt and penitence associated with the plague and other social crises. Popular preachers were sometimes preceded into town by women repenting their sins by self-flagellation. "Revivalist" meetings often ended with a bonfire of vanities and grand days of penance. It is rarely possible for us to distinguish between penitents atoning for lives sunk in vice and those repenting for tempting men with false hair or makeup.

Finally, nuns who had recourse to prayer as their only source of power and protection from violence tended to blame themselves for every disaster. One nun at Töss who, through negligence, failed to join in a special prayer to Saint Gertrude felt that she had cursed the whole community. Elisabeth Bechlin lived an irreproachable life. Yet, when the convent suffered a dearth of wine and corn while she was cellaress, she attributed it to her own ingratitude and could only complete her year in office after being reassured by an angel.[61] Women's self-accusations, penitence for guilt that did not always exist, contributed to an atmosphere of suspicion. The penitential stress on sins of intention and the dangers of temptation exposed them to severe self-doubt. To complicate things further, the most virtuous women made a specialty of repenting for the sins of others and suffering in their place.

God sometimes gave his favorites over to diabolic power to test and hurt them. Christine of Stommeln was assaulted night after night by demons who claimed that God had given them power to stuff poisonous toads and reptiles into her body, tear her apart and otherwise challenge her integrity.[62] Her triumph brought the release of hundreds of souls from purgatory. At the beginning of the schism, Pope Urban was threatened with violence. Catherine of Siena obtained his rescue by voluntarily giving the devil power to torment her. Heroic as these accounts were, they served to strengthen the image of religious women acting in the hands of the devil. For nuns, particularly those whose confessors were inadequate to their needs, fear of demoniac possession and diabolic temptation was ever present. Justified fear of rape easily extended to fear of their own attractive powers. Every nun guarded against the wiles of men. The wiles of the supernatural were even more terrifying. Nuns felt exposed to the ancient enemy, the old serpent in a whole series of new forms. Demons came seductively in the guise of saints and angels to trouble the dreams of unwary women. When the young Elisabeth of Schönau first started having visions, she took them for diabolic possession. Her first visions cast her into a state of torment and darkness. The devil's threatening appearances alternated with images of the blessed Virgin, who reassured and comforted her.

Even union with God became cause for suspicion. Nuns in their confessionals were vulnerable to the same sort of shaping and direction as heretics before inquisitorial tribunals. Moving back and forth, as they often did, between heterodox prophets and orthodox mystics, certain learned clergymen gradually formulated the concept of the Free Spirit heresy, a mixture of erotic mysticism, libertinism, and hypocrisy. The myth rested on false topoi imposed by inquisitors on the standard pieties of the *vita evangelica*. It was said to flourish in beguinages among devout men and women mystics whose desire to annihilate the soul in God resulted in excessive love. Passion led to libertinism and the orgies later associated with witch cults. Jean Gerson, chancellor of the University of Paris, charged that "some naive women" who confused divine love with carnal love, "through ignorance were more attached to God or to holy men by sensual affection than through love."[63] He quoted "Marie de Valenciennes" as claiming that anyone who achieved the state of divine love was free from all the commandments. Again, he implied, men can never safely associate with women because even love originating in the spirit tends to be consummated in the flesh.[64]

The idea of orgiastic women devoted to the Free Spirit no doubt pointed to the fantasy of devil-worshiping covens that seized the popular imagination at the end of the Middle Ages. Charges against nuns became increasingly vitriolic. Masuccio il Salernitano perfected a new genre when he accused them of unbridled license followed by abortions or infanticides, filling the sewers of nunneries with the skeletons of babies. We are suddenly but a short step to the ghastly tales of orgies and child murder that readily attached to medieval society's pariahs: prostitutes, usurious Jews, and finally witches. In the thirteenth century, Thomas Aquinas argued against the old *canon episcopi*, which rejected belief in witchcraft as a heresy.[65] The reality of the devil's power to do harm began to overshadow confidence in the protective power of prayer. Once it was established that devils could cause harm and prevent sexual intercourse, it was easy to argue that, with the devil's help, witches could reduce men to impotence, injure their sexual organs, or create an illusion of castration.

It took nearly two centuries, from the trials of the Templars in the early fourteenth to the publication of *Malleus Maleficarum* in the late fifteenth, to complete the identification of women and witchcraft. John XXII identified heresy with sorcery and women with both. Out of their experience in molding heresy, Dominican inquisitors like Johannes Nider began a systematic indictment of women as practitioners of witchcraft.[66] On December 5, 1484, Innocent VIII's bull, *Summis Desiderantes Affectibus*, proclaimed the real existence of witchcraft.[67] *Malleus Maleficarum*, written in the same year by the Dominican inquisitors Jacobus Sprenger and Heinrich Kraemer, proposed that both the devil and the witch did evil with God's permission. There remained only a hair's breadth of difference between the compliance of the witch and the submission of the saint to the power God gave the devil to test her endurance.

Sprenger and Kraemer directly confronted the question of women's peculiar susceptibility to diabolic temptations. The key to their thinking seems to be some growing fear of threats to male virility. Repeating the original drama of Eden, *Malleus* maintains that women are seduced by the devil, with whom they make a pact giving them the power to seduce men.[68] The authors offer the proof that witches are women because only men are rendered impotent. The seizures of lust and longing that afflicted men, their unbidden erotic surges, seemed to come from some outside source and that source was identified, explicitly or implicitly, as the wicked will of the woman who was its object. Prostitutes and aged women who became procuresses were also attacked during this period of growing hysteria. An old woman imprisoned in 1390 confessed after torture that she had conspired with the devil to assist a young prostitute bewitch her lover. She also confessed that the devil assisted her in healing a prostitute of various occupational diseases. Late 1459–60, in Artois, several prostitutes were burned for sorcery. The inquisition searched the ranks of the homeless in Paris rounding up numerous free-lance prostitutes. Thus we have cases linking sorcery and prostitution, procuresses and healing and charms. A Franciscan Tertiary, Belleza Orsini, accused of casting a spell on a young man in a group of pilgrims with whom she traveled to Rome, told her inquisitors that she knew many ways of healing but used them for nothing but good. Indeed, all these women may have experimented with the charms and spells and potions so universally credited with extraordinary power. Women's insatiable sexuality was the instrument that attracted the devil while their weakness and insecurity drew them to use the deceitful weapons he provided for vengeance.

Uncontrolled virginity was as dangerous as uncontrolled sexuality. The Beguines, who were persecuted and burned in the early fourteenth century, were accused of having embraced vows of chastity without ecclesiastical approval and supervision. At the Council of Constance, the Dominican Matthew Grabon demanded the restoration of this rule. This was, of course, the same council that burned John Hus for his radical anticlericalism. The whole group of reformers engaged in ending the schism and restoring the power of the hierarchy sought to silence men as well as women who preached too loudly against the moral failings of the clergy. Women were particularly offensive when they consciously opposed the example of their own virginity and austerity to priestly self-indulgence. One self-consecrated virgin even claimed that she bore the Holy Spirit within her as Mary had once borne Christ and that in due course she and her child would usher in the purified church of a new age.[69] The growing confidence of pure women in their own powers had spread from their convents out into the public world during the fourteenth century. Johannes Nider described the trial of a virgin of fifty-three, with a good reputation at Regensburg, during the Council of Basel. She said she had a spirit from God, divine revelations that instructed her not to obey the pope when he was wrong. She believed herself to be impeccable, the mother of the entire church of Christ represented at the Council of Basel. Chancellor Gerson took the lead in enlisting highly trained theologians to establish tests that could reliably distinguish true from false visions.

As a Frenchman, Gerson was willing to exempt Joan of Arc from his suspicions, but the English were not. They burned her for witchcraft. Nider noted other individuals and groups of women inspired to dress as men and imitate Joan who were tried and sometimes burned as witches. No saint was so reputable or so secure as to be safe from attack. Ursulina of Parma, whom God instructed to visit both popes to end the schism, barely escaped being tried for sorcery. Catherine of Siena also faced suspicions of sorcery when she tried to pursue the public mission to which her visions called her. The fifteenth-century reformer of the Franciscan order Saint Colette was accused "by people of every condition, even those who had known and loved her. . . . Some said she was a witch who cast lots and invoked the enemies from Hell. And they attempted . . . to push her into such infamy and vituperation that no one dared to receive her into their own hospice. At last with such many sided atrocious persecutions, they compelled her to go away quickly from her native land to foreign and distant parts."[70]

In this atmosphere, even the most scrupulous cloistering had its own dangers. Presumably imposed upon chaste unmarried women for their own protection, it was extended to prostitutes for the purported protection of respectable women. But the consistent subtext of the argument was that men were in danger from uncontrolled women, which in turn suggested that such women had some mysterious power stemming from their own inherent evil. Occasionally, religious women were criticized for avoiding men, using their vows to express their hatred of the opposite sex. Aelred, even more explicitly, warned that gossiping in the day would lead to entertaining even less reputable women at night. He reminded his sister that virginity can be lost with a member of one's own sex, a man for a man or a woman for a woman, "which meets with more relentless condemnation than any other crime."[71]

The idea of women concentrated together in highly charged spaces, bursting with barely controlled sexual desire, terrified men. Misogynist writers became obsessed with the idea of women's power. The good-natured Chaucer posed that question in *The Wife of Bath's Tale,* which concerns women's desire to rule over men through secret lore and cunning. Many nervous authors saw even women safely placed inside the household as sources of danger and disruption. The fifteenth-century, *Quinze joyes de mariage* depicted a wife, mother-in-law, and female servants plotting together, eating and drinking in the bridal chamber while neglecting the solitary husband, and even forcing him to do chores for his wife. Mothers were envisaged as enticing their daughters into sin. Women servants were relentlessly disciplined in the courts because they were uncontrolled by husbands. Plates given to congratulate new mothers often depicted such popular scenes as Phyllis riding Aristotle. Pamphlets and books warned men about widows who had to be prevented from lording it over their second husbands. Nigellus Wirecker, in *Brunellus,* accused nuns of using religion to express their hatred of men.[72]

The *Evangiles des quenouilles* pictures women spinning together, talking in secret, and telling stories related to the Decameron. They read chapters to each other and exchanged women's lore on fertility and other semioccult matters. These "gospels" depict means of control over animal husbandry and crops; the sexual act and birth. The women can make a husband prefer one child to another. They end by vowing to pass on what they learn from woman to woman but never divulge their secrets to men. The secretary recording their sayings remarks: "It seemed to them that, through these constitutions and chapters, the world should henceforth be governed and ruled by them."[73]

In the middle of the fifteenth century, when Johannes Busch and his cohorts set out to impose a uniform rule on all nuns in Saxony, they met with considerable resistance in convents long accustomed to formulating their own customs. Some convents locked their gates; some appealed to other superiors. Some nuns opposed them physically or persuaded their relatives to do so. In one convent, the horrified reformers burst into the chapel and found the nuns with arms outstretched in the form of a cross, clutching lighted candles and chanting the forbidden psalm, *In media vitae* (In the midst of life we are in death). They recoiled in fear from a ritual long associated with deadly curses.[74] This story foreshadows the covens of witches who danced through the nightmares of sixteenth- and seventeenth-century judges. The outcast women of the age melted together, haunting men as the seductress whose beauty covered the bones and worms of mortality or as the cloistered prostitute who exchanged secrets and brewed potions to control her lovers. Cloistered virgins might control even more terrible powers if one gave credit to their own tales of mystical marvels or to the reports of their critics.

The Middle Ages ended in war, plague, and famine. The apocalyptic horses rode roughshod over a cowering and penitent population. The modern age dawned with a new longing for order and authority as a solution to the horrors of medieval liberty. The values of the patriarchal household gained new respect, while unmarried women nuns and prostitutes alike were disciplined by secular and ecclesiastical authorities to ensure the safety of the new order.

IV

THE EARLY MODERN ERA

14

∴✦∴

Regular Lives

In 1437, Johan Nider, a prominent Dominican reformer, was just completing a book of popular theology, *Formicarius* (The ant hill). Criticisms of women religious garnered from his visitations of Dominican nuns preceded a description of the witch cult, which was just beginning to preoccupy social critics. He left the radical Council of Basel for Speyer to support a reforming mission headed by Peter de Gengenbach, a German provincial called vicar-general of reformed Preacheresses. Anticipating resistance from the nuns, the local margrave had assigned men-at-arms to the reformers and some of the burghers also gathered to help. Peter brought them to the convent of Hasepful just after the nuns had retired for the night and, unaccountably, climbed up into the room where the sisters were sleeping. When the nuns awoke to find their dormitory full of men, they ran screaming to the windows and roused the city. The watchman blew his trumpet and the confessor rang the bells. Townsmen rushing to the rescue were astounded to find Peter and the burghers there. Peter was bound and led through an angry crowd by torchlight to the court. The margrave's servants were locked up and the burghermeister was deposed from his office. Finally they were all told that the reform should be introduced by day and not by night.[1]

Despite continued threats of war, plague, and economic instability, the fifteenth century was an energetic period of reform. Satirists depicted monks as useless, greedy parasites and friars as fraudulent exploiters of gullible lay folk. Assuming the incorrigible frailty of women, they saw vanity and hypocrisy where outright sexual misconduct was not demonstrable. The most radical humanists, Wyclifites and Hussites, precursors of sixteenth-century Protestants, launched a broad attack against the whole monastic order, denying the very concept of chaste celibacy as a virtue. But most people still defined reform as the restoration of regulars to their pristine ideals. They sought the causes of monastic decay in transitory phenomena that could be corrected or reversed.

Popes, councils, bishops, and orders tried to enforce *Periculoso* and subject all religious women to a uniform way of life based on the Benedictine rule, with strict claustration. Reformers particularly opposed their tendency to live on private endowments and tried to force them to shift, willingly or unwillingly, to the common life. Reformers branded dowries simoniacal and blamed the prebend system for disunity, intrigue, and inequity among the nuns. They attributed the decline in the number of nuns who could be supported by an eroded endowment to self-indulgence and attacked secular abbesses for monopolizing the common funds entrusted to the abbatial mense. The complaints were not always unjustified. The abbess of Harcourt, for example, supported a hundred hunting dogs and four falconers, while the sisters had barely enough to eat.

Nuns retaliated with complaints on the conduct of the *cura*. Cluniac nuns of Feldbach repeatedly asked the order to replace their single French-speaking priest with German-speaking confessors. Dominicans of Strasbourg charged that the friars demanded money or jewelry in exchange for administering the sacraments to them. The Augustinian reformer Johan Busch admitted that the confessor of the Penitents of Hildesheim resigned when the restoration of common property stopped the flow of their customary gifts. Nuns particularly resented criticism from orders that had always been indifferent to their needs. In 1382, the chevalier of Eptingen, whose five daughters and two sisters-in-law dominated the community at Klingenthal, got the convent transferred to the bishop of Basel's jurisdiction, accusing the friars of neglecting their spiritual and temporal interests. The nuns of Meaux objected to obeying rules not current when they made their vows and continued to come and go freely as they had done since their profession. Canonesses protested that they had vowed neither poverty nor permanent chastity. Nuns often found themselves condemned for resisting reform when they did not consider themselves deformed. They resisted invasion by presumptuous strangers as fiercely as they could. At Markyate, they threw a copy of *Periculoso* at their bishop's departing back. The Cistercian nuns in Marienzee expected the bishop of Mynden to protect them from the duke of Braunschweig's attempt to force an Augustinian reform upon them. When he declined, one threw her headdress at his feet, saying: "You have always said I should not reform and now you want to force me to reform. There! take your veil and crown! I don't want to be a nun any more."[2] Was this hopeless corruption? Before we leap too swiftly to the bait, let us stop and consider whether it is a true measure of corruption that women failed to embrace vocations defined by men.

Some bishops acted in a realistic and genuinely paternal spirit toward the nuns in their charge. The bishop of Lincoln in 1432 issued a statute regulating the nuns of Godstow that required them to keep the canonical hours, share common meals in the refectory, and observe silence.[3] He sensibly limited and supervised trips out of the monastery and visitors within. In addition, he made some effort to curb the worst effects of the unequal distribution of income, which reproduced the class system in the monastery. The nuns were to be distributed in no more than three separate households, and private evening parties devoted to gossip and wine drinking were to be stopped. The dinner parties might have offset the imbalances in the resources of the community but they gave richer nuns a golden opportunity to patronize their own favorites and to form factions based on generosity with their food parcels from home or whatever else came into their hands. Instead, the bishop commanded that the nuns reinstate their old customary contributions to the general fund for the relief of destitute nuns. On the whole, the bishop, who knew the abbey and its inhabitants, provided them with a reasonable program for maintaining their social and spiritual responsibilities, while acknowledging their place in local society by accommodating relaxed claustration.

The papacy favored monastic union as a counter to episcopal autonomy and a resurgence of lay patronage. In the fourteenth century, Benedict XII promulgated a series of reforming statutes aimed at abolishing the worst deviations from the respective monastic rules and regularizing common mitigations. At the same time, he imposed constitutional unification on orders hitherto defined only by a common rule.[4] He grouped the Benedictines into thirty-five provinces and ordered them to hold regular chapter-generals. The Augustinians, too, were envisaged as an order rather than a series of communities using variations of the rule. Papal legates organized provincial chapter-generals and visited each house. This strengthened ordering checked abuses of abbatial power but it also threatened community autonomy, which had much more relevance to the structural conditions that governed women's position in the religious environment. Nuns never entered the broader network available to monks through university training, preaching, or other pastoral activity. They were never eligible for offices that would give them a broader view of the church or even their own order as an international community. Nor were they ever responsible for its governance at any level beyond their own convents.

In the twelfth and thirteenth centuries, women were eager to be partners with men in the formation of orders but they had been refused and marginalized. They had developed a religious life within a smaller and more intimate sphere, and in the fifteenth century they were reluctant to give up their autonomy for the supervision of strangers. Their lives remained closely interwoven with local society. They depended on their families and friends for economic and political support when their jurisdiction and their endowments were threatened. In return, they supplied pastoral and spiritual services. They were called home to help out in family crises and extended family influence by capturing monastic offices. Relatives or patrons who had bequests or privileges to give received hospitality and sometimes simply moved in. Abbesses took more liberty than strict claustration allowed to protect their rights and their property from their putative guardians. But resistance to *Periculoso* threatened their income and prestige by fueling the fires of scandal.

While the pope worked at unifying all the old independent houses under the banner of an order, nuns often used the confusion of jurisdiction between orders and bishops to maintain their own autonomy. In 1408, thirty nuns of Malquelt, who wore Cistercian habits while following the Cluniac rule in the precincts of Paderborn Cathedral, told a Cluniac visitor that they did not know what order they belonged to and refused to obey anyone who could not prove just rights over them. Nuns of Colmar used episcopal jurisdiction against the encroachments of the

Dominican order. Competent abbesses often profited from the relaxed grip of ecclesiastical authority in the late fourteenth century to guide their monasteries through the perilous decades of plague, war, and financial crisis. For them the breakdown of the papacy and its attendant institutions brought, perhaps, a welcome breathing space.

The autonomous abbey of Sainte-Croix exemplified the "corruption" that critics decried. It had been exceptionally well endowed at its foundation and the abbatial mense had kept a reasonable portion of its corporate wealth. The conventual mense was divided into prebends of unequal value to which each choir nun added her dowry. Income from autonomous priories held by the monastery was assigned to prioresses, who lived at Sainte-Croix and rarely visited their livings. In 1359, the monastery was seriously damaged by English pillagers after the battle of Poitiers. The community weathered the storm only to be devastated again during the French resurgence of the early fifteenth century, but the abbatial mense grew as land value increased. The conventual mense shrank as heritable prebends were eaten away by inflation and had to be combined, diminishing the number of nuns. The chapter, however, still had sufficient financial resources in the years 1439–1444 to fortify the villages on its estates.

Sainte-Croix survived—and still survives—maintaining an honorable place in the society of the countryside. Most of the nuns came from the petty nobility who dominated secular and clerical life in Poitiers, and they continued to cultivate the bonds of family. Individual sisters were often absent on personal or family business, such as lawsuits regarding legacies. The whole community regularly dispersed to the country when epidemic raged in the city, and individuals were frequently advised to take the waters or pursue other restorative regimens. When the war came too close, they returned home for safety or took refuge in a priory. Abbesses and prioresses took nuns, men-at-arms, and other attendants when they traveled on business, calling on vassals with hospitality duties to house and feed them. Reciprocally, they had to entertain visitors, sometimes for long sojourns, and they educated young girls, who brought contributions to supplement their income. On the Feast of Innocents, a nun was designated Abbess of Innocents and led the city's merrymakers. They shared the beauty of their elaborate services and their splendid altar fittings and vestments with the town and with pilgrims from afar through public processions and other liturgies celebrating feasts in honor of Radegund. The mandatum was observed on Holy Thursday, and alms of daily food with special distributions on her feast days commemorated Radegund in a more practical way. A special veneration of the relic of the cross linked the monastery to Good Friday.

Such women were not deaf to the voice of reform. Many houses eagerly joined reforming congregations or observant movements within their orders, and many undertook their own reform—not an easy process. Nuns were not so well linked as monks and found it difficult to get reforming nuns into their communities to train them. Few nunneries had regular contact, and cloister kept them tied to their own communities. They could rarely transfer permanently because, while they took the income from their dowries with them, the capital belonged to the original monastery. When ecclesiastical authorities took the initiative in imposing reform, nuns often refused to invade communities where they would be unwelcome. These were not unjustified misgivings, although some convents came to love their new sisters. The prioress Helena and procuratrix Geseke of Marienberg wrote lovingly to Ida, Thecla, and Aleida of Bronopia, who had come in with Johan Busch to reform their monastery. They thanked the reformers for their service and regretted that cloistering would mean that they could never hope to visit their newfound friends.[5]

Nuns who had been involved in reforming their own houses seem to have been willing to answer the request of a sister house for assistance. Twenty years after Peter's sophomoric attack, the nuns of Hasepful welcomed a group of reformed sisters from Worms. In broad daylight in the presence of the new father of the order and the burghers and lords of Speyer, the prioress handed over her keys, saying, "We all understand that you mean to lock us in and impose the observance." But patrons, family, and even the alms-seeking poor were not eager to see the cloister gates close or to encourage the austerity of the common life. A reforming nun of Saint Agnes of Strasbourg argued that even visiting family through the windows was inimical to chastity and to poverty. "So I see my mother, father, brother and sisters coming to me in their worldly finery and we are all human. I will make many distortions in my heart and desire or admire goods and serve God with singing and reading while I am becoming more worldly in dress and behavior, blighting true purity.

So I will become ashamed of my humble clothing and want all sorts of
fancy things. And so I will be ashamed in my work and every evidence
of poverty."[6] Possibly, other nuns did not mind escaping the constant
demands that accompanied the favor of their families. When the nuns at
Soleilmont chose to undertake strict cloistering, their families tried to
stop them. Soleilmont became a leader in the reform movement, but the
prescient reader may well wonder if reforms so unwelcome to their
supporters did not contribute something to the Reformation.

As early-fourteenth-century pressures relaxed, the numbers of Tertiaries, Beguines, Beatas, and recluses grew. The schism that divided the
papacy after Gregory XI's return to Rome from Avignon has often been
seen as medieval Catholicism's darkest hour. It widened the spaces where
corruption could take root, but it also made space for innovation. A
number of women tentatively organized communities and even small
congregations. The Sisters of the Common Life occupied Gerhard
Grote's house in Deventer about 1380, seeking to realize the principle
enunciated by many contemporary humanists that true nobility rested
upon character, not birth or personal wealth. Grote criticized convents
for excluding devout and accomplished women who were poor or common: "Poverty is condemned and despised by those for whom the love
of poverty is prescribed."[7] The Sisters adopted neither vows nor habits,
working for a living and pursuing a common life of service to God.
They paid for their own utensils, food, and clothing out of their earnings.
They prayed individually rather than doing common offices and tried to
maintain their fresh ardor by using the little things of daily life to
stimulate meditation on the life of Christ.

Their spirituality came to be known as the *devotio moderna*, emphasizing inward emotions and direct communication with God inspired by
reading Scripture rather than studying formal theology while retaining a
scrupulous orthodoxy in regard to the sacraments and indulgences.
Essentially monastic in nature, it inspired devotions compatible with
enclosure and, coincidentally, with feminine piety. By 1407, the devotion
was spreading to other towns. The Sisters associated with Brethren of
the Common Life, who acted as their confessors. Otherwise, they restricted their contacts with men and rarely traveled abroad but did not
attempt strict cloistering. Their earnings went into a common purse and
all shared equally, including the sick and infirm. When sisters died, their

property went to the community. Each house annually elected a "mistress" to administer the common property and distribute work to the inmates. She supervised their behavior and kept peace among them. They paid their local taxes and submitted to secular magistrates in external affairs. After the Council of Constance, in 1418, resolved the schism with the election of Martin V, popes and subsequent reforming councils revived the policy of unifying religious individuals in the regular life. The Sisters of the Common Life gradually turned into Augustinian nuns.

Nicholas of Cusa, as papal legate, attempted to organize the Beguines and distribute them among recognized orders. In 1451, John of Capistrano estimated that more than 600,000 Franciscan Tertiaries still lived in their own homes in Italy. The constitutions of the Carmelites, an order of male hermits, had long been used to regulate communities of Flemish Beguines, Tuscan Mantellati, Spanish Beatas, and Lombard Humiliati. A young childless widow whose marriage had been unhappy, the duchess of Brittany, Françoise d'Amboise, evaded a forced remarriage by publicly vowing chastity during mass. She had endowed several Franciscan and Dominican convents, but because of her attraction to the *devotio moderna*, she persuaded John Soreth, the Carmelite general from 1451, to compose a rule for a new convent she entered at Vannes. Another widow, Innocenza de Bartoli, founded a Carmelite group in Florence in 1450 and asked the chapter-general of 1452 for inclusion into the order. Nicholas V soon issued *Cum Nulla* recognizing the Carmelite second order and encouraged them to recruit "pious virgins, widows, beguines, mantellate, and others who (presently) wear the habit and are under the protection of the Blessed Virgin of Mount Carmel."[8] Each convent operated autonomously under the supervision of the first order's local provincial.

Angelina of Marsciano, also a young widow, eagerly took vows of chastity and organized local virgins under the Franciscan Tertiary rule. Wife-seeking young men soon broke up the group, accusing Angelina of heresy. In 1395, she was banished and a vision directed her to the friendlier environment of Foligno, where the famous mystic Angela of Foligno had set an example of Tertiary devotion at the beginning of the century. There Angelina founded the first of fifteen communities combining the Franciscan Tertiary rule with strict enclosure. She continued to be *ministra* with visitation rights in six houses until she died in 1435. In 1461, Franciscans organizing the Strict Observance revoked the privileges of Angelina's Tertiary houses and put an end to the office of *ministra*, though we find it still in use a century later in the Netherlands. Similar communities were independently attracted to the ideal of strict observance. Caterina of Bologna led Corpus Domini, an autonomous community following the Augustinian rule without formal vows. Her book, *Le sette armi spiritali*, written in 1438, is a metaphor of temptation and demonic attack, charting the struggle between her loyalty to the "mother" who trained her and the pull of the Clarisse observance. Ultimately, she became a leader in the movement to adopt Clara's original rule and Corpus Domini became a mission for Clarist reform in northern Italy.

In most cases, both reform and corruption tended to be intrusive. Reformers attributed the most immediate cause of decline to the influence of aristocratic families, who embroiled communities in faction fighting, election disputes, and even violence to secure offices for ambitious relatives. The abbot of Cîteaux complained at the chapter-general of 1494 that relatives and friends of the aristocracy cared nothing for the ordinances of abbots or visitors, denying that they were bound to obey them. Secularization continued to divert offices and prebends to royal pensioners or local nobles. When they were pursuing reforms, Martin V and his successors abrogated a community's right to elect its own officials and commended the appointments to bishops and legates. The reformers aimed to nullify local influences, particularly their resistance to the incorporation of houses under regular discipline. The mere threat of this *commenda* encouraged Benedictines, Cistercians, Augustinians, and mendicants to impose tighter discipline. Congregations often discarded the abbatial office in favor of priory status or replaced life tenure with three-year terms to make the offices less vulnerable to *commenda*.

They were right to be fearful: *commenda* was a tricky instrument. Cardinal Nicholas of Cusa, bishop of Brixen and papal legate in Germany in 1466, held four reforming councils to regulate priestly morals and attack popular "superstitions." For nuns, his first priority was reestablishment of claustration. After a brief period of grace to allow everyone to return to her monastery, he decreed that anyone going in or coming out of the cloister without authorization would be excommunicated. He forbade monks and nuns to reside outside their monasteries, even on granges, and abolished private ownership. A veteran of the

Common Life movement, he even tried to get at least one of his abbesses to open her doors to women of non-noble origin. These high-minded sentiments, however, did not prevent his own political maneuvering. He used his commendatory power to depose the administrator of the canonesses of Thorn and gave her prebend to the young daughter of a local baron whom the pope was later obliged to depose because her frivolity had a sorry influence on the sisters.

As bishop of Brixen, Cusa often resorted to intimidation and threats to enforce his demands on unwilling monastics. He took control of appointing visitors regardless of the rights and exemptions of orders and houses. *Commenda* thus deteriorated into an instrument in the power struggles of competing ecclesiastical powers. Cusa used his powers as papal legate to further his local ambitions as bishop of Brixen. His predecessors had long opposed the exemptions of Sonnenberg, a Benedictine convent whose wealth and juridical power went back to the eleventh century. In 1453, Cusa's episcopal court upheld some peasants who claimed that the abbess, Verena von Stuben, had usurped certain rights over them. At the crucial moment when the abbess was scheduled to defend her cause before the archduke, Cusa reissued his decrees on strict claustration. He appropriated control of their property and, according to one of his letters, would have given the whole of it to the monkery of Tegernsee, which he had already reformed, if the local nobles had not frustrated the plan because they looked upon the nunnery as a home for their daughters.

As it was, he appointed as their visitor the prior of Tegernsee, who claimed that Verena was a "true Jezebel," totally ignorant of the rule and obstinate besides. He blamed Verena for all the discontent in other forcibly reformed monasteries, both male and female, and used his legatine powers to excommunicate the nuns and depose Verena. The Salzburg Benedictines refused to replace her. Cusa forcibly blocked her access to the archduke to protest the financial damage caused by the excommunication. His troops drove out the soldiers she hired to collect their rents and stormed the convent, driving the nuns away while Cusa installed his own abbess. The archduke finally intervened to restore the nuns, but Verena had to retire before he would support the convent's appeal to Rome. A newly elected pope finally forced Cusa to lift the excommunication but, in the end, a new abbess was brought in from

Brixen. The nuns finally submitted to the reform with the provision that it would be supervised by monks of their own order. After six years of resistance they had lost many of their privileges and were impoverished. Verena died in exile. Did her old age resemble that of the anonymous old woman whom Johan Busch met a few years later in the convent of Dorstadt enduring regular whippings from a young nun as penance for resisting reform in another convent where she had once been abbess?

Possibly to avoid the unhappy effects of such strangely misplaced efforts at reform, many houses joined congregations with similar principles and cooperated on internal reform and external integrity. The Clarisses of Brixen successfully resisted Cusa despite his imposition of a new abbess and threats of interdict. Unlike the nuns at Sonnenberg, they had the support of the Observantine Franciscan movement for their appeal to Rome and thus escaped the slanders that destroyed Verena. Sisters and a new abbess from Nürnberg came to help them establish self-imposed reform without loss of their privileges and exemptions.

These new congregations, in dramatic contrast with the old networks like Cluny and Gorze, were willing, even determined, to incorporate women. The Cassinese congregation founded by Louis Barbo (d. 1443), for example, took over the direction of convents in Brescia, Vicenza, Milan, Ferrara, and Cremona. Prioresses with three-year terms replaced abbesses elected for life and submitted to the direction of the congregation. Congregations of Melk and of Kastel, based on older customs of Hirsau, began in 1450 to abolish individual prebends and noble exclusivity and to restore the common life. Their houses, spreading in Austria, Bavaria, and Swabia, followed uniform customs and liturgies but retained their autonomy. Melk "influenced" German convents, although—except for the small convent of Saint Peter Nonnberg in Salzburg—it did not incorporate them. In France, a few new communities formed, centered on the Paraclete. In 1425, several reformed Cistercian nunneries were welcomed into the predominantly male congregation of Sibculo. In 1503, Cardinal d'Amboise instituted a reform of Saint-Menoux under his sister Magdalena and of Charenton under his niece, who formed a small congregation.

One of the most successful Benedictine congregations was Bursfeld, founded in 1433, which ultimately extended to 136 male and 64 female monasteries. Abbesses were elected for life under oath to observe the Bursfelder statutes and submit to the visitor's supervision. The chapter could depose the abbess. To preserve the choir sisters' cloister, lay sisters, who took no vows except obedience to the abbess, controlled all outside communication. They said only simple prayers instead of the monastic offices. The nuns said the daily hours, confessed every week, and took communion on the first Sunday of every month and on feast days. They had to learn some skill to support the vow of poverty and were assigned housework, handiwork, and manuscript copying and illumination. They spoke nothing but Latin with the clergy or among themselves. Despite their claustration, many of the nuns corresponded with scholars and humanists, who commended their learning.

The strength of the congregations secured individual houses from the dangers of *commenda*. Their nuns' horizons even expanded with participation in the congregation itself. Abbesses could go out for chapter-generals and the vow of stability could always be abrogated when the nuns were needed elsewhere in the interests of reform. But many convents influenced by Bursfeld or Melk refused to be subjected to direct control. Many individual nuns resisted incorporation into the Bursfeld congregation and got help from their noble families. Some convents divided into reformed and unreformed nuns living side by side though always under the authority of a reformed abbess.

For abbesses, subjection to a male congregation meant a substantial loss of power not balanced by eligibility to be visitors or other officials of the congregation. A few solved the problem by forming independent female congregations. In 1437, Isingarde of Greiffenklau successfully reformed Marienberg in Boppard, reimposing cloister, common life, and observance of the vows of poverty and chastity. This convent grew to 150 nuns and sent sisters to introduce the reform at about a dozen other German convents.

Cistercian nuns also took some initiatives in the period of the schism. In Spain, in 1390, the abbess of Las Huelgas established a reformed convent in Valladolid. The nuns called themselves the Recollects, for their faithful observance of the Benedictine rule, and formed the Federation of Valladolid, which encompassed about twelve houses. In 1406, the abbess Marie de Bervier was given permission to transfer with like-minded nuns from Robertmont to Moulins in Namur, and the community attracted nuns from other houses. She sent reformers to other houses including her own former house. The growing movement came to be headed by Soleilmont, a seedbed of abbesses. The houses they founded formed a congregation that grew until 1450. The congregation adopted the plan of the Italian Cassinese in the early sixteenth century, with a central director and a three-year term for the abbess or prioress. Other congregations in Spain and Italy took up the same plan in the late sixteenth century.

It is not clear why fifteenth-century men so eagerly undertook the reform and spiritual direction of women that their predecessors had avoided so scrupulously. Johan Busch offered an "altruistic" solution.

> The feminine sex cannot long subsist in the due observance of the rule without proven and reformed men and their good counsel often calling them to the better. . . . Where nuns and devout sisters are not confessed at set intervals and do not communicate, and hold a chapter of guilt at least once a month and are not visited by their fathers every year as the pope ordered . . ., they fall from the observance of the rule and religious life into dissolute ways. . . . First through dissolute life they fall from fear of God to ownership of small things, and then greater things and finally in possession of money and declining dress standards they are dragged in succession to fleshly desires, incontinence of the external senses and finally nefarious acts spring forth with all uncleanness and filth.[9]

Busch's opinion was not a strictly objective one. He converted about twenty nunneries to the mild but uniform observance of the Windesheim congregation and found only two cases of apostasy and one of clear sexual transgression.[10] He claimed that some nuns of Dorstadt had not preserved their chastity but in view of their practice, which he found frequently in Saxony, of whipping one another daily to punish all transgressions, these lapses of chastity may have been no more than incautious conversation with visitors or similar breaches. Some nuns, in fact, were dismayed when he curbed their corporal punishments. "I was asked by several senior nuns that they might receive this discipline lest they should grow cold in their breasts."[11] He pursued their reform with steely resolve, though his only substantive charge was their refusal to wear the habit he prescribed.

When Dorstadt sent a dozen reforming nuns to Stendhal, Busch sourly described their enthusiastic reception in the town, saying they arrived "not in the black cape and great black veil over all their pepula but in white pepula that they called *claram*." He gleefully noted that, being without his support, they could not maintain the reform but succumbed to the gossip of lay sisters and involved themselves in local activities. When questioned, the prioress admitted that she knew nothing about the reform except that the sisters had to eat at one table and walk between the dormitory and the choir in a group. The Dorstadt nuns were sent home and sisters dressed in the prescribed Augustinian habit were brought in, who could count on Busch's direction.[12]

The willingness of male congregations to incorporate women's houses cannot have been based on altruism alone, but no one has yet studied the advantages they gained from undertaking the traditionally odious *cura mulierum*. The Dorstadt nuns accused Busch of stealing ten farms from their convent and giving them to his own reformed convent of Heyninghen. The congregations had the option of incorporating individual communities and, no doubt, shunned potentially burdensome poor houses. There must have been financial advantages in the obedience of well-endowed houses. Still, there is no compelling sign of the widespread transfer of endowments and properties from women to men that characterized the pre-Gregorian period and, later on, in the sixteenth century. It may have simply been the spirit of the times, a push for greater direction and control for all areas of the organized church, which would culminate in the extensive reforms of the Council of Trent.

During the latter half of the fifteenth century all the major orders sought to reform and strengthen themselves. They adopted the slogan "observance," meaning the restoration of strict rules. All religious were basically subject to one of three rules, the Benedictine, Augustinian, and Franciscan, which had been approved by the Fourth Lateran Council in 1215 and revised, mitigated, and reissued by Benedict XII. Benedictine observance usually meant the mitigated rule, though there were always some proponents of the original strict rule, especially among Cistercians.

Under the Benedictine rule, private property was banned as was the division of the monastery's income into prebends. Abstinence from meat was urged but not fully imposed. Stability was reaffirmed, though the monks did not observe the strict cloistering imposed on the nuns. Monks, but not nuns, were expected to participate in the provincial chapters grouped by Benedict XII. As we have seen, nuns participated in the chapters of some of the reforming congregations and could break their cloister to serve the order as reformers.

The rule of Saint Augustine, which had never been as detailed and institutionalized as that of Saint Benedict, was always modified by the particular constitutions of the orders and congregations that used it. In the fifteenth century, the most important of those were the Dominicans and the Windesheim congregation. Augustinian canons at Windesheim interpreted observance as a return to enclosure with a life of mortification and worship with community of property. Dominicans, who attended university and served in pastoral positions, sought to avoid relaxation of the rule in their busy life in the world. The rule also governed houses of canons and canonesses as well as many other autonomous houses.

The usual Franciscan rule was the mitigated rule of Gregory IX or the Urbanist rule for women. The question of poverty remained central to the fierce quarrels that ultimately split the order into Conventual and Observantine branches. Although established as a separate order with its own rule, the Clarisses were strictly subjected to legislation passed by the friars. They could not attend the chapter-generals nor hold chapters of their own. They had to maintain a substantial number of friars as chaplains, advisers, and lay brothers. The minister-general appointed friars as annual visitors. Clarisse abbesses were generally elected for three years to protect them from *commenda* but some continued in office for life. Some had very broad dispensations and one of them had even fallen heir to an abandoned abbey's privilege allowing her some episcopal prerogatives. Only Saint Damiens retained Clara's privilege of poverty though, ironically, even as the friars became less active mendicants, some desperately poor nuns of both the Franciscan and Dominican orders were permitted to break their claustration and beg for life's necessities. Most depended on income from wealthy women seeking entry into the convent. Individual sisters enjoyed their hereditary possessions, goods, and rights as though they had remained in the world. This property was managed by *conservatores*, sometimes lay women, as at Genoa, who had to consult the friars on all decisions about property and maintenance.

Colette of Corbie was a recluse who became the center of a local network attached to the monks of Corbie in 1402. Visions of Francis urging her to reform his order, reinforced by horrifying revelations of the hell prepared for the unreformed, drove her to a wider destiny.[13] Two important noblewomen and a Franciscan friar conducted her to the Avignonese pope in 1406, where she unveiled a reform plan disguised in ambiguous terminology. Francis had commanded her to reform "his" order, centered on a renewal of poverty. In her exposition to the pope, she argued that the rules of Francis and Clara were equally ordained by the Holy Spirit and therefore implied that they somehow constituted a single order. The pope consecrated her "to the full service of the Rule of blessed Clara . . . instituting her as Mother and Abbess."[14] Possibly to disguise the danger of reviving the conflict over poverty, which always threatened to disrupt the order, Colette placed her reformed houses under Clara's original rule with its privilege of poverty.[15] The pope authorized her to receive religious from other houses and Tertiaries and to reform "the diverse branches of the order."[16] Her mission thus spread to houses of brothers as well as sisters.[17] The "Cordeliers" or Colettans became an unstructured congregation within the "order" of Francis and Clara, distinguished by wearing a cord as revealed in a vision.

Colette always avoided using her title of "abbess" and forbade her flock to call her "mother." This laudable display of saintly humility also obscured the constitutional difficulties of her position as an unenclosed promoter of the hitherto virtually unobserved rule of Clara, which she was also imposing on communities of men. She classified herself as an enclosed Tertiary and her biographer said that was the status of Francis himself.[18] In 1408, her growing flock took over the Franciscan convent at Besançon, which had dwindled to two nuns. Her companion, Henri de Baume, took charge of the male convent of Dôle, which became the center for the friars' reform. Lay people as well as ecclesiastical supporters affected the cord and joined the reform as Tertiaries, almsgivers complementing the regulars, who were thus enabled to observe the poverty that distinguished their order from all others. This patronage pragmatically solved the problems caused by her commitment to strict poverty. The Colettans became a sort of triple monastery system, draw-

ing on small communities of reformed friars for their spiritual support
and associated Tertiaries for material aid. With their help, she established
seventeen convents in forty years. Colette's houses remained within the
body of the order, obedient to its provincials rather than to a separate
set of vicars. She had no direct jurisdiction over men's houses, but the
friars who worked with her as confessors in the women's houses carried
the spirit of her reforms into the first order. Henri de Baume became
vicar of the Burgundian province.

But the order as a whole was dubious. While Colette pursued her
Cordelier reform in France, Italian Observantines were organized by
preachers who established relations with a growing number of independently reforming Clarisse convents. In 1420, Paula Malatesta established an Observantine house in Mantua following Clara's rule. In 1422,
a house at Foligno adopted the same rule and sent out parties of sisters
regularly to reform other houses. Perugia became a similar center.
Bernardino of Siena alone claimed credit for the reform of two hundred
Clarisse houses in Italy.

After 1430, both female and male Italian, Flemish, and Spanish Observantine houses tended to function separately from the Conventuals
with their own vicars. In 1442, the famous Italian preacher John of
Capistrano tried to get Colette to soften her reform for the sake of unity.
She and her supporters embarked on a three-day prayer marathon at the
end of which he recognized her divine inspiration. However, his preaching continued to fold Observantine nuns into a close bond with friars in
pursuing the restoration of the order's ancient zeal. Many Benedictine
and Augustinian convents also adopted Clara's rule. In his constitutions
of 1440 for the Italian Observantines Bernardino of Siena sought to
avoid offending the Conventuals, but the emphasis even on moderate
poverty and humility in tune with Francis's ideals renewed the old strife
in the order. When Leo X split the order in 1517, he transferred the
Colettan houses to the Observantines.

In 1380, Catherine of Siena's disciple, Raymond of Capua, was elected
general of the Dominicans loyal to the Roman pope. Perhaps inspired
by his experiences with Catherine and other women, he determined to
establish an enclosed convent devoted to the strict observance of the
Augustinian rule upon which the Dominican constitutions were based in
every province of the order. Not surprisingly, in view of the monastic

character of his vision, most of the reformed convents he established as missionary centers for the reform were nunneries. His reform stressed solitude and meditation, which (oddly) precluded most of the dispensations necessary for the order's preaching mission but which particularly suited the women in the order. Observantine nuns were established in 1391 at Saint Dominic of Pisa. Further communities in Venice, Lombardy, Spain, Holland, France, and Germany were made independent of the provincials under their own vicars. Their direct dependence on the master-general was intended to enable him to multiply them without territorial constraint. Raymond spent the last years of his life in Germany spreading the observance among women. Possibly he hoped that once these centers were well rooted he could tie them to the active preachers on the model later established by the small convent of Guebwiller where, in 1461, the friars ceded all their goods to an associated community of nuns who managed their affairs in imitation of the early wandering friars and Prouille.[19]

Raymond achieved his local reforms without splitting the order, but after his death jealous Conventuals who lost control of reformed houses in their territories turned away from his reform. Neither the new master nor the provincials felt threatened by its spread among women. Many nuns held their course and even expanded the reform during those sterile years. A new female monastery in the Netherlands being recruited when Raymond died went forward. In 1395, Catherine of Burgundy (wife of the duke of Austria) gathered recruits from various orders for Schönensteinbach, an abandoned Augustinian convent in Alsace. In 1397, an admiring crowd attended their formal entry into the cloister as reformed "Preacheresses." Subsequently, despite their periodic eviction by marauding armies, the community became an exemplar and missionary center for the movement.[20]

Where nuns initiated their own reform, they usually sent to a friendly house for sisters to train them in the new discipline. In 1419, Unterlinden asked for reforming nuns and received thirteen recruits from Schönensteinbach. By 1426 Unterlinden had sent out two reforming colonies of its own. In 1423, Saint Mary Magdalene of Basel joined the reform; the convent remained a center of sanctity throughout the fifteenth century, receiving recruits from the best families of the city. Nuns took the initiative in reforming Sylo of Sélestat with the help of the town government. Three houses of Freiburg-im-Breisach embraced the observance despite the hostility of their Conventual superiors. The Dominican sisters always remained directly under their provincials, though the authority of the order over the various houses differed. Some Preachers complained that Observantine nuns were too great a burden on them as confessors and directors. But as the order reformed, Preachers took their nuns with them, sometimes even against the protests of the women.

In 1426, another reformer was elected master and his agents began to labor among nuns and friars, sometimes with the misplaced zeal of Peter Gengenbach. Johan Nider was roughly treated on several occasions. Once some nuns dragged him out of their convent on a table covered with dishes and pushed him into the river. Another group of nuns frightened him so that he was forced to slink through the fields in secular clothes and dared not go into the open streets.[21] But he believed that in the end even the sisters of Saint Catherine's at Nürnberg, who had been forced to submit to his reform, became fond of him. It was to the credit of the new prioress of Saint Catherine's that of the thirty sisters originally in the community all but two finally agreed to join the observance. The convent ultimately provided reforming sisters to convents in several other provinces.[22] There is indeed evidence that reformed women shared a special bond with reformed friars. The reformed had fewer litigations with their confessors over payment for services and loans of books than did the Conventuals. In 1458 the Colmar friars signed a confraternity of prayer and merits with the sisters. Johan Meyer undertook a far-reaching reform of the German province, but soon after he died in 1477 a master-general hostile to the observance forbade reforming nuns to accept invitations from convents hoping to introduce reform. Still, some deserted convents were repopulated with new nuns, and at the end of the century one colony of nuns even went into Bohemia, where the lingering flames of the Hussite rebellion still smoldered.

At the end of the century, provincials came from the observant ranks and still favored the reforms of nuns. Nearly all the communities of nuns were absorbed into the Observantine movement and firmly tied to the order. The observance was consolidated not only in Germany but in eastern Europe and Scandinavia, often associated with comprehensive reforms initiated by princes, towns, and bishops over all the orders. By

1516, only ten houses of Dominican Conventuals were left in Germany. Sprenger, provincial until 1496 and coauthor of the infamous *Hammer of Witches*, chose to be buried in the convent of Saint Nicholas-aux-Ondes in Strasbourg, among the nuns he particularly loved.

By the end of the fifteenth century, Observantine movements had succeeded in widespread reforms. Martin Luther himself was the product of the Windesheim congregation that had captured so many Augustinians. Two major reformers, Johan Busch of the Augustinian reform and Johan Meyer of the Dominicans, left detailed diaries of their experiences, allotting generous attention to the nunneries.[23] All the orders aimed to impose community property, cloister, and uniformity upon their female religious communities. In 1440, at Mary Magdalene near Hildesheim, Busch and his male companion, who had come without any reforming sisters, demonstrated the *Benedicite* at table and the chapter of guilt, two observances apparently unfamiliar to many nuns. They arranged the tables so that the nuns sat along the walls, not facing one another. When the whole community was arranged in prescribed order, the men began the proper chants. They may have been comically imitating female chant, for the sisters laughed at first but "when we came to the *Gloria Patri* they sang the rest with us with their heads bent and scapulars drawn in toward themselves."[24]

When he announced the chapter of guilt, the sisters asked whether it came from the gospel or from the Epistles of Paul. And Busch answered, "This chapter is about your own guilt, not a reading from Holy Scripture." Again, with some humor, the two brothers demonstrated the procedure. Busch's companion prostrated himself and confessed: "Dearest brother! I am guilty: I laughed in refectory when I ought to have read *Benedicite*. I looked around the table keeping bad charge of my eyes in choir and refectory. I came late to choir without licence. I broke silence and spent time at the window without permission talking to strangers. And in much else have I been negligent." Busch imposed a penance, explained the rest of the procedure to the sisters, and said they received his prescriptions cheerfully.

Busch scornfully recalled a community of sisters who met Johan Nider at their convent door and tried to stave off their reform by singing various chants to show their zeal for the spiritual life. Busch was a fierce critic of the musical embellishments practiced by nuns; he often described his efforts to teach nuns who "had forgotten" how to chant the offices and instead sang loud and elaborate forms he considered immodest and ill-becoming. On a softer note, Meyer, who was equally disapproving of the obtrusive way that nuns chanted, recalled Clara von Ostren, one of the original recruits for the Dominican reform at Schönensteinbach, who lovingly taught the younger sisters the singing of each note, attaching special devotional symbolism to her "do, re, mi" scale in a manner worthy of the movie nun Maria von Trapp. For seventeen years after her death they still did what she taught them.[25]

At the Cistercian convent of Wienhausen, Busch procured collects from the abbot of Marienrode so that they might take up the chanting of their own order, "omitting secular chant." The resentful Wienhausen chronicler looked back from a distant future and observed that in that time, "Fathers and preachers often came into the cloister without the bishop's permission and each of them under the appearance of reform introduced or abolished various improvements. Among other things that the High Mass should not be sung as before by the celebrants and virgins together but rather only by the virgins. Also that no organ or instrumental music should be heard any longer at Matins or Vespers."[26]

At Erford, Busch found that each sister stored images of Christ and the saints and sculptures and paintings in her choir stall to suit her private devotions. He confiscated them and placed them around the choir and church "so that they could be seen by everyone and devotion given to them in common and no longer as a private custom."[27] Again, the Wienhausen chronicler complained, "The pictures of the saints and their ornaments were damaged and many good ways and customs abolished and branded as foolish which before had freed many a troubled soul from sorrow and lightened their melancholy."[28]

All was not sweetness and light. The seventy-year-old Katharina von Hoya of the Cistercian convent at Wienhausen was one of many abbesses to resist the intrusive reformers. She maintained that she kept the order she found forty years earlier and wished to continue doing so.[29] Busch admitted:

The nuns had always observed chastity well. The old abbess had governed them strictly so that they held her in much reverence and fear and called her gracious lady by reason of her lineage. But each of the sisters had her own portion of her paternal inheritance, which supported her in the monastery with her own food and dress so that she bought whatever she wanted. They got food and drink from the prepository on certain days with an individual tray. They had a chest in common to which one sister had the key in which each sister laid her money in her own purse or case. When anyone wanted something she went to the key keeper and asked her to open the chest and she always agreed that she could take what she wanted from her own money for it was her property. Thus they thought they lived in common because they kept their private money in a common chest and ate in a single refectory what was given to them from the commune what they bought with their own money and what was sent them from friends and relatives. One thus had much and abundance and another sitting beside her had less and was poor. And indeed they were proprietors because they each had power over their own things.[30]

Busch reported that he removed all the officers and the abbess who refused to submit to his reform. Even her relative, the duke of Brunswick, assisted Busch in forcibly carrying them to Dernberg, a convent whose original nuns had already been forcibly dispersed. The new abbess of Dernberg cooperated with Busch and took charge of the remaining nuns. He claims they put their money into a common fund while the abbess's funds were sealed in a chest to await an accounting. He also said that they gave up their private cooking and eating vessels and placed everything safely under lock and key for common use. Finally, he maintained that the nuns then willingly elected the designated nun from Dernberg as their new abbess and thanked him for their reform. Abbess Katharina resigned voluntarily in exchange for restoration to her old home.

In this one precious instance, we have the nuns' own version of what happened. Katharina von Hoya had not been an easy abbess. Her original election had been disputed by some of the nuns, and when she resigned to avoid factionalism, she retired to a private house within the cloister, which she had enlarged and redecorated. During an illness, however, a vision of Saint Anne threatened her with purgatorial punishments for her luxuries. In 1442, she converted her house into a chapel for Saint Anne and endowed it with much of her own inheritance.[31] The chronicler lingered over her account of the religious pictures and vessels that the abbess bestowed on the community, including the great painted sepulcher, which still stands in the nuns' chapel. She secured spiritual wealth as well for her convent—rich indulgences brought by a visiting cardinal, an archbishop, and several bishops. At the dedication of the great bell named Maria in 1444, the lady and the whole community of virgins in their white cloaks threw costly things into the smelting furnace to the value of 200 marks.

Katharina was wealthy and well connected, but she constantly struggled with her noble relatives and the neighboring towns of Celle and Brunswick to defend and enlarge her rights. The pious chronicler noted that some burghers of Brunswick once tried to poison her because she would not tolerate their seizure of the abbey's corn tithe. The chronicler rejoiced that the unjust bishop of Celle got the drink by mistake and died of it.[32] In 1469, Otto of Brunswick commanded their reform. "In the last week before Advent, around two o'clock in the afternoon, the Duke came with a group of nobles and some town councillors, the oldest Preacher of Holmar, the Abbot of St. Michael and Godehart, the Abbess of Dernberg with several virgins and a person from Sulta."[33] They occupied the winter refectory and examined each nun separately, isolating the abbess and her officers from the rest of the community. Writing in later years, when the nuns of Wienhausen had accepted their reform, the chronicler explained: "They all stood by the abbess not, as one might think, because they were rebellious but rather to testify to their obedience to their mother superior, from whom they would not be divided in life or in death. Indeed a few of them were drawn to the other side but as soon as they saw their sisters holding with the abbess they drew back." The duke had come prepared, with two wagons. He tricked the abbess into coming out of the cloister, forcibly took her keys, deposed her, and forced her into a wagon. "She was driven until evening with neither food or drink to sustain her and with no change of clothing and no spiritual companion of her order."[34] She was confined, with her cellaress, at Dernberg, where she nearly died. The other officers were lured out and dispatched elsewhere, some of them never to return. Meanwhile, the sisters of the community knew nothing of what had become of them.

The prince with those reformers entered the cloister and told each conventual that he would take and use as he pleased all the cash, crockery and other things which they had possessed hitherto. And so saying, he had everything that had been given in memory of the dead and for the use of the monastery brought out of the abbey. From the summer refectory, they brought pottery, kettles and cauldrons and other utensils large and small, and the best cloths provided for God's service on feast days which had been collected with great labor. They filled receptacles with lamb and chestnuts alike. Like a thief, the Lady of Dernberg let her virgins and friends take some of these things and sell them. . . . These included silver bowls, golden rings and golden crowns before the pictures of saints Maria and Alexander and other saints.[35]

Although the nuns of Wienhausen came to embrace their reform and ultimately to defend it powerfully against the Lutherans, they never acknowledged that Busch or his tool, the abbess of Dernberg, deserved any credit. Instead, they attributed the success of the new regime to one of the nuns from Dernberg, Susanna Potstock, who risked the vengeful anger of her abbess to comfort Katharina on the fatal day.[36] Partly in gratitude and partly, perhaps, to spite the hated abbess of Dernberg, the Wienhausen nuns in 1470 elected Susanna as abbess. The deposed Katharina lived four years after her return to Wienhausen and died in 1474. At the beginning of her administration, thanks to the depredations of the reformers, Susanna found no food in the cloister.

Before the reformation each one supplied what she could with her own hands and whatever else she might be able to bring in, and also the convent goods had been in good condition. But now the abbess struggled to provide daily food, poor and mean at that. For more than three years they had to concoct a drink out of barley water for every meal and could get beer only on high feast days. But finally through God's care, the convent recovered, and the revenues were restored and things began to get back to their former condition.[37]

For thirty two years, she guarded them spiritually and materially, incurring no debts.

The *Chronicle of Wienhausen* is the clear and thoughtful testimony of the nuns themselves. More than a hundred years after these events, they still regarded themselves as the victims of violent men, secular as well as ecclesiastical, and their female tool. They had not seen themselves as having been in need of reform, and Busch himself did not question their moral integrity. In the face of a renewed assault from the outside by

Lutherans, they clung stoutly to their reform, but we may wonder how carefully they kept Busch's community property rules and how scrupulously they discarded their old and well-loved devotions. When Protestants stormed the cloister the nuns hid little pictures and books under their choir stalls where they remained until unearthed by twentieth-century decorators. Fifteenth-century Cistercians, sixteenth-century Augustinians, and the twentieth-century Lutherans who live there today all saw themselves as living devout and decorous lives loyal to their elected abbess and to one another.

The well-being of a local monastery was a matter of profound interest to the secular people in its vicinity. At Ursprung in Württemberg, the abbess Gredonna von Freyberg with the help of her relative, the duchess Mechthild, initiated a reform modeled on the nearby convent of Saint Walburg in Heggbach and received several nuns to help train her community. Rebellious nuns, led by Barbara von Stein, who preferred their old way of life, barricaded themselves in the infirmary prepared to repulse the reformers with sticks and stones. The duchess roused the local peasantry and they stoned the house, arresting the resisters and sending the obdurate nuns to other convents or to their relatives. Eventually most of them submitted and even Barbara returned and accepted the reform. When the abbess of Söfflingen and her entire convent resisted the Franciscan observance, the people and nobles of the town drove them out in favor of a new abbess and new nuns. They snatched up what they could and fled, and only those who submitted to reform ever returned.[38]

Noble families put a high value on their daughters' prebends. At Saint Nicholas of Strasbourg, in 1431, the unwilling Dominican sisters who were driven to find another convent demanded repayment for the dinners they had given their friends and made inroads on the stores and cellars they had inherited from previous holders of their prebends. They wanted compensation for all the goods the convent got when they were being educated. In all, those eight sisters collected more than 1,600 gold gulden over and above their personal dowries.[39] This was an investment worth defending. Some Saxon nuns got their families to ambush Johan Busch and he was nearly killed. A nun at Dernberg tried to kill the reformer by pushing him into the cellar and bolting the door.[40] The reformers retaliated by rounding up all the nuns while they were still in their night clothes and dispersing them without further ado to other monasteries, even monkeries. Most never saw their lost homes or their lost belongings again. The nuns of Marienzee climbed up the choir screen to escape the reformers. The duke ordered some of his serfs to put a ladder outside and pull them out by climbing to them under the roof. With that, they came down from the screen to the duke at the ambulatory gate as ordered and the abbess swore: "I will freely do all that you require."

Local city magistrates were often discontent with the old feudal powers of abbeys and their own lack of power to tax ecclesiastical institutions. This disgruntlement encouraged them to intervene. The nuns of Saint Catherine's at Nürnberg drowned out Raymond of Capua so that his instructions to reform could not be heard. The reformers threw flour into their faces to silence them but achieved nothing beyond confining them to their cloister. The nuns had thus escaped reform for twenty years until Nider got the town council to invite "Preacheresses" from Schönen-steinbach.[41] They were lodged in a townswoman's house for a week before the convent could be persuaded to admit them. As was typical of the reform movement, the old officials were deposed and the reform sisters put in charge. All the sisters already in the cloister were asked to remain and try to behave well. Those who clung to their own customs— eating meat, fasting little, keeping their own beds and clothing—were eventually moved into another community with their dowries, but the prebends stayed behind and were soon taken by wealthy new recruits.

Nider reported that at this troubled time the sisters of Saint Catherine's were attacked by restless spirits taking the shape of huge rats and cats whose noise kept them awake at night. One night, a spirit possessed a particularly disobedient and angry sister. It so tormented her and dragged her about that they all thought she would die that very day. Some of the sisters said, "this never happened when we were living in the old open way." But Nider argued that the spirit was trying to force or trick the ladies back into the old ways. And when they did not change, the manifestations ceased.[42]

Reform often became a confrontation for competing local interests: the families of the nuns, representing local power, contested broader royal or ecclesiastical interests. In 1464, Brid Melburgen, the young prioress of Saint Agnes, a convent in the fields outside Strasbourg, with

the town council's support, brought in reforming sisters from Unterlinden. When they arrived, they found most of the nuns determined to
resist. The streets were barricaded. The prioress and her three supporters
had been put out of the convent. Four rebellious preachers, the stadt-
master and his wife, whose daughter was a nun, and various other
well-wishers had barred themselves inside, where they shouted out the
windows and rang bells. In the morning, delegations from the concerned
parties confronted one another. The prioress and her little flock of three
nuns swore that no matter how they were threatened, they would go into
the choir and take up the Holy Sacrament and trust in God to support
their reform. Friends of the unwilling sisters complained that the reformers would throw them out of their livings and put new sisters in their
place. The reformers grudgingly agreed to give the unwilling sisters a
year to adjust. The old sisters who could not get used to claustration
could retain a little window to visit with their families. They would not
be forced into fasting and abstinence from meat or getting up for nightly
services.

Then the reforming sisters from Unterlinden arrived in a covered
wagon and entered the church, singing the correct antiphon of the day.
They took over the convent offices and drove out all intruders and
servants, locking the doors and cell windows. Eight nuns still protested
and would neither come to choir nor to the refectory, nor to the
dormitory at night. They begged to go out and passed messages through
secret holes in the ground. On the Feast of the Innocents, the eight of
them secretly met after mass and, with the help of a Conventual preacher
named Wolfhart, got out of the convent. They said they could not sleep
for fear that someone would set fire to the convent. They complained
that strange people came in at night and that they found lighted fires
under their dormitory, which they swept away. They appealed for pity
because they had to do the work of their vanished servants. They also
brought in the bishop, procuring a note by his sworn notary that they
were bound to him in obedience.[43]

The reformed sisters sent their advocate to the city council and
registered an appeal against the bishop. The council told Master Wolfhart
to stay away from the convent, but he retorted that the bishop had the
power to intervene and managed to get himself appointed vicar. The
prioress protested that she must have an Observantine vicar. Finally, the

provincial master came and imposed the reform. A decade later, the armies of Charles the Rash ravaged the fields outside Strasbourg and pillaged Saint Agnes. The sisters lived in the empty rooms for nearly a year "with the wolves entering in the winter," until they could gain entry into the reformed Augustinian house of Saint Marguerite in the town. The newly combined house became a bulwark of the Catholic faith when the town turned Lutheran.

Efforts at monastic reform never seriously flagged. In 1493, the whole Benedictine order mounted a general visitation to restore common life and property, impose cloister on the nuns, and separate choir and nave in monastic churches. Commendatory monasteries were to have resident vicars, and the king agreed to lend the support of the secular arm to enforce the reforms. The same general reform was enforced on Cluny and Tiron in 1494. Toward the end of the fifteenth century, the abbot of Cîteaux tightened attendance at chapter-generals and other reforms. And houses the orders reformed grew in size. New recruits and new endowments were never lacking. But the laity grew increasingly hostile to reform itself, turning away from the old monastic values. Charles IV initiated reform in Bohemia in the fourteenth century, stimulating support for the Hussites by the local nobility which had been deprived of its commendatory rights.

The most dramatic confrontations among nuns, their families, and reformers centered on the question of common property. Gerhard Grote believed the provision of dowries caused families to cut their monastic sons and daughters out of their inheritances, which ultimately impoverished the monastery more than the dowry enriched it. But the use of the dowry and prebend system ensured that each individual would have an adequate income despite the vagaries of fate. That, of course, was what their families intended for them with, perhaps, callous indifference to the corporate status of the monastery. When Busch tried to restore communal ownership, he systematically collected all the private utensils and furnishings and gave them over to the common treasury. Nuns locked up their goods and tried to conceal their money and called on their relatives for support. They frequently protested that they could only support themselves with their private incomes, which often proved true.

More than once, Busch had to preach to the neighboring towns to get charity for them.

Indeed, as the complaints of the nuns of Dorstadt and Wienhausen suggested, he may have tried to compensate reformed nuns from the goods of the unreformed. He certainly tried to force their relatives to give to a common fund.[44] When the Cistercian nuns of Saint George protested poverty, Busch threatened to reduce the community to the number of nuns the endowment could support.[45] By this means he used the nuns themselves to force their families to continue to send the supplementary supplies and income that had previously supported them privately to support the common life. But most families were unwilling to have their private indulgences made the object of common property.

Fifteenth century reformers agreed that *commenda* introduced the evils of venality and expectations into the monastic orders, while the multiplication of commended benefices led to absentee officials whose only purpose was to exploit the religious. Immediately after the schism ended, the popes apparently thought they could use the system to restore church order, but it soon became a two-edged weapon in the power struggles of the age. In 1434, the Council of Basel, competing with papal claims, appointed a visitor-general to Benedictine nuns and instigated reforms in Cologne and Trier claiming powers of *commenda* equal to those of the pope. In addition, various secular powers, kings, nobles, and town councils, whose incursions into the ecclesiastical sphere had grown during the schism, demanded commendatory rights comparable to the old proprietary church as the price of renewed obedience. The Pragmatic Sanction of Bourges of 1438 restored patronage rights over church offices to the French nobility in return for their recognition of the Roman pope. Commendators—nobles exercising their rights under the Pragmatic Sanction—disputed benefices with the elected officials and despoiled the monasteries. They sold off furnishings and diverted revenues, letting the fabric of the establishment fall into ruin. In 1481 and again in 1486 Cluny forbade *commenda* in all its houses. The French Commission d'enquête in 1493 reaffirmed that commendators were divorced from the life of the community and recommended their abolition.

Secular rulers were not necessarily indifferent to the affairs of their churches. The "new monarchs" of the early sixteenth century used reform as a tool for wresting control of the churches from the nobility.

In 1507, Louis XII entrusted a broad reform to his chief minister and papal legate, Cardinal d'Amboise. But reform faded after 1516, when Francis I signed the Concordat of Bologna giving him virtually unrestricted powers of appointment in the abbeys of France. In Spain, Ferdinand and Isabella inaugurated their newly unified rule by having the pope appoint Ximénes de Cisneros (1436–1517) as cardinal and legate to reform their churches. He imposed observance on Benedictines, Dominicans, and Franciscans. At least eight convents joined the reforming congregation of Castile. In 1484, Beatrice de Sylva abandoned her life at court to become a Cistercian in Toledo, where she founded the Congregation of the Immaculate Conception. Assisted by Ximénes, she transferred her houses in 1489 to the Observantines of the Order of Saint Clara. In 1511, the congregation was reestablished as the Conceptionist order, which spread through Spain, France, Belgium, Mexico, and Peru. Matthias Corvinus, likewise, instituted a sweeping reform in his two kingdoms of Bohemia and Hungary.

Charles VIII and Louis XII of France, following the advice of a royal commission of 1493, used *commenda* to reform Fontevraud. In 1458, Abbess Marie of Brittany asked the pope for visitors to help reform the abbey and repair the devastation of the Hundred Years' War. After investigation, they presented her with a new rule in 1462, claiming to follow the spirit of Robert rather than his words. Marie found the new rule too soft. With some like-minded nuns, she retired to the priory of the Magdalene at Orsan, where she established her own rule drawn from several traditional sources, including Robert's original, emphasizing restoration of cloister, poverty, and observance of the Benedictine rule. It was approved by the pope in 1476 and spread to two other priories, which attracted recruits from such unreformed convents as Sainte-Croix.

Marie's successor, Anne of Orléans, sister of the future Louis XII, used the royal power of *commenda* to become abbess of Sainte-Croix with the intention of imposing Marie's reform there. This act of gross pluralism and its attendant chronic absenteeism hopelessly mixed the twin streams of reform and corruption. In 1492 the community elected a nun of Sainte-Croix to succeed Anne, but Anne was reinstalled with the help of her brother's men-at-arms. A nun of Fontevraud who had been associated with Anne contested the election. Her brother's soldiers forced their way into the convent and remained there, eating at the community's expense and terrorizing the nuns who supported the elected abbess. The royal governor refused to dislodge the soldiers. After a year, the nuns bought them off with large financial concessions. But the new abbess had made lasting enemies. Through her twenty-year tenure, the respective brothers used their political offices and military power to make repeated attacks on her temporals and her agents. Perhaps in desperate response, she filled the convent offices with her own relatives.

Despite the considerable damage it had done to its sister convent, the "Fontevraud reform" flourished under another royal princess, Renée de Bourbon (1491–1534). In 1503, she imposed a grille on the nuns and monks at Fontevraud who had resisted the reform for years. The nuns enlisted men from the town to break it down. With the help of the Parlement of Paris, Renée expelled about 150 recalcitrants who still clung to the rule of 1462 and dispersed them among the reformed priories. The abbey submitted to enclosure in 1505. She used her royal influence to attach other convents to her order, including the Filles-Dieu in Paris, despite episcopal objections. By her death, Renée had reformed thirty-eight convents; twelve more were added under her successor, Louise de Bourbon.

Meanwhile, in 1509 some discontented nuns of Sainte-Croix sued the abbess Jeanne de Couhé for aggrandizing herself at the expense of the monastery. The Parlement of Poitiers sentenced her to give up a third of the revenues to the chapter and to eat with the community. With the support of Francis I, who visited the monastery in 1520, the Parlement virtually took Sainte-Croix into tutelage. It brought in a reforming Fontevrist, Isabeau de Beauvan, who imposed permanent cloister, community of life and goods, and newly introduced liturgies. The incumbent abbess was sent to Fontevraud. Ten other nuns were dispersed among Fontevrist foundations and their offices apportioned among those who remained. Jean Bouchet's *Annales d'Aquitaine* indicates that popular opinion opposed the expulsion of the abbess and her nuns, who had no reputation for scandal. Sainte-Croix, which had always been autonomous, ended up under the control of Fontevraud's reforming (and royal) abbesses. Through them, the king took control of the women's goods in a gross extension of his commendatory rights under the Concordat of Bologna.

Chelles, which had lost its exemption and was subjected to the bishop of Paris in 1196, provides a stunning example of skillful maneuvering among competing reformers. The bishop had substituted the Benedictine rule for their ancient Caesarian observance, but the nuns retained their white Caesarian habits until 1613. The bishop complained that they neither ate in common nor slept in the dormitory. Rich sisters wore jewels and received presents and visits, while the rest were barely able to buy bread. Nevertheless, the endowment continued to support a large community, though the prebends were divided in a highly complex manner. After being dispersed by war and plague, the community pulled itself back together. In 1499, it shifted from election of a life abbess to triennial elections. In 1504, the sisters vowed cloister and accepted a new set of statutes from the bishop while appealing to Renée of Bourbon for nuns from Fontevraud to put the reform into operation. In 1513, the abbess got an episcopal order suppressing "canons pretending to make up the community of Chelles" who were pressing claims against the monastery's goods. They were replaced by six Benedictines, who helped her make Chelles the center of a French congregation.

Chelles sent nuns to reform Montmartre, Jouarre, Saint Peter of Reims, Gif, Malnoue, Royal-Lieu, Val de Grâce, and Faremoutiers, whose nuns had had to take refuge in the village when soldiers pillaged the convent. After the nuns returned, contemporary documents record that they abandoned the common life. Their cloister destroyed, they tended to wander into the village for gossip. Neither meals nor choir were conducted regularly. The abbess Jeanne de Bautot abandoned the monastery altogether in 1454, stealing the linen, beasts, tin, and other goods. By 1511, only eleven nuns remained. But when the abbess, Jeanne Chrétien, attempted to reform them and restore the endowment, the bishop of Meaux refused his help, claiming that she herself was responsible for the disorder. He appealed to the Parlement of Paris for help in imposing his own reforms, accusing her of hunting regularly and other disorders. But the citizens and nuns of Faremoutiers testified on her behalf and praised her for the restoration of discipline and recovery of the monastery goods. Her successor, Marie Cornis, adopted the customs of Fontevraud and joined the union of Chelles, which strengthened her position against the bishop. After this flowering, however, Chelles lost its triennial system and fell to royal *commenda* with the Concordat of 1516.

Dangerous as the *commenda* system was for the independence and health of monasteries, the interest of the French monarchy in reform sometimes bore healthy fruit. Jeanne de Valois (1464–1505), eldest daughter of Louis XI, devoted herself to piety and charity before and during her unhappy marriage with Louis of Orléans (Louis XII). He was imprisoned during the reign of Charles VIII and Jeanne had a vision of the Virgin Mary while praying for his release. The Virgin prophesied that she would found a religious order. When Louis became king, he had the marriage annulled much to God's displeasure, as popular opinion interpreted an outbreak of miracles that surrounded the event. Taking advantage of her leverage, Jeanne obtained a large endowment from her former spouse with which to found the Order of the Annunciation in 1505. In her retirement in Bourges, she made the mother convent a center for charity and piety.

Clearly, the fifteenth century was a time of reform. During the schism, reform was often a feminine enterprise. The Sisters of the Common Life, Angelina Marsciano, Colette of Corbie, and the abbess of Las Huelgas headed fairly large enterprises. More often, reform was accomplished within individual houses or even, following the *devotio moderna,* within the individual breast. Thereafter, it became a masculine enterprise, and its genuine idealism was shaped and often warped by the ambitions of the pope and his legates, bishops, monastic orders, and secular magistrates. They often used the rhetoric of morality, ranting about loss of chastity and filthy depravities. But when they thrust themselves, often indecorously and sometimes violently, into women's communities, what they imposed was control. The property, the political authority, and the independence of female monastics was the chief target and the chief victim of these reformers.

Fifteenth century reformers, unlike their Gregorian predecessors, aggressively sought to take the *cura mulierum* into their own hands. They wanted to direct the spiritual life of women even at the cost of carrying the burdens of responsibility. Paradoxically, this trend came at a time when men appeared to be more actively afraid of women than they had ever been before. Twelfth-century reformers feared the seductions of Eve but felt confident that they could escape contamination by segregating themselves and cloistering women. Fifteenth-century reformers, men actively in the forefront of the movement, feared the maledictions and spells of witches. In a way, we might even admire their bravery in daring to confront these fears with such a resolute program of reintegrating women back into the regular orders. In the sixteenth century, the Protestant clergy married women and the Catholic clergy endured a more active syneisactic relationship with chaste unmarried women than it had countenanced for half a millennium.

15

✦

Defenders of the Faith

FOR FIFTEEN CENTURIES, aspiring women had maintained independence and authority, both temporal and spiritual, through heroic chastity. They had always found a creative response to reforms that restricted their influence. Cloister became a condition for cultivating the hidden life as a means to channel divine grace. They harnessed the power of self-denial to support the salvific mission of Christianity. Devout reception complemented priestly dispensation of the sacraments. The Observantine reforms silenced cynics who doubted women's capacity for virtue. But at last, the rhetoric of reform sharply reversed and nuns suffered a new and unpredicted assault. In 1517, Martin Luther, a German monk, posted his Ninety-five Theses, a broad challenge to the beliefs and institutions of the Catholic Church. He argued that Christ's sacrifice was sufficient atonement for the sins of those who believed unreservedly in his godhood. They needed only their faith in him to justify their salvation. Voices long silenced by monastic rhetoric rose to condemn celibacy as an occasion of sin and virginity itself as a crime against nature.

Protestantism attacked the spirituality most associated with women, denying the redemptive value of prayer and sacrifice. The mystical power nuns derived from reception of the Eucharist was scorned. Processions and chanting, the extrasacramental liturgies that accumulated indulgences, came under attack. The cult of relics, pilgrimages, and the intercession of saints became anathema to men who attributed all power

419

to a transcendent God, beyond the influence of human prayers or sacrifices. Human sacrifices intended to share the passion of Christ and incline God to mercy were stripped of their power. Thus the monastic life, based on the idea of saving souls still among the living or in purgatory through prayer and self-mortification, became a futile exercise.

Many nuns embraced the new ideas. Protestantism attracted women seeking an alternative to the cloister, though it is far from clear that they were longing to marry. The attack on celibacy and the sacraments (which had always been a male monopoly) held an inherent attraction for many women who had given time and thought to religious questions. In the first generation, when the Protestant churches had not yet become institutionalized, some nuns eagerly seized the opportunity to play a more active pastoral role. By 1528, Ursula zu Münsterberg, who had entered Mary Magdalene in Freiburg as a child, was bringing Luther's books into her convent with the help of a noble aunt. She secured the appointment of a new confessor who preached that good works were hypocrisy and the cloistered life worthless. Ursula and two companions escaped while the other nuns were in choir.

The partnership of reforming couples and the inclusion of a few women in embattled groups of reformers offered a fleeting renewal of the syneisactic ideal. Katherine von Bora, another child nun, was inspired by the reformers' ideas to escape with eight sisters from Numschen. Although their duke had made it a capital crime to help nuns leave their convents, Luther arranged for all nine to get out in a delivery wagon. He married Katherine and placed the rest in Protestant homes as wives or as servants, a courageous act in those early days when women who abandoned their profession were often scorned by their new neighbors. Another nun, Katherine Zell, based a vocation on her marriage with a sympathetic Protestant clergyman, the most liberal of the Strasbourg reformers. She interested herself in hospital reforms and education and edited a collection of hymns translated from Czech into German. She corresponded with some radicals whom more conservative ministers condemned and visited them when they were imprisoned for rabble-rousing. After her husband's death, she continued her charities, caring for reformers who had to flee their homes and writing a treatise of comfort for a quarantined leper. Delivering her husband's eulogy, she said, "I am not usurping the office of preacher or apostle. I am like the dear Mary

Magdalene who, with no thought of being an apostle, came to tell the disciples that she had encountered the lord."[1]

Catholic as well as Protestant humanists questioned the value of the contemplative life, equating the active life with secular civic service, from which women were barred. Where Protestantism prevailed, the regular life was condemned as unnatural, while monks converted to the new faith and were absorbed into the secular clergy, which retained an active ministerial role. Competition for ecclesiastical careers intensified among the younger sons of nobles, professional men, and the rising bourgeoisie. Many nuns, however, placed their communal life above their theological commitments. The abbess of Godstow hoped to save her community from Henry VIII's attack when she wrote that they did not respect pope or purgatory, did not pray to images, did not go on pilgrimage, and did not praise dead saints.[2] The Bourbon abbesses of Faremoutiers and the Paraclete did not disturb their comfortable celibate lives because they embraced Lutheran ideas. They simply remained abbesses over Catholic nuns while practicing the Protestant religion. During the ducal inquiry at Freiburg, it became clear that Ursula had persuaded about fifty of the Magdalene's seventy-seven nuns to become Lutheran. The remaining Catholics denounced the blasphemy of their preacher but in the end were apparently content to remain where they were under a Lutheran prioress. This choice existed only where Catholicism retained some authority. Elsewhere, endowments that maintained women's communities were transferred to men with no balancing compensation. Few female communities dissolved without a struggle or at least a protest. In some places, women waged heroic battles to save their way of life but most of them failed.

The theological revolution opened the festering wounds of old resentments. Peasants, bourgeois, nobles, and, above all, monarchs cast longing eyes upon monastic lands and wealth. They saw opportunities to regain patronage powers lost in the papal revolution. The fourteenth-century English writer John Wyclif argued that the reading and preaching of Holy Scripture offered a surer road to salvation than the sacraments. He advocated secular control of church property to ensure support of religion and charity free of clerical corruption. Wyclif's ideas, vulgarized by preachers called Lollards, inspired a peasant revolution that long alienated the nobility, but they still echoed in sixteenth-century religious

rhetoric. John Huss introduced Wyclif's critique of ecclesiastical property and exemptions at the University of Prague. He was burned by the
Council of Constance, but Bohemian Hussites rose up against both pope
and emperor in hopes of gaining control of the church in their own land.
Anticlerical ideas, including an attack on monasticism, spread into Germany with the Hussite armies.

The pope's expedient uses of *commenda* in the fifteenth century
stimulated resentment of "idle" religious. The kings of Sweden and
England, who did not enjoy the powers of appointment it conferred,
launched a frontal attack on the whole monastic system. In 1527, Gustavus Vasa began gradually to return monastic property, which had always
been exempt from taxation, to its donors in return for their agreement
to pay taxes on it. Mobs using Lutheran rhetoric gave him the necessary
moral support to carry out the program. At Stralsund, in 1525, the
populace pelted the Brigittine nuns with stones and mud at church
services, calling them "heavenly harlots."[3] They were driven out of their
convent, which was plundered and destroyed. Still, like a good Lutheran,
Gustavus tolerated the unobservant female communities so inimical to
Catholic notions of the regular life.

Luther scorned monastic pretensions to spiritual superiority or even
utility and affected profound horror of claustration as imprisonment. Yet
he approved of maintaining foundations where daughters of the nobility
could live honorably in scholarly and religious pursuits as long as they
agreed to attend Protestant preaching, gave up the sacraments, and
remained free to marry.[4] Despite evidence of popular hostility, the
Brigittine convents favored by the upper classes were the last to be
dissolved by the Swedish crown. Most of their nuns were pensioned off;
a few institutions, like Maribö in Denmark (which lasted until well into
the seventeenth century), were left to attrition.

The English Reformation, by contrast, was not Lutheran and, indeed,
under Henry VIII, was not even considered Protestant. To many Eng-
lishmen, starting with the king himself, monasteries represented an
untapped and virtually undefended source of wealth waiting to be
exploited. Papal efforts to consolidate tighter, better-disciplined orders
only angered the English. English monasteries had become isolated from

their Continental orders, and monies paid to their mother houses often looked like subsidies to England's enemies. At the end of the thirteenth century, Edward I's Statute of Mortmain prohibited legacies of land to the church without crown license. Parliament passed a series of antipapal bills in 1353 aimed at loosening the clergy's ties to the French popes. Tithes sent to Avignon seemed like a species of treason. As the schism weakened the papacy, knights, and burghers began to heed Wyclif's arguments for the disendowment of at least some of the monastic clergy. They did not understand reform in the same way that Continental critics did. Moral charges had disproportionate resonance in a country that produced no Colette of Corbie, no Catherine of Siena, no Birgitta of Sweden. As the Hundred Years' War heated up again, in 1408, the king appropriated the income of "alien priories," small cells of one or two foreign monks supervising estates and collecting revenue for their Continental abbeys, to the royal household. Henry V confiscated such revenues to finance several new English abbeys, the most important of which was Syon house, a Brigittine convent, offered thanks for his acquisition of the French crown. This flirtation with Continental reforms proved as brief and illusory as English rule over France.

English nunneries were rarely used to maintain the purity of the aristocracy by withholding noblewomen from the marriage market. The systematic application of primogeniture and entail kept family trees severely pruned so that the ruling class was smaller and wealthier than elsewhere. Heiresses to noble titles were royal wards and the king valued the opportunity to bestow them on his supporters. Nobles invested more cash in their daughters' dowries than in provision for younger sons. Many noble titles were not hereditary and the crown periodically dropped the weak and impoverished by failing to call them to Parliament, adding "new men." To avert degradation, nearly all nobles expected their daughters to marry and forge ties with these wealthy and influential courtiers.

The hungry younger sons looked to the church for benefices and, increasingly, for subsidies. As early as 1410, a bill in Parliament urged the use of church property to create lay baronies and to found colleges for the education of professionals and almshouses for the poor. The transfer of monastic property to colleges began in earnest in the 1430s. Tales of the immorality and financial incompetence of nuns served as an excuse to transfer their incomes to these ambitious men. For example, in 1497 the bishop of Ely closed Saint Radegund on the grounds that dissolute conduct had reduced the priory to poverty. In fact, the nunnery was not poor. Its income was sufficient to found Jesus College. It had, however, been reduced to only two nuns: one was already professed elsewhere while the other was an infant. In most convents, the nuns moved up a career ladder that gave them the experience they needed to deal effectively with administrative problems. With the same legatine powers so effectively employed by Ximénes in Spain and d'Amboise in France, Thomas Wolsey began attacking monasteries for faulty obser-vance in the 1520s, threatening them with Observantine reforms to force bribes out of them. He preferred to use reform as an excuse for dissolution, however, augmenting the income of colleges with the goods of supposedly corrupt or financially unsound monasteries. He endowed an Oxford college with the goods of a number of small nunneries whose inhabitants were few and, he said, immoral.

The process only accelerated when Henry VIII determined to divorce his queen. In 1535, Parliament declared him Supreme Head of the church in England. Wolsey's successor, Thomas Cromwell, mounted a general visitation of the monasteries, which coupled the *Valor ecclesiasticus,* a statement of church revenues, with the *Comperta,* a list of complaints against the immoral lives of monks and nuns. Cromwell's visitors made a systematic effort to document the lasciviousness of English nuns. Certainly, some women were dissolute. The prioress of Littlemore, for example, was bringing up her illegitimate child in the convent at the community's expense. The custom of hiding the shame of fallen gentle-women behind convent walls ensured similar problems in other houses. The visitors noted thirty-eight nuns who had borne children, but only twenty-seven were actually charged with incontinence and, of those, seventeen were later given crown pensions, which suggests that the charges were unfounded. More important, the figures do not disclose whether the nuns in question were one-time sinners or chronic cases. Often, a sin had long since been expiated and the nun had grown old in good repute. Moreover, the accused woman might have been a corody holder or a nun like Sister Ryvel at Denny, who went back to her husband and four children when the crown closed the monastery. Some convents, like Catesby in Northhamptonshire, were admitted to be "in very perfect order, the prioress a poor, wise, discreet and very religious woman, with nine nuns who were obedient, religious and devout and with as good obedience as we have in time past seen or be like to see."[5] The *Comperta* was challenged in the north, where the population resisted the dissolution and the nuns testified that Cromwell's agents had attempted both to seduce them and to suborn them to commit perjury in testifying against their sisters.

The absence of observance meant neglect of cloister. Many nuns were found living outside their convents when the visitors came. The common purse and table were apparently almost unknown, putting the abbess at a distance from the community. A nun at Rusper, for example, complained that the prioress wasted communal resources on lavish hospitality to her friends. Four nuns of Kildalliheen in Ireland accused their abbess of dissipating the communal property, forcing the nuns to choose between begging outside the cloister or starving within. A few nuns profited through chicanery. A niece of Queen Jane Seymour at Romsey married the steward after conniving at the dispersion of the community. A few noble abbesses in league with their families evaded the crown's grasp. Abbess Temmes of Lacock anticipated the dissolution in 1539 by leasing out all the property to her brothers and other relatives. She took her pension and her family continued to occupy the property. The abbess of Grane in Ireland took advantage of troubled political conditions to delay dissolution for two years while leasing out her rights.

The *Valor* and the *Comperta* targeted the weakest communities for dissolution. Only eighteen nunneries were eligible to survive the act of 1536 dissolving monasteries with less than £200 income. Twenty nunneries saved themselves by bribery from the first round, fleecing the nuns of their valuables. During the last years, the beleaguered women complained of neglect, debt, and lack of money because they had to bribe Cromwell's officers. In addition, they suffered harassment by royal officials and by the students they put in the place of absent or deposed abbesses. English nuns lacked the community solidarity created by observance, which enabled many Continental nuns to sustain an effective resistance. Few nuns protested Henry's claim to supremacy over the church. Some promised to abandon Roman devotions if they could remain in their communities. But Henry VIII moved against them with the same fierce self-righteousness that drove his relationships with his wives. Abbess Florence Bannerman of Amesbury was arbitrarily deposed when she protested and a pliant abbess installed. Resisters like the nuns of Romsey, who refused pensions for turning secular, were punished with confiscation of all their goods.

Most nuns in England came from insignificant families who could endow them modestly in neighborhood houses but could not defend their property against the combined forces of king and nobility. Eventually every house was closed and the nuns turned out without their dowries to seek shelter from their families or live as best they could on meager pensions. Henry distributed most of the monastic lands among his noble supporters. Royal commissioners took inventory. Lead was stripped from roofs and fittings and melted down with the bells. Relics and pictures were shipped to London for burning. Plate and jewels were also sent to London and dispersed. Furniture, utensils, and vestments were sold on the spot. The roofless and gutted buildings were left to decay.

The dispossessed nuns who did not resist these proceedings were given modest pensions, on the average about £3 (compared to between £4 and £5 for monks)—roughly equivalent to an unskilled laborer's wage. Small as they were, the pensions offered to most nuns may have cost the crown more than the paltry incomes that were confiscated, but they kept the women in permanent dependence. Henry VIII was no Lutheran and he furiously defended himself against any charge of countenancing sexual laxity. The Six Articles of 1539 declared it a felony to break a vow of chastity. An oft-quoted monk wrote that 10,000 former nuns lived in England after the suppression and none were allowed to marry.[6] Lay sisters and novices generally did not receive pensions because it was assumed they could marry. Hungry and abused, many nuns held out in their decaying buildings until forced away and still lived to return under Mary Tudor.

Neither the French nor Spanish monarchies had an interest in dissolving monasteries because they controlled them through the *commenda* system. They often promoted reform as a means of imposing royal appointments on convents accustomed to electing their own superiors, usually members of the local nobility. But some reformed communities attempted vainly to resist the imposition of unreformed royal abbesses who cared nothing for three-year limitations or prohibitions on pluralism and absenteeism. Loss of monastic patronage brought many nobles to the Protestant side when religious strife broke out in France and in the Spanish Netherlands, which were subjected to "reform" in the early sixteenth century. At Prouille, local nobles struggling to maintain the Pragmatic Sanction (which had recognized noble patronage privileges) against the Concordat of Bologna (which restored appointive power to the pope and through him to the king) supported the nuns' opposition to Francis I's nominations in 1538 and 1543, but in the end three of his Bourbon cousins succeeded one another as abbesses.

The Bourbon ladies were competent and pious, deploying their influence effectively to protect as well as exploit their nuns. But they reserved their community loyalties for their noble family, whose flexible attitude toward religion was symbolized by Henry IV's famous trade of Paris for a mass. They moved from order to order and house to house as family interests directed. Eléonore de Bourbon retained her abbatial office at Fontevraud while she governed Prouille through a vicar who, in turn, appointed her own vicar when she went to Jouarre as abbess. At Fontevraud, separate houses accommodated the suites of the Bourbon and Orange princesses who were educated there. Every house contained sumptuous quarters for visiting royalty. The many-branched house split religiously. Some of its abbesses became Lutheran and all remained in friendly correspondence with their cousins of Navarre, leaders of the Protestant force. Thus, in 1559, when Protestant troops controlled Poitiers, pillaging its churches and convents, Sainte-Croix was spared out of respect for Abbess Madeleine de Bourbon.

The Queen of Navarre, Jeanne d'Albret, was the acknowledged leader of the French Protestant cause. With most of their men fighting, and often dying, in the religious wars, the power of French noblewomen vastly expanded. Noble abbesses, supported by influential relatives, tried to steer a successful course through the storms of religious strife. In many cases, they took advantage of the breakdown of ecclesiastical authority to recapture their ancient autonomy, placing community values over sectarian loyalty. Remiremont and other old canonries broke from their orders, proclaiming themselves secular canonesses while maintaining the abbey's immunities from both lay and ecclesiastical power. They lived in private dwellings within the cloister, which they opened or closed at their pleasure. They gave parties and wore secular clothing. They claimed the right to leave and marry, though few of them did so. Yet, in 1613 when the abbess and nuns determined to reform, the papal visitor spoke well of their behavior and praised their charity. Thereafter they adopted a more sober form of life but did not resume a monastic rule. The nuns of La Déserte in Lyons also took to secular dress, singing their offices in the midst of the general congregation.

Needless to say, however, not all displays of independence were so innocent. In his embattled youth, Henry IV had veered back and forth between the two religions as political necessity and his personal survival required. Once he was crowned, he may have taken ironic delight in using his commendatory powers to benefit his mistresses. A famous ladies' man, his preference for convents as lodgings became a joke and a scandal. In 1590, he stayed at Montmartre and thanked the abbess Claude de Beauvilliers for her hospitality by adding Pont-aux-Dames to her benefices. He also allowed plural nominations at Amiens and Maubuisson to Angélique d'Estrées, sister of his mistress Gabrielle. Their double portrait, naked in the bath, still charms and amuses visitors to the Louvre. Angélique had twelve children by a number of lovers and entered them as nuns in her new establishment. Maubuisson became famous for its lavish hospitality until after Henry's death when the Cistercian abbot-general, Nicolas Boucherat, broke into the convent with his soldiers to remove Angélique.

Class overcame both religion and gender in the political and social calculations of the German nobility. The abbess of Kitzingen, Katharina von Fronhofen, humbly described her cloister as a hospice for noble-women in a dispatch in 1526–27 to the prince bishop of Würzburg seeking his support against burghers who had attacked the abbey. A few months later, she had so far recovered her authority that she could command the support of the margrave and the city council against the bishop's attempt to claim visitation rights over the convent. She was fighting for a complex of secular and ecclesiastical powers typical of the German prince-abbesses. They had minting rights and set weights and measures; they sat in court and in the imperial diet. In Kitzingen, the mayor and all the officials had to renew their oaths to the abbess publicly each year. She appointed the river master and collected tolls and customs duties. She had market rights and owned warehouses. She exercised the power to license weekend trading and ran bread and meat stalls. She imposed wine regulations and had a tavern. Proprietary rights over parish churches enabled her to give advantages to abbey services. Public processions and displays of relics lured worshipers and donors away from the local clergy. The burgermeister and council successfully appealed to the emperor Maximilian I in 1498 to relieve them of her right of pardon and asylum but the abbess did not comply. The ongoing logic of the Reformation eroded the abbesses' power over parish churches, but until 1803 the abbess of Quedlinberg still occupied the first place among her ecclesiastical sisters on the prelates' bench in the Reichstag.

For noblewomen, social realities remained unchanged by religious upheaval, which Luther recognized when he sanctioned continuation of the convent as an alternative to marrying renegade monks or lower class men. Even in threatened convents, it was they who tended to stay while middle-class women left. Despite the dangers of religious war and the spread of Protestantism in the area, Sainte-Croix received forty-five new nuns from local noble families in the last quarter of the century. Their endowments remained demonstrably smaller than dowries paid in the same families. Right up to the Reformation, the demand for places outstripped the convents' capacities. Competition among nobles and urban patricians for places in convents for their daughters was stiffened by their reduction under pressure of inflation. In Strasbourg, for example, the number of nuns who could be accommodated in the city's eight convents was halved by 1450. By 1500, many convents had only ten to fifteen sisters to ensure that the available prebends were generous.[7] The nobility were frequently placated for their loss of top offices by the exclusion of non-nobles from prebends, which in its turn fueled their resentment of monastic property and exemptions. No wonder the Protestant city council of Augsburg exiled "foreign" nuns from the rural nobility.

In the aftermath of the Hundred Years' War, growing nationalism defined many ruling-class women as "foreign." The political struggle that paralleled the religious struggle brought conflicting visions of a divinely constructed gender system into the fray. As fate would have it, the attack on unmarried and uncontrolled women came at a time when women were

exceptionally visible in the public arena. Catholic princes often preferred
to delegate authority to female relatives, foreigners to their subjects,
rather than to men who did not share their dynastic interests. Margaret
of Parma represented her nephew Philip II in the Netherlands. Mary of
Guise and Catherine de Médicis ruled as regents over their dead husbands' realms. Even more perversely, it seemed, nature had favored
several Catholic women with legitimate royal authority. John Knox, the
Scottish Calvinist, issued his *First Blast of the Trumpet against the
Monstrous Regiment of Women* condemning the unnatural queenship of
Mary Tudor and Mary Stuart over God-fearing men. Urban Protestants
singled out the authority of abbesses over towns as an affront to the
natural order. A memo of the Augsburg council, in 1534, scolded that
God made woman subject to man because of her weakness: "How should
it come to any good when women join themselves in a separate life so
that, contrary to the ordinance of God, yes against nature, they give
themselves into obedience to a woman who has neither reason nor
understanding either in spiritual or temporal matters, who ought not to
govern but to be governed."[8]

Burghers were often intrinsically hostile to religious life. Already in
the fifteenth century, cities tried to incorporate convents into the community by taxing them and increasing lay control over them. Burghers
resented the ecclesiastical tax exemptions convents enjoyed on property
they rented for income. The noble convents of Strasbourg speculated
successfully in the grain market and made a tidy income as moneylenders.
In 1465, the Strasbourg town council imposed guardians on widows and
orphaned girls to prevent them from taking their taxable property into
convents. A nun could take enough to support herself but could receive
no bequest over £50. Other town councils fixed maximum incomes for
individual nuns or taxed convents as corporate bodies. Prohibitions on
property purchases and even gifts and legacies limited the amount of
tax-free property they could have. By the sixteenth century these measures were undermining the convent economy and even ruining many of
them. Even so, there were always more applicants than places, and efforts
to limit the number of nuns never succeeded. The towns regulated the
reception of novices, forbade religious women to leave town, and imposed other restrictions. After the Reformation, where they could not
dissolve convents because of noble opposition or imperial intervention,

they stiffened their regulations. The Augsburg city council appointed prioresses and replaced male religious with secular guardians.

Craftsmen, who were pressed by a shortage of masterships, resented the competition of convents, which could employ many servants to engage in household enterprises. They also objected to the commitment of poorer religious to manual labor. The Sisters of the Common Life, Beguines, and Tertiaries competed in the Netherlands's textile trades by offering cheaper labor, precipitating industrial conflicts. Dutch towns passed ordinances limiting the number of looms in convents and forcing them to contribute to the expenses of appropriate guilds, though they could not be members. The Diet of Spires in 1526 attacked mendicants as parasites living on alms that would otherwise support the married poor. Guildsmen saw nuns and Beguines who supported themselves with manual labor as scabs, undercutting the wages of married men. Masters saw women's labor as demeaning to their own licensed skills and sought to relegate it to a subordinate position within the domestic workshop. A widespread body of late medieval literature equated women's economic aggressiveness with sexual aggressiveness. Fear of women as seductive and castrating monsters, ever seeking to place themselves out of men's control or even on top, fed the spreading flames of the witch craze.

In some cities, the burghers supported violent mobs that attacked church wealth. Nützel, a Nürnberg burgher, welcomed the rebellious peasants who, he thought, were doing God's work by looting cloisters and churches. The peasants who attacked Kitzingen appear to have been encouraged by radicals in the town who wanted to abolish the abbess's tax rights. A similar move against the Holy Sepulcher convent in Bamberg indicated resentment against the abbey as tithe holder. Armed bands of iconoclasts roamed around Switzerland destroying altars and statues and taking away altar vessels. In Zurich, the Frauenmünster was plundered and precious metal minted into coinage for the town. Similar destruction signaled the start of the Dutch revolt later in the century. In 1524–25, peasants swarmed about the newly Protestant lands in Germany destroying a hundred or more cloisters, including the venerable monastery of Helfta. They stole food and wine and made off with valuable objects. Where they did not steal, they destroyed relics, mutilated statues and pictures, and carried out other activities designed to show their scorn of Catholic "idolatry." In some cases, they simply held convents to ransom. The convent of Saint Clara in Heilbronn paid 5,000 gulden to be spared. The peasants boasted that they had turned out the entire clergy, monks and nuns, from the diocese of Mainz. At Auhausen, statues were smashed, tombs broken into, the books in the library torn to pieces and thrown into the river. Looting peasants often received arms and supplies from townspeople who were not unhappy to see their ecclesiastical rivals so damaged.

The peasants' war provided the ideal opportunity for secular princes to intervene in the religious anarchy and take charge of church offices and properties. The Diet of Augsburg in 1526 released a plan for the dissolution of ecclesiastical principalities and the secularization of church property. Protestant territories were released from Catholic discipline, and management of monastic goods passed to lords who openly declared themselves Lutheran. Monkeries were universally dissolved and prince abbots became secular princes. Abbesses had to play a subtler game to preserve a status that depended on the survival of their monasteries. Like other German nobles, they used proprietary power to determine the religion of their principalities. The abbess of Gernrode, Elisabeth von Weida, introduced Lutheran services and removed parish clergymen who refused to swear to perform their offices only according to the gospel. The disgruntled town of Herford became Lutheran but the abbess maintained control of the parish churches by changing her religion. Kitzingen also moved to take control of parish churches and established a common chest in 1523 to finance the schools, orphanages, and hospitals supported by the abbey. The abbess adjusted swiftly. As early as May 1524 she invited a lay peasant preacher to preach against the cult of the saints. Although she told the margrave that she was neutral toward Lutheran preaching, she convinced the townspeople that she was sympathetic.

Thus, many wealthy and powerful canoness institutes survived as protestant establishments. In 1536, the Wittenberg articles recognized that women could pass their lives in the cloister, as long as they remained pure in life and doctrine. While the legitimacy of the monastic life was in question, Quedlinberg remained Catholic. But in the 1540s the community accepted Protestantism, and the abbess continued to control local church officials and turned a Franciscan monastery into a school for girls. Gandersheim fought the Reformation for decades despite political and military pressure from the dukes of Braunschweig, who wanted the abbey land for their new university. With imperial support, they elected their own abbess, causing a schism in the abbey with the two abbesses competing for taxes and tolls. The abbess elected by the community was finally confirmed after the "discovery" of the birth of a child to the ducal appointee. The duke gave up his claim to their land and the abbess resumed her seat in the imperial diet. Having secured her authority, the next abbess, elected by the community in 1589, put politics over religion and embraced Protestantism.

The survival of these princely abbeys did not offend the Protestant principle that nature intended women for marriage. A succession of Anhalt princesses governed Gernrode, many leaving when they were old enough to get married. When the ladies did not marry, it was regarded as accident or anomaly. The handful of women set aside as too costly or highly placed for settlement had pleasant lives, but no one was encouraged to emulate them. Only Elizabeth of England transformed the ancient rhetoric on virginity into a justification of her peculiar secular power. The feat inspired political philosophers to brood over the intrinsic problems of gynocracy in a patriarchal world: How could a queen have the manly virtues needed to rule? How could a married queen satisfy the demands of nature by submitting to a husband? Yet how could she so flout them as to rule him? The virgin queen herself spent many years playing out elaborate charades of fickle femininity in the game of courtship and marriage forced upon her by her most loyal counselors. It was an unrepeatable performance. Protestants attacked the celibate ethic vigorously, urging nuns to marry and have children.

The issue of forced vocations had always disturbed the most ardent supporters of monastic life. In the first round of visitations, before the articles prohibiting their marriage were passed, Cromwell's men had some success in pensioning women who wished to renounce their unwilling vocations. In 1566, immediately after the Catholic Council of Trent decreed no woman should be admitted into a convent against her will, the abbess of Ligueux resigned, claiming that she had been coerced into taking religious vows. Some nuns at Freiburg testified that they had taken vows unwillingly or in ignorance. One said her mother had forced her into perpetual virginity to intercede for her in heaven under threat of depriving her of support on earth. Charlotte de Bourbon, abbess of Jouarre, was the fourth of five daughters and had been destined from birth to dedicate her life to prayer for her parents' souls. As abbess she energetically guided the spiritual life of her nuns and efficiently administered their temporals. But at the same time, she listened to Lutheran preachers as her mother and sister had done before her. In 1565, she attempted to gain release from her forced vocation, alleging both fraud and force against her father. In 1572, she left Jouarre on the pretext of visiting her Lutheran relative at the Paraclete and never came back. Several years later she married William of Orange, the leader of the Dutch revolt against the Hapsburgs. In 1581, the Spanish declaration of outlawry against him mentioned his marriage to an abbess as one of his crimes.

Not all women who left nunneries wanted to marry. About twenty of the fifty nuns of Sainte-Croix left in the first outbreak of the civil war; it is impossible to tell whether they left because of Protestant sentiments, a desire to marry, or for fear of attack by marauding soldiers. The destruction of their community certainly forced out some nuns. In 1562, Norman Huguenots attacked the abbey of Montivilliers. One nun escaped and passed through the armies to her parents in Paris, who signed a contract to provide her with support if her lost dowry could not be recovered, but eventually Catholic troops liberated the convent and she willingly returned. In other cases, nuns left the convent as they had entered it, in obedience to the head of their families. Philip of Hesse gave his sister Mechtild, who had been a nun at Weissenstein for thirty-three years, in marriage to the count of Tecklenburg to win him to the new religion. In 1527, the duke of Braunschweig had his sister Apollonia snatched by force from Wienhausen. Kept in the custody of a former nun married to an apostate monk, Apollonia accepted the "new learning" but never broke her vow of chastity.

Not only Protestants but Catholic humanists like Erasmus as well viewed celibacy as an offense against nature and prescribed marriage as a cure for clerical immorality. As popular religion turned away from the monastic image of celibate women as brides of Christ, the fearful vision of the witch as Satan's sexual partner arose in its place. As the battle between Christian camps heated up, contenders came to see diabolic characteristics in their sectarian opponents. Catholic practices were inverted to provide the elements of the Black Mass and other fantasies associated with the witch persecution. The suspicion of single women intensified. Attacks on convents paralleled the dissolution of public brothels, driving women out of shelter and, some would say, out of control. Fear of covens nursing a secret legacy of supernatural powers strengthened social pressures to secure women separately in well-ordered households.

The Reformation's syneisactic moment was brief and soon affirmed the limitation of women's roles to the family. Moreover, an early impulse toward conjugal egalitarianism gave way to gendered authoritarianism in the face of public demand. The enthusiastic women of the 1520s had stopped writing by the 1530s, and even Katherine Zell was increasingly marginalized. Contemporaries "blamed" her for her husband's tolerance of sectaries and separatists and accused her of aspiring to be "Doktor Katrina." Bucer, who had married a nun himself, called her "a trifle imperious."[9]

Lutheran teachings comfortably matched an ongoing trend to privatize women and their labor in a husband-headed household. Protestants even abolished the confessional, which had provided women with extrafamilial access to the clergy. Pamphlets focused on the dangers of alliances between women and priests against husbands and fathers. Luther taught Protestants to place all Christians in a secular hierarchy reaching from the prince through the patriarchal household, the foundation of civic order: wife subjected to husband; children to parents; servants to masters. Marriage guaranteed social responsibility, political maturity, and capacity for government in Catholic as well as Protestant cities. The presence of a wife proved masterhood, the passage from bachelor boyhood to adult manhood. In some German towns only married men could vote and hold office. At one point in the fifteenth century, the Augsburg council was even closed to widowers. In the Middle Ages, artisans were not considered ready for marriage until they had achieved the mastery of their craft, which enabled them to set up a household and workshop.

But by the fifteenth century, the family production unit was giving way to larger workshops that reduced the numbers of masters and households. As pressure on the crafts grew, most guilds closed membership to everyone but sons or sons-in-law. This system created a class of men who faced life as journeymen perpetually subordinate to a master. It also left many unmarried women working as servants in the enlarged households of the masters. Responsible burghers viewed the growing number of unmarried young people with mounting alarm as sources of violence and disorder. Particularly in the north, the money economy made the multiplication of nuclear households a practical possibility. A logical solution was the marriage of journeymen not only to servants but to those former nuns who would otherwise live alone or in groups free of male control.

These were not ideal conditions to re-create the household hierarchy among the humble, but town statutes and religious teaching provided powerful support to petty household tyrants. Between 1534 and 1537, Augsburg dissolved several convents and monasteries and forbade the released women to become householders, keeping them out of economic enterprises. Convent dowries were smaller than secular ones and nuns' pensions were very small indeed, but they encouraged poor men to marry them. As wives of journeymen, they still had to work outside the house, usually as servants, to secure sufficient income to support the family. The potentially subversive effect of this independence was countered by a series of laws to enforce marital discipline. Men were made responsible for their failure to master their wives as well as their daughters and authorized to punish them physically. Rape was redefined from a crime of violence to a crime of sex, an extension of seduction, which allowed some of the blame to fall on the woman. Gossip and suspicion of a widow's sexuality constantly pressured her toward remarriage. Nor were these measures confined to people with Protestant sympathies. When Augsburg returned to Catholicism after the imperial victory of 1548, the Protestant Discipline Ordinance remained in force.

The belief that women should marry and submit to the burdens of family life was a necessary complement to belief in the preeminence of men expressed in the literature associated with the *Querelle des femmes*, a fashionable literary exercise disputing the relative capacities of women compared to men. Protestant city fathers pressured individual nuns to leave their convents and marry, helping them to recover their dowries. The Genevan Poor Clare, Jeanne de Jussie, recounted with hot indignation how the apostate nun Sister Blesine tried to persuade the city syndics that she too was anxious to be "rescued" from her vocation.[10] As pressure to make nuns marry escalated from persuasion to coercion, many women were able to break their accustomed silence and take a partisan position in the celibacy controversy.

Marie Dentière, a former nun who married twice and achieved some fame as a pamphleteer, published an open letter to Marguerite of Navarre claiming that women were permitted by the gospel to write though not to preach. She stretched the proposition to include her "private" efforts to talk the nuns of Geneva into following her own example. She forced her way into local convents, haranguing the nuns that celibacy was hypocrisy and that they could not live a wholesome life without a husband and children. Jeanne de Jussie, encouraged by her superiors to write for the Catholic side, described Dentière as "a false abbess, all wrinkled and full of diabolical language."[11] She described the sisters as praying in tears for Catholic victory on a day of violence after they had been warned that the Protestants would make them marry. Anna Bijns, a celibate non-monastic Catholic polemicist in the early days of the Reformation in Antwerp, styled herself a knight and earned her living as a teacher. She wrote a poem, "They Covet Happy Nights and Lose Their Happy Days," urging nuns not to give up the steady meals and comforts of the monastery for the sorrows of marriage. Even a Protestant German widow, Anna Owena Hoyers, urged widows not to remarry but to retain their liberty.[12]

In rebuttal, male preachers attacked virginity itself as a selfish refusal to shoulder the burdens of home and family. Preachers complained that nuns lived in luxury on alms better earmarked for the needy poor. Female relatives visited many convents to harangue sisters to give up their "sinful" lives in favor of marriage and children. A tract of 1523 urged burghers to take their daughters out of the cloisters and teach them their duty as women, not even sparing widows until they were past childbearing and their children grown.[13] The convent of Saint Clara in Nürnberg was literally brought under siege. Friends and relatives charged the nuns with leading damnable lives, trying to persuade them to renounce their vows. When only one gave way voluntarily, the city council decreed that relatives could remove them by force because their vows were worthless. Sisters Margaret Tetzel, Catherine Ebner, and Clara Nützel wept and argued for over an hour before they were taken out of the convent by their mothers and their male friends.[14] It took four men to drag one girl out. They were stripped of their habits in front of the gathering crowd and forced to put on secular clothing. Even as they were driven away, the three girls continued to scream that they had been forced out against their will. The abbess, Caritas Pirckheimer, claimed that some onlookers were so moved to pity that they said they would have rescued the girls had they not feared the armed sergeants.[15]

To strengthen their attack, some reformers did not scruple to play upon the pervasive prurience of men who could not believe in the innocence of women living without men. In a treatise defending his decision to marry a former nun, Martin Bucer admitted that he had fornicated as a monk and said that his wife had had sexual relationships with other men while in the convent and that she had not even been freely seduced but pressured and deceived by her companions. Elizabethan authors frequently cited a record of monastic crime, *The Black Book*, which has turned out to be nonexistent.

Whatever they thought of such rumors, anxious parents became fearful for their daughters as attacks on convents by mobs escalated. The mother of one novice used the excuse of being chilled to penetrate the cloister at Wienhausen. Once inside, she let her servants in the window and they tried to kidnap the novice. In the uproar, the daughter hid herself, but the mother ran through the convent swearing that if the nuns did not surrender her daughter she would go to the duke, who had already kidnapped his own sister, Apollonia. The abbess reluctantly agreed to let the girl visit her parents, who deprived her of her habit and forbade her return. One day when they were still asleep, she got out of the house and walked through the forest to the convent. Finding the doors locked, she waded through the river and climbed up the wall to the choir where the nuns were chanting. When they saw the girl in secular clothing dripping with mud and water, some thought she was a diabolic apparition. But when they calmed down, they hid her until she could take her permanent vows.[16]

Pervasive fear and suspicion concerning what went on in cloisters, already evident in the aggressions of fifteenth-century reformers, spread. Towns sometimes opened the cloister on certain days, saying that townspeople had a right to assure that the nuns lived in poverty. At Wienhausen one of the cloister walls was broken down, and a man climbed through the choir window to see what was going on in the chapel. A nun of

Pforzheim wrote that the margrave's chancellor repeatedly came into the convent, rushing into the dormitory without notice. When the frightened nuns heard him shouting, they would run and hide. "Then he would tear from one cell to another like a maniac and behave in such a manner that our honor wouldn't have been safe if we had not protected one another."[17] The Nürnberg town council demanded that windows be installed in the convent of Saint Clara, making the nuns visible to their visitors, and encouraged men to call on the nuns and spread scandals about them. The abbess, Caritas Pirckheimer, wrote that men threw stones through the windows and forced their way into the convent, threatening the nuns even in the middle of the night. She complained that Protestant townspeople reacted to their bell with curses, brawling, and ribald songs and brought prostitutes to the convent to abuse the nuns verbally. "They look upon us as more despicable than the poor woman in the streets, for they preach openly that we are worse than these." When they appealed for protection, the town council replied that they had brought their troubles on themselves by provoking the people with their accursed manner of life.[18]

The power of the Catholic emperor and Catholic nobles prevented German Protestants from using the sweeping methods of Thomas Cromwell. Initially, at least, Protestants put their hopes in conversion and hoped to close the convents simply by allowing the nuns to leave. As we have seen, some of them did so in the early 1520s, and others were forcibly removed by their families. Strasbourg forbade Catholic worship, suppressed the cloisters, and dissolved the nuns' vows. Their families took them home. But the unhappy nuns and their unemployed servants successfully pressured the council through their relatives to reopen some convents. The nuns of Saint Katherinenthal near Diessenhofen appealed to "divine, federal and imperial justice" against local authorities attempting to convert them. The sisters declared: "our parents placed us in the convent to serve God in this holy order and we are determined not to forsake our Order but to live and die in it."[19]

The siege of resistant convents went on for decades and sometimes ended in victory for the nuns. In nearly all the convents of Upper Württemberg, the sisterhoods held firm and remained in their convents without changing their religion. In 1564 the Lutheran church councillors determined either to turn out those nuns who remained stubborn or to put them together in a single convent. But theologians and secular councillors agreed that it would be too dangerous. They wrote to the duke:

> It is to be feared that the nuns would not let themselves be removed to other places or put up in a separate convent, without offering resistance and raising a terrible feminine fuss; they would be sure to fly for help to their friends among the nobles and the burghers and to make appeal to the imperial privileges bestowed on their convent and their ecclesiastical colleges. . . . It is quite likely that they themselves or their relatives would take measures by which the matter might be brought before the emperor or the imperial chamber and grave complications might ensue. The best course is for the duke not only to forbid sternly the practice of all popish ceremonies but also to have their prayer books and reading books taken out of their cells and all images and books removed from their churches. In case of any nun falling ill, they must be made, under pain of civil punishment, to call in a preacher. They must be forbidden to elect any new abbess or prioress in future and they must be compelled to give up all secular administration.[20]

Clearly, they did not resist simply because they liked lives of ease and irresponsibility, as many Protestants charged. In Germany, site of an active confrontation between the two religions, the first generation of women spoke out articulately. They not only rejected the world; they rejected Protestantism. Protestant writers have seen the fifteenth-century reform as an arid overreliance on formality at the expense of inner religion. But the German Observantine convents enjoyed a sense of discipline and community that enabled them to hold together under assault and keep up some form of their religious services despite every effort to disrupt them. Nuns at these convents were more likely than the Conventuals to have chosen their communities themselves, but even in less thoroughly reformed areas like the Netherlands, evidence suggests that women were more often than not given some choice about the form of religious life they would enter. They were stiffened by writers like Jeanne de Jussie of Geneva, who maintained that women were truer Catholics than men. She recounted the trials of women whose husbands converted to Protestantism and who were beaten and abused by their husbands for their fidelity. She described Catholic women who organized to fight Protestant women in support of their men.[21]

The sisters of Saint Clara in Nürnberg submitted an informed state-ment of their faith. They protested that it was already their custom to read the Old and New Testaments regularly in Latin and German and that they also kept abreast of new religious ideas "except the libellous books which distress our consciences and in our opinion are not always in accordance with Christian simplicity." They also protested the charge of dependence on their own works to gain salvation, claiming a thorough understanding that none can be saved without faith. But they affirmed that faith is manifest in good works, which included a humble effort to follow the crucified Jesus by means of self-mortification.[22]

One abbess agreed to hear a Protestant preacher as long as he said nothing "against God's teaching." When he said that there were only two sacraments, the whole community walked out. The nuns of Ebsdorf claimed that Protestant preaching was not godly: instead of preaching the pure word of God, their preacher insulted their virginal glory, discipline, and honesty. They wanted no other church but the one that had endured from the time of the apostles.[23] Caritas Pirckheimer argued, as did many nuns after her, that Lutherans who preached Christian liberty should not coerce the consciences of nuns who were true to their ancient faith. She marked the disagreement among the Protestants and asked which of them she should believe when being urged to give up her own faith for the "truth." The nuns of Himmelskrone and Liebenau begged the elector Palatine not to "confuse them with all the different creeds being preached."[24] A nun from Pforzheim said that between 1556 and 1562, eighteen different preachers tried to persuade the nuns to break their vows with no success.

In 1525, the city council of Nürnberg ordered the Clarisse abbess to supply an inventory of the convent property and free her nuns from their vows. A skilled humanist, Caritas Pirckheimer responded that she had no power to revoke vows made to God but that, in any case, she exercised no coercion over her nuns and could not allow their relatives to interfere with their oath of obedience, which they had unanimously renewed in chapter.[25] One of the sisters, Felicitas Grundherr, wrote to her father on the town council and pleaded with him not to take her from the life she had freely embraced: "With the help of God, no one shall drag me out of my beloved cloister while I live. I will go further and say this much: if anyone abuses the monastic state as something terrible, I at least am of this mind: Had I still my free will I would again offer myself to God of that free will."[26]

Caritas accused the town council of being motivated by lust for the convent's property and argued that her nuns were less expensive to maintain where they were than they would be living privately on pensions. Wealth was clearly a primary concern for many of the Protestant lords as for Henry VIII and Gustavus of Sweden. The marauding soldiers of the duke of Braunschweig had already plundered Isenhagen and other convents, and in 1517–1519 he demanded subsidies from them in return for protection. The serious campaign against the convents in Braunschweig-Lüneburg began with the duke's demand for 4,000 gulden from every convent in 1524. In the following year, in the middle of the peasants' war, he demanded a larger portion of their goods and income, particularly from those in need of protection from the peasants. He insisted on removing their treasures to a "safe place" under the direction of a Lutheran jurist whose aim was to secularize all wealth in the duchy. He and other jurists also convinced the prince that he was the heir of the cloisters.

Religious harassment followed financial persecution. In 1528, the duke of Braunschweig began a visitation of his cloisters forcing the nuns to listen to a Protestant preacher, a former Dominican who had baptized his own children with well water. The six convents reformed by Meyer proved heroic in their determination to resist. The nuns of Medingen locked themselves away from him, and at Walsrode they shouted him down. The resistance spread and took firm hold. Frustrated preachers put notices on choir doors that everyone must listen attentively and took attendance from the pulpits. Their patrons stiffened their orders and increased the frequency of sermons. The Dominican prioress of Saint Margaret's in Strasbourg, Ursula Bock, set up dummies in the choir and behind the grille while a few aged nuns gave them an appearance of animation during the hours when Protestant preachers were talking. Once discovered, the sisters were forced to congregate in the nave, where they sometimes came to blows with their persecutors. At Lüne, the nuns, led by abbess Mathilde Willen, used smoke bombs made of old fur and rags to drive the preacher out of their church and persisted until the last nun died in 1562.

As time wore on, these nuns were soldiering along without the support of their own priests, who were forced from the convents or became

Protestants themselves. When the sisters of Saint Clara in Nürnberg heard of the threat to remove their confessors and "hand them over to the power of lawless priests and runaway monks," they signed a supplication to the city council. The cloister was opened nevertheless, the priests driven out, and the nuns deprived of their spiritual ministry even on their deathbeds. The chaplain of Saint Clare in Geneva fled in the night, fearing for his life.[27] The Clarisses of Pfüllingen were allowed to remain in their cloisters for eleven years under Lutheran stewards who abused and mocked them daily. They were deprived of mass, the sacraments, and their religious books. Eleven of them died without the last sacraments. The nuns of Isenhagen wrote to complain that the provost had robbed their convent of all its goods and fired the chaplain and the servants, thereby depriving the nuns of mass, the sacraments, and all Christian ceremonies. By action of the city councils, Lüne, Medingen, and Ebstorf lost their chaplains. Catholic confessors were replaced by Protestants who preached that all who embraced the cloistered life would be damned. Lutheran eavesdroppers listened to the confessions of the nuns at Wienhausen. Chapters were forbidden and the nuns could not speak with any spiritual counselor or associate with a relative, and if they spoke to one another there was always a spy nearby.

The nuns of Nürnberg complained to the city council, "no servants or beggars even are compelled to confess to priests chosen by their employers. We should be poorer than the poorest if we were obliged to confess to priests who themselves have no faith in confession; to receive the Holy Eucharist from people who commit such terrible abuses with regard to it would be a shame and disgrace; and to be obedient to men who themselves obeyed neither pope, bishop, emperor nor the holy Christian church; men who abolished the beautiful services of God and instituted others out of their own heads just as they liked."[28] The mass, the five sacraments, and other aspects of their divine services were prohibited. German was substituted for Latin at communion. Prayers to the saints were abolished and the *Salve Regina* prohibited.

Six Lutherans installed in the convent church forced the nuns of Isenhagen to take communion from them. "Therefore we were hard-pressed and said we could not and would not ever let them into our cloister. That it was against our consciences. It was a matter of life and death, fame and piety that we did not treat our holy Christian church and its sacraments so. And the Licentiate answered that he understood our feelings very well, that we would hold to the papacy and not to the truth."[29] The duke ordered the nuns of Wienhausen to begin taking communion in both kinds, under threat that he would have them put where neither the sun nor the moon would shine. He also ordered a sort of joint service with the nuns singing before and after the preaching. The chronicler laconically noted, "But this did not last long for the bad feeling between us and the preacher made joint services impossible."[30]

When the choir books were confiscated, the nuns of Medingen "hid as many as we could in corners and as best we could carried on the old customs."[31] The stouthearted abbess Catherine Remstede held Wienhausen together for fifteen years in these hostile conditions. In 1543, when the duke raided the convent, the sisters threw their prayer books and daily handbooks out the windows in the hope that friends would pick them up and restore them. But, to their dismay, their former confessor brought out hidden books and handed them over to the preacher. Commoners rudely searched out the relics and other holy things secured in the choir, smashed the glass cases, and destroyed the contents.

The Lutherans at Nürnberg proposed that the chapel door be removed so that the activities of the nuns inside could be public knowledge. At Saint Magdalene in Strasbourg, the sisters attended clandestine services and, after they were discovered, they celebrated the offices without a priest. At Medingen the chaplain openly conducted the old services until he was ejected by force from the church by the duke's chief officer. The nuns hid him in the cloister for some weeks, holding secret services and mass in the granary. On Easter night, 1530, the duke was caught in the bushes outside Wienhausen about to assault the convent and catch the nuns celebrating mass. The nuns huddled in one of the outbuildings until daybreak, singing and reading until the duke went back to town. Thereafter, they chanted and read with lowered voices so as not to be heard by the Lutherans who surrounded them.[32] When they could no longer chant the hours in the choir, they read them and tried to compensate by singing in the refectory. After they lost their priests, the nuns of Saint Nicholas, Augsburg, performed "dry mass" without bread or wine.

The instruments of devotion and the outward signs of communal life were attacked. At Medingen, the duke's men took the clapper from the bell and cut off the rope. Iconoclasts tore the habits from the nuns of Katherinenthal and stuffed them into sacks, which they burned in the town. The sisters who remained in Nürnberg were ordered to wear secular dress.[33] At Lüne, the nuns ignored an order to put off their habits and wear secular clothes. In Augsburg, the nuns of Saint Nicholas wore their habits under the new clothes the city imposed upon them. The prioress of Liebenau pleaded that her nuns could offend no one by their habits because they never went out. This symbolic stripping of religious women was associated with greater sexual violence. Nuns in the Netherlands were terrorized by rumors that the Calvinists paraded groups of naked nuns through their camps. In England, Catholics claimed that Cromwell's visitors often behaved roughly and actually attempted to seduce the nuns themselves. Steinheim-am-Murr was invaded in 1553 by sixty soldiers who broke the windows and exposed the nuns to the public. A nun at Pforzheim reported: "One of the preachers scolded us in the most abominable manner and called us all bad names and abused our Franciscan confessors worse, calling them stud stallions, stud bulls, mass sows, murderers of souls and other vile names, which would take too long to write. . . . All our works, he said, aimed at making people gape in wonderment, at skinning and fleecing the poor, for which we got great profit."[34]

As the decades went by, violence often escalated. Soldiers smashed the doors and gates to Medingen's cloister and broke a great hole in the wall of the choir exposing the convent to wind and rain. At Saint Margaret's in Strasbourg, provisions and furniture and even the chains and buckets from the wells were taken. At Easter in 1533, Protestant attackers demanded 700 gulden from Isenhagen and when the nuns refused, a choir dame wrote, "bread, drink, wood, butter, milk, coffee and everything which we held from our provost had to be put into carts. We had to send bread and drink to Uelzen and Lüneburg to friends and enemies. The wood we had to drag ourselves out of the fields through mud and filth for our shame. And this suffering went on for ten weeks." For all that, one "young person" declared herself for the reform and three "puellen" and two *conversi* followed her example.[35] Sisters at the Dominican convent of Marie Reuthin near Wildberg held out for years after the destruction of their services, priests, and religious articles. In 1556, their preacher got the duke's permission to force two of the most obstinate nuns out in hope that the rest would give in. In 1559, despite individual examination and private exhortation, they continued to resist.

In the aftermath of the peace of Augsburg, in 1556, the Palatinate Protestantized and the remaining cloisters were suppressed. At Gnadenburg confessors invaded the cloisters in November and denounced the nuns' vows. The abbess and the entire community replied: "in the outside world there was nothing but envy, hatred, persecution and faithlessness; vices innumerable multiplied daily; they themselves were old and useless persons; they had brought their little all into the convent and they intended to go on living up to their vows in willing poverty, fasting and prayer. They knew nothing else from the word of God but that their faith and religion were right and true and they pled that they might be left in the enjoyment of these things." The nuns were stripped of sacred accoutrements and their aged confessor was forced out into the cold. The nuns themselves were moved to a convent at Seligenparten, "which had just been protestantized," and their own goods were confiscated.[36]

At its core, this long struggle centered on the question of obedience, particularly the obedience of women to men. In Upper Württemberg, the royal chancellor wrote Duke Ulrich, "Even if the monks and nuns in the land of Württemberg were devils and not human beings, still duke Ulrich should not treat them in such an unchristian, inhuman and tyrannical manner."[37] The duke replied that they were his subjects and had no right to repudiate his religion. He resented the imperial interference and said that the convents did nothing but "breed apostasy and idolatry, scandal and offence to consciences." At Pfüllingen, preachers complained that "the Gospel made no headway with these stiff-necked blinded women."[38] In response to renewed ducal pressure, the nuns explained that they had been obedient in omitting the mass and other ceremonies and had borne the regular preaching of his deputies for four years and now asked only that he cease tormenting them with his unchristian talk and leave them to die in peace.

Protestants blamed their failure to convert nuns on the sisters' stiff-necked, disobedient attitude. They saw them as undisciplined womanhood, ever prone to rebellion against all authority. When the nuns of Saint Nicholas in Augsburg called for the duke of Bavaria's protection, they were carted into the city and housed with the nuns of Saint Katherine's, who in turn were accused of treason for trying to protect themselves with papal privileges and imperial letters. Granted it was a time of war and the Protestant cities and lords were engaged in deadly strife with the Catholic emperor and his supporters. Nuns were indeed partisans in the struggle. The reformer Rhegius lashed out against the nuns who resisted his preaching:

> There they stood on their Turkish absolution, nuns so convinced of their unbelief, that they did not believe in Christ. The whores thought to come brazenly into the heavenly kingdom like their impenitent saints. They obeyed their stinking rule and thought their pharisaical hypocrisy as high and worthy as the Passion of Jesus Christ and held themselves for reconciled women, mediatrices, do-gooderesses, who would rob and steal from Christ himself his godly glory. They had their ears stuffed with Pelagian free will so that they could hear nothing of God's grace in Christ. All their books and lessons were full of their own services and good works. They would come to God without Christ's mediation. I say Fooey! on this stinking convent holiness! How dare you place the devil's shit of your hypocritical works next to the unending service of Christ's bitter death? Now it was just a wonder that God was so long-suffering that he had not made the earth open against their choir as [it swallowed] Dathan and Abiron, and that God has not struck all that convent hypocrisy with thunder, lightning, hail, brimstone and pitch into the pit of hellfire. What are theft, robbery, whoring and such sins of the flesh compared to the diabolic sins of the convent? He who can be cool and patient here and not spit on this abomination does not hold Christ very dear or valuable. The convent is a house of sin and idolatry . . . and they have closed themselves in so tightly that no glimmer of Christ or the gospel can get in.[39]

The issue of obedience even affected relations between nuns and their Catholic superiors. In 1570, the Franciscans tried to take advantage of the Spanish occupation to undermine the privileges of a Tertiary community in embattled Utrecht. Bely Ruysch, the *ministra*, refused them admission and later complained to the duke of Alba that his troops used gunpowder to force open the cloister gates and climbed over the walls in pursuit of the nuns, chasing them through the convent when they tried to flee. The friars broke into the cloister and excommunicated the nuns, claiming that their resistance proved they had Protestant sympathies. In 1571, Bely and Mechteld Kuyff, superior of Bethlehem in the same city, organized a group of cloisters who agreed to support one another in retaining their privileges against the aggression of the post-Tridentine papacy.

Hundreds of nuns all over Germany were left homeless and without means of support. Cochlaeus's pamphlet on the peasant war lamented the lot of aged and indigent women who, after having prayed for their fellow creatures for decades, were forced out of their cloisters with nowhere to go and no bread to eat.[40] The religious wars had the same results in Germany, France, and the Netherlands. English nuns had to depend on their families or friends to supplement their pensions, when they got them. Some of them lived together in secular housing and returned to the new houses briefly established by Queen Mary in the 1550s. Early in the reign of Edward VI, when the act against breaking vows of chastity was rescinded, a fair number of them married. But as early as 1548, English nuns appeared on the Continent in houses of their orders. After the failure of Mary's restoration, houses exclusively composed of English nuns appeared in France and Belgium. Gaelic and Anglo-Norman lords in Ireland frequently forestalled the royal commissioners and took most of the profit from the dissolution. But they kept some of the monasteries alive into Elizabeth's reign, including at least one nunnery at Killone and most of the nunneries in Connacht.

Syon House was suppressed in 1539, but some members of the community managed to stay together in a series of rented houses under the abbess, prioress, and other officers. The rest went to Belgium, where the remaining members joined them after Mary's death. The site was unhealthy and hardship was intensified by the queen's embargo on supplies from England, which left them dependent on Philip II and the pope for charity. English merchants at Antwerp gave them a property near the city, but it was wrecked by Calvinists in 1571. In 1576 their refuge in Mechlin was pillaged by Calvinists in the wake of the Spanish sack of Antwerp. Abbess Catherine Palmer, who had led them throughout the sojourn in the Netherlands, died of shock. The older nuns fled to Antwerp and then to France, sending the younger sisters back to England for safety. Most of them were captured and taken into custody. Elizabeth Sander, who later entered the English College in Valladolid, was taken prisoner after serving the mission headed by Edmund Campion. After a series of escapes, concealments, and flights she finally rejoined the convent in Rouen, where she and others braved bombardment and hunger when the city was besieged by Henry of Navarre in 1591. Moreover, they attracted suspicion because, though Catholic, they were English. When the war was over, their support of the Catholic League with its Spanish connection exposed them to French hostility. They fled to Lisbon, where the archbishop refused to recognize a community so impoverished that it would probably depend on him for support. They finally gained papal recognition and determined to preserve their English character. With the death of their own confessor, they relied on priests sent to Lisbon as an offshoot of the English seminary in Douai. This independence of the Portuguese hierarchy enabled them to refuse the admittance of Portuguese nuns. Their presence inspired the foundation of a Spanish branch of the Brigittine order at Valladolid.

In German Protestant principalities Catholic recruits gradually dried up and Lutherans displaced them. In 1554, the first communion in both kinds was given at Medingen. Ebstorf became Lutheran at an unknown date. Anna von Langelen was the last Catholic abbess at Wienhausen. Lüne went on another decade but turned Lutheran by 1573. In 1540, the abbess of Isenhagen, Margaret of Boldessen, the prioress, and the sacristan were removed to Halberstadt and replaced with a Lutheran abbess. With the reformers ensconced, the old abbess came home and died there still firmly Catholic in 1554. A Protestant abbess was also installed in Walsrode until the old abbess was finally won over to the reform and restored to office. In 1529, the Strasbourg Dominicans were finally forced to give up Catholic worship until Louis XIV conquered Alsace. Augsburg and Ulm tacitly allowed female monastic communities that had been "secularized." At Saint Katherine's in Augsburg a Lutheran prioress was appointed and the sermons went on with some sisters attending and others devising private devotions of their own. In 1547, the Dominicans returned to Augsburg, deposed the prioress, and restored Catholicism to Saint Katherine's and Maria Stern. Most of the Protestants remained in the convent. This evidence that Catholic and Protestant women shared the same convents for years suggests that their collective devotional life meant more to them than confessional loyalty.

Unterlinden in Colmar managed to continue the cloistered life until 1789, when the convent was confiscated. Töss even maintained the cult of a local saint down to the seventeenth century. In 1602, Abbess

Elisabeth Tobings of Wienhausen, who was probably Lutheran, ordered that all the readings and the psalms be in German. The chronicler added the prayer that they would know how to praise God properly in that language.[41] Between 1616 and 1620, several modifications were made in their habits and they gave up the reading of the Hours. The number of recruits sharply increased: ten in 1629; ten more in 1643. The convent survives today. The Clarisses of Pfüllingen had been driven from their convent but came back despite the loss of their goods. In 1559, the abbess and fourteen or fifteen nuns were still holding out without sacraments despite the hostile preacher. The communities of Dominican nuns at Gnadenzell and at Weiler near Esslingen were equally unanimous. Throughout Protestant Germany convents survived, some Lutheran but many continuing to carry on Catholic services into the eighteenth century.

Throughout the wars, Dutch Catholic families continued to send their daughters to convents, though by the late sixteenth century most convents had suffered financial distress. Many nuns left to marry or were forced out by a convent's closing. Many women in the northern Netherlands who could not enter convents after 1600 became "klopjes" or "holy virgins" who undertook various charitable functions visiting the sick and dispensing charity. Throughout the Netherlands, notably in Utrecht and Amsterdam, klopjes continued to live together in small groups engaging in clandestine religious activities and taking roles formerly played by priests. They often came from wealthy patrician families who had originally endowed convent prebends and continued to nominate daughters to enjoy them. Many of the convents' charitable activities continued throughout the period: foundling homes, shelters for poor women. A group of nuns from Saint Martha's, a surviving convent in Amsterdam, contracted to undertake the care and supervision of poor girls, in effect a new sort of convent. In this sense, the Protestant reform undid centuries of Catholic reform in reopening a sphere of public service to uncloistered religious women.

And it gave new luster to the cloistered. Where the overwhelming majority of people worked enthusiastically to root out the monastic system, nuns stood alone and resisted the loss of their way of life. Despite this story of failure and loss, the honor of nunhood never gleamed more brightly than in those hours when their cloisters were broken and their habits stripped from them. In 1524, an admirer said of Caritas Pirckheimer and the nuns of Saint Clara: "The manly heart that nature refused them, Godly grace rendered them generously; they made their stand and held firmly to their vocation like so many monks."[42] In fact, he did them an injustice. Few monks stood as firmly to their vocation as nuns did.

16

Martha's Part

CAPITALIST ENTERPRISE generated suspicion among twelfth-century Christians accustomed to associate monetary profit with usury and greed. Increasingly they hesitated to entrust their salvation to the prayers of monks and nuns who claimed personal poverty while enjoying the fruits of corporate wealth. Guilt-stricken lay people often renounced the accumulated fruits of financial success in favor of a life of voluntary poverty or soothed their consciences with the less rigorous alternative of contributing generously to the mendicant orders. By the fourteenth century, however, women and men who responded literally to Jesus' admonition to the rich young man offended the growing numbers of Christians who had made peace with worldly prosperity. As plague, war, crop failure, and financial panic relentlessly battered Europe from end to end, people ceased to admire would-be saints who threatened to add to the burden of the proliferating poor. Disgust for beggars fueled growing contempt for the friars as useless parasites who diverted the gifts of the charitable from the truly needy. The proponents of apostolic poverty were condemned as heretics. Pilgrims were treated as vagabonds.

The idea of poverty as a crime and wealth as a reward for virtue spread. In the wake of the plague, legislation in England, Spain, and elsewhere attempted to force the able-bodied to work without satisfying their aspirations for higher wages or upward mobility. Unable to break guild monopolies, the poor were driven into homelessness and crime. The lurid visions of the dangerous late medieval underclass conjured up so starkly in the poetry of François Villon replaced the notion of God's beloved poor. Social reformers were linked to civil unrest. Evangelical reminders that the last shall come first came to have an ominous ring. Wyclif's admirers in England, Hussites in Bohemia and followers of the radical Dominican, Savanarola, in Italy led violent social revolutions and often burned at the stake for it. Protestants advocating social reform like Thomas Muntzer and the leaders of the peasants' war in Germany suffered no kindlier fate. Voluntary poverty was stigmatized as moral turpitude.

As always, women had a more ambivalent and difficult relationship to poverty. The feminization of poverty grew out of a consensus that poverty was in some way compatible with the meekness and modesty of women. Wage controls, for example, justified paying women half the salary of men on the grounds that women required only half as much food. The exclusion of women from guilds and professions was validated by the idea that women naturally depended on men. Women who accepted that lot seemed exceptionally worthy of charity and exceptionally desirable as advocates. The Sisters of the Common Life, who combined mystical meditation with a diaconate of service in the world, lived in communities with the dual characteristics of almshouses and convents. Most of the inmates were poor women repaying the charity of the wealthy with their prayers and spiritual services. Uncloistered religious women, who generally supported themselves and their charitable endeavors with cloth work, were caught between conflicting practical and ideological demands. Beguine regulations at Strasbourg and Basel, for instance, recommended spinning with the distaff rather than the more efficient wheel because the noise of the latter disturbed the silence. The regulations may also have been a deliberate effort to inhibit them from competing with guild workers.

The syneisactic character of the Common Life and its commitment to a public career of teaching and charity eventually provoked an inquisition that compelled some of the sister houses to adopt a Tertiary rule and others to become canoness institutes. The faint disapprobation that Jesus himself seemed to cast on Martha's labors was magnified by nervous misogynists who could see nothing but hypocrisy in the piety and charity of latter day "Marthas," as the directresses of beguinages or Sisters of the Common Life were apt to be called. In the wake of the Black Death, the Tertiary life represented by Catherine of Siena, who combined self-imposed poverty and suffering with care for those who suffered involuntarily, still received high praise. The great saint herself, however, was not immune to witchcraft charges when her public profile became uncomfortably high.

As the deserving poor were being distinguished from the undeserving by their ability or willingness to work, women presented an anomaly because, though systematically prevented from competing with men in the workplace, they remained able-bodied. The fifteenth-century monastic reformer Nider, in his notorious *Formicarius*, linked Beguines, recluses, Tertiaries, and secular canonesses with the able-bodied beggar. In the tightened economic conditions of the fifteenth century, guilds attacked the Beguine privileges of working without an apprenticeship and buying and selling freely. While still associated with the ideal of voluntary poverty, Beguines slipped so far down the social scale that they begged out of genuine need. As the witch craze developed in earnest, it tended to target old impoverished women, particularly those who reacted angrily when neighbors refused them an anticipated charity. As towns began to restrict begging, they were forced to the work they had once been denied. In the sixteenth century, the abandoned beguinages of Liège and the Netherlands were revived as asylums for aged women obliged to work as spinsters under the control of local merchants.

Battered by war and plague as well as secular ambitions, older monastic and quasi-monastic charitable enterprises collapsed. The laity acknowledged that care of the needy was a pragmatic responsibility but maintained that charity begins at home. Families were ashamed to allow relatives to go homeless or hungry. But downward mobility and involuntary poverty escalated with the wars, civil strife and proscription, bank failures, and the demands of greedy rulers for loans that they never repaid. A new class joined the ever-present poor—the embarrassed poor, people who lacked goods but not social status. The stability of the social order seemed to demand that they be prevented from contaminating themselves with manual labor.

Private and public charity worked to preserve the gulf that separated the embarrassed and respectable poor from the lazy and dangerous poor by matching the recipient's accustomed standard of living. The Venetian government used public offices to support impoverished patricians and granted them outright subsidies when that failed. Charity dowries for girls who could prove that they had never worked with their hands were twice as high as those given to working-class girls. Even the maintenance of the servants of the rich took priority over helping the unemployed. Similar measures were enacted elsewhere in Italy, Spain, France, and the Netherlands. Thus, nunneries for noblewomen were strong candidates for generous charity because inflation and overpopulation threatened the standard of living of their high-born inmates. By the same token, Beguines and Beatas, women who voluntarily crossed the deepening gulf between the classes, fomented the gravest social disorder.

Laymen preferred to support poor people with whom they felt kinship: residents of their town or parish, members of their own class or guild. They ran foundling homes, dowered poor girls, visited condemned prisoners, ransomed debtors, and buried the dead, but not indiscriminately. English prayer guilds provided nursing and burial to their own members. The Milan Misericordia explicitly put charity toward fellow members before the needs of other poor people. The Venetian *scuole* divided their membership between rich governors and poor charges. In northern Europe, hospices were restricted to local bourgeois who lost their fortunes. Craft guilds assisted sick members and their widows and orphans. The Lisbon Misericordia, founded in 1498, extended royal patronage to Portuguese in the colonies from Nagasaki to Bahía, joining nobles and plebs in a super-confraternity of spiritual and material aid. This arrangement set the European poor apart from the native poor and left slaves to organize their own confraternities.

The men who dominated confraternities saw the able-bodied poor not as images of Christ in need but as predators to be controlled. Protestantism, as such, had little impact on their social attitudes. Max Weber's thesis linking Protestantism and capitalism has weakened considerably as our knowledge of the medieval economy has improved.[1] The public charities of Catholic countries became equally grudging and repressive. Nevertheless, private charitable activities still reflected theological differences between the churches. The Catholic Church attempted to reform the corrupt indulgence system by promoting corporal as well as spiritual works of mercy. The clergy could offer spiritual benefits and personal satisfaction to women of means and social status who did not go to the extremes of joining the ranks of the poor but who sought to devote their energies to appropriate good works. At the same time, they could mix with the docile and virtuous women whom subtle social distinctions easily classed as embarrassed poor.

The pauperization of women was structural. War and the normal hazards of life deprived many women of their husbands, while social restraints and guild regulations hampered their ability to support themselves and their children without a husband. As almsgiving became masculinized and secularized, the anomaly of the female able-bodied beggar could be solved by employing poor women to share the physical labor of charity with richer volunteers under male direction. In 1530, the confraternity of Santa Caridad in Toledo added thirty Beatas as members, most of whom were probably widows of deceased brothers. These women were the principal recipients of the confraternity's charities. In return, they took over the physical labor in the confraternity's program of visiting and nursing the poor. In 1500, the magistrates of Cologne ordered the hospitals to refuse alms to Beguines unless they spent their mornings caring for the sick.

All over Europe, secular authorities controlled public begging by licensing the embarrassed poor, forcing the able-bodied to work, and criminalizing vagrants. In the 1520s, Nürnberg, Strasbourg, Mons, and Ypres pioneered "poor legislation," which was extended to the entire empire by Charles V and widely publicized in 1526, by Juan Luis Vives, *De subventione pauperum*. Vagabonds and "foreigners" were to be driven away and the able-bodied poor set to public works, reserving charity for those who could not work and were duly registered. Foundlings would be educated until able to work. Vives spoke for a powerful faction who favored secularizing charity and its potential for social control. He relegated the clergy's contributions to personal donations and blamed the friars for fomenting social disturbances. But then, as now, the intervention of the secular state was always limited by its unwillingness to pay the bill for caretaking. Cheap, preferably volunteer, labor demanded payment in a different coin. The ideals of the *devotio moderna*, however battered by distrust and even by an "enlightened" view that simple charity would not cure poverty, survived in the spirituality of female *dévotes*, married noblewomen who did not renounce their position in the world.

* * *

The Protestant revolution weakened the Catholic clergy's resistance to women's pursuit of an independent public life inspired by the apostolic ideal. Hospitals and other care-giving activities, often obscured by the lack of institutional records, had never ceased to attract devout women since the Middle Ages. Many tiny hospitals were the ephemeral creations of individual donors. They were often run by one woman, called a *hospitalaria*, or a married couple. The Hôtel Dieu of Villefranche in 1473 had six rooms, four dedicated to the sick and a chapel supported by a man and his wife, the hospitalers. At Lyons, a hospital for contagious diseases was granted to Huguette Balarin and her husband in 1474 to care for plague victims from the revenues of an old chapel. In the early sixteenth century, Catalina de Ribera transformed her house in Seville into a hospital for poor women.[2] The ancient gospel vision of the syneisactic life brightened once more and the cults of Martha and Mary, Paula, Melania, and other desert mothers enjoyed new popularity. Catholic women, like Protestants, were more likely to be pressured into marriage in the sixteenth century than in the twelfth, and they often sought an outlet for their frustrated vocations in charitable activity. Indeed, many worked with the poor as a first step toward the perfection of the cloister, which awaited women set free by widowhood.

Francesca da Romana was married against her will and tried to turn her home into a convent, where she promoted devotion to her Roman foremothers, Paula and Melania. When civic violence drove her husband into exile and war and plague claimed two of her children, she and her sister-in-law, Vanozza, with eight other noble Roman ladies, dedicated themselves as Oblates of Mary to the poor. Attached to the male Oblates of Mont Olivet, they lived at home, attended services together, made the pilgrim rounds of the Roman churches, and worked as nurses at the Hospital of San Spirito. There she became the center of a circle of nobles, poor people, and even Pope Eugenius IV, a member of the hospital's confraternity, who sought her pastoral counsel on the strength of her visions. In 1433, she secured papal approval to assemble fifteen consecrated women at Tor de Specchi, to lay the foundations for a permanent congregation. Until her husband's death in 1435, she spent as much time there as she could spare, performing various household tasks. Then she enclosed herself in the convent. The vows and rule of Tor de

Specchi excluded all the corporal works the oblates had originally undertaken. They abandoned hospital work, substituting daily chant as prescribed by the Benedictine rule with appropriate sacred reading and manual labor.[3]

Elsewhere broad networks formed to cope with the accumulating disasters afflicting Italy in the late fifteenth century: French and Spanish invasions causing famine and the spread of syphilis among abandoned women and children. Catherine Fieschi Adorno of Genoa had also been thwarted in her girlhood attempt to enter a convent and forced into a political marriage with a dissolute husband. In addition to personal penances and mortifications, she took up serving the poor. Eventually her husband, sobered by bankruptcy, joined her in vowing continence as a Tertiary. They spent the rest of their lives serving the sick at the Pammatone hospital in Genoa. In 1479 they moved into the hospital and she became director in 1490. During the plague of 1493, she transformed the square outside the hospital into a tent city and supervised doctors, nuns, priests, and Tertiaries. Until her death in 1509, Catherine was surrounded by disciples drawn to her teaching on the purifying values of purgatory.[4] She became part of a growing network of holy women who acted as "spiritual mothers" to reforming clergy, spearheading the Catholic reforms of the sixteenth century. Catherine's spiritual son, Ettore Vernazzo, founded the Oratory or Company of Divine Love in 1497, a group of priests working with pious lay people particularly concerned with care of the embarrassed poor.

The Company of Divine Love kept its membership secret and eschewed the public displays of religiosity that usually characterized lay confraternities. Combining asceticism, regular confession, and communion with charity, the group brought the reforming clergy together with the energetic lay charitable movement. Concurrently with the careers of Luther and the first Protestant generation, the company spread to Rome between 1514 and 1517 and infiltrated the curia itself. This first generation of monasticized priests who became the vanguard of the Counter-Reformation, continued the modified syneisactism of the early reform. Laura Mignani, an Augustinian nun who was spiritual mother to a company leader, Bartolomeo Stella, drew him into a network of Roman nuns of her order. Stella brought the company to Brescia, whose charitable circles included Angela Merici, spiritual mother of Francesco

Sforza. Probably influenced by the reputation of Osanna Andreazzi, a Dominican Tertiary and spiritual mother of Francesco Gonzaga, who had just been canonized and named patron of Mantua, Sforza put his city of Milan under Angela's spiritual protection, creating the tie that later bound Angela's Company of Saint Ursula with the reforming bishop Carlo Borromeo.

In Milan, Ludovica Torelli, countess of Guastalla, consecrated her widowhood to God and changed her name to Paula. Her chaplain created a congregation of priests, the Barnabites, to reform both clergy and laity and raise their moral standards. In 1549, she founded the Angelicas, who received exemption from episcopal authority to work with women under the direct supervision of the Barnabites. They supervised houses for repentant prostitutes in Vicenza. In Verona, they recruited women from the best families to run hospitals for orphans and foundlings. They attracted many wealthy patrons for Venetian hospitals. Unfortunately, the Milanese connection roused the suspicions of the Venetian government. In 1548, Paola Antonia Negri, an Angelica who had been venerated as a saint in Padua, came to Venice. Her arrogance alienated the aristocratic governors of the hospitals of Saints Giovanni and Paoli, who accused the Barnabites of using their close contact with the Angelicas to learn state secrets in the confessional. The incident probably contributed to the eventual cloistering of the Angelicas but when Ludovica died in 1559, they were still active in a variety of charitable works. The Venetian work was taken up by the Somaschians, women associated with the Theatines, another order of priests founded in 1526. They founded the Zitelle to shelter girls rescued from prostitution, governed by a female congregation that not only supervised the conditions of the house itself and the training and moral education of the girls but actively worked to secure them husbands or convent places as well. The governesses employed lawyers to free widows' dowries from their husbands' estates.

The most famous and successful of the priestly orders, the Company of Jesus, or Jesuits, took their first vows in 1534. At first, some sort of feminine counterpart seemed natural. Isabel Roser in sixteenth-century Rome and Eleanora Montalbo-Landi in seventeenth-century Bologna sought in vain to form female branches of the society. But, like medieval orders, the company resisted partnership with women and the dangers of scandal that invariably followed. As they had done before, women with similar vocations formed their own communities. The post-Tridentine church, however, was far more carefully organized than the medieval church had been. It kept the female companies juridically apart from the male, however similar their activities. The bishop usually provided the *cura*. The female companies, therefore, formed the base for multiple organizations that came within striking distance of being autonomous orders for women.

The foremost contender for Jesuit counterpart was the Company of Saint Ursula. Angela Merici spent her youth amidst the violence of foreign armies and civil strife in northern Italy. From *The Golden Legend*, she became acquainted with the heroic women of the early church and determined to reproduce their active lives. Pictures of Paula and Eustochium decorated the first Ursuline meeting room. At an early age, she had a vision of a heavenly ladder with maidens going up and down, singing, while a voice told her they would be members of the order she was to found. She vowed herself to virginity and took the habit of a Franciscan Tertiary organizing the plentiful supply of young widows around her home on the Lago di Garda to do relief work. In 1516, she went to live in Brescia, where she gained a reputation as arbiter among families who had been drawn into feuds and violence. But she found no way to reconcile her vision with the social work to which she felt called until very late in her life.

In 1525, she successfully applied to Rome for permission to establish a company of virgins devoted to teaching the young and caring for the sick. Her concern for women driven by poverty to prostitution and disease, brought Angela into the network of the Company of Divine Love working in the Hospital for the Incurable (syphilitics), and Elisabetta Prato gave her home as a meeting place. Angela determined to combine practical assistance with religious instruction to save young women from immorality. During the first century most Ursulines continued to be poor women closely connected to those they served. Some were rescued from a threatening home environment and housed as servants with wealthier members of the company or their sympathizers.

The Company of Saint Ursula took more formal shape after 1530, when Angela was nearly sixty years old. The rule approved in 1534 divided them into two tiers: virgins, usually from the lower classes, and matron widows, each with their own superiors. District leaders were eventually added as liaisons between the virgins devoted to individual care and instruction and the lady governesses whose administrative duties did not include direct visitations. Angela was mistress-general in charge of the distribution of alms and legacies under direct papal jurisdiction. She provided for corporate ownership of property, enabling the company to run orphanages and schools for abandoned girls and recovered prostitutes. A small number of men were appointed to assist orphaned members in gaining their inheritance and servants in collecting their wages or to resolve any other legal conflicts between members and their parents and guardians. A list of members in 1537 indicates that the majority were girls of humble background. They remained uncloistered and did not suffer the civil death, which accompanied religious vows. When Angela died in 1540, one of every four families in Brescia housed an Ursuline.

Angela's death nearly coincided with the beginning of the Council of Trent, which labored for twenty years to reform and reinvigorate the ancient church. The council redefined Catholicism to reinforce its institutional structure and strengthen clerical control of the faith. Yet in all of the exhaustive reexamination of doctrine, liturgy, and discipline, the fathers barely considered the situation of their consecrated sisters. Not a thought was spared for the besieged German nuns fighting so bravely for their rules. On December 3, 1563, as they were leaving the final meeting, the prelates hastily decreed that nuns were universally to observe strict enclosure according to Boniface VIII's *Periculoso*. They were forbidden to go out of their monasteries after their profession except with specific episcopal approval. In 1566, Pius V ruled that the law applied to all professed nuns, even Tertiaries who had made vows of chastity. Those who had not taken solemn vows were instructed to do so or have their communities closed, while women who were not nuns were forbidden to form communities. The hostile sentiments of fourteenth-century popes revived as though none of the bitter tests of intervening years had ever been passed.

The real issue was not cloistering but clerical control. Restriction on religious women previously left free for charitable work fitted into a larger pattern of restriction on private social enterprise. Protestant countries abolished confraternities and Catholic monarchs circumscribed them as potentially disruptive of the social order. In 1562–63, the Council of Trent subjected charitable organizations to episcopal visitation and gave bishops control over pious legacies. In this restricted context, the prelates promoted groups like the Jesuit-sponsored Company of the Holy Sacrament in France, which empowered Catholic laymen to police the poor in conjunction with government efforts. Their female relatives, the *dévotes,* formed auxiliaries that were encouraged to dispense charity and enforce their moral standards on other women.

Despite the seeming intransigence of the council, the new rules were not widely applied for some time. France resisted the publication of the Tridentine decrees throughout the religious wars. The internal missions of Europe and the broad foreign fields opened up by European explorers called for willing hands to reap the potential spiritual harvest. Catholic women in Protestant countries entered what has been termed a "matriarchal" phase of Catholicism, in which mothers and wives fostered the continuation of the religion. Possibly to protect their husbands, who were legally responsible for them, English Catholic wives often acted without their consent and with the encouragement of clandestine priests, organizing charity, assisting at childbirth (and baptizing sickly babies), and nursing the sick (and giving them spiritual comfort). They often sent their daughters to the Continent for a convent education. Many of them remained, despite the dangers of the religious wars, as enclosed nuns in English houses in the Spanish Netherlands and France. In exchange, some women came from the Continent to undertake an English mission.

Mary Ward, who had already established an English teaching community in Saint Omer, wrote to Paul V in 1616 to propose the formation of an English apostolate for ladies who would emulate the Jesuits by dressing and living as seculars though consecrated to the religious state. Like them, her ladies would obey only a single superior responsible to the pope:

> We propose to follow a mixed kind of life, such a life as we hold Christ our Lord and Master to have taught his disciples; such a life as his blessed Mother seems to have led . . . and many holy virgins and widows; . . . that we more easily instruct virgins and young girls from their earliest

years in piety, Christian morals and the liberal arts that they may afterwards, according to their respective vocations profitably embrace either the secular or the religious state.[5]

In the first years of his long pontificate (1605–1621), Paul sympathized with such schemes. He approved the institute and the English Ladies opened free public schools on the Continent in Liège, Cologne, Trier, Rome, Naples, Munich, Vienna, and Prague. Mary Ward tirelessly supervised them all. In 1619, she was arrested in England but freed through the influence of friends. The Jesuits, however, did not welcome association with these "galloping girls" and became increasingly hostile as the inevitable accusations of scandalous behavior surfaced. Ward was accused of too much intimacy with her Jesuit confessor and even of living, disguised as a man, in a Jesuit community. The real crime was that women were seen to be usurping the roles of priests in the evangelization of England. Opinion hardened in Rome and at last the pope ordered her to close her houses and schools. Mary Ward herself was condemned as a heretic because of her refusal to accept cloistering. The pope eventually lifted the personal excommunication but her work was destroyed.

Other isolated groups of "Jesuitesses" were dissolved. In 1631, Urban VIII wrote:

We have learned, not without great displeasure, that in several parts of Italy and beyond the mountains certain women or virgins take the name of Jesuitesses without any approbation from the Holy See. Being gathered for several years under pretext of living the religious life, they have usurped a particular habit distinct from others. They have founded buildings in the form of colleges; they have erected houses of probation. They have a superior general over their pretended congregation and have made vows in her hands of poverty, chastity and obedience in imitation of the solemn vows; that they go freely everywhere without respect for the laws of cloister under the pretext of working for the salvation of souls; and that they are accustomed to undertake and exercise several other works very little in conformity with the weakness of their sex and their spirit, with feminine modesty and above all with virginal shame, works which many highly distinguished in the science of sacred letters by their experience and by their innocence of life would only undertake with difficulty and with the greatest circumspection.[6]

The pope's aversion to would-be Jesuitesses reflected the post-Tridentine church's strengthened commitment to the clerical hierarchy. The geographical structure of the parish system under diocesan authority was intrinsically hostile to the cross-diocesan structure of religious orders. Bishops could incorporate women's communities into diocesan religious life and might even appreciate their services, as long as they remained under episcopal control and did not gain monastic exemptions. Ironically, this policy gave an advantage to religious women who were not tied to orders, but it meant that the charism, the particular cohesiveness of an order, would be lost or subsumed into the bishop's priorities. Angela Merici's warrant from Rome subjected her only to the pope. Mary Ward was also exempted from episcopal jurisdiction. Female orders with their own superiors and their own rules were, for the first time, a real possibility. One by one, the Ursulines, the Visitandines, the Daughters of Charity, and others strove for this independence. One by one they failed. But in their failure, they gained a versatility and value that women's communities had never enjoyed before.

Claustration for religious women was generally supported by secular magistrates and by the families of nuns who did not want to see inheritance patterns disrupted or social order threatened by undefined and ill-placed women. Angela Merici and some other prominent female religious leaders embraced the old apostolic ideal of becoming one with the poor they served. This philosophy in turn helped the poor to help themselves and to join as equals in the care of others. But in the second generation, the Ursulines were besieged by demands from the relatives of the members that they be cloistered. Angela's successor, Lucrezia Lodrone, imposed special clothing on the sisters, which then made it necessary to prohibit unauthorized women from adopting their dress and provoking scandal by unsuitable behavior. People jeered or gossiped about their appearance in the streets, hostility that became more threatening as postulants came from the higher classes and their educational mission began to focus on well-born girls.

Bishop Borromeo's first rule of 1567 for the Milan Ursulines suggested the possibility of permanent vows without imposing them; the second rule of 1582 isolated the matron widows as the Company of Saint Anne and implied that the Company of Saint Ursula should live in community. Again, the requirement was not imposed, although it had always been difficult to find suitable homes for women who could not live with their families. Borromeo urged some of the virgins to form an elite community isolated even from any boarding school attached to the convent.

In France, *dévotes* did much of the practical organization of educational and charitable activities. Those who wanted a more complete religious life often saw the convent, and enclosure, as the logical end of their spiritual development. They did not noticeably object to the requirements of Trent. By the 1630s it was clear that most upper-class women, from whom nuns were traditionally drawn, would pursue their vocations from a cloister, by their own choice as much as by canonical prescription.

Jeanne de Chantal, almost an exact contemporary of Mary Ward, perfectly exemplified this process and its subsequent jurisdictional complications. A noble widow with several children, she became attached to the reforming bishop of Geneva, François de Sales, through her charitable activity among the *dévotes* in Dijon. In 1607, he outlined his idea for an order that would combine Martha's charitable activity with Mary's contemplative virtue. Chantal responded by enclosing herself with two companions in a house at Annecy in his diocese, while keeping herself free to attend to the needs of her family and friends. We do not know to what extent she shared de Sales's vision of a Martha mission. After an initial year's trial of community life, the ladies added visits to the sick to their routine, but the charity was restricted to mature women judged capable of doing the work without detracting from their devotions.

The concept of the mission was basically spiritual, not medical, and de Sales connected it to the examples of the Milanese Ursulines and Francesca da Romana. His *Constitutions for the Order of the Visitation* (1613) eschewed formal vows and stated:

> This Congregation having two principal exercises: one, the contemplation and prayer which must chiefly be practiced within the house; the other, the service of the poor and sick, principally of the same sex, it has properly chosen for Patroness Our Lady of the Visitation, since in this mystery the most glorious Virgin visited and served Saint Elizabeth in the work of her pregnancy and at the same time composed the *Magnificat*, the sweetest and most elevated, spiritual and contemplative work ever written.[7]

In that year, Chantal went to start a new house in Lyons, where the bishop immediately prohibited the visitations to the sick, which he considered unsuitable for well-bred women in a large city. De Sales intervened with a historical argument resting on the more active secular life of the early church. But the bishop of Lyons retorted that the argument reinforced the Protestant rejection of monasticism, which rested on the claim that there was no cloister in the early church. De Sales, who was also a bishop, ceded to diocesan authority. The speedy abandonment of the visitations has occasioned much debate about the intentions of both founders. With all due respect to the respective champions of the active and contemplative sides of their vision, I would venture to say that the active apostolate seems to have been dearer to de Sales than to the ladies who had to carry it out.

Chantal herself seems to have been inclined toward the contemplative life and the old-fashioned embrace of voluntary poverty. She gave away her own wealth and depended on the annuities of new recruits for sustenance. In one of her exhortations, she reminded her sisters that, unlike the starving poor, they had enough to eat, if nothing superfluous. She also noted that they were sheltered from the harassment of married life, perhaps remembering her own sufferings with a husband who habitually gave way to his temper and even threw the dishes about and a stepmother who consistently turned her bad humor on her husband's daughter. Finally, they had priority status with some of the clergy and were not left unconfessed after waiting in line for hours.[8] The Visitand-ines abandoned the practice of charitable visiting and, like Francesca da Romana, Chantal ascended willingly to the "higher" contemplative state.

In 1615, despite de Sales's constitution for an informal congregation, the bishop of Lyons intervened again. He insisted that the sisters take formal religious vows and submit to enclosure, securing a more rigid rule approved by Rome. Accepting the demand, de Sales and Chantal both envisioned a centralized order with a uniform rule. When he died in 1622, de Sales had completed the *Constitutions*. In 1628, Chantal gained approval from the heads of approximately two dozen Visitandine insti-tutes for the *Coustumier et directoire pour les soeurs religieuses de la visitation de Saincte Marie*. She then attempted to influence the French bishops to act as a group in issuing a new edition, presumably to ensure uniformity of observance. They did so in 1637 but only after deleting de Sales's vital recommendation that the order as a whole be supervised by a single apostolic visitor. Such supervision would have provided uniform practice and enforcement. The censored customary strengthened the "bond of charity," which held the institutes together, but they remained under the authority of separate bishops. Despite her prestige as foundress and the influence she enjoyed among secular nobles as well as ecclesiastical leaders, Chantal found it impossible to maintain uniform discipline among the thirty-four houses of the order without a unifying administrative structure. The sisters of Grenoble refused to obey the injunction to elect a new prioress after two three-year terms, though the lady herself moved to the house at Aix to avoid breaking the rule. The Lyons sisters were cloistered but the bishop of Bordeaux licensed the order to run a school for girls in his diocese.[9]

The difficulties can best be summed up in the career of Marie-Aimée de Tertre, a widow of dissolute life who was received as a penitent (under threat of more forcible restraint) into the house at Moulins. After a period of defiance, she became excessively religious and goaded her superior into negotiating with people at Nevers to found a new house for her without informing Chantal or the patrons of the order at Moulins, who made a public outcry when they found out. Her continual intrigues with the local bishop for personal privileges within Moulins, including rights to receive her friends with no regard for enclosure, brought scandal on the whole order. As long as the bishop supported her, Chantal had no means but persuasion to control her wayward sister.[10] She was never free of the difficulties of imposing conformity within a decentralized system relying on willing obedience. On her deathbed, in 1641, she suggested the appointment of an inspector general, chosen by all the monasteries, who would advise the respective bishops on the condition and needs of monasteries in their jurisdiction. Her wish was unheeded. Episcopal interference in the affairs of individual houses remained a divisive force.

Though it has often been made the focus of Chantal's story, claustration was only a side issue. Well-bred women did not normally expect to mix too indiscriminately with people of lower standing. Nor were most of them anxious to run about the streets. In Italy, as in Lyons, it was simply not proper or even safe. The *Libro di Ricordanza* of the convent of Cavalieresse di Malta in Florence preserved the story of a young noblewoman of the Frescobaldi family who was so eager to become a nun that she escaped from the parental home to run across town to the nuns. During the brief but unfamiliar journey, she was abused by quarreling muleteers who were blocking the streets and threatened with physical injury. When she arrived, muddy and disheveled, the nuns would have turned her out if her sister had not vouched for her identity.[11]

The degree to which different communities would experience cloister ultimately depended on the bishop's perception of their mission. All over Europe, the Catholic Church was becoming painfully aware in the face of the Protestant challenge that all too many of their members had never been to confession and had never been instructed in the rudiments of their religion. They began to reach out for these threatened souls with missionary zeal. The Jesuits took the lead in devising a new Catholic pedagogy offering rigorous classical training to the elite. They combined preaching, popular reading, and simple catechisms with the extended use of the confessional to form a new Catholic conscience. Among them, the male orders did an excellent job of reaching men, but a combination of prudence, fear, and distaste moved them to keep their distance from women.

But women could not be left open to the snares of Protestantism without the sacrifice of their services as the mothers of future Catholic men. A general consensus emerged, partially shaped by the treatise on the education of women produced by Juan Luis Vives, that as far as possible women should learn the catechism and receive moral training buttressed by the rudiments of reading, writing, and arithmetic. Some upper-class women were even thought to need a more elaborate humanist education, though even the great educator of women, Mme. de Maintenon, eventually came to feel that she had made her pupils too clever for their own good. With some trepidation, the Catholic hierarchy determined that it was a risk that had to be taken. Moreover, it determined, probably for its own protection, that the best teachers of women and of children also were women.

At first, education appeared to be a simple pragmatic mission, like the "matriarchal" initiative of the English. Angela Merici informally catechized the poor whom she visited, particularly those who had fallen into sin or were being tempted. In 1536, the forerunners of the Angelicas, calling themselves "Daughters of Mary" and popularly known as the Guastallines began the education of orphans of noble birth, a vocation they continued after their claustration. The first archbishop of Mexico sent for nuns to assist in the work of converting the Indians. Dominican, Franciscan, and Augustinian nuns appeared with the friars in the wake of the Conquistadors. Generally working from a cloistered environment they helped to establish the first school system in Mexico City. By 1534, there were eight schools where Indian girls learned reading, writing, and arithmetic along with European household skills. The education of the poor and the education of the Indians provoked the same ambivalent feelings in their patrons. The generous impulse to reach out with access to the advantages of their class and caste warred with the self-protective instinct to pull away and close the door to strangers. The objects of this solicitude felt equally pushed forward by the ambition to enter a dominant group and pulled away by unwillingness to forsake their own kind.

In the post-Tridentine atmosphere, Carlo Borromeo, the reforming bishop of Milan, subsumed the Ursuline teaching mission into a larger plan of instruction for children and adults in Milan. By 1566, the company had added Schools of Christian Doctrine for girls to its hospital service, under the supervision of an overseer approved by the bishop. The virgins of the company still lived at home and scrupulously avoided the characteristics of a religious order. They still followed Angela's advice to dress soberly and behave discreetly. But their dress was not to resemble a religious habit and even their larger institutions were not to be cloisters. Locks and gates needed for security were not to inhibit the virgins from going out. Angela passionately stressed the voluntary nature of the life of virginity and service. Though her rule required obedience to the laws of God and the company, to parents and the state, she stressed the precedence of inspirations from the Holy Spirit in the individual soul.[12]

In 1567, Borromeo published his first rule for the Milan Ursulines. He empowered a father-general to determine which of the virgins' inspirations derived from the Holy Spirit. The position of mistress- or mother-general had died with Angela. Elisabetta Prato tried, in 1570, to generalize Angela's institutional structure to enable the Brescian group to form the core of a unified order. In 1580, Borromeo subjected the Milan company to episcopal jurisdiction, ignoring their pre-Tridentine papal privilege of autonomy. His rules were widely publicized but not imposed outside Milan. His initiative ensured that the Ursulines would lack a cohesive constitution.

In heavily Protestant southern France, Angela's *Counsels* inspired Françoise de Bermond to undertake an educational program guided by the Brothers of the Christian Doctrine in Avignon. In 1597, they adopted the Borromean rule for the Ursulines still living at home. They expanded rapidly by bringing Ursuline discipline to previously established groups of women. Noblewomen in northern cities were attracted to the new order, and their individual communities hived off into daughter houses bound by their peculiar customs and habits, frequently very jealous of their own peculiar practices. When the company was brought to Paris, in 1607, Bermond was unable to resist the demand of the noble foundress, Mme. de Sainte-Beuve, for a regular cloistered rule. By 1610, she had withdrawn and the house was cloistered. The Ursulines of Paris determined to protect their educational mission by adding a fourth vow: the free teaching of girls, which became the hallmark of the teaching sisters of every order. By 1658, the Paris model ruled nearly all the French houses. While the Ursulines always maintained day schools for poor girls, cloister and its expenses and restrictions forced them to favor wealthy boarders. In 1673 they began to require a dowry for entrance.

In 1639 Mme. de la Peltrie, a widow of Alençon, gave herself and her fortune to support the Canadian missions. She recruited Marie Guyart Marti, an Ursuline from Tours who adopted the religious name Marie de l'Incarnation, and a companion, a third nun from Dieppe; and two from Paris.[13] Though Marie always maintained that the five sisters never quarreled, she conceded that it was not easy for them to negotiate a common habit and devotional routine. The friction was continually revived by the interference of partisans of their respective houses in France. Like Chantal, Marie dreamed of a union of prelates supporting a single Ursuline constitution approved by the pope. Practically, she pushed for a specific constitution for her own house that would graft the Parisian fourth vow onto the liturgies of Tours. She wanted to gain official recognition before a Canadian diocese could be established because her experience in France had taught her that every new bishop was liable to subject nuns to capricious changes. Despite papal approval of their rule of 1647, Marie's fears were realized in 1661. The first bishop of Quebec sought to establish his authority by making changes "more suitable to Nuns of the Calvary or Carmelites than Ursulines."[14] Marie successfully resisted "to the limits of obedience" and saved her rule. But after she died, the bishop forced her followers to adopt the Paris constitution and pay for new habits from France.

Jeanne de l'Estonnac's Company of Notre Dame, chartered by the pope in 1607, was intended to become an order under a superior general on the Jesuit model. Throughout her life, she worked for papal approval for the company's self-government but was frustrated by episcopal influence. The communities maintained spiritual unity through the sharing of the rules and customs of the mother house in Bordeaux. In 1598, the Filles de Notre Dame, inspired by the life of the early church, developed a pedagogy for little girls. The foundress, Alix le Clerc, with her parish priest, Pierre Fournier, experimented with new educational techniques like the blackboard and letter cards and provided each child with newly accessible cheap books. Le Clerc and Fournier proposed a formal order with chapter-generals and a mother superintendent uniting their original three houses in three different dioceses. Cloistered houses for wealthier nuns were to support unenclosed schools with secular teachers too poor to supply dowries. But as the first generation passed away, the archbishop of Lorraine's ambition to establish his own authority over the whole order caused frictions with other bishops and a long delay. Finally, in 1628, the pope made approval contingent on acceptance of the Observantine Augustinian rule modified by the use of the fourth vow. The Filles failed to formalize their union and cloister restricted them to elite pupils.

Hospital sisters experienced similar problems. The town councillors "reformed" the Hospitalières de Dieppe, with the assistance of the archbishop of Rouen, who had designs on their temporals. Having been turned into regular canonesses, they submitted to wearing a habit and living in a cloister but continued their hospital work by bringing patients into the enclosure. In 1633, the duchess of Aiguillon raised money to send them to Canada. Their initial success as missionaries, however, was gradually restricted to the service of French settlers as episcopal priorities subsumed their own. Thus, claustration was in some respects an incidental issue confronting religious women in the seventeenth century. The real issue was jurisdiction.

Nevertheless, the issue of enclosure cannot be ignored as it developed in conjunction with the mania for order that characterized the seventeenth century. "The Great Confinement," as Michel Foucault called it, the building of barriers and restrictions, was a complex and pervasive feature of this "age of fear." Men became obsessed with the need to restore order to a civilization that had been torn by religious war for half a century. Class allegiance, the containment of the poor and the protection of the prosperous, became an overriding concern. The breakdown of the gender system, most notably evident in the "monstrous regiment of women—queens and dowager regents" who controlled so many of Europe's thrones and the rakish heroines of the French Fronde, a rather ineffectual rebellion against royal absolutism in defense of noble privileges—created a devouring anxiety that fueled the witch craze. The seductiveness of women irretrievably connected them to the devil. Their natural fragility threatened male honor. The overseas missions were poisoned at the well by the development of a universal and unreasoning racism. It perhaps seemed almost inevitable that the enclosing of women and the enclosing of the poor should follow complementary and sometimes intersecting tracks as a consensus developed that absorbed non-European populations into the stereotypes of the dangerous poor in Europe.

Catholic missionaries aimed at the conversion of non-Christians abroad and faulty Christians at home. The educational mission was logically tied to caretaking, for which they wished to pay as little as possible. Volunteers like the Beata Violante de Jesús, who worked as a nurse in the women's prison in Seville, gave simple sermons to the prisoners based on saints' lives, urging them to repent and shun the temptation of men who visited at the prison grille. The missionaries complemented secular efforts to convert the poor into productive citizens and the immoral into respectable members of society. The learning process intermingled charity and discipline including imprisonment and physical punishment. The Jesuits and other representatives of· the reformed priesthood worked closely with the laity in works of penance and social service, sponsoring confraternities for ruling-class men who used poor relief as an instrument of social control. The most powerful of these confraternities was the French Company of the Holy Sacrament, a secret society of priests and secular officials, founded in the late 1620s with numerous and varied auxiliary groups and sympathizers. They reached every corner of the country, progressively criminalizing the poor by combining moral policing with charity. Collecting money in a sort of United Way approach, they could channel the flow of alms to the embarrassed or virtuous poor while institutionalizing the rest.

Women vigorously claimed a role in Catholic evangelization through charity. They shared the growing tendency to place considerable distance between themselves and the poor they served. Hospital work, for example, became increasingly institutionalized and professionalized. In the fifteenth and early sixteenth centuries, the religious aspect of medicine, giving spiritual comfort to the sick and gaining spiritual merit in return, still attracted ladies of the highest class. In the 1520s, the Company of Divine Love centered its attention on syphilitics, the Incurabili, who had replaced lepers as the favored figures of the outcast poor.

In 1496, the Prioress of the Hôtel Dieu in Paris confused syphilis, brought back by French soldiers returning from war with Naples, with leprosy, which medievals also associated with illicit sex. The victims' character as the most godforsaken of the poor was underlined by popular attribution of the original infection to frightful strangers: European enemies, Jews exiled from Spain in 1492, and finally the American Indians. The care of syphilitics, therefore, combined corporal with spiritual works of mercy, the impulse that drove Counter-Reformation spirituality. In Venice, the company joined forces with two noblewomen, Maria Malipiera Malipiero and Marina Grimani, who took in syphilitic women from the streets. Adriana Contarini formed an apostolate to young penitents, adolescent girls who had been sold into prostitution, and established a shelter for them. The Hospital for the Incurable in Brescia was the common ground where Angela Merici met noble patrons like Elisabetta Prato and the countess Laura Gambara, who founded a shelter for homeless women. The life of Rose of Lima, a Dominican Tertiary who died in 1617, expressed these old-fashioned impulses. She modeled herself on Catherine of Siena, imposing ferocious physical sufferings upon her own body, while nursing sick women, native Peruvians as well as poor Spaniards in her home.

As charity became a manly pursuit and an instrument of social control, women who had traditionally bridged the gulf between rich and poor as care givers were gradually forced to one side or the other. The developing male medical professions attacked women's healing activities as ignorant and even harmful, while spiritual authorities took an increasingly suspicious view of their religious activities. Prudence as well as modesty caused Francesca da Romana to credit her healing miracles to a simple homemade ointment. In Spain, the nun Barbara María del Espiritu Santo was accused of involvement with the *alumbrados* ("enlightened"), a sort of Gnostic sect. Her healing, both medical and miraculous, was condemned as a device to make herself spiritual mother of her admirers. Inquisitors investigated other female healers for "incantations," which turned out to be prayers recited while administering medicine. Beatas were often obliged to work in hospitals and prisons in exchange for alms, but every effort was made to reduce their work to a menial and unprofessional status.

With the concept of contagion, the poor, the homeless sick, and particularly prostitutes were converted from agents of grace into plague carriers. The women who customarily provided their care risked being identified as "typhoid Marys." With state support, the charitable established hospitals for the Incurabili, which confined them as well as sheltered them. Gone were the days when virgins affirmed their purity by embracing the corruption of lepers. The hospital in Venice also provided a wing for repentant prostitutes, who in turn did much of the physical labor for the hospital. Fear of physical infection became entwined with fear of moral pollution and, possibly, even racial pollution as the century progressed. Unmarried women were vulnerable to scandals conflated with their handling of the bodies of the sick. They were constantly suspected of seducing their patients in order to get married, a charge that involved not only sexual misconduct but also the threat of misalliance. Their associations with charitable men were never free from scandal. François de Sales recognized this danger and restricted the Visitandines' contact with the sick to women except in a case where a man was so desperately ill as to be utterly helpless.[15]

In France, *dévotes* rarely stepped outside their own class. Mme. de

Sainte-Beuve, who brought the Ursulines to Paris, and Mme. Acarie, who sponsored the Carmelites, belonged to a close circle of influential ladies associated with French reformers. Mme. de Saint-Beuve was a cousin of Mme. de Villeneuve, who founded the Daughters of the Cross, using the original guidelines of François de Sales for the Visitation. She was in turn one of Chantal's benefactresses and lived in a Visitandine convent while establishing a small school in Paris that set an example for numerous autonomous "institutes" for charitable service. Mme. de Gondi patronized Vincent de Paul's Dames de Charité, wealthy women who organized charities at the parish level. Their societies were not uniform or organized efficiently but reflected the interests of the women who started them. Like the Dames de la Miséricorde, who visited the sick at home and in hospitals, they were principally occupied with the embarrassed poor and usually sent their servants to do the dirty work. It was they who demanded cloistering for girls' schools, which gradually separated girls of good family from lower-class girls, even in the schools where day pupils continued to be taken in. The school became a convent protecting young women from the threat of inappropriate men.

Poor women, begging women, abused women, and immoral women were a source of increasing anxiety. Controlling them became the key to the whole fabric of social control and the cloistered convent became the model for that control. Even the sorts of activities approved for the Italian Ursulines were condemned in Spain when they were undertaken by women who lived alone and uncloistered. In 1575, the Seville inquisitors investigated Beatas who provided shelter for women with marital troubles, rescued young girls from procuresses, and helped repentant women to marry or find employment as servants. They were condemned for moving about freely and for taking communion with improper frequency which, the inquisitors alleged, provoked false religious experiences. Out of prudence and out of fear, charitable women maintained the distance between themselves and those they wished to help. In Spain, social status and political office depended upon *limpieza de sangre*, purity of blood. As Spanish men went to the New World, they left their cities in the hands of women whose chastity was vital to the preservation of their social superiority. Civic leaders, fearful that prostitution would attract women of good family with insufficient dowries, debated whether loose women should be treated as prostitutes.

The trend was to mix and confuse enclosed women as prisoners, refugees from home, penitents, and genuine nuns. The Council of Trent excepted "Penitents or Convertites, who will hold to their own constitutions" from the general rule of claustration.[16] But in 1566, Pius V imposed cloister on Sisters of Penitence along with Tertiaries and all other religious women. Despite their universal dislike for convents that occupied tax-exempt ground, city officials encouraged houses for Convertites as a way to confine prostitutes, unmarried women and "badly married" women in danger of becoming prostitutes, and loose women, who were worse than prostitutes because they were not driven by economic need. Borromeo's Casa della Crucifix, founded in the 1560s in Milan, mixed virgins, penitents, and Tertiaries with a group of single and "badly married women" who lived in an unveiled state in a single "convent." The Santa Valeria, established in 1533 as a refuge for women wanting to return to an honest life, had become a house of confinement by 1579. Rehabilitated women were distinguished from penal women, including nuns being imprisoned for nonsexual infractions. But even the seasoned nuns could not ignore the bawdy behavior, escape attempts, and even suicides of women assigned there as a disciplinary measure, which disrupted their religious life.

The Jesuits, who consistently rejected partnership with virtuous women, took a particular interest in the conversion of fallen women, helping them to marry or enter service. In 1626, they established the house of Mary of Egypt in Avignon, confining penitents until they could respectably be disposed. The Malmaritate, founded in Florence in 1609, sheltered women threatened by poverty or abused by their husbands. Until they could be returned to their families, they lived the enclosed life of nuns, ironically supported by a fine on prostitution. In Toledo, Cardinal Quiroga founded Nuestra Señora del Refugio, a house where twenty-four lay women (widows, young women awaiting marriage, separated married women) were cloistered under the supervision of the Augustinian prioress of Santa Monica. In the Portuguese colony of Goa, the Misericordia maintained two retirement houses for "orphan girls" who included the daughters of colonial troops and girls sent from Portugal to marry colonial men but remaining unwed. They also housed white women of dubious virtue and widows. Stray women were a problem in Macao and in Africa. Misericordia hospitals accompanied the founding of most towns in Brazil.

Some women had probably tried to earn a living before entering a Malmaritate or a Convertite house. Some ex-prostitute nuns in Florence managed to retain their property and carry on their own business. The real object, however, was to discipline poor women as a cheap labor force, not turn them into economic competitors. By 1663, although women made up the bulk of Italian textile workers, their wages would not support an independent life without the supplement of occasional prostitution. The Italian Malmaritate institutes, the Jesuits, and the Company of the Holy Sacrament placed their women in jobs as servants when they could not marry them off. Convents themselves sometimes turned effectively into sweatshops. The Milanese sisters of the Casa della Crucifix spun silk and "worked with gold" (probably spinning gold thread). The archbishop's deputies acted as brokers with outside merchants. In effect, financial and civic pressures interfered with the spiritual life of the convent even as ecclesiastical pressures imposed heavier restrictions.

The enclosure of unmarried women was complemented by the tightening of marriage bonds at the Council of Trent. The most common pleas to justify annulment were eliminated by requiring a priestly witness and a written record to validate vows of marriage and the removal of affinity created by sexual intercourse. Catholic wives could thus be subjected to the same disciplines as Protestants. The religious control of women corresponded to secular movements for the enclosure of the poor. Many municipalities established offices for the distribution of poor relief from taxes, keeping a register of the residents who could not support themselves. In Lyons, which set the pattern for France, nearly all charities were absorbed by the Hôtel Dieu, which took in poor invalids, and the Aumône Générale, which sheltered male foundlings and educated them until they could be apprenticed. Girls went to a separate hospital governed by widows who taught them spinning and household skills. In this way the city could register the poor, sending strangers away or committing them to the hospital and putting the able-bodied poor to work.

With the growing perception of poverty as immoral, reformers argued that imprisonment of the poor benefited not only society but also the poor themselves by disciplining them to work, to practice their religion, and to respect public authority. Inspired by Protestant workhouses in the Netherlands, Mother Magdalene de San Jerónimo wrote a treatise in 1608 proposing the establishment of a prison-workhouse for wayward women in Madrid.[17] She intended to convert public corporal punishment for women into private incarceration, which might achieve reform through the harsh discipline of manual labor. Following her model, more than seventy females who wove and spun clothes for other city hospitals were placed in the Galera de Santa Isabel. In Rome, the pope undertook to organize the poor in spinning, weaving, and book making. The confraternities followed suit elsewhere in Italy. Venetian hospitals employed female inmates, who were also put to work caring for more helpless patients or at spinning and whose earnings went to support the institution. The matrons of the hospitals acted as placement agents, putting girls in domestic service and checking on them regularly to ensure their virtue. Lyons's Notre Dame de la Charité, a branch of the Aumône Générale devoted to the incarceration of the poor in 1622, supplied labor for the flourishing silk industry. Repentance was elicited by confining prostitutes either to the institution or in a separate house run by the Company of the Holy Sacrament. Street walkers, kept women, and "those who seduced and prostituted others" were imprisoned for two to three years and put to work sewing.

The institutions of Lyons were widely emulated in Marseilles, Toul, and other large towns under the influence of the company. The introduction to the charter establishing the Toulouse hospital set the tone by criticizing the idleness and immorality of the poor, "who by birth ought to serve the rich" but who are ruined by their own corruption.[18] The foundation in 1656 of the Hôpital Général des Pauvres in Paris was the proudest achievement of the Company of the Holy Sacrament. It imposed a harsh quasi-monastic schedule of hours for religious duties and work on the poor, which it enforced with whipping posts and dungeons. The founder of the charity in Seville described a hospital projected for Madrid as a prison. The imposition of the sacraments on each entrant to a hospital was stressed.

The workshops themselves proved costly and had to be subsidized, but they were defended as important for the teaching of discipline. They were not very effective economically or spiritually. In convents, poor diet inhibited the work of the nuns and their charges and lowered their productivity, while handiwork interfered with their devotions. Guilds saw them as undercutting wages and prices; customers complained of the shoddy work. Nevertheless, workhouses spread to England, Savoy, Germany, Austria, Poland, and Russia under Peter the Great. The most extreme effort to separate the poor from society transported them to the colonies. But the problem of poverty and begging was already plaguing Quebec in 1677, when the governor asked the king for permission to establish a general hospital to feed the poor, put them to work, and control public disorder.

In Canada, the French had undertaken an extensive mission under Jesuit direction to convert the native population. In 1632, Father Lejeune, like Saint Boniface many centuries before, put out a call for nuns to support their work. In Europe nuns already longed vainly to enter the mission field. In Tours, the young Ursuline Marie de Saint-Josèphe dreamed

> she was in a beauteous square, enclosed with fine houses and shops filled with vanities frequented by worldly people. She was reluctant to go in because she saw how the worldly people, and even a monk, were drawn to the vanities and lost themselves among them. As she hesitated to follow so dangerous a path, she saw that all along the square there were many young people dressed as natives divided into two sides like a pair of hedges, through which she could pass without peril. And as she passed, she heard them saying, "Through us you will be saved."[19]

Like Leoba and her eighth century companions, Marie de Saint-Josèphe and her superior, Marie de l'Incarnation, answered the Jesuit call to forsake their homeland and brave the hardships of the Canadian wilderness. The Ursulines sequestered themselves behind a wooden grille in their parlor so fragile that they broke through it easily to escape a fire in 1650. They took refuge with the Hospital Sisters from Dieppe, who had come to Quebec and built a hospital in 1640, and donned their hosts' habits instead of replacing their own.[20] The Hospitalières de Saint Jean, led by Jeanne Mance, arrived in 1659 with enough money to establish the Hôtel Dieu of Montreal to care for Indians as well as French settlers.

In her early years, Marie de l'Incarnation had high hopes of augmenting her order with native novices, whom she described as eager and adaptable to French customs.[21] Marie boasted that winter was their harvest time. Girls left behind by their parents during the winter hunt came into their enclosure, and the nuns competed for the humble task of scrubbing off the grease with which the Indians warded off the cold and the lice that fed on it.[22] They nursed their charges through smallpox and suffered hunger with them in times of famine. Marie spent winter mornings teaching the native languages to young French novices. She wrote an Algonquin dictionary and book on sacred history, and an Iroquois catechism. She kept the parlor open to Huron men, who received "the same charity" as their wives. Marie wrote that the Huron hunters treated Marie Josèphe as a mother, even making confession to her when a priest was not available.[23] She described the heroism of Huron women martyred by the Iroquois to her wealthy patronesses in France.[24]

In those first years, native girls lived and ate with French girls. But the latter eventually acquired their own instructors. As financial hardship bore ever more heavily upon the nuns, French girls who could pay their way gradually preempted most of the space. Despite her continuing admiration for the courage and devotion to the faith shown by many of her native catechists, Marie concluded toward the end of her life that Indian women were not suited to the religious life. "They cannot endure the cloister for they have a melancholy nature and their habits of liberty augment it."[25] In a particularly hard year, Marie wrote that they were reduced to sixteen French women and three natives of whom two were Iroquois captives assigned to them to learn French. The French girls, she maintained, needed the security of enclosure to guard against the danger of rape. Indian girls rescued from the same threat by the Jesuits stayed only briefly until the fathers could place them outside.

Her letters never betrayed the ebb of the Catholic commitment to native vocations. But as the church gradually discouraged indigenous clergy throughout the mission fields of the early modern period, it also excluded native women from the religious life. When Marie died in 1667, Quebec had become a city, and her pupils its foremost ladies. The governor was already laying plans for the enclosure of the poor. Marie stoutly maintained to the end of her life that her order steadily converted Indian women, but her own letters reveal her sensitivity to critics who condemned the enclosed nuns as worthless. Similarly, the Hospitalières de Montréal lost their mission to the Indians when, in 1669, the bishop insisted that they follow their French mother house, whose nuns had taken the habit and cloister to get papal sanction for their rule. Also in Montreal, Marguerite Bourgeoys, who clung to her secular status, was hard-pressed to keep contact with the Indians.

Thus, it was largely as care givers and teachers of Europeans that nuns still went to the overseas missions, though they took what opportunities were offered to work among other peoples. Marie de l'Incarnation wrote to the superior of the Ursulines of Saint Denis, in 1669, urging her to the Martinique mission promising the help of a contingent of Canadian Ursulines.[26] In 1687 the Ladies of Saint Maur sent a mission to Siam to work in the harem, though they were forced out when the king who had admitted them was overthrown. In 1688 the Spanish sisters of Bethlehem organized a hospital in Mexico. The king of France sent sisters of Saint Paul of Chartres to work in a hospital in Cayenne in 1727. Also in that year Marie Tranchepain de Saint Augustin with seven nuns and a novice from the Ursuline convent of Rouen established an Indian mission in Louisiana.[27] They opened a hospital, a school for poor children, and the first academy for women's education in the present United States.

Perhaps Marie de Saint-Josèphe, who died tragically of tuberculosis in the deadly Canadian cold, was indeed saved by the Indians of her dream. Perhaps they and the natives of other lands into which the church was then spreading could have saved their missionaries and the institutions they helped to plant from the deadly fruit of racism and colonialism, which the future held for them all. But the ancient experience of the European conversion—when the converted barbarians contributed their own talents and energies to the developing church—was not repeated. The few nuns who persisted in the missions were intent on socializing the Indians on the European model. They may not have been mistaken in trying to make their converts fit for life in a conquering culture, but in doing so they certainly sowed seeds of future discontent. Similarly, the European poor, perhaps in defiance of upper-class disdain or perhaps only as a figment of upper-class imagination, seemed to develop their own "culture of poverty."

* * *

In the cities of Europe, the distanced generosity of upper-class women did not always meet the immediate needs of the poor for physical and spiritual attention. Upper-class families became increasingly hostile to the idea of their uncloistered relatives appearing in the streets as paupers or even as benefactors. What was needed were women who could formulate a life of religion in the world. Vincent de Paul and Louise de Marillac, also known as Mlle. le Gras (the married name imposed on her by a perversely class-conscious custom that denied her the dignity of "Madame") jointly developed a plan. As the acknowledged illegitimate daughter of a noble, Marillac occupied a sufficiently ambiguous social position to bridge the developing gap between rich and poor without threatening the social order. Her aunt, a Dominican at Poissy under the abbess Jeanne de Gondi, brought her into the *dévote* circle. Early in her life, she experienced a revelation that she would serve God through assisting her neighbors. After her husband's death in 1624, she began to formulate a means to fulfill this destiny. De Paul guided her through the contradictions inherent in the imitation of Martha. He had already become aware of rural charitable networks operating on the estates of Mme. de Gondi. Marguerite Naseau, whom he described as "a poor uneducated cowherd," provided the labor for the first of his *charités*, rural poor relief societies staffed by peasants accustomed to the labor of nursing and funded by the wealthy Ladies of Charity. Marillac enlisted several "good country girls" as workers for the urban poor, whom the Ladies supported and educated to city ways. These Daughters of Charity enlisted the poor to care for their own neighbors. At first, de Paul assigned the care of the healthy poor to a male branch of the Charities but, when he realized the men could not be made to respect the women's authority over the sick, he cut them loose. Typically two Daughters, living together as a village community, could care for the sick, catechize children, and partially support themselves with manual labor.

Thereafter, the Daughters, under the protection of the Ladies, evolved toward religious status. De Paul strove to avoid the difficulties raised by the universal cloistering of nuns through use of the simple or private vow renewed annually, as opposed to the solemn vow of perpetual obedience which characterized the true nun. Vincent's famous formulation has guided his Daughters ever since: "having no monastery but the houses of the sick and the place where their superior lives, having no cell but a rented room, no chapel but the parish church, no cloister but the streets of the city, and no enclosure but obedience, they should go to the sick and to other places only when it is necessary for their service having the fear of God for a grille and holy modesty for a veil."[28]

In his three conferences explaining the rule, de Paul urged the Daughters to serve the souls as well as the bodies of the poor. Their uncomplicated and tentative sense of organization gave them enormous flexibility for a great diversity of social service tasks. He added a mission to the galley slaves imprisoned in Paris, always a constituency dear to Vincent de Paul, to their home visiting. In 1641 they opened catechism schools, *petites écoles,* for converting Protestants in Alsace Lorraine. They undertook the care of soldiers wounded at Sedan and thereafter became familiar figures on the battlefields of Europe. In 1651, when the parishes in and around Paris were short of food and stricken with epidemics, de Paul estimated that the Daughters were preparing and dispensing soup from Louise's house every day to 1,300 Parisians with 800 refugees from the country parishes. The work was not accomplished without a high price. Daughters frequently caught their patients' diseases and died or collapsed from overwork, leaving their aged parents for the society to support. On the other side some Daughters did not renew their vows and left to get married. But the society spread steadily. In the fall of 1651, the first mission of Daughters went out to Poland under the queen's patronage.

Since the Ladies of Charity numbered about a hundred of the noblest women in France, it was difficult to disabuse them of the idea that their donations entitled them to direct the work of the Daughters. They stemmed from old Catholic League families who had opposed the Bourbon succession and who would finally be heavily implicated in the Frondeur rebellion against the young Louis XIV. The *dévotes,* therefore, were clustered among aristocrats primarily concerned with preserving noble privileges. As in the case of a foundling home in Paris funded by the duchess of Liancourt, the Ladies were often insensitive to the practical difficulties encountered by the Daughters. Moreover, their interests were often at odds. The growing movement to enclose the poor engaged the support and interest of the *dévotes,* who steadily drew the Daughters in the direction of institutions that both de Paul and Marillac tended to oppose.[29] In Angers in 1640, a community of Daughters first became attached to a local hospital. Over the next twenty years, they both resisted the confinement of the poor against their will. In 1644, Marillac devised a system for separating feeding the poor, child care, nursing, and education, which pointed the way toward a more widespread and specialized charitable operation. She developed the idea of an alternative hospital system supplying voluntary shelter supported by voluntary alms. By 1653, Marillac planned to lodge twenty poor people of each sex in separate wings with a common chapel and refectory served by Daughters of Charity. Ideally the first beneficiaries would be skilled people who could teach newcomers to contribute to their expenses. Their time would be highly structured, following a monastic model. In its general form, the idea was highly successful. The Daughters established a house in Paris to train recruits to fill the growing number of requests from distant parishes. They chose not to emulate the Hôtel Dieu, which put each new girl in the charge of an older woman for instruction. A general novice mistress helped avoid special attachments among the women and guaranteed a uniform standard of training. In the course of the seventeenth century, religious workers replaced "mercenary" staff. The Daughters did not evade the enclosure of the poor but produced alternative institutions, which were more humane in character, and a second generation of hospitals grew from 1680 on.

The Charities were always subject to the bishop and under the direction of the parish priest unless he showed no inclination for the work, in which case the bishop appointed a chaplain to direct the enterprise. After the Fronde (1648–1653), many of the Ladies of Charity were impoverished and the Daughters moved out from under their wing. By 1655 they had permanent status as a branch under the Superior General of the Missions, thus getting the elusive unity of direction that partially countered the divisiveness of episcopal authority. At the same time, however, the bishop had the ultimate right to decide whether to call them into his diocese and what task they would undertake. They did not always start from scratch. As in the case of the Hôtel Dieu, there were often religious communities or individuals already in place who had long used the system of simple vows. In Lyons, widows and orphans from La Charité followed a quasi-religious rule but did not belong to an order or take permanent vows. The Filles-Hospitalières de Sainte Marthe, founded in 1443 to run the hospital in Beaune, formed communities all over Burgundy in the seventeenth century. At Angers and at Le Mans conflicts arose over the assimilation of these volunteers and earlier communities into the uniformity of the Daughters. As a result, instead of a tightly organized order, the Daughters of Charity tended to inspire a multitude of emulators, some of whom took the same rule but operated autonomously while others took different names and sometimes developed into small orders and congregations of a local nature.

By the end of the seventeenth century, at least one poorhouse stood in every French town with over five thousand people. They were all run by new orders of religious women: Sisters of Providence, Filles de la Sagesse, Paulines of Tréguier, Soeurs Chrétiennes de Nevers, Soeurs Hospitalières de Saint Alexis de Limoges, Soeurs Hopitalières de Saint Joseph du Puy, Sisters of Saint Thomas de Villeneuve. Some used a modified system of enclosure, which enabled them to take in patients or pupils. However they operated, they could never keep apace of the demand for service. The reverend mother of the Hôpital Général de Lamballe recorded her entrance in 1684 as a scene out of Dante. She entered a deserted hospital. At first no one answered her calls until a single head emerged from a heap of stinking rags and said in a fading voice, "In the name of God, help us." She "then discovered that these creatures that trembled and thrashed in the infected bed were the children of the hospital."[30] In Rodez, 4 nuns had to care for 472 poor people, about half of whom were helpless while the other half had to help with most of the work. Even considering how little most sisters got for their support, the hospitals were always trying to cut costs and always in debt. Thrifty or careless officials tended to blame the sisters as poor managers. The inevitable deaths of foundlings and patients was attributed to their lack of medical training. Despite the claims of "enlightened" critics, however, the evidence confirms that they were careful, thrifty to a fault, and sometimes heroic in their measures to raise money (like one superior who had the heads of every one in her hospital shaved to sell their hair for wigs).

Teaching sisters followed the same pattern. In Dôle, Anne de Xainctonge kept the original Ursuline rule as introduced into France by Françoise de Bermond and spread it to Switzerland and Dijon. In 1662, the Ladies of Christian Instruction followed suit as did the Beatas, Sisters of the Lost Villages, founded in 1668, and the Sisters of Christian Doctrine, founded in 1725. In 1677, the director of the diocesan schools in Lyons created a "Company of Ladies" to take over the city's girls' schools. The Trinitarian Tertiaries opened small private schools for hospital pensioners. This group was not a religious community but "a voluntary association of girls caring for pensioners" living in seven or more houses, combining prayer with aiding the sick, teaching the poor, and helping poor girls to marry, enter a convent, or learn a trade. The Filles de Saint Geneviève, founded in 1636 by Mlle. de Blosset for the relief and education of the poor, amalgamated to the Miramionnes in 1665.

The Sisters of Saint Joseph were founded in 1650 for the teaching and assistance of the poor in Le Puy and often combined hospital and educational work. The Charitable Sisters of the Infant Jesus began at Rouen for the purpose of teaching the lower classes, without vows or any constitution. Originally they founded *petit écoles* for boys and girls, but the boys' schools were subsequently taken into those founded by the Christian Brothers. The sisters combined the three r's with Christian doctrine. The sisters lived together and, as their movement spread, established a mother house to provide training and a central direction in Paris on the Rue Saint Maur, from which they subsequently took their name. They temporarily ran the famous school for young ladies founded by Mme. de Maintenon at Saint-Cyr but withdrew in 1694 when it became a cloister. In smaller towns, three to six sisters generally occupied a house and ran a school and gave home care to the poor. In small towns, they were often in charge of the whole Office of Charity, working with local benefactors.

Nuns who taught did not receive the advanced training available to brothers who taught. Moreover, nuns had to overcome real public resistance to the education of girls. In the eighteenth century, they were criticized for providing a narrow education with too much discipline and too little knowledge of the world. Nevertheless, they formulated an education specifically aimed at the formation of women. They adapted Jesuit pedagogy to the lowest levels of the primary school system where it could be spread by secular teachers. For all their inadequacies, they created a genuine profession: a school mistress was little better than a servant in 1600 but was a respected professional by 1700.

Other women, patterning their lives on the Daughters, took no vows and called themselves *filles seculières*, secular girls, who often got salaries from municipalities or sponsors of institutions to which they were attached. In 1653, Marguerite Bourgeoys, an extern of the Congregation of Notre Dame of Troyes with no official religious connection, came to Montreal to organize a school under civil contract. For eight years her teaching mission was frustrated by the high infant mortality rate of the colony. She lived in the fort and occupied herself with caring for the sick, laying out the dead, and washing the soldiers' linen. She aspired to found a community pursuing a third way between the contemplative Carmelites and the cloistered religious who served their neighbors like the Ursulines. Departing from the traditional choice between Mary or Martha of Bethany, she hoped to emulate the Blessed Virgin in her *vie voyagère*, her life as a pilgrim in the outside world.

By remaining in the world without habits, women without property could at last enjoy the religious life. The missionary Father Vimont praised the hospital and the Ursuline nuns for their love and care of the Indians, but he concluded that it was God's work because "their sex does not possess such consistency."[31] The first bishop of Quebec tried to turn the Ursulines into Carmelites. His successor attempted to turn Marguerite Bourgeoys's secular congregation into Ursulines. When she refused, he would give them no constitution. He was further displeased by her trip to France, which gave her firsthand observation of the multiplying communities of simple vows and strengthened her desire to avoid solemn vows and claustration. Only in 1671 did she succeed in establishing the *filles seculières*, who took only simple vows. The next bishop gradually imposed rules on the congregation that brought it closer to the Ursuline model. The women continued to resist and used the protection of royal letters patent, which the king had given Bourgeoys, prohibiting their transformation into a religious order. Finally in 1698 the bishop gave them a rule that respected their secular status. Marguerite Bourgeoys's Sisters of Notre Dame spread throughout Canada as teachers, though the bishops themselves tended to favor the Ursuline establishments.

In subsequent years, bishops continued to put their own priorities over the interests of the orders they employed. In America as in Europe, however, the popularity of service nuns for a variety of tasks continued into the nineteenth century. As the Enlightenment gained the support of fashionable intellectuals in the eighteenth century, the entire concept of the contemplative life came under attack. Even in Spanish and Portuguese America, there was great reluctance to open convents on the established model. As the power of the secular state deepened, the alternative power represented by the church and the great international orders it controlled came under suspicion. In the mid-eighteenth century the Jesuits were dissolved. The destruction of contemplative houses followed. But the work of nursing and teaching guaranteed a continuing place for these "useful" sisters. Moreover, while bishops wanted to control the sisters' missions and the expenses required from the diocesan church, they were gradually less concerned with the details of governance. The pope himself recognized women's limited right to self-governance in the eighteenth century. Clement II reconstituted Mary Ward's Institute in 1703, with the pregnant remarks, "Let the ladies govern themselves."[32] Bishops continued to dominate women's vocations but they grew increasingly willing to grant them broader responsibility especially in the mission fields, which opened vast new horizons to women religious. As Louise de Marillac wrote: "If the work to be done is considered political, it seems that men must undertake it; if it is considered a work of charity, then women may undertake it."[33]

17

---------------✦---------------

The Mystical Regiment

CLOTHED AS IT WAS in the imagery of war and military organization, the Counter-Reformation was thoroughly masculinized. Teresa of Avila spoke from a frustrated longing to participate actively in reformed Catholicism's Christianizing mission:

> As for a poor woman like myself, a weak and irresolute creature, it seems right that the Lord should lead me on with favors. . . . When I hear servants of God, men of weight, learning, and understanding worrying so much because he is not giving them devotion, it makes me sick. . . . They should realize that since the Lord does not give it to them, they do not need it. They should exercise control over themselves and go right ahead.[1]

Sixteenth-century Catholic rulers Christianized their subjects violently. The monarchs of newly unified Spain defined its very nationhood as Catholic, expelling Jews and Moors who refused to convert and demanding that the Indians of the New World convert in return for the limited liberty of life under Spanish rule. Spanish armies secured eastern Europe, large portions of Germany, and the southern Netherlands for the old religion. Mary Tudor introduced the Inquisition into England to support her short-lived effort to restore the church. In France, the Catholic League threatened to overturn the legitimate succession rather than allow the Protestant Henry of Navarre to take the throne. In the seventeenth

489

century, the crown restricted colonial emigration to Catholics and made conversion the centerpiece of French Indian policy.

Even at the height of the battle, the clerical hierarchy sometimes scorned women warriors and condemned their devotion as hysteria or even fraud. The Council of Trent's program of Christianization stressed conformity of belief and uniformity of worship by strengthening the ecclesiastical hierarchy. It put the primacy of the sacraments over all "profane" or "superstitious" manifestations of individual or collective devotion outside clerical control. The Inquisition burned women who dared follow their personal visions too far. In 1541, the Spanish Beata Magdalena de la Cruz was burned as an *alumbrado,* one who "falsely" claimed to achieve direct communication with God. Similarly, the Inquisition condemned Quietism, abandonment of the self entirely to God, as a form of the old Free Spirit heresy leading to the diabolic delusion that all consequent actions were justified. Around 1555, the Index of Forbidden Books included many popular books on devotion that had formerly stimulated lay piety. New religious orders, the Oratorians, Theatines, and Jesuits, made ordination a requirement of admission, implying that Christianization was a mission that only priests could undertake. The transfer of rural convents to urban sites ostensibly gave them the security of city walls but it tightened claustration dramatically. In 1612 Paul V reiterated this law, and in 1627 Urban VIII extended the same measure to convents in the Indies.

In this violent age, however, the maintenance of cloister often required heroic initiatives. Secular women of every sort took refuge in the monastery of the Lady Knights of Malta in Florence during outbreaks of civil strife. In 1530, the convent itself was absorbed into fortifications against the troops of Charles V and the nuns had to take shelter with relatives.[2] The explosion of a powder magazine collapsed part of the English convent at Gravelines. In 1562, Huguenots broke a cloister wall in Toulouse and chased the canonesses from their house. Years later, the broken wall still rendered their garden easily accessible to a pair of duelists, and the prioress feared that it would become a regular rendezvous for combatants. During the French siege of Turin in 1639, the nun who tended the vegetables at the Visitation became accustomed to waiting for the third shot before leaving her work even though a cannonball once shattered her basket.

When Marguerite de Quibly became abbess of La Déserte in Lyons,

> the vaults of this church were broken and the old building was utterly uninhabitable. The rents, the endowments, and the abbey rights were lost. As to spirituals, . . . there remained no hint that the Ladies of La Déserte had ever lived under any rule approved by the church . . ., no trace that their clothing was distinct from that worn in the world. The only observances of these ladies consisted of finding themselves in this church when it suited them and, without being separated from the people, to chant the canonical office as they pleased.[3]

Few of the nuns left in these ruins could have been leading a life of pleasure. Uniformity of habit and regularity of life were luxuries they could not afford. They wore the clothes their families provided and lived outside the convent to save money and secure themselves from marauders. Still, clearly, they tried to keep up their offices.

Fleeing from abbeys devastated by both Catholic and Protestant soldiers some communities survived on the roads. Anna van Aelst staved off Dutch raiders at Rosendael while her nuns fled out the back. For eighty years, they lived in rented rooms in various parts of Belgium. But they converted enough novices to preserve their community until they regained the abbey. While priests went under cover to keep Catholicism alive in England, English women crossed the channel to the war-torn continent to fight for the salvation of their lost country with prayer and voluntary hardship. The English nuns of Syon Abbey, among the last to be dissolved by Henry VIII, fled to the Spanish Netherlands. Driven from Holland by religious war, they ended up subsisting on the charity of English tourists in Lisbon until the French Revolution sent them back to England once more. New recruits for the three daughter houses of the English Poor Clares of Gravelines had to stop in a dirty inn "crowded with heretics who stayed up all night drinking and eating." They said their offices in the orchard while doing their laundry.[4]

In the middle of the seventeenth century, the desire to cloister women's bodies seemed to be paralleled by a desire to cloister their minds as well. The learning and devotion of the *Précieuses* was subjected to deadly ridicule. The *Querelle des femmes,* a literary polemic about the merits and demerits of women, ended by reinforcing ancient stereotypes. Catholics and Protestants alike reinforced the authority of masculinity by stressing the responsibility of the man as the head of the couple, the family, and the state. Even as the monstrous regiment of women gave way to the absolute monarchy of Louis XIV and his train of royal mistresses, the clergy churned out treatises suggesting that unbridled feminine desire frustrated every effort to secure women's chastity. Prescriptive literature urged that even secular women be cloistered at home with their heads covered, firmly subjected to men to protect them from their natural propensity to sin. Women's threat to male virtue and male honor was connected irretrievably to the devil, who seemed to walk the world in feminine guise.

The seventeenth-century practice of making written confessions, however, has uncovered childhood traumas that attracted women to the claustral ideal. Teresa of Avila was first placed in a convent to shield her from sexual scandal. She later wrote, however, that exposure of young women to visitors in the nunnery was so dangerous to their well-being that almost any marriage might be preferable. Her companion, Ana de Bartolomeo, probably suffered some sexual abuse in childhood that impelled her to make plans to disguise herself as a man and go away "where no one would know me as a woman, and everyone would despise me."[5] When Sister Marie de Saint-Josèphe, the Canadian missionary, was four, a man servant carrying her to her mother "touched her naked skin, either by accident or design." Some years later when "a man of quality, seeing her aversion for his sex, bent over her secretly wishing to divert himself," her screams forced him to retreat.[6] At a time of plague, Charlotte de Bréchard's father deserted her and a servant left her with a pair of grave diggers who endangered her life repeatedly by exposing her to diseased cadavers. She was one of the first recruits when her godmother, Chantal, established the Visitation. The widowed Chantal herself suffered atrocious abuse from her father-in-law's servant-mistress. Margaret-Mary Alacoque and her mother were also maltreated by relatives from whom they sought help in time of need.

As women within and without the cloister struggled to maintain some semblance of order in their lives, public preaching, private confession, and stern penitential practices disciplined Catholic Europeans and spread the faith around the globe. Covert missionaries began to shore up the Catholic families left in England after the accession of Elizabeth. Confessors, spiritual directors, and preachers became familiar and prestigious figures in courts, cathedrals, and public squares. Portuguese, Spanish, and French missionaries ventured into distant lands to win voluntary or involuntary converts who had never before heard of Christianity. The ambiguities of these conversions are dramatically illustrated by the Aztec noblewomen who defied Spanish stereotypes regarding the incapacity of their people for the consecrated life to form the community of Corpus Christi in Mexico. Their memoirs frequently offer thanksgiving that God had rescued them from the idolatry of their ancestors.[7] Like the women of barbarian Europe, they may well have found the alternative of cloistered virginity appealing in contrast to the demands of their own society.

Catholic women were no less enthusiastic than men and sought means of using their limited opportunities to serve a missionary vocation. Women who shrank from the terrors of family life willingly tested their strength against physical hardship. The traumatized Marie de Saint-Josèphe proved courageous enough to brave the hardships of Canada, despite the tuberculosis that ended her brief life. As we have seen, however, direct access to the foreign missions was soon denied to women. Their activity, therefore, derived from the concept of spiritual cooperation and support, the practical power of prayer that few women or men of the Counter-Reformation questioned.

Teresa sought to transform the cloister itself into a missionary field, using the image of the mystical body of Christ. As organs of the same body, she deployed her Carmelite sisters to support the more mundane labors of men for the salvation of endangered souls in France and Flanders, the Indies, and the Orient with their prayers and sacrifices. The Spanish Conceptionist María of Agreda was widely believed to have achieved so sublime a state of mystical ecstasy that she "flew" to isolated New Mexican villages where she inspired the Indians to seek out priests for baptism. Virile women recaptured the military qualities of monasticism and boldly occupied higher ground of the cosmic war, opposing the forces of evil with weapons of silence and self-mortification.

Carmelites from Spain went to reinforce the women of the Catholic League in a "mystical invasion" of France against the Protestants and *politique* Catholics who surrounded Henry IV.[8] Silencing the ghost of John Knox, a mystical regiment of women—under Catholic queens like Marie de Médicis and Anne of Austria—patronized the revival of decadent convents and encouraged spiritually talented women to act as advisers to their courtiers. Convents acted as missionary centers not only by educating young women but by holding retreats for secular patrons. The Visitation in Paris reserved cells for the queens. Fleeing from Cromwell's England, Mme. Henriette and Charles I's widow retired there. The heroines of the Fronde were daughters of Catholic League mothers, educated in convents. Many of the great French abbesses and their communities joined the French aristocracy's last stand against emerging royal absolutism.

Even after the defeat of their worldly armies, convents joined religious missions to the cultivation of personal piety. They ran retreats for ladies lasting for a week or more. Select groups would participate in systematic examinations of conscience and meditation on the pains of hell and the rewards of heaven to stimulate attrition and contrition. Nor did the cloister bar an educational mission to the neglected poor. The Visitand-ines of Lyons undertook to catechize vagabonds who fell outside the parish system. Sunday lessons in the convent parlors were followed by alms distribution under the supervision of the out-sisters. Chantal pre-scribed Thursdays, Sundays, and feast days in the rule for ladies and maidens to gather for conferences in the convent where the nuns exhorted them to charity as well as giving them simple catechism.

The Council of Trent's final session enjoined the monastic orders to practice "strict observance," which did not differ significantly from the goals of fifteenth-century reformers: enclosure and stability; the common chest and common table; uniformity of dress; austerity and self-mortifica-tion; and the faithful performance of liturgical offices. The rules of the various orders, however, had evolved over long periods of time with periodic refinements, mitigations, and reforms introduced in individual houses, provincial synods and chapters general. The observant movement produced bitter quarrels and even schisms over the rules' original content and application.

Teresa of Avila's mystical visions took institutional shape about ten years before the Council of Trent dealt with the question of monastic orders. The second Carmelite order had been founded by the reforming general John Soreth in 1452, to accommodate the irregular women grouped around his male monasteries. By the sixteenth century, however, male and female convents followed a mitigated rule that allowed ownership of private property and did not demand claustration. In her childhood, Teresa once ran away from home to seek martyrdom among the Moors. As a young woman, however, she was content in her mitigated convent, La Encarnación. Several nuns there had saintly reputations, including a second Teresa anxiously competing to fulfill the prophesy that the convent would produce the first saint by that name. All the nuns enjoyed the decorous company of relatives and *devotos* who brought them presents and gossip in exchange for uplifting conversation, refreshments, and a little music. When Teresa was about forty, however, a powerful conversion experience revived her old missionary fervor. Thereafter, she devoted her life to discovering the original unmitigated rule and bringing it to life.

Sor María de Jesús, who had once walked barefoot to Rome in search of a papal commission to establish strict observance, surprised Teresa with the information that the original rule forbade all property. At first, Teresa felt that lack of an economic base would prohibit the strict cloistering that she envisaged at the heart of her reform. A vision of Saint Clara, however, convinced her that the opposite was true. Teresa came to see poverty as the means to liberate women from slavery to fashion, to the Spanish obsession with "honor" measured by worldly prestige, and to the degrading need to flatter potential patrons.[9] The change enabled her to cut loose from dependence on donors, patrons, and even, to some degree, dowries. She rented a small house in Avila and moved in overnight with a couple of companions. The peal of their bells in the morning announced that San José, the first foundation of Discalced (Barefoot) Carmelites, had been born and was already pursuing its mission of salvation. This daring technique became Teresa's hallmark, blocking local opposition to supporting new convents and, ironically, stimulating the charitable.

Teresa's reform slowly spread to other communities within the Carmelite order while her broader ideas inspired women in other orders as well. Her bold determination to embrace poverty enabled her to recruit sisters with spiritual qualifications regardless of dowry, social status, or, most radically, racial background. At San José, she created a model egalitarian community, untainted by the pernicious principle of "pure blood," which permeated Spanish society.[10] Coming from a converted Jewish family with a recently purchased title of nobility, Teresa was painfully aware that family ties supported class divisions among nuns at the expense of community life. When she entered San José, she left her worldly self, Doña de Ahumada, behind her and became Teresa de Jesús. The Discalced uniformly adopted the occasional monastic custom of changing names to signify rebirth in religion. Abandonment of titles, polite forms of address, and family names obliterated ethnic and social distinction. The practice spread to most reforming congregations.

Except for this formal disguise of a nun's lineage, however, Teresa's vision died with her. Noble family connections and purity of blood not only returned to most of the Spanish convents but also infected the new communities of America. Even the Aztec convents of Mexico restricted their membership to noble or *cacique* women. Ana de Bartolomeo, Teresa's friend and most loyal successor, who introduced the Discalced rule into the Spanish Netherlands, became isolated from her sponsors and her sisters over her support of English Protestant converts who sought admission to their convent. She believed that Teresa's rejection of "pure blood" must extend to the English as well, but the community saw them only as foreigners. Bartolomeo was vindicated in the eighteenth century when the successors of these first English Carmelites established the order in their homeland and also in Maryland.

Initially at least, the principle of poverty fared somewhat better. Sisters with strong vocations believed that "the lord works among pots and pans," and gladly observed the old rule of sharing menial tasks. The same inspiration improved their chances of earning money through handiwork and even of attracting charity in recognition of their superior spirituality. Neither the time nor the content of meals was fixed in Teresa's rule so as to allow her nuns to take advantage of neighborly charity in supplying their daily food. English Poor Clares, also mindful of the inspiration of their foundress, gladly shared the austerity of former times with Flemish nuns in a poor Louvain convent. "Their ordinary fare was a mess of porridge made of herbs . . . to which they added at dinner a little piece of black beef or . . . half a herring . . . and some little portions of peas dressed with lamp oil." The English nuns, being young, acted as servants to the old Flemish women, many of whom were bedridden. Gentlewomen as they were, they took pride in being cheerful while washing clothes on rocks, though wash day left them sore in all their joints, with their fingers burned and peeling from lye. To support themselves they learned to weave linen, "a man's work and very hard for tender weak women."[11]

The Arnauld sisters at Port Royal took on the most humbling of domestic tasks and the most austere lifestyle to avoid asking financial help from their parents. Moreover, they freed communal resources for works of charity to the outside community. When Angélique Arnauld was charged with the reform of Maubuisson after the deposition of the scandalous Angélique d'Estrées, she "packed" the convent with thirty women whose only dowries were spiritual. She encouraged the poor to come to the grille, where she gave them food that the nuns denied themselves. She tended the sick, turning the abbess's apartment into an infirmary. In return, the people of the town helped Arnauld repel d'Estrées and her armed relatives when she attempted to drive the reformers from the abbey.

In that age of "Christianization," obedience was the most highly prized of the three monastic vows. But obedience to the rule, to the superior, and to ecclesiastical authority did not always work in harmony. Teresa reflected, "Needful as a spiritual director is, great care must be taken because some are inexperienced and afflict the penitent with too many exercises, which interferes with God's work. A foolish director may even tell a nun to put obedience to him over obedience to her superior."[12] Chantal suffered precisely this difficulty with her first spiritual director, who subjected her to capricious mortifications to test her obedience. Teresa, whose Jewish background rendered her particularly vulnerable to the Inquisition's scrutiny, struggled to bind her nuns closely into the ecclesiastical hierarchy. Hoping to shield them from accusations of heresy, witchcraft, or diabolical possession, she prescribed frequent and full confession as the best recourse for women who, she cunningly stressed, "have no learning."[13] Yet her writings chronicle multiple disappointments with confessors who were badly trained, unperceptive to spiritual subtleties, and too susceptible to the charms of their penitents.

Teresa was not alone in her complaints. Catherine of Lorraine found the male directors of Remiremont ignorant of the proper conduct of the sacraments, particularly penance. Cistercian houses were served by confessors and priests who had been admitted to the order and trained only for that purpose. The chapter-general of 1601 specified that elderly monks be delegated spiritual directors for nuns. Additionally, the order assigned inexperienced seminarians as preachers to nuns. Angélique Arnauld maintained that she was unable to obtain competent spiritual directors for Port-Royal because there were so few men with the talent to direct women and those few were overburdened already.[14] In 1679, the Dominican nuns of Santa Catalina in Quito complained to the bishop that the friars had not supplied them with confessors but left the work to an ignorant secular priest who did nothing but pry into their eating and dressing habits while the friars themselves went in and out of the cloisters at will, imposing intimate relationships on the nuns. The abbess determined to dramatize her dilemma. Carrying her processional cross, she was leading sixty nuns out of the church "to save their freedom of conscience," when the Dominican general attacked them with a small army of friars. The friars pursued the nuns with clubs and swords back into the cloister, where they destroyed the furniture and beat and even stabbed the nuns, who at last were placed under episcopal jurisdiction. On investigation, the bishop accused the friars of seducing four women who had previously led blameless lives and raping at least one.

Nevertheless, a choice of confessors from among brothers of the same order remained the best solution. The Carmelite general Giovanni Battista Rossi of Ravenna, who visited Spain in 1567, encouraged Teresa to establish communities of friars for the spiritual direction of her burgeoning convents. By 1581, with the approval of Pope Gregory XIII, the Congregation of Discalced Carmelites held their first chapter general and approved constitutions for both sexes. In keeping with Teresa's own principles of claustration and submission to ecclesiastical authority, nuns were excluded from the chapter but her influence was wielded through her confessor and partner, the provincial Gracián. Nevertheless, she complained that even Rossi would not listen to a woman when men advised differently. Foreseeing the difficulties her nuns would face after her death, she inserted protective provisions for them into the constitution. They were to be free to choose their own confessors. She exempted prioresses from the authority of local priors to safeguard them from orders in conflict with the constitution. The provincial, whose authority over the prioress might be open to abuse, could not also be confessor. Confessors were forbidden to encourage nuns to use the confessional for tattling on one another or the prioress.

In her last years, she suffered from the misogyny of Antonio de Jesús, the Discalced vicar provincial, who resented her moral authority. He was quick to entertain the foulest charges of her enemies, even looking into a complaint that she slept with "both black and white men" to satisfy her lusts. He encouraged the Inquisition to investigate the charges of a half-mad novice in the Seville convent that Teresa's confessor, Gracián, used to strip naked and dance before the assembled nuns before retiring for the night with the sixty-year-old abbess. While she was dying at Medina, Antonio spitefully commanded her to attend a pregnant noble-woman who had requested her prayers. To set the example of obedience to her nuns, she made no protest and died on the road in 1582.

In 1587, the Discalced got papal permission to separate from the mitigated Carmelites and form a new order. The surviving nuns struggled unsuccessfully to maintain Teresa's provisions for them. In 1591, their new general, Doria, threatened to cut the nuns loose from the friars if they did not accept his new and more authoritarian constitutions. Teresa's old supporters lost their offices. The brothers gained complete authority over the nuns. Ana de Bartolomeo, one of her closest companions, was virtually driven from Spain and went with Ana de Jesús to France in 1604. There they were awaited by the famous mystic, Barbe Acarie, who had had a vision of Teresa in 1601 urging her to train a group of girls in anticipation of the arrival of the Discalced in her country. Though the Queen of France and other noble ladies welcomed them enthusiastically, Cardinal Bérulle prevented Ana from bringing in Carmelite confessors and kept the French Carmelites subject to the *cura* of his own Oratorians. Ana's resistance in favor of the Teresian constitutions so angered him that he forbade the nuns of her house in Dijon to speak to her, "for your spirit is evil; we do not wish you to infect them for you have a demon and hatred against us."[15] As a result, the Discalced Carmelites broke up into separate congregations. Ana left France to bring the Carmelites to Belgium, and Gracián himself was ultimately forced to follow her there.

Carmelite observance spread to Italy in 1590 under the sponsorship of the widow Marguerite Spinola, whose house in Genoa mothered convents elsewhere in Italy, Avignon, and Vienna. A group guided by Teresa's writings established itself spontaneously in Rome. In 1600, the Italian congregation was separately chartered. In 1612, Discalced monks and nuns went to Poland. Before the end of the century there were nineteen provinces throughout Europe. By 1604, a group of wealthy Mexican women who had read of Teresa's accomplishments had received habits and a copy of the rule from Spain and the order began to spread throughout Mexico and into California, mobilizing the spiritual aspirations of women in the New World. European sisters, however, failed to overcome the hierarchy's resistance to their missionary vocations. Discalced men, originally organized only as confessors for the nuns, broke free of the Discalced women and went to the missions without them. As with the Cistercians, the nuns' confessors were isolated in *hospicios* attached to female monasteries, "a little extraneous to the juridical order but . . . fully observant."[16]

Fontevraud remained the one bastion where the abbess had the power to assure monks for the *cura*. In 1639, however, they challenged Jeanne-Baptiste de Bourbon's authority to assign them as confessors to various priories and parishes under her jurisdiction, and to organize funerals, baptisms, and even marriages in the abbey. They incorporated the abbess's assignment of fasts, liturgical direction, and blessing of nuns under the umbrella of priestly monopoly: "Women are in no way by common law capable of spiritual jurisdiction touching the sacraments." The abbess responded, "If men have published laws and the praises of a crucified God, women have done as much. . . . If doctors have served as lights to the church, they have borrowed these lights from women informed by the particular grace of God. . . . If men have converted peoples, women have converted entire kingdoms. If piety is accidental to men, it is natural to women."[17] The abbess's brother, Louis XIII, confirmed her authority, and the pope approved her new redaction of the rule.

A good abbess sought to mold her community to love obedience more than to fear disobedience. This obedience was twofold: to the rule and to the abbess as the legitimate interpreter of the rule. Cistercian abbeys that maintained their filiation principle might have either abbesses or abbots as spiritual directors. As the international discipline of the order split under provincialism, and different interpretations of the rule were adopted by various reforming groups, each abbess enjoyed the freedom to select a visitor, or spiritual director, whose interpretation of the rule conformed to her own. The abbess of Las Huelgas was "mother" of twelve Spanish monasteries of nuns and a royal hospital that had adopted a strict observant constitution first formulated in 1591, by the nuns of Gradefes. A number of other houses followed the constitutions of these Houses of Recollection, approved by the pope in 1606, without joining the congregation. In 1593, the abbess reinforced the strict observance at Valladolid with nuns from a mitigated house, though Las Huelgas itself remained under the mitigated "common observance." Other Recollect houses came under episcopal authority but referred to Las Huelgas in all matters concerning the observance. Similarly, a Portuguese congregation of four female convents was organized as "Discalced Recollects." The new Cistercian observances of 1601 integrated nuns for the first time: "Everything already enacted concerning vows, celebration of divine offices, regular observance, the reception of novices, should be applied to persons of both sexes."[18] The strict rules of claustration permitted nuns to leave the monastery only in life-threatening emergencies. They prohibited private property and encouraged the nuns to prefer *conversae* over lay servants.[19]

Throughout the century, nuns became embroiled in the quarrel between proponents of common versus strict observance, characterized by a vegetarian diet. In 1589, Anne de Polastron founded a community associated, through the visitor, with the strict observance house of Feuillant. The Feuillantines had three houses by 1620, but their expansion ended when the monks broke with the order and refused to recognize new nuns. Many French Cistercian nuns, conversant with the thought of Saint Bernard, embraced strict observance in his honor. The Congregation of Saint Bernard of the Cistercian Order, a group of strict observant nunneries, combined houses founded separately by Louise de Ballon and Mme. de Ponçonas and recognized by the pope in 1634. The Bernardine regulations included keeping matins at 2:00 A.M., abstaining completely from meat, wearing serge instead of linen, giving two hours a day to mental prayer, and doing handiwork. Rigorous silence was broken only by two recreations after meals. The congregation had thirty-two convents at the end of the century, most of which survived in good order until the French Revolution.

The first stirrings of the strict observance also inspired Angélique Arnauld of Port-Royal and her sister, Jeanne, to discover and practice the austerity of the original rule. On September 15, 1609, the "day of the grille," fainting with fright, Angélique refused to admit her visiting father and mother into the abbey. The nuns, supporting their young abbess against her powerful family, ceremoniously handed over their small possessions to the community. They forsook meat and stripped their habits of all frills. Conferences, recently introduced in most orders for the edification of nuns during their recreational periods, were abandoned in favor of silence, anticipating La Trappe by some decades. The abbess's search for the true rule, however, was not complete until the publication of the Customs of Port-Royal in 1648.

The Trappists, the most austere of the strict observance groups, rejected women from the beginning, but several nunneries adopted its customary and emulated its practice of silence. Angélique de Valençay chose Rancé, abbot of La Trappe, as spiritual director for Les Clairets, where the nuns gave up all recreation and conversation except for conferences, devoted to the discussion of sacred subjects (but not theology), for about an hour on Sundays. Rancé also directed Anne de la Vieuville in reforming Leyme in Cahors. Her nuns rebelled against the harshness of Trappist life, and she risked excommunication from the order to impose it. Conversely, the nuns of Saint Antoine of Paris rebelled against their abbess in favor of the Trappist reform and ultimately left to establish a new abbey. Maubuisson also came under Rancé's influence when he converted Abbess Louise-Hollandine, the Palatine princess, from Protestantism.

The mendicant orders also produced movements for strict observance tied together by common spiritual directors or common customaries. In 1538, at Naples, Marie Laurence Long founded the Capuchin Clarisses, or Daughters of the Passion, using the Rule of Saint Clara with the Collettine constitutions. They expanded in the north into France and Bavaria. The Urbanists also imposed strict cloister on their convents. When the wars were over, Philippe and Marguerite d'Arpajon revived the name and endowment of the dispersed house of Saint Praxède in Avignon and from there Dominican observance spread to more than twenty-five houses. The customary of Saint Catherine of Siena in Toulouse, using Gregory IX's rule for San Sisto, became the prototype for new Dominican convents of the seventeenth century. Sisters of neighboring Prouille, whose royal prioress, Eleonora de Bourbon, clung to *commenda* and mitigated the strict discipline, twice jumped over a broken wall to break into their cloister, where silence and humility reigned.

Systematic visitation was intended to ensure consistent regularity. But the international authority of most religious orders and even the pope to enforce observance was inhibited by *commenda* and by the vested rights of the nuns themselves. The Council of Trent attempted to eliminate pluralism, hereditary benefices, and *commenda* in favor of election by secret ballot and the three-year term. Abbesses were required to be at least forty years old, with eight years experience in the convent they were to rule and unsullied reputations. Age requirements for the novitiate were raised and the council sought to ensure willing vocations by restricting familial donations until the novice was consecrated. Still, Port-Royal was the exception rather than the rule in gaining royal consent to obey these laws. Most convents everywhere continued to be commendatory.

Even before the acceptance of the Tridentine decrees in France, in 1615, a generation of fervent abbesses studied the Benedictine observance and experimented with its practice. Abbesses at La Trinité of Caen and Sainte-Croix of Poitiers were among the first to reform and they undertook to train other abbesses in their methods. The reforming abbess of Montmartre, Marie de Beauvillier, successfully used the Jesuit system of spiritual exercises to train her nuns in Benedictine observance and sent them in their turn to colonize other abbeys. These abbesses were commendatory, often transferred into a strange community from other convents or orders. Youth gave them an advantage over the disgruntled older generation and their high birth gave them inherent power, but success was never assured. The nuns at Montmartre tried to poison their martinet abbess. Even the celebrated mystic Marguerite d'Arbouze, who chose Montmartre for its discipline, could not please her.

Marguerite herself faltered when she saw the nuns of Val de Grâce, beautifully gowned and jewelled, passing in review to welcome her as abbess. She decided not to coerce the elders but to set an example herself and impose the rule on all the newcomers; within two years, the whole community was exemplary. Jeanne de Courcelles, abbess of Tart, who had originally been a Clarisse, undertook a new novitiate to learn the Cistercian observance. But she allowed each nun to convert in her own good time, clipping her hair to signal her allegiance. When Marguerite du Saint Sacrament arrived as prioress at Beaune, one diarist said that they all expected a person of great dignity and vowed to treat her with cold reserve. But she embraced each and singled out the narrator, who had determined to hold herself apart: "passing her hand over my face, she said to me, 'Pride, pride, do not let it get the better of you.'"[20]

The spirit of any monastic law could be expressed only in the daily life unfolded behind the grille. Teresa was so concerned with this question of internal harmony that she prescribed that the nuns should be allowed a secret ballot before admitting any novice. That system could only work with new communities where older nuns were not entrenched and prebends did not give them hereditary rights. Reforming abbesses often encountered the resistance of nuns who had enjoyed relaxation. Maria Maddalena dei Pazzi wrote to comfort the observant Diamante Mazzinghi, whom "relaxed" nuns had alienated from the community: "This deprivation of the conversation of your sisters . . ., you must offer to your spouse in union with his own isolation from all his friends at the time of his Passion, which even caused him to cry out aloud to his eternal father, Why have you abandoned me? . . . When she speaks angrily, you must let it pass in holy silence and pray that she will learn to live like a true religious."[21]

Regular conferences within the community became a hallmark of the observant life. Chantal advised her monastic daughters:

> Have only Jesus in your thoughts, in your will have only longing for his love, and in your actions have only obedience and submission to his good pleasure by an exact observance of the rule, not only in externals but, much more, in your inner spirit: a spirit of gentle cordiality toward one another, a spirit of recollecting of your whole being before our divine master and that true sincere humility which makes us as simple and gentle as lambs. Finally, strive for that loving union of hearts which brings about a holy peace and the kind of blessing we should desire to have in the house of God and his holy mother.[22]

Influential women often looked for a spiritual director outside their own order. Antoinette of Orléans, foundress of the Daughters of Calvary in 1617, turned to Père Joseph, Louis XIII's Capuchin confessor, to organize spiritual conferences and compose several treatises for them.

The observant dominicans of Saint Catherine of Toulouse rejected the order's spiritual direction to be free of unreformed friars. A *conversa* sister had a vision of a friar in purgatory because his too-frequent visits with the sisters had discouraged their persistence. The sisters turned to secular priests appointed by the archbishop of Toulouse as confessors. In Santiago de Chile, the nuns of Santa Clara rebelled against the Franciscans and appealed for episcopal jurisdiction in 1656. They barricaded the convent against the friars who armed themselves and incited the male population to help them break into the nunnery. The nuns attempted to escape but were caught, physically abused and beaten, and dragged by the hair back to the convent. They remained virtual prisoners of the Franciscans until 1662, when a royal decree transferred them to episcopal authority.

In 1626, Tart got papal approval to remove from Cistercian jurisdiction and take Bishop Zamet of Langres as spiritual director. Zamet also undertook the direction of Port-Royal after Angélique Arnauld divorced the convent from the Cistercian order. Zamet even considered forming a congregation with Tart. In the end, however, Zamet came close to destroying Arnauld's reforms. He encouraged spectacular liturgies and severe mortifications and milked the community of nuns for a wealthy new convent devoted to the perpetual adoration of the Blessed Sacrament. Arnauld turned to a new director, the Abbot of Saint-Cyran, who confirmed her original dedication to Cistercian principles of internalized contemplation and physical moderation and, above all, undisturbed devotions within the silence of the cloister.

The cloister not only offered shelter from a hostile world, it offered access to the broader world of the spirit. At Saintes, Françoise de Foix

> spoke about the obligations of religious souls, about the true peace to be found in the way of the cross, and finally she spoke of truths so moving that the little flock enlisted wholly in her cause. They began to deprive themselves of commerce with worldly people . . . they dismissed all whose visits seemed useless and suspicious; they built parlors and closed the gates. The monastery was girded with strong walls. This house became the enclosed garden of the bride, the hidden fountain, the vine shrouded in the hedge to repel the boars; they began to entertain their Beloved in secret places and to enjoy divine caresses which never come in public, as Saint Bernard has said.[23]

A "do-it-yourself" system of spiritual development naturally resulted from priestly neglect of women and their own increased claustration. Many abbesses and even ordinary nuns with well-tested spiritual gifts were recognized as competent spiritual directors. Their natural talents were enhanced by training with "how-to" guides, such as the Jesuit *Spiritual Exercises* and Teresa's *Way of Perfection*. Teresa intended to demystify her mystical experiences in keeping with the scientific philosophy of the age, which sought to subdue the most passionate human experiences to predictable and methodical control. "Learned men," as Teresa generally characterized her inquisitors, were always busy testing spiritual motives with demands for lengthy written general confessions and examinations of conscience. The graduates of this exhausting school spread the benefits of their experiences in standardized workshops or retreats open even to the laity and to common people. Preaching, dramatizations, and other therapeutic methods were utilized to guide the penitent through a process of self-realization shocked by graphic threats of hell and finally comforted by the assurance of salvation.

The obsession with method occasionally threatened the spontaneity of genuine sanctity. The individual creativity associated with medieval worship aroused increasing suspicion in the Tridentine church. The adolescent Charlotte le Sergent made a direct leap to the mature mystical experience of compassion when she saw a poor charcoal seller weeping over the crucified Christ. Unable to accept the validity of her experience, her superiors subjected her to the Spiritual Exercises. The "gehennas and inconceivable torments" associated with the Jesuit system of afflicting the spirit with fear of hell to inspire appreciation of salvation afflicted her deeply. "In place of holy liberty which she had found for herself in the service of Our Lord, she found herself in strange servitude."[24] When she resisted the exercises and reverted to her original direct union with God, the rigid abbess of Montmartre, Marie de Beauvillier, who may have felt pressured to atone for the scandalous behavior of her relative, Henry IV's complacent abbess Claude, reprimanded her in full chapter. The more indulgent de Sales allayed the fear and anxiety provoked by thoughts of sin and encouraged his charges to conclude every meditation by recalling the certainty of salvation.

Systematic training greatly enhanced the Christianizing mission by reinforcing the Catholic principle of salvation through works. But it tended to provoke revelations and graces outside the clerical conduit, which always caused anxiety no matter how orthodox their content and how observant their messenger. The Protestant idea of a priesthood of believers renewed fears of prophecy once embodied in Maximilla and Priscilla. "More credit should be given to the revelations of men than those of women: because that feminine sex is weaker in the head, and they mistake natural things or diabolic illusions for those of heaven and God; they dream more than men and think their dreams are complex truths . . . they are more imaginative than men, and thus less judicious and reasonable and still less prudent, and so the Devil is more likely to deceive women."[25] The more impressive a woman's spiritual achievements, the greater the threat she posed to the hierarchy's monopoly of the channels of grace. The Inquisition accused Teresa of violating priestly prerogatives by hearing the confessions of her nuns. To protect herself from the charge of trying to teach men, Teresa addressed *The Interior Castle* to women only, but the Carmelite provincial restricted access to the book to "educated men" who might find it useful in understanding women's confessions.

Fear of the Inquisition or even of the unwelcome public attention connected with ecstasy reinforced a seventeenth-century tendency to privilege silence over the more elaborate liturgies previously associated with the monastic life. The Carmelite rule prescribed solitude and silence, to be broken only by the mass and Divine Office. The office itself, which lay at the very core of monastic spirituality, provoked criticism. Many reformers condemned the elaborate displays of musical talent customary in socially popular churches as encouragements to vanity. On the other side, Teresa and Chantal, among others, worried because so many nuns did not understand their offices, which resulted in a miserably poor quality of Latin as well as chanting performed by bored and careless nuns. The Visitation abandoned the office altogether in favor of low masses while the nuns pursued pious practices like saying the rosary. Some directors devised appropriate meditations for each part of the mass to infuse meaning into the routine.

Without the chant to focus the wandering mind, new spiritual disciplines had to be developed. In her *Life,* Teresa outlined a six-stage system of mental prayer, disciplined contemplation of the divine mysteries that cultivated the soul's capacity to appreciate God and ultimately approach that union with him which enables the religious to cooperate in his purposes.[26] The Ursuline Marie de l'Incarnation instructed her seminarian son on thirteen grades of prayer, which she had painstakingly distinguished from her own experience.[27] This systematic prayer began with "recollection," emptying the heart of all created things, focusing the senses by avoiding distraction and concentrating on one's past life and past sins and on the life of Christ.

This discipline produced individuals highly trained to seek out every imperfection and enhance every perfection through the examination of conscience associated with confessional practices in this period. The unpracticed meditator might be tempted to run too quickly through untutored application of the *Spiritual Exercises*. Teresa warned against letting self-satisfaction cause regression.[28] Without careful supervision, there was also danger of obsession with past sins and present imperfections. When two Carmelite nuns guided Chantal to the "second level" of prayer, where she could dispense with "preparation" and the use of the imagination, de Sales brought her back to the "safer" first level.

Spiritual directors periodically elicited a general confession from souls in spiritual difficulties, requiring them to go back to the beginning of consciousness and find every sin and every pattern of behavior that produced sin. The process could take weeks of intense individual work. In the form of written autobiographies these confessions could be used as guides to other struggling souls. They also served to detect weaknesses of character or, even worse, dogma. Spiritual directors associated discipline with beneficent violence. They applied the metaphor of cathartic medicine, enemas and purges, to the correction of women, children, servants, and the poor. Even "indulgent" spiritual directors like de Sales recommended frequent self-flagellation including public use of the "discipline," as the whips issued to every monastic were called. Teresa recommended the discipline to cure unregulated and proud spirits who disrupted the harmony of a community. Sor Juana de Jesus, a Clarisse of Morón de la Frontera, wrote: "Disciplines were very prolonged and vigorous so that the whole choir was bathed in blood and the higher dormitory also."[29] Self-inflicted violence, combined with mental prayer, enabled the disciplined practitioner to achieve a trancelike state. While being whipped, Sor Maria Garavito de San Juan Evangelista had a sense of entering into the work of Christ bleeding copiously while carrying the cross. In effect, the discipline contributed to the achievement of a higher spiritual state.

The effort to follow complex spiritual inspirations exposed novices to great dangers. María of Agreda's parents were both Tertiaries but practiced complementary, or competing, devotions: he reenacted the Crucifixion while she rehearsed death and decomposition. Obedient to a vision of the Blessed Virgin, the mother finally evicted her husband and two sons from the family home and turned it into a convent with her two daughters and three Clarisses imported from Burgos. Though none of them had experience with the rule, they decided to emulate the Conceptionists of Madrid. Without a competent spiritual director, the adolescent María tried to overcome diabolic assault and strong sexual temptations by indiscriminate self-tortures. She won no sympathy from the older nuns, who considered her an exhibitionist and possibly a half-wit or madwoman or both. When the diabolical attacks gave way to ecstasies, they made her into a profitable tourist attraction. Only her own innate sense of balance finally rescued her and, as she grew out of adolescence, she settled into a regular and fruitful mystical life.

In the immediate post-Tridentine period, suspicion tended to fall on every ecstatic as an *alumbrado* or false prophet. Mari Díaz, a holy woman of Avila, regarded the disappearance of her ecstasies as progress toward perfection. As late as 1575, "learned men" were still trying to persuade Teresa that her raptures and revelations were diabolical delusions. She struggled to control her mystical trances, complaining that they shamed her and robbed her of her wits. When they seized her in public, she tried unsuccessfully to conceal them. She began first to work with a Jesuit confessor who urged her to stave off mystical onsets by using the discipline and encouraged her to write out a general confession. A second Jesuit reversed the process and allowed her to welcome the mystical state. In 1559, Teresa's books and writings were confiscated, and her new confessor ordered her to give up the mental prayer despite her protests that it protected her from assault by demons. She then had to fend off diabolic assault with a crucifix and holy water. For two years, she obediently resisted ecstasy, but she said that God seized her ever more relentlessly and spoke to her whenever he pleased in any company.

The immediate agent of Teresa's possession was an angel who pierced her heart with a golden arrow. Guardian angels, messenger angels, and warrior angels populated the spiritual world of the seventeenth century in burgeoning numbers. However, as no one in the century of John Milton was liable to forget, angels could fall and even Lucifer had once had a high place in heaven. Père Coton, a Jesuit exorcist, argued that anyone who believed that demons served witches and sorcerers must believe in the good services of the angels. Isabel de Jesús, a Clarisse, saw angels supporting the other nuns in their self-inflicted mortifications. But the ability to discern good from evil spirits was a special gift. A young girl, Nicole Obry, claimed to be possessed by her grandfather, who favored her with heavenly visions. Under examination, she then claimed that his angel provided the visions. Exorcists finally convinced her that devils had deluded her. The process, however, could easily go astray, and self-inflicted violence might imperceptibly turn to fraud where women were cheated of the anticipated ecstasy. Around 1620, an Italian nun, Benedetta Carlini, claimed that she was possessed by an angel named Splenditello, who poured out divine revelations through her and ultimately involved her in the seduction of her companion nun. Once this strangely disguised eroticism had been exposed, she confessed that she had inflicted stigmata upon her own body. Benedetta, like many ambitious contemporaries, aspired to sainthood but ultimately her fantasy or her possessing agent drove her across the boundary separating ecstasy from possession.

Sometimes these incidents alerted inquisitors that mysticism was leading to heresy. As the seventeenth century progressed, the tendency to identify women as possessed by the devil rather than God increased. The power of Satan grew palpably greater as the intensity of the religious struggle increased. In the Protestant world, the devil seduced malicious women as partners in evil, and they were duly burned at the stake in great numbers. Catholics, who were never slow to burn heretics, seemed to lose more women to diabolic possession than to witchcraft, perhaps reflecting their commitment to the efficacy of works. The determination of monastics to confront and do battle with the forces of evil naturally drew unrelenting attacks. Marie Alvequin, abbess of the Augustinian convent of Saint Magloire, had the gift of discernment. At night she patrolled the house to console nuns whom she found in their cells, agitated and half-conquered by the violence of demonic attacks. The threat that the most glorious revelation might be a diabolic delusion inhibited the free spiritual development of many women who felt themselves already marginalized. The Aztec nuns of Corpus Christi in Mexico were under terrible pressure to prove their worth against critics who charged that Indians were incapable of the religious life because they were too prone to sexual incontinence, intellectual sluggishness, and emotional melancholy. Anxiety drove Sor Apolonia to work herself to death before she reached age thirty-five. When Sor Magdalena showed strong mystical talents, her sisters helped her suppress them for her own protection.

The situation of European nuns, particularly Ursulines whose original vocation to an out-reaching educational mission was being transformed into a more cloistered and restricted life, had many points of resemblance to these anxious women. Jesuit reports from Canada, eagerly read by nuns, noted that Huron communities balanced socially imposed "niceness" toward one another with ritualized madness, which freed frustrated spirits to behave extravagantly and command the attention and healing care of the community. Modern anthropologists have noticed similar effects, particularly among women, in other highly repressed communities. Missionaries abroad and spiritual directors in Europe encouraged Indian as well as European charges to direct their feelings of aggression and rage against themselves as sinners. When Huron women transformed their rage against enforced Europeanization into ritual madness, it was reinterpreted as diabolic possession. Jesuits in Europe recognized the same symptoms among women gripped by ecstasy.

Catholics and Protestants alike associated diabolic power with women, but the Catholic clergy never warmed to the idea of women making pacts with the devil. They tended to prefer the older concept of demonic possession, stressing the inherent weakness of the woman and enhancing the power of the priestly exorcist. Priests were often more comfortable with women who had been reduced to vessels for an outside power than they were with the genuinely knowledgeable women or women possessed by God. The devil himself was transformed. Bérulle wrote the *Traité des énergumènes* in 1599, republished after his death in 1631, arguing that God designed sorcery as a last resort for the education of disbelievers who could be taught neither by nature nor by Jesus.[30] Satan, no longer simply the father of lies, was held to be capable of a certain degree of truthful teaching, which a cunning exorcist could elicit, leaving the victim guiltless of the sorcery. Marie des Vallées, a country girl first exorcised in 1612, was possessed by a devil who answered questions in Latin, Hebrew, and Greek. She said that she knew she had never given herself to an evil spirit and therefore concluded that God had judged that the possessed state was necessary for her salvation. Like many possessed persons, Adrienne Dufresne also received divine revelations and, during her lucid periods, discussed their content with Coton. He thought that God had allowed her possession as a proof of the reality of evil in the world. Many skeptics who would have ignored a true ecstasy were drawn to observe her in that state. The power of priests over devils and the women they possessed was thus enhanced by their ability to discern whether spirits were good or evil, by their powers of exorcism, and by their ability to interpret and control the discourse between the devil and humanity.

At the same time, Catholic concepts of witchcraft often attributed the powers of sorcerers to priests. French cases of possessed nuns at Aix in 1611, followed by Loudun in 1631, and then Louviers in 1642 involved accusing a priest of seduction and witchcraft. In 1626, Jeanne des Anges, an ambitious nun who had failed to impress her fellow nuns with her efforts to become a new Teresa, secured an appointment to found an Ursuline convent at Loudun, and within a year she had been elected prioress. Years later, she admitted that she had employed "as many artifices as hypocrisy could devise" to become indispensable to the superior and popular among the influential citizens who came to her parlor. There she became conversant with the intrigues and idle gossip of the town and when she became prioress, she tried to secure a notorious clerical Don Juan, Urbain Grandier, as her convent's spiritual director. He rebuffed her, and she claimed that he caused her possession by seven demons. Other nuns caught the contagion. Grandier was tried and burned for sorcery by enemies swift to take advantage of the scandal.

For ten more years the nuns of Loudun continued to frighten and inspire the curious who attended their repeated displays of possession and exorcism. At one point, Jeanne suffered a false pregnancy and tried to cut out the baby with the intention of baptizing it and killing it and herself. In 1637, the practiced exorcist and spiritual director Jean-Joseph

Surin forced Jeanne to use mental prayer, meditation, and finally the discipline to regain control of herself. Ecstasies followed and her departing demons marked her with bloody stigmatas so dramatically regulated that it is almost impossible not to suspect self-infliction. In any case, the pain cured her. One by one the demons left her as her ambitions for sainthood revived. Saint Joseph replaced the devils in her fantasies. He gave her a shift smeared with miraculous healing balm. Her vow to make a pilgrimage to the grave of de Sales in Annecy finally released her from the last demon. In Tours, thousands came to view the miraculous marks that appeared on her hands and forehead. Back at Loudun with her great relic, she cultivated the career of a mystic and lived famed and respected for many years.

Despite the dangers, however, mental prayer and its mystical fruits became the preferred standard of devotion for the Counter-Reformation. The mother of historian Jacqueline de Blémur was chapelaine at La Trinité when the abbess Laurence de Budos undertook to learn the new devotions: "At that time, the very name of mental prayer was so unknown among our religious that they were afraid of it and, like the Israelites, they did not want God to speak to them because they were afraid they would die."[31] The abbess and her chapelaine went to chapel after the other sisters were in bed to attempt the technique. After experimenting for a year, Budos brought in a Jesuit to give an elite cadre of novices further instruction. When they were trained, she sponsored a ten-day retreat for the rest and established a group of Jesuit and Oratorian priests to serve the community with a missionary father for her own director.

   With practice, recollection brought the mind into the state of quiet and concentration needed for more advanced levels of prayer. The spirit was trained to progress from self-preoccupation to thoughts of God. The most expert practitioners would ultimately achieve confrontation with the divine and then union and finally submersion in God's love. Regularized in this manner, mental prayer became a standard practice in most reforming houses. The venerable Benedictine abbey of Sainte-Croix set aside ten days a year when Jesuit confessors led the community in the exercises, combining mental prayer, meditation on set themes, and the general and individual examination of conscience. The Dominican Customal of Saint Catherine, in Toulouse, provided two hours a day of mental prayer. The Franciscan chapter-general of 1639 (Chapter 10) ordered that, in addition to singing the Divine Office, all women of the order should practice mental prayer in a prescribed manner. In a well-disciplined early-seventeenth-century convent, it was not unusual to find a number of nuns capable of triggering ecstatic states routinely by recourse to certain well-considered prayers. Acarie's daughters testified that they became accustomed to continuing with their routine tasks when a prayer sent their mother off into a trance for hours at a time.

De Sales himself once wrote that he would far rather be taught by Acarie than attempt to give her guidance. The convent grille was often the scene of hushed devotional conversation between a nun and her male and female admirers. Louis XIII regularly consulted one Visitandine for her consolation and advice. Isabel de Jesús, a servant in another Augustinian convent, claimed that Christ used her as a vehicle for criticizing the errors of his people and some of the clergy, particularly those guilty of fornication. Marie de Valence had a particular devotion to Mary Magdalene, who often appeared to her criticizing preachers who dwelt with too much enthusiasm on the faults that God had forgiven. At the Ursuline convent in Paris, the accomplished mystic Marie de l'Incarnation (the former mistress of Louis XIV, Louise de la Vallière) inspired her one-time friends at court with the rewards of penitence.

Possession and mysticism alike posed great dangers in exposing nuns to intrusion from admirers, exorcists, and gawking spectators, depriving them of the centered peace that gave power to their spirituality. In that sense, these outbreaks signaled the disorder of a community. Wise abbesses and spiritual directors strove to impose a decorum that would discourage such outbursts. Père Coton praised Marie de Valence because the light she radiated during her ecstasies was soft, not blinding, and she never thrashed about indecently. Chantal wrote to the superior at Moulins in 1617, advising her to forbid the sisters to take unusual positions in the choir, preferring that they turn modestly and attentively toward the altar.[32] Teresa urged her nuns not to vie with one another in bizarre practices or spiritual gifts. Port-Royal's constitutions of 1648 emphasized moderation. Sisters were advised to spend time saved by their efficient completion of a task in helping one another rather than indulging in extra prayer. Above all, the cloister was to be their refuge against the violence of exorcists, promoters, sightseers, and even genuine devotees. At the Beaune Carmel, Marguerite du Saint-Sacrement told Anne of Austria: "Your Majesty does us great honor when she bothers to come among us but if she knew the effect that her visits makes upon us and the time that it takes us to recover from the impression that the fanfare which accompanies Your Majesty makes on our spirits, I think that she would have the goodness to leave us to our solitude."[33]

All devout people felt that prayer was an instrument of power and expected skilled practitioners to use their gifts in the public interest. Teresa fervently believed that the cloister was a staging ground for her missionary vocation.[34] The more strictly her nuns could fortify themselves behind their walls, the more effectively could they send their spirits soaring to heaven or out across the globe. Enclosure and silence, discipline and mental prayer were intended to train the nun as a militant participant in the Christianizing mission. The struggle with demons, the revelation of special graces, spiritual direction, and healing by miracle or by simple charity were all part of the mission. Devotions that began with visions within the cloister were refined into ceremonies that spread out through the chapel to embrace the enthusiastic laity.

For Catholics, renewal and validation of the sacraments remained the focus of the Christianizing mission. Before Trent, however, they were rarely enjoyed. The Easter duty imposed by the Fourth Lateran Council in 1215 still marked the outer limit of most Catholic experience. Angélique Arnauld recalled that she received no instruction before making her first communion. Few of the nuns at Port-Royal had been confirmed and most had not even heard of the sacrament. Trent ordered nuns to confess and take communion at least once a month, "so that armed with this salutary safeguard they may boldly overcome all attacks of the devil."[35] Seventeenth-century Catholic spirituality rested heavily on the idea of penitence. Confessional boxes that encouraged deep personal confidences between confessor and penitent without the distraction of human interchange were introduced into the churches. Nuns trained in mental prayer and the ceaseless examination of conscience published lengthy general confessions as guides to neophyte penitents.

When the Port-Royal reform was well under way, a Cistercian visitor prescribed that choir nuns take communion every Sunday and on feasts, observing the day as sacred to that activity. María Esaltata, chronicler of the Florentine Lady Knights of Malta, credited Maria Maddalena dei' Pazzi with a constitution of 1588 allowing them to partake freely of communion on Sundays and all feast days.[36] Blémur wrote that after the introduction of mental prayer at La Trinité, "the sacraments began to be frequent which had formerly been very rare."[37] Eventually, as the seventeenth century progressed, confession and communion became so frequent a practice among devout Catholics that some reformers began to argue for their restriction.

Drawing upon the idea of transferability of grace, some nuns extended the traditional feminine devotions associated with reception of the sacraments to other devotions designed to intensify their effect. Protestant denial of the real presence of Jesus in the Eucharist was countered by reparation: visits, forty hours of continuous devotion to the exposed sacrament, and even communion by proxy were instituted to make amends for the insult. Mère Agnès (Jeanne Arnauld) of Port-Royal described kneeling in the presence of the sacrament as a type of communion in which the worshiper participated not for herself alone but for the whole church.[38] Under Zamet's influence, Angélique Arnauld dedicated some of the Port-Royal nuns to a new Institute of the Blessed Sacrament, which became wildly popular in Catholic League Paris. Nuns from leading noble families practiced elaborate public liturgies, including daily communion, in penitential garments. Each day began with the admonition: "My sisters, remember that we are dedicated to God as victims to repair the outrages and profanations which are done incessantly to the most holy Sacrament of the altar."[39]

Reparation was most effectively accomplished when a trained individual voluntarily entered into the suffering and sacrifice of Jesus. Through mental prayer, meditation, and self-mortification, nuns struggled to achieve a state of compassion, to share the sufferings of the Redemption. The mystic's ego, dissolved into the divine intention, closed a circuit and conducted grace back to the troubled world. For the most favored individuals, the marks of compassion were spontaneously induced by concentrated prayer. Acarie described the results of her meditation on the Passion:

> Casting the exterior eye without design on a crucifix, my soul was touched
> so subtly, so vibrantly, that I could not even envisage it externally but

only internally. . . . This sight was so efficacious and had so much clarity that [my soul] could not consent and comprehend, that having so many other means to ransom the world He had wished to degrade something so worthy and so precious [as the second person of the Trinity] until it might please that same Lord to comfort the anguish in which she was . . . the pains at the extremities which we ourselves suffered for so many years (stigmatas) were rendered sweet and gentle however painful.[40]

Naturally, the clergy kept a stern control over these manifestations. Mexico's first mystic, Sor Maria Magdalena (1576–1636), was initially treated with bleeding and other medical methods and then by exorcists who took her ecstatic spasms for diabolical possession. Ultimately, after she joined a convent, the contemplative life disciplined her experiences and enabled her to live a fruitful pastoral life with the local community and souls in purgatory.

More commonly, however, self-inflicted suffering was required to induce a state of compassion, ever more pointedly linked to the much-disputed system of indulgences. Maria Angela Astorhc, foundress of the Capuchinas of Barcelona, wrote: "To exercise the whip, one must tie oneself to a column . . . and one or two nuns, sure and zealous, . . . whip her with the instruments we have discussed, treating her like a slaughterhouse." By meditation, the nun redirected her suffering to an identification with Jesus: "while suffering at the column, it is important to imagine that you have been punished for a crime you did not commit and that the pain of your body is doubled by the shame of your public torment."[41] In Pavia, Domitilla Galluzzi and her sisters followed a rigorous pattern of devotional prayer and meditation on the Passion, which resulted in four recipients of the stigmata and other outward signs of compassion. The Manifiesto de las cosas notables, from the Clarisse convent of Morón, describes one nun who shared the sufferings of purgatory. Another had such pains in the head from Thursday to Saturday that she could not eat. Every Friday, Sor Juana Pura de la Cruz devoted herself to the crown of thorns holding her head to the side, imitating the images of suffering Christ. The sisters said that often blood covered her eyes.

Some women claimed compassion with Jesus' humiliation as an infant because childhood represented the loss of wisdom, a vile and abject aspect of the human condition. Six months after she took her vows at Beaune, Marguerite du Saint-Sacrament was overcome with the divine power of the baby Jesus in the crib so that she seemed to be in the crib herself, like him. For several days she lay on the ground, crying and moving like a powerless baby. In 1658, Jeanne Perraud envisioned the child about three years old with the cross and instruments of his Passion, which he flung into her arms when he embraced her. The subsequent images imply that even in infancy Jesus knew and accepted the sufferings for which he was destined.

Penitential exercises released vast treasuries of indulgences to aid less zealous souls. Marie de Valence once had a vision of the souls whose sanctification depended on her prayers and penances. The whole of human society paraded before her in the hierarchy of the world: pope, cardinals, nuntios, bishops, heads of orders, kings, ambassadors, aristocrats, soldiers, judges, doctors, and surgeons. The bourgeoisie ranked as merchants, artisans, villagers, and common people. The whole chain then dissolved and reformed according to spiritual ranking, sinners, converts, penitents, innocents, the just, and finally the saints. Her own apostolate included 50,000 sinners to convert, 30,000 penitents to maintain in their firm purpose, and 15,000 just and 12,000 saints to maintain and increase.

The principle of garnering grace through works often involved elaborate public displays of penitence, concentration on Jesus' human sufferings and his ongoing bond with living humans. Some nuns refined the popular practice of following the way of the cross as a public liturgy. The Nazarenas of Peru devoted themselves to the Passion, wearing purple habits tied with a rope at the waist and a crown of thorns under their veils. Their day closed with each nun carrying a cross on her shoulder in a *via sacra* through the cloister. The abbess of Fontevraud commissioned a pilgrim to the Holy Land to measure the exact distances of the *via crucis* in Jerusalem, which were replicated by thirty-six stations incorporating spiritual landmarks in the abbey grounds. After preparing themselves before the exposed Eucharist with tears, prayers, and washing of feet, the nuns processed from one sacred image, crucifix, or chapel to another with prayers, psalms, scripture readings, and penances for each.

Catherine de Jesus of the Paris Carmel said: "God is my wisdom; God is my knowledge; God is my power . . . God took my whole spirit and drew it to himself so that I could not understand anything but that God wished to work something in me."[42] Seventeenth-century nuns recaptured many of the strands of piety associated with the humanity of Jesus, its expression in the Eucharist, and its extension through shared suffering that characterized late medieval female devotions. Although most seventeenth century nuns denied any learning, the republished writings of the great mystics of the Middle Ages made a profound impression on their meditations. Gertrude of Helfta's vision of divine love inspired Teresa's vision of an angel who pierced her heart with a golden arrow. In turn, Teresa's writings and example contributed greatly to the spread of mysticism in the early seventeenth century, giving revelations the imprimatur of consistency with one another and with Catholic dogma.

Mental prayer trained the mind for the reception of the inner truths of Catholic doctrine, which Teresa called mystical theology. "The soul is suspended so that it seems entirely outside itself. The will loves; the memory is, I think, almost lost, and the mind, I believe, though it is not lost, does not reason—I mean that it does not work, but stands as if amazed at the many things it understands."[43] With the guidance of their spiritual directors, hundreds of women developed a capacity to fall into trances on a daily basis. Disciplined through mortification and obedience to the rule and trained through the reading of prescribed literature, the performance of the spiritual exercises, and the painfully transcribed "general confessions" that opened their most intimate lives to the scrutiny of their spiritual directors—these prophetesses of Christianization contributed powerfully to the reinforcement of Catholic doctrine.

Revelations concerning the Incarnation and the attendant place of Mary in the process of redemption were inspired by the great medieval mystics, Gertrude, Hildegard, Mechthild, and Birgitta. The power of Mary received even greater exaltation in the late seventeenth century through the cult of Our Lady of Victory, established in the popular belief that the Virgin had personally intervened to save Christian Europe from the Turks at the battle of Lepanto. Marian devotion might be said to have reached New Spain with Columbus, but it was given a special American quality by the mestiza virgin of Guadelupe, who appeared at the cult site of the Aztec mother goddess Tonantzin. María of Agreda, popularly believed to have converted several tribes of Indians during her mystical "flights," was a Conceptionist nun, particularly devoted to the promotion of the doctrine of the Immaculate Conception, which the hierarchy continued to resist until the late nineteenth century.

María's *Mystical City of God*, a life of the Virgin claiming to be based on direct revelation from the Virgin herself, emphasized Mary's role as co-redemptress and co-judge. María used material from the Protoevangelion and other early Apocrypha to assert that the Virgin was present at the Transfiguration and ascended to heaven with Jesus at the Ascension. She told María that although she herself commanded the evangelists to conceal as much as possible of her role in order to highlight the Redemption, she was present in a vision when Jesus entered Jerusalem and for the Last Supper when Gabriel brought her the first piece of the consecrated bread to eat. She mitigated the pain of the Crucifixion by her compassion and shared her son's transfiguration at the moment of Resurrection. She then took over the direction of the primitive church, instructed secretly by Jesus, who often visited her from heaven after she had chosen to return to earth. She organized the first mass and edited the first Apostles' Creed, to which each apostle contributed a sentence. She persuaded the Trinity, with whom she consulted regularly, to convert Paul. Finally she organized Saint James's mission in Spain, and at Ephesus she overthrew the temple of Diana and converted its nine attendant virgins to the religious life, putting herself at the head of this first convent.[44]

Seventeenth century nuns not only amplified the role of the Virgin Mary in Christian history but actively sought to identify themselves with her salvific agency. The rule of the Annunciation nuns, published in 1681, is based entirely on the idea of imitation of Mary. Though it purports to restrict its inspiration to the Bible, it includes Mary's initial vow of virginity and her childhood sojourn cloistered in the temple drawn from the Protoevangelion. The rule of the Visitation included the Little Office of the Blessed Virgin Mary and encouraged its use in mental prayer. These ideas circulated broadly and provided a sense of empowerment to women. God assured Jeanne de Matel, founder of the Congregation of the Incarnate Word, that even if Adam had not sinned Jesus would have been born. He was created before Adam, and his mother had already been prepared as the unstained virgin, which tended to exonerate Eve's crimes by placing her deed in the necessary order of salvation. The divine intention was always to bring man to repair the loss of the angels. Jeanne-Baptiste de Bourbon decisively justified the powers granted the abbesses of Fontevraud over their monks on the basis of "Son behold your mother." She claimed that "if in the order of nature, God has given some preeminence to men rather than women, that was within limit and measure. But in the Order of Grace he has communicated his favors to women without restriction or limit such as in his elevation of the Virgin above all those who are not God."[45]

Meditation and evangelization reinforced each other in seeking the inner soul's perfection and the salvation of a society drifting away from the essentials of Catholic belief. Extrasacramental popular devotions flourished and many nuns campaigned to establish new feasts and liturgies. The idea of the Sacred Heart was deeply entwined with Visitandine spirituality. Gertrude of Helfta and other medieval mystics had reported the mystical exchange of hearts with Jesus, the ultimate expression of divine love. Chantal carved the name of Jesus on her breast with a heated knife to guard her from temptation. De Sales wrote to her in 1611 suggesting that the order use the image of a heart pierced with two arrows and enclosed in a crown of thorns, surmounted by a cross and engraved with the sacred names of Jesus and Mary, as its "coat of arms." Margaret-Mary Alacoque at Paray-le-Monial enjoyed a series of visions promising a blessing on all who displayed and honored the image of the Sacred Heart in particular ways. The manufacture of badges signifying allegiance to the devotion became a major Visitandine industry. The devotions were given liturgical shape at the Moulins house, to which Alacoque's superior had been transferred. The ordinaries included the feast as an option, and the practice of the nine First Fridays, which assured a final chance for salvation to the most hardened sinner, became one of Catholicism's most enduring popular devotions. Nuns everywhere took it up and promoted celebration of the feast and the formation of associated confraternities of lay people as instruments of Christianization. Several nuns at the Nantes Visitation had visions or revelations concerning the unification of their hearts with the Sacred Heart. In 1730, the entire community signed an act of consecration composed by the superior and placed it under the monstrance holding the exposed Eucharist, with a vow to make honorable reparation for themselves and all sinners.[46] One nun was delegated daily to receive communion on behalf of the whole community.

The hierarchy resisted the institution of feasts and special offices for the Immaculate Conception and the Sacred Heart. It accepted more readily the worship of the Incarnate Word, expressed in various Christmas liturgies. After a week of ecstasy, through which she did not lose the use of her senses, Marie de Sainte-Josèphe learned

> all the points of the spiritual life, particularly the mystery of the Incarnate Word. . . . One day while she was sharing the Credo with me [Marie de l'Incarnation], at the words *per quem omnia facta sunt*, she was filled with astonished joy to realize how her beloved created her and, as she nearly fell into insensibility at the thought of this kindness, she heard him say: "Yes, my daughter, all things were made by me but I myself will be re-made in you."[47]

Convents took great pains to reconstruct and honor the manger of the baby Jesus. At Saint Orsola in Florence it was surrounded by votive offerings and gifts and was continually requested at the bed of the sick and dying. Another, of sheepskin, in the pietà on Christmas night 1620 "changed miraculously." The sisters who went to kiss it one by one found that it had taken on the appearance of living flesh. The Mantellate sisters had a baby Jesus in their small choir held in great esteem by the Medici grand dukes because it blushed whenever it heard a prayer or granted a blessing.

Carmelites under Teresa's inspiration promoted the mysteries of the Holy Infancy with statues and special prayers. The Spanish widow of a Czech count gave the miraculous statue of the Infant of Prague to the Prague Carmel founded in 1624 to celebrate the Catholic victory over the Protestant nobility of Bohemia. One of the friars testified that it came alive and began to produce many miracles to assist the Christianization of Bohemia. At the Beaune Carmel, Marguerite du Saint Sacrament founded the Archconfraternity of the Baby Jesus. She claimed that Jesus directed the organization of the cult, which spread when the Holy Infant engaged himself to protect the entire kingdom if it enlisted in this devotion. On the twenty-fifth of every month, a small rosary of fifteen beads, called the Crown of the Holy Child, would be recited and the devotee would strive to enter into the "state" of the child by practicing humility and simplicity and by bringing the spirit of the Holy Family into her own family life. Marguerite established a small oratory, called her Nazareth, in the convent, and led the aristocratic members of the confraternity in the chaplet. When the Spaniards reached the borders of Burgundy and plague threatened Dijon, she took a straw from the crèche and predicted that it would be enough to rout both enemies. The desired result gave evidence to the prophecy.

All these elaborate ceremonial devotions had roots in the Jesuit system of stimulating popular piety. In seventeenth-century France, critics complained that too much reliance on prescribed liturgies encouraged mechanical participation in the sacraments in the hope of obtaining "easy" grace. The principles outlined in Miguel de Molina's *De concordia* (1588) were espoused by no less a person than Cardinal Richelieu, who maintained that a soul could be saved through attrition (fear of hell) if it lacked true contrition. In 1641, the Augustinian Cornelius Jansenius maintained that this Jesuit doctrine of sufficient grace was merely a prop to human vanity and that only the chosen few who "know the victorious delights of the spirit" would receive true saving grace.

While the Institute of the Blessed Sacrament foundered in excesses of dramatic liturgy and its own social success, Angélique Arnauld and Port Royal turned away from public display and even from the mysticism that courted public attention. She and her followers embraced silence, meditation, and mental prayer ever more passionately but resisted the rewards of ecstasy and revelation. They substituted all-night adoration of the sacrament in decorous silence for the glamorous public displays associated with the institute. The constitutions of 1648 stipulated that care and reverence accompany confession. Angélique Arnauld went so far as to defer communion from Easter to Assumption to take full advantage of the grace that followed Penance. Her brother, "the great Arnauld," in the book *Frequent Communion* argued that communion should never be taken until the soul was prepared with meditation and love of the crucified Christ. Jeanne Arnauld later said that her single object was to listen to God who prays within and to lose herself in his depths.

When the Port-Royal constitutions were finally published in 1648, they marked the end of an era of experimentation. With the end of the Thirty Years' War, Europe abandoned the struggle to impose religion by arms. The interests of the French state, so ardently defended by Cardinal Richelieu, had triumphed over Catholic Spain and Protestant Germany alike. Within France, the daughters of the Catholic League turned against their old friend and champion, Anne of Austria, and her son in defense of aristocratic liberties. The "war of the women," as the Fronde rebellion was sometimes called, ushered in a new era of repression associated with royal absolutism. An edition of the Benedictine rule adapted for women circulated widely in the mid-seventeenth century with the preface:

> Your sex is weak, fragile and inconstant, if the reins are left loose. . . . That is why it is necessary to give you Rules, Laws, Statutes and Ordinances to regulate your life . . . [and] necessary that you have as director and observer of your life and your morals a man of virtue, above reproach, who will make you practice your Rule and Statutes, and who will be entirely dedicated to the examination and investigation of your life.[48]

Louis XIV perceived the patronage of Frondeur leaders like the duchesse de Longueville, Mme. de Sevigné, Mme. de Lafayette, and others as implicating many reformed convents and particularly Port-Royal in their treason. They spoke no treason and no heresy, but the king was probably right to see their devotion to the cross and redemption by suffering as silent opposition to the Jesuit exaltation of royalty and absolutism. The purity of the nuns silently rebuked the corruption of the court. He demanded the elimination of Jansenism "for three reasons: the first, my conscience; the second, my honor; the third, the welfare of my state." Among the prominent men called *solitaires* attached to the convent were Pascal and Racine, who defended Jansenist principles for decades. The king required from the nuns a formal acknowledgment that the teachings advanced by their male associates were false. The abbess Jacqueline Pascal replied: "I know it is not the place of nuns to defend the truth," but "since the bishops have the courage of nuns, nuns must have the courage of bishops."[49] The nuns who remained silent in their cloister when the quarreling men went into exile refused to be bullied into acknowledging beliefs that they could not in their hearts accept.

In 1661, the king informed them that they must dismiss their pupils and receive no more novices. Angélique Arnauld died with a last prayer, "Lord have pity on us all. I say upon all, my God, upon all." The dwindling community led by Angélique de Saint Jean, continued to resist even despite excommunication. The sisters prostrated themselves on the floor during the part of the mass devoted to communion: "We are a hundred poor nuns who left everything to cleave to Christ, snatched from the foot of his altars, banished from his holy table—we who have devoted ourselves day and night to adoration of the Blessed Sacrament."[50] Their leaders were taken away into solitary confinement and pressured in isolation. In 1705, seventeen remaining nuns signed a document disclaiming any future submission that might be extorted from them out of age, frailty, or exhaustion.

The nuns of Port-Royal wrote no books. They resisted ecstasy and visions. They made no prophecies. They maintained that they knew no theology and could not say whether or not Jansen's work contained the heresies of which he was accused by the Jesuits. But they would not sign casuistic documents, and they would not let cardinals or kings or the pope himself tamper with "the truth" that they held in their devout hearts. As on the "day of the grille," they defended their cloister and when it was broken, they kept it in their hearts. In the end, the most absolute of monarchs feared that his power could never be secure while seventeen old women persisted in silent meditation and turned their backs on the created world, fixing their minds on eternity. In 1708, soldiers occupied the monastery. Even the graveyard was violated and the bones scattered so that no cult could form about their silent remains. The lieutenant of police, sitting in the abbess's chair, told the women that they would never see one another again. The last prioress, Mother du Mesnil, declared, "How blessed we are to be of little consequence in the eyes of this world; it makes it impossible for us to oppress anyone." She led her nuns in a final chant *Ad te, Domini, levavi*. As the soldiers carried her from the doomed monastery, the paralyzed Sister Robert decreed, "This is the day of man. The day of God will come in turn."[51]

18

The Sweetness of Life

THE DAY OF MAN had come indeed. After Louis XIV's revocation of the Edict of Nantes in 1685 and the savage repression of the Huguenots that followed, the republic of letters awoke to the horrors of religious persecution. Pierre Bayle, Richard Simon, and Benedict Spinoza laid the basis for a historical and critical examination of religious tradition aimed at discrediting the exclusive claims of various sects to divine revelation. Angels and devils, saints and witches receded into an outdated consciousness, a world of shadows that the new sciences of the Enlightenment hoped to dispel. People educated in the cosmos of René Descartes and Isaac Newton called into question the efficacy of prayer itself. The basic contours of the intellectual universe changed, undermining the fundamental doctrines of monasticism. The concept of human nature, grounded in original sin, redeemed only through tears and penitence, gave way to the *tabula rasa* of John Locke, a human nature that was fundamentally good and perfectible through social reform. *Philosophes* began to pride themselves on discovering the natural causes of what had hitherto seemed miraculous. Extravagant displays of mysticism and possession were viewed cynically by the sophisticated generations of a self-consciously "scientific" age. The mystical invasion shrank to a handful of women suffering convulsions in certain Parisian convents.

While disorderly houses became stricter under pressure from the post-Tridentine church, rigorously reformed communities softened under the influence of the Enlightenment. Growing skepticism pointed to the de-Christianizing programs of the French Revolution. Popular writers treated religious passion as neurosis and, sometimes, as a twisted sexuality grown from the frustration of natural impulses thwarted by unnatural burdens of chastity. When the occasional woman rebelled against confinement, her sad plight was broadly publicized. But within their cloister, most nuns lived a decorous and pleasant life. With their servants, their pets, their pastimes, and their visitors, they partook easily of that sweetness of life that the nostalgic Maurice de Talleyrand remembered as reserved to the generation fortunate enough to have matured before 1789. A few of the more ambitious addressed themselves to learning, the arts, or some profitable enterprise.

Their fate was tied to the class system of the ancien régime, in which most people derived their status from family connections. A series of hierarchies defined church, state, the workplace, and the family. Upward mobility was slow and laborious; downward fall was averted or at least retarded by government subsidy, community support, and a variety of private strategies. Since Paula's retreat to the desert, female monasticism had depended on generous subsidies from aristocratic donors—usually nuns themselves or their relatives. As we have seen, the most passionate reformers had consistently failed to inculcate egalitarian sentiments in their ranks. True aristocrats, nuns were able to live like paupers and even to humble themselves in the service of the poor. But they could not, would not, live on the same footing as upthrusting bourgeois women. And if they had proposed it, their horrified parents would soon have set them straight.

Parental control over children governed this system. A girl's future was hostage to her dowry. Despite literary pressures to recognize the demands of love and affection over class interest and worldly ambition, most families preferred to remove poorly dowered daughters from the marriage market. The early modern church and state added legal reinforcements. Spanish law recognized parental control over marriage arrangements and specifically forbade mixed marriage in the colonies. French parents could secure royal *lettres de cachet* giving them almost unlimited power over defiant children. The Council of Trent reinforced parental permission as a condition for the validation of marriage. Aristocratic families supported convents in return for having their daughters socialized to be docile or, if recalcitrant, disciplined by physical confinement. They did not pay to expose the girls to sororal relationships that might weaken their carefully constructed bastions of privilege and difference.

Aristocratic communities guarded their prebends fiercely from the ever ambitious daughters of the bourgeoisie who tried persistently to bribe their way into the company of their betters. Some convents were virtually family affairs where the nuns acted as vestals perpetually devoting vocal, public prayer to securing the salvation of deceased relatives ensconced in prestigious funerary chapels. Below the great noble abbeys, each community sought to restrict itself to the highest social level possible. At the same time, need for money forced convents to accommodate guests of dubious suitability. After the failure of the Jacobite uprising of 1715, for example, widowed English noblewomen sought refuge in Continental monasteries, though they had no intention of following the rule. Their money ensured their welcome in the economic climate precipitated by the collapse of John Law's monetary system.

Some nuns perhaps noticed the rumbles of distant drums as the eighteenth century wore on. But few could have predicted a coming day when the walls that sheltered them would be razed and their dream of an otherworldly life would turn to nightmare. Instead, despite the religious cooling of the age, convents were as popular as ever and, often, overcrowded. In Italy, so many girls pressed for entrance that bishops had to prohibit new novices and cap their numbers. The system expanded into new territories. A convent established in Dublin in the 1720s in defiance of the penal laws supported itself by educating young women. In 1727, French Ursulines from Rouen emigrated to New Orleans, the first convent on territory later destined to be part of the United States.

Conceptionist nuns came to New Spain in 1540 to take over the teaching of Indian women from the friars, Beatas, and Tertiaries who were being overwhelmed by the task. The needs of Creoles soon replaced those of the Indians, however. Instead of forming a network of female missions, as originally intended, Mexican convents devoted themselves to sheltering unmarried white women. When orders hesitated to undertake the *cura mulierum* in the colonies, women acted on their own initiative. In 1606, the widow Elvira de Padilla with her two daughters and two nieces established Santa Fe de Bogotá with two Conceptionists, who trained them using the rule and writings of Saint Teresa, softened to admit their personal maids. The convent soon produced daughter houses in other parts of Colombia. The Quito Carmel proliferated throughout Ecuador into the early nineteenth century. In 1613, Argentina convent life began with a peculiar community of Augustinians who wore the Dominican habit and used the rule of Saint Teresa. Convents appeared in Chile and Bolivia through the seventeenth and eighteenth centuries. By the middle of the seventeenth century, more than a fifth of the white female population of Peru was cloistered. Lima had thirteen convents, not counting houses of retreat, beaterios, and little informal groups. In 1724, the Clarisse convent of Corpus Christi was founded in Mexico City for Aztec noblewomen and soon had daughter houses in the provinces. They organized personal charities and a quiet pastorate for Indian women, but they were as adamant as their white sisters on their exclusivity.

Leading Brazilian families repeatedly petitioned the king for permission to establish a convent to secure their daughters from undesirable marriages. The Desterro, established in Bahía in 1677, had fifty places always in demand, and in 1717 the king was informed that eight to ten women left the city on each fleet to enter convents overseas. By 1750, most Brazilian cities had at least one convent whose eagerly sought places were reserved for white women. Black, Indian, and mulatto women nevertheless found it worthwhile to bear the expense of going to convents in Portugal or the Atlantic islands.

The fabric of the ancien régime contrasted sharply with the idea of ascetic individualism and the monastic common life. One finds a certain element of the masquerade in such hagiographical dramas as Marie de l'Incarnation's account of the ritual of Marie de Sainte-Josèphe's veiling. The girl had grown up in the convent in the expectation that she would become a nun. But before she could take her vows, "her mother determined to test her vocation. She withdrew her to a secular house where she tempted her with beautiful clothes and other delights of the secular life." After a charade of blandishment, her parents formally gave in to her entreaties to consecrate herself to God.

> On the day when she was to take the habit, her parents wanted her to be interrogated by the superior of the house in the external parlor. They came to witness the firmness of her vocation but a second attack occurred.

After her mother had dressed her to appear at the grille in clothes suitable to her rank, she took her into her arms. Overcome with sorrow at losing so dear a daughter she held her so long to her bosom that her father began to fear that some mischance had occurred and was forced to separate them. He brought his daughter to the enclosure where the community awaited her. Then realizing that this was where he must part with her finally, he was so stricken that he could not even speak to say goodbye.[1]

The family was acting out the liturgical rite of a girl's final passage into the cloister. Despite the pathos of their affectionate emotions, the parting was only a ritual; in reality their connection and concern would last a lifetime. Even when the saintly Josèphe had gone far away to die in the wilds of Canada, her family supported her with monetary contributions, publicity, and prayer.

The "day of the grille" at Port-Royal shocked all of France. But once Angélique Arnauld had made her point, her family continued to be her strongest protection against the hostility of the crown. The most determined reformers remained socially enmeshed in their familial networks. For example, Antoinette of Orléans, foundress of the Calvariennnes, was related by marriage to Mme. de Longueville, leader of the Fronde and protectress of Port-Royal, as well as of Saint Anne de Caumont. Two of her sisters, Catherine and Marguerite, founded the first French Carmel, while her niece became a Calvarienne. One brother-in-law was Cardinal de Retz and another was a patron of Vincent de Paul. Dominican priories like Prouille, Poissy, and Saint Pardoux-la-Rivière became the privileged prebendaries of the princes of the blood who ensconced their daughters there. The royal princesses who took over the ancient abbeys of France, sometimes ignoring the appeals of the nuns to follow the precepts of their rule and elect their own prioress, often lived luxuriously as strangers to the community. Others energetically fostered reform.

Families were intensely involved on both sides of the struggle at Remiremont. Catherine of Lorraine bypassed the electoral rights of the chapter to become abbess in 1611 through the influence of her brother, the duke of Lorraine. For fifteen years, the canonesses resisted her reforms and refused to yield their electoral prerogatives or rights over the community goods and seal. They appealed to their relatives, to the estates general of 1614, and Queen Marie de Médicis against claustration, which they interpreted as an insult to their honor. Their control of their prebends frustrated the abbess's effort to "pack" the chapter with observant Benedictines, and they instituted charivaris against the independent community she established. In the end, they maintained their cozy lives until the revolution. The canonesses held chapter meetings in the choir, ignoring the eucharistic presence. Meals were served in the sacristy or in the choir itself during long vigils and feast-day liturgies. The charcoal fire that burned in a brazier from October through Easter tempted the ladies to turn their backs on the tabernacle. They hardly ever sang matins (even when the office was set at daybreak rather than one o'clock in the morning). During other services they came and went, chatting and snacking, drawing a robe over their secular clothing at the door of the choir or bringing secular persons into the choir with them during services.

Common life in many convents extended only to a sewing room, chapel, and governance meetings. The nuns of the Immaculate Conception claimed that their rule did not include common meals. At Saumur the cellaress eventually had to forbid the older nuns to burden the community cooks with their private dinner orders, commanding them to eat what the others ate even if they would not come to table. Vincent de Paul accused the nuns of Longchamps of worldly clothing, visiting regularly at the grille, receiving their confessors at improper hours, and even visiting in Paris. Longchamps resisted reform, but a century later the community also fiercely resisted dissolution when the nuns were urged to return to the world.

In effect, women in the better convents adjusted themselves to a life that was not much different from the lives they would have led in the secular world. Class distinctions among the nuns replaced ranking by seniority. They were obsessed with "honor," pride in lineage, and prestige. Before her conversion, Teresa of Avila had a two-story apartment at La Encarnación with a kitchen, accommodations for a younger sister, and several other relatives as well as servants. The convent housed 120 nuns, each one living as well as her dowry would allow. Poorer nuns slept in a common dormitory. Cells, prebends, and offices were often hereditary in certain families. Family groupings formed blocs around a cell and within the community. Lawsuits sometimes arose over rights in the cell, a place viewed as collective family property.

Well-bred women were held to a standard of "ladylike" behavior that suited them equally for the domestic or the conventual life. Piety was an attribute cultivated by respectable matrons, while nuns were praised for their wit and talent. The daughters of the provincial nobility in France were raised in an atmosphere of learning and active religious work. Charity dominated their social life. They shared the professional education and religious activities of their husbands and brothers, and when they were widowed Chantal and other recruits brought young daughters with them into their convents and raised them among the other boarders. Barbe Avrillot, Mme. Acarie, was raised in a convent like hundreds of girls whose destiny as nun or matron largely depended on the will of their fathers. She taught her three daughters their catechism at home and trained them in deportment. As they testified at the hearings for her beatification, her tendency to drop unexpectedly into a state of ecstasy did not interfere with her domestic life.

Modified as it generally was, cloistering was not shockingly different from domestic discretion. Noblewomen of every country were protected from the accidents of common life. Spanish and Portuguese women were carefully guarded behind grilles at home as in the convent. Italian girls did not attempt the streets without trustworthy escorts. Nuns often took leaves from their convents to shoulder family responsibilities or relieve temporary financial pressures by living at home. The nuns of Aywières regularly took vacations at home. A popular nun like Teresa might be sent to stay with potential benefactors. Even reforming abbesses often retained their old customs of taking promenades either in the relatively isolated country surroundings or in towns. Thus in 1608, when de Sales delivered the Christmas sermon at Annecy, the Cistercian abbess of Saint Catherine attended with four nuns and four pensioners. In 1742, Benedict XIV complained that Portuguese nuns walked about in public places and attended spectacles in the theaters.

The convent itself was often uncomfortably open to the surrounding world. The cloister of the Visitation in Nantes bordered on a pleasure garden where local people had picnics and games, which sometimes involved scaling the low wall or jumping into the nuns' garden from a decorative building in the park. Once a fugitive murderer took refuge in the wine cellar and forced the nuns to hide him until nightfall. On another occasion, a whole troop of players climbed over the wall chasing one of their members. The broken garden wall of Saint Catherine's in Avignon was irresistible to duelists seeking isolated spots for their illicit meetings.

At La Concepción in Lima, a baker attacked a nun who refused to pay him because the bread he delivered was stale. Thieves occasionally broke into the enclosure at Sainte-Croix and robbed the gardens. A Peruvian novice at Saint Joseph was abducted late at night by a suitor who rushed in when several nuns stood at the open door conversing with a friend.

In many abbeys, the cloister ran for miles, surrounding forests and gardens where the nuns could walk freely. In 1790, for example, Bonlieu in La Sarthe covered 307 hectares with twelve farms and two mills. At Fontevraud, spacious apartments and a sumptuous refectory featuring paintings of the various royal abbesses in devotional attitudes were set in great gardens that accommodated outbuildings and a luxurious villa for royal pupils. The enclosure of Sainte-Croix opened on to the river, encompassing about thirty buildings for living, working, and worship. At San Gerónimo in Mexico City, commodious two-storied cells each had a bathroom, kitchen, and sitting room in addition to sleeping quarters. They surrounded a series of patios spacious enough to house three maids to each nun. The *conventos grandes* of Peru formed small towns within their walls. Individual nuns owned small houses with patios in back and an opening into a "street" within the cloister. They were furnished to taste and had room to accommodate visitors. A series of small cloisters, gardens, fountains, workhouses, a school, an infirmary and a jail were set apart with quarters for students and novices.

Individual nuns supported personal servants or slaves. Free women sometimes came in with their original mistresses. Others entered voluntarily as servants looking for a better alternative to the harsh world outside. Nuns with a maternal instinct often adopted abandoned babies. One Peruvian nun even arranged for a kidnapping, but the baby was ultimately found and returned to her own parents. The convents also housed lower-class girls born to the maids or, in Latin America, slaves of mixed, black, or Indian blood. In 1732, the king of Portugal rebuked the Desterro in Bahía for harboring the illegitimate children of well-born white girls, Creoles' colored mistresses, and even two children whose parents were a nun and a priest.

Economic activity kept nuns attached to the world at many points. Their lands and gardens and buildings were part of a complex economic enterprise that brought in a good income both by the sale of agricultural produce and the renting of urban land, which supported general servants and lay sisters. Individual nuns, with their separate prebends, had personal possessions, even jewelry, and transacted financial business through intermediaries. Each nun of the Desterro conducted her own business affairs. Abbesses actively participated in running their estates, supervising their accounts, and investing in the speculative enterprises that proliferated in these early capitalist centuries. Peruvian abbesses who had inherited their social prestige and political power from the conquistadores, invested the nuns' dowries and often loaned money from the profits to the viceroy in return for further privileges. Flandrine of Nassau, abbess of Sainte-Croix, applied herself to restoring the finances, introducing regular audits and a prompt settlement of bills. She actively used her influence with her powerful relatives at court to protect peasants on her domains from the effects of internal military movements of Richelieu and during a plague and famine generously cared for the indigent in Poitiers. She exercised her feudal rights of justice and collected her dues, collated her benefices, and managed her domains like any prudent landlord. She enjoyed good relations with other orders and gave hospitality to the first Carmelites, Ursulines, and Visitandines to enter the neighborhood.

Farms and their accoutrements had to be run to assure the food supply of rural convents. In towns, individual or communal gardens needed tending to supply vegetables, fruits, and medicinal herbs. Some nuns raised chickens to be killed and eaten privately. A wolf got into the henhouse of Santa Verdiana in Florence, and four factors with harquebuses tried unsuccessfully to shoot it before one of the *conversae* struck the death blow with a club. One Visitation convent raised eels until the fish pond froze in 1789 putting an end to the enterprise.

The nuns also devoted communal or individual efforts to other moneymaking schemes. Fine needlework was a specialty of many houses. At Malagón, Teresa brought in a "good Theatine" woman to teach the novices to sew and do other useful handiwork. In Florence alone, a variety of industries have been noted. Monticelli manufactured garlands of gold and lace. Savanarola thundered against the handiwork of the nuns of Murate as a snare for the vanity of ladies, though the nuns protested that it was their sole source of income. The Umiliate were known for the fine quality of their woolen cloth. San Jacopo was famous for typography; its codices and incunabula are still admired in museums. Ortensia Fedeli of Sant'Agata was a well-known painter, and Sister Plautilla Nelli received a notice in Giorgio Vasari's *Lives*. There were three sculptresses and two miniaturists among the sisters of the same convent.

Many other convents gained fame for their spices, herbs, and medicines. Santa Orsola gave its name to the pills dispensed by a Sister Benedetta, which Cosimo I favored. The Visitandines of Nantes grew tobacco for ointments. The rosewater of Longchamps was very popular among court ladies. The enterprising Françoise de Châtre, abbess of Faremoutiers, marketed water in which the foundress's relics had been soaked. Saint Fara's water had a particularly good record in healing "stone." Flowers laid out on the exposed sacrament at the same abbey were efficacious against migraines.

The practice of educating gentlewomen in convents spread among the upper classes throughout Europe and its colonies. Convents generally housed one or two dozen pupils. These girls and young women brought in relatives and friends to visit and further tightened the mesh that secured nuns to the social fabric. Nuns in larger cells in Mexico often had "favorites" or "nieces" entrusted to their care sometimes in infancy. They dressed in a modified habit, a uniform, taught female skills and graceful and submissive deportment considered suitable to either walk of life. Peruvian convents harbored the children of relatives or orphans of wealthy Creole families growing up to be nuns. Often babies were assigned to individual nuns and grew up in their cells.

Abbesses and prioresses energetically cultivated families that might provide well-endowed recruits. Alumnae were always working to secure desirable boarders for them. Mme. Roland remembered how her displays of adolescent piety drew the attention of such an abbess. In 1618, the Lady Knights of Malta decorated an apartment for a five-year-old Medici pupil with new windows and her arms on the balcony. She occupied it with her servants while three sisters attended to her education. Jeanne de Blémur described the luxury of Flandrine of Nassau's childhood at the Paraclete with her own little house and a retinue befitting a royal princess. Some of these great ladies grew up to become abbesses; others married but remained close to the nuns who had guided them through childhood. From 1558 forward, the abbess of Regina Coeli in Florence recorded the expenses of entertaining Giulia de Medici, who used the convent as a sort of club, visiting with her friends and relatives, freeloading meals, and sometimes making fairly long sojourns. She even brought her husband, her sons, and sometimes manservants. Eventually she left the city promising to repay the nuns for everything. Alas, no gifts from Giulia ever appeared in the abbess's scrupulous accounts.[2]

Girls being educated in the convent were expected to learn the social graces: dancing, singing, drawing, even acting. Hélène Masalska, a boarder at Abbaye-au-Bois, fondly remembered romping around the convent doing much mischief with her friends. On the Feast of Innocents, the girls performed role reversals, electing a girl abbess, and other pieces of harmless mischief. Saint Catherine's Day was a popular festival, devoted to spinsters seeking husbands. At Remiremont, nuns danced with the townsmen on the vigils of Saint John and of Saints Peter and Paul. The Monday after Pentecost they held a dance in the courtyard with the ecclesiastical officers of the abbey owing a certain number of dances to the ladies. At Sens, young nuns disguised themselves as shepherdesses to go out to village dances.

Women separated from their husbands paid large sums to rent a place in a convent where they gave parties and entertained and carried on their business. Mme. du Deffand, for example, regularly entertained Voltaire, Jean-Jacques Rousseau, and other leading figures of the Enlightenment in her two-story apartment in Saint Joseph's. The Calatravas were said to have the finest salon in Madrid. Devotees clustered around accomplished nuns dining in the reception hall while their hostess sat behind her grille conversing. The persistent efforts of supervisors, bishops, and even the pope to prevent visiting failed. The older Florentine nuns at San Jacopo resisted papal "excommunication" to maintain their right to frequent a little window or grotto in their church where they could entertain parents and friends, who often brought picnic meals and other treats to be shared with nuns short of food.

Many Latin American women lived in convents or beaterios until they married to protect their reputations and their chastity. An investigation of 1774 disclosed that about half of the 474 niñas in Mexican convents were too old to be returned to their families. They had simply stayed on when no suitable marriage developed. In general, the family decided whether a girl would marry or enter the cloister. Affectionate parents consulted their daughter's wishes in the decision-making process. But whether her choice was freely made or forced upon her by her guardians, her chances for happiness were about equally good in the convent as in an arranged marriage. Elaborate wedding ceremonies confirmed her decision to remain among her childhood friends in the lively schoolgirl world of the convent. The *Memoires* of Hélène Masalska, describe the profession of Mlle. de Rastignac:

Mlle. de Guignes carried her candle and accompanied her as her god-mother. The count of Hautefort was her knight. She took her place in the outside church on a prie-Dieu in a dress of white crepe embroidered in silver and covered with diamonds. She kept a calm face during the sermon of Abbé de Marolle, who was pleased to test her, to describe to her all that she would be giving up. After the sermon, the count of Hautefort took her hand and conducted her to the entrance of the cloister. As soon as she had passed through the door, they closed it with a great noise behind her and loudly threw the bolts. When she came to the choir grille, they commanded her to strip herself of her worldly ornaments. She had long blond hair. When it was loosened we all wanted to cry out that it should not be cut and all the pensioners muttered, What a pity! In a moment, the novice mistress put the scissors to it and she was shorn. The hair was put on a great silver tray and it was lovely to see. Then she was dressed in the habit of the order with the veil and a crown of white roses, and they opened the grille and presented her to the priest, who blessed her. On her knees before the abbess, who was seated near the grille, having her cross bearer and chaplainess by her side. She took her hands in her own and pronounced the formula of profession: "I vow to God between your hands, Madame, poverty, humility, obedience, chastity and perpetual cloister following the rule of St. Benedict, the observance of St. Bernard, the Order of Cîteaux, filiation of Clairvaux." Her emotion was so great that she was slow in speaking. The custom was then to embrace the knees of all the religious and pensioners. Finally she prostrated herself in the middle of the choir. They stretched a funeral cloth over her and chanted Lalande's *Miserere* and we then sang the *Dies Irae* and the *Libera* of the Cordeliers, which is superb music. The whole lasted an hour and a half ending with the prayers for the dead to remind her that she was dead to the world.[3]

Was she dead to the world outside? Possibly. But there was another world inside any convent where a woman was very much alive and had the opportunity to develop talents for which the secular world had little use. Teresa of Avila's generation benefited from the educational ideas of Vives, who dedicated his treatise to Catherine of Aragon. Defenders of female education in the *Querelle des femmes* tended to espouse the Platonic ideal that intellectual development inspired moral elevation. In the tradition of Christine de Pisan, María de San Jose cited a lineage of illustrious women claiming that the consecration of virgins was the single most important advance that Christianity made over Judaism. In her fictive dialogue, Sor Justa remarked that since women have been equal and even superior to men in learning, they have a duty to record the virtues and good works hidden from men. Sor Gracia agreed, noting that men "have gloried in holding women to be weak, inconstant, imperfect, useless and unworthy of any noble undertaking."[4] Other nuns used literature, particularly drama, to express their ambivalent feelings and dreams of escape from the very convent life that gave them their opportunity for self-expression.

Post-Tridentine ideology slowed the expansion of female education but, as we have seen, an impressive tradition of mystical prose grew out of the practice of writing spiritual autobiographies. Scholars have barely begun to uncover the wealth of poetry, drama, and other literature produced in baroque convents. Nuns often expressed worship in song and dance. Convents competed fiercely for good singers and often forgave them the dowry for the sake of their attraction for wealthy donors. Sister Sainte-Suzanne, the fictional heroine of Denis Diderot's novel *The Nun,* boasts that her fine voice and her ability to play the organ and the harpsichord won her a privileged place even though her stubborn resistance to the religious life made her an object of intense hostility in the community. In parlors, musically talented women regaled their admirers with little concerts from behind the grille, and splendid choral performances, written by the greatest musicians of the age, marked the public liturgies. François Couperin, for example, composed a Tenebrae for Longchamps and when, in 1727, the convent admitted the opera star Mlle. le Maure as a nun, her followers came to hear her sing. In Italy, music gave cloistered nuns an opportunity to communicate with the public world, first as "disembodied voices" and gradually as performers and even composers on festive occasions.

Sor Juana de la Cruz, a Mexican nun, achieved an international reputation. Having learned to read and write when she was six or seven, she badgered her mother vainly to let her go to a school or university. An illegitimate child with no dowry, she had limited prospects until her beauty and intellect attracted great admiration at the viceregal court. She might well have commanded a decent marriage, but in 1669, she entered San Gerónimo and later testified that aversion to marriage combined with love of learning had led her to the convent. "If true that I am female, none substantiate that state. I know that *uxor*, woman in Latin, designated only those who wed; and either gender may be virgin."[5] Clearly, she felt that virginity liberated her from gender constraints: "I will never be a woman who may serve a man as wife. I know only that my body is not inclined to either state, neuter, abstract, guardian of only what my soul consigns." In her *Response* of 1691, she testified: "Given the total antipathy I felt toward marriage, I deemed convent life the least unsuitable and most honorable I could elect if I were to ensure my salvation. To that end, was the matter of all the trivial aspects of my nature . . ., such as wishing to live alone, and wishing to have no obligatory occupation to inhibit the freedom of my studies."[6]

Sor Juana observed the rule about as well as anyone, though she complained about constant interruptions to her studies. Her library encompassed thousands of books in Latin, Spanish, and Portuguese. She read extensively in the medieval scholastics and contemporary Jesuit writers, though she later claimed that she avoided theology because her limitations might lead her into heresy and she did not wish to be involved with the Holy Office. She corresponded with like-minded people and held regular discussions and debates among her admirers. She wrote lyrics for convent performances and occasional poetry for public events. Her work included erotic poetry and sexual satires, didactic contemplations on a theme well-established in Western literature. She addressed three love poems to God employing much the same rhetoric as in her secular romances.

Eventually she became involved in local ecclesiastical politics. As the quarrel broadened, she was forced to defend her whole way of life. Attacks upon her secular work escalated as a misogynist bishop exercised his authority over a woman in a small provincial society whose fame and favor at court had overshadowed the prestige of the local clergy. Her position deteriorated with an uprising of 1692 against her protector, the viceroy. She defended her intellectual activity by proving that Paul did not forbid women to study and teach in private places. The *Response* incorporates a short history of learned women from the fallen Gnostic Ennoia (Helena) through Hypatia and the contemporary Swedish queen Christina. She saw herself as Catherine of Alexandria, the virgin persecuted for her learning: "There in Egypt, all the sages by a woman were convinced that gender is not of the essence in matters of intelligence. . . . It is of service to the church that women argue, tutor, learn; for he who granted women reason would not have them uninformed."[7] Under ecclesiastical pressure and, perhaps, a failure of nerve, she determined to renew her vows after twenty-five years in the convent by reentering religion in a new spirit. She surrendered her books and instruments and may have taken a vow to abandon study. Shortly thereafter she caught a sickness raging through the convent and died in 1695.

Virginia Woolf painted a dark and tragic picture of the probable fate of a fictional sister of Shakespeare, obliged to make her way in Elizabethan England. But if such a woman had had the fortune to be born in a Catholic country with enough money for a convent dowry, her fate might have been reasonably pleasant. Marcela de San Felix (1605–1687) entered a convent to cultivate the literary talent inherited from her father, Lope de Vega, and her mother, an actress. There can be little doubt that the huge output of convent drama now coming to light was the fruit of an unbroken tradition reaching back to Hroswit. In her *Foundations*, Teresa said the only cure for epidemics of melancholia, which attacked convents, is not to take oneself too seriously and to indulge in small celebrations, singing, and other acts of gaiety and recreation. In a letter from Antwerp, Ana de Bartolomeo described Carmelite theatricals as an integral part of the Teresian tradition.

Teresa's old companion encouraged her nuns and pupils to perform satires mocking her French antagonist, Cardinal Bérulle. Bartolomeo recalled that Barbe Avrillot's performance of Dionysia made everyone laugh, and Angelito's mock prioress for the Feast of Innocents was widely acclaimed.[8] Dramatic and musical performances helped solidify communities both through shared jokes and the bonding of joint endeavors. Italian nuns bought elaborate costumes, including male attire and even codpieces, to enhance their performances. Despite the bishop's prohibition, in 1631 the nuns of the Incarnation in Lima rode, dressed as men, through the cloisters in a donkey parade before a performance. In 1705, the nuns of the Conception dressed as men and remained in costume during the party after the play. They even accompanied the guests to the gates, displaying themselves to curiosity seekers gathered outside.

More ambitious drama was often written and produced. Marie-Alexis le Huédez, as a young pensioner at Nantes, wrote a series of burlesques about people she did not like. Marcela de San Felix's plays contained jokes and criticisms of community life but they also enabled the nuns to act out symbolic religious themes. Her *Six Colloquies*, simple spiritual conversations utilizing allegorical figures, were used to instruct novices. Mme. de Maintenon produced Racine's *Andromache* at Saint-Cyr and commissioned *Esther*, a more pious play that restricted her pupils' talents for displaying raging passion. The whole court attended the performances by the young amateurs.

Liturgical dramas and pastimes enhanced the theological education of most sisters. In 1657, Marie-Alexis le Huédez described her decision to enter the convent as a seduction by Jesus utilizing the diction of the Song of Songs. As a nun and mistress of novices, she wrote a series of rhymed prayers to be used as spiritual exercises at different points of the day (remembering that Visitandines did not chant the great offices). Nuns wrote dramas for the Nativity, Easter, and their consecration ceremonies. In Benedictine convents, each nun was assigned a role in the nativity pageant. Lines or business were sometimes provided for the animals, the stalls, and even the swaddling clothes, to ensure that everyone participated. Nuns in Madrid performed Christmas night services singing popular carols and dressing in secular costumes. The canonesses of Remiremont baptized the image of the infant Jesus on Christmas Eve. They pulled Christ on a wheeled donkey in Palm Sunday processions and on Candlemas, as the godmothers of Christ, they carried a statue into the crypt for an all-night vigil.

Convents customarily contributed to public celebrations and feasts. The Lady Knights of Malta celebrated the Feast of the Decollation of Saint John (their patron) with specially commissioned music.[9] They brightened their church with silken banners and even hung draperies and garlands in the streets outside. Eight novices led the procession in splendid black cloaks decorated with the great white cross of the Maltese Knights. When the sisters of Ognisanti moved, carrying their relics, to a new monastery, "the bells of all the churches began to ring, not by human hands, but by the holy angels and so did the bells of the new monastery until the sisters had entered and placed the most holy bones in the cemetery."[10] When a nun died, a solemn funeral was held with the participation of twenty or forty priests. The procession moved into the piazza to a "cheering" crowd while the four bells of the monastery rang. Similarly, the entrance of a new nun generated a public ceremony.

The archbishop of Florence celebrated his installation in the convent church of San Pier Maggiore. The procession of lords and clergy came into the lavishly decorated church where the abbess sat under a "minor canopy" near the altar representing the church of Florence in the ancient ceremony of the archbishop's espousal. When everyone was seated, she rose from her place opposite the choir where the nuns were ranged in their habits of black and white and went to the archbishop's seat. He raised her with his own hands and helped her to a seat next to him on his right. He placed a rich diamond at her feet and she responded with expressions of love, warmly commending the churches of Florence and particularly the convent church to him. She then returned to her own place and all the other nuns, one by one, came forward to kiss his hand and receive his benediction. The following day they sent the archbishop a wedding bed and returned the ring he had given to the abbess, saying that the archbishop could make better use of so beautiful a diamond. In gratitude, the bishop sent her a gift of 600 ducats.[11]

Other abbesses were imaginatively opportunistic in capitalizing on their festal celebrations. In addition to the universal feasts, Sainte-Croix instituted feasts consecrated to aspects of the Passion and to Radegund, Agnes, and Disciola. Around 1640, a number of miracles were attributed to Radegund, which encouraged pilgrimages, and the nuns revived their ancient custom of public processions. A new biography patronized by the abbess tied the Merovingian queen to other royal saints who high-lighted the intense Catholicism of Louis XIII. Special feasts also strengthened Fontevraud's peculiar attachment to the French crown: Saint Louis, Radegund, Jeanne de Valois, and Stephen of Hungary.

Nuns' spiritual contributions to the welfare of family, friends, and communities were highly valued. In 1525, the signoria gave the Lady Knights of Malta in Florence 10 scudi in alms because they had prayed for the city. Civic observances were taken so seriously that in 1770, the crown judged in favor of the abbess of Fontevraud who sued a citizen for his scandalous conduct in watching the convent's Corpus Christi procession from his window instead of joining the devotions in the street. Whenever a member of the royal family was ill, nuns in French convents were asked to undertake a forty-hour vigil. Similarly, special devotions were expected for military campaigns. Richelieu himself enlisted Madeleine de Saint-Joseph's prayers before the exposed sacrament to aid him in repelling an English attack in the Bay of Biscay and ascribed the French victory to her intervention. A royal recovery or victory or an event like a wedding called for a public act of rejoicing, the singing of *Te Deum*. When Louis XV died in 1774, the bells tolled thirty times at noon and evening.

In 1630, plague spread through Florence. The grand duke ordered processions and visits to all the holy images in the city and forty hours' devotion in all the churches during Holy Week. Everyday the people came out to say the Rosary in the streets and at their window. The chronicle of San Jacopo de Ripoli describes how the nuns opened their chapel to individuals ready to offer prayers before their miraculous crucifix. When there was a great flood in 1740 the nuns of Saint Anna were inspired to throw a piece of the veil that covered one of their holy images into the water, which immediately receded. In 1758, the whole city was saved when nuns poured oil from the lamp that burned before the crucifix into the drains. The crucifix of Regina Coeli had a reputation for answering prayers from some of the great families of Florence for children and even got credit for the birth of Ferdinand II of Austria.[12] In 1773, when the grand duchess of Tuscany was about to give birth, the nuns of Santa Verdiana sent her their pietà which was reputed to have miraculous powers, and she returned it after her successful delivery with gratitude.[13]

Perhaps the greatest effort of all was the concerted siege of heaven, which the nuns of France undertook to ensure an heir to the pious Anne of Austria. The queen made a pilgrimage to Radegund at Sainte-Croix and visited Val de Grâce in festive seasons. There she placed the Christ child in the crib on Christmas Eve. Marguerite du Sainte-Sacrament claimed that Jesus had revealed his love for France and promised a dauphin if she would pray to his Divine Infancy. In 1635, Jesus revealed the conception of Louis XIV to her even before the queen was sure of her success. The queen herself begged Marie Alvequin for prayers and credited her with the birth of Louis XIV. Jeanne des Anges lent the miraculous healing shirt of Saint Joseph to assist at the birth. On the night of Louis's birth Beaune made special devotions, supporting the queen's labors with prayers and offering the Christ child a crown. With the successful birth, enthusiastic subscribers to the cult of the Divine Infancy endowed a small chapel in the convent grounds to which public access through a window in the wall was guaranteed.[14]

All this color and pomp sometimes hid a darker side. In 1667, two pupils in the Rouen Poor Clare house came down with the plague. Their Jesuit adviser warned the abbess to conceal the outbreak, even at the cost of depriving the children of the last sacraments. The sisters buried the dead children by night in the cloister and suffered the spread of the plague among themselves for some weeks before admitting a doctor. The abbess's adviser informed her that other monasteries were keeping silent in the same circumstances because if the news were made public, the town officers would prohibit public prayers and shut up the churches and "that would greatly incense the people against us." As it was, the Poor Clares took their turn with the other monasteries of the city holding forty hours' devotions to "thank" God for the plague's ending. The chronicler wrote that the solemnities and crowds of people "augmented our affliction, we knowing that ourselves were the infected persons and had more need of the prayers of others than those who came with so much confidence to beg ours for their preservation."[15]

The skepticism of the Enlightenment made its heaviest impact among the charitable upper classes who came to believe that nuns lived frivolous and idle lives. Public performances of all kinds were increasingly viewed as sources of scandal. In 1717, a traveler in Brazil commented on the unseemly postures of the actors in plays at the Desterro. Even pious and innocent Nativity plays and Easter pageants elicited criticism. On the one hand, they distracted from the Counter-Reformation focus on the sacraments, and on the other they perfectly typified the superstitious mumbo-jumbo abhorred by the Enlightened. In some cases, abbesses themselves, driven by a mix of thrift and decorum, reacted positively to these criticisms. In 1726, the economical abbess of Regina Coeli resolved to cancel carnival celebrations, which involved entertaining masked guests with plays and refreshments. The convent's outspoken chronicler wrote that carnival was little enough diversion after eleven months of spinning. Ironically, many novices were attracted by the convent's "holy customs of not making Commedia." The bishop gave them the profitable privilege of weekly communion for the dead.[16] The three Benedictine convents of Florence, Pier Maggiore, San Ambrogio, and Santa Felicita, abolished the custom of giving dinner to their assembled priests on all principal feasts. Instead, each of the three took turns at celebrating particular feasts and distributed the food originally intended for the priests to the poor.[17]

Reformers sought vainly to keep unwilling and unsuitable women out of their communities. Nearly all sober monastic advisers warned against the bad effects of overly enthusiastic or unstable people within a community. Forty-one years old and inclined to her own eccentric religious practices, Marie-Françoise Hardouin entered the Visitandine convent of Nantes without a full novitiate because her sister had endowed the house. She lectured the novices while disdaining the common observance of the community. The community historian described her as a trial of their charity.

The fabric of community life was very delicate and easily torn even by well-intentioned women. The great reformer Marguerite d'Arbouze entered a second novitiate under Marie de Beauvilliers at Montmartre to develop her mystical gifts. But the two strong-minded women competing for religious leadership in the same house produced a rocky relationship despite their mutual admiration. Marie sent Marguerite to take charge of Val de Grâce, founded by the duchesse of Longueville. But when Marguerite began to attract too much attention from rich patrons, Marie ordered her to resign and return to Montmartre. Once she was installed again at the mother house, Marie complained that Marguerite's followers disrupted the routine.

A convent's economic well-being depended heavily on popular confidence in its nuns' prayers and ceremonies, confidence easily shaken when a community got involved in scandal. Loudun's financial resources dried up when reports of diabolic possession began to circulate. Their families disavowed the nuns and their pupils were whisked away. Even merchants who supplied the nuns with handiwork paid them less than the prevailing wage and charity ceased. Often they had no food but what they grew in their garden. But few convents could escape becoming a respectable prison for women who were no longer welcome in worldly society. Parents secured *lettres de cachet* to place disobedient adolescent daughters in the cloister, despite the objections of nuns who had to suffer the disruption and sometimes the scandal involved in an inevitable elopement.

Unwilling nuns often festered for years in a community, a trial to themselves and to their sisters. When Seville was flooded in 1626, a nun, anxious to be evacuated, was heard praying fervently that God not spare her convent. One nun became famous for her wit: upon being asked at her consecration what she desired, she answered, "The keys to this place so that I can leave." Some misguided reformers strengthened requirements for cloister to protect unwilling nuns from worldly temptation. One desperate girl punished her family for putting her in the convent by strangling herself while they visited her at the grille. Florent Boulenger used the poor girl's example as an argument against frequent family visits.[18] Courtesans and royal mistresses patronized convents in their successful years to secure a place of retirement when they were discarded. Sometimes, as in the case of Louise de la Vallière, whose repentance as the Ursuline Marie de l'Incarnation earned her beatification, the exchange of roles was a success. But when the fabled courtesan Ninon de l'Enclos was ordered to a convent, her admirers threatened to storm the cloister until she was transferred to a less rigorous house where she could hold court daily. In 1776, Jeanne de Valois, who had impersonated Queen Marie Antoinette in a scandalous scheme to steal a diamond necklace, was imprisoned at Longchamps. Women forced into the retirement house in Bahía by authorities who disapproved of their morals rioted against conditions, "not fit for white women."

Madwomen with enough property to secure them relatively humane institutional care commonly found homes in convents. Ana de Bartolomeo recalled nursing a violent woman, whom they had to beat into submission and lock in the jail until she was cured by a vision of Teresa. María Celeste, Galileo's daughter, had to share a cell with a woman who had tried to kill herself twice with a penknife. Isabella della Rena haunted her convent like a ghost, throwing off her clothing, sleeping where she fell, eating garbage, and proclaiming herself to be the Virgin Mary. A Lima community was enjoying a torchlight celebration featuring comic songs and jokes about life in the convent. The slaves and servants were dancing when Doña Ana de Frias attacked a slave, wounding her in the scalp. She tore off her clothing and ran through the cloister cursing and throwing stones until four servants confined her. For twenty years, her violent outbursts terrorized the convent, and finally she killed a nun. She remained in the convent jail for the rest of her life.

Many of the leading writers of the Enlightenment represented forced vows that confined "healthy" young women to an "unnatural" life of chastity as one of the great symbolic oppressions of the ancien régime. Diderot saw madness as an inevitable result of convent life. His famous novel *The Nun* was inspired by Mary Delamare, who appealed for dispensation from her vows in 1758 after twenty years at Longchamps, claiming to have been coerced into the convent by her parents. She lost her case despite the championship of many influential people. Diderot changed significant details of the case to shape a complaint against the heart of the monastic ideal, its commitment to chastity. For many "enlightened" men, the sweetness of life included a free run in a garden of women. Louis XV, aptly tagged "the well-loved," epitomized an age whose citizens considered a choice of bed partners as part of the good life. Casanova and his many fictional counterparts from Don Giovanni through the Chevalier de Valmont cultivated a reputation for sexually subduing women by seduction, fraud, or rape. A system that withheld women from male sexual ambitions was naturally abhorrent to them and to their emulators.

The *philosophes* targeted convents at many points. The construction of new forms of sexuality fascinated many trendy intellects. Parents considering consigning their daughters to convents were warned of dangers that might lurk within their mysterious walls. Writers like Marquis de Sade and Casanova discerned erotic elements in flagellation. The spinster wardens at the retirement house in Bahía were frequently accused of ill treating the girls. Diderot may have modeled his sadistic lesbian abbess in *The Nun* on Louise-Adelaïde of Orléans, abbess of Chelles, but his character was far kinkier and more aggressive than the rumors circulating about the real abbess. The endowment of lesbian sexuality with identifying social characteristics began seriously in the sixteenth century and achieved full definition by the eighteenth. The fashion was said to have been introduced into France by a "manly Italian woman," possibly Catherine de Médicis, who protected her modesty by wearing pants under her riding skirts. But even in that period men generally assumed it to be but a poor substitute for male love. The fantasies and wild fabrications of the failed mystic Benedetta Carlini revealed a quasi-lesbian love affair mingling erotic desire for Christ as spiritual bridegroom and a physical relationship with another nun when Benedetta was pretending to be possessed by the (male) angel Splenditello. The confessions of the possessed nuns at Loudun reveal some similar fantasies of lesbian behavior. By the eighteenth century, the condemnation of special friendship originally intended primarily to prevent monastics from indulging social favoritism was interpreted as a measure against the dangers of sexual familiarity.

Critics attacked the root idea of unworldly nuns preparing women to live in the world. In novels like Choderlos de Laclos's *Liaisons dangéreuses,* the naive convent-bred girl is shown to be no match for the experienced seducer Valmont. The extreme timidity and modesty the nuns cultivated left women defenseless against wily worldly men. Voltaire, Diderot, Jean d'Alembert, Rousseau, and others were convinced that the physical and moral weaknesses associated with women were the product of their education. They claimed that the convent's methods of personality formation produced ignorant, vain, self-absorbed women untrained in the use of their reason. New ideas about hygiene and exercise provoked criticism of the ascetic ways of the convents. At heart, these gifted men, thwarted by the social constraints of the ancien régime resented the deposit of wellborn girls and their attractive dowries in convents when they might have assisted the ambitions of upwardly mobile young men.

By the middle of the eighteenth century, a broad attack on the religious orders had begun with the dissolution of the Jesuits. A series of "reforms" aimed at reducing the numbers of institutions given over to the contemplative life followed. The leaders of the Enlightenment built up a humanitarian social vision that transformed the highest ideals of

Christianity into liberal secularism and obviated the connection with the redemptive work of the monastic order. Ironically, those religious carrying on the once despised active life fared best. The enemies of the contemplative life conceded that women who devoted themselves to nursing, teaching, and other social services were too useful to be dispersed. Moreover, the active sisters with their simple vows tended to be lower-class women, which made them more acceptable to political and social critics than aristocratic contemplative nuns. Like other members of their class, squeezed by a hostile monarchy and an ambitious bourgeoisie, they gradually lost the functions and professional services that justified their special privileges. The poor and the ambitious tended to look upon them as idle parasites. Their claim that they gave their prayers, as they gave their blood, for the service of their people only irritated a people learning to think that both were overpriced.

The persistent and increasing use of convents to withdraw desirable women from the marriage market and endow them with tax-exempt property was a growing irritation to the money-hungry states of the eighteenth century. French edicts of 1629 and 1666 forbade the establishment of new religious houses without royal permission. The Spanish king tried repeatedly to reduce the "burden to the republic." Portugal attempted to stabilize its colonial European population by prohibiting white women from leaving the colony. In a rare example of interference with parental rights, Joao V required in 1732 that every woman going to a convent be interrogated to ensure that she made her own choice. The convent population continued to grow through the early eighteenth century with little reference to the religious vocation of the women themselves.

Diderot's *Encyclopedia* attacked religious orders as superstitious and parasitical. It characterized the Jesuits as downright dangerous with their well-known political agenda and their virtually independent control of some colonial areas. In midcentury, they were exiled from Spain and its colonies. Other monarchs followed the same course until the papacy was forced to dissolve the entire order. This successful move encouraged monarchs vigorously to attack the monastic community at large as a repository of untaxed funds. In fact, though exempt from taxation, religious institutions paid dearly for the expenses of the state. In 1691, the French crown exacted so heavy a "gift" to defray the expenses of the wars that many convents had to sell portions of their silver. Similarly, vast amounts of land in the Hapsburg Empire were seen as "unproductively" invested in monastic establishments.[19] In the face of this propaganda, we should remember that regardless of ownership, this land supported villages and private farms. It was the royal treasury, not the economy in general, that suffered from the privileges of the religious. In 1749, the king of France forbade religious establishments to acquire free title to any real estate (thus taking it out of the taxable category). A memo of 1755 from the governor of the Austrian Netherlands bemoaned the "cupidity" of religious houses from which society and individual families were in need of protection. In fact, much of the profit from the land went to the people who actively exploited it. The rents and revenues of the monasteries, like those of other landlords, declined even as they paid heavy gratuities to the crown.

The Christianizing mission emphasized individual self-help centered on reception of the sacraments. Gradually, this idea eroded popular faith in the transferability of grace, and consequently the value of the prayers of religious deflated. In turn, widespread misgivings arose about the diversion of economic resources to the monastic enterprise. When convents became crowded beyond the capacity of their endowments to support the nuns or when religious poverty drove them to beg for alms, the concern spread. Even in the sixteenth century, local governments objected that the working population could not support so many "unproductive" members of society. Seventeenth century Spaniards ascribed the impoverishment of the countryside to emigration, vagabondage, and a surplus of religious vocations.[20] In 1619, the Council of Castile appealed to the king to reduce the number of religious houses and prevent the wholesale recruitment of novices into them. The Cortes in Madrid made the same complaints. The city council violently opposed the Visitation foundation at Riom because the town was too poor to support it.

Individual ideals wildly diverged from the social logic that allowed convents to be replenished with wellborn women who desired simply to live a comfortable life suitable to their station with or without being married. The failure of nuns to support themselves thwarted the religious ideal of social and racial egalitarianism. Teresa urged her nuns to earn money by spinning and sewing and to share the proceeds equally. But women could never earn enough to sustain a tolerable standard of living.

The nuns at Medina del Campo, for example, earned 11 reals a week and collected about 30 in alms, while the cost of food was 79 reals, forcing them to depend on gifts of food from friends and relatives. Donors objected to the surrender of their private property to communal funds. Families sought to limit the amount of money supporting their dependent relatives by investing in a more or less hereditary prebend, tax exempt but subject to inflationary pressures. As a result, the convent population continued to grow in the early eighteenth century, but the endowments that maintained buildings and service personnel were cruelly strained. In addition, inflation was eating at the best endowed. French economic disasters consequent to the failure of John Law's system stemmed the flow of recruits in midcentury. The legendary wealth of Flines Abbey in the Austrian Netherlands was unique.

The Cistercian chapter-general of 1738 proposed that a certain portion of all sales of the order's property be set aside for the relief of nuns without sufficient income to feed themselves. Rising dowry costs no doubt made the convent a less desirable alternative for thrifty parents. Las Huelgas originally supported two hundred nuns but only thirty remained, not living very well, in 1654. Often convents had trouble collecting dowries on a regular basis while they had to support their noble nuns in accustomed style. The elaborate apartments and servants required a dowry of 1,000 to 1,500 ducats. In 1780, the Clarisses of Morón wrote to the father provincial:

> The number of nuns is very small and many of them are old and invalid while others are occupied with the communal offices . . . for which reason there are very few left for the choir. The divine office and the cult have to be carried on in weakened form. There are several persons who have the will to dedicate themselves as nuns but because of the calamitous times they cannot raise the necessary dowry of 800 ducats. For this reason other convents, even in this town, have lowered that and therefore gained many entrants. We beg . . . that we may immediately admit 20 nuns with dowries of 700 ducats.[21]

To the contrary, the order raised the dowry from 800 to 1,000 in 1785 and with increasing inflation raised it again in 1797. Complaints arose throughout the Catholic world that the expense of religious dowries was too heavy a charge for families, dilapidating the patrimony.

In addition to the rising expense of supporting unmarried women in their own communities, parents may well have been swayed by the growing literature in praise of companionate marriage. Just as the passion for mysticism had drawn many young women and their families toward the convent in the seventeenth century, the sentimental love literature of the eighteenth must have had its effect on vocations. In the first half of the century monastic institutions were still spreading, with new Carmelite convents in Sicily, Italy, Austria, Germany, and Poland; but in the second half no new ones for either sex opened. The numbers of nuns in convents dramatically decreased in Peru as in Spain and France. The Cistercian order had to combine failing houses frequently in the latter part of the eighteenth century.

Toward the end of the century, a shift in the class pattern seems to have occurred. Some of the abbesses and officers of Sainte-Croix came from neighboring convents with strong ties to Poitiers. None were Bourbons. They came from local nobility or royal officials. In 1737, the daughter of an anonymous bourgeois of Poitiers was admitted as a choir nun. Some parents were newly ennobled during their daughters' tenure. The *conversae* seem generally to be the daughters of workmen or clerks attached to the abbey. At the time of the revolution thirty choir nuns (down from fifty in 1665) and thirteen *conversae* (down from thirty in 1665) remained. Of the former French nuns who petitioned to be absolved of their vows in 1801 and who mention family background, only one was noble and most were of poor backgrounds. These data may reveal only that after the dissolution of the convents noble families were better able to support their dependent former nuns than poor families. More likely, the numbers indicate that younger nuns of marriageable age in the 1790s were from poorer backgrounds than their noble elders.

Without strong support from the nobility, convents were exposed to the depredations of the hungry state. French royal commissions systematically suppressed poor or disorderly women's houses throughout the eighteenth century. A Commission des Réguliers headed by Cardinal Loménie de Brienne between 1766 and 1780 determined to suppress nine orders of both sexes and 450 houses. It raised the age of profession to eighteen for women and twenty-one for men. A house was to have a minimum of nineteen monks or fifteen nuns, and no order could have more than one house in a town. The cardinal entertained an additional project to convert as many nuns as possible into canonesses and thus secularize them. In the Austrian Netherlands, also, a new prejudice developed in favor of such secular institutes. Nearly all Cistercian monasteries in the empire were secularized. Herkenrode, a noble convent that prided itself on being unreformed, became a canoness institute and survived the general dissolution until the invasion of the French in 1797.

Loménie de Brienne's commission concentrated on convents that did not fulfill the social duties of educating children, nursing the sick, or ministering to the poor. Similarly, during Maria Theresa's reign, the Austrian Empire reorganized religious houses to provide social benefits. In 1771, the governor of the Austrian Netherlands tried to impede the establishment of new monasteries and prevent an increase in the goods of the old ones by reviving ancient canonical legislation that prohibited the dowry. The goods of communities ruined by restrictive new laws were diverted to support those deemed "useful" because of their charitable or educational work. A public subsidy of 1779 compensated "useful congregations" for the loss of the dowries. Contemplative communities scrambled to reestablish themselves as "useful." Many female houses had already opened schools. The Cistercian house of La Cambre, for example, survived and housed 150 girls in 1787 with 30 choir nuns and 23 lay sisters, mostly from bourgeois families. Some convents acted as houses of incarceration for criminal women or "protective institutions" for delinquent girls. Even more simply, houses went to court to prove that an incontestably "useful" community had wrongfully been entered on the lists to be infiltrated and suppressed. The superiors of the mendicant orders issued a joint plea in the cahiers of 1789 for relief from the unremitting campaign of slander, investigation, and dissolution that had plagued them for twenty-five years.

Joseph II began the suppression of the contemplative monasteries in Austria in 1781 and soon smaller states followed. At first, they proceeded only against male communities and small priories. Between 1782 and 1783, nuns of Vienna, Graz, Linz, Leopolis (Poland), Milan, Cremona, and Mantua were precipitately evicted and the convents closed. Louise of France (Louis XVI's niece) brought the Carmelites of Brussels to

Saint Denis at Paris and gave shelter to many other refugee nuns. In Italy, Joseph's brother, Grand Duke Leopold of Austria, restricted the number of nuns who could be professed and raised the age of profession to thirty. The Florentine nuns of San Ripoli recorded the increasingly restrictive laws that eroded their community from 1777 on. In 1785, Archduke Leopold of Austria ordered that every nun in Tuscany make a free declaration with a sealed statement whether she wished perfect community or *conservatorio* (giving her private property into the keeping of the superiors, as opposed to common life). The subsequent division along property lines destroyed the community. Leopold appointed himself conservator and instructed workmen to make disruptive repairs. His wife was provided with handsome apartments. In 1788, he reassigned the *conservatorio* to the Montalve sisters while the rump of the original community struggled to exist in the ruins of their former establishment.

Confiscated funds at first went to pay the parish clergy, replicating the Protestant pattern of transferring money from women to men. But communities that had been living very poorly since the attack on the dowry became very expensive when the nuns had to be pensioned. The poorest contemplative Benedictine and Annunciation houses were also the most crowded. When the communities were broken up, the outlay in pensions was larger than the community revenues. In 1784, the Austrian government showed a deficit of 100,000 florins. Finally, the list was divided between houses to be suppressed immediately and houses to be suppressed "later," which would receive the members of the first group. Most of the women, when given a choice, preferred to remain in their profession. Flemish resistance prevented most dissolutions until after Joseph's death, and Leopold gave them another decade. A further argument was made for the exemption of the English houses, which were supported from abroad.

Thus, at the time of the French Revolution, the attack on monasticism had somewhat modulated. In France, evidence suggests that after the reforms of the 1770s and 1780s vocations were on the rise. In Burgundy and Champagne, impoverished and failing houses had been weeded out by the royal commission of 1768. The seventy surviving female houses were not overfilled as in the beginning of the century. They had healthy complements of about thirty each. A majority of nuns were over fifty, but there were enough novices to secure a future. A letter from an unwilling nun propelled the National Assembly to suspend all monastic vows and dissolve all monasteries on February 13, 1790. But when officials visited each monastery and interrogated the nuns about their vocations, nearly all of them defended their vows. Only sixteen of the nuns who came forward a decade later to annul their vows took advantage of the opportunity to leave, though a much larger number said that they had taken their vows unwillingly. At the end of the century, when self-proclaimed "enlightened" thinkers who scorned the medieval nature of their faith tried to break open the cloisters that had confined them for so long, the vast majority of nuns fought to defend their freedom to be conservative, backward, and unenlightened. Women who had been idling away their time in elaborate rituals and mildly stimulating entertainments then found the courage of their ancient foremothers. The sweetness of life did not rob them of their ability to embrace the glory of martyrdom when their call came.

In 1790, the French National Assembly decreed the confiscation of all religious property, alleging the incompatibility of the monastic ideal with the modern social order and with public welfare. The helpless young nun, coerced by her parents, whose tyranny was reinforced by a brutal monarchy and a pitiless church, became a favorite symbol of oppression. The assembly claimed to be acting on behalf of imagined multitudes confined against their will. The nuns of the Visitation appealed with revolutionary rhetoric: "How many times have we, speaking of free choice of our way of life, said to ourselves: the defenders of liberty ought to be our champions! We who pray in the shadow of our altars for the fatherland and raise in our cloisters the subjects who are the hope of the nation."[22] They begged the representatives to be mindful of their charities—shelter for widows, invalids, and other helpless persons. They cited the sacred right of property secured by the Declaration of Rights. They claimed that they trained their pupils in the spirit of equality by teaching them to live without distinction of birth or wealth, each dressed in the same simple uniform.

On October 14, 1790, the wearing of religious habits was prohibited. In early 1791, visitors went to all the convents offering each nun a choice between liberty (with a pension) and staying in the convents. Occasionally whole communities took advantage of the offer of liberty, such as Notre Dame des Près in Troyes, where the abbess led the exodus. But most houses had few or no defections. Often the nuns responded by formally renewing their vows in the presence of the commissioners. Gradually the attack escalated. New vows were prohibited. Small or weak communities were dissolved, and the nuns who held to their profession were shunted into larger houses like Sainte-Croix, which became "houses of union," basically old age pensionaries, where they could finish their lives.

The houses that remained open tried to maintain their regular lives in a virtual state of siege. In Avignon, agents of the revolutionary government pillaged Saint Catherine's and robbed the nuns of their personal possessions. In July 1791, commissioners nailed up the church door of the English convent in Rouen. For a while, the nuns smuggled seculars in for private masses, but groups of hostile people began breaking in, particularly on Sundays, searching for arms, priests, and religious artifacts. In October, a mob broke in during mass and arrested the priest. The invaders locked up the sisters for hours while demanding their papers and forced them to take off their habits for secular clothing. The next day commissaries came and started a detailed inventory "even to counting the dirty dish-cloths in the kitchen." They informed the abbess that all the convent's goods belonged to the nation; the convent had become a prison. The nuns shared their food with growing numbers of English and émigré lady prisoners until it ran out. They felt obligated to wait upon them,

> though it was a very severe slavery at that time whilst we had the cruel task of changing our dress. It is not easy to conceive what a piece of work it was to clothe forty-two people from head to foot, especially as we had neither wherewithal to make clothes nor money to buy them. We were obliged to cut up the curtains of eleven beds and many large window-curtains to make gowns but these were far from supplying our necessities; the lady prisoners and other benefactors in the town were very charitable in giving us money, cottons and stuffs, otherwise we could never have compassed our task. We were obliged to work night and day for we were continually threatened with a more severe prison if we did not put off our religious habits.[23]

Most nuns tried to obey those laws that did not directly force them to deny their religious vows. They gave up their habits and accepted transfers to new houses. At first, nuns were excused from taking the Civil Oath of Loyalty to the Republic, a renunciation of papal authority imposed on the clergy, because they were perceived as having no public position. Abbesses strove to avoid relations with the constitutional clergy and were often pulled into "treasonable acts" by their efforts to secure the sacraments from priests who refused the oath and even to shelter them from the authorities. At least one Josephite sister devised a liturgical service for the dying to save them from the attentions of constitutional priests.[24] The constitutional priests attempted to take the place of dissolved canons and to implement visitation rights through the authority of revolutionary bishops. The revolution could not disband the active orders without demolishing the school and social services systems. Reluctantly, the republic put up with the continuing work of women religious, but sisters who taught were universally condemned for poisoning the minds of the young with seditious sentiments. The Ursulines of Chaumont were accused of using reactionary catechisms as readers.

As it became clear that nuns indeed held a kind of public position, they were required to take a milder Oath of Liberty and Equality in exchange for their pensions. At first, most of them did so, but gradually many nuns began to resist more firmly. In February 1792, the Dijon sisters of Refuge opened their chapel to the public to witness a formal renewal of vows by every sister of the community. The municipal government denounced the ceremony as counterrevolutionary and imposed penalties. The constitutional clergy attempted to force the nuns of Poitiers to display their relic of the cross in patriotic processions. Defending the honor of Radegund, the nuns refused this collaboration with the new authorities. The Franciscan nuns of the city were also attacked when they refused to carry the customary crown for the Virgin Mary in the same processions. Nuns everywhere refused the services of oath-taking clergy and harbored refugee priests in their cloisters. Some held semiclandestine services (admitting the public). When the Visitandines of Nantes celebrated the First Friday in January 1792, a crowd of people congregated outside the monastery to participate silently in the celebration. The commune of Auxerre nailed shut the outside doors of the Visitation to exclude the "secret" parish that had formed around the community's confessor. The Carmelites of Compiègne were accused of receiving persons into a confraternity of the scapular (a devotion promoted by Carmel, from the middle of the eighteenth century).

All over France, religion became more insistently counterrevolutionary as the revolution devoted itself more systematically to de-Christianization. With the institution of ceremonies in honor of the Supreme Being and the Goddess of Reason, royalists began to adopt the Sacred Heart, or the Rosary as their emblems. The nuns of Paray, where Margaret Mary Alacoque in the seventeenth century had a spectacular series of visions promising salvation through devotion to the Sacred Heart, distributed "prodigious numbers" of the condemned symbol. In Brittany, where armed resistance was organized, nuns were arrested for embroidering the emblems of the Sacred Heart which the royalists commonly wore. On the First Friday in March 1790, the Nantes Visitation renewed its consecration to the Sacred Heart. Each nun signed a vow to submit unconditionally "to the purposes for which they had been redeemed by its blood," promising special devotions, mortifications, and charities for the future in honor of the feast. It is no accident that the modern symbol of the Catholic resurgence in nineteenth-century France is the great church of Sacré Coeur, which floats over Paris from the heights of Montmartre.

As the danger of the situation became clearer, so the lure of martyrdom became stronger. The Ursulines of Valenciennes attempted to escape into the Austrian Netherlands when expelled from their convent in 1792. Having failed, they debated a future course in chapter and determined that their vows required them to die for their faith. They were guillotined in 1794. In the summer of 1792, Mme. Lidoine, prioress of the Compiègne Carmel, urged her flock to consecrate themselves as a "sacrifice to appease the anger of God, that the divine peace which His dear Son had come to give to the world would be restored to the church and to the state."[25] They felt that the ultimate act of compassion, to participate with their own sufferings in the continuing work of redemption, was in their grasp, and many nuns prepared to fulfill their ancient dream.

The Paris government decreed the final dissolution of all monastic houses, except for those used as hospitals, on August 17, 1792. Most of the service communities stayed together. Sometimes they took the necessary oaths of loyalty to maintain their schools and hospitals. The nuns of Saint Catherine in Toulouse were moved to the canoness institute next door while their convent was used as a prison for recusant priests. The last surviving nun addressed a letter to the Dominican general in Italy asking his permission to use her own discretion in trying to obey her vows in such changed circumstances.

As the armies of the republic and of Napoleon swept across Europe, they imposed the de-Christianization laws completing the secularization program of the Enlightened despots. A group of nuns from Annay took refuge in the Belgian houses, only to flee again before the revolutionary armies to Westphalia, where they were again forced to disperse in 1796. In Belgium, no convents were spared. In Italy, the more resistant people saved many convents during the initial attacks. German princes, encouraged by Napoleon in 1801 to repay their wartime losses with ecclesiastical property, expropriated eighty-three nunneries. In 1799, four days after the grand duchess had visited the holy sepulcher maintained at Santa Verdiana, the French entered Florence and billeted their troops in the convent, confiscating their money and altar goods. In 1810 the French suppressed all the monasteries. In France, in the wake of the revolution, the great old convents were demolished or their buildings were converted to social "usefulness." Fontevraud became a prison. Many Italian convents were put to the same use. San Jacopo di Ripoli, gutted by Leopold's *conservatorio*, became a barracks for military engineers.

The most common crime of nuns against the republic was their effort to continue to live by their rules as best they could. Ironically, once they went out in the world, their determination to keep the vow of chastity provoked the same popular hostility that once whispered of their secret vices. Their persistent chastity elicited complaints to the public authority. In addition, their tendency to maintain small communities in private housing laid them open to charges of treason. In 1792, Sainte-Croix's bells were confiscated and ninety-four soldiers were quartered on the community. The nuns were driven out and their property sold, but the abbess smuggled the relic, Radegund's legacy, out of the house saving it for the community, which reappeared years later. After their dispersal, the Carmelites of Compiègne split up into four houses. At first, they took the Oath of Liberty and Equality but later, receiving instructions for the clergy to resist the oath, they all retracted it and gave up their pensions.

In September 1792, the first of the massacres in the prison of Paris occurred. At Saint Antoine, the Cistercian nuns were presented with the head of their former pensioner, the princess of Lamballe. The Carmelites of Nantes were violently driven from their cloister by a mob bearing the bleeding bodies of their chaplains. At Bollène, nuns in a mixed group were arrested in a house they had rented together. They reorganized their conventual life in prison in Orange. Twenty-six Visitandines spent two years in jail with other women in the Good Shepherd at Nantes. One of the inmates wrote:

> A stingy portion of rice made up their daily diet and anyone who wanted more paid the jailor seven sous for an ounce of rice in water. They often stole the food that a few of us got from outside. Seven hundred of us were jammed into quarters intended for 200. Twenty or 40 women were put into a single small room. The beds were so close that one often found oneself under a neighbor's cover. The sick and dying were mixed with healthy people. I can't count the women who were infected thus and suffered and died at my side.[26]

The nuns had no money to buy extra food, and the republic canceled their pensions on the grounds that they received food and lodging in prison. The jailor enjoyed tormenting them by inserting their names on the list of women to be executed.

In 1794, the English nuns of Rouen were moved to a large convent where seven hundred nuns were collected. There was only a small kitchen fire to warm the four hundred nuns who were still there a year later. They received a half-pound of bad flour each day with some heavily watered cider. Many sisters sickened from the wormy flour and corn so bad that horses refused it. They were constantly terrorized by rumors of drownings and hangings, but their doughty wardress "was resolved to defend her prisoners at the cost of her own life. She never laid down for three or four nights, but carried several loaded pistols on her person. She secured the doors with new locks and made use of every means in her power to save us."[27] Imprisoned at Orange, two Cistercians, twelve Sacramentines, and fourteen Ursulines tried to turn their jail into a convent and went to the guillotine smiling, according to their guard. On February 9, 1794, six daughters of Saint Teresa in Paris were condemned to perpetual imprisonment and deported. On April 5 the prioress of Lyons, Magdalena de la Cruz, was executed with seven Carmelites and eleven Clarisses who had been living clandestinely together in a parish house at Ainay.

In Compiègne, the Committee of Surveillance indicated that former nuns, supported by their *dévotes*, were maintaining their communal life and rituals. The committee suspected that they were in criminal correspondence with "fanatics" in Paris and were perhaps holding meetings of their own "directed by fanaticism." In July 1794, the Carmelites were tried by the Committee of Public Safety. Accused of hiding arms in the convent, Mme. Lidoine drew out a crucifix and said, "Here are the only arms we have ever had in our house." She confessed to clandestine correspondence with their exiled chaplain, who continued to give her spiritual advice. And she added that the crime was hers alone, for the rule forbade the other nuns to carry on any correspondence except with the superior's permission.

The entire community, however, was ready for its moment of glory. When the tribunal accused the nuns of fanaticism, Sister Henriette proclaimed, "My dear Mother and my sisters, you have all heard our accuser declare to us that we are being condemned for our attachment to our Holy Religion. All we have desired we shall now obtain; immortal grace shall be rendered to him who puts us first on the road to Calvary. Oh! What joy! what joy to die for God!"[28] Arrested, brought to Paris, condemned for treason, the Carmelites sought to use their time in prison to convert their guards and their fellow prisoners. On the Feast of Our Lady of Carmel, July 16, they got a visitor to smuggle them some burned sticks with which they wrote a hymn on the prison wall to be sung to the tune of the Marseillaise.[29]

Marie de l'Incarnation, the natural daughter of the prince of Conti, was out of the house when the Carmelites were arrested. For years thereafter she wandered around France as a refugee and then into Switzerland, sometimes forced to eat grass to appease her hunger. She reentered the Carmel at Sens in 1823 and recorded various eye-witness accounts of her sisters' end. They had recovered their habits, or enough pieces of them to go as nuns to the guillotine, having cut their wimples around the neck so that the executioner need not touch them. As they mounted the tumbrils, they began to sing their offices. For once, the crowds of Paris were abashed. Onlookers testified to the silence as the chanting nuns were driven through the streets. Even the rattling drums that customarily celebrated the death of an aristocrat were silenced. Mme. Lidoine received permission to shepherd her flock before her. Each nun in turn renewed her vows of religion and asked her prioress for permission to mount the scaffold. The novice Constance went first, singing *Laudate Dominum omnes gentes*. Sister Julie, who feared the scaffold, refused her family's attempt to free her, proclaiming, "We are the victims of this age and we should sacrifice ourselves for its reconciliation with God."[30]

V

MODERN TIMES

19

Culture Wars

IT WAS 1797. Seven barges fled the French revolutionary armies down the Danube to Passau. A chorus of nuns sang their offices and the responses rang out across the water from the Trappist monks who had joined them in exile. A new order had arisen from the ruins of a dozen broken communities. Two recruits, the Benedictine Sister Saint-Maur Miel of the Little Calvary at Paris and a companion from Arcies, fled across revolutionary France with the help of strangers willing to risk their own safety. A Protestant innkeeper in Strasbourg, where they were stranded for lack of passports, found them refuge with two Catholic ladies who could also offer the sacraments, through a secret network of nonjuring priests and fugitive nuns. A sympathetic border guard let them pass as soldiers' wives going to their husbands. They joined the ragged assortment of nuns from various orders grouped around the old novice master of La Trappe, that stern Cistercian house which had always closed its doors to women.

In 1796, Stanislas Michel, from Sainte-Catherine d'Avignon, recorded the vows of eight nuns who formed the first Trappistine community. By the fall of 1797, forty or fifty nuns resided in the cloister, refugees from all orders and all classes, peasant and artisan included. All were called sister, and the distinction between choir and convert was dropped until a later date when the capacities of the various individuals could be clarified. Sister Sainte-Marie Bigaux, wrote:

> Having obtained the grace from my God of returning into my holy estate,
> I . . . can barely bring myself to recognize how great is that mercy . . .
> I am not alone in enjoying that peace. . . . Novices in my charge attest
> with me that they feel in entering here joy, peace, in a word happiness
> which was unknown to them until then. . . . I vow that it seems surprising
> that in a novitiate composed of persons of every age and condition,
> religious and seculars, all should be content.[1]

They were to suffer from shortages of food and from the Russian winter.
They would wander for years before they could finally take root and
expand their new order, which today flourishes in America and even
Japan. The adversity of their long flight and shared hardship welded the
male and female Trappists together into a more enduring partnership
than nuns and monks had established since the early Middle Ages.

Estimated numbers of nuns expelled from their communities range
from 30,000 to 55,000. Most of them sank into the unknown. Only 6,700
former nuns still living in 1800 resumed their vows. Some 356 nuns and
conversae are known to have married, mostly to priests combining their
poor pensions. Another 700 are known to have found secular employment
or otherwise settled in the world as single people and asked to be relieved
of their vows between 1800 and 1808. For the rest, we have only flashes
of information. Many of the oldest nuns died almost immediately after
expulsion. Some of the youngest were seduced or raped. Those who
could took refuge with their families, but older nuns often had no families
and others found their families had emigrated or had no use for them.
When their pensions were not paid, some starved.

Some took to wandering the roads and sheltered in the forests. Others
took refuge in foreign convents, only to be expelled anew by the invading
French armies that dissolved monasteries across Europe. Some died of
hunger, exposure, and violence. A whole community from Toledo lost
its meager belongings to highway robbers. Cistercian escapees, disguised
as peasants, made their way to Switzerland, where the congregation of
Wettingen was formed with three male houses and eleven female convents in 1806. English nuns fleeing the Terror or surviving it in 1795,
determined to go to England, where the Relief Act had granted Catholics
greater toleration, and begin the reestablishment of the monastic way of
life there.

As soon as order was restored, survivors began to return. By 1802, the nuns of Soleilmont in Belgium had managed to rent their old monastery. One of the oldest Italian communities, the Cistercian convent in Ivrea, dissolved in 1800, had some of its nuns back again by 1802. In Lerida, a nun who delayed flight too long was hanged from the curb of the well by French soldiers enthusiastically enforcing the suppression of the Spanish monasteries. As soon as the Napoleonic wars ceased, however, the abbess of Las Huelgas and the Recollects of Valladolid reopened their houses. The abbess of Quedlinberg would never again take her place in the diet of German princes, but in 1828, religious orders returned to Austria, Germany, and Holland. In France itself, at least a third of the old communities survived clandestinely. In 1810, on the anniversary of their first foundation, fifteen survivors of the Nantes Visitation followed their eighty-two-year-old superior back to their cloister and renewed their vows.[2] The nuns of Sainte-Croix brought their salvaged relic of the holy cross out of hiding, and in 1857 a solemn procession marked the thirteen-hundredth anniversary of Radegund's arrival in Poitiers. Camille of the Infant Jesus, a Carmelite, gathered the remnants of her order in Paris and lived to reestablish five Carmels. Even Compiègne was restored in 1866.

Cloistering became a daring and difficult vocation. Some nuns expelled from convents in revolutionary Europe carried their way of life to new territories. Led by Clare Joseph Dickinson, four refugees from the English Carmel in Antwerp crossed the Atlantic in 1790 to establish the first convent in the young United States at Port Tobacco, Maryland. Maintaining Teresa's principle of the hidden life, they firmly restricted their "usefulness" to prayers in support of the first bishop in the new United States, John Carroll. After the first generation they were obliged to add a boarding school, the nearest equivalent to cloister that the American church could or would support.[3] Many nuns found that they could not re-create the old traditions. Though few religious women who appeared before Cardinal Caprara to regularize their status after the Napoleonic Concordat in 1808 asked to be fully secularized, hardly any had enough money to recloister. About two-thirds of them asked for dispensation from the vow of poverty. Their endowments, their convents, and even their household furnishings were gone. The dowry system that had created them was ebbing. They could barely support themselves by making curative waters and salves or the apple jelly that the refugee

Clares from Rouen sold in London. At the least, they had to open their houses to boarding pupils.

Philippine Duchesne, who had been a novice at the Visitation of Grenoble before the revolution, devoted decades to the doomed dream of restoring the mother house. The scattered nuns were, for the most part, too old or ill or too involved with new responsibilities to return. Even when a core of former nuns from other orders gathered around the aged and infirm mother superior, they could not develop a rule that would serve their new circumstances. The community broke up in ill will and recrimination, and Duchesne was obliged to try a more public vocation as a teacher under the guidance of Sophie Barat, founder of the Religious of the Sacred Heart. On the American prairie where she established a string of schools, Duchesne still insisted that she belonged to a cloistered order, though she accepted that they could not install grilles and other restrictive devices.[4] She grieved for her solitude and even more for the abandonment of the Divine Office. The recitation of the psalmody and the observance of the horarium, the grand silence, the meditations, and the conferences, which were the very heart of the monastic life, could not be effectively fitted to the demanding schedule of teaching most contemplatives now kept.

Other contemplatives applied themselves to a lengthy process of reevaluating their constitutions to express a greater unity and a renewed charism. While under siege by the secular state that claimed Rome for its capitol, Pius IX lent a friendly ear to the mystic Maria Hesselblad, who was inspired to reunite the Brigittine order, which still survived in a few remaining nunneries in Syon, Valladolid, and Altomünster. They have since returned to Vadstena in Sweden and again occupy the Casa Brigitta in Rome. Benedicta Riepp, from the ancient monastery of Eichstätt, where Huneberc of Heidenheim once recorded the travels of Willibald, brought two sisters to Pennsylvania in 1853 to join the abbot Boniface Wimmer in a revival of the old partnership of Boniface and Leoba: double monasteries with a teaching mission and mitigated cloister. But ultimately conflict developed, as Wimmer intruded his authority into the domestic arrangements of the nuns, episcopal expedience frustrated the unified design that Riepp had hoped to implement, and the pope himself resisted recognizing unenclosed women who had no time to perform the full office as true Benedictines.

In the nineteenth-century culture war (to borrow the term *Kulturkampf*, so aptly coined by German anticlericals), critics reinterpreted the old ideal of self-mortification and discipline as unnatural and tyrannical. Nothing in the modern, individualistic, bourgeois world seemed more atrocious than cloistering unmarried women. In the old compounds of Eichstätt, the adaptation of the contemplative life to a sedate school for girls had been accomplished when the convent reopened in 1835. Riepp was unprepared for conditions in the United States, where she could not acquire the landed endowment that allowed her to wall up outdoor spaces for exercise, gardens, and storage. Simple tasks like fetching wood or water required breaking cloister. Duchesne's problems were multiplied by curiosity seekers, women and men who did not hesitate to walk into the unlocked house. Even sisters who did not define themselves as cloistered nuns often found it difficult to live without harassment. Traveling sisters avoided wearing their habits in public. In England they were forbidden to do so. Some communities countered these suspicions with invitations to the public to enter their forbidden precincts on special days. Frances Warde, who introduced the Sisters of Mercy to the United States in 1843, made reception of a novice into a public event as a way of soothing public fears.

Women living together hidden from the reach of men continued to be a magnet for prurient curiosity. When it was falsely rumored that Elizabeth Harrison, an Ursuline in Charlestown, Massachusetts, was being held against her will, a mob intent on "rescuing" her broke in and burned the convent down in 1835. Attacks in Baltimore, Frederick, Saint Louis, Galveston, and elsewhere followed. *The Awful Disclosures of Maria Monk*, a lurid tale of sex slavery and murder in a Montreal convent became a best-seller in 1836. In 1853, proposals were introduced in the British Parliament to investigate convents as places of confinement for unwilling girls. On the Continent, liberal revolutions were generally accompanied by the forcible "rescue" of nuns from their cloisters. In America, anti-Catholic Know-Nothings prevailed on several states to authorize civic officials to "inspect" convents and "liberate" unwilling inmates providing excuses for unruly men to break in without warning. Theresa Gerhardinger wrote that the School Sisters' house in Philadelphia had been threatened with burning and had to be closely guarded for a week, while the sisters slept in their street clothes. At the same time, however, she was preparing to transfer her mother house in Munich to the United States if its residents' safety was threatened by the militant hostility of the new German state under Bismarck. In 1909, Alejandro Lerroux urged anticlerical Spaniards to liberate nuns and "elevate them to motherhood."[5]

Despite sporadic rioting, the relatively peaceful atmosphere of the United States often provided a final refuge for nuns expelled from France, Italy, Germany, and other troubled nations. In 1820, Spain adopted a secularized constitution and attacked the monasteries. The Portuguese government suppressed religious orders in 1834, though it allowed women's convents to continue until the nuns died. Austria secularized schools in 1867, and in 1874 only Franz-Josef's veto averted suppression of the monasteries. In 1871, an English parliamentary committee urged the suppression of convents, which had been multiplying since the Catholic Emancipation Act of 1829. The Piedmontese Law of Convents in 1855, which extended to united Italy in 1860, abolished all religious orders except those actively engaged in charity and education and gave the state jurisdiction over their property. As Germany coalesced around Prussia, Christians likened Bismarck's *Kulturkampf* to Diocletian's persecutions. In 1873, all religious congregations but those caring for the sick were expelled.

The French *lois laïques* of 1880 imposed corporate taxes on religious communities, and in 1884 all church property was assessed as "capital" and therefore taxed more heavily than ordinary real estate. The diversion of public funds and even family fortunes to convents offended the deepest beliefs of modern social scientists, who not only detested the nuns' religion but considered their chastity aberrant and subversive. In the 1890s, the French Third Republic restricted religious orders, culminating in the law of July 1901, which dispersed about 30,000 religious (out of 200,000). Hundreds of English and Irish nuns in France and Belgium were assigned to foreign missions when those governments restricted teaching to citizens. Thérèse Martin entered the Lisieux Carmel in 1888, hoping to share the fate of the Compiègne martyrs: "We always lived as if we were in a volcano," she wrote.[6]

The same depressing rite of passage—the torture of women to appease social unrest—has repeated itself from Nero to the present. Men who were once their pupils apparently need to exorcise the fantasies of childhood through the eviction, humiliation, rape, or murder of nuns. Insurgents often seize nuns as the most available representatives of a hated ruling class even fueling their anger with resentment for their virtues. Latin American revolutionaries against Spanish authority in the 1820s closed and destroyed convents. The violence recurred in Mexico in the 1860s and the 1920s. Francesca Cabrini's school in Nicaragua was closed and the nuns expelled to Panama. As they settled into a new routine, they were again attacked by revolutionaries and fled to Argentina. Carmelite communities from Argentina spread to Uruguay, despite constitutional prohibitions in 1935, and into Paraguay in 1951. Alliance with colonial authorities often targeted nuns for revolutionary violence in mission areas. In 1870 10 French sisters were killed in anti-French rioting in China. Their martyrdom, even when it accounted for only a small percentage of atrocities, acquired immeasurable symbolic value to counterrevolutionaries. Nine sisters were killed by the Boxers in 1900, while thousands of Chinese Christians died. During six furious months of the Spanish Civil War in 1936, 283 nuns died among the thousands of clerical victims murdered.

The international press promoted lurid (but untrue) stories of nuns paraded naked in public and gang-raped by militiamen. They were, in fact, driven from their cloisters and sometimes imprisoned as subversives. Tombs were opened and nuns' bodies, exposed to mockery with cigarettes stuck in their mouths, obscenely handled. Though nuns were not specially targeted for attention, the Nazis killed 289 of them as against nearly 3,000 male clerics. News services highlighted violence against nuns in reporting the Mau-Mau terror in Kenya and the bloody aftermath of Belgian withdrawal from Congo. Three American nuns and a lay coworker raped and murdered in Salvador became symbols for uncounted victims of the roaming death squads there. Modern students of signs and significance have much to consider in this use of virgin women to stand both for oppressive male authorities and victimized institutions. Something in the very nature of their inaccessibility, their integrity, and their devotion seems to raise testosterone levels.

Nuns and their admirers often used the same imagery. They were never innocent victims but were actively and fully engaged in a mission. Thérèse of Lisieux's best-selling autobiography, *Story of a Soul,* reasserted the cloister's claim to be the incubator of virgin sacrifices ready to redeem a sinful age. The most popular saint of modern times, Thérèse, called the Little Flower, believed in the missionary power of prayer flowing from the hidden life. On the centenary of the execution of the Carmelites of Compiègne, she wrote that she "thought of those souls who offered themselves as victims to the justice of God so that by drawing it down on themselves they turned aside the punishment due to sinners." Her meditation led her to reformulate the need to sacrifice oneself not only to satisfy divine justice but also to unleash divine love upon the world, kindling it by her own immolation.[7] Inspired by Teresa of Avila's command, "Carmel's zeal must embrace the world," she shaped a concept of love binding all vocations within the mystical body of Christ. Through the "little way" of offering small daily trials, the consumptive girl, enclosed not only in a convent but in a failing body, believed that she could participate in the lives of warriors, priests, apostles, doctors of the church, martyrs, and missionaries: "I realized that love includes all vocations, that love is all things and that, because it is eternal, it embraces every time and place."[8]

The cloister's response to a world engulfed in violence was of necessity a response of the spirit whose practical effects were feeble at best. During World War II, the Vatican gave no unifying direction to its troops. Despite their fractured lines of communication, their isolation, and their enclosure, some convents offered refuge for Jews, especially children already resident as pupils. The Polish convents alone are credited with saving several thousand children and a few hundred adults. Matylda Getter, the provincial of the Franciscan Sisters of the Family of Mary organized nearly all the houses of her congregation to save almost a thousand Jews. The nuns of the Immaculate Conception hid Jewish girls in their boarding school. Similar isolated examples have been reported for France and Italy.

One of the few nuns who could recognize the threat before it fully developed was the philosopher Edith Stein, who strove to emulate Teresa of Avila in cultivating Christian spirituality from her Jewish roots.[9] She appealed repeatedly to Pius XI and other ecclesiastical dignitaries for an encyclical to mobilize Catholics. Hearing of the nuns murdered in Spain, she wrote that German sisters must be prepared for martyrdom in their turn. The principle of compassion, the offering of prayer and pain as a balance to the crimes of others, guided her final years. In 1933, before her entry into Carmel she prayed to carry the cross being laid upon the Jews in the name of all. On Passion Sunday 1939, she made formal offering of herself "to the Heart of Jesus as a sacrifice of atonement for true peace that if possible the reign of Antichrist might be broken without another World War and a new social order might be established." True to the tradition of her order, Stein sought to give meaning to her death in Auschwitz and give some healing to the dark world that engulfed her: "We are going for our people," she told her sister.[10]

Despite the bombs, food shortages, occupation, and internment as enemy nationals, World War II brought a sort of respite in the culture wars. When the Cold War developed, however, nuns became frontline troops in many capacities. Their social services proved invaluable in the struggle for hearts and minds in the "third world," and this contribution often made them the prime targets of guerrillas and death squads. When Soviet troops took hold of Eastern Europe, they forcibly entered convents and subjected the nuns to every sort of pressure to break their vows. The overwhelming majority appear to have stood fast and many spent the remainder of their lives in isolated monasteries converted into overcrowded, undersupplied internment camps that relied on the charity of a sparse local population for life itself. Others remained in the city, keeping up secret networks, pastoral services, and even a hidden communal life, while outwardly conforming to the secular world. Similarly, in communist Asia, Western sisters were expelled by Chinese, Vietnamese, and Korean authorities, while the indigenous sisters had to be left to their mercy. The women of those churches, however, already have a proud record of maintaining their religion and their vocations under the heaviest pressures.

The nuns of the last two centuries, like all their contemporaries throughout the world, have been forced to grope their way toward some moral ground where their own consciences can find rest without insult to other visions. Even compassion and self-sacrifice are contested ground in the culture wars of today. The Carmelites built a convent at Dachau and, within the spiritual tradition of their order, planned another at Auschwitz under the leadership of a nun distinguished for wartime resistance to the Nazis. The convent was to be named for Edith Stein, to extend her offering of self-sacrifice and prayer in atonement for the evil done in that place by Christians. But the language and the religious symbolism offended Jewish leaders, who particularly resented the impli-cation that Stein's conversion rewarded her with an immortality denied to other Jewish victims. In the end, the nuns had to withdraw the sacrifice that no one wanted to accept.

As the modern world ceased to value the spiritual productivity of cloistered women, it scorned them as useless parasites. No state would recognize their permanent civil death, and simple vows depended on the constancy of the votary herself for enforcement. The church was no longer part of the ruling establishment of any nation. The Vatican retained an influential but essentially marginal role in global politics, a shift that, ironically, demarginalized its religious women during its most embattled periods. Secular governments recognized the economic advan-tages of subsidizing their disciplined and self-sacrificing social services. These deceptively meek ladies with downcast eyes built an unparalleled network of educational and care-giving institutions. Serving their church as loyal soldiers, they remained strong-willed and fully focused on goals of their own.

I shall devote the next chapter to these spectacular achievements. At present, I want to explore the complexities of their institutional and cultural commitments in a world vastly different from the one that formed them. The institutional separation of church and state was replaced by a far more rigorous exclusion of religion itself from the modern secular state, whose ideology of nationalism and human perfecti-bility contest otherworldliness and universalism. Withdrawal of the state's coercive powers deprived the church of the means to support persecution and crusades. Once again, as in ancient times, its authority had to depend on moral strength alone. Women religious took the center point of the pope's battalions and became more intimately intertwined in its institutional structure than ever before. Everyone understood that they were not simple do-gooders but determined missionaries. Opponents of Catholicism recognized a formidable enemy:

When the demon wished to introduce evil into the world, he made use of woman to corrupt man; now, to introduce Catholicism to America, he makes use of nuns, true Eves, with their sweet and engaging manners, their knowledge and their attractions. The Jesuits are dangerous but the nuns are their agents and still more to be feared. Guard against sending your children to their schools and even against . . . servants trained by the sisters for they will instill their bad principles into the hearts of your children.[11]

The democratic aspirations of millions were tempered by religious faith. Freed by secularism from state interference with church administration, Catholicism became more ultramontane than ever before in its history. Papal adjustment of the diocesan system to national frontiers strengthened Rome's control of the hierarchy. North America received its organization directly from the pope without reference to the secular power. Rome reacted energetically when Bishop Carroll of Baltimore urged that American Catholicism reflect the spirit of the new country by reviving the local election of bishops that characterized the church in its first millennium. In 1790, the pope established a national hierarchy with the separation of the Archbishopric of Baltimore from London. Canadian and Australian churches soon followed. After the Emancipation Act of 1829, Cardinals Cullen in Ireland and Wiseman in England brought their long-isolated archdioceses into conformity with papal Catholicism. With the Papal State under siege by a newly unified Italy, the First Vatican Council proclaimed papal infallibility in 1870.

In non-Catholic countries, constitutional prohibitions against state support of any religion, as in the American Bill of Rights, worked in favor of Catholicism and other nonestablished churches. They learned to resist government regulation in the name of religious liberty. Demonstrations of popular piety were organized in response to anticlerical eruptions, fueled by well-publicized reports of Marian appearances at La Salette and Lourdes. The promulgation of the Immaculate Conception in 1854 underlined papal control of doctrine. The clergy retained confessional authority over the faithful. Though Liberal critics, like Michelet, saw the attachment between pious women and their confessors as a double treason against the authority of husbands and the state, Conservative politicians were impressed by the adherence of loyal Catholics to their embattled church and began to reassess the political value of such loyalty, making concessions to Catholics to strengthen their patriotism.

In England (and, consequently, Ireland) mid-eighteenth-century relaxation of anti-Catholic penal laws allowed nuns to form communities

and even to open schools. Their educational and devotional activities—
their social training of young girls and married women—among many
other activities created that disciplined and cohesive Irish Catholicism
which brought about the election of Daniel O'Connell to the English
Parliament in the early nineteenth century. In Napoleonic times, the
English Poor Clares from Rouen and the English Brigittines, whose
transplanted Syon in Lisbon was no longer a haven, turned home. The
Emancipation Act opened England to foreign nuns seeking refuge. The
Prussian constitution of 1848 gave Catholics freedom of worship and the
right to control benefices, establish religious orders, and communicate
with international superiors.

Teresa of Avila's vision of the cloister extending its spiritual power
throughout the world could be a metaphor for a church at once cloistered
by the hostile modern world and expansive in its missionary reach. In
1817, Pauline Jaricot organized the Society for the Propagation of the
Faith in Lyons to collect funds for foreign missions. It spread to many
countries in the 1830s as Gregory XVI created a worldwide network of
new bishoprics, completed in 1846 with the Vicariate of Japan. Pius IX
reinforced episcopal authority over most monastic personnel and bestowed exemptions on congregations in the mission fields directly under
his own authority even while he remained a "prisoner of the Vatican,"
refusing the slightest acknowledgment of the Italian state that had
engulfed Rome. Anticlerical governments like Spain and Germany took
advantage of Leo XIII's accession in 1878 to negotiate the restoration of
the religious orders. Although the question of the Papal State delayed
settlement with Italy until the 1920s, nuns expanded their work during
his regime and followed Italian immigrants to America. The Italian
Concordat was not untypical of the growing alliance between political
conservatives and the church. A right-wing Catholic nationalism entered
the international mainstream with Francisco Franco's victory in Spain
and flourished in the Cold War period. The apparition at Fatima enlisted
the Blessed Virgin's devotees in the war against "godless" communism
and the threat of a world revolutionary movement. After World War I,
when women gained suffrage in many countries, Benedict XV and his
successors through Pius XII marshaled nuns as voters against anticlerical
left-wing movements.

*   *   *

In the period bracketed by the First and Second Vatican Councils, Thomist theology and Tridentine discipline provided a bulwark against the rising floods of change. Leo XIII, in his *Testem Benevolentiae,* branded "Americanism" a quasi-heresy for attempting to adjust Catholic teaching to the democratic and secular values of the United States. Pius X further condemned individualism and relativism in his bulls against modernism, *Lamentabili* and *Pascendi* (1907). The church saw itself as the City of God, denying any possibility that time could affect eternal values. But it could not seal itself off from the agents of the times. Culture wars are intestinal. Throughout its long history, the church has awkwardly embraced both inquisitors and champions of the oppressed. Leo XIII's *Rerum Novarum* and other social encyclicals revived ancient visions of the apostolic life. The pope urged Catholics to redress imbalances in the distribution of wealth in the name of Christian charity. Martha's charitable and educational mission lent credibility to his message of social justice in a Christian context. Sisters pursuing a vocation of social service under simple vows emerged from the shadows of the cloister to become a palpable public presence.

The results were ideologically equivocal. Secularization of church land drove charities to solicit support from the monied middle class, which tended to see its institutions as instruments for the education and discipline of a work force for the industrial age. To achieve their own goals, many congregations tried to do without outside patronage, combining the need to earn a living with charity. In the Beguine tradition, they obtained work to do at home through the putting-out system and pooled their property and earnings. They taught children for free but accepted donations. Teaching "luxury" subjects like music was a common supplement. The Sisters of the Blessed Virgin Mary hired themselves out as farm laborers. American sisters in rural areas supplemented modest tuition fees by running farms. Convents doubled as small factories, manufacturing textiles, clothing, and other products. The Oblate Sisters of Providence, a Baltimore congregation founded by and for black immigrants from Haiti, supported themselves and their mission to educate black children with menial labor. Sisters became accustomed to raising money through raffles and outright begging. Catherine Mallon traveled through the western mining camps begging for the support of the community. The School Sisters of Notre Dame had to beg for money to repay a loan from the Redemptorist fathers and to supply their necessities since the low tuition in their school did not meet their expenses.

"Need brings out our talents," wrote Hyacinth Le Coniat. Theresa Gerhardinger boasted that her sisters in America cooked, gardened, painted, gilded, made and cobbled shoes, bound books, and did secretarial work. Fasting, scrimping on clothes, lodging, and other material comforts, and hard work in outside jobs funded their institutions. The self-sacrifice characteristic of the medieval poverty movement paired uneasily with conditions created by modern industrialization. Self-mortification sometimes led to capital accumulation. Many nuns prospered with investments and small enterprises in the developing capitalist world. Angela Sansbury's nine Kentucky Dominicans opened their first parish school in 1823; they farmed and made linen from their own flax. To build a three-story trade school, Blandina Segale inspired the citizens of Santa Fe to open a quarry, install a lime kiln, start a brick yard, and establish a lumber mill.[12] Joseph of the Sacred Heart, a Providence sister from Montreal, earned enough money in the Oregon Territory as an architect and contractor to found eleven hospitals, seven academies, five Indian schools, two orphanages, and an old age home by her death in 1902. Francesca Cabrini knew enough about surveying land to foil an attempt to swindle her by the owners of the North Shore Hotel in Chicago, which she bought for a hospital. When a dishonest contractor tried to cheat on the work, she took direct charge of its renovation and had the nuns do their own carpentry and painting.

While this commitment to honest labor and its rewards certainly followed in the best tradition of the Benedictine rule, it continued to raise the old question of the compatibility of profit and monastic poverty. Sisters were able to purchase estates and hotels at bankruptcy auctions and support extensive charities through a combination of begging, self-denial, and painstaking bookkeeping. Landed property and cash donations were supplemented by government subventions for their public work and private pensions. Businesses and private persons used the tax system to advantage by donating properties whose usefulness or supportability had declined. Ladycliff College was established in an outdated resort hotel. Abandoned mansions made good asylums, orphanages, or boarding schools.

Physical plants used for charitable purposes were only illusory assets.

Bequests entrusted to nuns for charitable purposes did not remain in their hands. Nevertheless, the trend toward having property and buildings distanced the sisters from the objects of their ministry. Despite unlimited self-sacrifice and hard work, their lives were often enviable. In the Western world, recruits from slums found relief in the consecrated life from the crowding and dirt of their home environment even if they continued to endure hardships in the form of heavy labor and insufficient food. Moreover, they were spared the burdens that family life laid on secular women. Catherine Mallon wrote from New Mexico that the sight of women with children, toiling in settlements far from their friends and families, moved her often to thank God for saving her from their fate.[13] In the non-Western world, the corporate property of a community, however poor by European standards, represented material wealth barely conceivable to most of the native novices. Thus, self-mortification became a psychologically complex process when conceived of as a dialogue between giver and receiver. The very process of "serving" the poor and unfortunate bespeaks the generosity of the privileged; humiliation, however successful, always implies a descent.

The missions were small in number; their leaders counted on the recruitment of native sisters wherever they went and rarely included lay sisters. The missions did not foster the Benedictine spirit of work for its own sake: rather, labor was pragmatic and geared toward human services. Farm produce fed them, their pupils, and their dependents and financed the sale of the services they had come to provide. But the sisters could not be spared for agricultural labor. Thus, in the American South or elsewhere in the world where free labor was not available, they became enmeshed in slave systems they knew to be evil.

It is a weary tale, well-known to American historians. Sisters coming from Europe learned to adapt to southern slavery and Americans were already accustomed to it. Novices often brought slaves as part of their dowry, and well-meaning patrons donated them to the sisters. Philippine Duchesne praised the honesty of a planter who gave her a slave to pay arrears on his daughter's tuition. Arriving in Louisiana from France, Hyacinth Le Coniat was shocked and horrified by the realities of American slavery: "They receive no attention or care. They are treated like beasts with little pity. And yet they are children of God!"[14] Within months, however, she was complaining about the cost of hiring slave labor and asking for servants from France. When at last the community bought a slave, she stanched her tears at having paid for human flesh with the thought that she could instruct him in religion. The war came and the slave ran away. His ingratitude dismayed Hyacinth.

The unquestioned class differences of the Old Regime affronted modern sensitivity toward the labor force. Irish sisters who set up school-workshops to train poor children to work and then started small industrial enterprises to employ them were actively participating in destroying the old Gaelic rural culture in favor of a modern, anglicized, working class. Their harshest critics sometimes said that well-meaning sisters trying to find a Christian solution to the dilemmas of capitalist society could only help to prolong the misery by making it more bearable. Throughout the industrial belt around Lyons, where silk production employed many women, Providences were established to provide work training and employment to women and orphans. The Providence of Red Cross in Lyons formed a self-contained community of working women supplied by the putting-out system. The work of the orphans and the austerity of the sisters produced a profit that could be invested for the future.

Other welfare workers, however, saw in the system nothing but exploitation of helpless children. In the paternalist vein that informed the early mill community at Lowell, Massachusetts, French industrialists sometimes put their working women under the supervision of sisters. Six hundred girls in the silk mills at Bourg-en-Bresse lived in community, while the Providence Sisters who had formed the cooperative found themselves effectively acting as managers for the mill owners. To the organizers of labor movements focusing on better wages and working conditions, this approach amounted to class betrayal, forcing the poor to put their families in the hands of the church because they could not command a living wage. In 1848, workers sacked and destroyed their physical plants. "The crisis demonstrated that solidarity itself and even charity could be an injustice when unreflecting."[15]

But as long as the male structures of industry and their political monopoly prevailed, the most energetic and powerful women could not have done more than ameliorate their effects on the poor and helpless. In Bavaria, for example, rural women without commercial training or education were sometimes driven out on the road, starving, to relieve local resources of their support. The textile industry shamelessly exploited their position when women lacking land or craft certificates could not even get a marriage license. If a group of sisters started a shelter that ultimately resembled a workhouse, they at least made an effort to provide help and a sympathetic environment. Moreover, we must not lose sight of the hardships for the sisters themselves. Even in Europe, but much more commonly in the missions, a community was generally very small. In rural areas and missions, education, medical help, and all sorts of other services were generally supplied by groups numbering less than a half-dozen women.

Even in enclosed convents, the culture wars went on as ancient rules bent before modern demands and sheltered women confronted the mysteries of otherness. In Old Regime Europe, most convents were stratified socially so that the inhabitants were spared the unpleasantness of cross-class accommodations. Homogeneity was strengthened where communities recruited locally and the members had strong family ties to support them. The Martin sisters, for example, threatened to overwhelm the Lisieux Carmel by sheer numbers. Lower-class women were clearly demarcated as servants or *conversae*. Among the sisters engaged in social services, class and education tended to go together. Lay sisters or even women who took no vows at all were attached to communities to do rough labor for sisters who could thus be freed for more extensive educational or medical services. An element of race was added in the missions. African women who joined European orders generally remained uneducated, since their superiors tended to be content with their household services.

Class distinctions carried over from Europe proved especially trying in the United States. With the decline of the dowry system and the rise of the active vocations that commanded regular, though pitifully small, salaries, religious vocations became steadily more accessible to working-class and peasant women. In Europe, most communities still made the distinction between lay and choir sisters, often modified by the insertion of a "middle class" of teaching nuns, but in the liberal atmosphere of the nineteenth century the practice caused discontent and guilt. Novice mistresses complained that recruits were becoming "susceptible, presumptuous, egotistical."[16] Rather than bring "mannish, rough nuns" from Germany to do the heavy labor of a community, Theresa Gerhardinger employed American women, but she was shocked by their laxity and aggressiveness. Her companion, Caroline Friess, who had a more positive attitude toward American ways, had to discipline her German choir nuns to treat the lay sisters as equals. Theodore Guérin was dismayed when her American postulants sided with a poor laundress whom she had excluded from the common table. Indigenous American congregations like the Sisters of Loretto never introduced the distinction, and many of the newer Saint Joseph congregations, like the Sisters of Saint Joseph of Cleveland, followed suit. Lay sisters at Carondelet resented their exclusion from elections and the civic life of the community. They complained about being made to wear a bonnet instead of a veil. Many American congregations never transferred the division between lay and choir sisters from Europe. At the beginning of the twentieth century many international congregations began to abolish it until it was finally swept away at the Second Vatican Council.

Traditional manners expressing subordination toward superiors continued to be instilled in the novitiate. Thérèse of Lisieux voluntarily kept the last place among the novices throughout her career to express the humility of the little way. In contrast, hostile accounts like *Miss Bunkley's Book* interpreted the ancient rites of humility and obedience as tyranny intolerable to the American spirit.[17] Even in America, however, ranking by seniority in the cloister was retained until well into the twentieth century. By 1929, when thirty-nine Mercy houses merged, many had already dropped the practice; the rest did not hesitate to follow. In time, the concept of sisterhood gave new meaning to their spirituality, though it took more than a century to create a classless community.

As Catholicism spread throughout the world, race did not prevent women from feeling a vocation to follow the religious life, though it often prevented its realization. We have already seen how many difficulties were placed in the way of Indian women in early French and Spanish American colonies. At best, they were recruited as lay sisters or formed segregated communities for a few well-endowed aristocrats. In the United States, segregation laws frustrated Henriette Delille's dream of establishing a branch of integrated Ursulines in New Orleans. Sisters of Loretto formed an auxiliary community of black sisters in their Kentucky community in 1824, but local prejudice and possibly their own indifference allowed it to wither. Theresa Maxis and another sister from the black congregation Oblates of Providence founded the Immaculate Heart of Mary Sisters in Michigan in 1845. They made no issue of their race; indeed, they refused to recruit additional black sisters and expunged the memory of Maxis's racial background from their official history until recently.[18]

Meanwhile, a global society was forming, driven by the upsurge of European imperialism. Christian missions outside Europe, even in Latin America, had only limited success until the nineteenth century. Then, particularly after 1860, they prospered with the military protection or administrative assistance of European colonial powers. Despite the growth of secular liberalism, the apparent decline of religious observance among the laity, and even violence against religious orders at home, colonial powers supported missions as ideological complements to their economic and political programs. The right to open missions was inserted into trade or settlement treaties between European governments and foreign potentates. Missionaries often acted as explorers and other agents for colonial powers in Africa, Asia, and the Pacific. This double service of God and Mammon seemed compatible to people who equated "Western civilization" with "Christian civilization," an incontrovertible vehicle of charity and progress.

Women were universally seen as the major civilizing force, and sisters were often the first white women into a new field. Few in numbers, they stinted nothing to support westernizing movements against foot binding, suttee, genital mutilation, and other abuses to women. Maryknoll sisters urged the advantages of a "healthy happy life" exemplified by American Catholic women to Chinese women. Lorettans instructed them to cut their hair as well as to unbind their feet, appear in public, and claim equal educational rights with men. Sisters had no doubts that their mission was a boon to distressed women throughout the world. In 1843, Aglaée Hamonet, one of the first sisters to venture from Bona into the African mountains to care for poor Arab women, wrote: "If you could see them, you would know how lucky we are not to be born to that sect [Islam]."[19]

European troops brought sisters with them into the harshest posts as nurses. In 1832, a few Sisters of Saint Joseph of the Apparition accompanied French troops to Algeria, and in 1890 five nuns from South Africa accompanied the British Pioneer Column into Zimbabwe. Finally, Pius XI ordered all religious congregations, including contemplatives, to maintain missionary communities. Notre Dame des Missions, founded in Lyons by Euphrasia Barbier in 1861, spread to Oceania. In 1875, the Daughters of Wisdom went to Haiti; in 1876, the Sisters of Portieux to Indochina and Manchuria; in 1877, the nuns of Chaufailles, a small house from Autun, to Japan. In America, in 1878, Frances Warde established a Sisters of Mercy convent among the Indians in Maine. The Ursuline Amadeus worked tirelessly among the Cheyennes, even after the Jesuits gave up the mission. Though crippled in a train crash in 1905, she led her sisters to Alaska, where she made her rounds among remote Eskimo settlements until she died.

Their deployment reinforced the Vatican's ultramontane policies by ignoring the nationalist claims of the imperialist map, mixing personnel from several nations or sending congregations from one nation into territory administered by a different secular government. After the Civil War, Sisters of Saint Joseph arrived from Le Puy to evangelize and educate southern blacks in the dioceses of Saint Augustine and Savannah. The English Mill Hill Sisters also set up schools for blacks in Baltimore in the 1880s. The Mill Hill Sisters also established themselves in a variety of African sites regardless of European claims. Colonial authorities and European settlers frequently resented the presence of these "foreigners," particularly when Catholic missionaries were working in territories claimed by Protestant powers. During World War I, foreign missionaries were interned as enemy nationals, a fate that fell with particular weight upon German nuns, who staffed many of the Catholic missions around the globe. After the war, the victorious allies exiled the defeated Germans permanently.

Even after the United States was officially removed from the list of mission fields in 1908, American blacks and Indians continued to be listed among the "pagan nations." Reservations and segregated neighborhoods continued to be targeted by foreign as well as domestic missions, and the religious women they produced were rarely assigned to serve white communities. In the early twentieth century, with legislation pending in

Georgia that would have removed white sisters from black schools, Elizabeth Williams founded the Handmaids of Mary, a community of black sisters, to teach the black children. When the laws failed to pass, the Handmaids transferred their mission to New York's Harlem, where so many southern blacks were emigrating. Starting there with a day-care center for working mothers, they expanded their work among American blacks and in the West Indies.

Native populations had their own interests. The ambitious Ibos of Nigeria considered the English language a mark of status and forced out the French Josephites of Cluny despite their charity and care of the sick. The opportunity for modern professional education open to English speakers persuaded the Chinese to tolerate foreign missions. However, nationalist pride and the secularism that grew out of the revolution in 1911 made the Chinese government extremely hostile to the westernizing, particularly the Christianizing, ambitions of mission schools. Right up to the Japanese invasions, the government issued and enforced regulations to confine that aspect of missionary work. The problem of "foreign" missionaries figured in a different scenario in Asia during World War II, when missionaries were overtaken by advancing Japanese armies. Some survived appalling hardships but many were interned and died in prison camps. The Sisters of Notre Dame de Namur at Okagama, Japan, had two Japanese sisters under perpetual vows in 1939. They carried on the school when the eleven American sisters and one Irish sister were interned and provided the prisoners with what comfort they could. Back at the home base in Waltham, Massachusetts, the American sisters did the same for the Japanese novices interned in the United States during the war.

Often forced to cope with an alien European colony as well as the alien culture they had come to confront, missionary sisters strengthened the ties that bound them to their own world. They concretized the theology of the mystical body of Christ by a variety of devices. The Maryknoll sisters, founded for the China missions in 1917, sent diaries and letters back to the training schools and to the homes of lay supporters, while cloistered communities of retired nuns at the mother house supported them with their prayers. Cloistered Carmelites had long maintained links among houses in Europe, America, Asia, and Africa and cultivated a strong spiritual syneisactism with missionary priests. In 1894,

Thérèse asked for assignment to one of Lisieux's daughter houses in Saigon or Hanoi. When her accelerating illness frustrated the project, she joined her prayers to the active mission of a pair of priest-brothers in China: "if I go to Heaven soon, I shall ask Jesus' permission to visit you in Su-Chuen and we shall continue our apostolate together."[20]

Sisters of European descent volunteered to serve non-Europeans in America and the rest of the world as soon as women were admitted to the mission fields. In the late nineteenth century, the Catholic hierarchy began to recruit and train native clergy and religious women intended ultimately to assume leadership of the young, non-Western churches. In Asia and Africa, the native clergy overtook and in many areas outnumbered the European. By 1923, the 190 female religious missions were still staffed by about 13,000 sisters coming directly from the West, but they were supplemented by an uncounted number of native sisters. By 1915, when the German Salvatorians were forced to leave India, they left 5,176 Catholics and 1,700 catechumens to the care of a congregation of native sisters. The Salvatorians the Lorettans, the Missionary Catechists of Mary, and the Sisters of Notre Dame des Missions all had native communities. In 1922, the Daughters of Saint Francis of Assisi began in Zimbabwe with 9 native postulants. In 1926, the Dominicans received 5 girls who provided the core of an African congregation. In 1923, the Trinity Sisters formed for African widows who preferred not to undertake a second marriage, organized by the bishop and modeled on sisters already established in Uganda. By 1932, they provided the model for the Little Children of Our Blessed Lady, who gathered sisters from all the Zimbabwe dioceses into a national order of African sisters. In 1912, the Sisters of the Divine Savior in Raliang (Bangladesh) began a society of native mission sisters whose own house was blessed in January 1914. In 1925, nearly half of the Third Order Regular of Mary were indigenous sisters in the missions in Oceania.

Indigenous sisters far outnumbered indigenous brothers in a 1925 survey. There is evidence that the example of Western nuns who sacrificed family life for divine service resonated deeply in Asia, where Buddhist spirituality presented a precedent. Legend has it that women forced their way into Asian monastic orders despite the reluctance of the

Buddha to allow their potentially corrupting presence.[21] In China, Confucianist patriarchs successfully countered the threat, but the sentiment remained, to be revived by Christianity. Fourteen Carmels appeared in India between 1870 and 1964 and others sprang up in Southeast Asia and Japan. There has also been an expansion of the Cistercian orders, particularly in Japan and the Philippines, spreading in the 1920s and 1930s to Ceylon, Malaysia, Thailand, Vietnam, Borneo, China, and Korea. These have been female foundations with few or no brothers attached to their *cura*.

Non-Western sisters have tended to be excluded from missions beyond their own homelands. Where they have formed their own communities, they have been bound by diocesan ties, leaving integrated branches of Western congregations to employ the African and Asian nuns as local workers. In 1867, the Presentandines established the Helpers of Holy Souls, Chinese women from the working classes who continued to wear Chinese clothing and work among peasants in schools and dispensaries. The Sisters of Loretto also formed Chinese congregations on the principle that they should retain their own culture and not westernize. The founder of the Maryknoll sisters, Josephine Rogers, determined that they would live among their converts. They recruited Chinese diocesan congregations to carry on local missions, running schools, dispensaries, orphanages, and crafts training while the Americans went to new fields. Only a few Chinese women left their homes for other distant missions. Appropriate as such strategies are to the goal of establishing local churches, one may reasonably question their implications for the place of the non-Western religious in the church universal.

At least one international order has sprung out of the needs of the third world and has now taken up an evangelical mission in the West. Agnes Bojaxhiu, an Albanian, joined the Irish Lorettans and did her novitiate in Darjeeling. In 1946, after twenty years in Calcutta, she felt "a call within a call" to leave the relatively secure convent and live among the poor. She abandoned the Lorettan habit for a white and blue sari pinned with a crucifix and, as Mother Teresa, established the Missionaries of Charity to serve the homeless. Indian women joined her mission to save women and babies from abandonment. Their numbers grew and the archbishop of Calcutta secured them a mother house. They raised funds for a hospice for the dying, an orphanage, and a leper colony maintained with active government assistance. Today the order has grown strong enough to send missionaries among the poor in the United States, and Mother Teresa holds a Nobel Peace Prize.

These non-Western Catholics were being recruited into a universal ultramontane church transcending national boundaries. Leo XIII and his successors sought direct diplomatic ties with non-Christian governments. In the missions, everyone else was auxiliary to the priests. The hierarchy directing them began with the pope and descended through the *Propaganda Fidei* and other agencies directed by cardinals and the heads of the orders, congregations, and societies supporting them. In the field, apostolic delegates, vicars, prefects, and superiors of missions governed each territory with visitation rights and rights to audit accounts and inflict sanctions. In effect, a mission became a religious colony governed by an institutional representative, which Monsignor Constantini, apostolic delegate to China, criticized in 1925 as territorial feudalism. Every Catholic mission was an extension of the Roman church, following its universal forms and norms. Catholic schoolchildren were taught to imagine a world in which Asians, Africans, Latin Americans, Australian aborigines, and even Martians, if such were ever encountered, would all regularly intone the same Latin mass every Sunday morning. Seminaries imposed a standardized Latin-based education on converted Christians in Asia and Africa, spurning efforts to achieve some harmony with their own cultural heritage. A gathering of church dignitaries in twentieth-century Rome now boasts prelates from every race and clime, but despite many cosmetic changes since Vatican II, their career success testifies to rigorous adherence to the tradition and hierarchy that defines itself as the voice of eternal and unchangeable truth.

From Europe to Japan, this stability and uniformity have had their attractions, but they were forged out of a thousand culture wars. Sisters stood on the front lines and opposed their discipline, their adherence to their rules and obedience to their superiors, to the hostility or simple fractiousness of the people they served and hoped to change. In non-Catholic countries and colonies, the mission extended to the conversion of Protestants. Sisters frequently provided the only education available on the American frontier and did not hesitate to combine the practical service with a certain amount of proselytizing. Philippine Duchesne wrote often to Sophie Barat of her disappointment when Protestant parents withdrew "promising" daughters from her American Sacred Heart Academies. Cardinal Vaughn brought Brothers and Sisters of Charity from Ghent to run a series of orphanages in England to take Catholic children from the workhouses (and thus save them from Protestant influence). A Presbyterian minister in Wisconsin anathematized parents who sent their children to Catholic school and encouraged boys to throw snowballs when the sisters walked out for mass.

Feminists who saw nuns as the overly-effective agents of an "unenlightened" church urged their sisters to follow their example. Catharine Beecher called for Protestant women to take up teaching to counter the subversive influence of convent schools on girls. The success of sisters in converting grateful clients helped to spark the caretaking vocations of Protestant women. A southern lady running a Tennessee hospital noted that Protestant women were reluctant to tend the sick in hospitals unless they were under the protection of a male relative on the staff: "I wonder if the Sisters of Charity have brothers, surgeons in the hospitals where they go? It seems strange that they can do with honor what is wrong for Christian women to do."[22] Protestant women organized charities to "Americanize" Catholic immigrants by combining social services for women with evangelizing in settlement houses and home visitations. Sisters from Europe were determined not to be engulfed by the same hostile ideology they were fleeing. When the *Kulturkampf* resulted in the dissolution of all religious orders in Germany in 1875, Theresa Gerhardinger made plans to bring her School Sisters to the United States. But a short stay convinced her that she hated the "unbridled freedom of the American people." She found that "The children attend school only on a voluntary basis and want to be entertained and given candy rather than disciplined. The parents refuse to allow them to be punished. The children won't do homework and refuse to learn German. The girls wear short dresses or pants and cross their legs. They talk and gossip and pass notes about boys and want to eat and drink at all hours."[23] Gerhardinger returned to Germany but never stopped warning the American superior, Caroline Friess, against assimilation. A common religion could not heal the deep differences among the immigrants. German congregations resisted the recruitment of Irish sisters, condemning them as ill-bred and (perhaps worse) English speaking. Swiss Benedictines hesitated to join the American Congregation of Saint Scholastica descended from the German community of Eichstätt.

The needs of immigrant groups in America were largely answered by sisters from among their own ranks. In 1793, several hundred Haitians fled the revolution and arrived in Baltimore. The first black congregation in the United States emerged to serve them. In 1829, Elizabeth Lange with three other black women began the Oblate Sisters of Providence. Approved by Gregory XVI, they ran the Saint Francis Academy for the education of black children. Black girls from all over the United States, Canada, Latin America, and the Caribbean came to the school, which eventually expanded into several schools and an orphanage. The Oblate Sisters joined other nuns in caring for the sick during the cholera epidemic of 1832 despite insults and open prejudice from fellow Catholics. Landlords refused them quarters and donations were hard to come by. Initially supported by the Sulpician order, they were ordered to disband in 1843 and had to turn to domestic service and laundry work to survive until 1852, when the Redemptorist Fathers took them up.

After the Civil War, immigrants flooded American cities and groups of sisters came with them to serve their own people. Schools were set up to preserve the language and culture of the immigrant populations. Sisters of Mercy, originally founded by Catherine McAuley in 1831 in Ireland, established hospitals in Pittsburgh, Chicago, and San Francisco. Germans from Aachen under Frances Schervier opened the hospital of Saint Francis in New York and Saint Mary's in Ohio. The Sisters of Saint Francis Seraph of Perpetual Adoration, the Hospital Sisters of Saint Francis of Springfield, the Franciscan Sisters, and the Daughters of the Sacred Hearts of Jesus and Mary all established hospitals and schools in German districts. The Polish order of the Holy Family of Nazareth, established by Frances Siedliska in 1874, sent sisters to minister to the Polish Catholics of Chicago in 1885. In the same city, Josephine Dudzik organized the Sisters of Saint Francis of Blessed Kunegunda (1894) to operate a home for the elderly. The Polish Felician Sisters were among 90 missionary and immigrant-aid societies active on Ellis Island until World War I. Leo XIII diverted Francesca Cabrini from her original ambition to be a missionary in Asia in favor of the United States. She brought the Missionary Sisters of the Sacred Heart in 1889, and they added health care to their primary educational mission. Soon they were staffing the Columbus Hospital for Italian immigrants in New York, to which the Italian government—to ensure the care of its seamen—contributed heavily. The Marianites staffed a French hospital in New York and French Sisters of Charity of Saint Augustine immigrated to Cleveland. The Sisters of Saint Casimir opened a hospital in Chicago primarily for Lithuanians. By 1871, nuns were running at least 70 hospitals. From 1876 to 1906, 270 more were opened to satisfy the needs of new Italian and Slavic immigrants.

Immediate needs reinforced national prejudices. Despite the universalist commitments of Catholicism, the shortage of nuns to serve the vast needs of the church tended to distract them from many broad designs. Repeatedly, sisters who started out in search of a wilderness to tame and savages to convert found that they could not get past the vices of baptized Christians. Philippine Duchesne originally came to America in 1818 to evangelize the Indians. From New Orleans she and her companions set out for Saint Louis and then to Saint Charles, where they opened a school for poor children but found themselves cut off from the near-by Indians. Each new school she founded was soon filled with white pupils whose parents objected to her efforts to include Indian and black girls. White American missions among the blacks became more concentrated in 1888 with the formation of the Mission Helpers of Saint Joseph's Guild, who established a school for girls, and Margaret Murphy's Sisters of the Holy Ghost, who opened schools for blacks in Texas, Louisiana, and Mississippi. Katharine Drexel established the Sisters of the Blessed Sacrament for Indian and Colored People in 1891.

In Shillong (Assam), settlers resisted the inclusion of native converts in religious services (especially those held in their homes). Tea planters in India, among others, resented the loss of labor when missionaries sought to bring religious services to their employees. Even Protestants gladly patronized Catholic girls' schools and hospitals for whites while opposing any interracial endeavor. Even priests in Bengal criticized Cecilia Vetz for her insistence on giving priority to the poor, and in 1887 she moved her whole congregation to Simulia and established a separate mission to outcastes in the villages. As non-whites were marginalized from white settlements, the sisters were pressured to give them less time and attention. The South Dakota Presentation sisters formed some associations with the Indians and educated individual families, but the demands of the parochial system diverted their efforts. Blandina Segale actively defended of the Indians against white thieves but still devoted the bulk of her social work to white frontiersmen. The Carondelet Saint Josephs set out primarily to convert Indians and Protestants, but bishops soon monopolized their services to educate Catholics.

As long as whites in the colonies or in the United States kept themselves segregated, individuals or small communities had virtually no chance to combine services to more than one group. Despite their intention to work among native non-Christians, missionary sisters all too often ended up serving white settlers in America, Africa, Asia, and the Pacific Islands. There were rarely more than three or four sisters to establish a religious framework in the mission fields, and they could not work at all without the financial and logistical support of whites who, in turn, claimed entitlement to their nursing and teaching services. Moreover, the white colonists required spiritual services perhaps even more urgently than the natives. Thecla, the provincial superior of the Daughters of Christian Doctrine in Algeria, wrote about 1850 of the need to "regenerate the Europeans who flooded into this country seeking their fortune."[24] Thus, convents often became part of a segregated white colony in an alien culture rather than points of passage between the cultures.

At the pope's orders, nearly every congregation found a handful of sisters to devote to the missions, though recorded numbers suggest that they were not always eager to follow his directive.[25] Some sisters later described the demand as an imposition or as an opportunity to remove difficult sisters from their communities with little regard for their qualifications.[26] The sisters went or accepted the decision not to allow them to go with little recorded expression of their own opinions on the subject. They went into the missions as they went into the slums of Europe and America, to serve the poor and to convert them, not to be converted to alien ways. The tight binding of nuns to their communities, their silence, their enclosure, and their obedience sent them out among strange peoples and at the same time insulated them from the impact of foreign cultures. Echoing medieval apostolic ideals, the ancient image of

the leper once more became part of the common discourse of the
missionary effort. Metaphorically, it extended to the native populations
of the mission fields and even, in peculiar ways, to pockets of the diseased
or unruly poor in Western societies. The segregation of nuns from all
unnecessary contact with the secular world helped to disguise (perhaps
even from themselves) the distance that often existed between them and
their clients. Exile among strangers was for many the expression of
self-sacrifice, "offering up" psychological as well as physical suffering to
God, while striving to maintain the image of a lily unspotted by the dirt
in which it grows.

This distancing was at least in part a lesson drawn from earlier mission
experiences. Centuries ago, Roman Christianity and Germanic Christianity guided by Gregory the Great showed the way in adapting harmless
pagan customs to Christian beliefs. Jesuits in the early modern missions
to China, however, became so exquisitely attuned to Mandarin culture
that they almost lost themselves within its un-Christian urbanities. The
best missionaries tended to be people aflame with their own self-righteousness, whose religious sensibilities resisted the tendency toward syn-
chretism inherent in any conversionary situation. But such fanaticism
precipitated the closing of the Asian monarchies to Christian proselytizing. Modern missionaries still confronted the questions that first haunted
Paul and his contemporaries. Sisters in Japan, for example, had to ask
themselves where they could draw the line between showing respect for
the emperor by displaying his picture in a convent and seeming to accept
the principle of his divinity. Even the sense of a divine ordering of the
world was thus subject to debate. How much could Christian churches
take from other cultures and still remain Christian? How much respect
should they show to customs that are flatly contradictory to Christian
doctrine? Though white congregations were not immune to Western
racism, they supported colonialist policies that ignored non-Western race
and class prejudices. The Indian orders recruited untouchables and
thereby contributed to the breaking down of the caste system. Anne-
Marie Javouhey, founder of Saint Joseph de Cluny in 1812, became a
major force in the European fight against the slave trade from her
missions in Senegal and Guinea, but the African seminarians that she had
trained in Europe found their careers hampered by their fellow Africans'
lack of sympathy with their new egalitarian ideals.

The spreading social strains of modern times could not command an adequate response from colonial or native governments far too impoverished to provide extensive care to the abandoned, a role that sisters had filled for so long in Europe. Again, however, their resources were severely limited in the face of endless need. This strain encouraged the practice of setting up schools and hospitals as centers in a missionary enclave. The widespread method of establishing Christian villages in the African mission fields was spurred by the need to protect converts from the African slave trade. In the wake of plague and famine in Algeria, Cardinal Lavigerie took charge of 1,800 orphaned children whose upbringing he entrusted to the sisters in his own centers. Javouhey's Cluny sisters particularly devoted themselves to the fight against the trade and to baptizing abandoned children, old women, widows, and sick women.

Gradually, havens developed for freed slaves and orphans drew in other Christians. The creation of Catholic villages was encouraged among mountain people in India, who tended to move their villages around to be near their crops. Chapel-farms formed a nucleus for Christian villages trained in European agriculture and technical skills. Though the intentions of the missionaries were no doubt sound and their actions perhaps inescapable, the villages segregated native Christians from their own people. This quarantine of non-Western converts from their natural environment enforced a cultural and psychological stratification of the foreign missionaries and their clients. Since World War II and before in many areas, centralized mission stations have replaced the Christian villages. But the dialogues and debates of segregation and integration are far from over.

Some missionaries believed that the conversion of women would ensure conversion of a nation and therefore made special efforts to bring young women into their schools. Where purdah was practiced and only women could penetrate the zenanas, the church was eager to make use of sister missionaries. Mission directors welcomed those African and American Indian women who could refuse property and status to Christian converts because of strong matrilineal traditions. The typical approach was to bring children and women to schools where they were taught European domestic skills and needlework. In 1896, the Salvatorian sisters in Shellah (Bangladesh) led by Bernarda Reichl, began running orphanages and educating girls to provide wives for male converts because the Khasi matrilineal system had caused widowed fathers to leave motherless children to non-Catholic maternal kin. The sisters at Shillong (Assam) often paid for orphans who had been sold into debt slavery to non-Catholics.

In modern times, with increased knowledge and more tender sensibilities, the debate over inculturation has grown ever more introspective and tortuous. Insofar as European culture is a product of Christianity, how successfully can Christian principles be isolated from it? And how far can Western civilization be divorced from Western domination? Following Paul's advice to Jewish Christians, the apostolic delegate Paolo Marella urged missionaries in the 1930s to learn the language and culture of their prospective converts, to embrace foreign cultures even at the expense of losing their own, believing that only a gospel stripped to its essence can really penetrate into alien cultures.[27] But again it must be the missionary who decides what the essence is. Western Christians who take pride in certain achievements of their own culture (for example, the abolition of the slave trade, forced marriage, or genital mutilation) can hardly be expected to hold back from including those agenda in a missionary program.

An iron logic in the dynamics of conversion inevitably leads to culture war. The wish to change others inescapably denigrates their original condition. Converts of necessity will be those who wish to escape some intolerable condition in their lives. The conversion of women and the role of women in missions are no exceptions, even when the converting culture has set up the conditions from which the convert feels obliged to escape. American Indian mothers often resisted a strategy that would turn their daughters into foreigners, lacking the instruction of women who could fit them into their tribal places. European domestic skills were useless in their native environment. European manners, dress, and language set them apart, and eventually most of them were forced to live among whites as servants or among Christian natives on mission lands. Often only the implicit threat of the girls' vulnerability to white men broke the maternal resolve. The same story was repeated in Asia and Africa, where mothers sometimes cooperated to save their daughters from brutal husbands but condemned them to a marginal life among whites.

Outside the West, nearly every society depends upon the family to supply social services to its own members. Christianity contributed to the tendency of colonialism and its economic demands to pull established family systems apart. It opposed polygamy and paternal control of marriages, with unanticipated social costs. Women were often the most numerous and enthusiastic of converts because they had the least to lose in discarding their own cultures. Sisters sometimes provided a supportive climate within the mission for women to deal with hostile husbands. Scholastica Hopfenmueller, for example, wrote that even at some risk to her mission, she had to give shelter to a woman whose husband, a pagan priest, accused her of neglecting her work and beat her, finally threatening her with an ax.[28]

Mission authorities had mixed feelings. They naturally welcomed converts and took seriously their responsibilities for the poor and rejected. But Christian efforts at redeeming slaves and at founding Christian villages for the most depressed and cast off members of the community whom they converted degraded them in the eyes of native ruling classes. Ambitious men tended to despise Christianity as a religion for old women, unless a mission education seemed to open career paths for them. They thus shared the attitude of secular European men, like the colonial official in French New Orleans who remarked that only women, blacks, and the governor's entourage attended mass.[29] It is an old Christian tradition.

Perhaps the most painful and perplexing efforts at conversion are those directed toward change in one's own society. Black American communities resisted secular racism and sometimes had to deal also with the hierarchy's failure to provide material or even moral support. When the New Orleans diocese approved Henriette Delille's all-black Community of the Holy Family in 1842, it forbade the sisters to wear their habits in public. They established a school for free girls of color and ran a hospice for the sick and an orphanage, but secular law frustrated their attempt to extend their educational services to slave children. Secular protests ended the efforts of the Sisters of Our Lady of Mercy and the Sisters of Saint Joseph to run schools for blacks before the Civil War. In 1866, the second plenary council of bishops in the United States decreed that the church should put its energy into the religious care and instruction of freed slaves, "which they so much stand in need of."[30] However, hostile lay patrons blocked the funding of integrated schools in the South and forced blacks into segregated communities in the North as well as in the South. In the West, Theresa Gerhardinger remarked that the "colored sisters'" school was even more impoverished than hers. At best, a few groups made a virtue of necessity. The Springfield Dominicans used the segregation of their hospital in Jackson Mississippi in 1940 to further the professional development of black employees. The Franciscan Tertiaries in Los Angeles used their segregated nursing home as a source of medical supplies for home visits to blacks. When the Olivetan Benedictines admitted black victims of a quarry disaster to their hospital in Jonesboro, Arkansas, however, all but one of the doctors resigned.

Even where no laws interfered, integration was slow. Blacks did not provide a large base of recruits for the religious life at any time, and the problems of cultural differences often alienated them within the convent. Sister of Mercy Martin de Porres was the first black woman to be accepted in a community that had rejected another applicant only two years earlier on racial grounds. After some years of trying to cope with racism as a personal cross to bear, she determined upon a more systematic approach. A survey revealed that few congregations in the United States had black sisters and that many had "lost" them during the novitiate. The pain and conflict behind those losses are all too apparent in her own account of her long apostolate for better racial understanding among her own sisters.[31] Racial prejudice could not have been ameliorated by pronounced behavioral differences in the tight and intimate conditions of the novitiate. The inherent process of homogenization applied to novices to fit them into the mold of self-denial that characterized convent life must have made the ordeal of community especially onerous for anyone who began community life with marked cultural differences from the other sisters.

Nevertheless, many congregations began to move toward integration by the middle of the century. An early champion of integrating Catholic higher education, Grace Dammann, president of Manhattanville College, answered her critics in a class-day address in 1938 that her admission of "a Catholic colored girl who meets the requirements of a Catholic college and applies for a Catholic education" was no more than her duty. She concluded, "The day has gone by when we Catholics can blithely live as compartmental Catholics, with our political, business, intellectual, social activities in an air-tight compartment functioning separately like parts of a well behaved machine. Catholicism is nothing if it is not a life, unified, coordinated to its end."[32]

In 1968, Sister Martin de Porres founded the Black Sisters Conference with over six hundred members. The largest contingent came, as might be expected, from the Sisters of the Blessed Sacrament, a congregation founded specifically to work among blacks and American Indians. The conference has steadily grown as sisters, like other Americans, have wrestled with new and broader perspectives on the world they live in. When Marie Dennis, the first black sister of Notre Dame de Namur, was assigned to teach math and science in Columbus, Ohio, in 1966, a cross was burned in front of the convent. The mother superior reacted effectively by threatening to expel any students who participated in an impending boycott. Both black and white nuns joined in the civil rights protests of the 1960s, and Judith, a white sister of the Blessed Sacraments, came to feel that the experience of being pulled by white men from an integrated bus consolidated her sense of sisterhood. Some black women simply dismiss white sisterhoods as irrelevant to their experience and others see conversion as a betrayal of black identity. But some remain anxious to claim their share of an experience that has empowered so many women for so long.

The last and most terrible of the culture wars is a *psychomachia,* the struggle within the secret soul itself. Religious women have always been inured to self-mortification, to sacrificing their own comfort to serve others. There has never been a shortage of heroines ready to embrace lepers in the name of Christ. But this very concept of self-sacrifice depends on a firm sense of difference between the saint and the leper. The great confinement has ended, at least for the moment. Nuns have emerged from their cloisters as the poor they served have emerged from the ghettos and the asylums where they were kept silent. Nineteenth-century labor movements, socialist politics, and the whole anticolonial and antiracist movement have forced an awakening to a world in which the poor do not bless their benefactors and the representatives of other cultures do not admit their inferiority. That is rude indeed.

Discarding habits and, often, common housing after the Second Vatican Council, sisters sought to redefine their vocations, exposing themselves physically and spiritually to the world around them. As they reduced the distance between themselves and the poor they served, setting up community groups and cooperative associations, they encountered the criticism and even unfairness of their clients. The old image of the "good sister," which had nourished their self-esteem, all too often collapsed before the counterimage of a condescending and unsympathetic stranger. The sense of spiritual superiority, which rewarded their sacrifices, fitted badly with the concept of entitlements developing in secular democracies. In recent years, literary speculation on the sex lives of nuns has given way to harsh criticisms of the education they once provided at such sacrifice to themselves. The crisis of conscience precipitated by these challenges has driven many women from their vocations and prevented many others from following a path rudely stripped of its mystique.

The battleground of the culture wars has largely been within the hearts and minds of all the participants, especially the extraordinary women who have pressed forward along the social and spiritual frontiers. Pursuing a two-thousand-year-old vocation, they have been among the first to deal with the problems of unity amid diversity that continue to beset our shrinking world.

Wars are not for the faint-hearted, and in battle she who hesitates is lost. Mistakes are made and even in victory friends are not always appropriately grateful. As representatives of an ancient and powerful church, sisters have represented a ruling hierarchy, sometimes perhaps masking harsh realities with soft charity. As members of silenced and oppressed classes and races, and a universally dominated gender, they have come forward to make their own claims in a clashing world. Through the nineteenth and into the twentieth centuries, they have systematically pursued their ancient mission of enlarging the vocational spaces belonging to women. In an age of emerging feminism, their voices were often drowned out by the more spectacular anthems of secular women, but no one who looks at the firm, steady advance of the sisters in those years can doubt that it is they who laid the foundation upon which the rest of us have built.

20

:✦:

The Feminine Apostolate

"MORE THAN EVER, the hope of salvation will be in the weaker sex. The men of our time are becoming women; transformed by faith, the women can become men."[1] The Terror had barely subsided but Madeleine Sophie Barat boldly adopted the badge of the Sacred Heart for her new community, to be devoted to the Christian education of women. In 1818, the Religious of the Sacred Heart sent their first mission to America under Philippine Duchesne. Barat bade them teach the girls of the New World to become "real women . . . (through) the full and harmonious development of their faculties, Christian women who shall be well informed and influential for good."[2]

Secularism complemented the democratic, capitalist, and scientific values increasingly identified with a masculine public sphere. In contrast, nineteenth-century women turned to the creation of a separate sphere, conceptualized as an outgrowth of the domestic realm. They used the idea of feminine virtues, drawn from the biological and psychological construct of wifehood and motherhood, to claim a voice in public policy. Religion became feminized in Protestant as well as Catholic societies, restoring a measure of authority and activity to women through a broad concept of social housekeeping that would eventually justify their demand for suffrage. The old image of feminine virility was transformed and ultimately discarded; nineteenth-century woman emerged fully conceptualized, claiming a sphere of her own. Finding their own voices, women developed the "cult of true womanhood" in novels, hymns, and poetry. This image enabled them to assert the claims of women within the church and society as a whole. The power of sweet virtue, the impenetrable shield of purity, and the invincible sword of moral rectitude armed the "good woman."

Adam Smith's masculine gospel of enlightened self-interest was balanced from the start by a feminine ideal of self-sacrificing women. Radical restructuring brought the ancient work of charity into conformity with the ideology of separate spheres. Under the Old Regime, the education and care of the poor had generally been delegated to religion. Established churches administered a vast array of institutions from old endowments and current alms. As we have seen, women did much of the administrative and physical labor, while funding and supervision usually came from men. Against the challenge of the Enlightenment, charity as a religious vocation took on new vigor. The pope himself, with the bull *Quamvis Justo* (1749), encouraged women taking simple vows under episcopal and parochial supervision to regard the Virgin Mary as a model for the active life. In 1748, with the first relaxation of the penal laws, Nano Nagle returned home to Ireland from a French convent to open a school for the poor, combining basic education with occupational training for boys as well as girls. Despite continuing legal restrictions and the disapproval of her parish priest, she lived and moved about the streets alone. Gradually other women joined her, forming the nucleus of the Presentation sisters.

With the disestablishment of the church, the property that sustained its educational and charitable apparatus vanished and the authority that assured its continuity collapsed. But the need for those services was stronger than ever. Nuns, Tertiaries, and secular women moved to the rescue. Even while French armies were suppressing old monasteries, communities under simple vows maintained their hospitals and asylums. They were soon supplemented by decloistered nuns and lay women. Charlotte Dupin was a priest's servant jailed during the Terror. After her release, she collected food, medicine, and other things for female prisoners in Lyons. When she died in 1805, about fifty "Charlottes" carried on the work. By 1811, they were distributing soup daily to about four thousand prisoners of both sexes.

The Napoleonic Concordat set a model for many modern governments. The church received modest compensation for its lost property and many buildings were restored. The papal legate Cardinal Caprara adjusted monastic vows for nuns who swore allegiance to the government, gave up their habits and their cloisters, and undertook to support themselves. The secular state even agreed to pay salaries to women religious who made themselves "useful" through their traditional activities of teaching and nursing.

As they freed themselves from a badly defined limbo between clergy and laity, women religious moved into the very center of religious public life. Even secular men who viewed religion as feminine, sentimental, and trivial relied on women to socialize virtuous citizens and care for the victims of unbridled industrial development. No longer recognizable as nuns in the traditional sense, many religious came to call themselves "sisters," while their superiors gave up the old aristocratic titles in favor of "Mother." The educational mission turned even contemplatives back to the ancient missionary tradition in which they were formed. As the century progressed, these vocations were transformed into professions, professions created by women and stamped with a peculiarly feminine character that betrayed their religious origins. Strengthened by their new prominence in the world at large, they were more articulate in expressing their own goals and convictions than they had been in the established churches of the *ancien régime*.

The boundary between the secular and the ecclesiastical established by the modern state disrupted the church's boundary between clergy and laity. Since the democratic revolution, priests have found themselves identified with an institution stereotyped as superstitious, undemocratic, and, increasingly, feminine. They could not prevent a popular perception of all habited personnel as "clergy." Sometimes reluctantly, sometimes enthusiastically, they moved toward a more syneisactic working relationship. After the French Revolution, the archbishop of Lyons wrote to Mother Saint-Jean Fontbonne: "We must have apostles for the children and the mothers of families and the aged, for everyone; the church is in need; the priesthood is too meager; follow St. Joseph and become the auxiliaries of the clergy."[3]

The embattled church of the nineteenth and early twentieth centuries was thus inclined to enfold nuns into the clerical population while rigorously maintaining their exclusion from the male priesthood. Religious women have been accorded most of the privileges and all of the penalties that the modern state reserves for the clergy. The hierarchy expects to dispose of their services and their resources as freely as it disposes of ordained personnel. The problems arising over their organization and jurisdiction mirror the problems of a church torn between local autonomy and international unity, conservative religion and progressive social action. Responding to her bishop's call for apostles, Fontbonne united forty-five informal charitable communities from villages in the diocese of Lyons under the aegis of Saint Joseph. When Louise Juliand decided to regularize the Charlottes, she adopted the same formula. This grouping of disparate communities into congregations became the institutional form that governed thousands of women in Europe, in America, and ultimately in the worldwide mission fields.

A congregation usually consisted of a number of small communities growing up in a single locality. A common novitiate in a common mother house formed their charism, that spiritual and vocational character that expressed itself outwardly in tailored devotional practices. A superior general coordinated a rule of life for all houses, which would enshrine their aspirations and guarantee their continuity. Victorine Barbin of the Good Shepherd, a reasonably typical founder, started with a group of independent village communities in Auvergne. She required locally recruited girls to be formed in a common novitiate at the mother house. She cultivated their families and friends and centralized deployment of their dowries. She regularly visited each house (sometimes without notification) and encouraged individual nuns to help her maintain extensive notes on individual characters and on feuds or tensions within the communities. Thus, the congregation developed a flexible and united sisterhood from a disparate set of local ties.

The local alliances and flexible service that contributed to their success often contradicted a congregation's expansionist ambitions while fostering commitment to a single charism. National boundaries often caused jurisdictional cleavages. Nevertheless, some congregations developed internationally. In 1873, three of the largest in England were French: the Sisters of Charity, the Little Sisters of the Poor, and the Faithful Companions of Jesus. Cornelia Connelly established the Sisters of the Holy Child Jesus in England, which expanded to her native America.

French congregations expanded into Belgium. Indeed, conflicts with an aggressive abbot drove Julie Biliart to transfer the Sisters of Notre Dame from France to Namur. Maria Theresia Scherer's Swiss Sisters of the Holy Cross provided social and educational services in industrial towns throughout central Europe. The Society of the Sacred Heart established a novitiate in America maintaining obedience to Sophie Barat in France, who furnished recruits. The American houses offered refuge when political turmoil threatened the French houses. As the nineteenth century progressed, some other congregations in North and South America maintained similar ties with their European sisters. The Sisters of Mercy preserved their union with the American missions through a constant stream of new recruits sent out from the mother country. Their worldwide expansion has been marked by a constant tension between the autonomy of single communities or diocesan groups and the sense of union intrinsic to their charism. By contrast, Elizabeth Seton, who introduced the rule of the Daughters of Charity to the United States resisted affiliation with the French congregation as long as she lived, though eventually the union was accomplished. Similarly, she did not seek to extend her authority over the Sisters of Charity of Nazareth, founded in Kentucky by Catherine Spalding, beyond sharing a copy of the rule and a translation of Vincent de Paul's *Conferences.*

Congregations sending missionaries from Europe fissioned institutionally while sharing common customs. Hyacinth Le Coniat's letters reveal the continuing problem of making the Daughters of the Cross in France understand conditions in Louisiana. They sent recruits too old or unqualified for the mission. They refused to lend her money or to let her borrow money in America to build suitable quarters. She complained about the failure of the mother house in Brittany to send annuity payments, and the two superiors continually haggled over the expenses of recruits from France.[4] The two communities finally separated but Le Coniat protected her buildings by flying the French flag during the Civil War.

Sometimes attachment to a European tradition was purely sentimental. Teresa Lalor, an Irish immigrant, opened a small school in Baltimore loosely connected to a convent of Poor Clare refugees who eventually went home to France. Inspired by a copy of the Visitandine rule she found in their discarded library, she organized the Georgetown nuns of the Visitation. The mother house at Annecy had yet to be refounded in the wake of the revolution and no other community would adopt an American house without a trained novice mistress. Lalor persisted and obtained papal approval to establish her house independently. As sisterhoods took root in the United States, however, their perception of themselves as American as well as the active intervention of the American clergy tended to cut them off from European ties.

The popularity of sisters as educational and charitable workers only increased conflict over their jurisdiction. In 1822, Angela Sansbury established a Dominican Tertiary mother house in Kentucky attached to a friendly friary. The original director, however, was replaced by a Spanish Dominican who neither appreciated the sisters' teaching mission nor approved of their uncloistered life in America. Refusing to honor the loan the former prior had guaranteed, he got an order from the bishop that they sell up, pay the debt, and dissolve the community. When they resisted on the grounds that they had approval from Rome, he deprived them of the sacraments in their own chapel, forcing them to attend the distant parish church. The bishop was no help. Without consulting the sisters, he tried to transfer them individually to Ohio parishes under his jurisdiction. The sisters vowed to pay the debt themselves and refused to disperse. They sold everything moveable and lived on the barest necessities until the arrival of a new prior. In 1830, they expanded to a new mother house in Ohio.

The Benedictine mission that began with such high hopes floundered with the open breach between Abbot Wimmer and Benedicta Riepp over the disposal of monetary donations and jurisdiction over the sisters. When Willibalda Scherbauer, founder of a daughter house at Saint Cloud, Minnesota, accused him of withholding money contributed by the king of Bavaria to the sisters, Wimmer wrote the king that he had mistakenly donated his money to a "group of undisciplined and adventurous nuns."[5] The founder of the men's college of Notre Dame did get control of the finances of the Sisters of the Holy Cross, which cost them their schools.

In Europe, most congregations were encapsulated within the ecclesiastical structure, grouped under a superior general at the diocesan level.

The medieval association of female communities with bishops adapted easily to a modern context of local needs and familial ties. In America, new dioceses were being organized simultaneously with the appearance or founding of congregations. It was not always clear who employed the sisters. Women of one congregation were often called to replace sisters favored by a former pastor. German clergy tried to discipline the Irish Sisters of Mercy, led by the strong-willed Austin Carroll, by cutting and then eliminating their salaries. She enlisted the support of an Irish bishop in appealing to Rome, but the pope did not exonerate her until after her death.

In 1847, Theresa Gerhardinger with Caroline Friess and three other School Sisters of Notre Dame from Germany answered the Redemptorists' request for nuns to teach the children of German immigrants in newly established parishes. The School Sisters replaced the Mercies in Philadelphia, but Gerhardinger forbade them to recruit locally because she wanted to avoid dealing with the archbishop until she could present their rule to him as approved by the bishop of Munich. Years later, however, when Friess had become thoroughly Americanized, she complained of the German tie.

Unlike nuns of earlier centuries, nineteenth-century sisters could make space in a widening world to develop their own visions. The Sisters of Mercy have always placed union at the center of the charism handed down by Catherine McAuley, as they state in their most recent governance plan. When they conflicted with their superiors, they moved or appealed to lay or papal supporters. Many sisters had sufficient worldly experience to use the tension produced by ultramontanism to widen their autonomy. They often secured an exemption from episcopal authority by trying to attach the congregation directly to Rome. Refugee French and Italian nuns established independent congregations in England under Cardinal Wiseman's patronage. The American Sisters of Saint Benedict transferred to pontifical jurisdiction. Mother superiors guided one another in seeking papal approval despite the hostility of the bishops. The Dominican Hyacintha of Racine, Wisconsin, wrote Pia of San Jose urging her to follow that road: "If a congregation is not recognized by Rome it is simply an episcopal association and depends in every respect upon the bishop of the diocese, who has full charge of the sisters and who can act at will in their regard."[6] Bishops, of course, understood full well what they were trying to do. The bishop of Wichita ruthlessly tried to wrest jurisdiction over the Sisters of the Sorrowful Mother from Rome, and Bishop England of Charleston refused to write to Rome for approbation of his rule for the Sisters of Our Lady of Mercy in 1829 because "I do not wish to make my institutions dependent upon superiors over whom I have neither control or influence."[7]

Thus, the development of international congregations ran athwart diocesan authority. Most American bishops followed Bishop Carroll's lead. In a letter of 1811, he urged Elizabeth Seton not to seek institutional affiliation with the French Daughters of Charity but to form an American sisterhood attached to American life. He further urged her congregation to control its own internal affairs and refuse ties to male communities. This course would leave them solely under episcopal authority. The Bishop of Saint Augustine, Florida, expressed the episcopal attitude: "I believe I see a necessity to have only sisters who are entirely diocesan, sisters who obey the Bishop of the Diocese."[8] Theodore Guérin, a French Sister of Providence, in 1840 established Saint Mary's-in-the-Woods at an Indiana farm. When she went to France in a vain attempt to maintain ties with the mother house, the bishop deposed her and refused to approve her new rule. Her continued efforts to assure the continuity of her institute provoked the bishop of Vincennes to denounce her as rebellious and ultimately to excommunicate her and try to expel her from her own community, writing: "To oppose the bishop was to revolt against God himself." Guérin was preparing to move her congregation to Detroit when the bishop was replaced.[9]

Most European congregations tended to lose the sisters assigned to missionary bishops. The Saint Josephs of Lyons sent communities to America and Australia, which used Fontbonne's customs, and the seven sisters who settled in 1836 at Carondelet in the diocese of Saint Louis viewed themselves as members of the Lyons congregation. As they expanded widely in the United States and Canada, their American superior, Celestine Pommerel, appointed the officers of their new communities, sent fresh recruits, and coordinated their activities. After her death in 1857, they attempted to give constitutional expression to this unity. American and Canadian bishops opposed the move vigorously.

Most Saint Josephs were transformed into independent diocesan congregations with only Albany and Saint Paul remaining attached to Carondelet. Whether the sisters or the bishops engineered the change is still disputed. A number of sisters transferred to these houses or otherwise registered protests against the "new rule."

The absence of state control gave the sisters broader opportunities to react to abusive church authorities. A number of them had a history of transfers, drifting from one diocese to another because of personality conflicts with their bishops. Since sisters generally did not take permanent vows, and indeed no women religious did so in the United States, they could also move from one community to another with relative ease or split off to found new congregations. The Sisters of Charity of Nazareth early established a pattern in maintaining a friendly relationship without a jurisdictional tie to Seton's Emmitsburg sisters. They split in turn when a group of the sisters withdrew to Kansas to escape the tyranny of the bishop of Nashville. Often they did not own the schools and charitable institutions they founded and staffed with hard labor and self-sacrifice and might lose them in a quarrel with the ecclesiastical or secular authorities who did. Frances Warde, who introduced the Sisters of Mercy to America, constantly struggled with bishops to preserve the unity of the congregation and defend its schools and hospitals in the dioceses of Pittsburgh, Philadelphia, Chicago, Cincinnati, and Maine against episcopal greed. Only rare heiresses like the Americans Katharine Drexel and Margaret Mary Healy-Murphy could emulate medieval canonesses and found their own orders, directing their money solely for the mission to black and Indian converts.

Women have also formed independent congregations either because they could not integrate or because they did not want to. Henriette Delille embraced this alternative for free women of color in Louisiana. After the American Civil War legal or de facto segregation shaped the vocations of many black women to devote themselves to an educational mission to their own people. The Oblate Sisters of Providence and the Sisters of the Holy Family, for example, ran black parish schools serving a majority of non-Catholic black pupils. Like so many of their constituents, the Handmaids of Mary, founded in Savannah by Elizabeth B. Williams, moved to Harlem in the 1920s. Catherine Sacred White Buffalo's Indian Congregation of American Sisters served as nurses in the

Spanish-American War. In western Kenya, African sisters took the initiative and formed their own novitiate as lay sisters guided by missionary priests. Lacking the canonical requirements for training by an established sisterhood, many of them were lost while others heroically withstood family pressures and loss of dowry. When the Mill Hill Sisters arrived to train them, the mature personalities of the novices clashed with the doctrines of humility and docility inculcated in the rule. The two groups eventually reached accommodations, however, and the sisterhoods expanded.

The First Vatican Council deprived most congregations of the flexibility to balance papal authority against episcopal authority. For the first time since the Gregorian revolution, the hierarchy began to treat women religious as at least auxiliary to the clerical elite, marking them off in a variety of ways from the rest of the laity. But even in the missions their subaltern status was confirmed by the reservation of the term "missionary" to ordained priests. Pius IX established a Committee on the Status of Regulars to reform established orders and organize autonomous houses into congregations under superiors appointed or approved by Rome. New congregations, especially of women, were subjected to the Roman Congregation of Bishops and Regulars, which aimed to fit their statutes into a common mold, often with little regard for their initial charism. The rule negotiated by Rome for the Cincinnati Daughters of Charity all but obliterated their historical link to Seton and diffused the tight linking of their lives and vocations to charity. A series of bulls distinguished sisters in simple vows from the traditional nun. At the same time, however, they tried to make their living patterns conform more closely. In 1869, the bull *Apostolicae Sedis* adjusted ancient regulations on enclosure to accommodate the need of teachers and nurses to perform their accustomed services. In 1889, Rome refused recognition to sisters who did not live in common and wear a habit.

In periods of stress, when clergymen were lacking or indifferent to some populations, sisterhoods formed to fill the needs in their own communities. Black sisterhoods in the United States responded to the needs of children for education and of the sick for care. Women made up a high percentage of the secret church that survived the closing of Japan, and they regularly performed its single sacrament, baptism. When the Jesuits returned to China after the treaty of 1842, the church of

Nanking under the leadership of a widow, Hou Ta-juan, numbered about 320,000. The Chinese Virgins, paired with catechists, had carried on the baptismal instruction entrusted to them since the seventeenth century. They even helped prepare candidates for priesthood, and during nineteenth-century persecutions they managed the local affairs of many churches and supported the scattered itinerant clergy.

The mere existence of the Chinese Virgins challenged traditional family-centered ideals and the church regulated them carefully: they could take simple vows for limited periods only after they were twenty-four years old. They could not wear a religious garb. They usually lived with their families and sometimes attended segregated religious gatherings. The instructions of the Propaganda emphasized that they could never preach or teach where men were present. The Chinese Virgins refused to yield their activities to the Jesuits until 1883, when the Propaganda ordered them to enter religious communities of European sisters "more easily to borrow the rules and advantages of the life of sanctity."[10]

Recruits in the mission fields were absorbed into Western congregations wherever possible. But a lack of sisters from Europe or America to train novices in disciplines conformable to Vatican prescriptions kept many recruits waiting for approval. The difficulty of assimilating black sisters in a French congregation serving an American school in the West Indies in the twenties was solved by sending them to a French novitiate. Thus, although the new sisters could pursue the religious life, their uniquely important contribution to the continuation and growth of the West Indian mission was lost. In the 1920s, Congolese women who made application to the Sisters of Notre Dame de Namur had to wait a decade before overcoming the objections of the Jesuit bishop of Zaire. Greed for dowry money in Africa and in India stiffened familial resistance to the loss of prospective brides. In Kenya, 30 prospective sisters waited more than a decade for episcopal approval, subsisting from their garden produce. The first superior, Teresa Nyambara, finally demanded direct payment of their teaching salaries, which had been going into general mission funds. With the monies, she financed their training in England and established a novitiate. Her congregation was 148 sisters strong before she died in 1988. Similarly, while Jamaican women in Kingston waited nearly ten years, until 1890, when the Sisters of Mercy of

Bermondsey sent 5 nuns and a novice to train them, they established an orphanage and expanded to industrial, primary and basic schools, a commercial school, and an academy. The founder of the first native Puerto Rican congregation in 1940 ran a religious goods shop from which she formed a network of charity workers in various parishes that received recognition only after attracting a wealthy patroness.

While the missionary clergy welcomed practical assistance, it had the same difficulties with the *cura* that have always plagued men who tend to trivialize women's aspirations. The priesthood was attempting to convert populations throughout the world where one form or another of the patriarchal family dominated. While they recognized the value of the sisters as coworkers, clerics wanted to limit the areas in which the religion they offered seemed to insult the established order of the prospective convert. Even within Catholicism, as we have seen repeatedly, the place of the consecrated unmarried woman was never uncontested. The ardent response of women throughout the world to the appeal of virginity arose from the desires for freedom and a wider range of opportunities that moved their long dead sisters in the West. Clerics, as always, were reluctant to disturb established marriage customs and challenge the authority of fathers over their daughters for the sake of gratifying female vocations. But when pressed, they could hardly deny the claims of religion.

The alternative of a celibate life in sisterhood serving God and the poor was gradually established in most twentieth-century societies. The Sisters of Saint Joseph de Cluny serving in North Africa, West Africa, Portuguese Congo, Madagascar, Seychelles, Hindustan, New Caledonia, Tahiti, the Marchesas, Fiji, and the Cook Islands eagerly recruited native sisters as Tertiaries, utilizing an ancient method of consecrating women without the formality of the novitiate. Marie de la Croix in 1874 brought three Tertiaries into her community, giving them a habit adapted from local dress:

> It is fresh, original and magnificent, simple and right for the country. Imagine our three black daughters with their heads bare and their hair forming a black halo around their black faces, a long floating dress in the fashion of the country but held at the waist by a belt with long sleeves and buttoned to the wrist (it is strange that all dresses among the blacks have short sleeves). They wear a bib like ours but similar to the dress;

our little white collar with blue cord and the medallion of the third order. This is the costume, all blue, the blue of the society.[11]

The congregation came close to capturing that elusive chimera, an order founded and administered by women. As secular women wrestled with the conflicting claims of family and society, sisters in religion experienced an ongoing ideological conflict between the humility and obedience expected of daughters of the church and the independence and authority of activists within the women's sphere, sometimes far in advance of their secular contemporaries. Their feminine culture conflicted with a masculine culture of authority and obedience. Nuns were doubly vulnerable to the enforcers of the traditional gender system because of the continuing difficulty of defining the virgin. Nineteenth-century women activists did not employ the imagery of virility. They preferred a more assertive conception of the virtues associated with womanhood. Unmarried women might aim to be sexless but never genderless. Thus, the first Zairian nuns fitted comfortably into the Western notion of the feminine sphere when they countered the men who jeered at them as "sterilized cows, barren women," by presenting themselves as spiritual mothers, addressed as Mama.

Many sisters felt themselves to be privileged in their freedom from marital authority, but they did not question the authority itself. The contradictions of the whole concept were dramatically illustrated when Cornelia Connelly's husband, who had separated from her to become a priest, attempted to pose as the founder of her community with power to administer her rule. When she successfully resisted, he enlisted an English court to retract the annulment of their marriage and got custody of her children. Nineteenth-century feminists knew all too clearly how abusive marriage could be and how much pain motherhood might bring with it. But the age did not produce a new Jerome to praise the power of virginity. Consecrated women were too deeply committed to the ideology of brides of Christ and mothers of his children. Clergymen all too willingly pushed their sisters/daughters into the roles fashioned for Victorian womanhood. Indeed, they were trained to regard nuns in their charge as childlike and deficient in judgment. Leo XIII himself, in 1896, used the ideology of separate spheres to keep women from ordination: "Woman is by divine council and decree of holy church formally

excluded from what directly regards the Adorable Body of Christ."
Though having "no part in the act by which, enveloped in a mysterious
cloud of faith and love, the Man-God daily renews the divine holocaust
of Calvary upon the cross," women were offered association with the
clergy through the preparation of the vestments, linens, and implements
of the sacrifice.[12]

The clergy treated them as glorified housekeepers, virtually volunteering their womanly talents to bring up a new generation of believers.
Rome set the pace by employing a congregation of sisters as housekeepers in the Vatican. Archbishop Corrigan of New York recruited nuns to
keep house at Dunwoodie Seminary because he imagined that men were
incapable of keeping things clean. Margaret Hallahan combined the jobs
of housekeeper to the bishop, sacristan, and head of the primary school
for girls at the Benedictine mission in Coventry, as though teaching were
simply an extension of her domestic responsibilities. The founder of
Notre Dame in Indiana diverted the assets of Angela Gillespie's Academy of the Sisters of the Holy Cross to his college and ordered the nuns
to supply it with domestics, which they successfully resisted. The bishop
of Dubuque demanded that the Sisters of the Blessed Virgin Mary work
as housekeepers, despite their objections to being exposed to sexual
harassment from a priest. In 1906, the sisters in the Zairian mission did
all the washing, ironing, and mending and sewing for the priests and
brothers. The community life of elementary school teachers was tightly
organized around the pastor. In her autobiography, Margaret Ann Cusack
recalled that the visiting priest of Kenmare habitually monopolized the
conversation during the nuns' recreation hour and spent hours in the
convent parlor expecting the sisters to bathe his sore feet and massage
them.

By implication, nuns were being realigned as subalterns at the lower
ranks of the clergy rather than being placed at the elite peak of the laity.
By the twentieth century, Rome was taking women religious more
seriously and spending more effort to define their position. The result
was a virtual ice age. In 1900, Leo XIII's *Conditae a Christo* recognized
active sisters as "real religious" despite their lack of cloister and solemn
vows. Episcopal control of the foundation and finances of congregations
of diocesan right was strengthened. The *Normae* of 1901 standardized
sisters' internal organization by imposing partial cloister and prohibited

them from going out alone. In 1906, Pius X established the Sacred Congregation for Religious with supervisory powers over congregations that had escaped diocesan control by direct ties to Rome. All religious communities were commanded to revise their constitutions to conform to the details of convent life prescribed in the new canon law code of 1917. The Cold War reinforced the church's siege mentality. In 1950, with the bull *Sponsa Christi* Pius XII again strengthened the rules of cloister as strictly as possible for active sisters.

Vocational conflict was probably one of the impelling motives for this repression. The need and desire for sisters to teach and care for the sick ensured them a welcome everywhere. But bishops and parish priests were not inclined to view this work as professional. Indeed, they tended to see it as a voluntary expression of natural womanly instincts. They did not refrain from employing rather unscrupulous tactics to get the most labor for the least money. Caroline Friess complained that new immigrants (whom she called "Bismarkerinnen," victims of the iron chancellor's anticlerical policies) were undercutting her School Sisters by their willingness to teach boys as well as girls and sometimes to throw in an infirmary at no extra cost.[13]

Of the many causes of friction perhaps the most common was clerical disapproval of sisters' devotion to a specifically feminine apostolate. Reformers gradually came to understand that middle-class morality, the virtue that shielded women against male vice, was not readily available to lower-class women. Nuns actively promoted a sexual ethic more favorable to women and more restrictive to men, attacking the double standard, prostitution, and drunkenness. Above all, they sought to avoid fixing the blame on women. In 1826, two free women of color, Henriette Delille and Juliette Gaudin, established the Holy Family Sisters as a religious alternative to the New Orleans tradition of quadroon courtesans. They urged their sisters to marry respectable, if poor, black men or to join the sisterhood and live in chastity. Theresa Gerhardinger, who had to add a soup kitchen to her first school, saw the charism of the School Sisters of Notre Dame as the transformation of society through the education of these poor women. Sisters of the Good Shepherd opened shelters for unwed mothers and their children. The Sisters of Divine Compassion organized a mission to fallen women and recruited those with a vocation to their order. Sisters of Mercy aimed to aid and protect "respectable" working women. Their social centers provided entertainment and a chance to attract a husband in a moral environment.

Occasionally, these feminine sensitivities may seem a bit ludicrous. Cabrini, for example, forbade any of her companions in Nicaragua to eat until the bare-breasted Indian servants could be suitably clothed because she refused to participate in what she felt was a demeaning exposure of their womanhood. But there was nothing false in their perception that the impoverishment and consequent immorality of women resulted from male domination of the sources of money and liberty. Middle-class sisters became sensitized to working women's vulnerability to sexual assault. As the idea began to clarify that male vice was the root of all the evils they were fighting, the mission to women expanded to militancy. The Sisters of Mercy in New York got city funding for a children's shelter and tried to convince the authorities to help unwed mothers. Austin Carroll's pastoral work with prisoners, especially on death row, involved her in the fight to provide female wardens for women prisoners. She helped run soup kitchens and a day-care center and opened a House of Mercy to teach women marketable skills and find them jobs. She started a college for women until opposition from local clergy terminated it. Experience as a probation officer inspired Blandina Segale to lobby for anti–white slave legislation. As "The Nun of Kenmare," Margaret Ann Cusack wrote in support of women's rights, convinced that moral reform must empower women with the suffrage. While working for the Land League, she called upon Irish women to demand equality and property rights. She fought against the economic disabilities that drove women into prostitution and the penalties of divorce. She championed equal pay for equal work and a wife's rights to control her income. She compared marriage to slavery and criticized women for socializing their daughters to accept it, advocating a thorough education for girls not only in classics and science but also in politics.[14] But she was ultimately forced to leave Ireland and found no warm welcome in New York.

Modern sister-historians, obeying the directive of Vatican II to recover their pristine charisms, have begun to recover a heritage of nineteenth-century feminism obliterated in official diocesan histories. The frequent overshadowing of a founder by an episcopal patron in male-oriented church histories became a recurring motif at the Conference on the

History of Women Religious at Marymount College in 1992. Male patrons even more commonly asserted control over a group's charism. Archbishop Hughes supported the Sisters of Mercy's program of training women for economic independence to avert prostitution and ordered special collections for them in New York churches. But he refused to support the Sisters of the Good Shepherd in their vocation to aid women whose purity had already been lost. In 1856, the Sisters of the Holy Cross left the diocese because of his interference in their industrial school for girls.

Following the time-honored military model, the vow of obedience threatened to subsume the other religious vows. The concept of the mystical body of Christ, used so creatively by missionaries to absorb the individual sister into the greater life of the whole, could also be used to imprison the personality. Superiors monitored letters and phone calls as well as visits. As most of the world developed more modes of communication, nuns were shut off from newspapers, radios, TV's, family visits, and even friendly conversation with fellow students or clients. Particular friendships were heavily policed to prevent personal factions or unions from interfering with communal commitments. Even memory and family ties eroded as canon law encouraged novices to put off the "old self" in favor of a "new self" modeled on the ideals of the Tridentine church. Like well-trained troops, nuns were expected to compensate for whatever violence they felt was done to their individuality, with esprit de corps and a sense of spiritual superiority.

Soldiers of God they had always been, but their appearance and their way of life had generally had more in common with lay women than with clerical men. Now, the characteristics of an army on active duty— their uniform dress, their disciplined manner, their common mess and barrack-like quarters—set them apart from lay women and marked them as part of the clerical force. As feminism and democracy impelled Western womanhood into a freer and more public sphere both socially and economically, the intervening authority of priest and bishop isolated nuns from their contemporaries.

The congregation provided sisters with a framework for their active mission and endowed them with an ill-defined set of powers to implement that mission. The two areas of teaching and nursing to which the sisters were generally restricted fitted the hierarchy's general assessment of the nurturing instincts of the feminine nature. The self abnegation instilled by the novitiate was dangerously stimulated by outsiders who tended to confuse sisters with benevolent wealthy ladies volunteering their services to the poor. People complained of paying them for their teaching and hospital activities. Convinced that they could not put a price on charity, sisters worked for free when they could, supporting themselves on donations and other labor.

Their self-sacrificing spirituality was perhaps the church's most effective weapon in the struggle for popular loyalty. In 1880, when the Australian government revoked its aid to Catholic schools, bishops recruited the teaching congregations to replace the secular teachers whom they could no longer pay. Catherine Spalding was obliged to ask the city of Louisville to pay for expenses for the Sisters of Charity of Nazareth in staffing their municipal hospital. She did, however, pointedly specify that they were not mercenaries and put no price on their own labors. Teaching congregations usually passed their fees from rich to poor students. Thecla Branlot at Bona in Africa determined to take gifts of food offered by grateful patients so as not to offend her converts. But she scrupulously used the money saved from the food budget to buy little gifts for the schoolchildren and other natives. Thus, women's work in the world tended to be defined by the ideal of femininity as self-abnegation, deference to male professionals, and a reluctance to demand money for service.

Typically, charitable sisters shared the poverty of their clients as part of their charism. Fontbonne's Saint Joseph houses were situated in the slums of Lyons. They revived the traditional ideals of labor and self-mortification as an enhancement of their mission. Jeanne Jugan, founder of the Little Sisters of the Poor, ran shelters for abandoned children and the aged poor on alms. Pairs of sisters publicly begging for support became a common sight, even in the mining camps of the American West. Josephine Bunkley, an American convert who abandoned her vocation and published a memoir of her "ordeal" in a Catholic convent, depicted the hardship of doing labor ordinarily imposed on servants as typical of the murderous sadism of the system.[15] Lack of heat and food and barely adequate shelter typified conventual conditions everywhere.

Journals and letters from the American frontier described log cabins with snow flying through the chinks and danger from fires, wolves and other wild beasts, and rapists and robbers. Scientists sometimes ascribed their high death rate to unnatural chastity, but harsh living conditions were the more likely cause.

Women who reshaped their vocations under the pressure of revolution or secularization often exacerbated their involuntary poverty by their inclination toward further self-sacrifice. This conflation of traditional spirituality with the demands of the active life killed many zealous women. Before Margaret Tobin rescinded the provision in the constitution of 1793 that encouraged liberal use of the discipline, many Presentation sisters had contracted severe health problems. The Sisters of Loretto kept an open grave at the entrance to their chapel to stimulate their otherworldly aspirations until 1824, when they finally modified a rule that killed half the sisters before they were thirty years old. In 1823, the Kentucky Dominicans were warned to cease trying to combine the rigorous prayer schedule of the cloistered second order with the physical labor appropriate to Tertiaries. American Benedictines never abandoned the effort to retain their status as full-fledged nuns despite their unenclosed apostolate. Slowly, a new spirituality emerged: Eugénie Millerest, founder of the Sisters of the Assumption, wrote to her director of conscience: "If you were a Trappist, then by God you could be as weak as you liked and try every means of being weaker yet; what would it matter to your vocation? . . . But I have never believed that perfection rests on what we eat and drink . . . but on poverty and obedience."[16]

Some nuns willingly played the role of angel at the clerical hearth. But in the nineteenth century no secular power would enforce their obedience. They could leave and some could even become famous and mildly lionized for their flight. At least one nun left religion when papal infallibility was proclaimed in 1870. Corrigan barred Margaret Ann Cusack from New York because of her outspoken books. In her *Autobiography,* she wrote of the New York cardinal's refusal to assist her work for immigrant women: "I was only a woman doing work for women. I had the approval of the pope and a letter from my own bishop recommending me to the kindness of the clergy wherever I went. What matter? Perhaps, even then, his Eminence was occupied too much with the affairs of the Knights of Labor to be concerned with the women of labor."[17]

By 1888 she had been forced out of her own community; ultimately, she left the church. A milder alternative, commonly used, was simply to move. Mary Clarke started as a Franciscan Tertiary in Dublin and took her band of sisters to the American West in 1833. For decades, they avoided the designs of various bishops to amalgamate them with other communities and kept moving westward, earning their own keep and recruiting American-born sisters. Finally, Clarke incorporated land originally bought in the name of individual sisters and got approval from Rome for an autonomous congregation, the Sisters of the Blessed Virgin Mary.

Nineteenth-century nuns experienced a double declaustration. Sister teachers and nurses often provided the closest contact that many people ever had with the church. Improvising on old models, they strengthened the links between wealthy secular women and poor religious. Convent schools had been consolidating this bonding since the Christianizing mission began in the seventeenth century. Older pupils who helped to oversee the less-advanced girls were often recruited to the convent. Alumnae who married contributed their energies and their husband's resources to their alma maters. Sisters became adept at collaborating with generous secular women in charitable enterprises. Thus Mme. Wallaert-Descamps, founder of the crèche movement in the 1860s, staffed nurseries with nuns, combining day care with religious education for poor children. Women who worked for a living as servants, like Margaret Hallahan, or were, like Julie Biliart, self-employed as dressmakers, cultivated relationships with influential women or clergy through charitable work and secured their patronage while advancing into the religious life. Mutual interests in charity or reform sometimes brought Protestant women together with Catholics and occasionally led to the conversion of prominent women like Rose Hawthorne Lathrop and Mary Danner Starr, who then founded new congregations.

The newly defined boundaries between church and state increased religious women's liberty to form independent charitable associations with direct access to funding from grateful pupils and patients, from private contributors, and even from governments. They adapted corporate property and contractual obligations between superiors and members to the requirements of modern civil law. Patient negotiation with local governments accommodated regulation of schools, hospitals, and other institutions to the religious mission. Developing public school systems throughout the world devised formulas for sharing funds, labor, and infrastructure so as to utilize their services. Even anticlerical governments like the French tried to avoid replacing sisters who worked so devotedly and so cheaply in schools and hospitals. Education was seen as essential to citizenship, and sisters developed a strong reputation for disciplining the minds and the manners of unruly children.

Catholic education was soon perceived as a powerful weapon against the crime and disorder of the urban working class. Napoleon subsidized sisters who staffed French schools. The Austrian archduke Maximilian Hapsburg revived the female auxiliary of the Teutonic Knights, believing that sisters would set examples of self-denial against the promiscuity and intemperance of the working classes, which he blamed for the crippled families of the industrial slums. The British state also subsidized sisters as a counterforce to the wildness of the culture of poverty. The small schools operated by nuns returning from the Continent after the French Revolution were supplemented by the Daughters of Mary Ward and other new congregations that offered secondary education. Teaching sisters were supposed to be restricted to instructing girls and young boys. In America, however, pragmatism often prevailed, and sisters took up secondary schools for young men where brothers were not available.

State funding for the education of girls developed particularly slowly. The Sisters of the Holy Child, founded by Cornelia Connolly in 1846, specialized in the education of Catholic girls. Nuns founded 30 percent of the women's colleges in the United States. Boarding schools turned out "accomplished" girls from important families whose tuition supported free day schools for the poor. These concurrent charity schools gave poor women domestic skills and middle-class manners, helping them to make a living in domestic service. It put them in touch with alumnae associations like the Children of Mary for referrals and assistance. The Ursulines of New Orleans imported this European system of pairing educational institutions to America in 1727. Eventually, many governments reached some compromise for subsidizing the Catholic school system. The fact that it was already in place and staffed with efficient, dedicated, and cheap labor made a persuasive argument to the most determined secularists. Many officials, in France for example, considered the sisters better role models for women than the secular "liberated woman."

Religious orders had such a strong influence on state schools in Prussia, Denmark, and Holland that it made Catholic schools unnecessary. In Belgium the congregations grew under the liberal constitution. The 1850 French Falloux Law gave the clergy an interest, sometimes even a controlling voice, in state schools by transferring many local schools to religious orders. Simultaneously, private Catholic schools multiplied. French novitiates doubled as normal schools giving the girls basic education and professional training to teach in secular schools. Their curricula generally retained a basic liberal arts "core" around which it offered vocational skills, tailored for boys and girls (who were taught commercially useful domestic skills, mainly needle work). Exported to America, this Catholic educational model resisted the native preference for change, experimentation, and individualism.[18]

In some areas, the church worked toward a separate Catholic school system in competition with public schools. By 1878, Dutch Catholics were strong enough to form a political party demanding Catholic education for Catholic children. In Ireland, before the emancipation, the Sisters of Charity and the Lorettos opened schools. Many Catholic educators there were reluctant to apply for the state grants made available in 1839 not only because it was not clear that Catholic schools were eligible but also because they feared government interference. In England, the Dominican Margaret Hallahan, who collaborated for twenty years with Bishop Ullathorne in establishing Catholic schools, wrote to one of her sisters calling subsidies a "deep-laid scheme of the devil,"[19] which would result in government action to undermine the faith. Her schools were brought into the government grant scheme only after her death in 1868.

In the United States, the strict separation of church and state made the church exceptionally anxious to develop a school system that would ensure the instruction of Catholics and sometimes act as a vehicle for the conversion of Protestants. In 1818, when only about 40 nuns resided in the United States, Elizabeth Seton opened the first free school associated with a parish. The first plenary council of Baltimore, in 1852, urged all bishops to attach schools to their churches. Sisters arrived from Europe to serve each new immigrant group, and new congregations were founded from among their ranks, moving west with Catholic settlers. By the end of the century, more than 40,000 nuns staffed 3,811 parochial schools and 663 academies for girls.[20] In 1884 the third council recommended that normal schools be established to train sisters.

The care of the sick was an ancient apostolate for women. In Europe in the nineteenth century the patchwork of hospitals and dispensaries, already in existence under dedicated congregations, was gradually regularized and expanded. Superiors persuaded local authorities to support small hospitals or shelters, which they staffed. Local governments contracted with communities of religious women to staff public hospitals. For example, Tertiaries known as the Merciful Sisters *(Barmherzige Schwestern)* were attached to various orders in the German states. Archduke Maximilian brought Agnes Weber, Franziska Weber, and Dominika Tamerle to Austria and incorporated them into the Teutonic Knights in the manner of the old canoness houses. They added a fourth vow to serve Christ in the persons of the sick and poor, modeling themselves on Elisabeth of Thuringia. From the medieval tradition of herbalists, sisters readily developed into modern pharmacists, and their dispensaries often represented the only health care facilities available in remote areas of the Western world as well as in non-Western mission stations.

Catholic hospitals grew in the United States along with state and county systems. In 1820, sisters in Saint Louis established the first Catholic hospital in the United States. In 1823, Emmitsburg sisters sent a colony at the invitation of the University of Maryland to take charge of the Baltimore infirmary. They opened eight wards with one for blacks and one for seamen as well as other local patients. The Sisters of Charity of Nazareth established an infirmary in Louisville. Saint Vincent's in New York was founded by Mary Angela Hughes in 1849. These free hospitals served the poor in partnership with secular governments under regulations ensuring religious freedom for the patients. To counter Protestant efforts to proselytize Catholic immigrants and bar their own institutions to priests, the Catholic hierarchy multiplied its hospitals in the cities in the 1850s.

The feminine apostolate was holistic. As active orders run by and for women, the sisters had to invent themselves as they went along. Though some practiced a specific charity, like the Peigneuses (combers), who washed and shampooed the sick in French hospitals, they rarely defined themselves within professional boundaries. The teaching Ursulines introduced themselves to New Orleans by running a hospital and routinely took in orphans and repentant prostitutes. Elizabeth Seton's Sisters of Charity ran schools, shelters, and medical facilities. Francesca Cabrini's Missionaries of the Sacred Heart founded orphanages, shelters, schools, and hospitals for Italian immigrants in North and South America. Austin Carroll and her Sisters of Mercy nursed yellow fever victims in New Orleans in 1832 and wounded soldiers during the Civil War. She herself taught in parish, industrial, and Sunday schools for forty years, establishing separate schools for blacks in Florida, Alabama, Mississippi, and Louisiana, while writing forty books and innumerable articles and pursuing a variety of reform projects.

The earliest congregations of women in America combined nursing with other charitable activities. Marguerite de Youville, a Canadian widow, formed the Grey Nuns in 1738, a congregation that took charge of the General Hospital in Montreal. In addition to the impoverished sick, she made room for repentant prostitutes, and eventually well-to-do women helped finance the charity. More commonly, however, nursing was undertaken when need arose. Two sisters of the old Rouen Poor Clares died from nursing small pox victims in their Northumbrian refuge. Mary Francis Clarke and a few other Franciscan Tertiaries in Ireland served in the cholera epidemic of 1831. Emmitsburg sisters went singly and in pairs to nurse victims of the cholera in 1832. Sisters of Our Lady of Charity fresh from Ireland, with their habits tied up at the waist and wearing oversized boots, lugged heavy baskets of food and medicine through the streets of Charleston to poor victims of the yellow fever epidemic. Many nuns began their nursing services among the immigrant poor on the boat and visited immigrant homes once they had landed in the United States. On new frontiers their ready attendance at the sick bed was often their first introduction to a suspicious community. In 1865, four Sisters of Charity arrived in Santa Fe to give medical care to laborers in the mining camps and on the railroad. Blandina Segale defended a threatened victim from a lynch mob, nursed a wounded member of Billy the Kid's gang, and persuaded the gunslinger not to shoot a doctor who had refused him treatment. Marianne of Molokai took over Father Damien's leper colony when he died and established a hospital for girls.

Protected by their habits, sisters felt they could move into all sorts of

areas never before open to respectable women, including the male world
of the battlefield. Through the French and Indian War, Marguerite de
Youville tended English prisoners as well as French wounded. Nuns at
the Hôtel Dieu of Quebec nursed American prisoners of war during the
Revolution. Wounded men left on the battlefield of Three Rivers were
nursed by sisters in Vermont, which may have inspired Ethan Allen's
daughter Fanny, who became a Hospital Sister of Saint Joseph in Canada.
The good press attending two dozen sisters from various congregations
who accompanied Florence Nightingale to the Crimea inspired American
church leaders to volunteer sisters for military hospitals during the Civil
War. Dorothea Dix, the strongly secularist organizer of the army nurses,
resisted the recruitment of sisters, but doctors made private arrangements
with sisters they had known before the war. Moreover, existing Catholic
hospitals were naturally incorporated into the war effort and convents
themselves served as makeshift hospitals. At Gettysburg and elsewhere
they gave first aid on the battlefield before the wounded could be brought
into neighboring houses for further treatment. Sisters of the Holy Cross
served the navy on the hospital boat *Red Rover.* Gonzaga Grace headed
ninety-one Sisters of Charity at Satterlee Military Hospital. Lincoln gave
the Sisters of Mercy in Washington free access to supplies and money
from the War Department.

Despite all this activity, a nun's profession remained what it had always
been, a religious vocation. Medical enterprises were bound together by
the need to keep the sacraments available to Catholic patients while
exerting influence on sick Protestants. Orphaned survivors had to be
assured a religious upbringing, and the poor had to be guarded from
irreligious influences. The Teutonic Sisters staffed workhouses, poor-
houses, orphanages, maternity and foundling homes, and hospitals. In
1814, Seton's community was asked for nuns to establish an orphanage
in Philadelphia and another in New York. In 1831, Mary Rhodes added
an orphanage to the Lorettan school, which expanded to care for the
children surviving the cholera epidemic of 1832 and added a hospital.
Sisters received little special training for their missions. The pope, the
Propaganda, bishops, or other superiors invited and dispatched nuns to
various fields and assigned them tasks with more regard for the needs of
the hierarchy or, perhaps, its assessment of the individual spiritual needs
of the sisters than for their qualifications in a foreign field. They almost

always arrived with no knowledge of local languages or customs, trusting God and their own spiritual zeal to carry them through. The Sisters of Notre Dame took over a school in Okagama, Japan, in 1924 with no training whatsoever in Japanese culture or language. Only in the 1920s were some of them trained in tropical medicine, handicrafts, and musical performance deemed to be useful. They expected to obey orders and to offer up their objections or dislike as self-mortification.

Thus, women disguised their entry into the professional world as a simple extension of the sphere of their natural feminine talents. Nursing sisters trained on the job in collaboration with doctors who appreciated their discipline, obedience, neatness, and above all their fearlessness in the face of contagious disease. In general, nineteenth century scientists considered their mysteries unfit for female understanding. Women responded with a social philosophy based on their own natural nurturing qualities, reinforced by their innate purity. Sometimes, their unique blending of womanly compassion with virile audacity gave them singular advantages in dealing with a hostile male environment. Rose Hawthorne Lathrop defended the indelicacy of her Saint Rose of Lima Dominicans in tending to male patients and then turned the argument upside down:

> A look of courteous disgust overspreads a man's face at the suggestion that his sex should be represented on any noticeable scale in the holy profession of tending sick men of destitute condition who are untended, rather than to study, or train souls at a fastidious distance from tragic complications. The vocation to nurse the sick male poor is so much beneath the notice of men today that they are willing to let women nurse poor men as well as poor women—and far worse than this contemptible neglect of their duties, they are willing to abandon poor men to any fate of entire neglect rather than to nurse them.[21]

By the end of the century, teaching and nursing were almost totally segregated as women's professions, oddly stamped with the character of religious vocations. Nuns like Caroline Friess, who conceived her teaching vocation as a mission to the poor, set the model for secular teachers, who were expected to attend church, uphold strict moral standards, and remain unmarried as long as they worked. Florence Nightingale was so impressed with their work that she considered becoming a nun and wrote to Caroline Manning, "No one can tell, no man can tell, what [the

Catholic Church] is to women, their training, their discipline, their hopes, their home . . . I have seen something of different kinds of nuns, I am no longer young and do not speak from enthusiasm but from experience. There is nothing like the training which the Sacred Heart or the Order of Saint Vincent gives to women."[22] Her guidelines for her London school incorporated a quasi-monastic attitude toward the life of the sisters and a persuasion that nursing was a spiritual activity. Even the veil or a modified cap and (in the British Empire) the appellation "sister" were transferred to secular nurses. Public tolerance depended on the understanding that they should not be greedy for money or ambitious for professional advancement applied.

In the nineteenth century, everyone with a stake in the services of sisters was in reasonably close agreement concerning their purposes. Principally, the sisters themselves saw their work as a religious vocation rather than a profession, though individual sisters no doubt varied in the degree to which professional ambitions and the desire to live on a broader scale motivated them. Parish priests and the clerical hierarchy were more concerned with getting sisters with a minimal education into the classroom than with their professional development. Sisters who taught struggled successfully to satisfy agencies' demands for a college education but they received little encouragement from disapproving clergymen who wanted them to go right into the classroom.[23]

Clerical suspicion that the intimacy of medical work was harmful to chastity restricted nursing vocations. Papal prohibition forbade sisters to work in obstetric units and nurseries. They were obliged to demand special contracts adjusting their care of patients to Vatican regulations, barring them from venereal wards and other threats to their sexual purity. Their participation in more sophisticated medical training in anatomy and surgical procedures was discouraged, but doctors still found that the sisters' discipline, cleanliness, and prompt obedience more than compensated. Nevertheless, building up their role as angels of mercy, congregations of nursing sisters took a lead in organizing training programs in their hospitals some decades before the rest of the profession initiated such programs. Saint Joseph of Cluny Sisters were the first nurses to use Louis Pasteur's precepts. They learned to give injections and tracheotomies in diphtheria cases. They were all vaccinated themselves and wore habits specially designed to discourage the accumulation of germs. One,

Sister Laure, remembered that they had to write for permission from Rome to wear short sleeves.

Nevertheless, they generally saw themselves as care givers more than professionals. Nursing, teaching, cooking and cleaning, religious instruction by word and deed, and begging money for the help of the poor, occupied them according to the needs of the moment. Above all they devoted themselves to prayer. This spiritual dimension gave meaning to work that might otherwise be classed as drudgery. As a lecturer on the problems of contemporary women, Edith Stein anticipated some of the modern debates on professionalization. She argued that intellect should be at the service of society and that the whole person should be actively involved with the life of the times. She defended the equality of professional women with men and hoped they would "feminize" the male professions with a holistic combination of humane sympathy and technical expertise.

Sisters gradually found themselves caught between the developing professional ideals of scientific method and intellectual rigor and their responsibilities in their communities including a schedule of prayer and meditation. But professional commitment increasingly required a distancing and a partitioning of functions that fitted badly with their spiritual outlook. Education became an additional burden to sisters with full schedules of prayer, community duties, and a job. Sometimes lasting twenty years, pieced together in odd hours and summer sessions, it rarely nurtured their capacities and only added stress.

By midcentury, it was clear that the whole question of the role of women religious in modern society had to be reconsidered. In 1948, the Conference of Catholic Schools of Nursing was formed in the United States to foster higher educational standards in conjunction with college programs. About 90,000 sisters teaching in American schools also needed to upgrade their credentials. By 1954, 150 centers had been established to assure that all teachers would receive bachelor of arts degrees before beginning their teaching assignments, putting them far in advance of their European counterparts. In 1954, the Sister Formation Conference was established in the United States with a newsletter and an annual conference to share ideas and expertise addressing the problem of advancing the spiritual and professional training of sisters. Thus, the sisters had already prepared themselves to reorganize their professional lives when *Sedes Sapientiae* (1956) summarized proposals for the training of novices. Sisters shifted from programs requiring twenty summers to get a degree to competitive professional training. They also worked to strengthen communal ties and avoid secular contamination from the college life around them. They persuaded themselves and the hierarchy that this upgraded education would not turn them into free-thinking intellectuals and would be used only for its practical applications.[24]

In the middle of the century, this movement galvanized the sisters themselves as they were brought into more active contact with one another and given a serious opportunity to take control of the shaping of their own lives in conformity with their vocations. Moreover, activity coming from Rome encouraged them. Sisters in the service congregations generally interpreted Pius XII's bull *Sponsa Christi* as an intentional sharpening of the distinction between the contemplative and active vocations and a recognition of the need for an apostolic spirituality to conform to their own charitable charisms. The pope presided over international conferences of superiors of congregations, urging them to adapt the rituals of daily life to the needs of professional standards. The International Congress of Mothers General was established. In 1952, the Conference of Major Superiors of Women formed a network in America, and in 1971 the group changed its name to Leadership Conference of Women Religious. Even with the steadily high number of vocations throughout the 1950s and early 1960s, sisters were overwhelmed by the demand for their services and the ratio of lay teachers and lay nurses to sisters increased in Catholic schools and hospitals. Neither the sisters nor their clerical superiors saw an insuperable conflict in the consequent linking of secular and religious professions. In 1954, the Sister Formation Bulletin began to explore an apostolate focused on inspiring and training lay professionals in the religious dimensions of social service vocations.

These discussions unexpectedly spread to questions concerning the anachronistic nature of nuns' appearance, life, and manners. Despite their credentials and even, perhaps, because of their devotion, sisters had to find a method of dealing with professions that men were beginning to define in terms of specialized training, professional associations, and a self-governing hierarchy. As work increasingly focused on results and acquired its own disciplined routines that precluded the demands of the religious life, the compatibility of the two vocations was strained. The gender separatism and communal solidarity of the sisters abraded against the individualism and professional hierarchies of their colleagues. Individual sisters began to take up specializations that brought them further into professional communities and distanced them from the conventual atmosphere. The integrity of their vocations as living exercises in Christian charity was threatened by the realities of modern social services as industries. Moreover, the traditional religious training in self-abnegation and obedience was challenged by professional demands for dignity and increased responsibility.

The care-giving professions that religious women invented and maintained for so many centuries have become secularized, and even Catholic institutions are increasingly staffed by secular workers. Federal programs mandating curricular standards and a secular bureaucracy have had a powerful impact on the atmosphere of parochial schools and Catholic charitable institutions. Federal monies disrupted community integrity as sisters with administrative tasks were classed as management in contrast to the nursing and teaching sisters. The tasks themselves had a corrosive effect on the spiritual life of administrators. In the 1950s the Sister Formation Bulletin focused on the dissonance between vocation and profession, "personal religious life and the active apostolate."[25] Audrey Kopp, who eventually became president of the National Coalition of American Nuns, wrote of the destructive effects of authoritarian bureaucracy in convent and church, arguing for the mystical body as a vehicle for collegiality. However powerfully the call to serve overrode professional ambition, vocations could not be undertaken without training. The conflict between the increasing costs of health care and its provision as charity set up tensions that remain unresolved. Sisters and secular colleagues have a common cause in expecting compensation for their services and their skills.

The Second Vatican Council firmly reminded women religious that they are not clergy and encouraged them to seek a new solidarity with the rest of the laity. Many sisters turned gladly away from their quasi-clerical isolation to embrace the church's "special option" for the poor.

They abandoned medieval habits for shorter skirts and streamlined veils, secular dresses and blue jeans. Apostolic sisters renounced their cloistered lifestyle and began to mingle socially and economically with fellow students and employees in schools, hospitals, and places of employment. There they could share their devotion to an active apostolate expressed in acts of caring and charity with their secular colleagues. The vision of holistic solutions revived in opposition to narrow specialization and the professional tendency to stratify. These changes have encouraged resistance to hierarchies beginning with those in the medical and educational bureaucracies and ending with the clergy itself. Sisters in hospital administration have experimented with methods to strengthen ties with patients. Mary Ignatia Gavin (d. 1966) was associated with the founders of Alcoholics Anonymous, and her hospital in Akron pioneered the care and treatment of alcoholism. The hospice movement has placed comfort and consolation against heroic medical treatment of the terminally ill, incorporating elements of a spirituality based on the in-working of the Holy Spirit. There is a growing sense that schools must provide moral (though not religious) guidance to their young charges. The whole complex of modern twelve-step programs relies on quasi-monastic combinations of prayer, humility, and self-control. In short, the viewpoint long associated with women's temperament has not been lost in the professionalizing of their apostolate. Indeed, the late-twentieth-century observer has reason to hope that, translated into feminist values, women's skills at networking, negotiating, and nurturing will come to permeate ever widening areas of the sphere once assigned to men.

Sisters in the professions and their lay colleagues share the problems facing modern feminists. They do not want to forgo their special sense of mission as women, their sense that they need not become men or submit to "masculine" definitions of their professional life. But neither do they wish to be confined by that separate, complementary feminine nature to which Pope John Paul II clings in his recent efforts to put the female genie back into her bottle. A holistic approach to human services of every sort well befits a new set of gender relations in which, at least in the vocational sphere of life, the separate spheres are abandoned and a syneisactic relationship is forged, transcending the power relations of masculinity and femininity. Most of the professions are already far along in this process. The Catholic clergy remains the last womanless space.

Conclusion: Toward a
Third Millennium

IN THE LAST DECADE of the twentieth century, with the median age of sisters now set at seventy and rising and no new generation of recruits in sight, the death of the feminine apostolate, at least in the United States and Europe, seems to be inevitable. As the vocation of service to the poor and suffering has been secularized, no fresh spiritual justification for pursuing it through the convent has been developed. By the 1950s, the structure that imposed so many clerical characteristics on the sisters without finally admitting them into the magic circle of the ordained was outdated. The position of the Catholic Church itself had changed as the world submitted to the realignment of the Cold War. In the Western world, the hostility of the secular state gave way to an ideological alliance against communism. The church's own monolithic face cracked as various factions debated its role in the late-twentieth-century world.

Pius XII, in *Sponsa Christi* and the papal conventions of the early fifties, sharpened the division between apostolic and monastic sisters, creating a closer analogy to the division between the secular clergy with its pastoral mission and the regular clergy. Establishment of the Conference of Major Superiors of Women encouraged the hope that stronger ties to Rome would reward women religious with greater access to the decision-making process. The Sister Formation movement and the intense debates and discussions that accompanied it prepared the sisters to take a broader role in the affairs of the church and the world in the years leading to the Second Vatican Council.

Women in the service orders who gave their religious profession priority over their secular professions held seminars and issued reports, seeking to define the nature of their pastorate. But the conference received no reply to its petition for representation at the Vatican council on questions regarding the lives of religious women. No women participated in the early meetings, and their role in the church was not discussed until the end of the sittings. Paul VI allowed a few female auditors to attend the third session without the right to speak. The conference president, Mary Luke Tobin, was the only representative of more than a million American sisters. In the end, Vatican II was no more creative than earlier councils in envisioning the role of women in a renewed church: *Perfectae Caritatis* (1965) challenged women religious to reassess their religious mission through a return to the sources of all Christian life and to their own original charisms.

Nuns had long been rigorously trained to have no history, personal or communal. The prescribed return to their roots paralleled the tumultuous experience of their present, leading them over several decades to a raised consciousness of their relationship with the male hierarchy. A massive operation of historical salvage and revisionism has revealed and corrected distortions and gaps in their history beyond anyone's imagination. A fruitful collaboration with feminist scholars seeking their own foremothers has already produced a wealth of books and articles on the ancient, medieval, and early modern periods. Sisters themselves have taken more active control of the histories of modern communities. A network devoted to the history of women religious has been formed with a newsletter, regular conferences, and a strong feminist sense of community. For the first time, women religious are uniting in self-conscious awareness of their own integrity. Having discovered their history, they seek new agenda for the future.

Vatican II, in the bull *Lumen Gentium*, asserted that religious were no longer an elite group set apart but rather members of an equally consecrated laity as distinguished from the clergy. Many women who had long imagined themselves attached to the clergy, albeit in an ancillary capacity, began to hope for restoring their sense of membership through ordination. Early in the 1970s, Protestant and Jewish women were beginning to make inroads into the sacred precincts of their respective religions. Catholic women took part in the liturgy as acolytes, eucharistic ministers, and lay readers. The idea of their ordination steadily gained acceptance among laity and some of the clergy, and an organizing conference met in 1975. They received only resolute discouragement from the Vatican. Paul VI's Commission on the Role of Women in Church and Society was instructed to respect the differences between male and female roles and, explicitly, to exclude ordination from consideration. Since 1977, the Vatican has repeatedly proclaimed that Christ established a bond between maleness and the priesthood that cannot be altered.

In 1979, soon after his election, John Paul II visited the United States. In a progress notable for the removal of altar girls and other women in liturgical functions from his sight, he permitted an address by Mary Theresa Kane of the Sisters of Mercy of the Union, president of the renamed Leadership Conference of Women Religious (LCWR). While the pope allowed his annoyance to show plainly before a television audience of millions, she made her plea:

> As I share this privileged moment with you, Your Holiness, I urge you to be mindful of the intense suffering and pain which is part of the life of many women in the United States. I call upon you to listen with compassion and to hear the call of women who comprise half of humankind. As women, we have heard the powerful messages of our church addressing the dignity and reverence for all persons. As women, we have pondered these words. Our contemplation leads us to state that the church in its struggle to be faithful to its call for reverence and dignity for all persons must respond by providing the possibility of women as persons being included in all ministries of our church. I urge you, Your Holiness, to be open to and respond to the voices coming from the women of this country who are desirous of serving in and through the church as fully participating members.[1]

Nothing of the sort was to happen. In 1982, at the assembly of male and female superiors, five women from the LCWR were publicly humiliated by Vatican officials who forbade them to take their places in a planned ritual in which they were to share with five male superiors in carrying consecrated bread and wine to the participants seated at their tables.

In Rome as elsewhere, the most stubborn resistance sometimes precedes the most revolutionary change. The worldwide shortage of priests has far more profound implications for the future of this church than the shortage of sisters. Even the ordination of women might not supply enough recruits to solve the problem. The simple fact is that for the last two centuries large numbers of Catholics have been forced to do without reliable reception of the sacraments that define the spirituality of their church. In times of revolution or culture war (including the long exiles of Catholics behind the iron and bamboo curtains), sisters and other lay people have managed with partial sacraments and substitute liturgies. In mission territories (including nineteenth-century America) sisters served as acolytes. They performed quasi-sacramental activities like blessing graves and developed alternative rites. Mental prayer, the monastic specialty, provided entrée to a level of existence that subsumed the priesthood, identifying its providers with Mary Magdalene, apostle to the apostles. The ideologically meek Thérèse of Lisieux wrote somewhat disingenuously of the Carmelite vocation to pray for priests as faulty human beings: "We offer our prayers and penance for God's apostles and we are their apostles, while by word and deed they bring the Gospel to our brethren."[2] Thérèse made herself part of the priesthood (and the better, spiritual, part at that) by binding herself to her spiritual brothers in the mystical body of Christ.

A less priest-centered church seems predicted by the demographics of declining male vocations and the refusal to recognize female vocations. Today, in many places, the priestly role has been reduced to the simple dispensation of sacraments to people whose daily pastoral care has been entrusted to others. Already, American bishops have endorsed rites for parishes without priests, which may be the norm for the future. Sisters have taken a leading role in nonsacramental pastoral ministry whenever the church has needed them. Long before the first black priest was ordained in America, the Oblates of Providence provided extrasacramental devotions for their own spiritual needs and for those of their flock. Similar arrangements endured for long periods of time in China and Japan. Priests, of course, still perform the central mission of appearing on some regular basis to administer the sacraments. But throughout the world sisters are the backbone of the parish system, performing all but the strictly delineated sacramental functions. In such a church, sisters cease simply to be subalterns to the "real" clergy and become leaders among the laity by virtue of their dedication and energy. At the 1994 Synod of Bishops, sisters in the young churches of Africa and Asia joined Americans in complaining about these limited capacities. An African nun lamented being forced to watch patients die repentant but unreconciled because of the absence of a priest.[3] It is hard to see how such a spiritual dilemma can be resolved without a less hierarchical and more holistic and syneisactic ministry.

Sacramental spirituality is not the only form of devotion. Sisters conducted perpetual adoration of the exposed Eucharist in attics during the French Revolution and on remote Indian reservations in the American West where lack of priests made communion impossible. The Catholic Church has always been rich in prayers and rituals, like the Rosary or the Stations of the Cross, that particularly appeal to women. Since 1960, Marian visions have proliferated in Africa as well as the United States. Votive rites centered on the Sacred Heart or the Immaculate Conception have multiplied. Local cults and practices, storytelling, and, of course, pastoral care are infinitely more compatible with the syncretic tendencies of grass-roots religion than the theologically correct liturgies of cathedral chapters.

Will the hierarchy ever accept such a solution? The path is far from straight. At the end of Vatican II, *Perfectae Caritatis* appeared to discard the Vatican I policy of cleaving to unchanging authority and tradition, urging reexamination and restructuring of congregational constitutions. Meetings on a community or regional level soon turned into passionate consciousness-raising sessions resonating with the debates and discoveries that were shaking women everywhere in the late sixties. Every order and congregation experimented with replacing the old hierarchy with a variety of leadership teams. They sought increased independence for individual sisters against the absolute authority that had marked religious communities as well as the church that harbored them. The Conference of Major Superiors of Women symbolized this conviction when it changed its name to the Leadership Conference of Women Religious. But while sisters have moved forward with a mandate that seemed so much in keeping with the spirit of the age, Rome has moved back toward the world view of Vatican I. The curia withheld approval of the name change for years and has gradually moved to isolate and undermine this organization of American sisters.

The complaints of women who invested a lifetime in the old routines of prayer and discipline and resisted every change have been reinforced by Vatican approval. The new ideals were explicitly and implicitly denied in John Paul II's letter *Essential Elements,* of 1983, launching an investigation of the condition of American sisters and seeking an explanation for the failure of vocations. The papal commission to reexamine the status of American women religious in 1989 stressed obedience as the chief vow and even flirted with a return to religious habits. The National Coalition of American Nuns responded that they were being criticized precisely because they had already obeyed the church's demand for renewal. By the nineties, a revived Conference of Major Superiors was recognized, representing about 6 percent of American sisters, arousing fears for the future of the Leadership Conference. The bull *Veritatis Splendor* (1993) restated the absolute authority of Christian tradition.

The number of nuns has continued to drop precipitately, raising doubts about whether the Western church could support the renewal of their vocations if it should occur. Poverty of an involuntary nature has all too sadly overtaken many an aged woman who has seen the assets of her community dwindle and discovered that the church has made no provision to cover her in old age.[4] Partly by choice and partly by necessity, sisters now face the prospect of supporting themselves and enduring illness and old age without firm institutional care. American congregations have reorganized their finances to provide pensions and qualify sisters for social security but most of their assets in land and buildings can be expected to support only the dying generation. More than one recent American nun-scholar has urged her readers to consider the probability that the sisterhood as it now exists will not survive into a new millennium.

If women are not to participate in a fully clerical vocation, they must renew the roots of their spirituality as laity. One choice that seems indicated by history is the monastic vocation, which has always been intrinsically laic and whose opposition to the secular clergy as a spiritual wellspring may well be ready for reassertion. The hidden life, the life of community and discipline, gains adherents as the active life collapses in the United States and Europe. Monasticism already has a deep kinship to the spirituality of Asia. Women who have always had difficulty maintaining their Buddhist sisterhoods may be one source of the recruits who are coming to the Carmelites and the Cistercians. The ancient virtue of chastity, the commitment that frees loving people from selfish commitments for altruistic service, remains the bedrock of their call. In Africa also, women who had never envisaged the choice of giving themselves wholly to meditation and prayer in a community of other women are enthusiastically embracing the opportunity. A comparison in one congregation of the sharp decline in vocations in the United States with the rise in vocations in Mexico suggests that the convent still presents a meaningful opportunity in societies with fewer alternatives for women. Thus, in all the disarray of modern times, the choir of virgins still gathers to offer that song that only they can sing and only God can hear.

The spirituality of monasticism may be a powerful response to the failure of sacramental spirituality, combining the spirit of community with the rituals of the office. Moreover, the direction of the age, which has multiplied the spaces where women and men can interact without sexual tensions, may favor the revival of its inherent syneisactism. In the end, the religious life is about worship and the positive benefits that worship brings to the world and its maker. The chants and processions that once occupied hundreds of lifetimes still retain the power to maintain women and men together on a spiritual plane. The premise of the contemplative life has always been that self-mortification informed by love of God and God's creatures can generate transferable grace. No other modern profession can supply this service. Unlike the apostolic congregations, the monastic life is hardly to be found outside the structure of the church, but it has never been integrated into the hierarchy. It may be that as Catholicism spreads beyond the Western world in modern times, it will become less centralized in response to the claims of distinct cultural traditions as well as the pressures of modern democratizing tendencies. Monasticism on the model of the first millennium church might prove again to be the ideal force around which Christian communities could be formed and nurtured. The commitment to manual labor as well as the traditional trade of spiritual services for financial donations have the capacity to free the community from dependence on the Vatican. A localized church might reflect the many peoples within it better than the present Rome-centered institution. The lack of hierarchy may allow better adaptation to a multicultural and more democratic world church.

If the system reverted to early medieval autonomy, it might also be prone to the divisions and petty power plays that branded the church of the first millennium as hopelessly decadent. The episcopal hierarchy has traditionally opposed the centralization of religious orders. As we have seen, however, the papacy has not been so rigid. The original process of ordering tended to bypass women, but in our time *Sponsa Christi* encouraged nuns to form federations to escape isolation, to support themselves by various enterprises, and to inform their spirituality with concern for the salvation of their neighbors. Unions such as the federation of twenty-six Spanish Cistercian houses in 1955 under the abbess of Las Huelgas and the federation of the Immaculate Heart of Mary in 1980 under the presidency of Jouarre formed. After 1965, contemplatives' efforts to meet were often blocked by reinforcements of enclosure. When they tried to form a seminar group, a papal letter, *Venite Seorsum*, demanded that they resign their community if they wished to experiment with alternatives. Nevertheless, in 1969 a group of American Carmelites took the lead in forming the Association of Contemplative Sisters. Their subsequent meetings have concentrated on bringing a feminist perspective to the contemplative life, relaxing the rules of enclosure to allow the nuns to hold regional meetings and general chapters. In the 1980s, when the Vatican reexamined the constitutions written by sisters over many years, contemplatives as well as active sisters suffered unilateral rejection of new rules that broke traditional molds. The painfully evolved constitution that had been forwarded to Rome with the approval of 80 percent of the world's Discalced Carmelite women was set aside and all sisters were informed that if they did not return to the old constitution, they would have to "find other forms of consecrated life."[5] If necessary, of course, they can simply do so.

The tie between monasticism and the secular clergy has weakened as priestly vocations have decreased and monks have ceased to seek advancement in the hierarchy. As a result, the authority and enterprise of women in nunneries serving as communal centers could revive. The commonality of nuns and monks has already begun to reassert itself in renewal of the old syneisactic ties, which have been so strained during the second millennium. Paired and complementary monasticism has a fair chance of success in a world where sexual barriers have become porous and thoughtful critiques of the gender system have exposed the corrosive workings of misogyny. The pope rechartered the three branches of the Cistercian order in the United States and Europe and fully incorporated the nuns into their branches. Monks and nuns cooperate on many economic ventures to support their communities.

Renewed study of the rule and its historical applications have encouraged Benedictines to ignore the pernicious heritage of *Periculoso*. Women in the Benedictine tradition today do not find a life of scholarship and spiritual direction incompatible with their commitment to the contemplative life. Moreover, they still offer the sorts of pastoral missions that distinguished medieval monasteries, reviving their ancient commitment to hospitality. Indeed, the future may well see a far more interactive relationship between practitioners of the active life and the contemplative life not unlike the mixed communities of the Middle Ages. They could expand a social mission based on retreat from the world, recuperation and spiritual renewal, borrowing from the charism of the ancient canonesses. In any case, where the need arises, women to fill it will never be lacking.

A second choice for spiritually inclined women remains a lay apostolate modeled on the Beguines, Tertiaries, and Beatas of times gone by rather than on the quasi-monastic congregations of the last century. Many sisters embraced the lay identification proclaimed by *Lumen Gentium*. Primed by their decade of professional renewal, they abandoned the habits and living conditions that separated them so decisively from the people they felt called to serve and took up a host of new missions. Sisters joined freedom riders and other demonstrators launching the American civil rights movement. They marched in the demonstrations demanding an end to the war in Vietnam and experimented with any number of community-service initiatives including helping prospective clients through the red tape of the public welfare system. In 1978, the Leadership Conference endorsed the idea that the apostolic life might be pursued through the American political system. Elizabeth Morancy served several terms in the Rhode Island House of Representatives, claiming that such political activism was part of the charism of the Sisters of Mercy. The pope, however, interpreted the boundary between church and state as a barrier to clergy (here including sisters) in political life. Arlene Violet, a candidate for Rhode Island attorney general, left her order when Rome refused to countenance her political activity.

Western women are now free of the compelling need for institutional validation and protection that forced women in earlier times to accept the restrictions the hierarchy imposed on them. They are no longer forced to marry and have the means of supporting themselves without family property. Motherhood is, or should be, a matter of choice. The decision to remain sexually inactive for a period or for life is also a choice and could be made at any stage in life. Moreover, women today are much better informed than in the past about the consequences of their choices. Once nuns tended to assume, and the world endorsed the assumption, that family violence, birth control, abortion, rape, and other problems of secular women had no relevance to them. Now they see themselves in solidarity with women to whom all these problems are daily burdens. They too must choose and then must minister to their sisters who have chosen differently. Through this female bonding a community of helping and receiving help could easily grow. Certain models found in halfway houses or the regular meetings embedded in twelve-step problems may point toward a new form of communal life. Again, however temporary the commitment of an individual may prove to be, chastity seems inevitable as the key to the requisite dedication.

American sisters have spent decades seeking a workable solution to the lay apostolate in their own country. A high number of departures from every community accompanied the steep decline in vocations. The Glenmary Sisters of Appalachia surrendered canonical status and became a lay community in 1965 seeking greater identity with the poor they served. Such groups have urged the church to cooperate in encouraging self-help actions for the poor and sponsoring multinational labor organizations to counter multinational corporations. In 1967, 400 of the 450 Immaculate Heart of Mary sisters followed Anita Caspary out of the diocesan schools rather than sacrifice curricular changes opposed by Cardinal McIntyre. They formed an alternative "community without walls" with married couples and male members, a syneisactic model of life that was promptly condemned by the hierarchy. Communities of this sort are probably not destined for institutional longevity, but there is no reason to dismiss an apostolate that springs up in answer to a need, dissolves, and reshapes itself as circumstances require.

American sisters have also been active in seeking bonds with communities throughout the world. In 1960, the Sisters of Mercy of the Union initiated a project through the Sisters Formation Conference Overseas Project to provide leadership training to sisters from Africa, Latin America, and India who would then carry the work back to their own countries. The project also sent American sisters to study formation in other countries, through which they also became cognizant of the conditions in which their fellow sisters served. As a result, they were ready to act in 1968 when 150 Latin American bishops meeting at Medellín condemned the institutionalized violence of modern society. Liberation Theology was born from this reassertion of the gospel message to the poor, as the assembled bishops disavowed the support of oppressive governments and vowed to devote themselves to the development of grass-roots human rights movements.

Sisters throughout the world took up the challenge and joined to promote the cause of the poor and abused. They were particularly active throughout Latin America in the formation of Christian base communities, communities of worship and social service working and living among the poor. The system has spread to many impoverished countries and the base communities have often played a prominent role in local struggles. During the 1970s many priests, nuns, and lay people throughout Latin America were attacked and some were killed for supporting land reform, trade unions, and peasant organizations. In Manila, Filipino nuns marched in the forefront of the crowds against Ferdinand Marcos's tanks. In Seoul in 1987, Korean nuns formed a prayer line to protect dissident students who sought asylum in Myongdong Cathedral. Thus, a Christian renewal based on the gospel has been linked to political and social activism and even revolution.

Since 1989, congregations of Catholic nuns who survived and recruited new members since the Russian Revolution have emerged from the ruins of the Soviet Union. Outlawed in 1950, Eastern European nuns in Poland, Czechoslovakia, Hungary and elsewhere maintained their congregations in secret and recruited novices on a regular basis, supporting themselves as practical nurses or in other jobs. When the Japanese interned missionaries during World War II, Japanese sisters carried on their work as did Chinese sisters and catechists in their own country. The communist government exiled the surviving Western sisters and imprisoned hundreds of Chinese sisters. Nevertheless, as late as 1973, the government sold a million copies of a booklet praising women of the People's Liberation Army for rescuing young girls from the clutches of nuns! Unknown numbers of Chinese Virgins and other sisters still continue their missions and recruit novices behind the bamboo curtain, not only in China but also in Vietnam, North Korea, and other areas presently inaccessible to church officials.

Despite the decrease of vocations in Europe and America by nearly 50 percent between 1965 and 1990, 960,991 of the remaining 1,190,272 religious in the world in 1993 were women.[6] The number of female vocations in the third world is rising steadily. Women's accomplishments will probably be the center of the history of the next millennium. At the 1994 Synod of Bishops, sisters from the "young" Asian and African churches maintained that they do not want to be dominated by a Western model. They may indeed reject the "feminist" model of the American church, but the hierarchical model of the Roman church is equally Western. Nuns in Africa and Asia and indeed nuns in America are still susceptible to negative male definitions of feminism, but they can be trusted to find their own way to its basic principles. In embracing the religious life, they clearly mean to repeat the effort to build a life on the gospel message as they understand it. Their work to date does not indicate that their understanding is unrecognizably at variance with that of their Western sisters.

The voice of a conservative multiculturalism seeks to discourage policies favoring women's rights because of their negative impact on the young churches where masculine authority through the family still reigns securely. However strenuously the Asian and African sisters and their clerical supporters seek definitions compatible with their native cultures, their very existence is an act of defiance against those cultures. They are already in the process of changing their worlds as their foremothers in the West did for so many centuries. Maintaining the traditional community life, including a habit and distinctive behavior patterns, only strengthens their identity. This deceptive conservatism pleases representatives of the hierarchy. But true traditionalism lies in the pressures on women to marry, to subject themselves to the will of parents and husbands, to shun personal ambitions. In brief, the conditions Asian and

African women are escaping make visible attachment to a powerful male institution a virtual necessity if they are to take the first steps to assure their own autonomy.

Some social activists call the struggle for inculturation "yesterday's battle" and feel that stressing multicultural values avoids the true challenge of poverty. All people of good will must be wary that abuse and oppression not be allowed to divide and conquer under the guise of respect for other peoples. As yet, we in the West are not well informed about the hopes and plans of the sisters in the young churches. Many of them are contemplative, but the fastest growing order in the world is Mother Teresa's Missionaries of Charity. In a world where so many nations have neither the money nor the tradition to develop a broad network of social services, the feminine apostolate still responds to the victims of dowry murders, child abuse, homelessness, addiction, and all the other ills of modern life. Indeed, impoverished India is restoring that apostolate to the West as secular social services crumble here and the needs of the homeless, the hungry, the abused, and the psychologically disabled far outstrip the willingness of taxpayers to provide the necessary assistance.

Institutionalization of the life of poverty and charity needs revision in the light of modern social policies. Like the virgins and widows of early Christianity, new communities may prefer to emphasize charity over poverty, particularly in relying on the financial resources of sisters drawing salaries from secular social services. Even so, future sisters will have to face a more precarious and perhaps more rewarding life exposed to the realities of the poor they serve, without institutional protection but also, like the original apostles, without institutional constraint. Individualistic capitalism releases most people from dependence on inherited wealth and status. Permanent vows once seemed necessary to prevent temporary enthusiasms from hopelessly entangling the lines of inheritance and status in the world. The apostolic sisterhoods have commonly relied on simple rather than permanent vows, and modern sensibilities certainly prefer the love and service given freely and freely renewed. In the future, the monastic or quasi-monastic life may be incorporated into a whole life pattern in which degrees and types of commitment shift with the lifecycle. Celibate chastity may be a life embraced for a period before or after a life of sexual and procreative involvement.

Modern nuns are still prepared to obey God speaking through their consciences, but they are less willing to admit that the pope and the rest of the male hierarchy speak for God. Paul VI confirmed the ban on birth-control first established by the church in 1895, to the shock and dismay of women all over the world. In 1983, Agnes Mary Mansour, whose post as Michigan's director of social services put her in charge of funding birth control programs, was forced to laicize rather than refuse state funds for legal abortions. Humility, the counterpart of obedience, used to be the center of all communal discipline. Girls brought up in a twentieth century democracy simply have no understanding or sympathy for the ceremonies of life developed for a millennium and a half by their predecessors. In the fifteenth century, abandonment of the common table was proclaimed a certain sign of corruption. Today most sisters remember it only as a pointless discipline from which they withheld inner self-identification. Silence, the discipline of deference and obedience, the public confession of faults and repentance all seem infantilizing and boring.[7] At least for women called to the lay apostolate as opposed to the contemplative life, it would seem that a whole new form of rule must be devised.

There has never been a Christianity that did not rely on the prayers and services of dedicated women. They were with Jesus before there was a church and devoted lives to prayer and service before men wrote rules and prelates enforced them. For two millennia, they have successfully responded to the challenges of history without losing fidelity to the ancient gospel. The world continues to change, but the turmoil that has marked the late twentieth century testifies that the regiments of sisters throughout the world are still needed on the battlefield where human frailty and human need face the powers and principalities of greed and oppression. As soldiers of Christ, they have fought honorably. Let us hope that in the third millennium the sisters will advance anew toward that vision where slave and free, male and female, are reconciled. As their struggle to affirm their own worth and answer their vocations continues, a larger global sisterhood promises to develop. Women from every culture will take their places in this long history of the warriors who found dignity and autonomy in dedication to God and to their neighbor, a noble purpose in life and a beneficent legacy in death.

NOTES

BIBLIOGRAPHY

INDEX

Notes

As this book grew in size and moved across many centuries, the apparatus of notes and bibliography threatened to overwhelm the publisher's capacity to confine it to a single volume. We settled on limiting the notes to primary sources and sources for direct quotations which are fully cited at first appearance in each chapter. These citations are not repeated in the bibliography section, though collections from which the individual sources were drawn are cited there, as are monographs that acted as the source for other information in the chapter. The bibliography accompanying each chapter includes all the secondary sources that contributed information and ideas directly to the text. In anticipation of a diverse audience for the book, I have cited English translations in preference to the foreign-language originals wherever possible.

Abbreviations

ANF	Alexander Roberts and James Donaldson, eds., *The Ante-Nicene Fathers*, (Grand Rapids, Mich.: W. B. Eerdmans, 1975–76).
AASS	J. Bollandus and G. Henschenius, *Acta Sanctorum . . . editio novissima*, ed. J. Carnandet et al. (Paris: Palmé, 1863–).
CCSL	*Corpus Christianorum Series Latina* (Turnholt: Brepols, 1972–1976).
CSEL	*Corpus Scriptorum Ecclesiasticorum Latinorum* (Vienna: Hölder, Pichler and Tempsky, 1981).
ER	Eudes of Rouen, *The Register of Eudes of Rouen*, ed. and trans. Sydney M. Brown (New York: Columbia University Press, 1964).
Hefele-Leclercq	Carl J. Hefele and Henri Leclercq, *Histoire des Conciles d'après les documents originaux* (Paris: Letousey and Ané, 1938).
HO	Jacques de Vitry, *Historia Occidentalis*, ed. John F. Hinnebusch, Spicilegium Friburgense 17 (Fribourg: University Press, 1972).
LCL	Loeb Classical Library.

MGH Capit.   *Monumenta Germaniae Historica Capitularia,* 2 vols. (Hannover, 1883–1897).

MGH Conc. 1   F. Maasen, ed., *Monumenta Germaniae Historica Concilia,* vol. 1 (to Aachen, 825) (Hannover, 1893–1906).

MGH Conc. 2   A. Wermgenhoff, ed., *Monumenta Germaniae Historica Concilia,* vol. 2 (Hannover, 1893–1906).

MGH Const.   *Constitutiones,* vol. 1 of *Monumenta Germaniae Historica Legum Sectio 3* (Hannover, 1893–1906).

MGH Epist.   E. Dümmler, ed., *Epistolae karolini aevi,* vols. 5–6 of *Monumenta Germaniae Historica Epistolae 5–6* (Hannover, 1885–1902).

MGH SS   *Monumenta Germaniae Historica: Scriptores.*

MGH SSRM   *Monumenta Germaniae Historica: Scriptores rerum merovingicarum.*

NPNF   Philip Schaff and Henry Wace, eds., *Nicene and Post-Nicene Fathers,* (Grand Rapids, Mich.: W. B. Eerdmans, 1979).

PL   J.-P. Migne, ed., *Patrologia Latina* (Paris: J.-P. Migne, 1844–1864).

SC   *Sources Chrétiennes.*

SWDA   Jo Ann McNamara and John E. Halborg, with Gordon Whatley, *Sainted Women in the Dark Ages* (Durham, N.C.: Duke University Press, 1992).

1. The Apostolic Life

1. This progression is elucidated by Elizabeth Schüssler Fiorenza, *In Memory of Her: A Feminist Theological Reconstruction of Christian Origins* (New York: Crossroad, 1983), 255, from Aristotle, *Politics,* 1.7, and extended beyond the Greco-Roman sphere through the use of two Jewish writers of the first century, Philo and Josephus, who insisted that Aristotle's vision of the family was also the model for Jewish community life.

2. Juvenal, Satire 6, 512–555, in *Satires,* LCL, ed. and trans. G. G. Ramsay (London: W. Heinemann, 1924).

3. Matt. 12:46–50. This and all subsequent biblical quotations have been taken from Herbert G. May and Bruce M. Metzger, eds., *Oxford Annotated Bible, Revised Standard Version* (New York: Oxford University Press, 1962).

4. The way of life revealed in Acts 4:32–38 and 10:36–44 is idealized by Paul, Gal. 3:28 and in many of the noncanonical gospels collected in Montague R. James, ed., *The Apocryphal New Testament* (Oxford: Clarendon Press, 1972), and in Edgar Hennecke and Wilhelm Schneemelcher, eds., *New Testament Apocrypha* (Philadelphia: Westminster Press, 1963–64). Syneisactism is even more pronounced in the Gnostic tradition that gives Mary Magdalene, Salome, and other gospel women key roles; see James M. Robinson, ed., *The Nag Hammadi Library* (San Francisco: Harper and Row, 1981).

5. Fiorenza, *In Memory of Her,* 250.

6. Luke (7:37–50) places the whole event in a different context from Matthew, Mark, and John and characterizes the woman as a prostitute.

7. Juvenal, Satire 6, 315–320.

8. Clement of Alexandria, in *Stromata*, 4.8, in *ANF*, 2:419.

9. Philo of Alexandria, *On the Contemplative Life*, 476.23–24, 481.22–24, 483.42, in *Works*, LCL, ed. and trans. F. H. Colson and G. H. Whitaker (Cambridge, Mass.: Harvard University Press, 1962). Josephus, *Jewish Antiquities*, 15.10.4, LCL, ed. R. Marcus (London: Heinemann, 1926), compared the Essenes with Pythagoreans perhaps as part of his plan to reconcile Jewish and Hellenistic traditions.

10. Pliny the Elder, a Roman observer, maintained that Essenes had no wives but were drawn from the ranks of men tired of life (*Natural History*, 5.16.4, LCL, ed. and trans. H. Rackham [Cambridge, Mass.: Harvard University Press, 1938–1963]), though there were women buried in their cemetery. Philo of Alexandria (*Hypothetica*, in *Works*, LCL, ed. and trans. F. H. Colson and G. H. Whitaker [Cambridge, Mass.: Harvard University Press, 1962]) agreed that they did not marry because, he thought, of the natural deficiencies of the female sex. Josephus claimed that a few members obeyed the commandment to be fruitful and multiply with women willing to minimize the inescapable pollution by extraordinary lustrations; see *The Jewish War*, 2.7, ed. and trans. G. A. Williamson (New York: Penguin Books, 1981), 129.

11. Charles T. Fritsch, *The Qum'ran Community: Its History and Scrolls* (New York: Macmillan, 1956), 104.

12. The Protoevangelion of James, in *ANF*, 8:363.

13. Juvenal, Satire 6, 525–530.

14. For example, Acts of Bartholomew 2, and others cited by James, *Apocryphal New Testament*.

15. Robinson, *Nag Hammadi Library*, 195–205.

16. See the story of Ananias and Sapphira, Acts 5:1–11.

17. Gal. 3:28.

18. "Clement of Rome," Second Epistle concerning Virginity, in *ANF* 8:63.

19. *Canones Apostolorum*, 1.51, in J. Mayer, ed., *Monumenta de viduis, diaconissis, virginibusque tractantia* (Bonn: Florilegium Patristicum, 1938).

20. Titus 2:1–5. "Paul" instructs deaconesses to teach young women sound doctrine and love for their husbands and children. For baptism, see *Constitutiones Apostolorum*, 2.15, in F-X. Funk, ed., *Didascalia et Constitutiones Apostolorum* (Paderborn: Ferdinand Schöningh, 1905).

21. Acts 16:13–40.

22. Acts 7.

23. Acts 9:36–43.

24. I Cor. 7:8–11; 39–40.

25. I Cor. 7:25–35.

26. I Cor. 7.

27. King James gives "virgin" as the translation here rendered as "betrothed." Some editors have construed the text to refer to daughters.

28. "Clement of Rome," First Epistle Concerning Virginity, 1.10, in *ANF*, 8.

29. Acts 21:8. Eusebius noted, in the fourth century, the belief advanced by Poly-

crates of Ephesus that Philip and his daughters were buried in Hierapolis; see Roy J. Deferrari, trans., *Ecclesiastical History,* 3:31.3–4 (New York: Fathers of the Church, 1955).

30. Philo of Alexandria, *Speculum Legibus,* 319f., in *Works,* LCL, ed. and trans. F. H. Colson and G. H. Whitaker (Cambridge, Mass.: Harvard University Press, 1962).

31. Clement of Alexandria, *Paedagogus,* 1.4, in *ANF,* 2.

32. Protoevangelion of James, 2, 8.

33. Acts of Bartholomew 2, and others cited by James, *Apocryphal New Testament,* 194–277.

34. Acts of Paul and Thecla, in Hennecke and Schneemelcher, *New Testament Apocrypha,* 2:355.

35. Acts of John 2, in James, *Apocryphal New Testament,* 266.

36. Acts of Paul, in James, *Apocryphal New Testament,* 5–12.

37. See especially the story of Drusiana and Callimachus in the Acts of John 51–63, which attracted the attention of the play-writing nun Hroswitha in the tenth century.

38. The Acts of Thomas (in James, *Apocryphal New Testament,* 82 ff.) provide a long and dramatic tale of a beautiful wife who dared prison and execution to escape from her conjugal duties.

39. Justin Martyr, *Apology to the Senate,* 2.2, in T. B. Falls, trans., *Works* (New York: Fathers of the Church, 1948).

40. Robinson, *Nag Hammadi Library.*

41. Epiphanius, *Adversus Haereses,* 1.45.2, in G. Dinfortius, ed., *Opera* (Leipzig, 1859–1862).

42. Irenaeus of Lyon, *Against Heresies,* 2.27, in *ANF,* 1.

43. Gospel of Philip, in Robinson, *Nag Hammadi Library,* 137.

44. Irenaeus, *Against Heresies,* 1.13.

45. Methodius, *The Symposium: A Treatise on Chastity,* in Herbert Musurillo, trans. *Ancient Christian Writers,* 27 (Westminster, Md.: Newman Press, 1958).

46. Tertullian, *On Prayer,* 21, in *ANF,* 3:687.

47. Tertullian *On the Veiling of Virgins,* 9, in *ANF,* 4.

48. An idea that was vigorously condemned by Hippolytus in *Against All Heresies* 5.8.44, in *ANF,* 6.

49. Robinson, *Nag Hammadi Library,* 130.

50. Eusebius, *Ecclesiastical History,* 5.18.4.

51. Epiphanius, *Panarion,* 49.2.1–5, cited by Fred C. Klawiter, "The Role of Martyrdom and Persecution in Developing the Priestly Authority of Women in Early Christianity," in David M. Scholer, ed., *Women in Early Christianity* (New York: Garland Press, 1993), 105–115.

52. Tertullian, *On Baptism,* 17, in *ANF,* 3.

53. Tertullian, *Veiling of Virgins,* 9, in *ANF,* 3.

54. Cyprian of Carthage, Letter 75.10, in R. Bernard, trans., *Letters* (Washington: Fathers of the Church, 1964).

55. Hippolytus, *Against All Heresies,* 8.12.

56. Irenaeus, *Against Heresies*, 1.12.7.

57. Tertullian, *Exhortation to Chastity*, 1, in *ANF*, 4; *To His Wife*, 2.8, in *ANF*, 4.

58. Tertullian, *On the Apparel of Women*, 1.1, in *ANF*, 4.

59. Ibid., 2.5.

60. Ibid., 1.2.

61. Eusebius, *Ecclesiastical History*, 5.1.42.

62. *The Passion of Perpetua and Felicity*, trans. W. H. Shewring (London: Sheed and Ward, 1931), 10.

63. Herbert Musurillo, *Acts of the Christian Martyrs* (Oxford: Clarendon Press, 1972).

64. Eusebius, *Ecclesiastical History*, 6.43.11.

65. Palladius, *Lausiac History*, 148, in Robert T. Meyer, ed. and trans., *Ancient Christian Writers*, vol. 34 (Westminster, Md.: Newman Press, n.d.).

66. DeLacy O'Leary, *The Saints of Egypt* (London: SPCK; New York: Macmillan, 1937), 65.

67. Palladius, *Lausiac History*, 146.

68. Gregory Thaumaturge, *Canonical Epistle*, 1 in *ANF*, 6.

69. *Vita Theodorae*, 3, in *AASS*, April 4, 572.

2. Cult and Countercult

1. Clement of Rome, *Address to the Greeks*, 40, in F. X. Cima, trans., *Fathers of the Church* (New York: Cima Publishing, 1947).

2. *Constitutiones Apostolorum*, 6.27, in F-X. Funk, ed., *Didascalia et Constitutiones Apostolorum* (Paderborn, Ferdinand Schöningh, 1905).

3. *Constitutiones Apostolorum*, 5.14.

4. "Clement of Rome," Second Letter concerning Virginity, 1–2, in *ANF*, 8.

5. Justin Martyr, *Apology to the Senate*, 1.13, in T. B. Falls, trans., *Works* (New York: Fathers of the Church, 1948).

6. Pliny the Younger, *Epistle* 96, in *Letters and Panegyrics*, LCL, ed. and trans. Betty Radice (Cambridge, Mass.: Harvard University Press, 1969).

7. *Constitutiones Apostolorum* 3.15.2.

8. *Constitutiones Apostolorum*, 3.3.6.

9. *Constitutiones Apostolorum*, 2.2.

10. Justin Martyr, *Dialogue*, 88.1, in *Works* (see n. 5).

11. Clement of Alexandria, *Stromata*, 4.1, in *ANF*, 2.

12. Clement of Alexandria, *Paedagogus*, 3.4, in *ANF*, 2.

13. Epistle to Diognetes, 5–6, in *ANF*, 1.

14. Clement of Rome, *Address to the Greeks*, 4. Unlike the two letters on virginity attributed to Clement, his authorship of this one is undisputed. Hermas was also disturbed by the difficulties of the Corinthian community and instructed a deaconess named Grapte to admonish the women there; see *Pastor*, 1.1–4, in *ANF*, 2.

15. Clement of Alexandria, *Stromata*, 3.6.

16. Ibid., 3.33.

17. Tertullian, *A Treatise on the Soul,* 9, in *ANF,* 3.

18. "Clement of Rome," First Epistle concerning Virginity, 1.10, in *ANF,* 4.

19. Ignatius of Antoich, To the Philadelphians, 4, in *Epistles,* in *ANF,* 1:45–127.

20. Ignatius of Antioch, Epistle to Polycarp, 5, in *Epistles,* in *ANF,* 1.

21. I Tim. 2:8.

22. Titus 2:1–5.

23. *Constitutiones Apostolorum,* 2.17.

24. Tertullian, *On the Apparel of Women,* 2.1, 2.8–9, in *ANF,* 4.

25. Tertullian, *On Prayer,* 25, in *ANF,* 4.

26. Cyprian, *De habitu virginum,* 5.15, in *CCSL,* 3.

27. Ibid., 14.

28. Victricius of Rouen, *De laude sanctorum,* 3, in Joyce N. Hilgarth, ed., *The Conversion of Western Europe, 350–750* (Englewood Cliffs, N.J.: Prentice-Hall, 1969) 23.

29. Palladius, *Lausiac History,* 46, in Robert T. Meyer, ed. and trans., *Ancient Christian Writers,* vol. 34 (Westminster Md.: Newman Press, n.d.).

30. Palladius, *Dialogue concerning the Life of Chrysostom,* 61, trans. Herbert Moore (London/New York, 1921).

31. John Chrysostom, *À une jeune veuve: sur le mariage unique* ed. and trans. B. Grilley, in *SC,* 138 (Paris: Editions du Cerf, 1968).

32. Chrysostom, *Life of Olympias* 9, in Elizabeth A. Clark, trans., *Jerome, Chrysostom, and Friends* (New York: Edwin Mellen Press, 1979).

33. Chrysostom, *Letters to Olympias,* in *Jerome, Chrysostom, and Friends* (see previous note), 298.

34. Gerontius, *The Life of Melania the Younger,* ed. and trans. Elizabeth A. Clark (Lewiston, N.Y.: Edwin Mellen, 1988).

35. Gregory of Nyssa, *Life of Saint Macrina,* in Virginia W. Callahan, trans., *Ascetical Works,* in *Fathers of the Church,* vol. 58 (Washington D.C.: Catholic University of America Press, 1966).

36. Palladius, *Lausiac History,* 148. Ibid., 137, on Olympias, who was also believed to have preserved her virginity throughout a brief marriage by unknown devices.

37. Jill Harries and Ian Wood, eds., *Codex Theodosianus,* 9.25.1 (Ithaca, N.Y.: Cornell University Press, 1993).

38. Constantine's abrogation of the Augustan marriage laws was incorporated into the *Codex Theodosianus,* 8.17, and Justinian recognized unmarried women's ability to control their own property in *Corpus Iuris Civilis,* 8.59.1.

39. Jerome, Epistle 122, *Ad Rusticum* 4, in *NPNF,* 6.

40. Palladius, *Lausiac History,* 41.2.

41. Jerome, Epistle 127, Ad Principiam 7, in *NPNF,* 6.

42. Gregory of Nyssa, *Dialogue of the Soul,* in Virginia W. Callahan, trans., *Ascetical Works,* in *Fathers of the Church,* vol. 58 (Washington, D.C.: Catholic University of America Press, 1966).

43. Egeria, *Travels to the Holy Land,* trans. John Wilkinson (n.p.: Ariel Publications, 1983).

44. Chrysostom, *Instructions and Refutation Directed against Those Men Cohabiting with Virgins*, in Elizabeth A. Clark, trans., *Jerome, Chrysostom, and Friends* (New York: Edwin Mellen Press, 1979).

45. Jerome, Epistola 22, *Ad Eustochium* 19, in *NPNF*, 6.

46. Gregory of Nyssa, *Life of Saint Macrina*, 47–48.

47. Jerome Epistola 22, *Ad Eustochium*, 21.

48. Jerome, *Dialogue against Helvidius*, 17, in *NPNF*, 6.

49. Augustine, *De sancta virginitate*, 4, in *CSEL*, 41, ed. J. Zycha (Prague/Vienna/Leipzig: F. Tempsky, 1902), 209–319.

50. Ibid., 5–6.

51. Ibid., 9.

52. Kenneth Holum, *Theodosian Empresses* (Berkeley: University of California Press, 1982), 157–163. For the importance of these councils, see W. H. C. Frend, *The Rise of Christianity* (Philadelphia: Fortress Press, 1984), 741–785.

53. Ambrose, *De virginibus*, 1.56, in *PL*, 16:187–232.

54. Chrysostom, *Instructions*, 9.

55. Canon 31 in Samuel Laeuchli, *Power and Sexuality: The Emergence of Canon Law at the Synod of Elvira* (Philadelphia: Temple University Press, 1972).

56. Sulpicius Severus, Letter to Bassula 4, in F. R. Hoare, ed., *The Western Fathers* (New York: Harper Torchbooks, 1965), 47–67.

57. Ambrose, *Liber de exhortatione virginitatis*, 5.6.7, in *PL*, 16, recalls the papal exhortation on that occasion.

58. *Life of Genovefa*, 6, in *SWDA*.

59. Basil, Epistola 199, c. 18 in *Letters*, trans. Agnes C. Way, (New York: Fathers of the Church, 1951).

60. Ambrose, *De virginibus*, 11.60.

61. Jerome, Letter 24, *Ad Marcellam* 3, in *NPNF*, 6.

62. Ambrose, Epistola 5, in *PL*, 16:929.

63. Tertullian, *Exhortation to Chastity*, 12, in *ANF*, 4.

64. Eusebius, *Ecclesiastical History*, 7.30.12–41, trans. Roy J. Deferrari (New York: Fathers of the Church, 1955).

65. Cyprian, Epistle 1.1, 3.3, 4.1.

66. Sulpicius, *Dialogue, Postumianus*, 21, in F. R. Hoare, ed., *The Western Fathers* (New York: Harper Torchbook, 1965).

67. Basil, *De virginitate tuenda*, in *Patrologia Graeca*, 30:669–810, cited by Peter Brown, *The Body and Society* (New York: Columbia University Press, 1988), 268, who notes the "studiously fostered" sexual alarm provoked by syneisactism.

68. Jerome, Epistola 52, in *NPNF*, 6.

69. Basil, Epistola 55, in Agnes C. Way, trans., *Letters*, (New York: Fathers of the Church, 1951).

70. Aphrahat, *Demonstratio*, 6.4, in *NPNF*, 6:366.

71. Sulpicius, *Dialogue, Postumianus*, 2.11, in Hoare, *The Western Fathers* (see n. 66).

72. Ambrose, Epistola 52, 5.6.11.

73. Chrysostom, *Instructions*, 11.

74. Constantius, *Life of Germanus*, in Hoare, *The Western Fathers* (see n. 66), 283–320.

75. Paulinus of Nola, Epistle 18, in *Letters*, in *Ancient Christian Writers*, vols. 35–36 (Mahwah: Paulist Press, 1966–67). See also Epistles 38, 39, and 44, to Aper and Amanda; and 51, to Eucherius and Galla, who lived in similar unions.

76. Augustine, Epistle 27, c. 33, in *CSEL*, 41.

77. Paulinus, Epistle 39.

78. For example, Council of Tours, 14, in C. Munier, ed., *Concilia Gallia*, in *CCSL*, 148:191.

79. Orange 1, 26, in *Concilia Gallia*.

80. Nîmes 2, in Hefele-Leclercq, 93.

81. Gelasius, *Epistola*, 1.14, in *PL*, 59.

3. The Discipline of the Desert

1. Athanasius, *Life of Antony*, 1, in *NPNF*, 4:189.

2. Sulpicius, *Postumianus*, 2.7, in F. R. Hoare, ed., *The Western Fathers* (New York: Harper Torchbooks, 1965), 116.

3. Ambrose, *Expositionis in evangelium secundum Lucam X*, 161, in *PL*, 15:1527–1858.

4. Jerome, *Commentarius in epistolam ad Ephesios*, 3.5, in *PL*, 26:567.

5. Eulogy for Gorgonia, in Rosemary R. Ruether, *Gregory of Nazianzus* (Oxford: Clarendon Press, 1969), 70.

6. Gregory of Nyssa, *The Life of Saint Macrina*, in Virginia W. Callahan, trans., *Ascetical Works*, in *Fathers of the Church*, vol. 58 (Washington, D.C.: Catholic University Press, 1966).

7. Paulinus of Nola, Epistle 29, in *Letters*, in *Ancient Christian Writers*, vols. 35–36 (Mahwah: Paulist Press, 1966–67).

8. Jerome, Epistola 108, in *NPNF*, 6.

9. Jerome, Epistola 77, *Ad Oceanum*, 3–4, in *NPNF*, 6.

10. Chrysostom, *Instructions and Refutation Directed against Those Men Cohabiting with Virgins* 7, in Elizabeth C. Clark, trans. *Jerome, Chrysostom, and Friends* (New York: Edwin Mellen Press, 1979).

11. Sulpicius, *Chronica*, 2.50, ed. A. Lavertujon (Paris: Librairie Hachette, 1899), 114.

12. Basil, Epistola 169, in Agnes C. Way, trans., *Letters* (New York: Fathers of the Church, 1951).

13. Augustine, Epistola 35, c.2, in *CSEL* 88, ed. J. Divjak.

14. Gerontius, *Life of Melania the Younger*, 21, trans. and ed. Elizabeth A. Clark (Lewiston, N.Y.: Edwin Mellen, 1988).

15. *Pelagia of Antioch*, in Sebastian P. Brock and Susan Ashbrook Harvey, trans., *Holy Women of the Syrian Orient* (Berkeley: University of California Press, 1987), 43.

16. Ambrose, *De institutione virginitatis*, 4, in *PL*, 16:305–334.

17. *The Life of Thaïs the Whore*, in Benedicta Ward, trans., *The Harlots of the Desert* (Kalamazoo, Mich.: Cistercian Publications, 1987).

18. *Life of Susan*, in Brock and Harvey, *Holy Women* (see n. 15), 137.

19. *Mary of Egypt*, 9, in Ward, *Harlots* (see n. 17).

20. L. Clugnet, ed., *Vie de l'abbé Daniel le Scétiote* (Paris: Bibliothèque hagiographique orientale, 1901).

21. A. J. Wensinck, ed., *Legends of the Eastern Saints*, vol. 2 (Leyden: Brill, 1913).

22. Anan-Isho, *Paradise of the Fathers*, trans. Ernest A. Wallis Budge (London: Chatto and Windus, 1907), 29.

23. Palladius, *Lausiac History*, 32, in Robert T. Meyer, ed. and trans., *Ancient Christian Writers*, vol. 34 (Westminster, Md.: Newman Press, n.d.).

24. Ibid., 63. Rousseau sees Pachomius's biography as a weapon for the instruction of monks on how to relate to the patriarch; see A. N. Athanassakis, trans., *Vita Prima Graeca*, in *The Life of Pachomius* (Missoula, Mont.: Scholars Press, 1975).

25. See the anonymous *Bohairic Life of Pachomius*, 32, trans. Armand Veilleux, in *Pachomian Koinonia I* (Kalamazoo, Mich.: Cistercian Publications, 1980).

26. Palladius, *Lausiac History*, 34.

27. Ibid., 59.

28. Ibid., 33.

29. Egeria, *Travels to the Holy Land*, trans. John Wilkinson (n.p.: Ariel Publications: 1983), 22.

30. Palladius, *Lausiac History*, 2.6.

31. Ibid., 132.

32. Council of Gangra, in Hefele and Leclercq, 1/2:1031f., 1038f., 1040

33. Jerome, Letter to Eustochium 17, in *NPNF*, 6.

34. Jerome, *Against Helvidius: Book on the Perpetual Virginity of the Blessed Mary*, 21.12, in *NPNF*, 6.

35. Jerome, Epistola 30, c.4, in *NPNF*, 6.

36. Augustine, Epistola 150, in *CSEL*, 88.

37. Gregory of Nyssa, *Life of Saint Macrina*, 170.

38. *Life of Febronia*, in Brock and Harvey, *Holy Women* (see n. 15), 150–176.

39. Gregory of Nyssa, *Life of Saint Macrina*, 177. See also Basil, Epistola 223 (in Agnes C. Way, trans., *Letters* [New York: Fathers of the Church, 1951]), who mentions the word "canonesses," though he does not define it.

40. Chrysostom, *Life of Olympias*, 6, in Elizabeth A. Clark, trans., *Jerome, Chrysostom, and Friends* (New York: Edwin Mellen Press, 1979).

41. Gregory of Nyssa, *Life of Saint Macrina*, 167.

42. Chrysostom, *Life of Olympias*, 13–15.

43. Jerome, Letter to Eustochium, 14.

44. *Life of Susan*, in Brock and Harvey, *Holy Women*, 135.

45. Jerome, Epistola 108, c.20.

46. Gerontius, *Life of Melania the Younger*, 21.

47. Gregory of Nyssa, *Life of Saint Macrina*, 183.

48. Ibid., 170–171.

49. Jerome, *Epistola* 108, c.6.

50. Gregory of Nazianzus, *Eulogy for Gorgonia*, 71.

51. Cassian, *Conférences*, 18.14, E. Pichery, ed. and French trans., *SC*, vols. 42, 54, 64 (Paris: Editions du Cerf, 1955–1959).

52. Jerome, *Epistola* 108, c.6.

53. Sozomen, *Church History from A.D. 323–425*, 8.9.1, in *NPNF*, 2. Palladius, *Dialogue*, 117, in *Ancient Christian Writers* (see n. 23).

54. Jill Harries and Ian Wood, eds. *Codex Theodosianus*, 16.2.27 (Ithaca, N.Y.: Cornell University Press, 1993); ibid., 16.1.17 prohibits deaconesses from leaving their property to the church instead of relatives.

55. Sergia, "Narration concerning St. Olympias," in Elizabeth A. Clark, trans., *Jerome, Chrysostom, and Friends* (New York: Edwin Mellen Press, 1979).

56. Dorothy de F. Abrahamse, "Byzantine Asceticism and Women's Monasteries in Early Medieval Italy," in John A. Nichols and Lillian Thomas Shank, eds., *Medieval Religious Women*, vol. 1, *Distant Echoes* (Kalamazoo, Mich.: Cistercian Publications, 1984), 40–41.

57. Augustinian rule, first mentioned by Eugippus about 530, represents a collection of various pieces addressed to men and to women, sometimes repeating the same prescriptions and apparently intended to be used by persons of both genders equally. A sensible and persuasive account of its development may be found in George Lawless, *Augustine of Hippo and His Monastic Rule* (Oxford: Clarendon Press, 1987).

58. Augustine, *Epistola* 211, in *CSEL*, 88.

59. Gerontius, *Life of Melania the Younger*, 49, 56.

60. In a letter to Radegund of Poitiers, Caesaria II (second abbess of Arles) relayed the same advice; see *SWDA*, 112–118.

61. Jerome, *Epistola* 122, *Ad Rusticum* 4.

4. The Power of Prayer

1. Sulpicius Severus, *Postumianus*, 8, in F. R. Hoare, ed., *The Western Fathers* (New York: Harper Torchbooks, 1965), 77.

2. John Cassian, *Institutions Cénobitiques*, 10.23, in J. C. Guy, ed. and French trans., *SC*, 109 (Paris: Editions du Cerf, 1965).

3. Gregory of Tours, *Glory of the Confessors*, trans. Raymond van Dam (Liverpool: Liverpool University Press, 1988), 30–31.

4. "The Thuringian War," a poem attributed to Radegund, in *SWDA*, 65–70.

5. Christine Fell, *Women in Anglo-Saxon England and the Impact of 1066* (Bloomington: University of Indiana Press, 1985), 66, notes that the name of Hrothgar's queen in *Beowulf* (who is described as a noblewoman wearing gold and giving rings), Wealhtheow, means "foreign slave." Her apparent dignity, therefore, may be only the dignity of a trophy for, as Fell says, the meaning of her name would not be lost on an Anglo-Saxon listener.

6. See particularly the extended imagery of the *Life of Aldegund*, in *SWDA*, 245.

7. *Life of Eustadiola*, in *SWDA*, 106–111.

8. *Life of Genovefa*, 1.3, in *SWDA*.

9. *Life of Genovefa*, 2.6, indicates that there was an established liturgy, but the only details provided concern the ranking of the candidates in order of age.

10. *Life of Genovefa*, 7.39–40.

11. For inconsistencies and difficulties in Clothild's story, see *SWDA*, 38–50.

12. Gregory of Tours, *History of the Franks*, 2.42, trans. Lewis Thorpe (New York: Penguin, 1974). The story is expanded in the ninth century *Vita Chrothildis*, in *SWDA*, 48.

13. Radegund's life is remarkable for the richness of the sources. It was outlined by Gregory of Tours in his *History of the Franks* and recounted in detail by Fortunatus, whose biography was further expanded by Baudonivia, one of the nuns of Poitiers. Finally, we have a lengthy poem, possibly written by Radegund herself. These three accounts are available in *SWDA*, 60–105.

14. Caesarius of Arles, *Rule for Nuns*, trans. Mary Caritas McCarthy (Washington, D.C.: Catholic University of America Press, 1960).

15. A century later, things had not improved when Sadalberga abandoned her original convent for a safer site within the citadel of Laon; see *SWDA*, 186.

16. Caesarius, *Rule*, art. 2, 36–40.

17. Baudonivia, *Life of Radegund*, 2.18–19, in *SWDA*.

18. Gregory the Great, *Dialogues 2: The Life of Saint Benedict*, 33, trans. O. J. Zimmerman (New York: Fathers of the Church, 1959).

19. Leander of Seville, *Regula sive de institutione virginum et contemptu mundi*, in *PL*, 72:866–898.

20. Bede, *A History of the English Church and People*, 4.19, trans. Leo Sherley-Price (Baltimore: Penguin Books, 1968). Eddius Stephanus, *Life of Wilfrid*, ed. and trans. J. F. Webb, in D. H. Farmer, ed., *The Age of Bede* (New York: Penguin, 1983), 105–183, blames Jurmenberg for the bishop's exile and makes no mention of Etheldreda.

21. A. W. Haddan and William Stubbs, *Councils and Synods with Other Documents Relating to the English Church to 870* (Oxford: Oxford University Press, 1964), 3:199 (decree of Theodore of Tarsus).

22. Aldhelm, *On Virginity*, in Michael Lapidge and Michael Herren, eds., *The Prose Works* (Totowa N.J.: Rowman and Littlefield, 1979), 51–135.

23. Jonas of Bobbio, *Vita Columbani Abbatis disciplinorumque eius, Liber II*, 19, in Bruno Krusch, ed., *MGH SSRM*, 7. The section covering the life of Burgundofara has been translated in *SWDA*, 155–175.

24. Gregory of Tours, *History of the Franks*, 10.8.

25. H. Leclercq, ed., *Concilia Gallia*, in *CCSL*, 148A (Second Tours) (Turnholt: Brepols, 1963).

26. Florentius, *Life of Rusticula*, 10, in *SWDA*, 128.

27. Continuator, *Life of Gertrude*, 3, in *SWDA*, 230.

28. Advocates like Genovefa continued the activity even after death. Queens like

Radegund had the power to issue orders. Other women acting under miraculous conditions freed condemned men from a distance or acted as agents for others like the anonymous virgin to whom Saint Martin appeared in a vision instructing her to fear nothing and free a prisoner; see Gregory of Tours, *Liber de Miraculi S Martini, libri quatuor*, 21, in *PL*, 71:913–1008.

29. Gregory of Tours, *History of the Franks*, 5.24.

30. Ibid., 6.12.

31. Ibid., 4.13 and 4.39.

32. Ibid., 7.4.

33. Agde, 10–11, *Concilia Gallia*, (*CG* in this note), in *CCSL*, 148, 199; Orléans, 29, *CG* 148A, 170–172; Epaone, 20, *CG* 148, 159–172; Clermont, 16, *CG* 148, 94–111; Orléans, 3, *CG* 148, 25–35.

34. Gregory I, *Dialogues 1*, 54.3.7.

35. Tours, 14, *Concilia Gallia* 183.

36. Jonas of Bobbio *Vita Columbani Abbatis* 2:7.

37. Council of Orléans (541) 17 ordered clerical couples to live in continence and to occupy separate chambers, *Concilia Gallia*, in *CCSL*, 148.

38. Gregory of Tours, *Glory of the Confessors*, 77.

39. *Life of Gertrude*, 6. *Life of Aldegund*, 22.

40. Fortunatus, *Life of Radegund*, 36.

41. Baudonivia, *Life of Radegund*, 1.

42. *Life of Balthild*, 14.

43. Bede, *History*, 2.9.

44. W. Levison, ed., *Vita Odiliae abbatissae Hohenburgensis*, in *MGH SS*, 6 (Hannover-Leipsig, 1913), 24–50.

45. Gregory of Tours, *History of the Franks*, 9.31.

46. Ibid., 4.26.

47. Ibid., 6.16.

48. Ibid., 9.31.

49. *Life of Austreberta*, 12, in *SWDA*. The story of the poison is a doublet also found in Gregory's life of Benedict.

50. Gregory of Tours, *History of the Franks*, 14.

51. Ibid., books 9 and 10.

52. In addition to rules already cited, see Benedict of Nursia, *The Rule of Saint Benedict*, ed. A. C. Meisel and M. L. de Mastro (New York: Doubleday, 1975); *Regulae S. Columbani*, in *PL*, 80; Adalbert de Vögué, ed., *The Rule of the Master* (Kalamazoo, Mich.: Cistercian Publications, 1980); and JoAnn McNamara and John E. Halborg, *The Ordeal of Community: The Rule of Donatus of Besançon and the Rule of a Certain Father to the Virgins* (Toronto: Peregrina Publishing, 1993).

53. Leander of Seville, *Regula*, 7.

54. Gregory I, *Dialogues 2*, 19.

55. Gregory I, *Letters*, in *NPNF*, 12:73–243, has numerous references.

56. *Life of Sadalberga*, 11.

57. Fortunatus, *Life of Radegund*, 30.

58. *Life of Monegund*, 3, in *SWDA*.

59. *Life of Austreberta*, 2.4.

60. Columbanus, *Regula*, in *PL*, 80, links this at length to humility

61. Baudonivia, *Life of Radegund*, 12.

62. *Life of Austreberta*, 2.16.

63. *Life of Sadalberga*, 17.

64. *Life of Eustadiola*, 3.

65. Jonas of Bobbio, *Vita Columbani Abbatis*, 2:16.

66. *Life of Austreberta*, 1.15.

67. *Life of Rictrude*, 26, in *SWDA*.

68. *Life of Austreberta* 2.3.

69. *Life of Leoba*, in C. H. Talbot, *The Anglo-Saxon Missionaries in Germany* (London and New York: Sheed and Ward, 1954), 208.

70. Gregory I, *Dialogues 2*, 33.

5. The Frontier Outpost

1. Patrick's *Confession* (31.50), in Liam de Paor, *Saint Patrick's World: The Christian Culture of Ireland's Apostolic Age, Translations and Commentaries* (Notre Dame: University of Notre Dame Press, 1993), praises his female converts who risked every danger for virginity. Irish hagiography soon abounded in this topos.

2. Cogitosus, *Vita sanctae Brigidis*, in *AASS*, February 1, 119–135.

3. Cited from Donncha O hAodha, ed., *Bethu Brigte* (Dublin, 1978), 6, 24, by Lisa M. Bitel (unpublished paper, "Bishop Brigit and the Christianizing Women of Early Ireland," delivered at the annual meeting of the American Historical Association, December 1990).

4. Jonas of Bobbio, *Life of Columbanus*, 1.8, trans. William C. McDermott, in Edward Peters, ed., *Monks, Bishops, and Pagans: Christian Culture in Gaul and Italy* (Philadelphia: University of Pennsylvania Press, 1975).

5. Jonas of Bobbio, *Columbanus* I.11. The impression of a pagan wilderness is confirmed also for Frankland by the sixth-century experience of Radegund, who broke up a pagan festival one day while on her way to visit a friend; see Baudonivia, *Life of Radegund*, 2, in *SWDA*.

6. Jonas of Bobbio, *Columbanus* I.17.

7. *Life of Sadalberga*, 15, in *SWDA*.

8. Donatus of Besançon, *Regula ad virgines*, Introduction, in Jo Ann McNamara and John E. Halborg, *The Ordeal of Community: The Rule of Donatus of Besançon and the Rule of a Certain Father to the Virgins* (Toronto: Peregrina Publishing, 1993).

9. *The Rule of a Certain Father*, in McNamara and Halborg, *Ordeal of Community*, 75–103.

10. Bede, *A History of the English Church and People*, 3.8, trans. Leo Sherley-Price (Baltimore: Penguin Books, 1968).

11. Ibid., 4.23.

12. Gregory of Tours, *History of the Franks*, 4.36, trans. Lewis Thorpe (New York: Penguin, 1974).

13. Gregory I, *Dialogues 2*, 19, trans. O. J. Zimmerman (New York: Fathers of the Church, 1959).

14. Bede, *Life of Cuthbert*, 37, in J. F. Webb, trans., *The Age of Bede* (New York: Penguin Books, 1983), 89.

15. Ephraim Emerton, ed. and trans., *The Letters of Saint Boniface* (New York: Octagon Books, 1973), 36 (letter 6).

16. W. Levison, ed., *Vita Odiliae abbatissae Hohenburgensis*, 22, in *MGH SS*, 6 (Hannover-Leipsig, 1913), 24–50.

17. Emerton, *Letters of Boniface*, 36 (letter 6).

18. Patrick J. Geary, *Aristocracy in Provence: The Rhône Basin at the Dawn of the Carolingian Age* (Philadelphia: University of Pennsylvania Press, 1985), 115.

19. J. Guérout, "Le testament de sainte Fare: Matériaux pour l'étude et l'edition critique de ce document," *Revue d'histoire écclésiastique*, 60, 3–4 (1965): 761–821.

20. Caesarius of Arles, *Rule for Nuns*, 5, trans. Maria Caritas McCarthy (Washington, D.C.: Catholic University of America Press, 1960).

21. Florentius, *Life of Rusticula*, 3, in *SWDA*.

22. Jonas of Bobbio, *Vita Columbani Abbatis disciplinorumque eius, Liber II*, 7, in Bruno Krusch, ed., *MGH SSRM*, 7:113–152.

23. *Life of Sadalberga*, 12, in *SWDA*.

24. *Life of Anstrude*, 5–6, in *SWDA*.

25. *Life of Sadalberga*, 18.

26. *Life of Aldegund*, 1.4, in *SWDA*.

27. *Letter to Egbert*, in James Campbell, ed., *Bede* (New York: Washington Square Press, 1968) 325.

28. Fructuosus of Buaga, *Regula communis*, in Lucas Holstenius *Codex Regularum Monasticarum et Canonicarum*, vol. 1 (Graz, 1957), 208–219. This Spanish family type has been called "vicinal monasticism" by C. J. Bishko, *Spanish and Portuguese Monastic History, 600–1300* (Leiden: Brill, 1984), 20.

29. A. C. Meisel and M. L. del Mastro, trans., *The Rule of Saint Benedict*, 48 (New York: Doubleday, 1975).

30. *Life of Gertrude, continuation*, 11, in *SWDA*.

31. *Life of Gertrude*, 3.

32. Rudolf of Fulda, *Life of Leoba*, in C. H. Talbot, *The Anglo-Saxon Missionaries in Germany* (London and New York: Sheed and Ward, 1954).

33. The letter with a few other letters by nuns has been translated by Marcelle Thiébaux, *The Writings of Medieval Women*, 2d ed. (New York: Garland Publishing, 1994).

34. Huneberc, *Hoedoporicon*, in Talbot, *Anglo-Saxon Missionaries* (see n. 32), 153.

35. Baudonivia, *Life of Radegund*, 26.

36. *Life of Glodesind*, 28, in *SWDA*.

37. W. W. Heist, *Vitae Sanctorum Hiberniae* (Brussels: Société des Bollandistes, 1965), 129.

38. *Life of Aldegund,* 16.

39. Jonas of Bobbio, *Vita Columbani,* 2:22.

40. *Life of Leoba,* 219–220.

41. Donatus, *Rule,* 16.

42. Jonas of Bobbio *Vita Columbani,* 2:12.

43. Donatus, *Rule,* 24 and 26.

44. *Life of Aldegund,* 22.

45. *Life of Austreberta,* 1.10, in *SWDA.*

46. *Life of Monegund,* 9–10.

47. *Life of Gertrude, continuation,* 2.

48. Emerton, *Letters of Boniface,* 2.

49. Theodore, *Penitential,* II.7.1, in John T. McNeill and Helena M. Gamer, *Medieval Handbooks of Penance: A Translation of the Principal Libri Poenitentiales and Selections from Related Documents* (New York: Columbia University Press, 1938).

50. *Life of Balthild,* 7–10, in *SWDA.*

51. *Life of Gertrude,* 2.

52. Jonas of Bobbio, *Vita Columani,* 2:13.

53. Gregory of Tours, *Life of the Fathers,* 9.1, trans. Edward James (Liverpool: Liverpool University Press, 1986).

54. Ludwig Bieler, ed., *Patrician Texts from the Book of Armagh* (Dublin, 1979), 132, cited in Lisa M. Bitel, "Women's Monastic Enclosures in Early Christian Ireland," *Journal of Medieval History* 12 (1986), 17, who analyzes the problem of inheritance.

55. Emerton, *Letters of Boniface,* 34.

56. *Life of the Fathers,* 6.1.

57. Ibid., 6.7.

58. James, note to *Life of the Fathers,* 1.3.

59. Gregory of Tours, *History of the Franks,* 7.1.

6. The Bonds of Castimony

1. Amalarius of Metz, *Regula sanctimonialium,* 8, in *PL,* 105:935–976.

2. E. Emerton, ed. and trans., *Letters of Saint Boniface* (New York: Columbia University Press, 1940), 126–128 (letter 57).

3. Leandri Episcopi, *Regula sive de institutione virginum et contemptu mundi,* in *PL,* 72:866–898.

4. Cloveshoe, 20, in A. W. Haddan and William Stubbs, *Councils and Synods with Other Documents Relating to the English Church to 870* (Oxford: Oxford University Press, 1964), 363.

5. Council of Frankfort (anno 794), 12, in *MGH Conc.* 1.

6. Council of Soissons, 5, in *MGH Conc.* 2.

7. *Capitularia regum francorum*, 1, ed. A. Boretius and V. Krause, in *MGH Capit.*, 347–348.

8. Cloveshoe, 22, in Haddan and Stubbs (see n. 4), 3.

9. *Vita Bertae viduae sanctimonialis Blangiaco in Artesio*, in *AASS*, July 26, 47–60.

10. Council of Chalons, in *MGH Conc.* 1, 55–57.

11. Amalarius, *Regula*, 10.

12. Council of Verneuil, 5, in *MGH Conc.* 1.

13. Benedict of Aniane, *Codex Regularum*, in *PL*, 103:393–422; Benedict, *Codicis Regularum pars tertia: Regulae ss. patrum ad virgines*, in *PL*, 103:663–700.

14. Bede, *A History of the English Church and People*, 4.35, trans. Leo Sherley-Price (Baltimore: Penguin Books, 1968).

15. Isidore of Seville, *De ecclesiastici officiis*, in *PL*, 83:737–826.

16. Cogitosus, *Vita sanctae Brigidis* in *AASS*, February 1, 119–135.

17. Contrary to the claim of Mary Bateson, "Origin and Early History of Double Monasteries," *Royal Historical Society Transactions* 13 (1899), 163, this did not include a direct attack on the double monastery, which was perhaps not actually recognized as an institution at all in the west. The "second council of Nice, 787," which she cited is, in fact, the Second Council of Nicaea, whose prohibitions strengthened those already imposed by Justinian in the sixth century upon the Byzantine empire. It is unlikely that either of these decrees had much effect on the Latin church.

18. Council of Friuli, 12, in *MGH Capit.* 2, 134.

19. Council of Friuli, 6.

20. *Vita Leobae* in C. H. Talbot, *The Anglo-Saxon Missionaries in Germany* (London and New York: Sheed and Ward, 1954), 216–218.

21. Conc. Latunense, in Carlo de Clercq, ed., 12, *Concilia Galliae* 2, in *CCSL*, 148A:316: all widows wishing to veil themselves must enter a monastery; and, in 755, Council of Verneuil, 11, in *MGH Conc.* 1: all virgins were added.

22. J. D. Mansi, *Sacrorum conciliorum nova et amplissima collectio*, vol. 12 (Venice: A. Zata, 1759–1798), 365.

23. *Capit. Francicum* 18, in *MGH Capit.* 2, 38.

24. Council of Soissons, 6, 20, 21–26, reiterate that nuns and monks must observe the rule.

25. Council of Friuli, 41–44; Council of Paris, 11.

26. *Capitularium ab episcopis in placito tractanda*, 4, in *MGH Capit.* 2, 7; Hrabanus Maurus, *Epistola Fuldensium fragmenta*, 6, in *MGH Epist.* 5, *Karol. aevi* 3, 518.

27. Emerton, *Letters of Boniface*, 26 (letter 8).

28. Council of Chalons, 10, 26.

29. Council of Chalons, 54.

30. Paschasius Radbertus, *Life of Wala*, 2:4–5, trans. Allen Cabaniss, in *Charlemagne's Cousins* (Syracuse, N.Y.: Syracuse University Press, 1967).

31. Monachus Marchianensi, *Historia Miraculorum S. Rictrudis*, in *AASS* May 12, 92.

32. In the encyclical to the archbishops, setting the agenda for Aachen, Louis the

Pious stated, "Quamquam enim nonnulli clerici monasteria puellarum et nonnulli laici monasteria virorum etiam et puellarum habeant" (Even though a number of clergy may have monasteries of girls and a number of lay people monasteries of men and of girls); *MGH Conc.* 1, 462.

33. Maximilian Quantin, *Cartulaire général de l'Yonne* (Auxerre, 1854–860).

34. Fructuosus of Buaga, *Regula communis,* in Lucas Holstenius, *Codex Regularum monasticarum et canonicarum* (Graz, 1957), 1:208–219.

35. H. Petzholt, "Abtei Kitzingen," *Jahrbuch für frankische Landesforschung* 15 (1955), 69–83.

36. Notker the Stammerer (Monk of Saint Gall), *Life of Charlemagne,* 1.4, trans. Lewis Thorpe (Baltimore: Penguin, 1969).

37. Ardo, *Life of Benedict, Abbot of Aniane and of Inde,* in Thomas F. X. Noble and Thomas Head, eds. *Soldiers of Christ* (University Park: Pennsylvania State University Press, 1995), 39.

38. Council of Tours, 813, 23.

39. Amalarius, *Regula,* 9, 13.

40. Ibid., 18.

41. Council of Aachen 2 (836), 13 in *MGH Conc.* 2.

42. In 836 the Council of Aachen 2.12 ordered the investigation of nunneries "quae in quibusdam locis lupinaria potius videntur esse" (which in some places appear rather to be brothels). For fornication in convents, see *Epistola Fuldensium fragmenta,* 6, in *MGH Epist.* 5; for prostitution, Jonas of Orléans, *De institutione laicali,* 2:16, in *PL,* 106: 121–278.

43. Mary Skinner, "Benedictine Life for Women, in Central France, 850–1100: A Feminist Revival," in John A. Nichols and Lillian T. Shank, eds., *Medieval Religious Women,* vol. 1, *Distant Echoes* (Kalamazoo, Mich: Cistercian Publications, 1984), 90, nn. 21–22.

44. Amalarius, *Regula,* 16–22.

45. *Vita Hunegundis virginis in Coenobio Humolariensi in Veromanduis,* 14, in *AASS,* August 25, 223–236.

46. *Vita Bertae,* 5.

47. Monachus Marchianensi, 13–14.

48. Roger of Wendover, *Flowers of History,* vol. 1, trans. J. A. Giles (London: George Bell and Sons, 1892), 191–192.

49. Carl Horstmann, ed., *Lives of the Women Saints of Our Contrie of England, de sancta Ebba* (London: Early English Text Society, 1886).

50. G. N. Garmonsway, trans., *Anglo Saxon Chronicle,* 1.192, 2.80 (London: J. M. Dent, 1955).

51. Peter H. Blair, *Anglo Saxon England,* 2d ed. (Cambridge: Cambridge University Press, 1977), 172–73.

52. *Collectio de raptoribus,* in *PL,* 126:1017–1036.

53. Hubert, *Vita de S. Gudilae virgine Bruxellis in Belgio,* 9, in *AASS,* January 8, 513–530.

7. Family Ties

1. W. Levison, ed., *Vita Odiliae Hohenburgensis*, 16, in *MGH SS*, 6 (Hannover-Leipsig, 1913), 24–50.

2. Council of Mainz, 13, in *MGH Conc.* 1.

3. Council of Tours, 24. A number of words were used rather indiscriminately in contemporary texts: *sanctimonial, nonna,* and *monacha* generally designated women living the monastic life.

4. Johannes Salernitensis, *Vita Odonis*, 1.36, in *PL*, 133:43–86.

5. Benedict of Aniane, *Institutio sanctimonialium*, in *MGH Conc.* 2, 284–285.

6. Council of Aachen, 7, 8: abbesses should live the life of the canonesses, the same habit and meals, stay in the cloister and not go out; 10: it is forbidden to speak with men except for necessary business with three or four witnesses; 11: the cloister must be walled with only a single entrance; 27: only a priest, deacon, or subdeacon can enter the cloister to say mass or to give sacraments to the sick.

7. Hoebanx, *L'abbaye de Nivelles des origines au XIVe siècles*, 46, argues for an earlier date from linguistic hints in the *Virtutum Continuatio* of the late eighth century. On 171, he further cites Baudouin des Hayes, who said that all the abbesses refused to embrace the rule or to take vows of chastity noting that des Hayes, writing for the abbess Marguerite de Hennin in the seventeenth century, relied on a source falsified or wholly forged by fourteenth-century nuns trying to give ancient sanction to their way of life.

8. Aachen, 9, in *MGH Conc.* 1.

9. Aachen, 20, though the rule demands that they be kept under strict watch to avoid "undue familiarities."

10. Johannes of Gorze, *Vita*, in *MGH SS*, 4:350–358.

11. *Vita Popponis*, in *MGH SS*, 11:299.

12. *HO*, 26, brothers called "of the Sword" (Santiago).

13. Eugen Ewig, in Friedrich Kempf, Hans-Georg Beck, and Josef A. Jungmann, eds., *The Church in the Age of Feudalism* (New York: Seabury Press, 1980), 106.

14. *Diplomata Ottonis*, 1, 89, in *MGH Const.*, 1:1.

15. Aachen, 9, 11, tries to impose equality of stipend for everyone, but it is only too probable that whether or not that was accomplished, it was a bare minimum that had to be supplemented by private means.

16. Agius, *Vita Hathumodis*, in *MGH SS*, 6:165–189.

17. Hroswitha, *Carmen de Primordiis Coenobii Gandersheimensis*, in *MGH SS*, 4:306–317.

18. Ibid., 93. Hroswitha was probably being deliberately naive about the bishop's claims because she was writing during the convent's struggle with him.

19. Thomas Symons, ed., *Regularis Concordia Anglicae Nationis monachorum sanctimonialiumque*, 9, (London: Thomas Nelson and Sons, 1953).

20. *ER*, 48 (1249).

21. Thietmar, *Chronicon*, 4.57, ed. J. A. Wagner (Nuremberg: L. S. Lechner, 1807),

196, says that such a marriage caused great scandal even when done "for the good of the country."

22. Hroswitha, *Carmen*, 310.

23. Odilo of Cluny, *Epitaphium Adalheidae Imperatricis*, in *PL*, 142:971–975.

24. Liutprand of Cremona, *Antapodosis*, 2.48, 3:42–46 (New York: E. P. Dutton, 1930).

25. *Vita Mahthildis Reginae*, 10–11, in *MGH SS*, 4:282–302.

26. Gratian, *Decretum*, c. 18, q. 2, c. 25.

27. G. H. Pertz, ed., *Annales Quedlinburgensis*, in *MGH SS*, 3:75–76.

28. Pertz, *Annales Quedlinburgensis*, 82.

29. *Miraculi S. Verenae*, in *AASS*, September 1, 164–168.

30. G. H. Pertz, ed., *Vita sanctae Liutbirgae*, in *MGH SS*, 4:158–164.

31. Synod of Mainz, 847, 16, in *MGH Conc.* 2.

32. Bertha of Willich, *Vita Adelheidis Abbatissae Vilicensis*, 6, in *MGH SS*, 15/2: 754–763.

33. *Expositio in Psalmum XLIV*, in *PL*, 120:923–941.

34. Hroswitha, *Plays*, trans. Christopher St. John (New York: Benjamin Blom, 1966), pref.

8. The World, the Flesh, and the Devil

1. *HO*, 31.

2. The *Vita Mahthildis Reginae*, in *MGH SS*, 4:282–302, makes the connection explicitly.

3. Hroswitha, *Carmen de Gestis Oddonis I Imperatoris*, in *MGH SS*, 4:328–329, was not the only one to promote the fame and sanctity of the empress. The story was also told by Odilo of Cluny in his *Epitaphium Adalheidae Imperatricis*, 3, in *PL*, 142, and the normally misogynist Liutprand of Cremona was grudgingly complimentary in *Antapodosis*, 4.13, trans. F. A. Wright (New York: E. P. Dutton, 1930).

4. *Vita sanctae Cunegundis: Imperatricis, virginis, coniugis, viduis, demum sanctimonialis Benedictina, Confugiae et Bambergae in Germania*, 7, in *AASS*, March 3, 265–280.

5. Thomas Symons, ed., *Regularis Concordia Anglicae Nationis Monachorum Sanctimonialiumque*, 2 (London: Thomas Nelson and Sons, 1953).

6. Abbo of Fleury, *Collectio canonum*, in *PL*, 139:473–508.

7. Symons, *Regularis Concordia*, 10.

8. Agius, *Vita Hathumodis*, 5–6 in *MGH SS*, 6.

9. Ibid., 15.

10. Bertha of Villich, *Life of Adelheid Abbess of Vilich*, 6, in Madelyn Bergen Dick, trans., *Mater Spiritualis* (Toronto: Peregrina Publishing, 1994).

11. Symons, *Regularis Concordia*, 10. Prudently, the synod added that while all monks and nuns were to be assigned service in the hospice, they were not to eat there themselves but take their own meals in the common refectory.

12. *MGH Conc.* 1, 27 and 28. The hospital was to be outside the cloister, but there would be room for widows and poor women within the cloister.

13. Rutebeuf, "Li Dit des Beguines," in Achille Jubinal, ed., *Oeuvres complètes* (Paris: Bordas, 1874).

14. G. H. Pertz, ed., *Vita sanctae Liutbirgae,* in *MGH SS,* 4:158–164.

15. Jotsaldus, *Vita Odilonis,* 2.13, in *PL,* 142, ascribes the idea to a hermit who told him Odilo had a vision of devils complaining that Cluny's prayers freed so many souls.

16. Thietmar, who was not always kind to the vocations of widows, compared her to Hannah and Judith; see J. A. Wagner, ed., *Chronicon* (Nuremberg: L. S. Lechner, 1807), 7.3.

17. *Vita Mahthildis,* 19.

18. Agius, *Vita Hathumodis,* 15–20. Indeed the last rites involved the nuns processing around the deathbed in communal order: first the prioress, then the decana, and the custodian followed by the rest of the nuns, presumably in order of seniority.

19. Joannes of Salerno, *Vita Odonis,* in *PL,* 133.

20. Hugh of Cluny, *Exhortatio,* in *PL,* 159:949.

21. Odo of Cluny, *Life of Gerald of Aurillac,* 9, in Thomas F. X. Noble and Thomas Head, eds., *Soldiers of Christ* (University Park: Pennsylvania State University Press, 1995).

22. Christopher St. John, *The Plays of Roswitha* (New York: Benjamin Blom, 1966).

23. W. Levison, ed., *Vita Odiliae abbatissae Hohenburgensis,* in *MGH SS,* 6.

24. Agius, *Vita Hathumodis,* 7.

25. This is probably the citation from Jerome's letters incorporated into the Aachen rule. Heinrich Schäfer, *Die Kanonissenstifter im deutschen Mittelalter: Ihre Entwicklung und innere Einrichtung in Zussamenhang mit dem altchristlichen Sanktimonialentum* (Stuttgart: Kirchenrechtliche Abhandlungen 43–44, 1907), 79, simply dismisses the rule as nonexistent but J. Siegwart, *Die Chorherren und Chorfrauen-Gemeinschaften in der deutschsprachigen Schweiz vom 6 Jahrhundert bis 1160; mit einem überlich über die deutsche Kanonikerreform des 10 und 11 Jh.* (Fribourg: Studia Friburgensia, 1962), 114–115, gathers other references tying it to Aachen and even to Vilich by way of a manuscript in the Spanish convent of Bobatella, which could have been known to Bertha of Vilich's brother, the abbot of Brauweiler, who is known to have used the Spanish Fructuarian rule.

26. Idung of Prüfenung, "An Argument concerning Four Questions," in J. Leahey and G. Perigo, trans., *Cistercians and Cluniacs: The Case for Citeaux* (Kalamazoo, Mich.: Cistercian Publications, 1977), 143–192.

27. Hroswitha, *Carmen de Primordiis Coenobii Gandersheimensis,* in *MGH,* 4:306–317.

28. This identification was postulated by Bernard Hamilton, "The House of Theophylact and the Promotion of the Religious Life among Women in Tenth Century Rome," in *Monastic Reform, Catharism, and the Crusades, 900–1300* (London: Variorum Reprints, 1979), who noted that Alberic and his cousins the senatrices Marozia the Younger, Stephania, and Theodora took the lead in establishing the Cluniac movement not only in Rome but elsewhere in Italy as well.

29. M. Gonsalva Wiegand, trans., *The Non-dramatic Works of Hroswitha* (Saint Louis: Abbey Press, 1937).

30. Dyan Elliot has woven the accusations of adultery against Queen Edith in England and Empress Cunegund in Germany into the entire redefinition of marriage as an institution that accompanied the Gregorian revolution; see *Spiritual Marriage* (Princeton: Princeton University Press, 1993), 127ff.

31. Hugh of Cluny, *Exhortatio*, in *PL,* 159:949.

32. Peter the Venerable, *De miraculis*, 1.22, cited by Noreen Hunt, *Cluniac Monasticism in the Central Middle Ages* (n.p.: Shoestring Press, 1974), 188.

33. See Gilo, *Vita Hugonis*, in *PL,* 159:586; Raynaldi, *Vita Hugonis*, in *PL,* 159:899. Later Cistercians criticized the Cluniacs for including women, then used the austerities of the women to criticize the men, and finally turned to Marcigny as a model for their own houses.

34. Hugh of Cluny, *Imprecatio*, in *PL,* 159:951–954.

35. The nun Elsendis, who compiled a necrology listing thousands of names to be commemorated in prayer by the Cluniac monks, added the names of sixty nuns apparently on her own initiative. In all probability, these are the nuns of Marcigny, deceased at the time of compilation. Only ninety other female names were included. Joachim Wollasch, "A Cluniac Necrology from the Time of Abbot Hugh," cited in Hunt, *Cluniac Monasticism* (see n. 32), 141–190.

36. Hefele-Leclercq, 4:1177.

37. Lateran Council, 26, in Carl Josef von Hefele, *Conciliengeschichte,* (Freiburg-im-Breisgau: Herder, 1886), 5:442.

38. Ibid., 441–442.

39. *HO,* 15.

40. Caesarius of Heisterbach, *Dialogue of Miracles* (London: George Routledge and Sons, 1929), 1:353.

41. Again, the Lateran Council of 1139 prohibited nuns or canonesses from singing in chorus with monks or priests; see 27, in Hefele, *Conciliengeschichte,* 5:442.

42. Joan Morris, *The Lady Was a Bishop: The History of Women with Clerical Ordination and the Jurisdiction of Bishops* (New York: Macmillan, 1973), 10, citing the Chartes du Chapitre de Ste. Waudru de Mons (Brussels: Archives de Hainaut et Mons, Archives de l'etat, 1884–1906).

43. Ivo, Epistola 70, to the bishop of Meaux, said he heard from a monk at Tours, who was informed in a letter from the venerable countess Adelheid, "that now it should be called not a place of nuns but a whorehouse for demon women prostituting their bodies for the use of every sort of evil known to man"; in *PL,* 162:90.

44. Jean Guérout, "Le monastère à l'époque Carolingienne," in Yves Chaussey, ed., *L'abbaye royale de Notre Dame de Jouarre* (Paris: Bibliothèque d'Histoire et d'Archéologie Chrétienne, 1961), 83.

45. Giovanni D. Mansi, *Sacrorum Conciliorum . . .* (Florence, 1759–1927), 21:714–715.

46. Jean de la Croix Bouton, ed., *Les moniales cisterciennes, I: Histoire externe, pt. I,*

jusqu'à la fin du XVe siècle (Grignan: Commission d'histoire de l'ordre de Cîteaux, 1985), 146.

47. J. Ch. Harenberg, *Historia Gandershemensis diplomatica* (Hannover, 1734), cited in H. E. Weirauch, "Die Grundbesitz des Stiftes Quedlinburg im Mittelalters," *Sachsen und Anhalt* 14 (1938), 133.

48. *Annalista Saxo, Monumenta Germaniae Historica Scriptores* 8.739, cited in Hans Schulze, Reinhold Specht, and Günter Vorbrodt, *Das Stift Gernrode: Mitteldeutsche Forschungen,* vol. 38 (Graz: Böhlau Verlag, 1965), 9.

49. Martin Luther, *An Open Letter to the Christian Nobility of the German Nation,* in *Three Treatises by Martin Luther* (Philadelphia: Muhlenberg Press, 1943), 64.

50. Betty Radice, trans., *The Letters of Abelard and Heloise* (Baltimore: Penguin Books, 1974), 97.

51. Bernard, Epistola 48, in *PL,* 182:154.

52. Ivo, Epistola 70, in *PL,* 162:90; see also his criticism of nuns of St. Avitus, Epistola 10, in *PL,* 162:23.

53. *ER,* 591.

9. The Imitation of Christ

1. Hugo of Floreffe, *De B. Yvetta vidua reclusa Hui in Belgio,* 31, in *AAAS,* January 13, 863–886: "And because it was seen to be good and useful to placate the offended God whom inoffensive she had offended; she began first to restore to God in the poor what she feared she had taken from others less justly, keeping nothing for herself that she could give to others."

2. Jacques de Vitry, *The Life of Marie d'Oignies,* 2.44, trans. Margot H. King (Saskatoon: Peregrina, 1986).

3. Betty Radice, trans., *The Letters of Abelard and Heloise* (Baltimore: Penguin Books, 1974), letters 6, 7.

4. Goscelin of Saint Bertin wrote her a devotional volume admitting that in embracing the solitary life she had become his superior in sanctity: "The *Liber Confortatorius,*" in M. M. Lebreton, J. Leclercq, and C. H. Talbot, eds., *Analecta Monastica* (Rome: Studia Anselmiana, 1955), 45.

5. Jacques de Vitry, *Life of Marie,* 69.

6. Hildegard of Bingen, Epistola 116, in *PL,* 197:336–338.

7. C. H. Talbot, ed., *The Life of Christine of Markyate: A Twelfth-Century Recluse* (New York: Clarendon Press, 1987), 20–21.

8. Ibid., 49–50.

9. Jacques de Vitry, *Life of Marie,* prologue.

10. *HO,* 17.

11. Matthew Paris, *Chronica Maiora,* 4.278.1243, ed. H. R. Luard (London: Longman, 1872–83): Communities of women calling themselves "religious, have so multiplied within a short time that two thousand have been reported in Cologne and the neighboring cities."

12. Herbert Grundmann, *Religiöse Bewegungen im Mittelalter: Untersuchungen über die geschichtlichen Zusammenhänge zwischen der Ketzerei, den Bettelorden und der religiösen Frauenbewegung im 12 und 13 Jahrhundert* (Berlin: Historische Studien, 1935), 170.

13. Grimlaic, *Regula Solitariorum*, 17, in *PL*, 103:572–664.

14. J.-H. Albanes, *La vie de Sainte Douceline, fondatrice des Béguines de Marseille* (Marseilles: Etienne Camoin, 1879).

15. Aelred of Rievaulx, *A Rule of Life for a Recluse*, trans. Mary Paul MacPherson, in *Treatises: The Pastoral Prayer, Works*, vol. 1, ed. David Knowles, (Spencer, Mass.: Cistercian Publications, 1971).

16. Aelred, *Rule*, 4.

17. William Dugdale, *Monasticon Anglicanum: A History of Abbies and Other Monasteries, Hospitals, Friaries, and Cathedral and Collegiate Churches with Their Dependencies in England and Wales*, 6:2.9–12 (London: James Bohn, 1846).

18. Hermann of Tournai, *Miraculae S. Mariae Laudunensis*, 3.7, in *PL*, 156:996–997.

19. Andreas of Fontevrault, *Vita Altera B. Roberti de Arbrissello*, 5, in *PL*, 162:1058–1078.

20. Albert Huyskens, ed., *Der sogenannt Libellus de dictis quatuor ancillarum s. Elisabeth confectus* (Kempten/Munich: Kösel, 1911).

21. Prior of Steinfeld, *Epistola* 472, in *PL*, 182:676–689.

22. Talbot, *Life of Christine*, 10.

23. Agnes de Harcourt, *Vita Isabellae*, in *AAAS*, August 31, 798–808.

24. Giles Constable and B. Smith, ed. and trans., *Libellus de diversis ordinibus et professionibus qui sunt in aecclesia* (Oxford: Oxford University Press, 1972).

25. Juncta Bevagnate, *De B. Margarita Poenit. Tert. OSF de Cortona*, 26–27, in *AAAS*, February 22, 308–309.

26. Bernard of Clairvaux, *Sermon on the Song of Songs*, 65, trans. Kilian Walsh and Irene M. Edmonds (Kalamazoo, Mich.: Cistercian Publications, 1979), 179–189.

27. Paschal II, in *PL*, 163:80.

28. J. S. Brewer, J. F. Dinock, and G. R. Warner, eds., *Giraldi Cambrensis Opera* (London: Rolls Series, 1861–1890), 4.183.

29. Marbod of Rennes, Letter, 33, in J. von Walter, *Die ersten Wanderprediger Frankreichs: Robert von Arbrissel* (Leipsig: Studien zur Geschichtes der Theologie und Kirche, 1903), 182.

30. Radice, *Letters of Abelard and Heloise*, 148 (letter 4).

31. Talbot, *Life of Christine*, 70: "Like another Jerome and Paula, though each had been praised separately for chastity, together they incurred slander."

32. Raynaldi, *Alia Vita Hugonis*, 2, in *PL*, 159:900.

33. Aelred, *Rule*, 32.

34. Ibid., 2–4.

35. Innocent III, *Nova quaedam nuper*, Epistola 137, in *PL*, 216:356.

36. Stefanus de Bourbon, *Anecdotes*, 292, in Johann J. Döllinger, *Beiträge zür Sektengeschichte des Mittelalters* (New York: Burt Franklin, 1960), 2:6.300.

37. Ibid., 296.

38. Alain de Lille, *Contra haereticos libri quattuor*, 1.2, in *PL*, 210:379.

39. There were a few exceptions: Ubaldesca of Pisa, 1136–1207, a sister of the Hospital of Saint John, was authorized by her superior (*AAAS*, May 6, 844–847) as was Claire of Montefalco, who had also entered a convent and did not plan to combine a wandering and preaching life with her begging (Isidore Mosconi, *Vita Clarae de Cruce Virgine prope Montem-Falconis in Umbria, ex vetustissimis codicibus extracta*, in *AAAS*, August 18, 664–688).

40. *HO*, 29.

41. Dugdale, *Monasticon Anglicanum*, 6:615, 653.

42. Baldric of Dol, *Vita B. Roberti de Arbrissello*, 4.22, in *PL*, 162:1047–1049.

43. Rule of the Teutonic Knights, 31, cited by Erentraud Gruber, *Deutschordensschwestern im 19. und 20. Jahrhundert: Widerbelebung, Ausbreitung und Tätigkeit* (Bonn-Godesberg: Verlag Wissensahftliches Archiv, 1971), Introduction.

44. J. M. Upton-Ward, ed. and trans., *The Rule of the Templars*, 70, (Woodbridge and Rochester, N.Y.: Boydell and Brewer, 1992).

45. *ER*, 38.

46. Ibid., 115.

47. Rotha Mary Clay, *The Medieval Hospitals of England* (New York: Barnes and Noble, 1966), 140 ff., gives examples of hospital regulations.

48. *ER*, 151.

49. Ibid., 319.

50. Ibid., 471.

51. Ibid., 614.

10. Cura Mulierum

1. This fate flooded local Flemish churches with widows in 1070, according to L. Vander Kindere, ed., *La chronique de Gislebert de Mons* (Brussels, 1904), 10–11.

2. ER, 430, 722.

3. Ibid., 187.

4. This old generalization has never been seriously challenged. Where close comparisons have been made, it has recently been confirmed, notably by Penelope D. Johnson, *Equal in Monastic Profession: Religious Women in Medieval France* (Chicago: University of Chicago Press, 1991), 219, comparing the net worth of male and female establishments in mid-thirteenth century Normandy: the mean for nunneries is £60 against £394 for monkeries.

5. Cited by Rose Graham, *Saint Gilbert of Sempringham and the Gilbertines* (London: Elliot Stock, 1901), 92.

6. *ER*, 383.

7. Cited by H. E. Weirauch, "Die Grundbesitz des Stiftes Quedlinburg im Mittelalters," *Sachsen und Anhalt* 14 (1938), 203.

8. Joseph H. Lynch, *Simoniacal Entry into Religious Life, 1000–1260* (Columbus: Ohio State University Press, 1976), 6.

9. *De rebus alsaticis,* in *MGH SS,* 17, 232–237.

10. *ER,* 401.

11. Ibid., 434.

12. *Register of Thomas Corbridge, Archbishop of York, 1300–1304* (London: Surtees Society, 1925), #70, July 20, 1300.

13. George F. Duckett, *Visitations and Chapter Generals of the Order of Cluny in Respect of Alsace, Lorraine, etc., 1269–1529* (London 1893).

14. Ulysse Chevalier, *Visites de l'ordre de Cluny dans la province de Lyon* (Paris, 1891).

15. *Corbridge,* #499, November 5, 1302: to the prior and convent of Watton.

16. Andrew Clark, ed., *The English Register of Godstow Nunnery* (London: Early English Text Society, 1905), Prologue (ca. 1460).

17. Ibid., #124, #130, #142.

18. The Roman Synod of 1059 attacked the capitularies of 816 authorizing private property, see Hefele-Leclercq, 4/2:1135–1179.

19. Antonio Garcia y Garcia, ed., *Constitutiones Concilii quarti Lateranensis una cum commentariis glossatorum (Monumenta Iuris Canonici, A: Corpus Glossatorum, 2)* (Vatican City: Biblioteca Apostolica Vaticana, 1981), Canon 64. However, Lynch, *Simoniacal Entry,* 193–194, points out: "Not one of the instances reported by the laws of Alexander III, Clement III, or Innocent III involved female religious." He found only one official complaint before 1215: Nun Coton visited by Hugh of Lincoln between 1186 and 1200. But after that, nuns were the focus of the concern.

20. Clark, *Godstow,* pt. 3, Introduction.

21. *De rebus alsaticis,* 17:232–237.

22. *Corbridge,* #41, #73. Other examples from the same register include #374: Queen Margaret appeals to the archbishop to receive a lady as a nun at Arden and the nuns there are ordered to admit her; #402: the prioress of Wilberfosse is to receive a relative of the chancellor of York as a nun; #476: nuns of Swine must receive a knight's daughter.

23. *ER,* 353 (1258); 470 (1261); 649 (1266).

24. Ibid., 199.

25. Barbara Newman, trans., *Life of Juliana of Cornillon,* 2:2, 5, 6 (Toronto: Peregrina, 1988).

26. Christine de Pisan, *Le livre du dit de Poissy,* in Maurice Roy, ed., *Oeuvres poétiques* (Paris: Johnson Reprint, 1965). 2:159–222, describes in warm detail such a visit to her daughter, who was a nun in Poissy, where Christine herself later retired.

27. Caesarius of Heisterbach, *Dialogue of Miracles* (London: George Routledge and Sons, 1929), 1:42.

28. *Vita de Veronica de Binasco,* 9.2, in *AASS,* January 13.

29. *Vita de Venerabili Virgine Gertrude ab Oosten Beghina Delphensi in Belgio,* in *AASS,* January 6, 348–353.

30. *ER*, 129 (1249); 225 (1254); 285 (1256); 411 (1259); 470 (1261); 676 (1267).

31. Jeanne Ancelet-Hustache, ed., "Les vitae sororum d'Unterlinden, Edition critique du manuscrit 508 de la Bibliothèque de Colmar," 12 in *Archives d'histoire doctrinale et littéraire du moyen age* 5 (1930), 361.

32. Elsbet Stägel, *Das Leben der Schwestern zu Töss*, 11, ed. F. Vetter (Berlin: Weidmannsche Buchhandlung, 1906), 37.

33. Guibert of Gembloux, *Vita Hildegardis*, ed. J-B. Pitra *Analecta Sanctae Hildegardis* (Monte Cassino: Analecta Sacra, 1882).

34. Die Nonne von Engelthal, *Buchlein von der Genaden Uberlast*, ed. Karl Schroder (Tübingen: Bibliothek des litterarischen Vereins in Stuttgart 1871), 264.

35. Ibid., 304.

36. *Archivum Franciscanum Historicum*, vols. 14 and 15 (1938 and 1939), give this rule and also me for Bavarian sisters placed under Franciscan direction in 1315.

37. Petrus de Vaux, *Vita Coletae*, 28, in *AASS*, March 6. "Certain notable merchants, who diligently kept their word, decided to give all profit from anything sold on Sunday or a feast day to the poor for God's sake. But . . . she would not consent to receive such things . . . asserting that they were neither justly nor reasonably acquired."

38. L. Hollman, ed., *Den heliga Birgittas Revelaciones Extravagantes*, 2.20 (Uppsala: Samlingar Utgivna av Svenska Fornskriftsällskapet, 1956). All the goods of the community were to be redistributed on All Souls Day to ensure that each nun had enough to see her through the year and no one, or the community as a whole, had more than strictly needed for the year. Every offering, no matter how needed, had to be scrutinized to be sure that no taint attached to it.

39. Elizabeth Lipsmeyer, "The Imperial Abbey and the Town of Zurich: Benedictine Nuns and the Price of Ritual in Thirteenth, Fourteenth, and Fifteenth-Century Switzerland," in Elspeth Durie and Dewey Kramer, compilers, Margot King, ed., *On Pilgrimage*, (Toronto: Peregrina, 1994), 365–376.

40. *Gertrude ab Oosten*, 22.

41. Ibid., 24.

42. Engelthal, *Buchlein*, 264–269.

43. Ibid., 272.

44. Ancelet-Hustache, "Unterlinden," 5, prologue.

45. Stägel, *Töss*, 13.

46. Ibid., 5, Ida von Wezzikon.

47. Ibid., 33.

48. Hugo of Floreffe, *De B. Yvetta vidua reclusa Hui in Belgio*, 31, in *AASS*, January 13, 863–886.

49. Thomas de Cantimpré, *Life of Lutgard of Aywières*, 2.11, ed. and trans. Martinus Cawley (Lafayette, Ore: Guadalupe Translations, 1987).

50. Sister Anna Mechthild Fuaza, *De B. Aemilia Biccheria*, 16, in *AASS*, May 3, 557–571.

51. Ibid., 19.

52. Stägel, *Töss*, 23.

11. Disordered Women

1. Betty Radics, trans., *The Letters of Abelard and Heloise* (Baltimore: Penguin Books, 1974), 161 (letter 5).

2. Ibid., 160.

3. Ibid., 212 (letter 7).

4. Ibid., 231.

5. Ibid., 216.

6. Penny S. Gold, "Male/Female Cooperation: The Example of Fontevrault," in John A. Nichols and Lillian T. Shank, eds., *Medieval Religious Women*, vol. 1, *Distant Echoes* (Kalamazoo, Mich,: Cistercian Publications, 1984), 151–168, points out that of the three surviving versions of the rule of Fontevraud none appears to be the original covering speech, acts, food, and clothing as Andreas of Fontevraud described it in the *Vita Altera B. Roberti de Arbrissello,* in *PL,* 162:1058–1078.

7. *Regulae Sanctimonialium Fontis Ebraldi,* 17–18, in *PL,* 162:1079–1082.

8. *Regulae,* 25–28.

9. Andreas, *Vita Altera,* 3.

10. Hugh V, *Statutes,* 20, cited in Giles Constable, "Monastic Legislation at Cluny in the Eleventh and Twelfth Centuries," in *Cluniac Studies* (London: Variorum, 1982).

11. *HO,* 15.

12. J. Caley, H. Ellis, and B. Bandinel, eds., *Vita Gilberti,* in William Dugdale, *Monasticon Anglicanum: A History of Abbeys and Other Monasteries, Hospitals, Friaries, and Cathedral and Collegiate Churches with Their Dependencies in England and Wales,* 6:2 (London: James Bohn, 1846).

13. J. M. Canivez, *Statuta Capitulorum Generalium Ordinis Cisterciensis ab anno 1116 ad annum 1786* (Louvain: Bureaux de la revue d'histoire ecclésiastique, 1933–1941), 1134 (statute 29).

14. See, for example, Louis Lekai, *The Cistercians: Ideals and Reality* (Kent, Ohio: Kent State University Press, 1977), specifically, his chapters devoted to the male branch of the order.

15. *HO,* 15.

16. According to Sophie von Stolberg's account, cited by Jeanne Ancelet-Hustache, *Mechtilde de Magdebourg* (Paris, 1926).

17. Canivez, *Statuta,* 1190 (statute 27).

18. This provoked a bull of Innocent III, Epistola 188, in *PL,* 216:356.

19. *HO,* 32.

20. Thomas of Celano, *Life of Saint Clare,* 7–8, ed. and trans. P. Robinson (Philadelphia: Dolphin Press, 1910).

21. Ibid., 24.

22. Ibid., 117.

23. Ibid., 14, says that no one had made such a request of the Holy See before.

24. Luke Wadding, *Annales minorum* (Lyons: 1628–1635), 1:1731, p. 311, n. 44.

25. Celano, *Saint Clare*, 12: "She had promised obedience to the blessed Francis and never departed in the slightest from that promise."

26. *Bullarium Franciscanum Romanum Pontificum*, 4 vols. (St. Bonaventure, N.Y.: Franciscan Institute, 1983), 1, 38, 73, 141. In 1232, a similar struggle began in Spoleto.

27. Hugolino's rule, *Bullarium Franciscanum*, 1.263–267.

28. Regis J. Armstrong and Ignatius C. Brady, "The Rule of Saint Clare," in *Francis and Clare: The Complete Works* (New York: Paulist Press, 1982), 209–225.

29. But by the time Ubertino Casale visited there, many of their papers had already been scattered and lost; see *Arbor Vitae Crucifixae Jesus*, 5.5 (Venice, 1485).

30. Celano, *Saint Clare*, 37.

31. Ibid., 14.

32. The correspondence is available in Armstrong and Brady, *Francis and Clare*.

33. Ibid., 15.

34. Her life was written by Agnes de Harcourt, abbess of Longchamps, originally her maid of honor: *Vita Isabellae*, in *AASS*, August 31, 798–808.

35. *Bullarium Franciscanum*, 5.164–336; 6.118, 119, 181.

36. Jordan of Saxony, *Libellus de principiis ordinis Praedicatorum*, ed. H. C. Scheeben, p. 39, in *Monumenta Ordinis fratrum Praedicatorum Historica* (Rome, 1935), 16.1–88.

37. See the letters incorporated into the history of Sister Cecilia of San Sisto, *Miracula beati Dominici*, in A. Walz, ed., *Miscellanea Pio Paschini* (Rome, 1949), 1:306–326.

38. Ibid., 391–393. The same portrait was moved to their new quarters in the sixteenth century and again in 1931.

39. Ibid., 310–311.

40. T. Ripoll and A. Bremond, eds., *Bullarium ordinis fratrum Praedicatorum* (Rome, 1729–1740), 1:183–186.

41. Epistola 17, in A. Walz, ed., *Monumenta Ordinis Pradicatorum Historica*, vol. 23 (Rome, 1951).

42. *De rebus alsaticis*, in *MGH SS*, 17:234–235.

43. Ibid., 235.

44. L. Hollman, ed., *Den heliga Birgittas Revelaciones Extravagantes*, 2.20 (Uppsala: Samlingar Utgivna av Svenska Fornskriftsällskapet, 1956).

45. Ibid., 10.

46. Ibid., 19.

47. Ibid., 16.

48. Consalvus Durantus, ed., *Revelationes S. Brigittae Card. Turrecremata*, 30 (Rome: Apud Stephanum Paulinum, 1606), 754–770.

49. Isak Collijn, ed., *Acta et processus canonizationis beatae Birgitte*, 21 (Uppsala: Almqvist and Wiksells, 1924–1931), 230. Nicholas of Nola testified, "She often asked for confirmation from Urban V of her monastery and constitutions which had been divinely revealed to her. The pope gave him those constitutions, ordering that they be examined by good and worthy men. Since they did not conform to the modern style of the Roman curia, he had them re-drafted and Lady Birgitta approved them. But

afterwards they were modified by certain masters and theologians named by the pope and issued as constitutions under the Rule of Saint Augustine."

50. Ibid., 101.

51. *Vadstena Klosters Minnesbok: Diarium Vazstenense* (Stockholm: P. A. Norstadt and Soners Forlag, 1918). My thanks to Father John E. Halborg for guiding me through the Swedish.

52. H. J. Cnattinguis, *Studies in the Order of St. Bridget of Sweden, I: The Crisis in the 1420's* (Uppsala: Stockholm Studies in History, 1963), 115.

53. For example, Hildegard of Bingen, Epistolae 190, 196, 210, in *PL*, 197.

54. Aelred of Rievaulx, *A Rule of Life for a Recluse*, trans. Mary Paul MacPherson, 2.14, in *Treatises: The Pastoral Prayer, Works*, vol. 1, ed. David Knowles (Spencer, Mass.: Cistercian Publications, 1971).

12. The Alchemy of Mysticism

1. Jeanne Ancelet-Hustache, ed., "Les vitae sororum d'Unterlinden, Edition critique du manuscrit 508 de la Bibliothèque de Colmar," 3, in *Archives d'histoire doctrinale et littéraire du moyen age*, 5 (1930).

2. Martinus Cawley, ed. and trans., *The Life of Alice the Leper (Vita B. Aleidis Scharembecunae)*, (Lafayette, Ore.: Guadalupe Translations, 1987).

3. Micheline de Fontette, *Les religieuses à l'age classique du droit canonique* (Paris: J. Vrin, 1967).

4. Der Nonne von Engelthal, *Büchlein von der Genaden Uberlast*, ed. Karl Schröder (Tübingen: Bibliothek des litterarischen Vereins in Stuttgart, 1871), 264.

5. Ibid., 278.

6. Ancelet-Hustache, "Unterlinden," 2.

7. J.-H. Albanes, ed., *La vie de Sainte Douceline, fondatrice des Béguines de Marseille* (Marseilles: Etienne Camoin, 1879).

8. Engelthal *Büchlein*, 271.

9. Anton Birlinger, "Leben heiliger alemannischer Frauen des 14/15 Jahrhunderts, V: Die Nonnen von St. Katharinenthal bei Diessenhofen," *Alemannia* 15 (1887), 157.

10. Ibid., 162.

11. Ancelet-Hustache, "Unterlinden," 12.

12. Ibid.

13. Ibid., 22.

14. J. B. Tolhurst, ed., *The Ordinale or Customary of the Nuns of Barking Abbey* (London: Bradshaw Society, 1927), 1.

15. *Die Visionen und Briefe der heiligen Elisabeth*, F. W. E. Roth, ed., (Brunn: Studien aus dem Benedictiner- und Cistercienser-Orden, 1884).

16. Elsbet Stägel, *Das Leben der Schwestern zu Töss*, 2, ed. F. Vetter (Berlin: Weidmannsche Buchhandlung, 1906).

17. Isidorus de Isolanis, *De B. Veronica de Binasco, Virgine mediolani* 7.7, in *AASS*, January 13.

18. Thomas de Cantimpré, *Life of Lutgard of Aywières*, ed. and trans. Martinus Cawley (Lafayette, Ore.: Guadalupe Translations, 1987).

19. Herrad of Landsberg, *Hortus Deliciarum*, ed. and trans. A. D. Caratzas (New Rochelle: Caratzas Bros., 1977).

20. Ancelet-Hustache, "Unterlinden," 28.

21. C. H. Talbot, ed., *The Life of Christine of Markyate: A Twelfth-Century Recluse* (New York: Clarendon Press, 1987).

22. Isidorus, *Veronica*, 9.10 and 21.27.

23. Birlinger, "Katharinenthal," 151–153.

24. Ancelet-Hustache, "Unterlinden," 3.

25. Cantimpré, *Life of Lutgard*, 1.22.

26. Anton Birlinger, ed., "Leben heiliger alemannischer Frauen des 14/15 Jahrhunderts, IV: Die Nonnen von Kirchberg bei Hagerloch," *Alemannia* 11 (1883), 1.

27. Ancelet-Hustache, "Unterlinden," 8.

28. L. Hollman, ed., *Den heliga Birgittas Revelaciones Extravagantes*, 2.5 (Uppsala: Samlingar Utgivna av Svenska Fornskriftsällskapet, 1956).

29. Ibid., 19.

30. Roger de Ganck, trans., *The Life of Beatrice of Nazareth*, 2.7–8 (Kalamazoo, Mich.: Cistercian Publications, 1991).

31. Ancelet-Hustache, "Unterlinden," 12.

32. Engelthal, *Büchlein*, 304.

33. Birlinger, "Kirchberg," 11.

34. Stägel, Introduction, p. 14. *Töss*.

35. Birlinger, "Katharinenthal," 158.

36. Isidorus, *Veronica*, 11.13.

37. Ancelet-Hustache, "Unterlinden," 48.

38. Stägel, *Töss*, 24.

39. Ancelet-Hustache, "Unterlinden," 23. She left her husband and children to enter the convent, but he then became a Dominican and brought their infant daughter to her convent.

40. Philipp Strauch, ed., *Die Offenbarungen der Margaretha Ebner und der Adelheid Langmann*, 10–15, trans. Josef Prestel (Weimar: H. Böhlaus Nachfolger, 1939), 90: "Soon after that there came to me the Sister whom I know well and who has written this to me: 'I offered you in this night your child, and that was a living child. You took it from me with great desire and took it to your heart and wanted to suckle it which surprised me. Are you so blind that you are not ashamed?'"

41. Engelthal, *Büchlein*, 273.

42. Stägel, *Töss*, 84.

43. Birlinger, "Katharinenthal," 160.

44. Stägel, *Töss*, 32.

45. Ancelet-Hustache, "Unterlinden," 6.

46. Cecilia of San Sisto, *Miracula beati Dominici*, in A. Walz, ed., *Miscellanea Pio Paschini* (Rome, 1949), 1:306–326.

47. Stägel, *Töss,* 23.

48. Hollman, *Revelaciones Extravagantes,* 2.6.

49. De Ganck, *Life of Beatrice,* 2.11.

50. Birlinger, "Katharinenthal," 158.

51. Herrad, *Hortus Deliciarum.*

52. Engelthal, *Büchlein,* 19

53. Ibid., 318.

54. Ancelet-Hustache, "Unterlinden," 11.

55. Hildegard of Bingen, *Scivias,* Declaration, trans. Columba Hart and Jane Bishop (New York: Paulist Press, 1990), 59.

56. Humbert of Romans, *Treatise on the Formation of Preachers,* 12.135, in Simon Tugwell, ed. and trans., *Early Dominicans* (New York: Paulist Press, 1982).

57. Trotula of Salerno, *The Diseases of Women,* trans. Elizabeth Mason-Hohl (Los Angeles: Ward Ritchie Press, 1940).

58. Roth, *Die Visionen,* 3.4.

59. Joseph L. Baird and Radd K. Ehrman, trans, *Letters of Hildegard of Bingen,* vol. 1 (New York: Oxford University Press, 1994), 200 (letter 89).

60. Ancelet-Hustache, "Unterlinden," 36

61. Birlinger, "Katharinenthal," 163.

62. Ancelet-Hustache, "Unterlinden," 5.

63. Thus Mechtild von Stanz saw Jesus lying on the cross during the Good Friday services at Töss when the nuns were flagellating one another but asked that the consequent stigmata be concealed; Stägel, *Töss,* 24.

64. Jesus gave her a gift of healing, which, after suffering the distractions of requests from the sick, she returned, asking instead for the gift to understand the Latin chant. She found that also distracted her and asked finally to exchange and mingle hearts, Cantimpré, *Life of Lutgard,* 1.12.

65. Gertrude of Helfta, *The Herald of Divine Love,* 4.4.1–4, in William J. Doheny, trans., *Revelations of Saint Gertrude,* (privately circulated, 1978).

66. *ER,* Bival, 541.

67. Engelthal, *Buchlein,* 267.

68. Ibid., 278.

69. Talbot, *Life of Christine,* 78.

70. *Vita de Venerabili Virgine Gertrude ab Oosten Beghina Delphensi in Belgio,* 23, in *AASS,* January 6, 348–353.

71. Gertrude, *Revelations,* 2.6.

72. Anelet-Hustache, "Unterlinden," 36.

73. Isidorus, *Veronica,* 14.17.

74. Ancelet-Hustache, "Unterlinden," 24.

75. John Coakley, "Friars as Confidants of Holy Women in Medieval Dominican Hagiography," in Renate Blumenfeld-Kozinski and Timea Szell, eds., *Images of Sainthood in Medieval and Renaissance Europe* (Ithaca, N.Y.: Cornell University Press, 1991), 222–246.

76. *De operatione dei*, 2.5.46, in *PL*, 197:952.

77. Aelred of Rievaulx, "The Nun of Watton," trans. Jo Ann McNamara, *Magistra* 1 (1995), 122–138.

78. Engelthal, *Büchlein*, 303.

79. Stägel, *Töss*, 26.

80. Ancelet-Hustache, "Unterlinden," 23.

81. Gertrude, *Revelations*, 2.8.

82. Marta Powell Harley, *A Revelation of Purgatory by an Unknown Fifteenth Century Visionary: Introduction, Critical Text, and Translation* (Lewiston, N.Y., and Queenston, Ont.: Edwin Mellen Press, 1985).

83. Isak Collijn, ed., *Acta et processus canonizationis beatae Birgitte* (Uppsala: Almqvist and Wiksells, 1924–1931), 84.

84. Cantimpré, *Life of Lutgard*, 2.11.

85. Isidorus, *Veronica* 3.6.

86. Hugo of Floreffe, *De B. Yvetta vidua reclusa Hui in Belgio*, 81–82, in *AASS* January 13, 863–886.

87. Ibid., 96.

88. Cited by Barbara J. Newman, "O Feminea Forma: God and Woman in the Works of St. Hildegard (1098–1179)" (Ph.D. diss., Yale University, 1981), 321–323.

89. Elizabeth A. Petroff, ed., *Medieval Women's Visionary Literature* (New York and Oxford: Oxford University Press, 1986), 159.

90. Anton Birlinger, ed., "Leben heiliger alemannischer Frauen des 14/15 Jahrhunderts, IV: Die Nonnen von Kirchberg bei Hagerloch," 4, in *Alemannia*, vol. 11 (Bonn, 1883), 4.

91. *Cum de quibusdam*, in Hefele-Leclercq, 6/2:681–682.

92. F. Baethgen, ed., *Chronica Provincia Argentinensis* (Berlin, 1955), 73–74.

13. The Tears of the Magdalene

1. See for example gossip by Giraldus Cambrensis, *Jewel of the Church*, 4, trans. J. J. Hagen (Leiden: Brill, 1979), 185.

2. William A. Hinnebusch, *The History of the Dominican Order* (New York: Alba House, 1965), 1:389.

3. A. Barthelmé, *La réforme dominicaine au XVe siècle en Alsace* (Strasbourg, 1930), 94.

4. Barbara Newman, trans., *Life of Juliana of Mont Cornillon*, (Toronto: Peregrina, 1988).

5. For example, documents 77, 169, 565, appealing to the pope for help, collected by H. Denifle, *La désolation des églises, monastères, hôpitaux en France vers le milieu du XVe siècle*, 3 vols. (Macon, 1897–1899).

6. Denifle, *Désolation*, #49.

7. Ibid., #371.

8. Ibid., #736.

9. E. Coyecque, *L'Hôtel Dieu de Paris au moyen age: Histoire et documents* (Paris, 1889–1891).

10. *ER,* 158, 384, 477, 559, 595, 649, 687.

11. Guido Ruggiero, *The Boundaries of Eros: Sex, Crime, and Sexuality in Renaissance Venice* (New York: Oxford University Press, 1985), 84.

12. Guy de Valous, *Le monachisme clunisien des origines an XVe siècle* (Paris: Picard, 1970), 390.

13. Marta Powell Harley, *A Revelation of Purgatory by an Unknown Fifteenth Century Visionary: Introduction, Critical Text, and Translation* (Lewiston, N.Y. and Queenston, Ont.: Edwin Mellen Press, 1985), 120.

14. Christine de Pisan, *Le livre du dit de Poissy,* in Maurice Roy, ed., *Oeuvres poétiques* (Paris, 1886; Johnson Reprint, 1965) 2:159–222.

15. Andrew Clark, ed., *The English Register of Godstow Nunnery,* pt. 3, 81–94 (London: Early English Text Society, 1905).

16. *ER,* 252.

17. Der Nonne von Engelthal, *Büchlein von der Genaden Uberlast,* ed. Karl Schröder (Tübingen: Bibliothek des litterarischen Vereins in Stuttgart, 1871), 289

18. Elsbet Stägel, *Das Leben der Schwestern zu Töss,* 3, ed. F. Vetter (Berlin: Weidmannsche Buchhandlung, 1906).

19. C. H. Talbot, ed., *The Life of Christine of Markyate: A Twelfth-Century Recluse* (New York: Clarendon Press, 1987), 33.

20. Engelthal, *Büchlein,* 294.

21. Eckberti, *Vita Sanctae Elisabeth,* 7.97, in *PL,* 195; Hildegard of Bingen, *Scivias,* 1.2.15–20, trans. Columba Hart and Jane Bishop (New York: Paulist Press, 1990).

22. *De periculis,* read at an assembly of the clergy of Sens and Rheims in 1256: H. Bierbaum, *Bettelorden und Weltgeistlichkeit an der Universität Paris. Texte und Untersuchungen zum literarischen Armuts- und Exemtionsstreit des 13. Jahrhunderts (1255–1272)* (Munster-in-Westfalia, 1920).

23. Rutebeuf, *32 propriétés de la béguinage* and *L'evangile as fames,* in Léon LeGrand, *Les béguines de Paris* (Paris, 1893), 19–20.

24. Jean de Meun, *The Romance of the Rose,* 5.56, trans. Harry Robbins (New York: E. P. Dutton, 1962).

25. Engelthal, *Büchlein,* 276.

26. Betty Radice, trans., *The Letters of Abelard and Heloise* (Baltimore: Penguin Books, 1974), 146 (letter 4).

27. James A. Brundage, *Law, Sex, and Christian Society in Medieval Europe* (Chicago: University of Chicago Press, 1987), 385, quotes the *Glossa Palatina,* ch. 32, q. 5, c. 9, v: If a woman's hymen was broken by a hand she could be consecrated as a virgin; but if it was broken by a penis, however slightly, she could not.

28. *ER,* 470.

29. For example, Clark, *Register of Godstow,* pt. 3, 81–94: Mary Browne, a nun of Godstow, was pregnant *(aliquibus officiariis exterioribus vel interioribus).*

30. *ER,* 359.

31. *Register of Thomas Corbridge, Archbishop of York, 1300–1304*, 2.101, 102, 104, 108 (London: Surtees Society, 1925).

32. *ER*, 48.

33. Newman, *Life of Blessed Juliana*, 91.

34. Agnes de Harcourt, *Vita Isabellae*, 43, in *AASS*, August 31, 798–808.

35. Jeanne Ancelet-Hustache, ed., "Les vitae sororum d'Unterlinden, Edition critique du manuscrit 508 de la Bibliothèque de Colmar," 43, in *Archives d'histoire doctrinale et littéraire du moyen age*, 5 (1930).

36. Thomas de Cantimpré, *Life of Lutgard of Aywières*, 1.7, ed. and trans. Martinus Cawley (Lafayette, Ore.: Guadalupe Translations, 1987).

37. Aelred of Rievaulx, *On the Nun of Watton*, trans. Jo Ann McNamara, *Magistra* 1 (1995), 122–138.

38. *Corbridge*, #506.

39. Ibid., #319.

40. William Dugdale, *Monasticon Anglicanum: A History of Abbies and Other Monasteries, Hospitals, Friaries, and Cathedral and Collegiate Churches with Their Dependencies in England and Wales*, 2:318 (London: James Bohn, 1846).

41. Caesarius of Heisterbach, *Dialogue of Miracles* (London: George Routledge and Sons, 1929), 1.503. In the late 1950s the same story, updated to the Napoleonic period, was made into a movie called *The Miracle*.

42. Johannes Busch, *Chronicon Windeshemense und Liber de reformatione monasteriorum*, 1.4, ed. Karl Grube, Geschichtsquellen der Provinz Sachsen 19 (Halle: Druck und Verlag Otto Handel, 1886).

43. Cantimpré, *Life of Lutgard*, 1.21.

44. Busch, *Chronicon*, 2.19.

45. Hugo of Floreffe, *De B. Yvetta vidua reclusa Hui in Belgio*, 62, in *AASS*, January 13.

46. *ER*, 300, 402, 597.

47. Busch, *Chronicon*, 2.3.

48. Denifle, *Desolation*, #556, p. 250: monastery of nuns of Bono Loca or Vinegolio O Cist, Maguelonne.

49. Ibid., #897, #898–899, #900.

50. Ibid., #902.

51. Ibid., #891.

52. For example, see third day, first story, p. 144, and ninth day, second story, p. 539, in Giovanni Boccaccio, *The Decameron* (New York: Modern Library, 1955).

53. William of Malmesbury, *Chronicle of the Kings of England*, ed. and trans. J. A. Giles (London: Henry G. Bohn, 1847), 469: "He erected near a castle called Niort, certain buildings after the form of a little monastery and used to talk idly about placing therein an abbey of prostitutes, naming several of the most abandoned courtesans, one as abbess, another as prioress and declaring that he would fill up the rest of the offices in like manner."

54. Exemplum 80, in Thomas F. Crane, ed. and trans., *The Exempla, or, Illustrative Stories from the Sermones Vulgares of Jacques de Vitry* (London, 1890), 36.

55. *Opus restitutionum*, 52–53, in Brundage, *Law, Sex*, 523.

56. *De rebus alsaticis ineuntis saeculi XIII, Monumenta Germaniae Historiae Scriptores*, 17:234–235, written ca. 1260, describes introduction of the Penitents in Germany.

57. Pierre de Vaux, *Vie de Soeur Colette*, 10, ed. Elisabeth Lopez (Saint-Etienne: CERCOR Travaux et Recherches, 1994).

58. Ibid., 16.

59. C. 2, cited in Pierre Pansier, *L'oeuvre des répenties à Avignon du XIIIe au XVIII siècle* (Paris: Recherches historique et documentaires sur Avignon, 1910), 40.

60. Hugo, *Yvetta*, 80.

61. Stägel, *Töss*, 32.

62. Peter of Dacia, *Vita Christinae Stumbelensis*, ed. Isaac Collijn (Stockholm: University of Stockholm Press, 1982).

63. Jean Gerson, *De distinctione verarum visionum a falsis*, 75, ed. and trans. Paschal Boland, (Washington D.C.: Catholic University of America Press, 1959).

64. Ibid., 81.

65. Alan Kors and Edward Peters, eds., *Witchcraft in Europe, 1100–1700* (Philadelphia: University of Pennsylvania Press, 1972), 72: *Quodlibet XI*, 10.

66. Nider, *Formicarius*, briefly excerpted in Kors and Peters, *Witchcraft*, 102–104.

67. Kors and Peters, *Witchcraft*, 107.

68. Jacobus Sprenger and Heinrich Krämer, *Malleus Maleficarum*, q. 6, trans. Montague Summers (London: Folio Society, 1968).

69. William H. May, ed., "The Confession of Prous Boneta, Heretic and Heresiarch," in John H. Mundy, Richard W. Emery, and Benjamin N. Nelson, eds., *Essays in Medieval Life and Thought Presented in Honor of Austin Patterson Evans* (New York: Columbia University Press, 1955).

70. De Vanx, *Colette*, 42.

71. Aelred, *A Rule of Life for a Recluse*, 1, 15, in Mary Paul MacPherson, trans., *Treatises: The Pastoral Prayer*, vol. 1 of *Works*, ed. David Knowles (Spencer, Mass.: Cistercian Publications, 1971).

72. Nigellus Wirecker (Nigel Longchamps), *Mirror of Fools, or, The Book of Burnel the Ass* (Oxford: Blackwell, 1961), 85.

73. Jacques Lacarrière, ed. and trans., *Les evangiles des quenouilles* (Paris: Editions Imago, 1987).

74. Busch, *Chronicon*, 2.11. I am indebted to Father John E. Halborg for the information that the *In media vitae* was sung by priests attending the duke of Oldenburg in 1234, when he massacred an army of rebel subjects. Regarded as a hexing psalm, its singing without episcopal permission was forbidden by a Synod in Cologne in 1316; Johan Beckman, *Den Nya Swenska Psalmboken* (Stockholm: P. A. Norstedt, 1845), 100.

14. Regular Lives

1. John Nider's account from *Formicarius*, incorporated into the account of Johan Meyer, *Buch der Reformacio Predigerordens*, 2.48–49, in Benedictus M. Reichert, ed.,

Quellen und Forschungen zur Geschichte des Dominikanerordens in Deutschland (Leipzig: Otto Harrassowitz, 1909).

2. Johan Busch, *Liber de reformatione monasteriorum*, 2.3, in Karl Grube, ed., *Geschichtsquellen der Provinz Sachsen*, vol. 19 (Halle: Druck und Verlag Otto Handel, 1886).

3. Andrew Clark, ed., *The English Register of Godstow Nunnery*, pt. 3, 81–94 (London: Early English Text Society, 1905).

4. The "three great orders of monks and canons"—Augustinians (*Ad decorem,* 1339), Cistercians, (*Fulgens sicut stella,* 1335), and Benedictines (*Summi magistri,* 1336)—were extensively reorganized. More limited statutes reformed the Cluniacs and Franciscans: Henri Marc-Bonnet, *Histoire des ordres religieux* (Paris: Presses Universitaires de France, 1968), 67.

5. Their letters are reproduced by Busch, *Liber,* 2.27.

6. Meyer, *Buch der Reformacio,* 2.65.

7. Gerardi Magni Epistolae, in W. Mulder, ed., *Ons Geestelijk Erf* (Antwerp, 1933), 167–168, cited by R. R. Post, *The Modern Devotion: Confrontation with Reformation and Humanism* (Leiden: Brill, 1968), 68.

8. Peter-Thomas Rohrbach, *Journey to Carith: The Story of the Carmelite Order* (Garden City, N.Y.: Doubleday, 1966), 128.

9. Busch, *Liber,* 2.587.

10. At Weerder, see ibid., 2.5.

11. Ibid., 2.37.

12. Ibid.

13. Pierre de Vaux, *Vie de Sainte Colette,* 2.12, ed. Elisabeth Lopez (Saint-Etienne: CERCOR Travaux et Recherches, 1994).

14. Ibid., 2.39, but abbess of what he did not say.

15. Ibid., 2.38.

16. P. Ubald d'Alençon, "Documents sur la réforme de Ste. Colette en France," *Archivum Franciscanum Historicum* 2 (1909), 447–456; 600–612; ibid., 3 (1910), 82–97.

17. De Vaux, *Colette,* 2.30, Francis presented Colette to Christ as the second founder of his order. Ibid., 2.32, makes it clear that she was to reform men and women.

18. Ibid., 2.19.

19. Annette Barthelmé, *La réforme dominicaine au XVe siècle en Alsace* (Strasbourg, 1930), 88.

20. Meyer *Buch der Reformacio,* 3.40–60.

21. Ibid., 2.20.

22. Ibid., 2.19.

23. Ibid., 2.54, includes biographies of women associated with the reform.

24. Busch, *Liber,* 2.9.

25. Meyer, *Buch der Reformacio,* 2.59–61.

26. *Chronik und Totenbuch des Klosters Wienhausen* (Wienhausen, 1986), 26.

27. Busch, *Liber,* 2.20.

28. *Wienhausen,* 23.

29. Busch, *Liber*, 2.32.

30. Ibid., 2.48, describes the same practice at the Cistercian house of Lübeck, which he also reformed.

31. *Wienhausen*, 15.

32. Ibid., 14.

33. Ibid., 19: the nun who wrote this account never deigned to mention Busch by name.

34. Ibid., 21.

35. Ibid., 22–23: the Lutheran deaconesses who now live at Wienhausen still point out to visitors the scars of this looting in their chapel.

36. Ibid., 24.

37. Ibid., 26. A list of goods, ornaments, and clothing that this abbess brought into the cloister follows through pages 27 and 28.

38. Felix Fabri, *De Civitate Ulmensi*, ed. Veesenmeyer (Stuttgart: Liter. verein, 1889), 180ff., cited by Lina Eckenstein, *Women under Monasticism* (Cambridge: Cambridge University Press, 1990), 427.

39. Meyer, *Buch der Reformacio*, 2.31.

40. Ibid., 2.14.

41. Ibid., 2.8.

42. Ibid., 5.19.

43. Ibid., 5.48.

44. Busch, *Liber*, 2.37.

45. Ibid., 2.7.

15. Defenders of the Faith

1. Roland H. Bainton, *Women of the Reformation*, (Minneapolis: Augsburg Publishing House, 1977), 1:67.

2. John Gairdner, ed., *Letters and Papers Foreign and Domestic of the Reign of Henry VIII* (London, 1880), 13:2, 758.

3. Johannes Janssen, *History of the German People at the Close of the Middle Ages* (New York: AMS Press, 1966), 5:119.

4. Martin Luther, "Open Letter to the Christian Nobility of the German Nation," 15–22, in *Three Treatises by Martin Luther* (Philadelphia: Muhlenberg Press, 1943).

5. Geoffrey Baskerville, *English Monks and the Suppression of the Monasteries* (London: Jonathan Cape, 1937), 215.

6. John Hooper, who is generally agreed to be vastly exaggerating, makes the point, in Baskerville, *English Monks*, 205.

7. Miriam U. Chrisman, "Women of the Reformation in Strassburg, 1490–1530," *Archiv für Reformationsgeschichte* 63:2 (1972), 143–168.

8. Lyndal Roper, *The Holy Household: Religion, Morals, and Order in Reformation Augsburg* (Oxford: Oxford University Press, 1989), 221–222.

9. Bainton, *Women of the Reformation*, 1:63.

10. Jeanne de Jussie, *Le levain du Calvinisme ou Commencement de l'heresie de Geneve*, ed. Ad.-C. Grivel (Geneva, 1865), 174.

11. Ibid., 164.

12. Katharina Wilson, ed., *Women Writers of the Renaissance and Reformation* (Athens: University of Georgia Press, 1987), 260–283, for Dentière (by Thomas Head); 304–326 for Hoyers (by Brigitte Archibald); 365–397 for Bijns (by Kristiaan Aercke).

13. Mathias Wurm, *Trost Clostergefängner*, 25–26, cited by Chrisman, "Women of the Reformation in Strassburg," 164.

14. Presumably Clara Nützel was related to the secular manager of the convent, who claimed that looting cloisters and churches was God's work: Caritas Pirckheimer, *Die "Denkwurdigkeiten" der Caritas Pirckheimer*, ed. Josef Pfanner (Landshut, 1962), 42.

15. Ibid., 97–107.

16. *Chronik und Totenbuch des Klosters Wienhausen* (Wienhausen, 1986), 68–69.

17. F. J. Holzwarth, *Katholische Trösteinsamkeit*, vol. 12 (Mainz: Verlag Franz Kirchheim, 1858), 12.

18. Pirckheimer, *Denkwürdigkeiten*, 83–93.

19. Janssen, *History of the German People*, 5:142.

20. Ibid., 7:89.

21. De Jussie *Le levain du Calvinisme*, 106 and 55.

22. Janssen, *History of the German People*, 4:66.

23. N. Paulus, "Glaubenstreue der Lüneberger Klösterfrauen im 16. Jahrhundert," *Historische-politische Blätter* 112 (1893), 641.

24. Janssen, *History of the German People*, 7:317.

25. Pirckheimer, *Denkwürdigkeiten*, 30.

26. L. Lochner, "Letter of Felicitas Grundherr," *Historisch-politische Blätter* 44 (1859), 442–455.

27. De Jussie, *Le levain du Calvinisme*, 141.

28. Janssen, *History of the German People*, 4:70.

29. Paulus, "Glaubenstreue," 643.

30. *Wienhausen*, 76.

31. J. L. Lussman, *Historische Nachricht von dem Kloster Meding* (Halle, 1772), 141.

32. *Wienhausen*, 70–71.

33. Pirckheimer, *Denkwürdigkeiten*, 30.

34. Holzwarth, *Katholische Trösteinsamkeit*, 12.

35. Paulus, "Glaubenstreue," 639.

36. Janssen, *History of the German People*, 7:60.

37. Ibid., 5:422.

38. Ibid., 413, claims that convents were more violently handled than monasteries.

39. "Eine ungeheure wunderbarliche Absolution der Klosterfrauen in Fürstenthum Lüneberg," 1532, cited in Paulus, "Glaubenstreue," 638.

40. Franz L. Baumann, *Quellen zur Geschichte des Bauernkriegs in Oberschwaben* (Tübingen: Litterarischer Verein, 1876), 685.

41. *Wienhausen*, 84.

42. Kaspar Schetzger, "Von dem waren Christlichen Leben," cited in Paulus, "Glaubenstreue," 625.

16. Martha's Part

1. Max Weber, *The Protestant Ethic and the Spirit of Capitalism* (New York: Charles Scribner's Sons, 1958).

2. Mary E. Perry, *Gender and Disorder in Early Modern Seville* (Princeton: Princeton University Press, 1990), 153.

3. P. T. Lugano, ed., *I Processi inediti per Francesca Bussa dei Ponziani (Francesca Romana), 1440–1453* (Vatican City: Biblioteca Apostolica Vaticana, 1945), 252, stresses her complete adherence to the Benedictine rule in its original purity.

4. Her teachings were compiled by her disciples in 1522; see *Purgation and Purgatory*, trans. Serge Hughes, introduction by Benedict Groeschel (New York: Paulist Press, 1979), 1–67.

5. Marie B. Rowlands, "Recusant Women," in Mary Prior, ed., *Women in English Society, 1500–1800* (London: Methuen, 1985), 169.

6. Marguerite Jean, *Evolution des communautés religieuses de femmes au Canada de 1639 à nos jours* (Montreal: Fides, 1977), 27. The sentiments differ only in insignificant detail from Clement V's *De quibusdam:* see p. 317.

7. François de Sales, *Oeuvres*, ed. André Ravier and Roger Devos (Paris: Desclée de Brouwer, 1980), 25:211–214.

8. Jeanne-Françoise Frémyot de Chantal, *Sa vie et ses oeuvres*, vol. 2 (Paris: Plon, 1842), exhortation 6.

9. Her anxiety over possible conflicts among bishops is scarcely veiled in her letter to the superior in Lyons; see Francis de Sales and Jane de Chantal, *Letters of Spiritual Direction*, ed. Wendy M. Wright and Joseph F. Power, trans. Péronne M. Thibert, (New York: Paulist Press, 1988), 231.

10. Ibid., 219.

11. Enrica Viviani della Robbia, *Nei monasteri fiorentini* (Florence: Sansoni Editore, 1946), 128–130.

12. Rule, 9, in Teresa Ledochowska, *Angela Merici and the Company of St. Ursula according to the Historical Documents*, trans. Mary Teresa Neylan (Rome: Ancora, 1969), 148.

13. Marie of the Incarnation, *Relation of 1654*, in Irene Mahoney, ed., *Selected Writings* (New York: Paulist Press, 1989), 117–118.

14. Guy Oury, ed., *Marie de l'Incarnation, Ursuline (1599–1672): Correspondance* (Solesmes: C d S-P, 1971), #171 (p. 574); #100 (p. 294); and #193 (p. 652).

15. De Sales, *Oeuvres*, 25:232.

16. Chapter 18 of session 25, in Hefele-Leclercq, 10:1, *Les décrets du Concile de Trente*, 602.

17. *Razón y forma de la Galera real* (Salamanca, 1608), which popularized the name *la galera* (the galley) for workhouses for women.

18. Cited by Emmanuel Chill, "Religion and Mendicity in Seventeenth-Century France," *International Review of Social History* 7 (1962), 410.

19. Marie de l'Incarnation, Letter on the Life of Marie de Saint-Josephe, in Oury, *Marie de l'Incarnation,* p. 445.

20. Ibid., #132 (p. 408).

21. Ibid., #41, (p. 91).

22. Ibid., p. 97.

23. Ibid., #97 (pp. 277, 285).

24. Ibid., p. 98.

25. Ibid., #209 (p. 718).

26. Ibid., #253.

27. The novice, Sister Madeleine Hachard, wrote *Une relation du voyages des religieuses Ursulines de Rouen à la Nouvelle Orléans, 1727,* ed. Dasson Baudry (Rouen: Boissel, 1865).

28. Vincent de Paul, *Oeuvres,* ed. Jean François Coste (Paris: Gabalda, 1920–1925), 10:661.

29. In correspondence with the duchesse of Aiguillon, de Paul expressed his reservations about the whole scheme of the General Hospital; see *Oeuvres,* 6:245, 250–251, 257.

30. Cited in Olwen Hufton, *The Poor in Eighteenth Century France* (Oxford: Clarendon Press, 1974), 188, n. 1.

31. Cited by Karen Anderson, *Chain Her by One Foot: The Subjugation of Women in Seventeenth Century New France* (New York: Routledge, 1991), 55.

32. *Lasciate governare le donne della donne,* cited by Ruth P. Liebowitz, "Virgins in the Service of Christ: Dispute over an Active Apostolate for Women during the Counter-Reformation," in Rosemary R. Ruether and Eleanor C. McLaughlin, eds., *Women of Spirit* (New York: Simon and Schuster, 1979), 152, n. 53.

33. Cited by Elizabeth Rapley, *The Dévotes: Women and Church in Seventeenth Century France* (Montreal: McGill-Queen's University Press, 1990), 92.

17. The Mystical Regiment

1. Teresa of Avila, *The Life of Saint Teresa of Avila,* trans. J. M. Cohen, (London: Penguin, 1957), 81.

2. Enrica Viviani della Robbia, *Nei monasteri fiorentini* (Florence: Sansoni Editores, 1946), 116–119.

3. Cited from her funeral eulogy by Henri Brémond, *Histoire littéraire du sentiment religieux en France,* vol. 2, *L'invasion mystique* (Paris: Bloud and Gay, 1925), 399.

4. Ann M. C. Foster, "The Chronicles of the English Poor Clares of Rouen, I," *Recusant History* 18 (1986), 61–62.

5. Electa Arenal and Stacey Schlau, *Untold Sisters: Hispanic Nuns in Their Own Works, 16th–18th Centuries* (Albuquerque: University of New Mexico Press, 1989), 55.

6. Guy Oury, ed., *Marie de l'Incarnation, Ursuline (1599–1672): Correspondance*

(Solesmes: C d S-P, 1971), #140 (the life and death of Mother Marie de Saint Joseph), p. 437.

7. Arenal and Schlau, *Untold Sisters*, 357.

8. This is the apt phrase employed by Brémond.

9. Teresa, *Life*, 1.

10. Ibid., 258.

11. Philip Caraman, *The Other Face: Catholic Life under Elizabeth I* (New York: Sheed and Ward, 1960).

12. Teresa, *Life*, 94.

13. Ibid., 185. Diabolic attacks and visions of hell accompanied the ever-present charges of the Inquisition. For example, see *Life*, 223 and 234.

14. A letter of 1653 called "Raisons qui ont porté le Mère Angélique á sortir de la Jurisdiction de l'ordre de Cisteaux," cited by F. Ellen Weaver, *The Evolution of the Reform of Port-Royal: From the Rule of Cîteaux to Jansenism* (Paris: Beauchesne, 1977), 59–60.

15. Arenal and Schlau, *Untold Sisters*, 62.

16. Alberto de la Virgen del Carmen, *Historia de la Reforma Teresiana (1562–1962)* (Madrid: Editorial de Espiritualidad, 1968), 178.

17. Patricia Lusseau, *L'abbaye royale de Fontevraud aux XVIIe et XVIIIe siècles* (Paris: Herault Editions, 1986), 65.

18. Chap. 30, cited by Jean de la Croix Bouton, ed., *Les moniales cisterciennes* (Grignan: Commission pour l'histoire de l'ordre de Cîteaux, 1987), 1/2:65–71.

19. Bouton, *Les moniales*, 1/2:73

20. Brémond, *Histoire littéraire*, vol. 2, bases his chapter "Les grandes abbesses" on the *Eloges* from two quarto volumes by Jacqueline Bouëtte de Blémur, a nun whose mother was in the forefront of the first mystical wave. She obtained memoirs from several abbeys for her collection, which therefore represented the whole Benedictine movement.

21. Viviani, *Nei monasteri*, 133–135.

22. Letter of Direction to the Sisters of Annecy, 1619, in Francis de Sales and Jane de Chantal, *Letters of Spiritual Direction*, ed. Wendy M. Wright and Joseph F. Power, trans. Péronne M. Thibert, (New York: Paulist Press, 1988), 239.

23. Blémur, *Eloges*, 1:561–562, cited by Brémond, *Histoire littéraire*, 2:423.

24. Jacqueline Blémur, *Abrégé de la vie de la V. M. Charlotte Le Sergent* (Paris, 1685), 14–16, cited in Bremond, *Histoire littéraire*, 2:469.

25. Gaspar Navarro, *Tribunal de la superstición ladina . . .* (Huesca, 1631), fol. 32, cited by Jose Sánchez Lora, *Mujeres, Conventos y Formas de la Religiosidad Barroca* (Madrid: Fundación Universitaria Española, 1988), 31, exemplifying guides commonly used by Spanish directors.

26. Teresa, *Life*, 187.

27. Marie of the Incarnation, *Relation of 1654*, in Irene Mahoney, ed., *Selected Writings* (New York: Paulist Press, 1989).

28. Teresa, *Life*, 104.

29. Sánchez Lora, *Mujeres* (see n. 25), 245: the same women applied the principle of violent pedagogy to their novices.

30. Michel Carmona, *Les diables de Loudun: Sorcellerie et politique sous Richelieu* (Paris: Fayard, 1988), 33.

31. Brémond, *Histoire littéraire*, 2:438 (citing Blémur).

32. De Sales and Chantal, *Spiritual Direction*, 235.

33. Brémond, *Histoire littéraire*, 2:360.

34. Teresa, *Life*, 236.

35. Hefele-Leclercq, 10/1:607–609.

36. Viviani, *Nei monasteri*, 130.

37. Brémond, *Histoire littéraire*, 2:439 (citing Blémur).

38. Jeanne Arnauld, *The Perfect and the Imperfect Religious*, cited in Ethel Romanes, *The Story of Port-Royal* (London: John Murray, 1907), 411.

39. Cited by Weaver, *Reform of Port-Royal*, 55.

40. Brémond, *Histoire littéraire*, 2:231.

41. *Vida y Virtudes de la V. Madre Sor Maria Angela Astorhc, capuchina descalʒa*, book 2, c. 7, cited in Sánchez Lora, *Mujeres* (see n. 25), 141.

42. Brémond, *Histoire littéraire*, 2:334–335.

43. Teresa, *Life*, 71.

44. María de Jesus Agreda, *The Mystical City of God*, trans. Fiscar Marison (Washington N.J.: Ave Maria Institute, 1971).

45. Lusseau, *L'abbnye royale*, 186.

46. Etienne Catta, *La vie d'un monastère sous l'Ancien-Régime. La Visitation Sainte-Marie de Nantes (1630–1792)* (Paris: Vrin, 1954) 465–466.

47. Oury, *Marie de l'Incarnation*, 454.

48. Weaver, *Reform of Port-Royal*, 53.

49. Marc Escholier, *Port Royal: The Story of the Jansenists* (New York: Hawthorn Books, 1968), 129.

50. Ibid., 144.

51. Ibid., 290.

18. The Sweetness of Life

1. Guy Oury, ed., *Marie de l'Incarnation, Ursuline (1599–1672): Correspondance* (Solesmes: C d S-P, 1971), 440–441.

2. Enrica Viviani della Robbia, *Nei monasteri fiorentini* (Florence: Sansoni Editores, 1946), 237–252.

3. Lucien Pérey, *Histoire d'une grande dame au XVIIIe siècle, la princesse Hélène de Ligne (1892)*, cited by Jean de la Croix Bouton, ed., *Les moniales cisterciennes* (Aiguebelle: Commission pour l'histoire de l'ordre de Cîteaux, 1987), 2:145.

4. Electa Arenal and Stacey Schlau, *Untold Sisters: Hispanic Nuns in Their Own Works, 16th-18th Centuries* (Albuquerque: University of New Mexico Press, 1989), 38, citing Sor Gracia, *Libro de recreaciones*, 106.

5. Cited by Octavio Paz, *Sor Juana, or, The Traps of Faith* (Cambridge, Mass.: Harvard University Press, 1988), 221.

6. *Response to Sor Filotea*, from Margaret Sayers Peden, trans., *A Woman of Genius: The Intellectual Autobiography of Sor Juana Inés de la Cruz* (Salisbury, Conn.: Lime Rock Press, 1982).

7. Paz, *Sor Juana*, p. 435.

8. Arenal and Schlau, *Untold Sisters*, 72.

9. Viviani, *Nei monasteri*, 141–143, from the chronicle by Suor Maria Esaltata Ridolfi, 1684–1750.

10. Ibid., 6.

11. Ibid., 281–283.

12. Ibid., 257.

13. Ibid., 171.

14. Cited by Henri Brémond, *Histoire littéraire du sentiment religieux en France*, (Paris: Bloud and Gay, 1925), 3:546.

15. Ann M. C. Foster, "The Chronicles of the English Poor Clares of Rouen, I," *Recusant History* 18 (1986), 71–76.

16. Viviani, *Nei monasteri*, 260.

17. Ibid., 289.

18. Cited in Geneviève Reynes, *Couvents de femmes: La vie des religieuses cloîtrées dans la France des XVIIe et XVIIIe siècles* (Paris: Fayard, 1987), 43.

19. The estimate of H. van Houtte, *Histoire économique de la Belgique à la fin de l'Ancien Régime* (Ghent, 1920), 426–427, is that three-quarters of the land in Belgium belonged to the church and two-thirds of that to monasteries.

20. Jose Sánchez Lora, *Mujeres, Conventos y Formas de la Religiosidad Barroca* (Madrid: Fundación Universitaria Española, 1988), 108–109, cites a census of 1591 showing 20,369 nuns in Castile to 20,697 monks, a large expansion from an earlier survey of 1528–1536, which listed about 28,000 of both sexes. In the course of the sixteenth century, the Clarisses, the most numerous feminine order, established about 83 convents.

21. Ibid., 114.

22. Cited in Etienne Catta, *La vie d'un monastère sous l'Ancien-Régime. La Visitation Sainte-Marie de Nantes (1630–1792)* (Paris: Vrin, 1954), 502.

23. Ann M. C. Foster, "The Chronicles of the English Poor Clares of Rouen II," *Recusant History* 18 (1986), 154–158.

24. Patricia Byrne, "'Priestesses of the Day': Sisters of St. Joseph and the French Revolution," paper presented at the History of Women Religious Network Conference, Cardinal Stritch College, Milwaukee, June 1995.

25. Bruno de Jesus Marie, *Le sang du Carmel* (Paris, 1954), 28.

26. Catta, *La vie d'un monastère*, 542.

27. Foster, "The English Poor Clares, II," 158.

28. Bruno, *Le sang du Carmel*, 469.

29. Livrons nos coeurs à l'allégresse / Le jour de gloire est arrivé, / Loin de nous

toute faiblesse / Voyant l'étendard arrivé (bis) / Préparons-nous en vrai conquérant / Sous les drapeaux d'un Dieu mourant / Courons, voulons tous à la gloire; / Ranimons notre ardeur, / Nos corps sont au Seigneur / Montons, montons à l'échafaud / Et rendons-le vainqueur.

30. Bruno, *Le san du Carmel*, 477.

19. Culture Wars

1. Marie de la Trinité Kervingant, *Des moniales face à la Révolution Française. Aux origines des Cisterciennes-Trappistines* (Paris: Beauchesne, 1989), 98.

2. Etienne Catta, *La vie d'une monastère sous l'Ancien-Régime. La Visitation Sainte-Marie de Nantes (1630–1792)* (Paris: Vrin, 1954), 556.

3. Constance FitzGerald, ed., *The Carmelite Adventure: Clare Joseph Dickinson's Journal of a Trip to America and Other Documents*, Carmelite Source Series 2 (Baltimore: Carmelite Sisters, 1990).

4. This is a repeated theme in her letters, quoted extensively by Louise Callan, *Philippine Duchesne: Frontier Missionary of the Sacred Heart, 1769–1852* (Westminster, Md.: Newman Press, 1957).

5. Joan C. Ullman, *The Tragic Week: A Study of Anticlericalism in Spain, 1875–1912* (Cambridge, Mass.: Harvard University Press, 1968), 88.

6. Guy Gaucher, *The Story of a Life: St. Thérèse of Lisieux* (New York: Harper and Row, 1988), 174.

7. Thérèse of Lisieux, *The Story of a Soul*, trans. John Beevers (Garden City, N.Y.: Image Books, 1957), 111–114.

8. Ibid., 155.

9. Edith Stein, *Collected Works*, vol. 1, *Life in a Jewish Family*, ed. L. Gelber and R. Leuven (Washington, D.C.: ICS Publications, 1986).

10. Waltraud Herbstrith, *Edith Stein* (San Francisco: Harper and Row, 1985), 73. Susanne M. Batzdorff, a relative who survived the Holocaust, still wrestles with the mystery of Stein's conversion and the nature of her sacrifice; see "A Martyr of Auschwitz," *New York Times Magazine*, April 12, 1987.

11. A sermon by an apostate monk in Cincinnati, cited by Mary Ewens, "The Leadership of Nuns in Immigrant Catholicism," in Rosemary R. Ruether and Rosemary S. Keller, eds., *Women and Religion in America*, vol. 1 (San Francisco: Harper and Row, 1981), 135–137.

12. Blandina Segale, *At the End of the Santa Fe Trail* (Milwaukee: Bruce, 1948).

13. Thomas Richter, ed., "Sister Catherine Mallon's Journal," *New Mexico Historical Review* 52 (1977), 141–147.

14. Dorothea Olga McCants, *They Came to Louisiana: Letters of a Catholic Mission, 1854–1882* (Baton Rouge: Louisiana State University Press, 1970), 28.

15. Yvonne Turin, *Femmes et religieuses au XIXe siècle. Le féminisme en religion* (Paris: Nouvelle Cité, 1989), 163.

16. Marie-Emilie Hervier, superior general at Clermont in 1870, cited in ibid., 122.

17. Josephine Bunkley, *Miss Bunkley's Book: The Testimony of an Escaped Novice from the Sisterhood of St. Joseph, Emmettsburg Maryland, the Mother House of the Sisters of Charity in the United States* (New York: Harpers, 1856), the account of a protestant convert who "escaped" the confinement of a Daughters of Charity community.

18. Compare the cautious whitewashed version of this history by a member of the Scranton community, *The Immaculate Heart of Mary* (New York: P. J. Kennedy, 1924), with the more modern and feminist version reported by Nancy Sylvester, Connie Supan, and Joan Glisky on behalf of the Claiming Our Roots Collective at the Second Conference of the History of Women Religious at Marymount College, Tarrytown, N.Y., June 28, 1992. My thanks to Margaret Susan Thompson, personal communication, for helping me untangle this story.

19. Turin, *Femmes et religieuses,* 217.

20. Gaucher, *St. Thérèse,* 175.

21. Karma L. Tsmomo, ed., *Sakyavhitä: Daughters of Buddha* (Ithaca, N.Y.: Snow Lion Publications, 1988), gives a variety of views on Buddhist nuns.

22. Mary Ewens, "Removing the Veil: The Liberated American Nun," in Rosemary Reuther and Eleanor McLaughlin, *Women of Spirit* (New York: Simon and Shuster, 1979), 271.

23. Ewens, "Leadership," 127.

24. Turin, *Femmes et religieuses,* 209–210, quotes letters from Africa from women who reassured themselves that the choice was confirmed by happiness in their work.

25. Bernard Arens's detailed survey, *Manuel des missions catholique* (Louvain: Editions du Museum Lessianum, 1925), showed how few the numbers of sisters sent to the missions were, relative to those kept at home, except in congregations specifically formed for the task. Indeed, some congregations appear to have satisfied the order by reporting preparations to send a sister or two, which apparently lasted for years.

26. The complaint of a mission representative of the Sisters of Notre Dame de Namur in America—that too many women sent to the missions were misfits in their American communities and racist to boot (in the 1970s)—is noted by Barbara Ferraro and Patricia Hussey with Jane O'Reilly, *No Turning Back: Two Nuns' Battle with the Vatican over Women's Right to Choose* (New York: Poseidon Press, 1990), 137. Similar difficulties are exposed in interviews from several congregations collected by Sara Harris, *The Sisters: The Changing World of the American Nun* (Indianapolis: Bobbs Merrill, 1970).

27. Angelyn Dries, "Uncondemned Americanism: The Rise of a Foreign Mission Impulse among U.S. Roman Catholics, 1893–1925," *Records of the American Catholic Historical Society of Philadelphia* 103 (1992), 27–39.

28. C. Becker, *History of the Catholic Missions in Northeast India (1890–1915)* (Calcutta: Firma KLM Private, 1980), 244–245.

29. Cyprian Davis, *The History of Black Catholics in the United States* (New York: Crossroad, 1990), 73.

30. Peter Guilday, ed., *The Major Pastorals of the American Hierarchy, 1792–1919* (Westminster, Md.: Newman Press, 1954), 221.

31. Harris, *The Sisters,* 245.

32. Mary J. Oates, ed., *Higher Education for Women: A Historical Anthology* (New York: Garland Press, 1987), 377.

20. *The Feminine Apostolate*

1. Madeleine Sophie Barat, cited in Yvonne Turin, *Femmes et religieuses au XIXe siècle; Le féminisme en religion* (Paris: Nouvelle Cité, 1989), 5.

2. Barat, cited in Susan C. Peterson and Courtney Vaughn Roberson, *Women with Vision: The Presentation Sisters of South Dakota, 1880–1985* (Urbana: University of Illinois Press, 1988), 40.

3. Turin, *Femmes et religieuses,* 70.

4. Dorothea Olga McCants, *They Came to Louisiana: Letters of a Catholic Mission, 1854–1882* (Baton Rouge: Louisiana State University Press, 1970), 53.

5. Ephrem Hollermann, *The Reshaping of a Tradition: American Benedictine Women, 1852–1881* (St. Joseph, Minn.: Sisters of the Order of St. Benedict, 1994), 154.

6. Mary Ewens, "The Leadership of Nuns in Immigrant Catholicism," in Rosemary Ruether and Rosemary S. Keller, eds., *Women and Religion in America,* vol. 1 (San Francisco: Harper and Row, 1981), 131.

7. Ibid., 114.

8. Patricia Byrne, "Sisters of Saint Joseph: The Americanization of a French Tradition," *U.S. Catholic History* 5:3–4 (1986), 241–272.

9. Eugenia Logan, *The History of the Sisters of Providence of St. Mary of the Woods, Indiana,* 2 vols. (Terre Haute, Ind.: Moore Langan, 1978).

10. Susan Bradshaw, "Religious Women in China: Understanding of Indigenization," *Catholic Historical Review* 68 (1982), 32. By the 1930s there were 42 Chinese congregations. Fifty foreign congregations numbered 1,016 Chinese sisters to 1,693 foreigners. And 6,211 virgins worked independently as catechists and teachers; ibid., 36.

11. Turin, *Femmes et religieuses,* 256, n. 1.

12. Quoted from Margaret Susan Thompson, "Women and American Catholicism, 1789–1989," chap. 5 in Stephen J. Vicchio and Virginia Geiger, eds., *Perspectives on the American Catholic Church* (Westminster, Md.: Christian Classics, 1989), 135.

13. Barbara Brumleve, ed., *The Letters of Mother Caroline Friess, School Sisters of Notre Dame* (Saint Louis: School Sisters of Notre Dame, 1991), 290 and 291.

14. Cusack, *Woman's Work in Modern Society,* cited by Irene ffrench Eager, *Margaret Ann Cusack* (Dublin: Arden House and Woman's Press, 1979) 84.

15. Josephine M. Bunkley, *Miss Bunkley's Book: The Testimony of an Escaped Novice from the Sisterhood of St. Joseph, Emmittsburg Maryland, the Mother House of the Sisters of Charity in the United States* (New York: Harpers, 1856).

16. Turin, *Femmes et religieuses,* 326.

17. Margaret Ann Cusack, *The Nun of Kenmare: An Autobiography* (Boston: Houghton Mifflin, 1889).

18. Angelyn Dries, "Living in Ambiguity: A Paradigm Shift Experienced by the Sister Formation Movement," *Catholic Historical Review* 79:3 (1993), 478–487.

19. Edward Norman, *The English Catholic Church in the Nineteenth Century* (Oxford: Oxford University Press, 1984), 160.

20. In comparison, about 10,000 priests served 102 academies for boys. See Mary Ewens, *The Role of the Nun in Nineteenth Century America* (New York: Arno, 1978).

21. Diana Culbertson, ed., *Rose Hawthorne Lathrop: Selected Writings* (New York: Paulist Press, 1993), 202.

22. Mary Ewens, "Removing the Veil: The Liberated American Nun," in Rosemary R. Reuther and Eleanor C. McLaughlin, *Women of Spirit* (New York: Simon and Schuster, 1979), 259.

23. Mary Jo Weaver, *New Catholic Women* (San Francisco: Harper and Row, 1986), 79. Despite the difficulties, a survey of 1927 disclosed that 57 percent of the sisters met a standard of two years of education beyond secondary schools, while only 50 percent of the secular teachers did. By the 1930s many were getting degrees from secular colleges.

24. These conclusions are shown in the results of a 1955 survey of clerical attitudes and spiritual and intellectual elements in the formation of sisters reported in Ritamary Bradley, ed., *The Spiritual and Intellectual Elements in the Formation of Sisters,* (New York, 1957), 170–173.

25. Mary Emil Penet, in, Ritamary Bradley, ed., *The Mind of the Church in the Formation of Sisters,* (New York: Fordham University Press, 1956), 2.

Conclusion

1. Quoted from Barbara Ferraro and Patricia Hussey with Jane O'Reilly, *No Turning Back: Two Nuns' Battle with the Vatican over Women's Right to Choose* (New York: Poseidon Press, 1990), 153.

2. Thérèse de Lisieux, *The Story of a Soul*, trans. John Beevers (Garden City, N.Y.: Image Books, 1957), 76.

3. Synod of Bishops, IX, Ordinary General Assembly: "The Consecrated Life and Its Role in the Church and in the World," October 2–29, 1994. This and other references to the proceedings are drawn from a roundtable discussion among a group of observers held at the Third Conference of the Network for the History of Women Religious, Cardinal Stritch College, Milwaukee, June 1995.

4. See the detailed story of nuns on welfare in the *Wall Street Journal*, May 19, 1986.

5. Mary Jo Weaver, *New Catholic Women* (San Francisco: Harper and Row, 1986), 232, n. 5. By 1989, the pope had softened somewhat toward American religious and reaffirmed the authority of the LCWR despite its liberal feminism. But he warned them against a radical stance that might lead them to challenge the basic teachings of the church as interpreted by the papacy; see the *New York Times*, April 21, 1989.

6. Helen R. F. Ebaugh, *Women in the Vanishing Cloister: Organizational Decline in*

Catholic Religious Orders in the United States (New Brunswick, N.J.: Rutgers University Press, 1993), 47, reporting on an update of Marie Augusta Neal, "The Sisters' Survey, 1980: A Report," *Probe* 10:5 (1981).

7. See, for example, the reminiscences of Pam Doyle, in Sara Harris, *The Sisters: The Changing World of the American Nun* (Indianapolis: Bobbs Merrill, 1970), 112. Similar stories are repeated in most of the many books by nuns who have left the convent.

Bibliography

1. The Apostolic Life

Achelis, Hans. *Virgines subintroductae.* Leipzig, 1902.

Boswell, John E. "Expositio and Oblatio: The Abandonment of Children and the Ancient and Medieval Family." *American Historical Review* 89:1 (1984): 10–33.

Brock, Sebastian P. "Early Syrian Asceticism." *Numen* 20:1 (1972): 1–14.

Brown, Peter. "Aspects of the Christianization of the Roman Aristocracy." In *Religion and Society in the Age of Augustine,* 161–182. London: Faber and Faber, 1972.

———. *The Body and Society: Men, Women, and Sexual Renunciation in Early Christianity.* New York: Columbia University Press, 1988.

Burrows, Millar. *The Dead Sea Scrolls.* New York: Viking Press, 1955.

Davies, Stevan. *The Revolt of the Widows: The Social World of the Apocryphal Acts.* Carbondale: Southern Illinois University Press, 1980.

Elliott, Dyan. *Spiritual Marriage.* Princeton: Princeton University Press, 1993.

Fiorenza, Elizabeth Schüssler. *In Memory of Her: A Feminist Theological Reconstruction of Christian Origins.* New York: Crossroad, 1983.

Fritsch, Charles T. *The Qum'ran Community: Its History and Scrolls.* New York: Macmillan, 1956.

Funk, F.-X. ed. *Didascalia et Constitutiones Apostolorum.* Paderborn: Ferdinand Schöningh, 1905.

Gaius. *Institutes.* Oxford: Clarendon Press, 1946.

Guignebert, Charles. *The Jewish World in the Time of Jesus.* New York: University Books, 1959.

Harnack, Adolph. "Probabilia über die Addresse und den Verfasser des Hebräerbriefes." *Zeitschrift für Neutestamentliche Wissenschaft* 1 (1900): 16–41.

Haskins, Susan. *Mary Magdalen: Myth and Metaphor.* New York: Harcourt, 1994.

Hennecke, Edgar, and Wilhelm Schneemelcher, eds. *New Testament Apocrypha.* Philadelphia: Westminster Press, 1963–64.

Hoppin, Ruth. *Priscilla, Author of the Epistle to the Hebrews.* Philadelphia: Exposition Press, 1969.

James, Montague R., ed. *The Apocryphal New Testament.* Oxford: Clarendon Press, 1972.

Klawiter, Fred C., "The Role of Martyrdom and Persecution in Developing the Priestly Authority of Women in Early Christianity." In David M. Scholer, ed., *Women in Early Christianity,* 105–115. New York: Garland Press, 1993.

Kuryluk, Ewa. *Veronica and Her Cloth.* Cambridge, Mass.: Basil Blackwell, 1991.

Labriolle, Pierre de. "Le mariage spirituel dans l'antiquité chrétienne." *Revue historique* 137 (1921): 204–225.

Legrand, Lucien. *The Biblical Doctrine of Virginity.* New York: Sheed and Ward, 1963.

Lightman, Marjorie, and William Zeisel. "Univira." *Church History* 46:1 (1977): 19–32.

MacMullen, Ramsay. "Women in Public in the Roman Empire." *Historia* 29 (1980): 208–218.

Mayer, J., ed. *Monumenta de viduis, diaconissis, virginibusque tractantia.* Bonn: Florilegium Patristicum, 1938.

McNamara, Jo Ann. "Matres Patriae/Matres Ecclesiae: Women of the Roman Empire." In Renate Bridenthal, Claudia Koonz, Susan Stuard, eds., *Becoming Visible: Women in European History,* 2d ed., 107–130. Boston: Houghton Mifflin, 1987.

———. *A New Song: Celibate Women in the First Three Christian Centuries.* New York: Haworth Press, 1983.

———. "Wives and Widows in Early Christian Thought." *International Journal of Women's Studies* 2:6 (1977): 575–592.

Meeks, Wayne A. *The First Urban Christians: The Social World of the Apostle Paul.* New Haven: Yale University Press, 1983.

———. "The Image of the Androgyne: Some Uses of a Symbol in Earliest Christianity." *History of Religions* 13:3 (1974): 165–208.

Miles, Margaret R. *Carnal Knowing: The Religious Meaning of Female Nakedness.* Boston: Beacon Press, 1989.

Moltmann-Wendel, Elisabeth. *The Women around Jesus.* New York: Crossroad, 1982.

Musurillo, Herbert. *Acts of the Christian Martyrs.* Oxford: Clarendon Press, 1972.

O'Leary, DeLacy. *The Saints of Egypt.* London: SPCK; New York: Macmillan, 1937.

Peterson, Joan M. "House Churches in Rome." *Vigiliae Christianae* 23 (1969): 264–272.

Pomeroy, Sarah B. *Goddesses, Whores, Wives, and Slaves.* New York: Schocken, 1975.

Ramsay, William. *The Church in the Roman Empire before A.D. 170.* London: Hodder and Stoughton, 1899.

Robinson, James M., ed. *The Nag Hammadi Library.* San Francisco: Harper and Row, 1981.

Robinson, John A. T. *Re-dating the New Testament.* London: SCM Press, 1976.

Scholer, David M., ed. *Women in Early Christianity.* New York: Garland Press, 1993.

Scroggs, Robin. "Paul and the Eschatological Woman Revisited." *Journal of the American Academy of Religion* 42 (1974): 536.

Shewring, W. H., trans. *The Passion of Perpetua and Felicity.* London: Sheed and Ward, 1931.

Swidler, Leonard. *Biblical Affirmations of Women.* Philadelphia: Westminster Press, 1979.

Theissen, Gerd. *Soziologie der Jesus Bewegung.* Munich: Kaiser, 1977.

Voöbus, A. *A History of Asceticism in the Syrian Orient, Subsidia 14.* Louvain: Corpus Scriptorum Christianorum Orientalium, 1958.

2. Cult and Countercult

Achelis, Hans. *Virgines subintroductae.* Leipzig, 1902.

Andrieu, Michel, ed. *Les Ordines Romani.* Louvain: Spicilegium Sacrom Lovaniense, 1956.

Barnes, Timothy D. *Tertullian.* Oxford: Clarendon Press, 1971.

Brock, Sebastian P. "Early Syrian Asceticism." *Numen* 20:1 (1972): 1–19.

Brown, Peter. "Aspects of the Christianization of the Roman Aristocracy." In *Religion and Society in the Age of Augustine,* 161–182. London: Faber and Faber, 1972.

———. *The Body and Society: Men, Women, and Sexual Renunciation in Early Christianity.* New York: Columbia University Press, 1988.

Burtchaell, James T. *From Synagogue to Church: Public Services and Offices in the Earliest Christian Communities.* New York: Cambridge University Press, 1992.

Clark, Elizabeth A. *Jerome, Chrysostom, and Friends.* New York: Edwin Mellen Press, 1979.

Courcelle, P. "Paulin de Nole et Saint Jérôme." *Revue des études latines* 25 (1947): 250–280.

Davies, Stevan. *The Revolt of the Widows: The Social World of the Apocryphal Acts.* Carbondale: Southern Illinois University Press, 1980.

Elliott, Dyan. *Spiritual Marriage: Sexual Abstinence in Medieval Wedlock.* Princeton: Princeton University Press, 1993.

Elm, Susanna. *'Virgins of God': The Making of Asceticism in Late Antiquity.* Oxford: Clarendon Press, 1994.

Fiorenza, Elizabeth Schüssler. *In Memory of Her: A Feminist Theological Reconstruction of Christian Origins.* New York: Crossroad, 1983.

Frend, W. H. C. "Blandina and Perpetua: Two Early Christian Heroines." In David M. Scholer, ed., *Women in Early Christianity,* 87–97. New York: Garland Press, 1993.

Hillgarth, Joyce N. *The Conversion of Western Europe, 350–750.* Englewood Cliffs, N.J.: Prentice-Hall, 1969.

Hoare, F. R., ed. *The Western Fathers.* New York: Harper Torchbooks, 1965.

Holum, Kenneth. *Theodosian Empresses: Women and Imperial Dominion in Late Antiquity.* Berkeley: University of California Press, 1982.

Jerome. *Principal Works.* In Philip Schaff and Henry Wace, eds., *NPNF,* vol. 6. Grand Rapids, Mich.: W. B. Eerdmans, 1979.

Joannou, Perikles. *La législation impériale et la christianisation du l'empire romain (311–476)*. Rome: Pontificium Institutum orientalium Studiorum, 1972.

Koch, Hugo. *Adhuc Virgo: Mariens Jungfrauschaft und Ehe in der alt kirchlichen Uberlieferung bis zum Ende des 4. Jahrhunderts*. Tübingen: Verlag J. C. B. Nohr, 1929.

Labriolle, Pierre de. "Le mariage spirituel dans l'antiquité chrétienne." *Revue historique* 137 (1921): 204–225.

Laeuchli, Samuel. *Power and Sexuality: The Emergence of Canon Law at the Synod of Elvira*. Philadelphia: Temple University Press, 1972.

Mayer, J. *Monumenta de viduis, diaconissis, virginibusque tractantia*. Bonn: Florilegium Patristicum, 1938.

McNamara, Jo Ann. "Chaste Marriage and Clerical Celibacy." In Vern L. Bullough and James Brundage, eds., *Sexual Practices and the Medieval Church*, 22–33. Buffalo: Prometheus Books, 1982.

———. "Cornelia's Daughters: Paula and Eustochium." *Women's Studies* 11 (1984): 9–27.

———. "Muffled Voices: The Lives of Consecrated Women in the Fourth Century." In John A. Nichols and Lillian Thomas Shank, eds., *Medieval Religious Women*, vol. 1, *Distant Echoes*, 11–30. Kalamazoo, Mich.: Cistercian Publications, 1984.

———. *A New Song: Celibate Women in the First Three Christian Centuries*. New York: Haworth Press, 1983.

———. "Sexual Equality and the Cult of Virginity in Early Christian Thought." *Feminist Studies* 3:3/4 (1976): 145–158.

———. "Wives and Widows in Early Christian Thought." *International Journal of Women's Studies* 2:6 (1977): 575–592.

McNamara, Jo Ann, and John E. Halborg, with Gordon Whatley. *Sainted Women of the Dark Ages*. Durham: Duke University Press, 1992.

Meeks, Wayne A. *The First Urban Christians: The Social World of the Apostle Paul*. New Haven: Yale University Press, 1983.

Metz, René. *La consecration des vièrges dans l'église romaine*. Strasbourg: Bibliothèque de l'Institut du Droit Canonique de l'Université de Strasbourg, 1954.

Noonan, John T., Jr. "Marital Affection in the Canonists," *Studia Gratiana* 12 (1967): 479–509.

Oost, Stewart I. *Galla Placidia Augusta*. Chicago: University Press, 1968.

Pagels, Elaine. *The Gnostic Gospels*. New York: Random House, 1979.

Reynolds, Roger E. "*Virgines subintroductae* in Celtic Christianity." *Harvard Theological Review* 61 (1968): 549–566.

Rousseau, Philip. *Ascetics, Authority, and the Church in the Age of Jerome and Cassian*. Oxford: Oxford: University Press, 1978.

Scholer, David M., ed. *Women in Early Christianity*. New York: Garland Press, 1993.

Theissen, Gerd. *Studien zur Soziologie des Urchristentums*. Tübingen: Mohr, 1979.

Weaver, P. R. C. *Familia Caesaris: A Social Study of the Emperor's Freedmen and Slaves*. Cambridge: Cambridge University Press, 1972.

3. The Discipline of the Desert

Abrahamse, Dorothy de F. "Byzantine Asceticism and Women's Monasteries in Early Medieval Italy." In John A. Nichols and Lillian Thomas Shank, eds., *Medieval Religious Women*, vol. 1, *Distant Echoes* Kalamazoo, Mich.: Cistercian Publications, 1984.

Anson, John. "The Female Transvestite in Early Monasticism." *Viator* 5 (1974): 1–32.

Boswell, John E. "Expositio and Oblatio: The Abandonment of Children and the Ancient and Medieval Family." *American Historical Review* 89:1 (1984): 10–33.

Brock, Sebastian P., and Susan Ashbrook Harvey, eds. *Holy Women of the Syrian Orient.* Berkeley: University of California Press, 1987.

Brown, Peter. *The Cult of the Saints.* Chicago: University of Chicago Press, 1981.

———. "The Patrons of Pelagius." In *Religion and Society in the Age of Saint Augustine*, 208–226. London: Faber and Faber, 1972.

———. "The Rise and Function of the Holy Man in Late Antiquity." In *Society and the Holy in Late Antiquity*, 103–152. Berkeley: University of California Press, 1979.

Bullough, Vern L. "Transvestitism in the Middle Ages." In Vern L. Bullough and James A. Brundage, eds., *Sexual Practices and the Medieval Church*, 43–54. Buffalo: Prometheus Books, 1982.

Bullough, Vern L., and Bonnie Bullough. *Cross Dressing, Sex, and Gender.* Philadelphia: University of Pennsylvania Press, 1993.

Cassian, John. *Institutions Cénobitiques*, ed. and French trans. J. C. Guy, *SC*, vol. 109. Paris: Editions du Cerf, 1965.

Chadwick, Owen. *John Cassian.* London: Cambridge University Press, 1968.

Chitty, Derwas J. *The Desert a City: An Introduction to the Study of Egyptian and Palestinian Monasticism under the Christian Empire.* London: Mowabray, 1977.

Clark, Elizabeth A. "On Friendship between the Sexes." In *Jerome, Chrysostom, and Friends*, 35–106. New York: Edwin Mellen Press, 1979.

Elm, Susannah. *"Virgins of God": The Making of Asceticism in Late Antiquity.* Oxford: Oxford University Press, 1994.

Frend, W. H. C. *The Rise of Christianity.* Philadelphia: Fortress Press, 1984.

Haskins, Susan. *Mary Magdalen: Myth and Metaphor.* New York: Harcourt, 1994.

Heffernan, Thomas J. *Sacred Biography: Saints and Their Biographers in the Middle Ages.* New York: Oxford University Press, 1988.

Hilpisch, Ferdinand (P. Stephanus). "Die Döppelklöster: Enstehung und Organisation." Diss., Münster in Westfalia, 1928.

Hoare, F. R., ed. *The Western Fathers.* New York: Harper Torchbooks, 1965.

Holum, Kenneth. *Theodosian Empresses: Women and Imperial Dominion in Late Antiquity.* Berkeley: University of California Press, 1982.

Ladeuze, P. *Etude sur le cénobitisme Pakhomien pendant le IVe siècle et la première moitié du Ve.* Frankfurt: Minerva, 1961.

Lawless, George. *Augustine of Hippo and His Monastic Rule.* Oxford: Clarendon Press, 1987.

Lorenz, Rudolf. "Die Anfänge des abendlandischen Mönchtums im 4 Jahrhundert." *Zeitschrift für Kirchengeschichte* 77 (1966): 1–61.

McNamara, Jo Ann, and John E Halborg, with Gordon Whatley. *Sainted Women of the Dark Ages.* Durham: Duke University Press, 1992.

Patlageon, Evelyne. "L'histoire de la femme déguisée en moine et l'evolution de la sainteté féminine à Byzance." *Studi Medievali,* ser. 3, 17:2 (1976): 597–623.

Pomeroy, Sarah B. *Goddesses, Whores, Wives, and Slaves.* New York: Schocken, 1975.

Rader, Rosemary. "The Role of Celibacy in the Origin and Development of Christian Heterosexual Friendship." Ph.D. diss., Stanford University, University Microfilms, 1978.

Rousseau, Philip. *Ascetics, Authority, and the Church in the Age of Jerome and Cassian.* Oxford: Oxford University Press, 1978.

———. *Pachomius: The Making of a Community in Fourth Century Egypt.* Berkeley: University of California Press, 1989.

Ward, Benedicta. *The Harlots of the Desert.* Kalamazoo, Mich.: Cistercian Publications, 1987.

Watson, Alan. *Roman Slave Law.* Baltimore: Johns Hopkins University Press, 1987.

4. The Power of Prayer

Abrahamse, Dorothy de F. "Byzantine Asceticism and Women's Monasteries in Early Medieval Italy." in John A. Nichols and Lillian Thomas Shank, eds., *Medieval Religious Women,* vol. 1, *Distant Echoes.* Kalamazoo, Mich.: Cistercian Publications, 1984.

Bitel, Lisa. "Sex, Sin, and Celibacy in Early Christian Ireland." *Proceedings of the Harvard Celtic Colloquium* 6 (1986): 65–95.

———. "Women's Monastic Enclosures in Early Ireland," *Journal of Medieval History* 12 (1986): 15–36.

Fell, Christine. *Women in Anglo-Saxon England and the Impact of 1066.* Bloomington: University of Indiana Press, 1985.

Griffe, E. *Le Gaule Chrétienne à l'époque romaine,* vol. 2, *L'église des Gaules au Ve siècle.* Paris: Picard, 1957.

Hochstetter, Donald Dee. "The Meaning of Monastic Cloister for Women according to Caesarius of Arles." In Thomas F. X. Noble and John J. Contreni, eds., *Religion, Culture, and Society in the Early Middle Ages,* 27–40. Kalamazoo, Mich.: Medieval Institute Publications, 1987.

Hollis, Stephanie. *Anglo-Saxon Women and the Church: Sharing a Common Fate.* Woodbridge, Eng.: Boydell Press, 1992.

McNamara, Jo Ann. "Chaste Marriage and Clerical Celibacy." In Vern L. Bullough and James A. Brundage, eds., *Sexual Practices and the Medieval Church,* 22–33. Buffalo: Prometheus Books, 1982.

———. "Chastity as a Third Gender in the Work of Gregory of Tours." In Kathleen Mitchell and Ian Wood, eds., *Gregory of Tours Anniversary Volume.* Forthcoming.

———. "*Imitatio Helenae:* Sainthood as an Attribute of Queenship in the Early Middle

Ages." In Sandro Sticca, ed., *Saints: Studies in Hagiography.* Binghamton, New York: Medieval and Renaissance Texts and Studies, 1996.

———. "A Legacy of Miracles." In Julius Kirschner and Suzanne Wemple, eds., *Women of the Medieval World: Essays in Honor of John Mundy,* 36–52. New York: Basil Blackwell, 1985,

———. "Living Sermons." In John A. Nichols and Lillian T. Shank, eds., *Medieval Religious Women,* vol. 2, *Peace Weavers,* 19–38. Kalamazoo, Mich.: Cistercian Publications, 1987.

McNamara, Jo Ann, and Suzanne Wemple. "The Power of Women Through the Family." In Mary Erler and Maryanne Kowaleski, eds., *Women and Power,* 83–101. Athens: University of Georgia Press, 1983.

McNamara, Jo Ann, and John E Halborg, with Gordon Whatley, *Sainted Women in the Dark Ages.* Durham: Duke University Press, 1992.

Nolte-Wolf, Cordula. "Conversio und Christianitas: Frauen in der Christianisierung vom 5. bis 8. Jahrhundert." Diss., Freie Universität, Berlin, 1993.

Prinz, Friedrich. *Frühes Mönchtum im Frankreich.* Munich and Vienna: R. Oldenbourg Verlag, 1965.

Rosenwein, Barbara H. *To Be the Neighbor of Saint Peter: The Social Meaning of Cluny's Property, 909–1049.* Ithaca, N.Y.: Cornell University Press, 1989.

Russell, James C. *The Germanization of Early Medieval Christianity: A Sociohistorical Approach to Religious Transformation.* New York: Oxford University Press, 1992.

Talbot, C. H. *The Anglo-Saxon Missionaries in Germany.* London and New York: Sheed and Ward, 1954.

Vogüé, Adalbert de. "Nouveaux aperçus sur un règle monastique du VIe siècle." *Revue d'ascetique et de mystique* 41 (1965): 19 54.

Wallace Hadrill, J. M. *The Frankish Church.* Oxford: Oxford University Press, 1984.

Wittern, Susanne. *Frauen, Heiligkeit und Macht: Lateinische Frauenviten aus dem 4. bis 7. Jahrhundert.* Stuttgart and Weimar: Verlag J. B. Metzler, 1994.

Wood, Ian N. "Gregory of Tours and Clovis." *Revue belge de philologie et d'histoire* 63 (1985): 249–272.

5. The Frontier Outpost

Bateson, Mary C. "Origin and Early History of Double Monasteries." *Royal Historical Society Transactions* 13 (1890): 137–198.

Bishko, C. J. *Spanish and Portuguese Monastic History, 600–1300.* Leiden: Brill, 1984.

Bitel, Lisa M. *Isle of the Saints: Monastic Settlement and Christian Community in Early Ireland.* Ithaca, N.Y.: Cornell University Press, 1990.

———. "Women's Monastic Enclosures in Early Ireland." *Journal of Medieval History* 12 (1986): 15–36.

De Paor, Liam. *Saint Patrick's World: The Christian Culture of Ireland's Apostolic Age, Trans. and Commentaries.* Notre Dame, Ind.: University of Notre Dame Press, 1993.

Folz, Robert. "Remiremont dans le mouvement colombanien." In Michel Parisse, ed.,

Remiremont: L'abbaye et la ville, 15–20. Nancy: Service des publications de l'Université de Nancy, 1980.

Geary, Patrick J. *Aristocracy in Provence: The Rhône Basin at the Dawn of the Carolingian Age.* Philadelphia: University of Pennsylvania Press, 1985.

Gougaud, Louis. *"Mulierum consortia:* Etude sur le syneisaktisme chez les ascètes celtiques." *Erice* 9 (1921): 147–156.

Guérout, J. "Le testament de sainte Fare: Matériaux pour l'étude et l'édition critique de ce document." *Revue d'histoire écclésiastique* 60:3–4 (1965): 761–821.

Herlihy, David. "Church Property on the European Continent, 701–1200." *Speculum* 36 (1961): 81–105.

Hillgarth, Joyce N. "Popular Religion in Visigothic Spain." In Edward James, ed., *Visigothic Spain,* 3–60. Oxford: Clarendon Press, 1980.

Hilpisch, Ferdinand (P. Stephanus). "Die Döppelklöster: Enstehung und Organisation." Diss., Münster in Westfalia, 1928.

Hollis, Stephanie. *Anglo-Saxon Women and the Church: Sharing a Common Fate.* Woodbridge, Eng.: Boydell Press, 1992.

Lesne, E. *La propriété écclésiastique en France aux époques romains et mérovingienne.* Lille: Giard, 1910.

McNamara, Jo Ann. "A Legacy of Miracles." In Julius Kirschner and Suzanne Wemple, eds., *Women of the Medieval World: Essays in Honor of John H. Mundy,* 36–53. Oxford: Basil Blackwell, 1985.

———. "Living Sermons." In John A. Nicholls and Lillian T. Shank, eds., *Medieval Religious Women,* vol. 2, *Peace Weavers,* Kalamazoo, Mich.: Cistercian Publications, 1987.

———. "The Need to Give: Economic Restrictions and Penitential Piety among Medieval Nuns." In Renate Blumenfeld-Kozinski and Timea Szell, eds., *Images of Sainthood in Medieval and Renaissance Europe,* 199–221. Ithaca, N.Y.: Cornell University Press, 1993.

McNamara, J. Ann and John E. Halborg, with Gordon Whatley. *Sainted Women of the Dark Ages.* Durham: Duke University Press, 1992.

McNeill, John T., and Helena M. Gamer. *Medieval Handbooks of Penance: A Translation of the Principal Libri Poenitentiales and Selections from Related Documents.* New York: Columbia University Press, 1938.

Moreau, Edouard de. *Histoire de l'église en Belgique,* 2d ed., 2 vols. Brussels: L'Edition Universelle, 1945.

Nicholson, Joan. *"Feminae gloriosae:* Women in the Age of Bede." In Derek Baker, ed., *Medieval Women,* 15–29. Oxford: Basil Blackwell, 1978.

Nolte-Wolf, Cordula. "Conversio und Christianitas: Frauen in der Christianisierung vom 5. bis 8. Jahrhundert." Diss., Freie Universität, Berlin, 1993.

Richards, Jeffrey. *Consul of God: The Life and Times of Gregory the Great.* London: Routledge and Kegan Paul, 1980.

Rosenwein, Barbara H. *To Be the Neighbor of Saint Peter: The Social Meaning of Cluny's Property, 909–1049.* Ithaca, N.Y.: Cornell University Press, 1989.

Ryan, John. *Irish Monasticism: Origins and Early Development*. London: Longmans, Green, 1931.

Schmitz, Philibert. *Histoire de l'Ordre de Saint Benoit*, 2d ed., vol. 7. Maredsous: Editions de Maredsous, 1948–1956.

Talbot, C. H. *The Anglo-Saxon Missionaries in Germany*. London and New York: Sheed and Ward, 1954.

Theis, Laurent. "Saints sans famille? Quelques remarques sur la famille dans le monde franc à travers les sources hagiographiques." *Revue historique* 255 (1976): 3–20.

Thiébaux, Marcelle. *The Writings of Medieval Women*, 2d ed. New York: Garland Publishing, 1994.

Wallace-Hadrill, J. M. *The Frankish Church*. Oxford: Oxford University Press, 1984.

Wittern, Susanne. *Frauen, Heiligkeit und Macht: Lateinische Frauenviten aus dem 4. bis 7. Jahrhundert*. Stuttgart and Weimar: Verlag J. B. Metzler, 1994.

Wood, Ian N. *The Merovingian Kingdoms, 450–751*. London and New York: Longman, 1994.

———. "The Mission of Augustine of Canterbury to the English." *Speculum* 69 (1994): 1–17.

6. The Bonds of Castimony

Bateson, Mary. "Origin and Early History of Double Monasteries." *Royal Historical Society Transactions* 13 (1899): 137–198.

Berlière, Ursmer. *L'ascèse bénédictine des origines à la fin du XIIe siècle*. Maredsous: Editions de Maredsous, 1927.

Bishko, C. J. *Spanish and Portuguese Monastic History, 600–1300*. Leiden: Brill, 1984.

Blair, Peter Hunter. *Anglo-Saxon England*, 2d ed. Cambridge: Cambridge University Press, 1977.

Borst, A. *Mönche am Bodensee (610–1525)*. Sigmaringen: Jan Thorbeke, 1978.

Cowdrey, H. E. J. *The Cluniacs and the Gregorian Reform*. Oxford: Clarendon Press, 1970.

Dulcy, Suzanne. *La Règle de Saint Benôit d'Aniane et la réforme monastique à l'époque carolingienne*. Nîmes: A. Larguier, 1935.

Geary, Patrick J. *Furta Sacra: Thefts of Relics in the Central Middle Ages*. Princeton: Princeton University Press, 1978.

Guérout, Jean. "Le monastère à l'époque Carolingienne." In Yves Chaussey, ed., *L'abbaye royale de Notre Dame de Jouarre*. Paris: Bibliothèque d'Histoire et d'Archéologie Chrétienne, 1961.

Hamilton, Bernard. "The House of Theophylact and the Promotion of the Religious Life among Women in Tenth Century Rome." In *Monastic Reform, Catharism, and the Crusades, 900–1300*. London: Variorum Reprints, 1979.

Heineken, Johanna. *Die Anfänge der sachsischen Frauenklöster*. Göttingen: Kaestner, 1909.

Herlihy, David. "Church Property on the European Continent, 701–1200." *Speculum* 36 (1961): 81–105.

Hilpisch, Ferdinand (P. Stephanus). "Die Döppelklöster: Enstehung und Organisation." Diss., Münster in Westfalia, 1928.

Hlawitschka, Eduard. "Zur Klösterverlegung und zur Annahme der Benediktsregel in Remiremont." *Zeitschrift für die Geschichte des Oberrheins* 109 (1961): 249–269.

Lesne, Emile. *L'origine des menses dans le temporel des églises et des monastères de France au IXe siècle*. Lille: Giard; Paris: Champion, 1910.

Levison, Wilhelm. *England and the Continent in the Eighth Century*, Oxford: Clarendon Press, 1946.

McNamara, Jo Ann, and Suzanne Wemple. "Marriage and Divorce in the Frankish Kingdom." In Susan M. Stuard, ed., *Women in Medieval Society*, 95–124. Philadelphia: University of Pennsylvania Press, 1976.

Metz, René. "La consecration des vièrges dans l'église franque d'après la plus ancienne vie de sainte Pusinne (VIII-IXe siècle)." *Revue des sciences religieuses* 35 (1961): 32–48.

Moreau, Edouard de. *Histoire de l'église en Belgique*, 2d ed., 2 vols. Brussels: L'Edition Universelle, 1945.

Paxton, Frederick S. *The Creation of a Ritual Process in Early Medieval Europe*. Ithaca, N.Y.: Cornell University Press, 1990.

Petzholt, H. "Abtei Kitzingen." *Jahrbuch für frankische Landesforschung* 15 (1955): 69–83.

Schmitz, Philibert. *Histoire de l'Ordre de Saint Benoit*, 2d ed., vol. 7. Maredsous, Editions de Maredsous, 1948–1956.

Schulenberg, Jane T. "Sexism and the Celestial Gynecaeum, 500–1200." *Journal of Medieval History* 4:2 (1978): 117–133.

———. "Strict Active Enclosure and Its Effects on Female Monastic Experience (ca. 500–1200)." In John A. Nichols and Lillian T. Shank, eds., *Medieval Religious Women*, vol. 1, *Distant Echoes*, 51–86. Kalamazoo, Mich.: Cistercian Publications, 1984.

Skinner, Mary. "Benedictine Life for Women in Central France, 850–1100: A Feminist Revival." In John A. Nichols and Lillian T. Shank, eds., *Medieval Religious Women*, vol. 1, *Distant Echoes*, 87–114. Kalamazoo, Mich.: Cistercian Publications, 1984.

Störmer, Wilhelm. *Früher Adel: Studien zur politischen Führungsgeschichte im frankischen-deutschen Reich vom 8. bis 11. Jahrhundert*. Stuttgart: A. Hiersemann, 1973.

Talbot, C. H. *The Anglo-Saxon Missionaries in Germany*. London and New York: Sheed and Ward, 1954.

Van der Straeten, J. "Sainte Hunegonde d'Homblières, son culte et sa vie rhythmique." *Analecta Bollandiana* 71:3–4 (1953): 39–74.

Voigt, Karl. *Die königlichen Eigenklöster im Langobardenreiche*. Darmstadt: Wissenschaftliche Buchgesellschaft, 1969.

Wemple, Suzanne F. "S. Salvatore/S. Giulia: A Case Study in the Endowment and Patronage of a Major Female Monastery in Northern Italy." In Julius Kirshner and Suzanne F. Wemple, eds., *Women of the Medieval World: Essays in Honor of John H. Mundy*, 85–102. Oxford: Basil Blackwell, 1985. 85–102.

————. *Women in Frankish Society: Marriage and the Cloister, 500–900*. Philadelphia: University of Pennsylvania Press, 1981.

7. Family Ties

Backmund, Norbert *Die Kollegiat- und Kanonissenstifte in Bayern*. Windberg, 1973.

Bishko, C. J. "The Pactual Tradition in Hispanic Monasticism." In *Spanish and Portuguese Monastic History, 600–1300*, 31–41. Leiden: Brill, 1984.

Borst, Arno. *Mönche am Bodensee (610–1525)*. Sigmaringen: Jan Thorbeke, 1978.

Burton, Janet. *Yorkshire Nunneries in the Twelfth and Thirteenth Centuries*. York: Borthwick Papers, 1979.

Hamilton, Bernard. "The House of Theophylact and the Promotion of the Religious Life among Women in Tenth Century Rome." In *Monastic Reform, Catharism, and the Crusades, 900–1300*. London: Variorum Reprints, 1979.

————. "The Monastic Revival in Tenth Century Rome." In *Monastic Reform, Catharism, and the Crusades, 900–1300*. London: Variorum Reprints, 1979.

Heineken, Johanna. *Die Anfänge der sachsischen Frauenklöster*. Göttingen: Kaestner, 1909.

Heinrich, Mary. *Canonesses and Education in the Early Middle Ages*. Washington D.C.: Catholic University Press, 1924.

Hlawitschka, Eduard. Studien zur Abtissinnenreihe von Remiremont (7–13 Jh.). Saarbrucken: Veroffentlichung des Instituts fur Landeskunde des Saarlandes, 1963.

Hoebanx, Jean Jacques. *L'abbaye de Nivelles des origines au XIVe siècle*. Brussels: Memoires de l'académie royale de Belgique: Classe des Lettres et des Sciences Morales et Politiques, 1952.

Holtzmann, Robert. *Geschichte der sächsischen Kaiserzeit*, 3rd ed. Munich: G. D. W. Callwey, 1955.

Hörger, Karl. "Die reichrechtliche Stellung der Fürstabtissinnen." *Archiv für Urkundenforschung* 9 (1926): 195–270.

Hubert, Jean. "Les cathédrals doubles de la Gaule." *Mélange Louis Blondel, Ganava* 11 (1963): 105–125.

Hunt, Noreen. "Notes on the History of Benedictine and Cistercian Nuns in Britain." *Cistercian Studies* 8 (1973): 166.

Kempf, Friedrich, Hans-Georg Beck, and Josef A. Jungmann. *The Church in the Age of Feudalism*. New York: Seabury Press, 1980.

Kroll, Hildegard. "Zum Charakter des Prämonstratenzerordens in den ersten Jahrzehnten seines Bestehens." *Analecta Praemonstratensia* 56:1–2 (1980): 36–37.

Lesne, Emile. *L'origine des menses dans le temporel des églises et des monastères de France au IXe siècle*. Lille: Giard; Paris: Champion, 1910.

————. "Les ordonnances de Louis le Pieux." *Revue d'histoire de l'église de la France* 6 (1920): 161–175; 321–338; 449–493.

Leyser, Henrietta. *Hermits and the New Monasticism: A Study of Religious Communities in Western Europe, 1000–1150*. New York: St. Martin's, 1984.

Leyser, Karl J. "The German Aristocracy from the Ninth to the Early Twelfth Century: A Historical and Cultural Sketch." *Past and Present* 41 (1968): 25–53.

———. *Rule and Conflict in an Early Medieval Society: Ottonian Saxony.* Bloomington: University of Indiana Press, 1979.

Linage Conde, Jose A. *Una regula monástica riojana feminina del siglo X: El 'libellus a Regula sancti Benedicti subtractus.'* Salamanca: Universidad Pontificia, 1973.

Meyer, Marc Anthony. "Patronage of the West Saxon Royal Nunneries in Late Anglo-Saxon England." *Revue Bénédictine* 91:3 (1981): 332–358.

———. "Women in the Tenth Century English Monastic Reform." *Revue Bénédictine* 87:1–2 (1977): 34–61.

Millinger, Susan. "Anglo-Saxon Nuns in Anglo-Norman Hagiography: Humility and Power." In John A. Nichols and Lillian T. Shank, eds., *Religious Women*, vol. 1, *Distant Echoes.* Kalamazoo, Mich.: Cistercian Publications, 1984.

Moreau, Edouard de. *Histoire de l'église en Belgique*, 2d ed., 2 vols. Brussels: L'Edition Universelle, 1945.

Morris, Joan. *The Lady Was a Bishop: The History of Women with Clerical Ordination and the Jurisdiction of Bishops.* New York: Macmillan, 1973.

Parisse, Michel. "Les chanoinesses dans l'Empire germanique (IX-XIe siècles)." *Francia* 6 (1979): 107–126.

———. *Les nonnes au moyen age.* Le Puy: Christine Bonneton, 1983.

Parsons, David, ed. *Tenth Century Studies.* London: Phillimore, 1975.

Rosenwein, Barbara. *Rhinoceros Bound: Cluny in the Tenth Century.* Philadelphia: University of Pennsylvania Press, 1982.

Schäfer, K. Heinrich. *Die Kanonissenstifter im deutschen Mittelalter: Ihre Entwicklung und innere Einrichtung im Zussamenhang mit dem altchristlichen Sanktimonialentum.* Stuttgart: Kirchenrechtliche Abhandlungen, 1907.

Schulze, Hans, Reinhold Specht, and Günter Vorbrodt. *Das Stift Gernrode. Mitteldeutsche Forschungen*, vol. 38. Graz: Böhlau Verlag, 1965.

Skinner, Mary. "Aristocratic Families: Founders and Reformers of Monasteries in the Touraine, 930–1030." In *Benedictus: Studies in Honor of St. Benedict of Nursia*, 81–98. Kalamazoo, Mich.: Studies in Medieval Cistercian History, 1981.

———. "Benedictine Life for Women in Central France, 850–1100: A Feminist Revival." In John A. Nichols and Lillian T. Shank, eds. *Medieval Religious Women*, vol. 1, *Distant Echoes*, 87–114. Kalamazoo, Mich.: Cistercian Publications, 1984.

Störmer, W. *Früher Adel: Studien zur politischen Führungsgeschichte im frankischendeutschen Reich vom 8. bis 11. Jahrhundert.* Stuttgart: A. Hiersemann, 1973.

Verdon, Jean. "Les moniales dans la France de l'Ouest sur XIe et XIIe siècles: Etudes d'histoire sociale." *Cahiers de civilisation médiévale* 19:3 (1976): 247–264.

Weirauch, H. E. "Die Grundbesitz des Stiftes Quedlinburg im Mittelalters." *Sachsen und Anhalt* 14 (1938): 203.

———. "Die Güterpolitik des Stiftes Quedlinburg im Mittelalter." *Sachsen und Anhalt*, 13 (1937): 117.

Wemple, Suzanne F. *Women in Frankish Society: Marriage and the Cloister, 500–900.* Philadelphia: University of Pennsylvania Press, 1981.

8. The World, the Flesh, and the Devil

Albers, B. "Hirsau und seine Grundungen." In *Festschrift zum 1100 Jahrigen Jubiläum des deutsches Campo Santo in Rom*, 115–129. Rome, 1897.

Backmund, N. *Die Kollegiat und Kanonissenstifie in Bayern*. Windberg, 1973.

Benson, Robert L., and Giles Constable. *Renaissance and Renewal in the Twelfth Century*. Cambridge, Mass.: Harvard University Press, 1982.

Bishko, C. J. "The Pactual Tradition in Hispanic Monasticism." In *Spanish and Portuguese Monastic History, 600–1300*, 31–41. Leiden: Brill, 1984.

Bouton, Jean de la Croix, ed. *Les moniales cisterciennes, I: Histoire externe. pt. I, jusqu'à la fin du XVe siècle*. Grignan: Commission d'histoire de l'ordre de Cîteaux, 1985.

Bullough, Donald A. "The Continental Background of Reform." In David Parsons, ed., *Tenth Century Studies*. London: Phillimore, 1975.

Constable, Giles. *Cluniac Studies*. London: Variorum, 1982.

Corbet, Patrick. *Les saints ottoniens: Sainteté dynastique, sainteté royale et sainteté féminine autour de l'an Mil*. Sigmaringen: Thorbecke Verlag, 1986.

Dereine, Charles. *Les chanoines reguliers au diocèse de Liège avant S. Norbert*. Brussels: Académie Royale de Belgique, 1952.

Elliott, Dyan. *Spiritual Marriage: Sexual Abstinence in Medieval Wedlock*. Princeton: Princeton University Press, 1993.

Esposito, M. "La vie de Ste. Wulfhilde par Goscelin de Canterbory." *Analecta Bollandiana* 32 (1913): 10–26.

Farmer, D. G. "The Progress of Monastic Revival." In David Parsons, ed., *Tenth Century Studies*. London: Phillimore, 1975.

Favreux, Robert. "Heurs et malheurs de l'abbaye XIIe-XVe siècle." In Edmond-René Labande, ed., *Histoire de l'abbaye Sainte-Croix de Poitiers: Quatorze siècles de vie monastique*. Poitiers: Société des Antiquaires de l'Ouest w/CNRS, 1986.

Feierabend, H. *Die politische Stellung der deutschen Reichsabteien während des Investitur-streites: Historische Untersuchungen*, 3, Breslau: Marcus, 1913.

Galli, André. "Faremoutiers au moyen age." In *Sainte Fare et Faremoutiers*, 37–56. Faremoutiers, 1956.

Gilchrist, Roberta. *Gender and Material Culture: The Archaeology of Religious Women*. London: Routledge, 1994.

Guérout, Jean. "Le monastère á l'époque Carolingienne." In Yves Chaussey, ed., *L'abbaye royale de Notre Dame de Jouarre*. Paris: Bibliothèque d'Histoire et Archeologie Chrétienne, 1961.

Hallinger, Kassius. *Gorze-Kluny: Studien zu den monastischen Lebensformer und Gegensätzen im Hochmittelalter*. Roma: Studia Anselmiana, 1950.

Hamilton, Bernard, "The House of Theophylact and the Promotion of the Religious Life among Women in Tenth Century Rome." In *Monastic Reform, Catharism, and the Crusades, 900–1300*. London: Variorum Reprints, 1979.

Hefele, Carl Josef. *Conciliengeschichte*, vol. 5. Freiburg-im-Breisgau: Herder, 1886.

Heinrich, Mary. *Canonesses and Education in the Early Middle Ages*. Washington D.C.: Catholic University Press, 1924.

Hlawitschka, Eduard. "Studien zur Abtissinnenreihe von Remiremont (7–13 Jh.)." Saarbrucken: *Veroffentlichungen des Instituts fur Landeskunde des Saarlandes,* 1963.

Hoebanx, Jean Jacques. *L'abbaye de Nivelles des origines au XIVe siècle.* Brussels: Memoires de l'académie royale de Belgique: Classe des Lettres et des Sciences Morales et Politiques, 1952.

Holtzmann, Robert. *Geschichte der sächsischen Kaiserzeit,* 3rd ed. Munich: G. D. W. Callwey, 1955.

Hörger, Karl. "Die reichrechtliche Stellung der Fürstabtissinnen." *Archiv für Urkunden-forschung* 9 (1926): 195–270.

Hunt, Noreen. *Cluniac Monasticism in the Central Middle Ages.* N.p.: Shoestring Press: 1974.

———. *Cluny under Saint Hugh, 1049–1109.* Notre Dame, Ind.: University of Notre Dame Press, 1968.

Kempf, Friedrich, *The Church in the Age of Feudalism.* New York: Crossroad, 1982.

Lesne, Emile. *Histoire de la propriété ecclésiastique en France aux époques romaine et mérovingienne.* Lille: Giard, 1910.

Leyser, Karl J. *Rule and Conflict in an Early Medieval Society: Ottonian Saxony.* Bloomington: University of Indiana Press, 1979.

Lipsmeyer, Elizabeth, "The Imperial Abbey and Town of Zurich: The Benedictine Nuns and the Price of Ritual in 13th, 14th, and 15th Century Switzerland." In Elspeth Durie and Dewey Kramer, compilers, Margot King, ed., *On Pilgrimage,* 365–376. Toronto: Peregrina, 1994.

Localetti, René. "L'implantation cistercienne en Bourgogne." *Cahiers d'histoire* 20:2 (1975): 166–224.

McNamara, Jo Ann. "Canossa: The Ungendered Man and the Anthropomorphized Institution." In Donald Treadgold and Sabrina Petra Ramet, eds., *Render Unto Caesar.* Washington, D.C.: American University Press, 1995.

———. "Chastity as a Male Virtue in Odo of Cluny's Gerald of Aurillac." In George Ferzoco, ed., *The Construction of Sanctity.* Brussels: Brepols, forthcoming.

———. "*Imitatio Helenae:* Sainthood as an Attribute of Queenship in the Early Middle Ages." In Sandro Sticca, ed., *Saints: Studies in Hagiography.* Binghamton, N.Y.: Medieval and Renaissance Texts and Studies, 1996.

Meyer, Mark A. "Patronage of the West Saxon Royal Nunneries in Late Anglo-Saxon England." *Revue Bénédictine* 91:3 (1981): 332–358.

Miller, Maureen C. *The Formation of a Medieval Church: Ecclesiastical Change in Verona, 950–1150.* Ithaca, N.Y.: Cornell Univerity Press, 1993.

Morris, Joan. *The Lady Was a Bishop: The History of Women with Clerical Ordination and the Jurisdiction of Bishops.* New York: Macmillan, 1973.

Petroff, Elisabeth A. *Body and Soul.* Oxford: Oxford University Press, 1994.

Rosenwein, Barbara. *Rhinoceros Bound: Cluny in the Tenth Century.* Philadelphia: University of Pennsylvania Press, 1982.

———. *To Be the Neighbor of Saint Peter: The Social Meaning of Cluny's Property, 909–1049.* Ithaca, N.Y.: Cornell University Press, 1989.

Schäfer, K. Heinrich. *Die Kanonissenstifter im deutschen Mittelalter: Ihre Entwicklung und innere Einrichtung im Zusammenhang mit dem altchristlichen Sanktimonialentum.* Stuttgart: Kirchenrechtliche Abhandlungen, 1907.

Schmitz, Philibert. *Histoire de l'ordre de Saint Benoît,* 2d ed. Maredsous: Editions de Maredsous, 1948–1956.

Schulenberg, Jane T. "Strict Active Enclosure and Its Effects on Female Monastic Experience (ca. 500–1200)." In John A. Nichols and Lillian T. Shank, eds., *Medieval Religious Women,* vol. 1, *Distant Echoes,* 51–86. Kalamazoo, Mich.: Cistercian Publications, 1984.

Schulze, Hans, Reinhold Specht, and Günter Vorbrodt. *Das Stift Gernrode: Mitteldeutsche Forschungen,* vol. 38. Graz: Böhlau Verlag, 1965.

Siegwart, J. *Die Chorherren und Chorfrauen-Gemeinschaften in der deutschsprachigen Schweiz vom 6 Jahrhundert bis 1160; mit einem überblich über die deutsche Kanonikerreform des 10 und 11 Jh.* Fribourg: Studia Friburgensia, 1962.

Skinner, Mary. "Benedictine Life for Women in Central France, 850–1100: A Feminist Revival." In John A. Nichols and Lillian T. Shank, eds., *Medieval Religious Women,* vol. 1, *Distant Echoes,* 87–114. Kalamazoo, Mich.: Cistercian Publications, 1984.

Smith, L. M. *Cluny in the Eleventh and Twelfth Centuries.* London: Philip Allan, 1930.

Stein, Frederick M. "The Religious Women of Cologne, 1120–1320." Ph.D. diss., Yale University, 1977.

Stenton, Frank M. *The Anglo-Saxons.* Oxford: Clarendon Press, 1971.

Valous, Guy de. *Le monachisme clunisien des origines au XVe siècle.* Paris: Picard, 1970.

Verdon, Jean. "Les moniales dans la France de l'ouest aur XIe et XIIe siècles. Etudes d'histoire sociale." *Cahiers de civilisation médiévale* 19:3 (1976): 247–264.

Weirauch, H. E. "Die Grundbesitz des Stiftes Quedlinburg im Mittelalters." *Sachsen und Anhalt* 14 (1938): 203.

———. "Die Güterpolitik des Stiftes Quedlinburg im Mittelalter." *Sachsen und Anhalt* 13 (1937): 117.

Ziegler, Joanna E. "Secular Canonesses as Antecedent of the Beguines in the Low Countries: An Introduction to Some Older Views." In J. A. S. Evans and R. W. Unger, eds., *Studies in Medieval and Renaissance History.* New York: AMS Press, 1992.

9. The Imitation of Christ

Ackerman, Robert W., "The Liturgical Day in Ancrene Riwle," *Speculum* 53:4 (1978): 734–744.

Berman, Constance H. "Men's Houses, Women's Houses: The Relationship between the Sexes in Twelfth-Century Monasticism." In Andrew Macleish, ed., *The Medieval Monastery,* 43–52. St. Cloud, Minn.: North Star Press, 1988.

Bienvenu, Jean-Marc. "Aliénor d'Aquitaine et Fontevraud." *Cahiers de la civilisation medievale* 29:1–2 (1986): 15–27.

————. *L'étonnant fondateur de Fontevraud, Robert d'Arbrissel.* Paris: Nouvelles Editions Latines, 1981.

Bitel, Lisa. "Women of Eriu: Tales of Sex and Gender from Barbarian Ireland." Unpublished manuscript.

Blevec, Daniel le. "Le rôle des femmes dans l'assistance et la charité." *Cahiers de Fanjeaux* 23 (1988): 180.

Bolton, Brenda. "Innocent III's Treatment of the Humiliati." *Church History* 8 (1971).

————. *The Medieval Reformation.* London: Edward Arnold, 1983.

Boswell, John E. *Christianity, Social Tolerance, and Homosexuality: Gay People in Western Europe from the Beginnings of the Christian Era to the Fourteenth Century.* Chicago: University of Chicago Press, 1980.

Brune, P. *Histoire de l'ordre hospitalier du Saint-Esprit.* Paris, 1892.

Casagrande, Carla, ed. *Prediche alle donne del secolo XIII: Testi di Umberto da Romans, Gilberto da Tournai, Stefano di Borbone.* Milan: Bompiani, Nuova Corona, 1978.

Clay, Rotha Mary. *Hermits and Anchorites of England.* London: Methuen, 1914.

————. *The Medieval Hospitals of England.* New York: Barnes and Noble, 1966.

Coakley, John. "Friars as Confidants of Holy Women in Medieval Dominican Hagiography." In Renate Blumenfeld-Kosinski and Timea Szell, eds., *Images of Sainthood in Medieval Europe*, 222–246. Ithaca, N.Y.: Cornell University Press, 1991.

Constable, Giles. "Renewal and Reform in Religious Life: Concepts and Realities." In Robert L. Benson and Giles Constable, eds., *Renaissance and Renewal in the Twelfth Century.* Cambridge, Mass.: Harvard University Press, 1982.

Dalarun, Jacques. *L'impossible sainteté: La vie retrouvée de Robert d'Arbrissel (v. 1045–1116) fondateur de Fontevraud.* Paris: Cerf, 1985.

Dauphin, Hubert. "L'érémitisme en Angleterre aux XIe et XIIe siècles." In *L'éremitismo in Occidente nei secoli XI e XII*, 271–310. Milan: Vita e Pensiero, 1965.

Demaitre, Luke. "The Description and Diagnosis of Leprosy by Fourteenth Century Physicians." *Bulletin of the History of Medicine* 59 (1985): 327–344.

Dereine, Charles. "Le premier ordo de Prémontré." *Revue Bénédictine* 58 (1948): 84–92.

Doerr, Otmar, *Das Institut der Inklusen in Süddeutschland. Beiträge zur Geschichte des alten Mönchtums und des Benediktiner Ordens.* Münster: Aschendorff, 1934.

Eckenstein, Lina. *Women under Monasticism, 500–1500.* Cambridge: Cambridge University Press, 1896.

Elkins, Sharon K. "The Emergence of a Gilbertine Identity." In John A. Nichols and Lillian Thomas Shank, eds., *Medieval Religious Women*, vol. 1, *Distant Echoes*, 169–182. Kalamazoo, Mich.: Cistercian Publications, 1984.

————. *Holy Women of Twelfth Century England.* Chapel Hill: University of North Carolina Press, 1988.

Ell, Stephen R. "Blood and Sexuality in Medieval Leprosy." *Janus: Revue internationale de l'histoire des sciences de la médicine de la pharmacie et de la technique* 71 (1984): 156–163.

Elliott, Dyan. *Spiritual Marriage: Sexual Abstinence in Medieval Wedlock.* Princeton: Princeton University Press, 1993.

Elm, Kaspar. "Die Stellung der Frau in Ordenswesen, Semireligiösentum und Häresie zur Zeit der heiligen Elisabeth." In *Sankt Elisabeth, Fürsten, Dienerin, Heilige.* Sigmaringen: Jan Thorbeke Verlag, 1981.

Fontette, Micheline de. *Les religieuses à l'age classique du droit canonique.* Paris: J. Vrin, 1967.

Graham, Rose. *Saint Gilbert of Sempringham and the Gilbertines.* London: Elliot Stock, 1901.

Greven, Joseph. *Die Anfänge der Beginen: Ein Beitrag zur Geschichte der Volksfrömmigkeit und des Ordenswesens im Hochmittelalter* (Vorreformationsgeschichtliche Forschungen 8). Munster: Aschendorff, 1912.

Gruber, Erentraud. *Deutschordensschwestern im 19 und 20 Jahrhunderts: Widerbelebung, Ausbreitung und Tätigkeit* (Quellen und Studien zur Geschichte des Deutschen Ordens 14). Bonn-Godesberg: Verlag Wissenschaftliches Archiv, 1971.

Grundmann, Herbert. *Religiöse Bewegungen im Mittelalter: Untersuchungen über die geschichtlichen Zusammenhänge zwischen der Ketzerei, den Bettelorden und der religiösen Frauenbewegung im 12 und 13 Jahrhundert.* Berlin: Historische Studien, 1935.

Heimbucher, M. *Die Orden und Kongregationen der Katholischen Kirche.* Paderborn: Ferdinand Schöningh, 1896.

Herlihy, David. *Medieval Households.* Cambridge, Mass.: Harvard University Press, 1985.

Holdsworth, Christopher J. "Christina of Markyate." In Derek Baker, ed., *Medieval Women,* 185–204. Oxford: Basil Blackwell, 1978.

Huyghebaert, Nicholas. "Les femmes laiques dans la vie religieuse des XIe et XIIIe siècle dans la province ecclésiastique de Reims." In *I Laici nella "Societas Christiana" dei secoli XI e XII,* 346–395. Milan: Pubblicazioni dell'universita cattolica del Sacro Cuore, Miscellanea del Centro di Studi Medievali, 1968.

Kosofsky Sedgwick, Eve. *Between Men: English Literature and Male Homosocial Desire.* New York: Columbia University Press, 1985.

Leclerc, J. "Reclus et recluses." *Revue de l'église de Metz* 23 (1952): 315–362; (1953) 21–24.

Lemaître, Henri. "Statuts des religieuses du Tiers Ordre Franciscain dites Soeurs Grises Hospitalières (1483)." *Archivum Franciscanum Historicum* 4 (1911): 713–731.

Little, Lester K. *Religious Poverty and the Profit Economy in Medieval Europe.* Ithaca, N.Y.: Cornell University Press, 1978.

Marc-Bonnet, Henri. *Histoire des ordres religieux.* Paris: Presses Universitaires de France, 1968.

Mayr-Hartung, H. "Functions of a Twelfth Century Recluse." *History* 60 (1975): 351.

McDonnell, Ernest W. *The Beguines and Beghards in Medieval Culture with Special Emphasis on the Belgian Scene.* New Brunswick, N.J.: Rutgers University Press, 1954.

McGuire, Brian Patrick. "The Cistercians and the Transformation of Monastic Friendships." *Analecta Cisterciensia* 37:4 (1981): 1–63.

McLaughlin, Mary M. "Peter Abelard and the Dignity of Women: Twelfth-Century

'Feminism' in Theory and Practice." In *Pierre Abelard, Pierre le Venerable*. Paris: Colloques internationaux du Centre de la Recherche Scientifiques, 1975.

McNamara, Jo Ann. "*De Quibusdam Mulieres:* Reading Women's History from Hostile Sources." In Joel Rosenthal, ed., *Women and the Sources of Medieval History*, 237–258. Athens: University of Georgia Press, 1990.

———. "The Herrenfrage: The Restructuring of the Gender System, 1050–1150." In Claire Lees, ed., *Medieval Masculinities*, 3–29. Minneapolis: University of Minnesota Press, 1994.

———. "The Need to Give: Economic Restrictions and Penitential Piety among Medieval Nuns." In Renata Blumenfeld-Kosinski and Timea Szell, eds., *Images of Sainthood in Medieval and Renaissance Europe*, 199–221. Ithaca, N.Y.: Cornell University Press, 1993.

———. "The Rhetoric of Orthodoxy." In Ulrike Wiethaus, ed., *Maps of Flesh and Light: The Religious Experience of Medieval Women Mystics*, 9–27. Syracuse, N.Y.: Syracuse University Press, 1993.

Miller, Maureen C. *The Formation of a Medieval Church: Ecclesiastical Change in Verona, 950–1150*. Ithaca, N.Y.: Cornell University Press, 1993.

Neel, Carol. "Origins of Beguines." *Signs* 14:2 (1989): 321–341.

Newman, Barbara. "Authority, Authenticity, and the Repression of Heloise." In *From Virile Woman to WomanChrist: Studies in Medieval Religion and Literature*, 46–75. Philadelphia: University of Pennsylvania Press, 1995.

Petit, F. *La spiritualité des Prémontrés aux XIIe et XIIIe siècles*. Paris: Vrin, 1945.

Philips, Dayton. *Beguines in Medieval Strasbourg*. Palo Alto, Calif.: Stanford University Press, 1941.

Pullan, Brian. *Rich and Poor in Renaissance Venice: The Social Institutions of a Catholic State*. Oxford: Basil Blackwell, 1971.

Riley-Smith, Jonathan. *The Knights of Saint John of Jerusalem and Cyprus*. New York: St. Martin's, 1967.

Roper, Lyndal. *The Holy Household: Religion, Morals, and Order in Reformation Augsburg*. Oxford: Oxford University Press, 1989.

Rubin, Miri. *Charity and Community in Medieval Cambridge*. Cambridge: Cambridge University Press, 1987.

Stein, Frederick M. "The Religious Women of Cologne, 1120–1320." Ph.D. diss., Yale University, 1977.

Thompson, Sally. *Women Religious: The Founding of English Nunneries after the Norman Conquest*. Oxford: Clarendon Press, 1990.

Vauchez, André. "Charité et pauvreté chez sainte Elisabeth de Thuringe d'après des acts du Procès de canonisation." In Michel Mollat, ed., *Etudes sur l'histoire de la pauvreté*, 2 vol. I, 163–173. Paris: Publ. Sorbonne, Etudes 8, I-II, 1974.

Walter, J. von. *Die ersten Wanderprediger Frankreichs: Robert von Arbrissel*. Leipsig: Studien zur geschichtes der theologie und kirche, 1903.

Warren, Ann K. *Anchorites and Their Patrons in Medieval England*. Berkeley: University of California Press, 1986.

Ziegler, Johanna E. "The Curtis Beguinages in the Southern Low Countries and Art Patronage: Interpretation and Historiography." *Bulletin de l'Institut Historique Belge de Rome* 57 (1987): 31–70.

———. "Secular Canonesses as Antecedent of the Beguines in the Low Countries: An Introduction to Some Older Views." In J. A. S. Evans and R. W. Unger, eds., *Studies in Medieval and Renaissance History.* New York: AMS Press, 1992.

10. Cura Mulierum

Aïtoff, Sr. Marie-Serge. *Ste. Françoise Romaine.* Bec-Hellouin: OSB, 1983.

Berman, Constance H. "Cistercian Nuns and the Development of the Order: The Abbey at Saint-Antoine-des-Champs outside Paris." Unpublished manuscript.

———. "Early Women's Houses in the Cistercian Order and a Comparison of Their Endowment and Economic Practice to That of Houses for Men." Paper presented at the Twenty-second International Conference on Medieval Studies, Kalamazoo, Mich., 1987.

———. "Economic Activities of Early Cistercian Houses for Women." Paper presented at the Sixth Berkshire Conference on the History of Women, Smith College, 1984.

———. *Medieval Agriculture, the Southern French Countryside, and the Early Cistercians: A Study of Forty-Three Monasteries.* Philadelphia: Transactions of the American Philosophical Society, 1986.

———. "Monks and Nuns in a Mediterranean Landscape: The Cistercian Expansion into Southern France, 1119–1249." Unpublished manuscript.

———. "Women as Donors and Patrons to Southern French Monasteries in the 12th and 13th centuries." In Constance H. Berman, Charles W. Connell, and Judith Rice Rothschild, eds., *The World of Medieval Women: Creativity, Influence, Imagination,* 53–68. Morgantown: West Virginia University Press, 1985.

Bienvenu, Jean-Marc. *L'étonnant fondateur de Fontevraud, Robert d'Arbrissel.* Paris: Nouvelles Editions Latines, 1981.

Bourdillon, A. F. Claudine. *The Order of Minoresses in England.* Ridgewood N.J.: Gregg Press, 1965.

Bouton, Jean de la Croix, ed. *Les moniales cisterciennes, I: Histoire externe. pt. I, jusqu'à la fin du XVe siècle.* Grignan: Commission d'histoire de l'ordre de Cîteaux, 1985.

Boyd, Catherine. *A Cistercian Nunnery in Medieval Italy: The Story of Riffredo in Saluzzo, 1220–1300.* Cambridge, Mass.: Harvard University Press, 1943.

Burton, Janet E. *Yorkshire Nunneries in the Twelfth and Thirteenth Centuries.* York: Borthwick Papers, 1979.

Chojnacki, Stanley. "Dowries and Kinsmen in Early Renaissance Venice." In Susan M. Stuard, ed., *Women in Medieval Society.* Philadelphia: University of Pennsylvania Press, 1976.

Cooke, Kathleen. "Kings, Knights, and Abbesses: Shaftesbury Abbey in the Twelfth

Century." Paper presented at the Nineteenth International Congress on Medieval Studies, Kalamazoo, Mich., 1984.

Freed, John B., "Urban Development and the Cura Monialium in Thirteenth Century Germany." *Viator* 3 (1972): 311–327.

Galli, André. "Faremoutiers au moyen age." In *Sainte Fare et Faremoutiers*, 37–56. Faremoutiers, 1956.

Gilchrist, Roberta. *Gender and Material Culture: The Archaeology of Religious Women*. London: Routledge, 1994.

Gold, Penny Schine. *The Lady and the Virgin: Image, Attitude, and Experience in Twelfth Century France*. Chicago: University of Chicago Press, 1985.

Graham, Rose. *St. Gilbert of Sempringham and the Gilbertines*. London: Elliot Stock, 1901.

Graves, Coburn V. "Stixwould in the Market Place." In John A. Nichols and Lillian Thomas Shank, eds, *Medieval Religious Women* vol. 1, *Distant Echoes*, 213–216. Kalamazoo, Mich.: Cistercian Publications, 1984.

Grundmann, Herbert. *Religiöse Bewegungen im Mittelalter: Untersuchungen über die geschichtlichen Zusammenhänge zwischen der Ketzerei, den Bettelorden und der religiösen Frauenbewegung im 12 und 13 Jahrhundert*. Berlin: Historische Studien, 1935.

Hajnal, J. "European Marriage Patterns in Perspective." In David V. Glass and David E. C. Eversley, eds., *Population in History*, 101–143. London: Edward Arnold, 1965.

Hall, Edwin, and James Ross Sweeney. "An Unpublished Privilege of Innocent III in Favor of Montivilliers: New Documentation for a Great Norman Nunnery." *Speculum* 69 (1974): 662–679.

Hefele, Carl J., and H. Leclercq. *Histoire des Conciles*. Paris: Letouzey and Ané, 1910.

Heimbucher, M. *Die Orden und Kongregationen der Katholischen Kirche*. Paderborn: Ferdinand Schöningh, 1896.

Herlihy, David, and Christiane Klapisch-Zuber. *The Tuscans and Their Families: A Study of the Florentine Catasto of 1427*. New Haven: Yale University Press, 1985.

Hoebanx, Jean Jacques. *L'abbaye de Nivelles des origines au XIVe siècle*. Brussels: Memoires de l'académie royale de Belgique: Classe des Lettres et des Sciences Morales et Politiques, 1952.

Hörger, Karl. "Die reichrechtliche Stellung der Fürstabtissinnen." *Archiv für Urkundenforschung* 9 (1926): 195–270.

Johnson, Penelope D. *Equal in Monastic Profession: Religious Women in Medieval France*. Chicago: University of Chicago Press, 1991.

Kieckhefer, Richard. *Unquiet Souls: Fourteenth Century Saints and Their Religious Milieu*. Chicago: University of Chicago Press, 1984.

LeGoff, Jacques. *The Birth of Purgatory*, trans. Arthur Goldhammer. Chicago: University of Chicago Press, 1986.

Lipsmeyer, Elizabeth. "The Imperial Abbey and Town of Zurich: The Benedictine Nuns and the Price of Ritual in 13th, 14th, and 15th Century Switzerland." In Elspeth Durie and Dewey Kramer, compilers, Margot King, ed., *On Pilgrimage*, 365–376. Toronto: Peregrina, 1994.

Lynch, Joseph H. *Simoniacal Entry into Religious Life, 1000–1260.* Columbus: Ohio State University Press, 1976.

McDonnell, Ernest W. *The Beguines and Beghards in Medieval Culture with Special Emphasis on the Belgian Scene.* New Brunswick, N.J.: Rutgers University Press, 1954.

McLaughlin, Mary Martin. "Looking for Medieval Women: An Interim Report on the Project 'Women's Religious Life and Communities, AD 500–1500.'" *Medieval Prosopography* 8 (1987): 61–91.

McNamara, Jo Ann. "The Need to Give: Economic Restrictions and Penitential Piety among Medieval Nuns." In Renate Blumenfeld-Kozinski and Timea Szell, eds., *Images of Sainthood in Medieval and Renaissance Europe,* 199–221. Ithaca, N.Y.: Cornell University Press, 1993.

Morris, Joan. *Against Nature and God: The History of Women with Clerical Ordination and the Jurisdiction of Bishops.* London: Mowbrays, 1973.

Oliva, Marilyn. "The Convent and the Community in the Diocese of Norwich from 1350 to 1540." Ph.D. diss., Fordham University, 1991.

Parisse, Michel. *Les nonnes au moyen age.* Le Puy: Christine Bonneton, 1983.

Philips, Dayton. *Beguines in Medieval Strasbourg.* Palo Alto, Calif.: Stanford University Press, 1941.

Power, Eileen. *Medieval English Nunneries, 1275–1535.* Cambridge: Cambridge University Press, 1922.

Quéguiner, Jean. "Jouarre au XIIe et XIIIe siècles." In Yves Chaussey, ed., *L'abbaye royale Notre-Dame de Jouarre.* Paris: Bibliothèque d'Histoire et d'Archéologie Chrétienne, 1961.

Rosof, Patricia J. F. "The Anchorite Base of the Gilbertine Rule." *American Benedictine Review* 33:2 (1982): 182–194.

Schulze, Hans, Reinhold Specht, and Günter Vorbrodt. *Das Stift Gernrode Mitteldeutsche Forschungen,* vol. 38. Graz: Böhlau Verlag, 1965.

Senn, F. *L'Institution des Avoueries écclésiastiques en France.* Paris, 1903.

Stein, Frederick. "The Religious Women of Cologne, 1120–1320." Ph.D. diss., Yale University, 1977.

Stuckert, Howard M. *Corrodies in the English Monasteries: A Study in English Social History of the Middle Ages.* Philadelphia, 1923.

Valous, Guy de. *Le monachisme clunisien des origines au XVe siècle.* Paris: Picard, 1970.

Waldman, Thomas G. "Abbot Suger and the Nuns of Argenteuil." *Traditio* 41 (1985): 239–272.

Warren, Ann K. *Anchorites and Their Patrons in Medieval England.* Berkeley: University of California Press, 1986.

Weirauch, H. E. "Die Grundbesitz des Stiftes Quedlinburg im Mittelalters." *Sachsen und Anhalt* 14 (1938): 203.

Wood, Susan. *English Monasteries and Their Patrons in the Thirteenth Century.* Oxford: Oxford University Press, 1955.

11. Disordered Women

Albers B. "Hirsau und seine Grundungen." In *Festschrift zum 1100 Jahrigen Jubiläum des deutsches Campo Santo in Rom*, 115–129. Rome, 1897.

Ancelet-Hustache, Jeanne. *Mechtilde de Magdebourg.* Paris, 1926.

Barrière, Bernadette. *L'abbaye cistercienne d'Obazine.* Tulle: 1977.

Berman, Constance. "Men's Houses, Women's Houses: The Relationship between the Sexes in Twelfth Century Monasticism." In Andrew MacLeish, ed., *The Medieval Monastery*, 43–52. St. Cloud, Minn.: North Star Press, 1988.

Bourdillon, A. F. Claudine. *The Order of Minoresses in England.* Ridgewood, N.J.: Gregg Press, 1965.

Bouton, Jean de la Croix, ed. *Les moniales cisterciennes, III: Histoire interne.* Grignan: Commission d'histoire de l'ordre de Cîteaux, 1987.

Brooke, Rosalind B., and Christopher N. L. Brooke, "St. Clare." In Derek Baker, ed., *Medieval Women*, 275–288. Oxford: Basil Blackwell, 1978.

Bugge, John. *Virginitas: An Essay in the History of a Medieval Ideal.* The Hague: Martinus Nijhoff, 1975.

Buhot, Jacqueline. "L'abbaye Normande de Savigny, chef d'ordre et fille de Cîteaux." *Moyen Age* 7 (1936): 1–19, 104–114, 178–190, 249–272.

Cnattinguis, H. J. *Studies in the Order of St. Bridget of Sweden, I: The Crisis in the 1420's.* Uppsala: Stockholm Studies in History, 1963.

Conner, Elizabeth. "The Royal Abbey of Las Huelgas and the Jurisdiction of Its Abbesses." *Cistercian Studies* 23:2 (1988): 128–155.

Constable, Giles. *Cluniac Studies.* London: Variorum, 1982.

Creytens, J. Raymond. "Les constitutions primitives des soeurs dominicaines de Montargis." *Archivum Fratrum Praedicatorum* 17 (1947): 42–44.

———. "Les constitutions primitives." *Archivum Fratrum Praedicatorum* 17 (1947): 50–55.

———. "Les convers des moniales dominicaines au moyen age." *Archivum Fratrum Praedicatorum* 19 (1949): 5–48.

Dalarun, Jacques. *L'impossible sainteté: La vie retrouvée de Robert d'Arbrissel (v. 1045–1116) fondateur de Fontevraud.* Paris: Cerf, 1985.

Dimier, Anselme. "Chapitres généraux d'abbesses cisterciennes." *Cîteaux* 11 (1969): 268–275.

Elkins, Sharon K. "The Emergence of a Gilbertine Identity." In John A. Nichols and Lillian Thomas Shank, eds., *Medieval Religious Women*, vol. 1, *Distant Echoes*, 169–182. Kalamazoo, Mich.: Cistercian Publications, 1984.

Escriva de Balaguer, Jose Maria. *La Abadesa de las Huelgas: Estudio Teologico Juridico*, 2d ed., Madrid: Ediciones Rialp, 1972.

Esser, Kajetan. "Die Briefe Gregors IX an die Hl. Klara." *Franziskanische Studien* 35, *Die heilige Klara von Assisi zu ihrem 700 Todestage* (1953): 274–295.

Fontette, Micheline de. *Les religieuses à l'age classique du droit canonique.* Paris: J. Vrin, 1967.

Gold, Penny S. *The Lady and the Virgin: Image, Attitude, and Experience in Twelfth Century France*. Chicago: University of Chicago Press, 1985.

———. "Male/Female Cooperation: The Example of Fontevrault." In John A. Nichols and Lillian Thomas Shank, *Medieval Religious Women*, vol. 1, *Distant Echoes*, 151–168. Kalamazoo, Mich.: Cistercian Publications, 1984.

Graham, Rose. *Saint Gilbert of Sempringham and the Gilbertines*. London: Elliot Stock, 1901.

Grundmann, Herbert. *Religiöse Bewegungen im Mittelalter: Untersuchungen über die geschichtlichen Zusammenhänge zwischen der Ketzerei, den Bettelorden und der religiösen Frauenbewegung im 12 und 13 Jahrhundert*. Berlin: Historische Studien, 1935.

Heimbucher, M. *Die Orden und Kongregationen der Katholischen Kirche*. Paderborn: Ferdinand Schöningn, 1896.

Hinnebusch, William A. *The History of the Dominican Order*, vol. 1, *Origins and Growth to 1500*. New York: Alba House, 1965.

Koch, Gottfried. *Frauenfrage und Ketzertum im Mittelalter*. Berlin: Akademie-Verlag, 1962.

Koudelka, V. J. "Le 'Monasterium Tempuli' et le fondation dominicaine de San Sisto." *Archivum Fratrum Praedicatorum* 31:1 (1961): 69.

Kuhn-Rehfus, Maren. "Zisterzienserinnen in Deutschland." In *Die Zisterzienser: Ordensleben zwischen Ideal und Wirklichkeit*, 125–148. Cologne: Rheinland-Verlag, 1981.

Lefèvre, Placide. "Le problème des soeurs aux origines de l'abbaye d'Averbode." *Analecta Praemonstratensia* 52:1 2 (1976): 38–43.

Lekai, Louis. *The Cistercians: Ideals and Reality*. Kent, Ohio: Kent State University Press, 1977.

L'Hermite-Leclercq, Paulette. *Le monachisme féminin dans la société de son temps*. Paris: Cujas, 1989.

McGuire, Brian Patrick, "The Cistercians and the Transformation of Monastic Friendships." *Analecta Cisterciensia* 37:4 (1981): 1–63.

McLaughlin, Mary M. "Peter Abelard and the Dignity of Women: Twelfth-Century 'Feminism' in Theory and Practice." In *Pierre Abelard, Pierre le Venerable, Colloques internationaux du Centre de la Recherche Scientifiques*. Paris: Editions du centre national de la recherche scientifique, 1975.

Meerseman, Giles G. "Frères prêcheurs et mouvement dévot en Flandre au XIIIe siècle." *Archivum fratrum Praedicatorum* 18 (1948): 118–119.

Moorman, John. *A History of the Franciscan Order*. Oxford: Clarendon Press, 1968.

Nichols, John A. "The Internal Organization of English Cistercian Nunneries." *Citeaux: Commentarii Cistercienses* 30 (1979): 23–40.

Parisse, Michel. *Les nonnes au moyen age*. Le Puy: Christine Bonneton, 1983.

Redpath, H. M. D. *God's Ambassadress: Saint Bridget of Sweden*. Milwaukee: Bruce, 1947.

Roggen, Héribert. "Les deux abbesses: Histoire et leçon d'une longe résistance." *Etudes Franciscaines* 19:50 (1969): 201–210.

Roisin, Simone. "L'efflorescence cistercienne et le courant féminin." *Revue d'histoire écclésiastique* 39 (1943): 342–378.

Scheeben, Heribert C. "Die Anfänge des zweiten Orden." *Archivum Fratrum Praedicatorem* 2 (1932): 284.

Sevesi, P. "Il monastero delle Clarisse in S. Apollinare di Milano." *Archivum Franciscanum Historicum* 18 (1942) 226–247; 19 (1943): 248–264.

Simon, A. *L'ordre des Pénitentes de Sainte-Marie Madeleine en Allemagne au XIII siècle.* Fribourg, 1918.

Thompson, Sally, "Why English Nunneries Had No History: A Study of the Problems of the English Nunneries Founded after the Conquest." In John A. Nichols and Lillian Thomas Shank, *Medieval Religious Women,* vol. 1, *Distant Echoes,* 131–150. Kalamazoo, Mich.: Cistercian Publications, 1984.

12. The Alchemy of Mysticism

Bynum, Caroline W. "Did the Twelfth Century Discover the Individual?" In *Jesus as Mother: Studies in the Spirituality of the High Middle Ages,* 82–108. Berkeley: University of California Press, 1982.

———. *Holy Feast and Holy Fast: Religious Significance of Food to Medieval Women.* Berkeley: University of California Press, 1987.

———. "Women Mystics in the Thirteenth Century: The Case of the Nuns of Helfta." In *Jesus as Mother: Studies in the Spirituality of the High Middle Ages.* 170–261. Berkeley: University of California Press, 1982.

Coakley, John, "Friars as Confidants of Holy Women in Medieval Dominican Hagiography." In Renate Blumenfeld-Kosinski and Timea Szell, eds., *Images of Sainthood in Medieval Europe,* 222–246. Ithaca, N.Y.: Cornell University Press, 1991.

Delaruelle, Etienne, E. R. Labande, and Paul Ourliac. *L'église au temps du Grand Schisme et de la crise conciliaire (1378–1449),* vol. 14 of *Histoire de l'église,* pt. 2. Brussels: Bloud and Gay, 1964.

Eckenstein, Lina. *Women under Monasticism, 500–1500.* Cambridge: Cambridge University Press, 1896.

Finnegan, Mary Jeremy. *The Women of Helfta.* Athens: University of Georgia Press, 1991.

Fontette, Micheline de. *Les religieuses à l'age classique du droit canonique.* Paris: J. Vrin, 1967.

Goodich, Michael. "Childhood and Adolescence among Thirteenth Century Saints." *History of Childhood Quarterly* 1:2 (1974): 285–309.

Jacquart, Danielle, and Claude Thomasset. *Sexuality and Medicine in the Middle Ages.* Princeton: Princeton University Press, 1988.

Kieckhefer, Richard. *Unquiet Souls: Fourteenth Century Saints and Their Religious Milieu.* Chicago: University of Chicago Press, 1984.

Klapisch-Zuber, Christiane. *Women, Family, and Ritual in Renaissance Italy.* Chicago: University of Chicago Press, 1985.

McDonnell, Ernest W. *The Beguines and Beghards in Medieval Culture with Special Emphasis on the Belgian Scene.* New Brunswick, N.J.: Rutgers University Press, 1954.

McNamara, Jo Ann. *"De Quibusdam Mulieres:* Reading Women's History from Hostile Sources." In Joel Rosenthal, ed., *Women and the Sources of Medieval History,* 237–258. Athens: University of Georgia Press, 1990.

———. "The Rhetoric of Orthodoxy." In Ulrike Wiethans, ed., *Maps of Flesh and Light: The Religious Experience of Medieval Women Mystics,* 9–27. Syracuse, N.Y.: Syracuse University Press, 1993.

Morris, Colin. *The Discovery of the Individual, 1050–1200.* New York: Harper Torchbooks, 1972.

Newman, Barbara J. "O Feminea Forma: God and Woman in the Works of St. Hildegard (1098–1179)." Ph.D. diss., Yale University, 1981.

———. "On the Threshhold of the Dead: Purgatory, Hell, and Religious Women." In *From Virile Woman to WomanChrist: Studies in Medieval Religion and Literature,* 108–137. Philadelphia: University of Pennsylvania Press, 1995.

———. *Sister of Wisdom: St. Hildegard's Theology of the Feminine.* Berkeley: University of California Press, 1987.

Paris, Gaston. "La vie de Ste. Catherine de Soeur Clemence de Barking." *Romania* 13 (1889): 400–440.

Petit, F. *La spiritualité des Prémontrés aux XIIe et XIIIe siècles.* Paris: Vrin, 1945.

Petroff, Elizabeth A., ed., *Medieval Women's Visionary Literature.* New York: Oxford University Press, 1986.

Roisin, Simone. *L'hagiographie cistercienne dans le diocèse de Liège au XIII siècle.* Louvain: Bibliothèque de l'Université, 1947.

Roth, F. W.E ., ed., *Die Visionen der Heilige Elisabeth und die schriften der Äbte Ekbert und Emecho von Schönau.* Brunn: Studien aus dem Benedictiner- und Cistercienser-Orden, 1884.

Schmitz, Philibert. *Histoire de l'Ordre de Saint Benoit,* 2d ed., vol. 7. Maredsous: Editions de Maredsous, 1956.

Scholz, Bernhard W. "Hildegard von Bingen on the Nature of Women." *American Benedictine Review* 31 (1984): 361–379.

Thurston, Herbert. *Lent and Holy Week.* London: Longmans Green, 1904.

Underhill, Evelyn B. *Mysticism: A Study in the Nature and Development of Man's Spiritual Consciousness.* New York: New American Library, 1974.

Weinstein, Donald, and Rudolph Bell. *Saints and Society: The Two Worlds of Western Christendom, 1000–1700.* Chicago: University of Chicago Press, 1982.

13. The Tears of the Magdalene

Barthelmé, Annette. *La réforme dominicaine au XVe siècle en Alsace.* Strasbourg: 1930.

Beckman, Johan W. *Den Nya Swenska Psalmboken.* Stockholm: P. A. Norstedt, 1845.

Bell, Rudolph M. *Holy Anorexia.* Chicago: University of Chicago Press, 1986.

Bierbaum, H. *Bettelorden und Weltgeistlichkeit an der Universität Paris. Texte und Unter-suchungen zum literarischen Armuts- und Exemptionsstreit des 13. Jahrhunderts (1255–1272)*. Münster in Westfalia: Asschendorff, 1920.

Brundage, James A., *Law, Sex, and Christian Society in Medieval Europe*. Chicago: University of Chicago Press, 1987.

————. "Rape and Seduction in the Medieval Canon Law." In Vern Bullough and James Brundage, eds., *Sexual Practices and the Medieval Church*, 141–148. Buffalo: Prometheus Books, 1982.

Cohn, Norman. *Europe's Inner Demons. An Enquiry Inspired by the Great Witch Hunt.* New York: Basic Books, 1975.

Coulton, G. G. *Five Centuries of Religion.* Cambridge: Cambridge University Press, 1923.

Coyecque, E. *L'Hotel Dieu de Paris au moyen age: Histoire et documents.* Paris, 1889–1891.

Daichman, Graciela S. *Wayward Nuns in Medieval Literature.* Syracuse, N.Y.: Syracuse University Press, 1986.

Delaruelle, Etienne, E. R. Labande, and Paul Ourliac. *L'église au temps du Grand Schisme et de la crise conciliaire (1378–1449);* vol. 14 of *Histoire de l'Eglise*, pt. 2. Brussels: Bloud and Gay, 1964.

Geremek, Bronislaw. *The Margins of Society in Late Medieval Paris,* trans. Jean Birrell. New York: Cambridge University Press, 1987.

Gill, Katherine. "Open Monasteries for Women in Late Medieval and Early Modern Italy." In Craig A. Monson, ed., *The Crannied Wall: Women, Religion, and the Arts in Early Modern Europe,* 15–47. Ann Arbor: University of Michigan Press, 1992.

Graham, Rose. *Saint Gilbert of Sempringham and the Gilbertines.* London: Elliot Stock, 1901.

Grundmann, Herbert. *Religiöse Bewegungen im Mittelalter: Untersuchungen über die geschichtlichen Zusammenhänge zwischen der Ketzerei, den Bettelorden und der religiösen Frauenbewegung im 12 und 13 Jahrhundert.* Berlin: Historische Studien, 1935.

Herlihy, David, and Christiane Klapisch-Zuber. *The Tuscans and Their Families: A Study of the Florentine Catasto of 1427.* New Haven: Yale University Press, 1985.

Hinnebusch, William A. *The History of the Dominican Order,* vol. 1, *Origins and Growth to 1500.* New York: Alba House, 1965.

Hughes, Diane Owen. "Distinguishing Signs: Earrings, Jews, and Franciscan Rhetoric in the Italian Renaissance City." *Past and Present* 112 (1986): 3–59.

Johnson, Penelope D. *Equal in Monastic Profession: Religious Women in Medieval France.* Chicago: University of Chicago Press, 1991.

Karras, Ruth M. "The Regulation of Brothels in Medieval England." *Signs* 14:2 (1989) 399–433.

Kieckhefer, Richard. *Unquiet Souls: Fourteenth Century Saints and Their Religious Milieu.* Chicago: University of Chicago Press, 1984.

Klapisch-Zuber, Christiane. *Women, Family, and Ritual in Renaissance Italy.* Chicago: University of Chicago Press, 1985.

Labande, Edmond-René, ed., *Histoire de l'abbaye Sainte-Croix de Poitiers: Quatorze siècles de vie monastique*. Poitiers: Société des Antiquaires de l'Ouest w/CNRS, 1986.

Lea, Henry Charles. *A History of the Inquisition of the Middle Ages*. New York: Russell and Russell, 1958.

LeGrand, Léon. *Les béguines de Paris*. Paris, 1893.

Lerner, Robert E. *The Heresy of the Free Spirit in the Later Middle Ages*. Berkeley: University of California Press, 1972.

McDonnell, Ernest W. *The Beguines and Beghards in Medieval Culture with Special Emphasis on the Belgian Scene*. New Brunswick, N.J.: Rutgers University Press, 1954.

Oliva, Marilyn. "The Convent and the Community in the Diocese of Norwich from 1350 to 1540." Ph.D. diss., Fordham University, 1991.

Otis, Leah Lydia. *Prostitution in Medieval Society*. Chicago: University of Chicago Press, 1985.

Pansier, Pierre. *L'oeuvre des répenties à Avignon du XIIIe au XVIII siècle*. Paris: Recherches historique et documentaires sur Avignon, 1910.

Parisse, Michel. *Les nonnes au moyen age*. Le Puy: Christine Bonneton, 1983.

Pasztoi, Edith. "I papi del duecento e trecento di fronte alla vita religiosa femminile." In Roberto Rusconi, ed., *I movimento religioso femminile in Umbria nei secoli XIII-XIV*. Florence and Perugia: Atti del Convegno internazionale di Studio nell'ambito delle celebrazione per l'VIII centenario della nascità di S. Francesco d'Assisi, 1984.

Power, Eileen. *Medieval English Nunneries, 1275-1535*. Cambridge: Cambridge University Press, 1922.

Régnier-Bohler, Danielle. "Imagining the Self." In Georges Duby, ed., *A History of Private Life*, vol. 2, *Revelations of the Medieval World*, trans. Arthur Goldhammer, 313-393. Cambridge, Mass.: Harvard University Press, 1988.

Ruggiero, Guido. *The Boundaries of Eros: Sex, Crime, and Sexuality in Renaissance Venice*. New York: Oxford University Press, 1985.

———. *Violence in Early Renaissance Venice*. New Brunswick, N.J.: Rutgers University Press, 1980.

Russell, Jeffrey B. *Witchcraft in the Middle Ages*. Ithaca, N.Y.: Cornell University Press, 1972.

Saxer, Victor. *Le culte de Marie Madeleine en Occident des origines à la fin de moyen age*. Paris: Librairie Clavreuil, 1959.

Simon, A. *L'ordre des Pénitentes de Sainte-Marie Madeleine en Allemagne au XIII siècle*. Fribourg, 1918.

Sperling, Jutta. "Potlatch alla Veneziana: Noble Women in Venetian Convents." Paper presented at the American Renaissance Society, New York, April 1995.

Stein, Frederick M. "The Religious Women of Cologne, 1120-1320." Ph.D. diss., Yale University, 1977.

Trexler, Richard C. "Le célibat à la fin du moyen age." *Annales: Economies, société, civilisation* 27 (1972): 1329-1350.

Valous, Guy de. *Le monachisme clunisien des origines au XVe siècle*. Paris: Picard, 1970.

Wiethaus, Ulrike. "Cathar Influences in Hildegard of Bingen's Play *Ordo Virtutum*." *American Benedictine Review* 38:2 (1987): 192–203.

14. Regular Lives

Barthelmé, Annette. *La réforme dominicaine au XVe siècle en Alsace*. Strasbourg, 1930.

Coudanne, Louise. "Le temps des Réformes." In Edmond-René Labande, ed., *Histoire de l'abbaye Sainte-Croix de Poitiers: Quatorze siècles de vie monastique*. Poitiers: Société des Antiquaires de l'Ouest w/CNRS, 1986.

Delaruelle, Etienne, E. R. Labande, and Paul Ourliac. *L'église au temps du Grand Schisme et de la crise conciliaire (1378–1449)*, vol. 14 of *Histoire de l'église*, pt. 2. Brussels: Bloud and Gay, 1964.

Delumeau, Jean. *La peur en occident, XIVe–XVIIIe siècles*. Paris: Fayard, 1978.

Eckenstein, Lina. *Women under Monasticism, 500–1500*. Cambridge: Cambridge University Press, 1896.

Favreau, Robert. "Heurs et malheurs de l'Abbaye, XIIe–XVe siècles." In Edmond-René Labande, ed., *Histoire de l'abbaye Sainte-Croix de Poitiers: Quatorze siècles de vie monastique*. Poitiers: Société des Antiquaires de l'Ouest w/CNRS, 1986.

Galli, André. "Faremoutiers au moyen age." In *Sainte Fare et Faremoutiers*, 37–56. Faremoutiers, 1956.

Hilpisch, Stephanus. *A History of Benedictine Nuns*, trans. M. Joanne Muggli. Collegeville, Minn.: St. John's Abbey Press, 1958.

Hofmeister, Philipp. "Les statuts du monastère des bénédictines de Marienberg in Boppard, 1437." *Revue Bénédictine* 46 (1934): 439–455.

———. "Die Verfassung der Bursfelder Kongregation." *Studien und Mitteilungen zur Geschichte des Benediktiner ordens* 53 (1935): 63–76.

———. "Die Verfassung der Kongregation der Benediktinerinnen von Kalvarienberg." *Studien und Mitteilungen OSB* 50 (1932): 249–277.

Imbart de la Tour, P. *Les origines de la reforme*, 2 vols. Melun: Librairie d'Argences, 1946–1948.

Klueting, Edeltraud. "Les pouvoirs des abbesses dans les couvents de femmes de la congrégation de Bursfeld." In *Les religieuses dans le cloître et dans le monde*. Saint-Etienne: CERCOR Travaux et Recherches, 1994.

Lekai, Louis. *The Cistercians: Ideals and Reality*. Kent, Ohio: Kent State University Press, 1977.

Lemoine, Robert. *L'époque moderne, 1563–1789: Le monde des religieux*, vol. 15:2, *Histoire du droit et des institutions de l'église en Occident*, ed. Gabriel LeBras and Jean Gaudemet. Paris: Editions Cujas, 1976.

Lopez, Elisabeth. *Culture et sainteté: Colette de Corbie (1381–1447)*. Saint-Etienne: CERCOR Travaux et Recherches, 1994.

Marc-Bonnet, Henri. *Histoire des ordres religieux*. Paris: Presses Universitaires de France, 1968.

McLaughlin, Mary M. "Creating and Recreating Communities of Women: The Case of Corpus Domini, 1406–1452." *Signs* 14:2 (1989): 293–320.

Moorman, John. *A History of the Franciscan Order.* Oxford: Clarendon Press, 1968.

Oakley, Francis. *The Western Church in the Later Middle Ages.* Ithaca, N.Y.: Cornell University Press, 1979.

Palastre, Bernard. "Anne d'Orléans." *Revue des questions historiques* 66 (1899): 210–217.

Post, R. R. *The Modern Devotion: Confrontation with Reformation and Humanism.* Leiden: Brill, 1968.

Power, Eileen. *Medieval English Nunneries, 1275–1535.* Cambridge: Cambridge University Press, 1922.

Rapp, Francis. *L'église et la vie religieuse en Occident à la fin du Moyen Age.* Paris: Presses Universitaires de France, 1971.

Rohrbach, Peter-Thomas. *Journey to Carith: The Story of the Carmelite Order.* Garden City, N.Y.: Doubleday, 1966.

Roisin, Simone. "Sainte Colette de Corbie." In *Dictionnaire d'histoire et de géographie écclésiastique,* 13:239–246.

Ubald d'Alençon, P. "Documents sur la Réforme de Ste. Colette en France." *Archivum Franciscanum Historicum* 2–3 (1909–10): 447–456, 600–612, 82–97.

Uzureau, François. "La reforme de l'ordre de Fontevrault (1459–1641)." *Revue Mabillon* 49 (1923): 141–146.

Valous, Guy de. *Le monachisme clunisien des origines au XVe siècle.* Paris: Picard, 1970.

Vansteenberghe, Edmond. *Le Cardinal Nicolas de Cues (1401–1464).* Frankfurt: Minerva, 1963.

Vaux, Pierre de. *Vie de Soeur Colette,* ed., Elisabeth Lopez. Saint-Etienne: CERCOR Travaux et Recherches, 1994.

Vital Wilderink, O. *Les constitutions des premières carmélites en France.* Rome: Institutum Carmelitanum, 1966.

Zumkeller, Adolar. *Augustine's Rule.* Villanova: Augustinian Press, 1987.

15. Defenders of the Faith

Aston, Margaret. *Lollards and Reformers: Images and Literacy in Late Medieval Religion.* Ronceverte, Eng.: Hambledon Press, 1984.

Bainton, Roland H. *Women of the Reformation,* vol. 1: *Germany and Italy;* vol. 2, *France and England;* vol. 3, *From Spain to Scandinavia.* Minneapolis: Augsburg Publishing House, 1977.

Barthelmé, Annette. *La réforme dominicaine au XVe siècle en Alsace.* Strasbourg, 1930.

Baskerville, Geoffrey. *English Monks and the Suppression of the Monasteries.* London: Jonathan Cape, 1937.

Beech, Beatrice. "A Nun of Montivilliers." In John R. Sommerfeldt, ed., *Erudition at God's Service,* 339–348. Kalamazoo, Mich.: Studies in Medieval Cistercian History, 1987.

Bourdillon, A. F. Claudine. *The Order of Minoresses in England*. Ridgewood, N.J.: Gregg Press, 1965.

Bradshaw, Brendan. *The Dissolution of the Religious Orders in Ireland under Henry VIII*. Cambridge: Cambridge University Press, 1974.

Chojnacki, Stanley. "Political Adulthood in Fifteenth-Century Venice." *American Historical Review* 19 (1986): 791–810.

———. "Subaltern Patriarchs: Patrician Bachelors in Renaissance Venice." in Clare A. Lees, ed., *Medieval Masculinities*, 73–90. Minneapolis: University of Minnesota Press, 1994.

Chrisman, Miriam U. "Women of the Reformation in Strassburg, 1490–1530." *Archiv für Reformationsgeschichte* 63:2 (1972): 143–168.

Coudanne, Louise. "Le temps des reformes." In Edmond-René Labande, ed., *Histoire de l'abbaye Saint-Croix de Poitiers: Quatorze siècles de vie monastique*, 221–307. Poitiers: Société des Antiquaires de l'Ouest w/CNRS, 1986.

Davis, Natalie. "City Women and Religious Change." In *Society and Culture in Early Modern France*, 65–94. Stanford: Stanford University Press, 1975.

———. "Women on Top." In *Society and Culture in Early Modern France*, 124–151. Stanford: Stanford University Press, 1975.

Delaborde, Jules. *Charlotte de Bourbon, Princesse d'Orange*. Paris: Fischbacher, 1888.

Demandt, Dieter, and Hans-Christoph Rublack. *Stadt und Kirche in Kitzingen: Darstellung und Quellen zu Spätmittelalter und Reformation*. Stuttgart: Klett-Cotta, 1978.

Douglass, Jane D. "Women and the Continental Reformation." In Rosemary R. Reuther, ed., *Religion and Sexism*, 292–318. New York: Simon and Schuster, 1974.

Eckenstein, Lina. *Women under Monasticism, 500–1500*. Cambridge: Cambridge University Press, 1896.

Foucault, Michel. *Discipline and Punish: The Birth of the Prison*, trans. Alan Sheridan. New York: Vintage Books, 1979.

Gasquet, Francis A. *Henry VIII and the English Monasteries*, 2 vols. London: J. Hodges, 1888–89.

Hilpisch, Stephanus. *A History of Benedictine Nuns*, trans. M. Joanne Muggli. Collegeville, Minn.: St. John's Abbey Press, 1958.

Höfler, Constantin. "Der Hochberühmten Charitas Pirckheimer, Abtissin von S. Clara zu Nürnberg, Denkwürdigkeiten aus dem Reformationszeitalter." In *15. Bericht über das Wirken des historischen Vereins zu Bamberg*. Bamberg: Reindl, 1852.

Holzwarth, F. J. *Katholische Trösteinsamkeit*, vol. 12. Mainz: Verlag Franz Kirchheim, 1858.

Howell, Martha C. *Women, Production, and Patriarchy in Late Medieval Cities*. Chicago: University of Chicago Press, 1986.

Janssen, Johannes. *History of the German People at the Close of the Middle Ages*, vol. 5. New York: AMS Press, 1966.

Kaminsky, Howard. *The History of the Hussite Revolution*. Berkeley: University of California Press, 1967.

Kieckhefer, Richard. "The Holy and the Unholy: Sainthood, Witchcraft, and Magic in Late Medieval Europe." *Journal of Medieval and Renaissance Studies* 24:3 (1994): 355–385.

Knowles, David. *The Religious Houses of Medieval England*. London: Sheed and Ward, 1940.

Lekai, Louis. *The Cistercians: Ideals and Reality*. Kent, Ohio: Kent State University Press, 1977.

Lemoine, Robert. *L'époque moderne, 1563–1789: Le monde des religieux*, vol. 15:2, *Histoire du droit et des institutions de l'église en Occident*, ed. Gabriel LeBras and Jean Gaudemet. Paris: Éditions Cujas, 1976.

Marc-Bonnet, Henri. *Histoire des ordres religieux*. Paris: Presses Universitaires de France, 1968.

Marshall, Sherrin D. *The Dutch Gentry: 1500–1650*. Westport, Conn.: Greenwood Press, 1987.

Oliva, Marilyn. "Aristocracy or Meritocracy: Office-holding Patterns in Late Medieval English Nunneries." *Ecclesiastical History Society Papers* (1990): 197–208.

———. "The Convent and the Community in the Diocese of Norwich from 1350 to 1540." Ph.D. diss., Fordham University, 1991.

Paulus, N. "Glaubenstreue der Lüneberger Klösterfrauen im 16. Jahrhundert." *Historische-politische Blätter* 112 (1893): 625–649.

Post, R. R. *The Modern Devotion: Confrontation with Reformation and Humanism*. Leiden: Brill, 1968.

Roelker, Nancy. "The Role of the Noblewomen in the French Reformation." *Archiv für Reformationsgeschichte* 63 (1972): 168–194.

Roncière, Charles de la. "Tuscan Notables on the Eve of the Renaissance." In Georges Duby, ed., *A History of Private Life*, vol. 2, *Revelations of the Medieval World*, trans. Arthur Goldhammer, 157–309. Cambridge, Mass.: Harvard University Press, 1988.

Roper, Lyndal. *The Holy Household: Religion, Morals, and Order in Reformation Augsburg*. Oxford: Oxford University Press, 1989.

Rubin, Miri. *Charity and Community in Medieval Cambridge*. Cambridge: Cambridge University Press, 1987.

Schulze, Hans, Reinhold Specht, and Günter Vorbrodt. *Das Stift Gernrode: Mitteldeutsche Forschungen 38*. Graz: Böhlau Verlag, 1965.

Vierling, Josef F. *Das Ringen um die letzten dem Katholizismus treuen Kloster Strassburgs*. Strasbourg: Herdersche Buchhandlung, 1913.

Wiesner, Merry E. *Women and Gender in Early Modern Europe*. Cambridge: Cambridge University Press, 1993.

———. "Women's Defense of their Public Role." In Mary Beth Rose, ed., *Women in the Middle Ages and the Renaissance*, 1–27. Syracuse, N.Y.: Syracuse University Press, 1985.

———. *Working Women in Renaissance Germany*. New Brunswick, N.J.: Rutgers University Press, 1986.

Wiesner, Merry E., ed. *Convents Confront the Reformation: Four Texts by Early Modern German Women.* Milwaukee, Wis.: Marquette University Press, 1996.

Wyntjes, Sherrin Marshall. "Women and Religious Choices in the Sixteenth Century Netherlands." *Archiv für Reformationsgeshichte* 75 (1982): 396–405.

16. Martha's Part

Aïtoff, Marie-Serge. *Ste. Françoise Romaine.* Bec-Hellouin: OSB, 1983.

Anderson, Karen. *Chain Her by One Foot: The Subjugation of Women in Seventeenth Century New France.* New York: Routledge, 1991.

Blevec, Daniel Le. "Le rôle des femmes dans l'assistance et la charité." *Cahiers de Fanjeaux* 23 (1988): 171–190.

Bossy, John. *Christianity in the West, 1400–1700.* New York: Oxford University Press, 1985.

————. "The Counter-Reformation and the People of Catholic Europe." *Past and Present* 47 (1970): 51–70.

————. *The English Catholic Community, 1570–1850.* New York: Oxford University Press, 1976.

Boxer, C. R. *The Church Militant and Iberian Expansion, 1440–1770.* Baltimore: Johns Hopkins University Press, 1978.

Brundage, James A. *Law, Sex, and Christian Society in Medieval Europe.* Chicago: University of Chicago Press, 1987.

Burns, Patricia. "Aux origines de la Visitation: La vraie pensée de St. François de Sales." In *Les religieuses dans le cloître et dans le monde.* Saint-Etienne: CERCOR Travaux et Recherches, 1994.

Caraman, Phillip G. *St. Angela: The Life of Angela Merici, Foundress of the Ursulines, 1474–1530.* New York: Farrar, Strauss, 1964.

Carmichael, Ann. *Plague and the Poor in Renaissance Florence.* Cambridge: Cambridge University Press, 1987.

Chatellier, Louis. *The Europe of the Devout: The Catholic Reformation and the Formation of a New Society.* Cambridge: Cambridge University Press, 1989.

Chill, Emmanuel. "Religion and Mendicity in Seventeenth-Century France." *International Review of Social History* 7 (1962): 400–425.

Christiani, L. *L'église à l'époque de Concile de Trente,* vol. 17 of *Histoire de l'église,* ed. Auguste Fliche and Victor Martin. Paris: Bloud and Gay, 1948.

Cohen, Sherrill. "Asylums for Women in Counter-Reformation Italy." In Sherrin Marshall, ed., *Women in Reformation and Counter-Reformation Europe: Private and Public Worlds,* 166–188. Bloomington: Indiana University Press, 1989.

————. *The Evolution of Women's Asylums since 1500: From Refuges for Ex-Prostitutes to Shelters for Battered Women.* New York: Oxford University Press, 1992.

"Compagnie du Divine Amour." In *Dictionnaire de Spiritualité,* 531–533. Paris: Beauchesne, 1917.

Costa, Milagros Ortega. "Spanish Women in the Reformation." In Sherrin Marshall, ed., *Women in Reformation and Counter-Reformation Europe: Private and Public Worlds,* 89–119. Bloomington: Indiana University Press, 1989.

Delumeau, Jean. *Le peur en occident, XIVe–XVIIIe siècles* Paris: Fayard, 1978.

Devos, Roger. "Le testament de Ste. Jeanne-Françoise de Chantal et l'affaire du visiteurs apostolique." *Revue d'histoire de spiritualité* 48 (1972): 453–476; 49 (1973): 199–226, 341–366.

———. *Vie religieuse féminine et société: L'origine social des Visitandines d'Annecy aux XVIIe et XVIII siècles.* Annecy: Académie Salésienne, 1973.

Dirvin, Joseph I. *Louise de Marillac.* New York: Farrar, Straus and Giroux, 1970.

Flynn, Maureen. *Sacred Charity: Confraternity and Social Welfare in Spain, 1400–1700.* Ithaca, N.Y.: Cornell University Press, 1988.

Foucault, Michel. *Discipline and Punish: The Birth of the Prison,* trans. Alan Sheridan. New York: Vintage Books, 1979.

Gibson, Wendy. *Women in Seventeenth Century France.* New York: St. Martin's, 1989.

Goyau, Georges. *La femme dans les missions.* Paris: Ernest Flamarion, 1933.

Gutton, Jean-Pierre *La société et les pauvres: L'exemple de la généralité de Lyon, 1534–1789.* Paris: Société d'edition "Les Belles Lettres," 1971.

———. *La société et les pauvres en Europe, XVIe–XVIIIe siècles.* Paris: Presses Universitaires de France, 1974.

Howell, Martha C. *Women, Production, and Patriarchy in Late Medieval Cities.* Chicago: University of Chicago Press, 1986.

Hufton, Olwen H. *The Poor in Eighteenth Century France.* Oxford: Clarendon Press, 1974.

Imbert, Jean. *Droit hospitalier de l'ancien régime.* Paris: Presses Universitaires de France, 1993.

Jean, Marguerite. *Evolution des communautés religieuses de femmes au Canada de 1639 à nos jours.* Montreal: Fides, 1977.

Jones, Colin. *Charity and Bienfaisance: The Treatment of the Poor in the Montpellier Region, 1740–1815.* New York: Cambridge University Press, 1982.

Jütte, Robert. *Poverty and Deviance in Early Modern Europe.* Cambridge: Cambridge University Press, 1994.

Ledochowska, Teresa. *Angela Merici and the Company of St. Ursula according to the Historical Documents,* trans. Mary Teresa Neylan. Rome and Milan: Ancora, 1969.

Liebowitz, Ruth P. "The Convertites of Santa Valeria." Paper presented at the Sixth Berkshire Conference on the History of Women, Smith College, 1984.

———. "Virgins in the Service of Christ: The Dispute over an Active Apostolate for Women during the Counter-Reformation." In Rosemary R. Ruether and Eleanor C. McLaughlin, eds., *Women of Spirit,* 131–152. New York: Simon and Schuster, 1979.

Lemoine, Robert. *L'époque moderne, 1563–1789: Le monde des religieux.* vol. 15:2, *Histoire du droit et des institutions de l'église en Occident,* ed. Gabriel LeBras and Jean Gaudemet. Paris: Editions Cujas, 1976.

MacFarlane, Alan. *Witchcraft in Tudor and Stuart England*. New York: Harper Torchbooks, 1970.

Martz, Linda. *Poverty and Welfare in Hapsburg Spain: The Example of Toledo*. Cambridge: Cambridge University Press, 1983.

Miller, Robert R. *Mexico: A History*. Norman: University of Oklahoma Press, 1985.

Monica, Sr. M. *Angela Merici and Her Teaching Idea, 1474–1540*. New York, 1927.

Pansier, Pierre. *L'oeuvre des répenties à Avignon du XIIIe au XVIII siècle: Recherches historique et documentaires sur Avignon*, 5. Paris: Campion, 1910.

Perry, Mary E. *Gender and Disorder in Early Modern Seville*. Princeton: Princeton University Press, 1990.

Post, R. R. *The Modern Devotion: Confrontation with Reformation and Humanism*. Leiden: Brill, 1968.

Pullan, Brian. *Rich and Poor in Renaissance Venice: The Social Institutions of a Catholic State*. Oxford: Basil Blackwell, 1971.

Quetel, Claude. *Le mal de Naples*. Paris: Seghers, 1986.

Rapley, Elizabeth. *The Dévotes: Women and Church in Seventeenth Century France*. Montreal: McGill-Queen's University Press, 1990.

Roper, Lyndal. *The Holy Household: Religion, Morals, and Order in Reformation Augsburg*. Oxford: Oxford University Press, 1989.

Rowlands, Marie. "Recusant Women." In Mary Prior, ed., *Women in English Society, 1500–1800*. London: Methuen, 1985.

Russell-Wood, A. J. R. *Fidalgos and Philanthropists: The Santa Casa de Misericordia of Bahia, 1550–1755*. Berkeley and Los Angeles: University of California Press, 1968.

Sánchez Lora, José L. *Mujeres, Conventos y Formas de la Religiosidad Barroca*. Madrid: Fundación Universitaria Española, 1988.

Sanders, E. K. *Sainte Chantal, 1572–1641: A Study in Vocation*. London: SPCK, 1918.

Schmitt, Jean-Claude. *Mort d'une hérésie: L'église et les clercs face aux béguines et aux beghards du Rhin supérieur au XIVe au XVe siècle*. Paris: Civilisations et sociétés, 1978.

Trexler, Richard C. "Charity and the Defense of Urban Elites in the Italian Communes." In Fred Jaher, ed., *The Rich, the Well-born, and the Powerful*, 64–109. Urbana: University of Illinois Press, 1974.

Weber, Max. *The Protestant Ethic and the Spirit of Capitalism*. New York: Charles Scribner's Sons, 1958.

Wiesner, Merry E. *Women and Gender in Early Modern Europe*. Cambridge: Cambridge University Press, 1993.

―――. *Working Women in Renaissance Germany*. New Brunswick, N.J.: Rutgers University Press, 1986.

Zarri, Gabriella. "Ursula and Catherine: The Marriage of Virgins in the Sixteenth Century." In E. Ann Matter and John Coakley, eds., *Creative Women in Medieval and Early Modern Italy*, 237–278. Philadelphia: University of Pennsylvania Press, 1994.

17. The Mystical Regiment

Alacoque, Marguerite-Marie. *Vie et oeuvres*, 3 vols., ed. Mgr. Gauthey. Paris: 1922.

Alberto de la Virgen del Carmen. *Historia de la Reforma Teresiana (1562–1962)*. Madrid: Editorial de Espiritualidad, 1968.

Anderson, Karen. *Chain Her by One Foot: The Subjugation of Women in Seventeenth Century New France*. New York: Routledge, 1991.

Auclair, Marcelle. *Saint Teresa of Avila*. Petersham, Mass.: St. Bede's Publications, 1988.

Bilinkoff, Jodi. *The Avila of Saint Teresa: Religious Reform in a Sixteenth Century City*. Ithaca, N.Y.: Cornell University Press, 1990.

Bougaud, E. *St. Chantal and the Foundation of the Visitation*. New York: Benziger Brothers, 1895.

Bouton, Jean de la Croix, ed. *Les moniales Cisterciennes, I: Histoire externe, pt. II, du XVIe siècle à nos jours*. Grignan: Commission pour l'histoire de l'ordre de Cîteaux, 1987.

Brown, Judith C. *Immodest Acts: The Life of a Lesbian Nun in Renaissance Italy*. New York: Oxford University Press, 1986.

Carmona, Michel. *Les diables de Loudun: Sorcellerie et politique sous Richelieu*. Paris: Fayard, 1988.

Catta, Etienne. *La vie d'un monastère sous l'Ancien-Régime: La Visitation Sainte-Marie de Nantes (1630–1792)*. Paris: Vrin, 1954.

Coudanne, Louise. "Le temps des reformes." In Edmond René Labande, ed., *Histoire de l'abbaye Sainte-Croix de Poitiers: Quatorze siècles de vie monastique*, 221–307. Poitiers: Société des Antiquaires de l'Ouest w/CNRS, 1986.

Delumeau, Jean. *Sin and Fear: The Emergence of a Western Guilt Culture*. New York: St. Martin's, 1990.

Diane du Christ. *Foyer de spiritualité dominicaine au XVII siècle: Le monastère Sainte Catherine de Sienne à Toulouse*. Toulouse: Privat, 1976.

Escholier, Marc. *Port Royal: The Story of the Jansenists*. New York: Hawthorn Books, 1968.

Huxley, Aldous. *The Devils of Loudun*. New York: Harper and Row, 1971.

Kendrick, T. D. *Mary of Agreda: The Life and Legend of a Spanish Nun*. London: Routledge and Kegan Paul, 1967.

Kervingant, Marie de la Trinité. *Des moniales face à la Révolution Française: Aux origines des Cisterciennes-Trappistines*. Paris: Beauchesne, 1989.

Kessel, John L. *Kiva, Cross, and Crown: The Pecos Indians and New Mexico, 1540–1840*. Albuquerque: University of New Mexico Press, 1987.

Krailsheimer, A. J. *Armand-Jean Rancé, Abbot of La Trappe: His Influence in the Cloister and the World*. Oxford: Clarendon Press, 1974.

Lekai, Louis. *The Cistercians: Ideals and Reality*. Kent, Ohio: Kent State University Press, 1977.

Lewis, Ioan M. *Ecstatic Religion*. Baltimore: Penguin Books, 1971.

Lusseau, Patricia. *L'abbaye royale de Fontevraud aux XVIIe et XVIIIe siècles.* Paris: Herault Editions, 1986.

Maravall, José Antonio. *Poder, honor y élites en el siglo XVII.* Madrid: Revista de Occidente, 1979.

Martín, Luis. *Daughters of the Conquistadores. Women of the Viceroyalty of Peru.* Albuquerque: University of New Mexico Press, 1983.

Matter, E. Ann. "Interior Maps of an Eternal External: The Spiritual Rhetoric of Maria Domitilla Galluzzi d'Acqui." In Ulrike Wiethaus, ed., *Maps of Flesh and Light,* 60–73. Syracuse, N.Y.: Syracuse University Press, 1993.

Messing, Susan. "Group Therapy and Social Status in the Zar Cult of Ethiopia." *American Anthropologist* 60 (1958).

Muriel, Josefina, ed. *Las indias caciques de Corpus Christi.* Mexico: Universidad Autónoma Nacional de Mexico, Publicaciones des Instituto de Historia, 1963.

Nemec, Ludvik. *The Infant of Prague.* New York, 1958.

Reynes, Geneviève. *Couvents de femmes: La vie des religieuses cloîtrées dans la France des XVIIe et XVIIIe siècles.* Paris: Fayard, 1987.

Rohrbach, Peter-Thomas. *Journey to Carith: The Story of the Carmelite Order.* Garden City, N.Y.: Doubleday, 1966.

Romanes, Ethel. *The Story of Port-Royal.* London: John Murray, 1907.

Sanchez Lora, José L. *Mujeres, Conventos y Formas de la Religiosidad Barroca.* Madrid: Fundación Universitaria Española, 1988.

Vital Wilderink, O. "Las Monjas Carmelitas hasta Santa Teresa de Jesus." *Carmelus* 10 (1963): Número extraordinario conmemorativo del IV Centenario de la Reforma Teresiana, 1–312.

Walker, D. P. *Unclean Spirits: Possession and Exorcism in France and England in the Sixteenth and Seventeenth Centuries.* Philadelphia: University of Pennsylvania Press, 1981.

Weaver, F. Ellen. *The Evolution of the Reform of Port-Royal: From the Rule of Cîteaux to Jansenism.* Paris: Beauchesne, 1977.

Willaert, Léopold. *La restauration catholique, 1543–1648,* vol. 18 of *Histoire de l'église.* Paris: Bloud and Gay, 1960.

Wright, A. D. *The Counter Reformation: Catholic Europe and the Non-Christian World.* New York: St. Martin's, 1982.

18. The Sweetness of Life

Alberto de la Virgen del Carmen. *Historia de la Reforma Teresiana (1562–1962).* Madrid: Editorial de Espiritualidad, 1968.

Arnemann, C. *Les bienheureuses Soeurs de Bolléne martyrisées à Orange.* Fribourg, 1965.

Auclair, Marcelle. *Saint Teresa of Avila.* Petersham, Mass.: St. Bede's Publications, 1988.

Bougaud, E. *St. Chantal and the Foundation of the Visitation.* New York: Benziger Brothers, 1895.

Boussoulade, J. *Moniales et hospitaliéres dans la tourmente révolutionnaire: Les commu-*

nautés de religieuses de l'ancien diocése de Paris de 1789 à 1801. Paris: Letouzey et Ané, 1962.

Bouton, Jean de la Croix, ed. *Les moniales cisterciennes, III: Histoire interne.* Grignan: Commission d'histoire de l'ordre de Cîteaux, 1987.

Brémond, Henri. *Histoire littéraire du sentiment religieux en France.* Paris: Bloud and Gay, 1925.

Brown, Judith C. *Immodest Acts: The Life of a Lesbian Nun in Renaissance Italy.* New York: Oxford University Press, 1986.

Carmona, Michel. *Les diables de Loudun: Sorcellerie et politique sous Richelieu.* Paris: Fayard, 1988.

Catta, Etienne. *La vie d'un monastère sous l'Ancien-Régime. La Visitation Sainte-Marie de Nantes (1630–1792).* Paris: Vrin, 1954.

Denuit, B. *Blanches Dames d'Aywières: Six siècles de vie monastique.* Brussels: Les Editions de Belgique, 1976.

Diane du Christ. *Foyer de spiritualité dominicaine au XVII siècle: Le monastère Sainte Catherine de Sienne à Toulouse.* Toulouse: Privat, 1976.

Dinet, Dominique. "Les communautés religieuses féminines de Bourgogne et de Champagne face à la Révolution." In Bernard Plongeron, ed., *Pratiques religieuses dans l'Europe Révolutionnaire (1770–1820),* 474–484. Brussels: Brepols, 1988.

Escholier, Marc. *Port Royal: The Story of the Jansenists.* New York: Hawthorn Books, 1968.

Graham, Ruth. "Married Nuns before Cardinal Caprara: A Sociological Analysis of Their Petitions." In Bernard Plongeron, ed., *Pratiques religieuses dans l'Europe Revolutionnaire (1770–1820),* 321–331. Brussels: Brepols, 1988.

Kervingant, Marie de la Trinité. *Des moniales face à la Révolution Française: Aux origines des Cisterciennes-Trappistines.* Paris: Beauchesne, 1989.

Kreiser, B. Robert. *Miracles, Convulsions, and Ecclesiastical Politics in Early Eighteenth Century France.* Princeton: Princeton University Press, 1978.

Laenen, J. "Etude sur la suppression des couvents." *Annales de l'académie d'archéologie de Belgique* 57 (1905).

Lávrin, Asunción. "Women in Convents: Their Economic and Social Role in Colonial Mexico." In Berenice Carroll, ed., *Liberating Women's History: Theoretical and Critical Essays,* 250–277. Urbana: University of Illinois Press, 1976.

Lusseau, Patricia. *L'abbaye royale de Fontevraud aux XVIIe et XVIIIe siècles.* Paris: Herault Editions, 1986.

Marcadé, Jacques. "L'age classique: Sainte-Croix aux XVIIe et XVIIIe siècles." In Edmond-René Labande, ed., *Histoire de l'abbaye Sainte-Croix de Poitiers: Quatorze siècles de vie monastique,* 335–434. Poitiers: Société des Antiquaires de l'Ouest w/CNRS, 1986.

Martín, Luis. *Daughters of the Conquistadores: Women of the Viceroyalty of Peru.* Albuquerque: University of New Mexico Press, 1983.

Matter, E. Ann. "Discourses of Desire: Sexuality and Christian Women's Visionary Narratives." *Journal of Homosexuality* 18 (1990): 119–131.

Monson, Craig A. "Disembodied Voices: Music in the Nunneries of Bologna in the Midst of the Counter-Reformation." In Craig A. Monson, ed., *The Crannied Wall: Women, Religion, and the Arts in Early Modern Europe*, 191–201. Ann Arbor: University of Michigan Press, 1992.

Muriel, Josefina. *Conventos de monjas en la Nueva España*. Mexico: Editorial Santiago, 1946.

Paz, Octavio. *Sor Juana, or, The Traps of Faith*. Cambridge, Mass.: Harvard University Press, 1988.

Pernot, Michel. "Catherine de Lorraine, Abbesse de Remiremont: Réflexions sur l'échec d'un réforme." In Michel Parisse, ed., *Remiremont*. Nancy: Service des publications de l'Université de Nancy, 1980.

Polt, Manuel Maria. *La familia de Santa Teresa en America*. Fribourg, 1905.

Reynes, Geneviève. *Couvents de femmes: La vie des religieuses cloîtrées dans la France des XVIIe et XVIIIe siècles*. Paris: Fayard, 1987.

Russell-Wood, A. J. R. "Female and Family in the Economy and Society of Colonial Brazil." In Asunción Lavrin, ed., *Latin American Women. Historical Perspectives*, 60–100. Westport, Conn.: Greenwood Press, 1978.

Sanchez Lora, José L. *Mujeres, Conventos y Formas de la Religiosidad Barroca*. Madrid: Fundación Universitaria Española, 1988.

Schepper, G. de. "Marie Thérése et Joseph II: Leur politique à l'égard des maisons religieuses dans les pays-bas." *Revue d'histoire écclésiastique* 35:3 (1939): 509–529.

Soeiro, Susan A. "The Feminine Orders in Colonial Bahia, Brazil: Economic, Social, and Demographic Implications, 1677–1800." In Asunción Lávrin, ed. *Latin American Women. Historical Perspectives*, 173–197. Westport, Conn.: Greenwood Press, 1978.

Theillier, Marc. *Les Ursulines sous la Terreur*. Valenciennes, 1986.

Van Houtte, H. *Histoire économique de la Belgique à la fin de l'Ancien Régime*. Ghent, 1920.

Vovelle, Michel. *Religion et révolution: La déchristianisation de l'an II*. Paris: Hachette, 1976.

Weaver, Elissa B. "The Convent Wall in Tuscan Convent Drama." In Craig A. Monson, ed., *The Crannied Wall: Women, Religion, and the Arts in Early Modern Europe*, 73–86. Ann Arbor: University of Michigan Press, 1992.

———. "Spiritual Fun: A Study of Sixteenth-Century Tuscan Convent Theater." In Mary Beth Rose, ed., *Women in the Middle Ages and the Renaissance*, 173–206. Syracuse, N.Y.: Syracuse University Press, 1985.

29. Culture Wars

Alberto de la Virgen del Carmen. *Historia de la Reforma Teresiana (1562–1962)*. Madrid: Editorial de Espiritualidad, 1968.

Arens, Bernard. *Manuel des missions catholique*. Louvain: Editions du Museum Lessianum, 1925.

Aubert, Roger. *The Church in a Secularized Society*, vol. 5, *The Christian Centuries*. New York: Paulist Press, 1978.

Bartoszewski, Wladyslaw T. *The Convent at Auschwitz*. New York: G. Braziller, 1990.

Bartoszewski, Wladyslaw, and Z. Lewin, eds. *Righteous among Nations*. London: Earls Court Publications, 1969.

Batzdorff, Susanne M. "A Martyr of Auschwitz." *New York Times Magazine*, April 12, 1987.

Becker, C. *History of the Catholic Missions in Northeast India (1890–1915)*. Calcutta: Firma KLM Private, 1980.

Bouton, Jean de la Croix, ed. *Les moniales cisterciennes, I: Histoire externe, pt. II, du XVIe siècle à nos jours*. Grignan: Commission pour l'histoire de l'ordre de Cîteaux, 1987.

Bradshaw, Susan. "Catholic Sisters in China: An Effort to Raise the Status of Women." *Historical Reflections/Reflexions Historiques* 8 (1981): 201–213.

Bullough, Vern L. *The Subordinated Sex*. Athens: University of Georgia Press, 1987.

Byrne, Patricia. "Sisters of St. Joseph: The Americanization of a French Tradition." *U.S. Catholic Historian* 5:3–4 (1986): 241–272.

Callan, Louise. *Philippine Duchesne: Frontier Missionary of the Sacred Heart, 1769–1852*. Westminster, Md.: Newman Press, 1957.

Catta, Etienne. *La vie d'une monastère sous l'Ancien-Régime. La Visitation Sainte-Marie de Nantes (1630–1792)*. Paris: Vrin, 1954.

Curb, Rosemary, and Nancy Manahan. *Lesbian Nuns: Breaking Silence*. Tallahassee: Naiad Press, 1985.

Dachs, A. J. and W. F. Rea. *The Catholic Church and Zimbabwe, 1879 1979*. Gwelo: Mambo Press, 1979.

Davis, Cyprian. "Black Catholics in Nineteenth Century America." *U.S. Catholic Historian* 5:1 (1986): 1–18.

———. *The History of Black Catholics in the United States*. New York: Crossroad, 1990.

Detiège, Audrey M. *Henriette Delille, Free Woman of Color*. New York, 1976.

Devens, Carol. "If We Get the Girls, We Get the Race: Missionary Education of Native American Girls." *Journal of World History* 3 (1992): 219–237.

Dinet, Dominique. "Les communautés religieuses féminines de Bourgogne et de Champagne face à la Révolution." In Bernard Plongeron, ed., *Pratiques religieuses dans l'Europe Revolutionnaire (1770–1820)*, 474–484. Brussels: Brepols, 1988.

Donovan, Mary Ann. "Spirit and Structure: Historical Factors Affecting the Expression of Charism in an American Religious Congregation." *U.S. Catholic Historian* 10:1/2 (1991): 1–12.

Dries, Angelyn. "Uncondemned Americanism: The Rise of a Foreign Mission Impulse among U.S. Roman Catholics, 1893–1925." *Records of the American Catholic Historical Society of Philadelphia* 103 (1992): 27–39.

Ellis, John Tracy. *American Catholicism*, 2d ed. rev. Chicago: University of Chicago Press, 1969.

Ewens, Mary. "The Leadership of Nuns in Immigrant Catholicism." In Rosemary R. Ruether and Rosemary S. Keller, eds., *Women and Religion in America*, 1:101–144. San Francisco: Harper and Row, 1981.

―――. "Removing the Veil: The Liberated American Nun." In Rosemary Ruether and Eleanor McLaughlin, eds., *Women of Spirit*. New York: Simon and Schuster, 1979.

―――. "Saint Stalin." Paper presented at the Second Conference of the Network for the History of Women Religious, Marymount College, June 1992.

―――. "Women in the Convent." In Karen Kennelly, ed., *American Catholic Women*, 17–47. New York: Macmillan, 1989.

Farnham, Janice. "Charity or Justice? Sisters and Workers' Uprisings in Nineteenth Century Lyon." Paper presented at the Third Conference of the Network for the History of Women Religious, Cardinal Stritch College, Milwaukee, June 1995.

Ferraro, Barbara, and Patricia Hussey with Jane O'Reilly. *No Turning Back: Two Nuns' Battle with the Vatican over Women's Right to Choose*. New York: Poseidon Press, 1990.

Fletcher, John Rory. *The Story of the English Bridgettines of Syon Abbey*. Syon Abbey: Burleigh Press, 1933.

Foster, Ann M. C. "The Chronicles of the English Poor Clares of Rouen II." *Recusant History* 18 (1986): 149–191.

Gaucher, Guy. *The Story of a Life: St. Thérèse of Lisieux*. New York: Harper and Row, 1988.

Gazeau, Roger. "Une nouvelle vie." In Edmond-René Labande, ed., *Histoire de l'abbaye Sainte-Croix de Poitiers: Quatorze siècles de vie monastique*. Poitiers: Société des Antiquaires de l'Ouest w/CNRS, 1986.

Goyau, Georges. *La femme dans les missions*. Paris: Ernest Flamarion, 1933.

Graham, Ruth. "Married Nuns before Cardinal Caprara: A Sociological Analysis of their Petitions." In Bernard Plongeron, ed., *Pratiques religieuses dans l'Europe Revolutionnaire (1770–1820)*, 321–331. Brussels: Brepols, 1988.

Harrington, Ann M. *Japan's Hidden Christians*. Chicago: Loyola University Press, 1993.

Harris, Sara. *The Sisters: The Changing World of the American Nun*. Indianapolis: Bobbs Merrill, 1970.

Herbstrith, Waltraud. *Edith Stein*. San Francisco: Harper and Row, 1985.

Isichei, Elizabeth. *A History of Christianity in Africa*. Grand Rapids, Mich.: Eerdmans, 1994.

Kennedy, Camilla. *To the Uttermost Parts of the Earth: The Spirit and Charism of Mary Josephine Rogers*. Maryknoll, N.Y.: Maryknoll Sisters, 1987.

Kervingant, Marie de la Trinité. *Des moniales face à la Révolution Française: Aux origines des Cisterciennes-Trappistines*. Paris: Beauchesne, 1989.

Kloczowski, J. "The Religious Orders and the Jews in Nazi-Occupied Poland." *POLIN* 3 (1988): 241.

Kottopallil, George. *History of the Catholic Missions in Central Bengal, 1855–1886*. Shillong: Vandrame Institute, 1888.

Langlois, Claude. *Le catholicisme au féminin: Les congrégations françaises à supérieure générale au XIX siècle.* Paris: Editions du Cerf, 1984.

Lannon, Frances. *Privilege, Persecution, and Prophecy: The Catholic Church in Spain, 1875–1975.* New York: Clarendon Press, 1987.

Leflon, Jean. *La crise révolutionnaire, 1789–1846,* vol. 20 of *Histoire de l'église,* ed., August Fliche and Victor Martin. Paris: Bloud and Gay, 1944.

Li, Xiaoqing. "American Missionary Sisters in China, 1920–1953: Educational Work and Medical Missions in the Context of Chinese Nationalism." Paper presented at the Third Conference of the Network for the History of Women Religious, Cardinal Stritch College, Milwaukee, June 1995.

Marcadé, Jacques. "L'age classique: Sainte-Croix aux XVIIe et XVIIIe siècles." In Edmond-René Labande, ed., *Histoire de l'abbaye Saint-Croix de Poitiers: Quatorze siècles de vie monastique,* 335–434. (Poitiers: Société des Antiquaires de l'Ouest w/CNRS, 1986.

Maol-Iaso. *Franciscan Missionary Sisters of the Sacred Heart in the United States, 1865–1926.* Peekskill, N.Y.: Mount St. Francis, 1927.

Member of the Scranton Community. *The Immaculate Heart of Mary.* New York: P. J. Kennedy, 1924.

Muehlenbein, M. Wibora. *Benedictine Mission to China.* St. Joseph, Mo.: Benedictine Convent, 1980.

Murthy, B. Srinivasa. *Mother Teresa and India.* Long Beach, Calif.: Long Beach Publications, 1983.

Neill, Stephen. *A History of Christian Missions.* New York: Penguin Books, 1979.

Norman, Edward. *Anti-Catholicism in Victorian England.* London: Allen and Unwin, 1968.

———. *The English Catholic Church in the Nineteenth Century.* Oxford: Oxford University Press, 1984.

Oates, Mary J., ed. *Higher Education for Women. A Historical Anthology.* New York: Garland Press, 1987.

Peckham, Mary L. "Women Religious and the Nineteenth Century Transformation of Irish Catholic Culture." Paper presented at the Third Conference of the Network for the History of Women Religious, Cardinal Stritch College, Milwaukee, June 1995.

Peterson, Susan C., and Courtney Vaughn Roberson. *Women with Vision: The Presentation Sisters of South Dakota, 1880–1985.* Urbana: University of Illinois Press, 1988.

Prevedello, M. A. *L'istituto delle Suore di Carita.* Venice, 1937.

Rohrbach, Peter-Thomas. *Journey to Carith: The Story of the Carmelite Order.* Garden City, N.Y.: Doubleday, 1966.

Sanchez, José M. *The Spanish Civil War as a Religious Tragedy.* Notre Dame, Ind.: University of Notre Dame Press, 1987.

Schneider, Maxyne D., Nancy Tallmire, and Pamela M. Cobey. "Hungarian Sisters and Soviet Occupation, 1950–1989." Paper presented at the Third Conference of the

Network for the History of Women Religious, Cardinal Stritch College, Milwaukee, June 1995.

Stepsis, M. Ursula, and Dolores Liptak. *Pioneer Healers: The History of Women Religious in American Health Care*. New York: Crossroad, 1988.

Sutera, Judith. *True Daughters: Monastic Identity and American Benedictine Women's History*. Atchison, Kan.: Mount St. Scholastica, 1987.

Takagi, Takako Frances. *A History of the Sisters of Notre-Dame de Namur in Japan, 1924–1978*. Washington D.C.: Port City Press, 1987.

Thompson, Margaret Susan. "Cultural Conundrum: Sisters, Ethnicity, and the Adaptation of American Catholicism." *Mid-America* 74:3 (1992): 205–225.

———. "Sisterhood and Power: Class, Culture, and Ethnicity in the American Convent," *Colby Library Quarterly* 25:3 (1989): 149–175.

———. "To Serve the People of God: Nineteenth-Century Sisters and the Creation of an American Religious Life." Cushwa Center, Notre Dame: Working Paper Series 18:2, 1987.

———. "The Validation of Sisterhood: Canonical Status and Liberation in the History of American Nuns." In Margot King, ed., *A Leaf from the Great Tree of God: Essays in Honour of Ritamary Bradley*, 38–78. Toronto: Peregrina Publishing, 1994.

Tjader, Marguerite. *Mother Elisabeth: The Resurgence of the Order of St. Birgitta*. New York: Herder and Herder, 1972.

Tsmomo, Karma I., ed. *Sakyavhita: Daughters of Buddha*. Ithaca, N.Y.: Snow Lion Publications, 1988.

Turin, Yvonne. *Femmes et religieuses au XIXe siècle: Le féminisme en religion*. Paris: Nouvelle Cité, 1989.

Ullman, Joan Connelly. *The Tragic Week: A Study of Anticlericalism in Spain, 1875–1912*. Cambridge, Mass.: Harvard University Press, 1968.

Welter, Barbara. "From Maria Monk to Paul Blanshard: A Century of Protestant Anti-Catholicism." In Robert N. Bellah and Frederick E. Greenspahn eds., *Uncivil Religion: Interreligious Hostility in America*, 43–71. New York: Crossroad, 1987.

20. *The Feminine Aposolate*

Arens, Bernard. *Manuel des missions catholique*. Louvain: Editions du Museum Lessianum, 1925.

Aubert, Roger. *The Church in a Secularized Society*, vol. 5, *The Christian Centuries*. New York: Paulist Press, 1978.

Baur, John. *The Catholic Church in Kenya*. Nairobi: St. Paul Publications, 1990.

Beck, G. A., ed. *The English Catholics, 1850–1950*. London: Burns, Oates, 1950.

Bradley, Ritamary. *The Mind of the Church in the Formation of Sisters*. New York: Fordham University Press, 1960.

Bradley, Ritamary, ed. *The Spiritual and Intellectual Elements in the Formation of Sisters*. New York: Fordham University Press, 1957.

Bradshaw, Susan. "Religious Women in China: Understanding of Indigenization." *Catholic Historical Review* 68 (1982): 28–45.

Byrne, Patricia. "Sisters of Saint Joseph: The Americanization of a French Tradition." *U.S. Catholic Historian* 5:3–4 (1986): 241–272.

Charmot, François. *In the Light of the Trinity: The Spirituality of Blessed Julie Billiart, Foundress of the Sisters of Notre Dame de Namur.* Westminster, Md.: Newman Press, 1964.

Clear, Caitriona. *Nuns in Nineteenth-Century Ireland.* Washington, D.C.: Catholic University of America Press, 1988.

Code, Joseph B. *Great American Foundresses.* Freeport, N.Y.: Books for Libraries Press, 1929.

Darcy, Catherine C. *The Institute of the Sisters of Mercy of the Americas.* Lanham, Md.: University Press of America, 1993.

Darrah, Mary C. *Sister Ignatia: Angel of Alcoholics Anonymous.* Chicago: Loyola University Press, 1991.

Davis, Cyprian. *The History of Black Catholics in the United States.* New York: Crossroad, 1990.

De Cock, Mary. "Turning Points in the Spirituality of an American Congregation: The Sisters of Charity of the Blessed Virgin Mary." *U.S. Catholic Historian* 1011/2 (1991): 59–70.

Diner, Hasia R. *Erin's Daughters in America: Irish Immigrant Women in the Nineteenth Century.* Baltimore: Johns Hopkins University Press, 1983.

Donovan, Grace. "Women of Holy Union in the West Indies, 1890–1929." Paper presented at the Third Conference of the Network for the History of Women Religious, Cardinal Stritch College, June 1995.

Donovan, Mary Ann. "Spirit and Structure: Historical Factors Affecting the Expression of Charism in an American Religious Congregation." *U.S. Catholic Historian* 10:1/2 (1991): 1–12.

Dries, Angelyn. "Living in Ambiguity: A Paradigm Shift Experienced by the Sister Formation Movement." *Catholic Historical Review* 79:3 (1993): 478–487.

Eager, Irene ffrench. *Margaret Ann Cusack.* Dublin: Arden House and Woman's Press, 1979.

Ewens, Mary. "The Leadership of Nuns in Immigrant Catholicism." In Rosemary Ruether and Rosemary S. Keller, eds., *Women and Religion in America,* 1:101–144. San Francisco: Harper and Row, 1981.

———. "The Native Order: A Brief and Strange History." In Jerome D. Lamb, ed., *Scattered Steeples: The Fargo Diocese, a Written Celebration of its Centennial.* Fargo, N.D.: Burch, Londergan and Lynch, 1988.

———. "Removing the Veil: The Liberated American Nun." In Rosemary Ruether and Eleanor McLaughlin, eds., *Women of Spirit.* New York: Simon and Schuster, 1979.

———. *The Role of the Nun in Nineteenth Century America.* New York: Arno, 1978.

———. "Women in the Convent." In Karen Kennelly, ed., *American Catholic Women,* 17–47. New York: Macmillan, 1989.

Fitzgerald, Maureen. "The Perils of 'Passion and Poverty': Women Religious and the Care of Single Women in New York City, 1845–1890." *U.S. Catholic Historian* 10:1/2 (1989): 45–59.

Gibson, Ralph. *A Social History of French Catholicism, 1789–1914.* New York: Routledge, 1989.

Goyau, Georges. *La femme dans les missions.* Paris: Ernest Flammarion, 1933.

Gruber, Erentraud. *Deutschordensswestern im 19 und 20 Jahrhunderts: Widerbelebung, Ausbreitung und Tätigkeit. Quellen und Studien zur Geschichte des Deutschen Ordens,* 14. Bonn-Godesberg: Verlag Wissensahftliches Archiv, 1971.

Healy, Kathleen, ed. *Sisters of Mercy: Spirituality in America (1843–1900).* Mahwah: Paulist Press, 1992.

Hervier, Marie-Stéphanie. *La congrégation de Saint-Joseph de Lyon.* Paris: Les organizations religieux, 1927.

Hollermann, Ephrem. *The Reshaping of a Tradition: American Benedictine Women, 1852–1881.* St. Joseph, Minn.: Sisters of the Order of St. Benedict, 1994.

Isichei, Elizabeth. *A History of Christianity in Africa.* Grand Rapids, Mich.: Eerdmans, 1994.

Keneally, James J. *The History of American Catholic Women.* New York: Crossroad, 1990.

Knibiehler, Yvonne. *Cornettes et blouses blanches: Les infirmières dans la société française, 1880–1980.* Paris: Hachette, 1984.

Langlois, Claude. *Le catholicisme au féminin: Les congrégations françaises à supérieure générale au XIX siècle.* Paris: Editions du Cerf, 1984.

Lannon, Frances. *Privilege, Persecution, and Prophecy: The Catholic Church in Spain, 1875–1975.* New York: Clarendon Press, 1987.

Lanslots, Ildephonse. *Handbook of Canon Law for Congregations of Women under Simple Vows.* New York, 1919.

Logan, Eugenia. *The History of the Sisters of Providence of St. Mary of the Woods, Indiana,* 2 vols. Terre Haute, Ind.: Moore Langan, 1978.

Mary Teresa. *The Fruit of His Compassion: The Life of Mother Mary Veronica, Foundress of the Sisters of the Divine Compassion.* New York: Pageant Press, 1962.

Milient, P. *Jeanne Jugan.* Paris: Le Centurion, 1978.

Murthy, B. Srinivasa. *Mother Teresa and India.* Long Beach, Calif.: Long Beach Publications, 1983.

Neal, Marie Augusta. *From Nuns to Sisters: An Expanding Vocation.* Mystic, Conn.: Twenty Third Publications, 1990.

Norman, Edward. *The English Catholic Church in the Nineteenth Century.* Oxford: Oxford University Press, 1984.

Nourisson, Paul. *Histoire légale des congrégations religieuses en France depuis 1789.* Paris, 1928.

Osborne, Francis J. *The History of the Catholic Church in Jamaica.* Chicago: Loyola University Press, 1988.

Peterson, Susan C., and Courtney Vaughn Roberson. *Women with Vision: The Presen-*

tation Sisters of South Dakota, 1880–1985. Urbana: University of Illinois Press, 1988.

Ranger, T. O., and J. Weller. *Themes in the Christian History of Central Africa*. Berkeley: University of California Press, 1975.

Sanchez, Julio A. *Community of the Holy Spirit: A Movement of Change in a Convent of Nuns in Puerto Rico*. Lanham, Md.: University Press of America, 1984.

Smith, Bonnie G. *Ladies of the Leisure Class: The Bourgeoises of Northern France in the Nineteenth Century*. Princeton: Princeton University Press, 1981.

Sutera, Judith. *True Daughters: Monastic Identity and American Benedictine Women's History*. Atchison, Kan.: Mount St. Scholastica, 1987.

Stepsis, M. Ursula, and Dolores Liptak. *Pioneer Healers: The History of Women Religious in American Health Care*. New York: Crossroad, 1988.

Takagi, Takako Frances. "Inculturation and Adaptation in Japan before and after Vatican Council II." *Catholic Historical Review* 79:2 (1993): 246–266.

Thomas, M. Evangeline. *Footprints on the Frontier: A History of the Sisters of St. Joseph of Concordia, Kansas*. Westminster, Md.: Newman Press, 1948.

Thompson, Margaret Susan. "Discovering Foremothers: Sisters, Society, and the American Catholic Experience." *U.S. Catholic Historian* 5 (1986): 273–290.

———. "The Validation of Sisterhood: Canonical Status and Liberation in the History of American Nuns." In Margot King, ed., *A Leaf from the Great Tree of God: Essays in Honour of Ritamary Bradley*, 38–78. Toronto: Peregrina Publishing, 1994.

———. "Women and American Catholicism, 1789–1989." Chap. 5 in Stephen J. Vicchio and Virginia Geiger, eds., *Perspectives on the American Catholic Church*. Westminster Md.: Christian Classics, 1989.

———. "Women, Feminism, and the New Religious History: Catholic Sisters as a Case Study." In Philip R. Vandermeer and Robert P. Swierenga, eds., *Belief and Behavior: Essays in the New Religious History*, 136–163. New Brunswick, N.J.: Rutgers University Press, 1991.

Turin, Yvonne. *Femmes et religieuses au XIXe siècle: Le féminisme en religion*. Paris: Nouvelle Cité, 1989.

Vovelle, Michel. *Religion et révolution: La déchristianisation de l'an II*. Paris: Hachette, 1976.

Weaver, Mary Jo. *New Catholic Women*. San Francisco: Harper and Row, 1986.

Welter, Barbara. "The Cult of True Womanhood, 1800–1860." In *Dimity Convictions*, 21–41. Athens: Ohio University Press, 1976.

———. "The Feminization of American Religion, 1800–1860." in Mary Hartman and Lois Banner, eds. *Clio's Consciousness Raised*. New York: Harper and Row, 1974.

Conclusion

Anderson, Gerald H., and Thomas F. Stransky, eds. *Mission Trends, 4: Liberation Theology*. New York: Paulist Press, 1979.

Beane, Marjorie Noterman. *From Framework to Freedom: A History of the Sister Formation Conference.* Lanham, Md.: University Press of America, 1993.

Bouton, Jean de la Croix, ed. *Les moniales cisterciennes, III: Histoire interne.* Grignan: Commission d'histoire de l'ordre de Cîteaux, 1987.

Bradshaw, Susan. "Religious Women in China: Understanding of Indigenization." *Catholic Historical Review* 68 (1982): 28–45.

Curran, Patricia. *Grace before Meals: Food Ritual and Body Discipline in Convent Culture.* Urbana: University of Illinois Press, 1989.

Dodson, Michael, and Laura Nuzzi O'Shaughnessy. *Nicaragua's Other Revolution: Religious Faith and Political Struggle.* Chapel Hill: University of North Carolina Press, 1990.

Ebaugh, Helen Rose Fuchs. *Women in the Vanishing Cloister: Organizational Decline in Catholic Religious Orders in the United States.* New Brunswick, N.J.: Rutgers University Press, 1993.

Egler, Monika. "Papst und Päpstin." *Die Zeit,* March, 1989.

Ewens, Mary. "Women in the Convent," In Karen Kennelly, ed., *American Catholic Women,* 17–47. New York: Macmillan, 1989.

Ferraro, Barbara, and Patricia Hussey with Jane O'Reilly. *No Turning Back: Two Nuns' Battle with the Vatican over Women's Right to Choose.* New York: Poseidon Press, 1990.

Harris, Sara. *The Sisters: The Changing World of the American Nun.* Indianapolis: Bobbs Merrill, 1970.

Isichei, Elizabeth. *A History of Christianity in Africa.* Grand Rapids, Mich.: Eerdmans, 1994.

Neal, Marie Augusta. *From Nuns to Sisters: An Expanding Vocation.* Mystic, Conn.: Twenty Third Publications, 1990.

———. "The Sisters' Survey, 1980: A Report." *Probe* 10:5 (1981).

O'Connor, Francis Bernard. *Like Bread Their Voices Rise! Global Women Challenge the Church.* Notre Dame, Ind.: Ave Maria Press, 1993.

Quiñonez, Lora Ann, and Mary Daniel Turner. *The Transformation of American Catholic Sisters.* Philadelphia: Temple University Press, 1991.

Smith, Brian H. *The Church and Politics in Chile: Challenges to Modern Catholicism.* Princeton: Princeton University Press, 1982.

Sutera, Judith, *True Daughters: Monastic Identity and American Benedictine Women's History.* Atchison, Kan.: Mount St. Scholastica, 1987.

Thompson, Margaret Susan. "Discovering Foremothers: Sisters, Society, and the American Catholic Experience." *U.S. Catholic Historian* 5 (1986): 273–290.

Weaver, Mary Jo. *New Catholic Women.* San Francisco: Harper and Row, 1986.

Wittberg, Patricia. *The Rise and Fall of Catholic Religious Orders: A Social Movement Perspective.* Albany: State University of New York Press, 1994.

Index